Why Do You Need This New Edition?

The overarching theme of *Human Communication in Society* is the interaction between the individual and society. In this third edition, we've enhanced this theme by adding new examples, illustrations, and pedagogical materials that connect the more traditional individual-centered, functionalist approach—that is, "who you are affects how you communicate"—with more contemporary critical approaches, which focus on the impact of societal structures and history on communication outcomes. By highlighting this tension between individual and societal forces, we encourage students to recognize the value of multiple perspectives in understanding communication.

Human Communication in Society, Third Edition, like previous editions, covers the full range of topics addressed in existing introduction to communication survey textbooks. Highlights of this new edition include:

1. The Human Communication in Society Model has been renamed "The Synergetic Model" in order to highlight the interactions among individual and societal forces and their effects on communication. This model extends the more traditional transactional model by emphasizing that all communication interactions are influenced by the intersection of individual and societal factors, are embedded in culture, and occur in specific contexts.

2. We have increased our emphasis on critical thinking. In this new edition, the "Alternative View," "Communication in Society," and "Did You Know?" features all include critical thinking questions to challenge students to evaluate the material in light of chapter concepts and their own personal values and beliefs. The ethics section of each chapter has been revised to present the material in a less prescriptive manner, instead engaging students in thinking critically about their own ethical practices. The reflection questions in the margins have also been modified to elicit critical thinking more explicitly.

3. We have increased opportunities for self-study by including "Test Your Knowledge" questions at the end of every major section within each chapter.

4. Chapter 2 has been revised to focus on the recent history of the communication field (rather than ancient history) and to highlight the major theoretical perspectives as well as their assumptions, values, and methods.

5. We have enhanced coverage of listening by adding a new chapter, Listening and Responding (Chapter 7).

6. Chapters 13 and 14 (Mass Media and Communication, Communication and New Technologies) have been updated and revised to more clearly differentiate between communication processes that occur in mass media and new technologies, respectively.

7. References in each chapter have been updated to reflect the most recent available research on the topics addressed.

PEARSON

Human Communication in Society

Edition 3

Jess K. Alberts
Arizona State University

Thomas K. Nakayama
Northeastern University

Judith N. Martin
Arizona State University

Boston   Columbus   Indianapolis   New York   San Francisco   Upper Saddle River
Amsterdam   Cape Town   Dubai   London   Madrid   Milan   Munich   Paris   Montréal   Toronto
Delhi   Mexico City   São Paulo   Sydney   Hong Kong   Seoul   Singapore   Taipei   Tokyo

Editor-in-Chief, Communication: Karon Bowers
Senior Acquisitions Editor: Melissa Mashburn
Director of Development: Eileen Calabro
Development Editor: Elsa Peterson
Editorial Assistant: Megan Hermida
Marketing Manager: Blair Zoe Tuckman
Associate Development Editor: Angela Mallowes
Senior Digital Editor: Paul DeLuca
Digital Editor: Lisa Dotson
Associate Managing Editor: Bayani Mendoza de Leon
Production/Project Manager: Raegan Keida Heerema
Project Coordination, Text Design, and Electronic Page Makeup: Integra
Senior Cover Design Manager/Cover Designer: Nancy Danahy
Cover images (from left to right): © Anton Gvozdikov/Fotolia; © moodboard/Alamy;
    © Radius Images/Alamy; © Corbis/ Fotolia; © Yuri Arcurs/Fotolia
Manufacturing Manager: Mary Ann Gloriande
Printer/Binder: Quad/Graphics, Dubuque
Cover Printer: Lehigh

Credits and acknowledgments borrowed from other sources and reproduced, with permission, in this textbook appear on the appropriate page within text or on pages C1–C2.

Library of Congress Cataloging-in-Publication Data

Alberts, Jess K.
    Human communication in society/Jess K. Alberts, Thomas K. Nakayama, Judith N. Martin.—3rd ed.
        p. cm.
    ISBN-13: 978-0-205-02938-9
    ISBN-10: 0-205-02938-8
    1. Communication—Social aspects. I. Nakayama, Thomas K. II. Martin, Judith N. III. Title.
    HM1206.A43 2013
    302.2—dc23

                                                                2011049484

10 9 8 7 6 5 4 3 2 1—V042—14 13 12

www.pearsonhighered.com

ISBN 10:   0-205-02938-8
ISBN 13: 978-0-205-02938-9

Brief Contents

v

Contents

PART II Developing Effective Human Communication Skills

PART III   Communicating in Context

Preface

As experienced researchers and instructors in the field of communication, we continue to be impressed by the breadth and depth of scholarship in our discipline; we also recognize that this scholarship presents challenges for students and instructors in the introductory survey course. For example, which research traditions should be covered: the traditional functionalist and psychological perspectives, the interpretive-qualitative perspectives, or the more recent critical and postmodern perspectives? Which subfields should be covered: intercultural communication, communication technologies, nonverbal communication, or rhetorical studies? Should instructors focus primarily on helping students develop communication skills or should they focus primarily on theories and inquiry?

Our struggle to answer these questions led us to write the first edition of this text, which we believe met the goals we established early on: first, to expose beginning students to the breadth and depth of our discipline's scholarship, and second, to provide a balance between theory and application. Finally, our third goal was to present a lively overview of the discipline, to meet students "where they live," and to engage them in exploring the implications of communication in their daily lives.

Our overarching theme for the first edition was the interaction between the individual and society. In this third edition, we've enhanced the emphasis on this theme, adding new examples, illustrations, and pedagogical materials that connect the more traditional individual-centered, functionalist approach—that is, "who you are affects how you communicate"—with more contemporary critical approaches, which focus on the impact of societal structures and history on communication outcomes. By highlighting this tension between individual and societal forces, we encourage students to recognize the value of multiple perspectives in understanding communication.

Human Communication in Society, Third Edition, like previous editions, covers the full range of topics addressed in existing textbooks but also introduces some useful innovations. We begin by describing the theoretical foundations of the study of communication, including models of communication, historical and contemporary approaches, and the role of identity in communication. We present the factors of perception, verbal and nonverbal communication, and listening and responding. We then explore communication in various contexts such as culture, close relationships, small groups, and organizations. Ours is the first book to provide comprehensive coverage of rhetoric (Chapter 12), and we devote full chapters to communication and mass media (Chapter 13) and to communication and new technology (Chapter 14). Overall, we discuss the full range of paradigmatic approaches in the field, offering a balance between theory and practice.

NEW TO THIS EDITION

In this edition, general changes have been integrated across the chapters as well as changes specific to each chapter (described in the next section).

- We have clarified the organization of the chapters by grouping them into three parts: Part 1, composed of Chapters 1–4, provides an overview of the book and outlines its theoretical foundations. Part 2, consisting of Chapters 5–7, introduces the fundamental concepts for the study of human communication. Part 3 includes Chapters 8–14 and explores the various contexts in which human communication occurs.

- The Human Communication in Society Model has been renamed "The Synergetic Model" in order to highlight the interactions among individual and societal forces and their effects on communication. This model extends the more traditional transactional model by emphasizing that all communication interactions:

- are influenced by the intersection of individual and societal factors,
- are embedded in culture, and
- occur in specific contexts.

■ We have increased our emphasis on critical thinking in several ways. In this new edition, the "Alternative View," "Communication in Society," and "Did You Know?" features all include critical thinking questions to challenge students to evaluate the material in light of chapter concepts and their own personal values and beliefs. The ethics section of each chapter has been revised to present the material in a less prescriptive manner, instead engaging students in thinking critically about their own ethical practices. The reflection questions in the margins have also been modified to elicit critical thinking more explicitly.

■ In response to instructor feedback, we have added a chapter that focuses specifically on listening, Chapter 7, Listening and Responding.

■ In response to instructor feedback, we have incorporated the material on public speaking into the chapter on rhetoric (Chapter 12) and deleted the chapter focused solely on public speaking.

■ Chapter 2 has been revised to focus more on the recent history of the communication field (rather than ancient history) and to highlight the major theoretical perspectives as well as their assumptions, values, and methods.

■ Chapters 13 and 14 (Mass Media and Communication, Communication and New Technologies) have been updated and revised to more clearly differentiate between communication processes that occur in mass media and new technologies, respectively.

■ References in each chapter have been updated to reflect the most recent available research on the topics addressed.

■ The "Test Your Knowledge" questions have been moved so that they're no longer at chapter end; instead, one or more "Test Your Knowledge" questions appear at the end of each major section within each chapter.

■ Updated examples that address contemporary events and trends will help students connect the concepts to their personal experiences and concerns.

CHAPTER-BY-CHAPTER CHANGES

Part 1

Chapter 1 explains the theme of this book—the interaction between the individual and society—as well as introducing important communication concepts and models. This edition presents the **Synergetic Model,** which depicts communication as occurring when two or more people create meaning as they respond to each other and their environment. It incorporates the roles of individual and societal forces, contexts, and culture in the communication process. This more explicit discussion of communication clarifies it as a process and stresses that it is more than a set of skills. Using a central organizing example of a conversation between a father and daughter, the chapter illustrates the Synergetic Model by introducing and explaining basic communication concepts and the tensions between aspects of the individual and society. It also includes a more developed discussion of the constitutive meanings of messages and a streamlined presentation of the use of symbols during communication.

Chapter 2 focuses on current research paradigms and methods. In this edition, the emphasis on history has been reduced. Additional research-based examples have been added, while a new opening example on conflict in a romantic relationship, revisited throughout the chapter, illustrates the applicability of theories/methods to everyday communicators' lives.

Chapter 3 explores the relationship between communication and identities. This edition includes updated discussions of contemporary identity issues (e.g., a new section and material on disability identity) as well as current research and examples such as the new Indian Census that offers a third choice for gender identity; Chaz Bono's change in gender identity; and Caster Semenya, the South African runner whose sex was questioned by athletic competition authorities.

Chapter 4 focuses on communication and perception. Changes include a revised and updated discussion of selection in perception and a tighter and clearer discussion of cognitive structures.

Part 2

Chapter 5 outlines the elements of verbal communication. New sections have been added on power and identity labels as well as on hate speech. We have also clarified the discussions of the California and Northern Cities Vowel Shifts.

Chapter 6 addresses issues of nonverbal communication. The section on "What Is Nonverbal Communication?" has been restructured to assess both of the prevailing views on this topic in a detailed and even-handed manner. The discussion of power and nonverbal communication also has been expanded.

Chapter 7 is a new chapter, created in response to instructor feedback, devoted to listening and responding. Chapter coverage includes: six important reasons for improving listening and responding skills, a description of the process of listening and responding, and a discussion of the influences and barriers to effective listening. We also discuss the role of societal forces in listening, ethical issues related to listening, and suggestions for becoming a more effective listener.

Part 3

Chapter 8 explores communication across cultures and includes a new discussion on Diasporas in the section on "Increased Opportunity for Intercultural Contact." It also offers an enhanced discussion of the history of interracial marriage/miscegenation laws and their relevance to current intercultural encounters, as well as a new "Alternative View" box focused on issues of assimilation and language learning patterns of contemporary immigrants. Finally, it offers updated statistics on U.S. ethnic and racial demographics, migration patterns, refugee trends, tourism travel, and intercultural encounters.

Chapter 9 discusses communication in close relationships. This edition focuses more explicitly on the communicative nature of close relationships. In addition, the material on models of relationship development has been divided into two sections—one on theories and the other on models. This enables more discussion of relationship developmental processes and leads to a streamlined discussion of stage models. A discussion of Uncertainty Reduction Theory and Predictive Outcome Value has been added to the section on theories of relationship development. New material on hurtful messages and how to deliver them has been added, as well as new features on "Is Dating Dead?" and preventing sexual coercion.

Chapter 10 explores small group communication. New and expanded material on the concept of teamwork as it relates to small group interaction, a new discussion of why leadership is important, new material on shared leadership and servant leadership, and an expanded

discussion of ethical issues in small group communication are key updates in this edition. The material relating to technology and small group communication (i.e., effective virtual teamwork) has also been expanded and updated.

Chapter 11 explores organizational communication. Overall, the new edition of this chapter is tighter and more streamlined. To do this, a less detailed discussion of organizational assimilation is provided, though new material offering a more critical perspective on assimilation research has been added. The discussion of organizational culture has been expanded, as has the material on contingent workers. The discussion of supervisor-subordinate communication has been pared back, and the material on negotiation has been replaced with a discussion of strategic conflict management at work.

Chapter 12 covers the area of public communication. Rhetoric is presented with emphasis on its historical, theoretical, societal, and ethical aspects. In response to instructor feedback, the material on public speaking (formerly a separate chapter) is streamlined and placed in the skills development section of this chapter, where its relevance to rhetoric is most evident.

Chapter 13 discusses communication and mass media. In this edition, we make a clearer distinction between mass media and new media. We also include recent scholarship on the relationships among politics, economics, and the media, as well as current examples such as the News Corp scandal.

Chapter 14 covers new media and communication. This chapter offers new material on mobile technologies as well as a more developed discussion of social media (e.g., Facebook, Twitter) and the increasingly important role these networks play in people's lives, an enhanced discussion of blogs, and new material on the "new" digital divide based on income, education, and rural/urban demographics. The chapter also includes updated examples, statistics, and research findings reflecting current scholarship and trends in new media use, more focus on the role and function of new media, and a more developed discussion of ethical issues regarding new media use (e.g., online dating, online anonymity).

FEATURES

Key features retained in this new edition reflect our four goals for this textbook.

ACCESSIBLE PRESENTATION OF COMMUNICATION THEORY.

In addition to using a down-to-earth writing style and providing plenty of examples, *Human Communication in Society*, Third Edition, offers specific tools throughout the text to help students understand the theory and key concepts:

■ Visual summaries illustrate theories and connections among key concepts.

■ Key terms are glossed in the margins of the page where the term is first used and defined, listed at the end of each chapter with the page number where the term and definition can be found, and compiled in a convenient Glossary at the end of the text.

■ Chapter summaries conclude each chapter.

---

stem, much like a religious system or faith does. In the academic belief systems **paradigms** (Burrell & Morgan, 1988). Each ap-carries with it a set of assumptions about knowledge, the nature n nature; these assumptions guide research and theory develop-7). For example, most social scientists endorse a paradigm which is external to individuals, that it persists across time and groups, edict future behavior based on observations of past or present they believe knowledge can be best acquired through observing

paradigm
belief system that represents a particular worldview

theory
a set of statements that explains a particular phenomenon

methods
the specific ways that scholars collect

KEY TERMS

paradigm 33	behaviorism 35	humanism 41
theory 33	naturalistic 35	qualitative methods 42
methods 33	quantitative methods 35	content analysis 42
rhetoricians 34	demand-withdrawal 35	ethnographic 43
elocutionist 34	attachment 36	rhetorical analysis 43
social science	interpretive approach 41	critical approach 45
approach 35	rhetoric 41	textual analysis 45

SUMMARY

Perception plays an important role in everyday communication. People use three perceptual processes to manage the vast array of sensory data in their environments: selection, organization, and interpretation. From all the sounds, sights, smells, tastes, and textures available, people choose only a few to focus on. Once we attend to particular sensory information, we organize it to make sense of it. Two of the cognitive processes we use to organize information are cognitive representations and categorization. Finally, after we perceive and organize sensory information, we assign meaning to it using frames and attributions.

In addition, the sensory data we select to attend to, how we organize it, and the interpretations we assign are all influenced by our individual characteristics, such as physical abilities and differences, cognitive complexity, and any personality and individual differences. In addition, perception processes are affected by one's position in the power hierarchy, culture, historical events during one's lifetime, and social roles.

Because people vary so much in their perceptions, no one should assume that what he or she perceives is the same as what others perceive. Instead, we all must

EMPHASIS ON ETHICS IN COMMUNICATION. Each chapter includes one or more detailed sections discussing ethical issues relevant to that chapter's communication topic.

TEST YOUR KNOWLEDGE
- What is the digital divide? What are the most important factors that determine whether one has access to new media?
- What are some suggestions for closing the digital divide?

ETHICS AND NEW MEDIA

One message we hope you take from this chapter is that CMC, in itself, is neither better nor worse than FtF communication. It is simply different. However, these differences can allow for irresponsible, thoughtless, or even unethical communication. How can you become an ethical user of new media? There are at least three areas of ethical consideration: 1) presentation of identity online, 2) privacy issues, and 3) building online relationships.

Ethics and Online Identity

As we discussed earlier, the issue of identity and ethics online is complex, and one can take various positions on the issue. An extreme position would be that one should never misrepresent oneself. On the other hand, some new media (e.g.,

OPPORTUNITIES TO APPLY WHAT WAS LEARNED. We advocate a hands-on approach to the study of communication. For this reason, we've added features throughout the text that will help bring the theory home for students:

■ **Skills improvement sections.** Chapters 3–14 conclude with a section providing practical guidelines for applying chapter material to everyday communication.

IMPROVING YOUR VERBAL COMMUNICATION SKILLS

When considering the ethics of language use, you should think about the effectiveness of your verbal choices. What are some guidelines for engaging in more effective verbal communication? We describe two ways in which you might improve: You can work on using "I" statements and also become more aware of the power of language.

"I" Statements

One type of disconfirming message involves making negative generalizations about others. Although you recognize that people are complex and variable, have you nevertheless found yourself making negative generalizations such as those listed here?

"You are so thoughtless."

"You are never on time."

As you can see, negative generalizations (which also are called "you" statements) are typically disconfirming. But, in the real world everyone lives in, some people

■ **Exercises and activities.** "Test Your Knowledge" questions distributed within each chapter and end-of-chapter **"Apply What You Know"** questions encourage students to work through challenging concepts.

Now that you understand the process of listening, the next section sho[w] an individual's personal characteristics influence listening and responding. describe how different situations require different types of listening skills.

TEST YOUR KNOWLEDGE
- What is a definition of listening?
- What are the four stages of listening?
- What is the role of critical thinking in the process of listening?

LISTENING AND THE INDIVIDUAL

Do you have any friends who are especially good listeners? Any who are good? Do you yourself find it easier to listen in some situations than in othe[r] While some studies have identified general listening skills (see *Did You The "Big Five" of Listening Competence*), there are many factors that i[n]

APPLY WHAT YOU KNOW

1. Research a popular media text—for example, a magazine, television show, or newspaper—that targets an identity group different from your own. What elements do you find in this text that differ from a text targeted at one of your identity groups?

2. Select and study a media event such as the Super Bowl, Miss America Pageant, or a famous mur-

3. Select a media activist group to study. Go to their Web page and identify their concerns about media. What strategies do they use to promote their messages? Who is their audience? How do they plan to change media in the ways that concern them?

4. Pick a major media event (whether a ritual event or a natural disaster) and compare how it was covered by

STUDENT ENGAGEMENT. We like to think that we have translated our commitment to the field and our love of teaching into a text that will engage students. We encourage this involvement with the following pedagogical features:

■ **"It Happened to Me"** boxes offer real-life accounts of student experiences that provide a "hook" to important communication concepts.

shock or reentry shock—a sort of culture shock in one's own count gone for a significant amount of time, aspects of one's own culture r what foreign, as the student Maham discovered on his return ho after living in the United States for four years (see *It Happened to M*

Most travelers eventually adapt to the foreign culture to some stay long enough and if the hosts are welcoming. This is often the ca Europeans who visit or settle in the United States. Sometimes peop

ence culture sh move from on United States t as someone w Boston to Birm Honolulu to M evacuation of te of African Ame ers from New Hurricane Katr this experience

It Happened to Me: *Maham*

I would say that I experienced culture (reentry) shock when I visited Pakistan after moving away from there four years ago. In those four years, I had basically forgotten the language and became very unfamiliar with the culture back home. Even though I enjoyed my visit to Pakistan a lot, I had problems adjusting to some of the ways of life. I was not familiar with the bargaining system… where people can go to the store and bargain for prices. I felt very out of place…. As I spent more time there, I got adjusted and used to how people did things there.

■ **"Alternative View"** boxes offer perspectives that challenge mainstream thinking or offer an interpretation of a chapter-related topic counter to conventional wisdom.

Alternative **VIEW**
Census in India Includes a Third Gender Choice

As the official record of a nation's population, what information should any census seek? What categories should the census use?

The United States is just one of many countries that conduct a census at regular intervals. Census forms typically ask for basic personal data like age, race, and gender. In 2000, the U.S. census made history by allowing respondents to check multiple race/ethnicity categories. In the 2010 census, the form was designed to "give the nation's more than 308 million people the opportunity to define their racial makeup as one race or more" (El Nasser, 2010). The 2011 ─── in India also made history, as its

"Male," "Female," or "Other." In India, individuals who are biologically male and adopt female gender identity are considered a third gender known as *hijra*; they face severe discrimination in mainstream Indian society (Venkat, 2008). The 2011 census will "give India a firm count for its 'third-gender' hijra community—the origins of which go back millennia to a time when transsexuals, eunuchs and gays held a special place in society backed by Hindu myths of their power to grant fertility" (Daigle, 2011).

To view a copy of the 2011 census form for India, see: http://www.censusindia.gov.in/2011-Schedule/Shedules/English_Household_schedule.pdf

To view a copy ─ the 2010 census form for the United

■ **"Communication in Society"** boxes serve to reinforce the connection between the individual and society as applied to chapter-related topics.

COMMUNICATION IN SOCIETY
Watching or Not Watching the British Royal Wedding

What were your most noteworthy reasons for deciding to watch or not watch the broadcast of the British royal wedding? What might have interested those Americans who watched the ceremony? Why might other Americans have ignored or avoided this media event?

When Prince William and Catherine Middleton were

population at about 6.9 billion, did over 28 percent of the world watch the royal wedding?

After the wedding, audience estimates fell dramatically. Nielsen Media Research estimated that 22.8 million Americans watched the royal wedding over 11 different U.S. media networks (Schucker, 2011). This represents a little over 7 percent of the total U.S. population of more than 308 million. In other ─── the ─────────── ─ snooze for

■ **Reflection questions,** placed in the margins at strategic intervals, encourage students to reflect on how major concepts connect with their everyday experiences.

■ **"Did You Know?"** boxes offer examples of chapter-related material that students may find surprising or unfamiliar.

audiovide

Speak those who as boring worked to *Stood Stil* each word notice this imprecisel not with h combined nizable to

Think back to the last time you encountered someone you could tell was truly happy to see you. How could you tell? What nonverbal behaviors communicated the other person's happiness to you?

Vocaliza

Did You Know?
The Ringtone Adults Cannot Hear

Are you familiar with Mosquito Ringtones? What are the implications of the Mosquito Teen Repellent and Mosquito Ringtone for communicating, perceiving, and understanding?

The Mosquito Ringtone is based on technology created by Britain Howard Stapleton, who developed a device described as the Mosquito Teen Repellent. The device emitted a high-pitched frequency tone that adults could not hear but that teenagers found annoying. It was used by shopkeepers to disperse teenagers from public spaces where they congregated.

A Word About Language

The text's commitment to presenting comprehensive coverage of the complex field of communication carries with it a responsibility to use language thoughtfully. We recognize the fact that, for complex historical and political relations, identity labels carry strong denotative meanings that may vary from person to person and across time. We have made an effort to use inclusive terms to represent the heterogeneity of opinions within various ethnic and racial groups.

For example, the term Hispanic was created and used in 1980 by the U.S. government for the census and other purposes of collecting census statistics. However, many individuals of Spanish descent prefer Latina/o, as do we. We endeavor to use the latter to refer to U.S. Americans of Spanish descent from a specific ancestral nation like Argentina, Mexico, or any country in Latin America or Spain. We also use Mexican American when referring to individuals coming more directly from Mexico, or Chicana/o to designate a more political consciousness among persons of Mexican descent.

Similarly, we use the inclusive term Asian American unless the context refers to individuals with a specific national origin (e.g., Japan or the Philippines). We use African American or Black interchangeably, recognizing that some individuals (often those from the Caribbean) prefer the more inclusive term Black, whereas others prefer African American. We also use Native American and American Indian interchangeably, recognizing that individuals are divided in their preferences for each of these terms.

We should also note that we use both White (which emphasizes race) and European American (which emphasizes ethnicity) to refer to U.S. Americans of European ancestry. At the same time, we recognize that some individuals prefer to emphasize their more specific origins (Japanese American rather than Asian American, Yaqui rather than Native American, or German American rather than White).

Finally, we are learning to think more internationally in our use of language. Many of our neighbors in Latin and South America, as well as in Canada, find it offensive when we use the term American to refer to ourselves. (After all, these people are Americans as well.) Therefore, we prefer the term U.S. American, in recognition of the fact that we are only one society out of many that make up the continents of North and South America.

The following pages highlight all of the support available when you adopt our book.

Resources in Print and Online

Name of Supplement	Available	Instructor or Student Supplement	Description
Instructor's Manual and Test Bank	Online	Instructor Supplement	The Instructor's Manual and Test Bank, prepared by Lauren Amaro, Arizona State University, includes recommendations on how to incorporate media into the course as well as a detailed sample syllabus. There is also a wealth of chapter-by-chapter resources including learning objectives, lecture outlines, key terms, and application/exploration exercises that can be used in class or as out-of-class assignments. There are also a variety of fully reviewed test bank questions for each chapter. Instructors can select from multiple choice, true/false, short response, and essay questions referenced by page and topic. Available for download at www.pearsonhighered.com/irc (access code required).
MyTest	Online	Instructor Supplement	This flexible, online test-generating software includes all questions found in the printed Test Bank, allowing instructors to create their own personalized exams. Instructors can also edit any of the existing test questions and even add new questions. Other special features of this program include random generation of test questions, creation of alternate versions of the same test, scrambling of question sequence, and test preview before printing. Available at www.pearsonmytest.com/irc (access code required).
PowerPoint™ Presentation Package	Online	Instructor Supplement	This text-specific package, prepared by Lauren Amaro, Arizona State University, consists of a collection of lecture outlines and graphic images keyed to every chapter of the text. These are available electronically through Pearson's Instructor's Resource Center at www.pearsonhighered.com/irc (access code required).
Pearson's Introduction to Communication Video Library	VHS/DVD	Instructor Supplement	Pearson's Introduction to Communication Video Library contains a range of videos from which adopters can choose. The videos feature a variety of topics and scenarios for communication foundations, interpersonal communication, small group communication, and public speaking. Please contact your Pearson representative for details and a complete list of videos and their contents to choose which would be most useful to your course. Some restrictions apply.
Lecture Questions for Clickers for Introduction to Communication	Online	Instructor Supplement	Prepared by Keri Moe, El Paso Community College, this assortment of questions and activities covering culture, listening, interviewing, public speaking, interpersonal conflict, and more is presented in PowerPoint™. These slides will help liven up your lectures and can be used along with the Personal Response System to get students more involved in the material. Available at www.pearsonhighered.com/irc (access code required).
A Guide for New Teachers of Introduction to Communication, Fourth Edition	Online In Print	Instructor Supplement	Updated by Christine North, Ohio Northern University, this guide is designed to help new teachers effectively teach the introductory communication course. It is full of basics for course planning and management, first day of class tips, great teaching ideas for both traditional and hybrid/online courses, a guide to Pearson resources including MyCommunicationLab, and sample activities, handouts, and assignments. Available at www.pearsonhighered.com/irc (access code required).
Preparing Visual Aids for Presentations, Fifth Edition (ISBN: 020561115X)	In Print	Student Supplement	Prepared by Dan Cavanaugh, this 32-page visual booklet provides a host of ideas for using today's multimedia tools to improve presentations, including suggestions for planning a presentation, guidelines for designing visual aids and storyboarding, and a walkthrough that shows how to prepare a visual display using PowerPoint™ (available for purchase).
Pearson's Introduction to Communication Study Site (Open access)	Online	Student Supplement	This open-access, student resource features practice tests, learning objectives, and Web links organized around the major topics typically covered in the Introduction to Communication course. Available at www.pearsonintrocommunication.com.
Public Speaking in the Multicultural Environment, Second Edition (ISBN: 0205265111)	In Print	Student Supplement	Prepared by Devorah A. Lieberman, Portland State University, this booklet helps students learn to analyze cultural diversity within their audiences and adapt their presentations accordingly (available for purchase).
The Speech Outline (ISBN: 032108702X)	In Print	Student Supplement	Prepared by Reeze L. Hanson and Sharon Condon of Haskell Indian Nations University, this workbook includes activities, exercises, and answers to help students develop and master the critical skill of outlining (available for purchase).
Multicultural Activities Workbook (ISBN: 0205546528)	In Print	Student Supplement	By Marlene C. Cohen and Susan L. Richardson of Prince George's Community College, Maryland, this workbook is filled with hands-on activities that help broaden the content of speech classes to reflect the diverse cultural backgrounds. The checklists, surveys, and writing assignments all help students succeed in speech communication by offering experiences that address a variety of learning styles (available for purchase).
Speech Preparation Workbook (ISBN: 013559569X)	In Print	Student Supplement	Prepared by Jennifer Dreyer and Gregory H. Patton of San Diego State University, this workbook takes students through the stages of speech creation—from audience analysis to writing the speech—and includes guidelines, tips, and easy-to-fill-in pages (available for purchase).
Study Card for Introduction to Speech Communication (ISBN: 0205474381)	In Print	Student Supplement	Colorful, affordable, and packed with useful information, the Pearson Allyn & Bacon Study Cards make studying easier, more efficient, and more enjoyable. Course information is distilled down to the basics, helping students quickly master the fundamentals, review a subject for understanding, or prepare for an exam. Because they're laminated for durability, they can be kept for years to come and pulled out whenever students need a quick review (available for purchase).
MyCommunicationLab (New text packaged with MyCommunicationLab ISBN: 0205843697; Standalone Access code card ISBN: 0205850669)	Online	Instructor & Student Supplement	MyCommunicationLab is a state-of-the-art, interactive and instructive solution for communication courses. Designed to be used as a supplement to a traditional lecture course or to completely administer an online course, MyCommunicationLab combines a Pearson eText, MySearchLab™, MediaShare, Pearson's class preparation tool, multimedia, video clips, activities, research support, tests and quizzes to completely engage students. See next page for more details.

The moment you know

Educators know it. Students know it. It's that inspired moment when something that was difficult to understand suddenly makes perfect sense. Our MyLab products have been designed and refined with a single purpose in mind—to help educators create that moment of understanding with their students.

The new MyCommunicationLab delivers **proven results** in helping individual students succeed. It provides **engaging experiences** that personalize, stimulate, and measure learning for each student. And it comes from a **trusted partner** with educational expertise and a deep commitment to helping students, instructors, and departments achieve their goals.

MyCommunicationLab can be used by itself or linked to any learning management system. To learn more about how the new MyCommunicationLab combines proven learning applications with powerful assessment, read on!

MyCommunicationLab delivers **proven results** in helping individual students succeed. Pearson MyLabs are currently in use by millions of students each year across a variety of disciplines. MyCommunicationLab works—but don't take our word for it. Visit our MyLab/Mastering site (www.pearsonhighered.com/mylabmastering) to read white papers, case studies, and testimonials from instructors and students that consistently demonstrate the success of our MyLabs.

MyCommunicationLab provides **engaging experiences** that personalize, stimulate, and measure learning for each student. MyCommunicationLab is available for Introduction to Communication, Interpersonal Communication, Mass Communication, and Public Relations courses.

- **The Pearson eText:** Identical in content and design to the printed text, the Pearson eText lets students access their textbook any time, anywhere, and any way they want—including downloading to an iPad. Students can take notes and highlight, just like a traditional book.

- **Assessments:** Pre- and Post-Tests for each chapter enable students and instructors to track progress and get immediate feedback. Results from the Pre- and Post-Tests generate a personalized study plan that helps students master course content. Chapter Exams allow instructors to easily assign exams online. Results feed into the MyLab grade book.

- **MediaShare:** This comprehensive file upload tool allows students to post speeches, outlines, visual aids, video assignments, role plays, group projects, and more in a variety of formats including video, Word documents, PowerPoint, and Excel. Structured much like a social networking site, MediaShare can help promote a sense of community among students. Uploaded files are available for viewing, commenting, and grading by instructors and class members in face-to-face and online course settings. Integrated video capture functionality allows students to record video directly from a webcam to their assignments, and allows instructors to record videos via webcam in class or in a lab and attach them directly to a specific student and/or assignment. Instructors also can upload files as assignments for students to view and respond to directly in MediaShare. Grades can be imported into most learning management systems, and robust privacy settings allow instructors and students to ensure a secure learning environment.

- **Videos and Video Quizzes:** Interactive videos provide students with the opportunity to watch and evaluate multimedia pertaining to chapter content. Many videos are annotated with critical thinking questions or include short, assignable quizzes that report to the instructor's grade book.

- **Class Preparation:** Collects the very best class presentation resources in one convenient online destination so instructors can keep students engaged throughout every class.

- **MyOutline:** This valuable tool provides step-by-step guidance and structure for writing an effective outline, along with a detailed help section to assist students in understanding the elements of an outline and how all the pieces fit together. Students can download and email completed outlines to instructors, save for future editing, or print—even print as note cards. Instructors can choose from our templates or create their own structure for use.

- **Topic Selector:** This interactive tool helps students get started generating ideas and then narrowing down topics. Our Topic Selector is question based, rather than drill-down or simply a list of ideas, in order to help students really learn the process of selecting their topic. Once they have determined their topic, students are directed to credible online sources for guidance with the research process.

- **MyPersonalityProfile:** Online resources that provide students with opportunities to learn about the various communication styles of themselves and others are housed in MyPersonalityProfile, Pearson's online library for self-assessment and analysis. Instructors can use these tools to show learning and growth over the duration of the course.

- **MySearchLab:** Pearson's MySearchLab™ is the easiest way for students to start a research assignment or paper. Complete with extensive help on the research process and four databases of credible and reliable source material, MySearchLab™ helps students quickly and efficiently make the most of their research time.

- **Audio Chapter Summaries:** Every chapter includes an audio chapter summary, formatted as an MP3, perfect for students reviewing material before a test or instructors reviewing material before class.

MyCommunicationLab comes from a **trusted partner** with educational expertise and a deep commitment to helping students, instructors, and departments achieve their goals.

- Pearson supports instructors with workshops, training, and assistance from Pearson Faculty Advisors—so you get the help you need to make MyCommunicationLab work for your course.

- Pearson gathers feedback from instructors and students during the development of content and the feature enhancement of each release to ensure that our products meet your needs.

No matter what course management system you use—or if you do not use one at all, but still wish to easily capture your students' grade and track their performance—Pearson has a MyCommunicationLab option to suit your needs. A MyCommunicationLab access code is no additional cost when packaged with print versions of select Pearson Communication texts. To get started, contact your local Pearson Publisher's Representative at www.pearsonhighered.com/replocator.

ACKNOWLEDGMENTS

We are once again grateful to all the students and instructors who have provided invaluable feedback to us as we wrote the first and second editions of *Human Communication in Society*. Unfortunately we are unable to list here all of the students who participated, but we would like to acknowledge the instructors who have helped to shape and define all three editions of our book.

Reviewers (First Edition)

Bob Alexander: University of Louisiana–Monroe
Isolde K. Anderson: Hope College
Jay Baglia: San Jose State University
Cheryl L. Bailey: Western Illinois University
John R. Baldwin: Illinois State University
E. Tristan Booth: Arizona State University
Joseph Bridges: Malone College
Lynn S. Cockett: Juniata College
Elisia L. Cohen: Saint Louis University
Lisa Coutu: University of Washington
Peter A. DeCaro, PhD: California State University–Stanislaus
Aaron Dimock: University of Nebraska–Kearney
Donald G. Ellis: University of Hartford
Larry A. Erbert: University of Texas at El Paso
Marty Feeney, PhD: Central College
Dr. Charles Feldman: George Washington University
Sarah L. Bonewits Feldner: Marquette University
Karen A. Foss: University of New Mexico
Kenneth D. Frandsen: University of New Mexico
John Gareis: University of Pittsburgh
Sonja M. Brown Givens: University of Alabama in Huntsville
Carroll Glynn: Ohio State University
Beryl S. Gutekunst: Chestnut Hill College
Thomas Edward Harkins: New York University
Carla Harrell: Old Dominion University
Brian L. Heisterkamp: California State University, San Bernardino
Dr. Patrick J. Hérbert: University of Louisiana–Monroe
Christine Courtade Hirsch: State University of New York–Oswego
Dr. John Katsion: Hannibal-LaGrange College
Joann Keyton: University of Kansas
Larry J. King: Stephen F. Austin State University
Thomas J. Knutson: California State University, Sacramento
Peter Lah: Saint Louis University
William A. Lancaster: Northeastern University
Sara McKinnon: Arizona State University
Jennifer Mease: Arizona State University
Diane Millette: University of Miami

Todd Norton: University of Utah
Shirley Oakley: Coastal Georgia Community College
Richard K. Olsen, Jr: University of North Carolina–Wilmington
Karen Otto: Florida Community College at Jacksonville–North Campus
Frank G. Pérez: University of Texas at El Paso
Linda Pledger: University of Arkansas–Little Rock
Steven B. Pratt: University of Central Oklahoma
Leanne Stuart Pupchek, PhD: Queens University of Charlotte
John C. Reinard: California State University–Fullerton
Brian Reynolds: State University of New York–Buffalo
Scott J. Robson: Washburn University
Pamela Schultz: Alfred University
Dr. David Schulz: California State University–Stanislaus
Kristina Horn Sheeler: Indiana University Purdue University Indianapolis
Deborah Shelley: University of Houston–Downtown
Nancy J. Street: Texas A&M University
Crispin Thurlow: University of Washington
Sarah Tracy: Arizona State University
April Trees: University of Colorado, Boulder
Kathleen J. Turner: Davidson College
Kyle Tusing: University of Arizona
Sam Wallace: University of Dayton
Toni S. Whitfield: James Madison University
Bill Yousman: University of Hartford

Reviewers (Second Edition)

Marcia S. Berry: Azusa Pacific University
Lynn S. Cockett: Juniata College
Larry A. Erbert: University of Colorado, Denver
Emma K. Gray: Portland Community College
Carla J. Harrell: Old Dominion University
Christine Courtade Hirsch: SUNY Oswego
Heather A. Howley: Cazenovia College
Thomas J. Knutson: Sacramento State University
Joanna Kostides: Holyoke Community College
Tema Milstein: University of New Mexico
Cynthia Ridle: Western Illinois University
Renee Beth Stahle: Aquinas College
Jenny Warren: Collin College

Reviewers (Third Edition)

Erin Baird, University of Oklahoma
Anthony Hurst, California State University, San Marcos
Dr. Vicki L. Karns, Suffolk University
Dan Lair, University of Denver
Valerie L. Manusov, University of Washington
Tema Milstein, University of New Mexico
Shane Semmler, University of South Dakota
Dr. Caitlin Wills-Toker, University of Georgia

xxiv   PREFACE

ADDITIONAL ACKNOWLEDGMENTS

We would also like to thank our colleagues and students for their invaluable assistance and moral support: a special thanks to Professor Pauline Cheong for providing foundational ideas for our revised chapter on computer-mediated communication, Professor Clark Olson who generously contributed his knowledge on small-group communication, Professor Karen Ashcraft (University of Utah) for her substantial assistance with the organizational communication chapter, and Professor Angela Trethewey for her support and help throughout this project.

And, of course, we need to thank the many, many students, both at Arizona State University and elsewhere, who have good-naturedly provided invaluable feedback on the first and second editions, helping us to make the necessary changes in the third edition.

Thanks also to our editorial assistants, Charee Mooney and Lauren Amaro, who spent hours searching for (and finding) the most recent and relevant research articles. They also successfully persuaded fellow graduate student instructors and their students to provide us with updated examples and contemporary margin material. We especially appreciate their assistance given that they had their own work to do.

Thanks to the team at Pearson who made it all happen. Thanks to Editor-in-Chief Karon Bowers and Senior Acquisitions Editor Melissa Mashburn. We could not have managed without their expertise, patience, and practiced hand guiding us through a rather complicated publishing process. Thanks also to Elsa Peterson, development editor, for her enthusiasm and hard work. We want to acknowledge the work of project managers Raegan Hereema at Pearson and [TK], who kept us on track. Thanks, too, to our marketing manager Blair Tuckman, editorial assistant Megan Hermida, Director of Development Eileen Calabro, and Associate Development Editor Angela Mallowes.

Finally, to our partners—James LeRoy, David Karbonski, and Ronald Chaldu, who continue to tolerate our frequent absences with good grace. We give them our deepest thanks for their support throughout this and many other projects.

About the Authors

Jess Alberts is President's Professor in the Hugh Downs School of Human Communication at Arizona State University. She is an interpretive scholar who focuses on interpersonal communication and specializes in the study of conflict. **Thomas Nakayama** is a professor in the Department of Communication Studies at Northeastern University. He is a critical scholar who focuses on rhetoric and intercultural communication. **Judith Martin** is a professor in the Hugh Downs School of Human Communication at Arizona State University. She is a social scientist whose expertise is in intercultural communication.

Jess Alberts   **Thomas Nakayama**   **Judith Martin**

Part

UNDERSTANDING HUMAN COMMUNICATION PROCESSES

1 Introduction to Human Communication

2 Perspectives On Human Communication

3 Communicating Identities

4 Communicating, Perceiving, and Understanding

*W*hy are some people excellent communicators while others struggle to make themselves understood? Are good communicators born, or can people learn to be better communicators?

1

Introduction to Human Communication

On her way to class, Adela called her father to let him know what time she would meet him that afternoon; she then texted a friend to arrange to meet at the cafeteria for lunch. Taking her seat in class, she checked her email and chatted with classmates. When the class began, she turned off her phone and listened attentively.

Most people, like Adela, exist in a sea of communication. They watch television; spend time (perhaps too much time) on Facebook; attend class lectures; phone, email, and text message their friends and family; and are inundated by messages over loudspeakers as they shop for groceries or use public transportation. Given all of this, it is hard to imagine that only seventy-five years ago most communication occurred either face to face or via "snail" mail. But in fact, throughout much of human history, individuals lived very close to the people they knew. They conducted commerce and maintained relationships primarily with the same small group of people throughout their lives. Today, people maintain relationships with individuals thousands of miles away, and they buy and sell products halfway around the globe on eBay. This instant and widespread access to the world has its benefits, but it also has its costs.

With so many communication options, people need a wider range of communication knowledge and skills than ever before. Successful communicators must converse effectively face to face; correspond clearly via email; learn when it is appropriate to use text messaging; and absorb the norms and etiquette surrounding cell phones, chat rooms, video conferencing, and Facebook posts. Becoming an effective communicator involves both understanding the components and processes of communication and putting them into practice. As you work in this course to improve your communication knowledge and skills, you may see positive changes in your relationships, your career, your engagement in civic life, and even your identity. How many other courses can claim all that?

Once you have read this chapter, you will be able to:

- Discuss the importance of studying human communication.
- Define communication.
- Name and explain the seven primary components of communication.
- Explain the Synergetic Model of Communication.
- Understand the ethical responsibilities of speakers and listeners.
- Formulate your own communication ethic.

THE IMPORTANCE OF STUDYING HUMAN COMMUNICATION

As you begin this book, several questions may arise. First, you may wonder exactly how the study of human communication differs from other studies of humans, such as psychology. Communication differs from other social science disciplines because it focuses exclusively on the exchange of messages to create meaning. Scholars in communication explore what, when, where, and why humans interact (Emanuel, 2007). They do so to increase our understanding of how people communicate and to help individuals improve their abilities to communicate in a wide variety of contexts. In addition, unlike most social sciences, the study of communication has a long history—reaching back to the classical era of Western civilization when Isocrates, Plato, and Aristotle wrote about the important role of communication in politics, the courts, and learning (National Communication Association, 2003; Rogers & Chafee, 1983). However, the ability to speak effectively and persuasively has been valued since the beginning of recorded history. As early as 3200–2800 BCE, the Precepts of Kagemni and Ptah-Hopte commented on communication (NCA, 2003).

Second, you may question why anyone needs to study communication; after all, most people have probably been doing a reasonably good job of it thus far. And isn't most communication knowledge just common sense? Unfortunately, it is not. If good communication skills were just common sense, then communication would not so often go awry. We would live in a world where misunderstandings rarely occurred; conflicts were easily resolved; and public speakers were organized, clear, and engaging. Instead, communication is a complex activity influenced by a variety of factors, including cultural differences, cognitive abilities, and social norms. (If you would like to discover how much you already know about communication, go to http://www.mindtools.com/pages/article/newCS_99.htm and take the fifteen-item Communication Quiz located on that page.) Good communication is not a cure-all for every relationship and career ill, but it can help attain goals, establish relationships, and develop one's identity.

Is it possible to have too much communication? To learn how one pair of communication scholars would answer this question, see *Alternative View: Too Much Communication as Bad as Not Enough*.

Finally, you may think of communication as a set of skills that are easily learned and wonder why there is an entire course (even a major!) that focuses on communication. Although it is true that every day people use communication to accomplish practical goals such as inviting a friend to see a movie, resolving a conflict with a colleague, or persuading the city council to install speed bumps in their neighborhood, communication is more than just a set of skills, like baking, that one can use in a variety of contexts and settings with little alteration. Rather, communication is a complex process whose effective performance requires an in-depth understanding of how it works and the ability to apply one's critical thinking skills to communication experiences to learn from and improve them.

Critical Thinking: A Key to Successful Communication

Critical thinking requires that one become a critic of one's own thoughts and behavior. That is, rather than responding automatically or superficially, critical thinkers reflect upon their own and others' communication, behavior, and ideas before responding (Paul & Elder, 2008). Scholars have proposed various definitions of critical thinking; the one we advocate describes it as a process that involves the following steps (Passer & Smith, 2004):

1. Identify the assertion or action.
2. Ask, "what is the evidence for and against the assertion or action?"
3. Ask, "what does the bulk of evidence point to?"
4. Ask, "what other explanations or conclusions are possible?"
5. Continue to keep an open mind for new evidence and new ways of evaluating the assertion.

Alternative **VIEW**
Too Much Communication as Bad as Too Little

When people engage in communication for its own sake, they are likely to communicate poorly and excessively. At least, communication professors André-A. Lafrance and François Lambotte think so. A review of their book Arrêter de communiquer: vous en faites trop! [Stop Communicating: You're Overdoing It!] *explains:*

Technology has greatly facilitated communication. But there's a hitch: communication networks are often used simply because they are available and not to satisfy a need or to communicate a pertinent message. It is communication for the sake of communication. This observation applies to both technological tools and traditional ones such as group meetings. "There is a lot of information but very little communication," says Lafrance. "Communication requires interaction between the communicator and the receiver, and the message must be tailored to the reaction of the other."

The book, written for communication students with an eye to the general public, has three premises: [1] All communication aims to bring about change in the receiver: change in knowledge, attitudes or practices; [2] All change comprises a risk to the person concerned: lack of expertise, an unreasonable amount of effort required or a questioning; and [3] The communicator must have more power than the receiver in order to convince him or her of any change.

Do you agree with Professors Lafrance and Lambotte that communication is sometimes overdone? What evidence is offered in this review to support their claim? Do you believe there is value in communicating with no particular goals, such as posting on Facebook? What value might communication add to one's life other than to "satisfy a need or communicate a pertinent message"?

SOURCE: Baril, D. (English adaptation by M. Tulin). (January 29, 2009). *News Digest*. Montreal: University of Montreal. Retrieved February 20, 2010, from **http://www.nouvelles.umontreal.ca/udem-news/news-digest/too-much-communication-as-bad-as-not-enough.html**

How might one apply this process to communication interactions? Let's explore this with a simple and common example. Imagine that you send a text message to your romantic partner on a Friday evening, but hours later have not heard back (Step 1: identify the action). How should you interpret the lack of reply and, consequently, how should you respond? If you were thinking noncritically, you might interpret the behavior negatively (my partner is cheating on me!) even though you have little or no evidence to support this interpretation. You then might respond by dashing off an accusatory text.

However, more critical thinkers evaluate their interpretations and beliefs before responding by asking themselves, "what evidence do I have for this belief or interpretation?" (Step 2). Thus, if their first impulse was to doubt their partner, they would ask themselves, "what evidence exists that my partner is cheating?" (Does failing to return a text necessarily mean the partner is intentionally refusing to respond? Even if the partner is purposely refusing to respond to a text, does that mean the reason for refusing is unfaithfulness?)

The critical thinker would then question whether this interpretation is supported by sufficient evidence and experience (Step 3: What does the bulk of the evidence point to—for example, has my partner cheated before? Does my partner usually respond quickly to texts? Is my partner normally trustworthy?). Next he or she would consider what other explanations are possible. (Step 4: What other conclusions are possible—for example, my partner's phone battery ran down; my partner fell asleep early and didn't receive my texts; my partner is studying and turned off his or her phone.)

If your romantic partner doesn't answer a text message, it could be because she is studying and has turned off her phone.

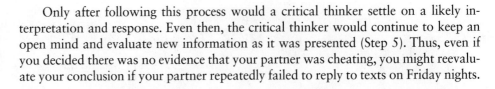

Now that you have reviewed the steps involved in critical thinking, would you consider yourself high or low in critical thinking skills? What topics or situations are most likely to cause you to use your critical thinking skills? What can you do to improve these skills?

Only after following this process would a critical thinker settle on a likely interpretation and response. Even then, the critical thinker would continue to keep an open mind and evaluate new information as it was presented (Step 5). Thus, even if you decided there was no evidence that your partner was cheating, you might reevaluate your conclusion if your partner repeatedly failed to reply to texts on Friday nights.

Advantages of Studying Human Communication

Studying human communication conveys a number of advantages. Individuals use communication to meet people, to develop professional and personal relationships, and to terminate dissatisfying ones. Communication scholar Steve Duck argues that relationships are primarily communicative (1994). Moreover, the relationships we have with others—including how we think and feel about one another—develop as we communicate. Through communication interactions, relationship partners develop shared meanings for events, explanations for their shared past, and a vision of their future together (Alberts, Yoshimura, Rabby, & Loschiavo, 2005; Dixon & Duck, 1993). So, if you tell your romantic partner, "I have never loved anyone as much as I love you, and I never will," you are simultaneously redefining your past romantic relationships, creating shared meaning for the present relationship, and projecting a vision of your romantic future together. Similarly, through communication with friends, coworkers, and acquaintances, we all define and redefine our relationships.

Perhaps most fundamentally, your communication interactions with others allow you to establish who you are to them (Gergen, 1982; Mead, 1934). As you communicate, you attempt to reveal yourself in a particular light. For example, when you are at work, you may try to establish yourself as someone who is pleasant, hardworking, honest, and competent. With a new roommate, you may want your communication behavior to suggest you are responsible, fun, and easygoing. However, at the same time that your communication creates an image of who you are for others, *their* communication shapes your vision of yourself. For example, if your friends laugh at your jokes, compliment you on your sense of humor, and introduce you to others as a funny person, you probably will see yourself as amusing. In these ways, communication helps create both our self-identities and our identities as others perceive them.

Communication has the potential to transform your life—both for the better and for the worse. (To read how one student's communication created a transformation, see *It Happened to Me: Chelsea*). As many people have discovered, poor or unethical communication can negatively affect lives. How? Communicating poorly during conflict can end relationships, inadequate interviewing skills can result in unemployment, and negative feedback from conversational partners can lessen one's self-esteem. Sometimes communication can have even more significant effects. In 2004, author and television hostess Martha Stewart was sent to jail not for insider trading but for lying (and thereby obstructing justice) when her case was being

It Happened to Me: *Chelsea*

When the professor asked us to identify a time when communication was transformative, many examples came to mind. Finally, I settled on one involving a negative relationship. In high school there's usually one person you just don't get along with. Boyfriend drama, bad-mouthing, you name it. I remember dreading seeing this one girl, and I'm sure she felt the same about me. Graduation came and went, and I completely forgot about her. A year later, I came across her Web page as I was searching for old classmates online. As I thought about how petty our arguments were and how cruel we were to each other, I felt smaller and smaller. So I decided to end it. I used email to apologize for my bad behavior because with email I felt safer. I could compose my thoughts, avoid a direct confrontation, and give her time to respond. A couple days later I received an email from her saying she felt the same way and was also sorry for the way she acted. Next week we're going to have a cup of coffee together to really put the past behind us. Maybe to some people that doesn't seem all that life changing, but after hating this girl for two years, it's an amazing transformation for me.

investigated. Thus she was imprisoned for a specific unethical (and illegal) communication act (McCord, Greenhalgh, and Magasin, 2004).

As you can see from Chelsea's story, developing excellent communication skills also can transform your life for the better. The three authors of this book have all had students visit months or years after taking our communication classes to tell us what a difference the classes have made in their lives. A student in a public-speaking class reported that, because of her improved presentation skills, she received the raise and promotion she had been pursuing for years; another student in a conflict and negotiation class revealed that her once-troubled marriage became more stable once she learned to express disagreements better. A third student felt more confident after he took a persuasion class that taught him how to influence people.

Studying human communication may also benefit you by opening doors to a new career path. A degree in communication can prepare you for a wide variety of communication careers. For more information, see *Did You Know? Careers Opportunities with a Communication Degree.*

Did You Know?

Career Opportunities with a Communication Degree

Majoring in communication can open up many career paths, as you can see from the list that the Career Services Network of Olivet College in Michigan has compiled from professional associations and other authoritative sources. The list contains job titles that former graduates with communication majors hold. We suggest you use it to generate ideas, remembering that it represents some, but certainly not all, of the careers you might consider. Be aware, too, that some careers may require additional education.

Business:

Management

Personnel Recruiter

Trainer

Admissions Counselor

Sales Representative

Public Information Officer

Negotiator

Newsletter Editor

Mediator

Manager

Vice President Human Resources

Director of Training and Development

Benefits Administrator

Executive Manager

Industrial and Labor Relations

Customer Service Representative

Human Resources Manager

Buyer

Advertising:

Advertising Specialist

Copy Writer

Media Planner

Creative Director

Public Researcher

Marketing Specialist

Account Executive Manager

Media Buyer

Media Sales Representative

Communication Education:

Language Arts Coordinator

Drama Director

School Counselor

Audiovisual Specialist

Director of College News

Educational Fundraiser

High School Speech Forensics/Debate Coach

Speech Communication Department Chairperson

Education Researcher

Educational Administrator

Educational Tester

Alumni Officer

(continued)

Did You Know?   *(continued)*

Electronic Media/Radio/Television/Broadcasting:

Broadcasting Station Manager	Director of Broadcasting
Film/Tape Librarian	Community Relation Director
Unit Manager	News Writer
Transmitter Engineer	Technical Director
Advertising Sales Coordinator	Market Researcher
Actor/Actress	Announcer
Disc Jockey	News and Relation Manager
Comedy Writer	Casting Director
Producer	Business Manager
Floor Manager	Talk Show Host

Journalism (Print or Electronic):

Reporter	Editor
Newscaster	Author
Copy Writer	Script Writer
News Service Researcher	Technical Writer
Acquisitions Editor	Media Interviewer

Public Relations:

Publicity Manager	Advertising Manager
Marketing Specialist	Lobbyist
Corporate Public Affairs	Specialist
Account Executive	Development Officer
Sales Manager	Media Analyst
Media Planner	Creative Director
News Writer	Public Opinion Researcher

Theatre/Performing Arts:

Performing Artist	Script Writer
Arts Administrator	Performing Arts Educator
Costume Design	Scenic Designer
Lighting Theatre Critic	Makeup Artist
Stage Manager	Model
Theatre Professor	Casting Director

Government/Politics:

Public Information Office Writer	Legislative Assistant
Campaign Director	Research Specialist
Program Coordinator	Elected Official

High Technology Industries:

Trainer for Communication Tech.	Circuit Television Producer/Director
Systems Analyst	Technical Copywriter
Language Specialist	Cognition Researcher
Audio & Visual Computer Display Specialist	

Communication and Health Care:

Health Educator	School Health Care Administrator
Medical Grants Writer	Hospital Director of Communication
Clinic Public Relations Director	Health Communication Analyst
Research Analyst	Medical Training Supervisor
Health Personnel Educator	Medical Center Publications Editor
Hospice Manager	Heath Care Counselor
Activities Director	Marketing Director

Did You Know? *(continued)*

International Relations and Negotiation:

On-Air International Broadcasting
Translator
Diplomat

Corporate Representative
Student Tour Coordinator
Foreign Correspondent

Law:

Public Defender
District Attorney
Legal Researcher
Legal Secretary
Legal Educator

Corporate Lawyer
Private Practice Lawyer
Mediation & Negotiation Specialist
Legal Reporter

Social and Human Services:

Public Administrator
Recreation Supervisor
Community Affairs Liaison
Religious Leader

Social Worker
Human Rights Office
Park Service Public Relations Specialist
Mental Counselor

SOURCE: Olivet College (2010). *What career opportunities are with a communication degree?* Retrieved February 15, 2011, from http://web.olivetcollege.edu/careerdev/communication.htm

TEST YOUR KNOWLEDGE

- How does the study of communication differ from other social science disciplines?
- Why is communicating a complex activity?
- The process of critical thinking involves what five steps?

WHAT IS HUMAN COMMUNICATION?

Even though you have been communicating for your entire life, you probably have not given much thought to the process. You may question why we even need to provide a definition for something so commonplace. Although communication is an everyday occurrence, the term covers a wide variety of behaviors that include talking to friends, broadcasting media messages, and emailing coworkers. Because the term *communication* is complex and can have a variety of definitions, we need to acquaint you with the definition we will use throughout this text.

Broadly speaking, human communication can be defined as a process in which people generate meaning through the exchange of verbal and nonverbal messages. In this book, however, we emphasize the influence of individual and societal forces and the roles of culture and context more than other definitions do. Because we believe these concepts are essential to understanding the communication process completely, we developed a definition of human communication that included them. Accordingly, we define **human communication** as a *transactional process in which people generate meaning through the exchange of verbal and nonverbal messages in specific contexts, influenced by individual and societal forces and embedded in culture*. In the following sections, we will illustrate our definition of human communication and explore the meaning of each these concepts and their relationships to one another. To do so, we first look at the basic components of communication as highlighted in current definitions. Then, we examine the way these components serve as the building blocks of our own model of human communication in society, the Synergetic Model. Finally, we explain how individual and societal influences as well as culture and context contribute to an understanding of the communication process.

human communication
a process in which people generate meaning through the exchange of verbal and nonverbal messages in specific contexts, influenced by individual and social forces, and embedded in culture

messages
the building blocks of communication events

encoding
taking ideas and converting them into messages

decoding
receiving a message and interpreting its meaning

symbol
something that represents something else and conveys meaning

Components of Human Communication

Consider the following scenario:

Adela grew up in the United States; her parents are from Mexico, where her grandparents and many other relatives still live. Adela needed to talk to her father about her desire to live in the dorms at college rather than commuting from home. She was worried; she was the first member of her family to attend college and would be the first single family member to live away from home before marriage. She hoped to convince her father that it was a good idea for her to live in the dorms while also displaying respect for him as her father as well as her commitment to her family. To ensure that the conversation would go well, she decided they should meet at his favorite neighborhood café in the early afternoon so they could talk privately. She rehearsed how she would convey information that he might not be happy to hear and practiced responses to the objections she expected him to raise.

As this example reveals, communication is a complex process that can require considerable thought and planning. The complexity inherent in communication is due in part to the variety of factors that compose and influence it. The seven basic components of communication to consider in planning an interaction are *message creation, meaning creation, setting, participants, channels, noise,* and *feedback.* Each of these features is central to how a communication interaction unfolds. To help you understand this process, we analyze Adela's experiences with her father.

Message Creation **Messages** are the building blocks of communication, and the process of taking ideas and converting them into messages is called **encoding** (receiving a message and interpreting its meaning is referred to as **decoding**). Depending on the importance of a message, people are more or less careful in encoding their messages. In our example above, Adela was very concerned with how she encoded messages to her father (and that is why she rehearsed what she would say). She particularly wanted to communicate to her father that they would remain close, both to persuade him that she should live on campus and to assure him that her leaving would not change her relationship with their family. To accomplish this, she decided to encode this idea into her message: "I'll still be able to come over to the bakery whenever you need me; you'll see me all the time!"

When we communicate, we encode and exchange two types of messages—verbal and nonverbal—and most of these messages are symbolic. A **symbol** is something that represents something else and conveys meaning (Buck & VanLear, 2002). For example, a Valentine's Day heart symbolizes the physical heart, it represents romantic love, and it conveys feelings of love and romance when given to a relational partner. The verbal system is composed of linguistic symbols (that is, words) while the nonverbal message system is composed of nonlinguistic symbols such as smiles, laughter, winks, vocal tones, and hand gestures.

When we say *communication is symbolic,* we are describing the fact that the symbols we use—the words we speak and the gestures we use—are arbitrary, or without any inherent meaning (Dickens, 2003). Rather, their meaning is derived as communicators employ agreed-upon definitions. For instance, putting up one's hand palm forward would not mean "stop" unless people in the United States agreed to this meaning, and the word *mother* would not mean a female parent unless speakers of English agreed that it would. Because communicators use symbols to create meaning, different groups often develop distinct words for the same concept. For instance, the

What symbolism do you see in a Valentine's Day heart?

common word for a feline house pet is *cat* in English, but *neko* in Japanese. Thus, there is no intrinsic connection between most words and their meanings—or many gestures and their meanings.

Because human communication is predominantly symbolic, humans must agree on the meanings of words. Consequently, words can, and do, change over time. For example, the term *gay* typically meant happy or carefree from the seventeenth century through much of the twentieth century. Although the term was occasionally used to refer to same-sex relationships as early as the 1800s, it has come to be used widely only since the late 1990s, when users agreed to this meaning and usuage. Nonetheless, people may have different meanings for specific symbols or words, especially if they come from different ethnic or national cultures. Read about one student's difficulties communicating while on a trip to Europe in *It Happened to Me: Alyssa.*

As Alyssa's experience reveals, though most people recognize that cultures vary in the words they use for specific ideas and items, they don't always realize that nonverbal gestures can have varied meanings across cultures as well. Creating messages is the most fundamental requirement for communication to occur, but it certainly is not enough. Messages also create shared meanings for everyone involved in the interaction.

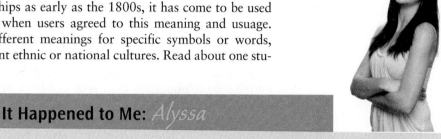

It Happened to Me: *Alyssa*

Recently I traveled in Europe; I had no idea how difficult it would be to communicate, even in England. I spent the first few days navigating London on my own. It was so hard! People tried to help, but because of the differences in word choice and accents I couldn't fully understand their directions. After London I went to Italy, where I had an even harder time communicating due to the language barrier. So I resorted to using nonverbal gestures such as pointing, smiling, and thumbs up and down. However, I ran into problems doing this. One night I ordered wine for a friend and myself. The bartender looked uncertain when he brought the two glasses of wine I'd ordered, so I gave him a "thumbs up" to mean okay, that he had it right. However, to him the gesture meant "one," so he thought I only wanted one glass, and he took the other away. It took us a while to get the order straight.

Meaning Creation The goal of exchanging symbols—that is, of communicating—is to create meaning. The messages we send and receive shape meaning beyond the symbols themselves. We also bring to each message a set of experiences, beliefs, and values that help shape specific meanings. This is why people can hear the same message but understand it differently. Adela was aware of this as she planned the conversation with her father. She knew they didn't always have precisely the same meanings for every word. For example, the word "independent" carried positive meanings for her, but she knew it carried more negative and potentially upsetting meanings for her father. Therefore, when talking to her father, she would never argue that living in the dorm was a good idea because it would make her more independent.

Meaning is made even more complex because, as the example above suggests, each message carries with it two types of meaning—content meaning and relationship meaning. **Content meaning** includes denotative and connotative meaning. Denotative meaning is the concrete meaning of the message, such as the definition you would find in a dictionary. Connotative meaning describes the meanings suggested by or associated with the message and the emotions triggered by it. For example, denotatively the word *mother* refers to one's female parent, while connotatively it may include meanings such as warmth, nurturance, and intimacy. **Relationship meaning** describes what the message conveys about the relationship between the parties (Robinson-Smith, 2004; Watzlawick, Beavin, & Jackson, 1967). For example, if a colleague at works told you to "run some copies of this report," you might become irritated, but you probably wouldn't mind if your boss told you to do the same thing. In both cases the relationship message may be understood as "I have the right to tell you what to do," which is appropriate if it comes from your supervisor—but not if it comes from a peer.

content meaning
the concrete meaning of the message, and the meanings suggested by or associated with the message and the emotions triggered by it

relationship meaning
what a message conveys about the relationship between the parties

Finally, communication helps create the shared meanings that shape families, communities, and societies. Specifically, the meanings we have for important issues including politics, civil behavior, family, and spirtuality—as well as for less important concerns such as what food is tasty or what type of home is desirable—are created through people's interactions with one another. For example, if you were asked what your family "motto" is (that is, what is important in your family) what would you say? Some people might say it is "family first" while others declare it is "do the right thing." How do families come to have these shared beliefs and meanings? They do so through the countless interactions they have with one another; through these conversations and everyday experiences they create a meaning for what is important to their family. What do you think happens when two people marry, one of whom believes "family first" and another who thinks "do the right thing" is more important than even family? Like the families they grew up within, they will interact, live together, and jointly develop shared meanings for their family beliefs. A similar process occurs when people come together to form groups, organizations, communities, and societies. In sum, our relationships, our understanding of the world, and our beliefs about life and death are created through the interactions we have with others.

Setting The physical surroundings of a communication event make up its setting. **Setting** includes the location where the communication occurs (in a library versus a bar), environmental conditions (including the temperature, noise, and lighting), time of day or day of the week, and the proximity of the communicators. Together these factors create the physical setting, which affects communication interaction.

Why do you think Adela chose to meet in midafternoon at her father's favorite café as the setting for their conversation? She did so for several reasons. First, her father would be more likely to feel relaxed and in a good mood in a familiar location that he liked. Second, she selected the middle of the afternoon because it was the most relaxed time of day for him; she knew that the family bakery business involved strenuous morning preparation and evening cleanup. Finally, she chose a public setting because she believed her father would remain calmer in public than in a private setting, such as at home; it would also give them more privacy and fewer interruptions. As you can see, Adela carefully selected a comfortable setting that she believed would enhance her chances of being successful.

Participants During communication, **participants**—two or more people—interact. The number of participants, as well as their characteristics, will influence how the interaction unfolds. Typically, the more characteristics participants share (cultural, values, history), the easier they will find it to communicate, because they can rely on their common assumptions about the world.

As Adela planned her conversation, she recognized that she and her father shared a number of important characteristics—commitment to family, concern with finances, and a desire for harmony. However, she also realized that they differed in important ways. Although she was close to her family, she desired more independence than her father would want for himself or for her. In addition, she believed it was acceptable for young, single women to live away from their families, a belief she was sure her father didn't share.

The type of relationship communicators have and the history they share also affect their communication. Whether communicators are family members, romantic partners, colleagues, friends, or acquaintances affects how they frame, deliver, and interpret a message. Since Adela was talking with her father rather than her boyfriend, she focused on displaying respect for his position as her father and asking (rather than telling) him about wanting to live on campus.

As we have suggested already, the moods and emotions that communicators bring to and experience during their interaction influence it as well. Since Adela

setting
the physical surroundings of a communication event

participants
the people interacting during communication

wanted to increase the likelihood that the conversation with her father would go well, she tried to create a situation in which he would be in a calmer and happier frame of mind.

Channels For a message to be transmitted from one participant to another, it must travel through a channel. A **channel** is the means through which a message is conveyed. Historically, the channels people used to communicate with one another were first face to face, then written (for example, letters and newsprint), and yet later electronic (for example, telephone calls, radio, and television). Today, thanks to technology, we have many more communication channels—email, instant messaging, mobile instant messaging, social networks such as Facebook and MySpace, and videophones, to name just a few.

The channel a person selects to communicate a message can affect how the message is perceived and its impact on the relationship. For example, if your romantic partner broke up with you by changing his or her Facebook relationship status instead of by talking to you face to face, how would you respond? Because Adela was sensitive to the importance of the communication channel she used with her father, she elected to communicate with him face to face because it was a channel her father was familiar with and would find appealing.

Text messaging is one channel of communication. What other channels do you often use?

Noise Noise refers to any stimulus that can interfere with, or degrade, the quality of a message. Noise includes external signals of all kinds: not only loud music and voices, but also distracting clothing or hairstyles, uncomfortably warm or chilly temperatures, and so on. Noise can also come from internal stimuli, such as hunger or sleepiness. Semantic interference, which occurs when speakers use words you do not know or use a familiar word in an unfamiliar way, is another form of noise. If you have ever tried to have a conversation with someone who used highly technical language in a noisy room while you were sleepy, you have experienced a "perfect storm" of noise.

How did the noise factor affect Adela's choices? She chose to meet at a café in the middle of the afternoon, avoiding the crowded lunch and dinner hours. There would be fewer competing voices and sounds, and the wait staff would be less likely to interrupt with meal service, so there would be fewer distractions. By choosing a setting that minimized interference, she improved the chances that her message would be clear.

Feedback Finally, the response to a message is called **feedback**. Feedback lets a sender know if the message was received and how the message was interpreted. For example, if a friend tells you a joke and you laugh heartily, your laughter serves as feedback, indicating that you heard the joke and found it amusing. Similarly, if you fall asleep during a lecture, you provide feedback to your professor that either you are very tired or you find the lecture boring. Thus your feedback serves as a message to the sender, who then uses the information conveyed to help shape his or her next message.

Although Adela wasn't sure what type of feedback her father would provide or what type she would need to give him, she did spend time anticipating what they each would say. She also knew that she would need to be sensitive to his messages and be prepared to offer feedback that was both supportive and persuasive.

How do you choose which channel to use when you communicate with others? Do you consider who they are, the topic, the importance of the message, or something else? Overall, do you think you pick the best channel most of the time? If not, what do you need to do to select more appropriately?

TEST YOUR KNOWLEDGE

- How do the authors define human communication?
- What are the seven basic components of the communication process?
- In what ways does communication create meaning?

channel
the means through which a message is transmitted

noise
any stimulus that can interfere with, or degrade, the quality of a message

feedback
the response to a message

VISUAL SUMMARY 1.1   Seven Basic Components of Human Communication

Participants—two or more people who interact; the number of participants, as well as their characteristics, will influence how interaction

Channel—the means through which a message is conveyed

◀ ••••••••••••••••••••••••••••••• ▶

Setting—the physical surroundings of a communication event

Let's meet at the cafe on 10th Street.

Messages—the building blocks of communication; the process of taking ideas and converting them into messages

I can come over after class.

How about three O'clock?

Noise—any stimulus that can interfere with, or degrade, the quality of a message

What did you say? You're breaking up.

Are you still there?

OK, I'll see you there at three.

I'll be there.

Feedback—lets a sender know if the message was received and how the message was interpreted

◀ ••••••••••••••••••••••••••••••• ▶

Meaning Creation The goal of exchanging symbols—that is, of communicating—is to create meaning

A MODEL OF HUMAN COMMUNICATION: THE SYNERGETIC MODEL

Synergetic Model of Communication
a transactional model based on the roles individual and societal forces, contexts, and culture play in the communication process

To help people understand complex processes, scientists and engineers, among others, create visual models to show how how all components of a process work together. Scholars of human communication have done the same. They have developed models to reveal how the seven components described above work together to create a communication interaction.

The first such model of human communication depicted communication as a linear process that primarily involved the transfer of information from one person to another (Eisenberg, Goodall, & Trethewey, 2010; Laswell, 1948; Shannon & Weaver, 1949). In this model, communication occurred when a sender encoded a message (put ideas into words and symbols) that was sent to a receiver who decoded (interpreted) it. Then, the process was believed to reverse: The receiver became the sender, and the sender became the receiver (Laswell, 1948). This model (see Figure 1.1) also included the components of "noise" and "channel." Since that time other, more complex models, such as our Synergetic Model, have been created to show a greater variety of factors that interact with one another to influence the communication process.

The **Synergetic Model** is a transactional model that, like most previous models, depicts communication as occurring when two or more people create meaning as they respond to each other and their environment. In addition, it is based on a belief in the important roles of individual and societal forces, contexts, and culture in the communication process. We discuss each of these topics in detail below, and to help clarify the the concepts, we revisit Adela's interaction with her father once again to illustrate how they function during the communication process.

After carefully planning for the interaction with her father about her desire to leave home to go to graduate school, Adela engaged in the following conversation with him:

Adela: *Dad, guess what! Purdue, Illinois, ASU, and Texas all let me in.* (Then, noticing a quizzical look on her father's face, she continues) *I mean, they all admitted me to their undergraduate programs.*

FIGURE 1.1: A Linear Model of Communication
Early models depicted communication as a linear process that primarily involved the transfer of information from one person to another

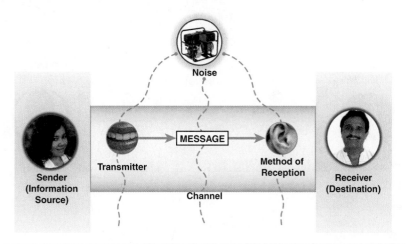

Father: Oh. How many did you apply to?

Adela: Just four. They all accepted me.

Father: I always knew I had a smart daughter! But (frowning, speaking uncertainly), *what does that mean for next year?*

Adela (cautiously): Well, I was thinking of staying here and attending ASU.

Father (smiling): Good! So it won't be any different from having you in high school—you'll still be at home when you're not in class.

Adela (hesitantly): Well, that is something I wanted to talk to you about. I would like to live in one of the dorms on campus instead of living at home.

Father (firmly, shaking his head): Oh. No, I don't think that is a good idea. We can't afford to pay for room and board, and we need you to help out with the accounts for our bakery.

Adela: Well, what I didn't mention before is that I've been offered a scholarship to cover my room and board, so we'll actually save money if I live on campus—plus I won't have to have a car to commute to school.

Father (looking doubtful): Well, this is something to think about. But what about your responsibility to do the accounts for the bakery?

Adela: I'll still be able to come over to the bakery whenever you need me; you'll see me all the time! I can take the light rail near campus. If I live on campus I can still be here when you need me, plus I'll save money and will have more time to study since I won't be stuck in traffic during my commute.

Father: I guess you make some good points. But I don't know if I am ready to see you move out of the house.

Communication Is Transactional To say that *communication is a transaction* (see Figure 1.2) captures the fact that (1) each communicator is a sender and receiver *at the same time*, (2) meaning is created as people communicate together, (3) communication is an ongoing process, and (4) previous communication events and relationships influence its meaning (Warren & Yoder, 1998; Watzlawick, Beavin, & Jackson, 1967). What does this mean?

FIGURE 1.2: Communication Is Transactional
Transactional models express the idea that meaning is created as people communicate.

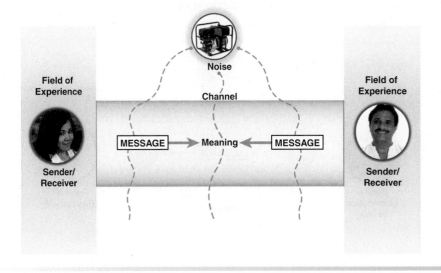

First, all participants in a communication event both receive and send messages simultaneously, even if those messages are sent only nonverbally. As you may have noted, as Adela explained that she was "let in" to four universities, she realized from her father's nonverbal behavior that he was confused. That is, she received his message even as she talked, and he sent a message even as he listened.

Second, as the example above suggests, meaning is not something one person creates and then sends to another person via a message. If that were true, Adela's father would not have been confused by the expression "let in"; Adela's initial message would have been sufficient. Rather, meaning was created as Adela and her dad communicated together; she made a statement, he showed his lack of understanding, and Adela offered more information until they shared similar understandings or meaning.

Third, describing communication as ongoing highlights the fact that it is a process whose specific beginnings and endings can be difficult to discern. All the interactions one has had with individuals in the past influence one's communication in the present, just as a person's current communication affects his or her expectations for and experiences of future interactions. For instance, Adela planned her interaction and communicated with her father based on her previous experiences with him. Specifically, she knew he would disapprove of her living on campus, so she was prepared to offer arguments for why living in the dorms was a better choice. Her experiences with her father, then, affected the messages she crafted for their conversation. In addition, she recognized that their conversation would influence how they communicated with each other in the future. If he became angry, he likely would communicate with her less or more negatively. This, in turn, would influence her future messages to him, and so on.

Finally, because communication is ongoing and interactive, when people communicate, they and their conversational partner(s) reaffirm or alter their identities and relationships. Thus, Adela's conversation with her father is likely to change how they see each other. He might see her as more adult and independent because of her desire to leave home, or he may now perceive her as a less loving child. Similarly, she may view him as less of an authority figure and more of a peer, or she might believe he is even more authoritarian and rigid than she previously thought.

Communication Is Influenced by Individual Forces The individual is a primary focus in communication. Many separate individual forces or characteristics contribute to your identity, and these in turn affect your communication. Individual forces include your demographic characteristics such as age, race, ethnicity, nationality, gender/sex, sexual orientation, regional identity, and socioeconomic class, as well as such factors as personality and cognitive and physical ability. In addition, individual forces include your **field of experience**, such as your education and experiences.

For example, Adela is female, eighteen, and about to become a college student, while her father is male, is in his late forties, and owns and runs a bakery. Each of these individual factors influences the way they communicate as well the ways others communicate with them and about them. Because of her experiences as a potential college student, Adela knows what "let in" means and understands the benefits of living on campus. On the other hand, her father is not aware of this information, and based on his culture and his experiences, he understands that commitment to family is paramount.

The combination of these individual characteristics is unique for every person, so people communicate in distinctive ways. However, every society places limits on the variations that are deemed acceptable. For example, not all men speak assertively, enjoy talking about sports, or "high five" one another. In mainstream U.S. culture, though, many people consider these behaviors as normal for males. Speaking in a more "female" style, such as speaking very quietly or politely, talking about fashion, or using "effeminate" nonverbal gestures, is typically considered inappropriate for men and boys. Those who veer somewhat from the norm may

field of experience
the education, life events, and cultural background that a communicator possesses

culture
learned patterns of perceptions, values, and behaviors shared by a group of people

be seen as odd, or they might be shunned; those who veer too far from the norm may be labeled as mentally ill. So while we are each individuals, society places constraints on the range of our individualism, a topic we will explore later.

Communication Is Influenced by Societal Forces As we suggested just above, individual differences are not value free. They are arranged in a hierarchy in which some individual characteristics are more highly valued than others. For example, being white is often advantageous in U.S. society, being young has advantages over being old, and being physically able is more advantageous than having a disability. How society evaluates these characteristics affects how we talk to—and about—people who display them.

The political, historical, economic, and social structures of a society influence this value hierarchy and affect how we view specific individual characteristics. The historical conditions under which many U.S. racial and ethnic groups arrived in the United States, for instance, continue to affect their identities. For example, many of the earliest Vietnamese immigrants who moved to the United States during and shortly after the Vietnam War had very strong work ethics but were not fluent in English, so they created businesses of their own—as restaurant owners, nail technicians, and other service professionals. Consequently, many people still fail to realize that Vietnamese Americans also work as lawyers, professors, and physicians. Similarly, even though Barack Obama was elected President of the United States, the fact that many African Americans are descendants of people who came to the United States as slaves continues to influence the ways people think and talk about him.

The values attributed to individual characteristics such as age, sexual orientation, and sex also come from these larger societal forces—whether communicated to us through the media, by our friends and family, or by organizations such as schools, religious institutions, or clubs. For example, the teachings of religious groups shape many people's views on sexual orientation, and because most societies historically have been patriarchal, they continue to value women in the public realm less than they do men.

In Adela's case, two societal forces at work in her interaction with her father are how society views women and parent/child interactions. Her father was raised in a culture where males held considerably more power than females, and parents were assumed to know what was best for their children even when the children were grown. Consequently, he tends to hold the belief that fathers should have considerable decision-making power over their children, especially their unmarried female children. On the other hand, Adela grew up in a culture where men and women are seen as more equal and parents exert less control over their children's lives as the children grow up.

Social hierarchies wherein men are more valued than women, or older people's opinions are considered more worthwhile than younger people's, arise from the meanings that societal structures impose on individual characteristics, and communication maintains these hierarchies. For example, cultures that value maleness over femaleness have many more stereotypes and negative terms for women than they do for men. Moreover, these cultures value certain types of communication over others. Thus men in leadership positions are expected to communicate decisively and avoid appearing "weak" by apologizing or admitting mistakes, while the same is not usually true for women. We will explore social hierarchies in more detail in later chapters.

Being gay is both an individual and cultural factor.

Communication Is Influenced by Culture Communication also is embedded in culture. **Culture** refers to the learned patterns of perceptions, values, and behaviors shared by a group of people. Culture is dynamic and heterogeneous (Martin & Nakayama, 2005), meaning that it changes over time and that despite commonalities, members of cultural groups do not all think and behave alike. You probably belong to many cultures, including those of your gender, ethnicity, occupation, and religion, and each of these cultures will have its own communication patterns.

When you identify yourself as a member of a culture defined by age, ethnicity, or gender, this culture-group identity also becomes one of your individual characteristics. For example, as people move from their teen years into young adulthood, middle age, and old age, they generally make a transition from one age-related culture to another. Since each cultural group has a unique set of perceptions, values, and behaviors, each also has its own set of communication principles. As you become an adult, then, you probably stop using language you used as a teenager. And even though changing your language is an individual decision, it is influenced by cultural and societal expectations as well.

Culture affects all or almost all communication interactions (Schirato & Yell, 1996). More specifically, participants bring their beliefs, values, norms, and attitudes to each interaction, and the cultures they belong to shape each of these factors. Cultural beliefs also affect how we expect others to communicate. As we discussed above, because he is Mexican, Adela's father values family closeness, loyalty, and the role of the father as head of the family. Because she is Mexican American, Adela holds many of these same beliefs, but she also values independence and individuality in ways that her father does not.

In addition to participants' cultural backgrounds, the culture in which a communication event takes place influences how participants communicate. In the United States, politicians routinely mention religion in their public addresses and specifically refer to God; however, in France, because of a stricter separation between church and state, politicians typically do not mention religion or deities in their public communication and would be criticized if they did. Regional culture can also affect participants' expectations for appropriate communication behavior. For instance, southerners in the United States tend to be more nonverbally demonstrative and thus might hug others more than do northeasterners (Andersen, Lustig, & Andersen, 1990). Of course, other cultural differences (ethnic background, religious background) might influence these nonverbal behaviors as well.

Communication Is Influenced by Context Each communication interaction occurs in a specific context. Context includes the setting, or aspects of the physical environment, in which an interaction occurs. It also includes which and how many participants are present, as well as the specific occasion during which the interaction unfolds (for example, a Sunday dinner or a birthday party). Context can exert a strong influence on how people communicate with one another. For example, you could argue with your close friend in private when just the two of you are present, during a social event when you are part of a group, during a staff meeting at work, on a television talk show about feuding friends, or in the mall. Can you imagine how each of these contexts would influence your communication? You might be more open if the two of you are alone and in private; you may try to get others involved if you are with friends; you could be more subdued at the mall; you might refrain from mentioning anything too negative on television; or you might be more hostile in an email. It is because context strongly affects individuals' interactions that Adela arranged to talk with her father at his favorite café in the afternoon.

The tensions that exist among individual forces, societal forces, cultures, and contexts shape communication and meaning. To help clarify this tension, let's return yet again to Adela's conversation with her father. Their conversation was influenced by the context (a restaurant), multiple individual forces (each person's age, sex, cultural background, and education), multiple societal forces (the value placed on education, family, sex, and age) as well as their cultures (the meanings of independence, loyalty, and family). Thus, in the conversation between Adela and her father, the context in which the conversation occurred, their individual experiences with

FIGURE 1.3: The Synergetic Model
The Synergetic Model presents communication as a transactional process in which meaning is influenced by cultural, societal, and individual forces.

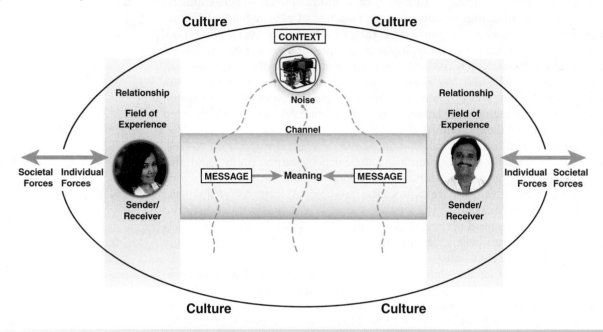

higher education, and the cultural meaning of the parent-child relationship all came together to influence the communication interaction. These components and their relationships to one another are depicted in Figure 1.3, the Synergetic Model.

As we stated at the beginning of the chapter, and as is revealed in our model, for us, communication is a transactional process in which people generate meaning through the exchange of verbal and nonverbal messages in specific contexts, influenced by individual and societal forces and embedded in culture. This is the definition and model of communication that will guide you as you explore the remainder of this book. After you complete this course, we recommend that you return to this section to assess how your own understanding of the communication process has changed and deepened.

Our goal in developing this model is to provide a framework for students to organize, read, and understand this complex process we call communication. However, before moving on, we need to discuss one more essential concept that frames and guides all of your communication efforts—ethics.

TEST YOUR KNOWLEDGE

- How does the linear model of communication depict the communication process?
- What does it mean that communication is a transactional process?
- According to the Synergetic Model, what are the individual factors that influence the communication process?
- According to the Synergetic Model, what are the social factors that influence the communication process?

COMMUNICATION ETHICS

In the United States, we appear to be in the midst of a crisis with regard to ethical communication. In the business world, investment executive Bernard Madoff was found guilty of running a Ponzi scheme in 2008 (Leventhal, 2011), and Red Cross

CEO Mark Everson was dismissed from his job in 2009 when he was accused of having a personal relationship with a subordinate (Jones & Koppel, 2010). The world of politics does not seem to be faring much better: In 2010 former presidential candidate John Edwards admitted to fathering a child with a campaign worker while still married to his ill (now deceased) wife; and former U.S. House Majority Leader Tom DeLay was convicted of money laundering (FoxNews.com, 2010).

Individuals' personal lives are apparently in a state of ethical disarray as well: Approximately 85 percent of surveyed daters admitted having lied to their partners in the previous two weeks (Tolhuizen, 1990), while 74 percent of students admitted to cheating on exams and 84 percent to cheating on written assignments (McCabe & Trevino, 1996). And it isn't only college students who admit to deceiving their partners. In a survey conducted by the National Endowment of Financial Education, 31 percent of respondents confessed to lying to their marital and living partners about money, often with disastrous consequences. To discover the five most common money lies, see *Did You Know? Breakdown of Money Lies*.

Given examples such as these, one may wonder if a communication ethic still exists. We strongly believe that it does. Even if unethical communication is widespread, and some people get away with their misbehavior, most people are still held

Did You Know?

Breakdown of Money Lies

Financial infidelity may be the new normal. In a recent survey, one in three Americans (31%) who have combined their finances admitted lying to their spouses about money, and another one-third of these adults said they'd been deceived.

The online poll, commissioned by ForbesWoman and the National Endowment for Financial Education (NEFE) and conducted by Harris Interactive, surveyed 2,019 U.S. adults. [Among the couples who experienced] financial infidelity, 67% said the deception led to an argument and 42% said it caused less trust in the relationship. Perhaps most alarming, 16% of these respondents said the money lie led to a divorce and 11% said it led to a separation" (Goudreau, 2010).

Breakdown Of Money Lies

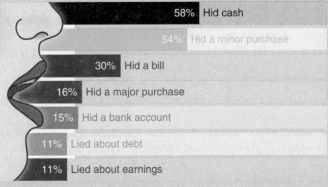

58%	Hid cash
54%	Hid a minor purchase
30%	Hid a bill
16%	Hid a major purchase
15%	Hid a bank account
11%	Lied about debt
11%	Lied about earnings

SOURCE: Goudreau, J. (2010, January 13). Is your partner cheating on you financially? Financially fit. Retrieved February 17, 2011, from **http://shine.yahoo.com/event/financiallyfit/is-your-partner-cheating-on-you-financially-31-admit-money-deception-2439792**

responsible for the messages they create (Barnlund, 1962; Christians & Traber, 1997; Johannesen, 1990). If you spread gossip about your friends, lie to your employer, or withhold information from your family, justifying your behavior by pointing to the ethical failures of others will not excuse you. Those who know you and are close to you still expect you to meet basic standards for ethical communication.

Why are communication ethics so important? First, they sustain professional success. Yes, unethical people may prosper in the short run, but over time unethical practices catch up with the people who engage in them. To a great extent, your reputation as a person of integrity determines whether others want to hire you, work for you, or conduct business with you. Once that reputation is damaged, it can be difficult if not impossible to regain; consequently, communicating and behaving ethically is just good business.

Communication ethics are vital to personal relationships as well. Maintaining intimate and caring relationships can be difficult, but they become virtually impossible if one communicates unethically by lying, manipulating, or verbally abusing friends and lovers. Intimate relationships are grounded in trust. Without trust, people can't be open and vulnerable with one another, behaviors which are essential to intimacy. When one person abuses that trust by his or her unethical conduct, the other party often is deeply wounded and finds it difficult to ever again be intimate within the relationship. Imagine, for example, how Adela's father would have reacted to her proposal to live in the dorms if in the past she had been caught lying to him about spending the night at a friend's house. Far too many people have learned the hard way that a lack of ethics destroys relationships.

As a communicator, you will face many ambiguous and difficult choices of both a professional and a personal nature. If you develop your own set of communication ethics you will be better prepared to face these difficult choices. Therefore, in this section we provide some basic principles of ethical communication for you to consider as you critically review your own ethical standard.

Fundamentally, individuals, groups, and communities develop ethical codes to reflect their beliefs and values. Clearly the guidelines we offer reflect our own communication ethics. We do not expect you to adopt our beliefs wholesale. Rather, we present this information so that you can analyze it critically to determine to what extent it reflects your own beliefs and behavior, what evidence supports it, and what other guidelines may be as useful or more useful for you. Thus, we want you to use your critical thinking skills specifically to critique our claims here and to use that analysis to form your own ethical code.

Defining Your Communication Ethic

Ethics can be defined in a variety of related ways. Most basically, it refers to a system of moral principles by which actions are judged as good or bad, right or wrong. It also has been defined as the rules of conduct recognized by a group, class, or individual; and as a belief system in which the determination of what is right is based on what promotes the most good or the common good. After reading these definitions, which one do you believe is the best explanation? Which one most closely reflects your current perspective?

Communication ethics describes the standards of right and wrong that one applies to messages that are sent and received. When you hear the term *communication ethics*, you might think we are simply referring to whether messages are truthful. Although truthfulness is one of the most fundamental ethical standards, communicating ethically requires much more than simply being truthful. It also involves deciding what information can and should be disclosed or withheld, and assessing the benefit or harm associated with specific messages. Individuals have a responsibility to evaluate the ethics of their own and others' communication efforts. Similarly, corporations ought to weigh the ethics of sharing or withholding information that

What are three specific communication behaviors you believe are unethical? What principles guide your decisions regarding whether a given communication behavior is ethical or unethical?

ethics
standards of what is right and wrong, good and bad, moral and immoral

communication ethics
the standards of right and wrong that one applies to messages that are sent and received

might affect the value of their stock shares, and media companies should decide whether it is ethical to report private information about individuals. Let's look at some of the issues you need to reflect on as you develop your code of ethics.

Truthfulness Truthfulness plays a fundamental role in ethical communication for two reasons: First, others expect messages to be truthful, and second, messages have consequences. Because people inherently expect speakers to be truthful, we actually may make it easier for them to deceive us (Buller & Burgoon, 1996). If an audience is not suspicious, they probably won't look for cues that the speaker is lying (McCornack & Parks, 1986). However, because of the implicit contract to be honest, discovery of deception can severely damage relationships. The more intimate the relationship, the greater the expectation people have that their partners will be truthful, and the more damaging any deception will be.

As we've implied, people rely on messages to be truthful because they have consequences. One's communication can influence the beliefs, attitudes, and behaviors of others. For example, an individual's communication could persuade a customer to purchase an item, a friend to lend money, or an acquaintance to become romantically involved with him or her. The more consequential the outcome of your message, the more likely you will be held accountable to the truth. You might not be criticized too harshly for exaggerating your salary during a flirtation with a stranger, but an employer will most likely consider it unethical if you lie about your salary on a job application.

Sharing or Withholding Information A related fundamental principle of ethical communication concerns what information should be divulged and what can be withheld. When is withholding information a matter of legitimate privacy, and when is it a matter of inappropriate secrecy? Thus, you have to determine whether to tell your romantic partner how many sexual partners you have had; media organizations have to decide whether to reveal the identity of confidential news sources; and physicians have to choose how much information to tell patients about the possible side effects of a prescribed drug.

In our view, a message can be considered legitimately private when other parties have no right to expect access to it. Inappropriate secrecy, on the other hand, occurs when other parties might legitimately expect access to a message that is withheld. This distinction is important because it is generally ethical to maintain privacy, but it may be unethical to engage in secrecy.

What's the difference between privacy and secrecy? We believe communicators have an ethical responsibility to share information that other people require to make informed decisions. For example, if you have only dated someone once or twice, you may choose to keep private that you have a sexually transmitted disease. However, if the two of you consider becoming sexually intimate, you probably have an ethical obligation to reveal the information. Without this information, your partner cannot make an informed decision about whether to engage in sexual contact. What will happen to your relationship if you withhold the information and your partner contracts your disease—and finds out later that you withheld the information? Similarly, your friends may not need to know why you were fired from your last job, but your new boss may have a legitimate need for access to this information.

On the other hand, revealing information can sometimes be unethical. For example, if you have agreed to maintain confidentiality about a topic, it could be considered unethical to reveal what you know. However, if you violate a confidence because of a higher ethical principle, most people would likely consider your behavior ethical. For example, if you have a duty of confidentiality to your employer, but your company engages in illegal toxic dumping, it likely would be more ethical to break

Is it ethical to gossip or share others' private information?

this confidence. Here, the ethic of protecting the public health likely supersedes the ethic of keeping a confidence. These are not easy decisions, but they reflect the type of complex ethical choices that people have to make.

Now that you have read our guideline for differentiating secrecy and privacy, do you find yourself agreeing or disagreeing with it? Can you think of situations in which it would not apply? Can you think of a better principle one could use to make decisions about whether to withhold or reveal information? Again, it is not important that you adopt our guideline but that you think through and develop one that is in line with your own ethical code.

You can begin to think through your position on this issue by exploring an important trend in job searches—the growing use of Internet searches by corporations to gather information on potential or current employees as well as the practice of potential or current employees hiding Facebook information from employers. To do so, see *Communication in Society: Young Job Seekers Hiding Their Facebook Pages.*

When individuals hide information on Facebook, do you believe they are engaging in secrecy or privacy attempts? How would you defend your position to someone who disagrees with you? That is, what evidence and examples would you use to argue for your belief? What arguments might someone make who disagrees

COMMUNICATION IN SOCIETY
Young Job Seekers Hiding Their Facebook Pages

Justin Gawel says there's nothing too incriminating on his Facebook page.

"There are a lot of pictures of drinking [but] nothing naked or anything—at least I don't think so," he said jokingly.

Even so, the Michigan State University junior recently changed his Facebook display name to "Dustin Jawel" to keep his personal life from potential employers while applying for summer internships.

Although Gawel ditched his rhyming alias after two weeks when he realized Facebook users also can be searched by e-mail address, school and network, he is not alone in his efforts to scrub his online résumé. Many students and recent graduates say they are changing their names on Facebook or tightening privacy settings to hide photos and wall posts from potential employers.

And with good reason.

A recent survey commissioned by Microsoft found that 70 percent of recruiters and hiring managers in the United States have rejected an applicant based on information they found online.

What kind of information? "Inappropriate" comments by the candidate; "unsuitable" photos and videos; criticisms of previous employers, co-workers, or clients; and even inappropriate comments by friends and relatives, according to the survey report, titled "Online Reputation in a Connected World."

Such prying into his online life makes Gawel uncomfortable.

"I understand that when [employers look] at someone's Facebook page, they're just trying to paint a bigger picture of the people they're hiring—so they're not just a name on a résumé," he said. "But that doesn't demonstrate whether they can do the job. It shouldn't matter what someone does when they're not in the office."

Gawel said he's not sure that employers would object to the information on his Facebook page. For him, it's more about personal privacy.

"Too many people take pictures of you. I didn't want to go through and 'untag' all of them," he said. "There's nothing illegal or too ridiculous in the photos...but people don't take pictures of people studying or doing school work. They take pictures of people at parties and doing silly things."

For better or worse, online screenings may be a permanent part of the 21st-century hiring process. The Microsoft survey found that 79 percent of U.S. hiring managers have used the Internet to better assess applicants.

SOURCE: Goldberg, S. (2010, March 29). CNN Tech. Retrieved February 21, 2011, from http://articles.cnn.com/2010-03-29/tech/facebook.job-seekers_1_facebook-hiring-online-reputation?_s=PM:TECH

with you? To what extent does the context of Facebook communication influence your response?

Benefit and Harm of Messages To determine the most ethical choice, you also should consider the benefit or harm associated with your messages. A classic example concerns whether it is right to lie to a potential murderer about the whereabouts of the intended victim. A principle of honesty suggests that you should tell the truth. But in this case, once you evaluate the potential harm of sharing versus withholding the information, you might well decide to withhold the information.

More typically, issues of harm and benefit are less clear. For example, if you discover your best friend's romantic partner is being unfaithful, should you share that information? Will it result in more harm or more benefit? If you know that a relative cheated on her taxes, should you report her to the IRS?

Think again about Adela's conversation with her father. If she had told her father that she wasn't accepted at ASU, then he would think she would *have* to live away from home to go to college. In that scenario, she wouldn't have had to worry as much that he would try to persuade her to live at home. However, because honesty in close relationships is part of her ethical standard and she understands the consequences that unethical behavior can have on relationships, she chose to be open and honest with her father regarding her options.

Because many communication events are complex and the underlying ethical principles are not definitive, you will need to gradually develop your own philosophy of ethical communication and apply it on a case-by-case basis. This is one requirement of being an effective communicator. However, just as you develop your own ethical standards and decisions, others will do so as well, which means you and others in your life may not always agree.

Absolutism versus Relativism A fundamental decision in communication ethics concerns how **absolute** or **relative** your ethical standards will be. Will you use the same absolute standards for every communication interaction, or will your ethical choices be relative and depend on each situation? The Greek philosopher Plato and the German philosopher Immanuel Kant conceptualized the absolutist perspective (Kant, 1949), and both believed there is a rationally correct, moral standard that holds for everyone, everywhere, every time. Relativists such as French philosopher Jean-Paul Sartre, on the other hand, hold the view that moral behavior varies among individuals, groups, and cultures. They argue that since there is no universal standard of morality, there is no rational way to decide who is correct (Sartre, 1973).

If you hold to the absolutist perspective that lying is always wrong, then in the earlier example regarding the potential murderer, you would be obligated not to lie about the whereabouts of the intended victim. But if you adhere to a relativistic position regarding truth and deception, you would decide in the moment what the most ethical choice is based on the specific circumstances. You might tell a lie to save a life.

In reality, few people develop an ethical standard that is completely absolute or relative. Instead, absolutism and relativism are the opposite ends of a continuum, and most people's standards lie somewhere along that continuum (see Figure 1.4).

The issue for you is to decide how absolute or relative your ethical standards will be. If you strongly believe that deception is wrong, you may choose the path of deception only when you believe the truth will cause great harm—a standard that

absolute
pertaining to the belief that there is a single correct moral standard that holds for everyone, everywhere, every time

relative
pertaining to the belief that moral behavior varies among individuals, groups, and cultures and across situations

---

FIGURE 1.4: Absolutism versus Relativism
Where would you place yourself on this ethics continuum?

Absolutism ⟵──────────────────────────────⟶ Relativism

falls toward the absolutist end of the continuum. However, if you favor a more relative view, you will consider a variety of factors, in addition to harm, as you make your decisions.

Communication Ethics in Practice

In this discussion of ethics, we have offered guidelines for creating your own communication ethics. However, in practice many situations arise that are ambiguous, complex, and multilayered. At times you may not see how you can be ethical and accomplish important goals at the same time. For example, if you know that a friend and classmate has plagiarized a paper, what should you do? Should you keep quiet and maintain your friendship, or should you maintain your personal ethics and tell the instructor? Similarly, if you are a salesperson, how do you respond if a potential client asks whether a competitor's product is as good as yours, and you believe it is? Do you tell the truth and thus jeopardize a potential sale? People who tend toward an absolutist view say that you must always tell the truth, so you should only sell a product you truly believe is superior. Others may tell you that no one expects salespeople to be completely truthful in this context; therefore, you are not bound to share your opinion (Diener, 2002; Wokutch & Carson, 1981).

Should a salesperson admit that a competitor's product might be as good as the product he or she is selling?

We believe that all communicators need to create an ethical stance based on their own beliefs, values, and moral training. Once *you've* established your ethical stance, you will be prepared to make thoughtful and deliberate communication choices.

For further guidance in creating your own communication ethic, please see *Communication in Society: Making Ethical Decisions*

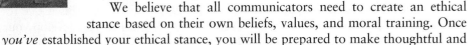

COMMUNICATION IN SOCIETY
Making Ethical Decisions

Making good ethical decisions requires a trained sensitivity to ethical issues and a practiced method for exploring the ethical aspects of a decision and weighing the considerations that should impact our choice of a course of action. Having a method for ethical decision making is absolutely essential. When practiced regularly, the method becomes so familiar that we work through it automatically without consulting the specific steps.

The more novel and difficult the ethical choice we face, the more we need to rely on discussion and dialogue with others about the dilemma. Only by careful exploration of the problem, aided by the insights and different perspectives of others, can we make good ethical choices in such situations.

We have found the following framework for ethical decision making a useful method for exploring ethical dilemmas and identifying ethical courses of action.

A Framework for Ethical Decision Making

Recognize an Ethical Issue

1. Could this decision or situation be damaging to someone or to some group? Does this decision involve a choice between a good and bad alternative, or perhaps between two "goods" or between two "bads"?

2. Is this issue about more than what is legal or what is most efficient? If so, how?

Get the Facts

3. What are the relevant facts of the case? What facts are not known? Can I learn more about the situation? Do I know enough to make a decision?

4. What individuals and groups have an important stake in the outcome? Are some concerns more important? Why?

5. What are the options for acting? Have all the relevant persons and groups been consulted? Have I identified creative options?

Evaluate Alternative Actions

6. Evaluate the options by asking the following questions:
   - Which option will produce the most good and do the least harm? (The Utilitarian Approach)
   - Which option best respects the rights of all who have a stake? (The Rights Approach)
   - Which option treats people equally or proportionately? (The Justice Approach)
   - Which option best serves the community as a whole, not just some members? (The Common Good Approach)

   - Which option leads me to act as the sort of person I want to be? (The Virtue Approach)

Make a Decision and Test It

7. Considering all these approaches, which option best addresses the situation?

8. If I told someone I respect—or told a television audience—which option I have chosen, what would they say?

Act and Reflect on the Outcome

9. How can my decision be implemented with the greatest care and attention to the concerns of all participants?

10. How did my decision turn out and what have I learned from this specific situation?

SOURCE: Markkula Center for Applied Ethics (2010). A framework for thinking ethically. Retrieved March 9, 2010, from **http://scu.edu/ethics/practicing/decision/framework.html**. This framework for thinking ethically is the product of dialogue and debate at the Markkula Center for Applied Ethics at Santa Clara University. Primary contributors include Manuel Velasquez, Dennis Moberg, Michael J. Meyer, Thomas Shanks, Margaret R. McLean, David DeCosse, Claire André, and Kirk O. Hanson.

TEST YOUR KNOWLEDGE
- Why is developing one's own code of communication ethics important?
- What are the three definitions offered for ethics?
- What is the difference between privacy and secrecy?
- What is the difference between an absolutist versus a relativistic view of ethics?

SUMMARY

Studying human communication can enrich and transform your life professionally and personally. *Critical thinking*, which involves reflection and weighing evidence, is a key to successful communication. Communication skills are crucial in developing relationships, establishing identity, and opening career doors.

The *process of communication* involves seven basic components: message creation, meaning creation, setting, participants, channels, noise, and feedback. Communication has been described in the past as a linear process between sender and receiver; more recently a transactional model was introduced. The *Synergetic Model* views communication as a transactional process; it emphasizes that all communication interactions are influenced by the intersection of individual and societal forces, that they are embedded in culture, and that they occur in specific contexts.

The *ethics* of individual communication choices are another essential feature of communication. This is a topic we will return to throughout the book. Key aspects of communication ethics to consider as you make decisions include truthfulness, decisions regarding sharing or withholding information, and the benefit and harm associated with one's choices. Communicators' ethical choices are affected by their position on the continuum of absolutism versus relativism, which in turn influences their language use and how they receive and how they respond to others' communication efforts.

HUMAN COMMUNICATION IN SOCIETY ONLINE

To review this chapter, use the MyCommunicationLab Web site to test your understanding of the following key terms, record your answers to the chapter review questions, and complete the suggested activities. Expand your learning and understanding of chapter concepts by completing additional activities and exercises online. Access code required. Go to www.mycommunicationlab.com for more information or to purchase standalone access.

KEY TERMS

human communication 9
messages 10
encoding 10
decoding 10
symbol 10
content meaning 11
relationship meaning 11

setting 12
participants 12
channel 13
noise 13
feedback 13
Synergetic Model
  of Communication 15

field of experience 17
culture 18
ethics 22
communication ethics 22
absolute 25
relative 25

APPLY WHAT YOU KNOW

1. **Guidelines for Responding to Electronic Communication**
   Much debate has raged over whether it is appropriate to talk on one's cell phone in restaurants, in front of friends, or in the car. The Federal Aviation Administration is considering whether to allow airline passengers to use their cell phones during flights—and many people are already complaining about the possibility. The widespread use of instant text messaging and the ability to access our email almost anywhere have made the issues surrounding the appropriate use of electronic communication even more complex. To focus the discussion and guide your own decisions regarding your responses to these types of electronic communication, develop a list of rules for how, when, and with whom it is appropriate to use the various types of electronic communication.

2. **Creating a Communication Ethic**
   Interview three people and ask them to describe the underlying ethic(s) that guide their communication choices. Then write a brief statement that describes your own communication ethic.

3. **Communication Ethics in the Media**
   Watch television for one evening and observe the number of ethical dilemmas related to communication that people and characters confront. Note their response to each dilemma. How many people/characters make choices that you consider ethical? How many do not? What justifications or reasons do people/characters give for their choices? What consequences, if any, are portrayed? What conclusions can you draw about the portrayal of communication ethics on television?

EXPLORE

1. Make a list of all of the careers that you believe require good communication skills. Then, locate a list of careers from a university career center, such as North Carolina Wilmington's Career Center or Western Washington University Department of Communication's Career Information page, and examine the site's list of careers for which a communication degree prepares students. What careers did you list that are not listed on a university's career website? Why do you think the differences exist? Finally, create a list of careers you would post if you were responsible for creating such a site for your university.

2. Go to the National Communication Association's "Famous People with Degrees in Communication" site. After reading the page, develop a list of at least 10 different careers that famous people have pursued after obtaining degrees in communication. Locate a website that discusses how to develop authentic communication skills, such as the site Authentic Communication or Hodu.com. After reading the suggestions and strategies described on the website, answer the following questions: When are you most likely to lie? What benefits do you think you will accrue if you lie? What can you do to increase how authentic you are when you communicate with others?

2

Perspectives on Human Communication

Nadia and Ben have been together for about a year. While they get along really well most of the time, Nadia has noticed that whenever they have serious disagreements about something, like future plans or how much time they spend with each other's friends, Ben gets really quiet and just doesn't say much. This frustrates Nadia. The more she tries to get him to talk, the quieter he gets. It's getting to the point where they don't seem to even talk about anything where they might have disagreements; as a result, the relationship seems less satisfying for both of them.

Nadia is a communication major, and she's started to wonder about their pattern of conflict communication. Why does Ben get so quiet? Why does it bother her that he doesn't seem to engage in disagreements? Is it because they come from different family backgrounds and each learned different ways of dealing with conflict? Is it a reaction to Nadia, specifically? Are they having more conflict because, with midterms coming up and no employment yet for summer, they both are having a lot of other stresses in their lives?

Nadia does not want her relationship with Ben to end. She starts to think about how best to approach this communication dilemma. She wonders if any of the communication experts and theorists might have suggestions to help her and Ben communicate more effectively.

Believe it or not, these are the types of real-life dilemmas that lead communication professors and scholars to develop theories about everyday communication. Theories are sets of statements that explain a particular phenomenon. In this case, as we'll see in this chapter, there are communication theories that can explain Ben's and Nadia's relationship challenges and could ultimately help them work through their conflicts. In fact, research shows that learning how to manage conflict effectively leads to more satisfying relationships. Communication theories, then, are not just academic exercises; they explain and offer insight into one's own and others' communication (Craig, 1999; Milburn, 2010).

In this chapter, we will explore how communication scholars approach the study of communication and how this systematic study of communication differs from just making theories up out of thin air, or making generalizations from a few personal experiences. You will see that communication scholars do not all agree on how to best approach the study of communication! We'll also address larger questions, such as: how do we know what we know about communication? and how do communication scholars decide what to study in the first place? We want to introduce material that will show you the broad range of communication theories and lead to an exploration of the role of societal and individual forces in the communication process.

In this chapter we'll explain three major theoretical approaches in the communication discipline: the social science, interpretive, and critical approaches. As you will see, social science and interpretive theories take a more individual approach to the study of communication, while the critical takes a more societal approach. To help you understand these three approaches and how they arose, we'll also incorporate some description of the development of the communication discipline.

Once you have read this chapter, you will be able to:

■ Describe the underlying assumptions of three contemporary approaches to the study of communication.

■ Identify theories and methods of each of the three approaches.

■ Identify ethical concerns of each approach.

■ Describe the strengths and limitations of each of these three approaches.

■ Understand the role of paradigm, theory, and methods in communication studies.

■ Describe the major historical influences in communication studies: rhetoric and behaviorism.

CONTEMPORARY APPROACHES TO STUDYING HUMAN COMMUNICATION

How might different communication experts investigate Nadia's communication dilemma? What type of expert information is out there that explains Nadia and Ben's pattern of communication, taking into consideration the larger contexts and forces that might influence their relationship? What type of expert information would *you* trust to provide insight and guidance about interpersonal relationships and the larger contexts?

There are a number of ways to investigate the topic of interpersonal conflict. One might systematically interview men and women about their behavior during conflict, or observe cross-sex couples during conflict in natural settings or laboratories. Or one could even create and test some hypotheses—perhaps speculating that men physically react more negatively to conflict or just can't deal with it. To test this hypothesis, one could measure couples' heart rates, blood pressure, and cortisol levels during conflict interactions. Or one could take a step back and examine Nadia's and Ben's family and cultural backgrounds to discover if these conflict patterns lie not in their individual personalities, but rather in the ways they were each socialized. Or one could study the contexts in which these disagreements occur and identify situational elements that seem to trigger or exacerbate the conflict.

Communication researchers use various approaches and methods to understand human communication.

The ways of investigating we have just described represent three contemporary approaches to studying human communication: the social science approach, the interpretive approach, and the critical approach. Each of these approaches to understanding the situation is actually represented by contemporary scholars conducting real research. Each approach also reflects very different assumptions about the nature of human behavior and the best way to obtain insights and build knowledge about human behavior. And each represents a particular historical tradition, some hundreds of years in the making.

Paradigms, Theories, and Methods

Before we discuss the various approaches to studying human communication, we need to answer a basic question: What do we mean by an *approach*? Each approach represents a belief system, much like a religious system or faith does. In the academic world we call these belief systems **paradigms** (Burrell & Morgan, 1988). Each approach or paradigm carries with it a set of assumptions about knowledge, the nature of reality, and human nature; these assumptions guide research and theory development (Mumby, 1997). For example, most social scientists endorse a paradigm which assumes that reality is external to individuals, that it persists across time and groups, and that one can predict future behavior based on observations of past or present behavior. Therefore, they believe knowledge can be best acquired through observing the behavior of a group of individuals and generalizing from it. Using this approach, one might predict, for example, that males and females will consistently use different strategies to manage conflict across many different conflict situations. Interpretivists, in contrast, assume that reality is socially constructed and, therefore, is internal to individuals and groups; thus it may not be consistent from group to group. They believe they can best acquire knowledge by understanding the perspectives and experiences of individuals and groups, although such knowledge may not be generalizable.

A **theory** is a set of statements that explains a particular phenomenon. Scholars develop theories in an attempt to explain why people communicate as they do. **Methods** describe the specific ways in which scholars collect and analyze data, the results of which are used to test their theories. For example, if researchers wanted to test whether men and women used different types of conflict communication strategies, a method could be to place males and females in conversational groups and ask them to discuss a very controversial topic. Researchers could observe their behaviors over a period of time and determine whether there was a difference in the way males and females approached conflict management. Another method would be to ask the men and women to imagine a conflict situation and then ask them to complete a survey containing questions about how they would prefer to approach the conflict situation. Researchers also use many other types of methods, including interviews, focus groups, and analyses of texts (such as speeches).

How does a researcher decide which method to use? The method depends on her paradigm or approach to the study of human communication. For example, if she believes the best explanations (or theories) of communication behavior come from examining the behaviors of many people, a survey would be the most likely method, allowing her to collect information or data from a lot of people. Scholars often disagree about the virtues or faults of a particular method. Thus, some claim that survey studies have limited usefulness, as they can only tell us how *most* people behave, and not much about an individual person. Others find interview methods inadequate because one cannot easily interview large numbers of people, making universal generalizations very difficult. Like religious belief systems, these paradigms also include ethical beliefs about the right (and wrong) ways to study communication. For example, some scholars find it objectionable to conduct large-scale surveys because they feel that researchers are usually too distant and unfamiliar with the groups they are studying and often do not understand the individuals well enough to adequately interpret the results.

Why do communication experts disagree about the best way to study communication? Part of the reason lies in the fact that the communication discipline is interdisciplinary in nature—its paradigms, theories, and methods have been influenced by different disciplines over the years. The earliest influence was from the study of rhetoric (public speeches), whereas later influences came from the fields of sociology and psychology. The *Did You Know?* feature shows how these disagreements developed and persist to this day.

As a way of understanding the differences among the three contemporary approaches, let us examine how each might view Nadia and Ben's communication dilemma. Before we begin, however, we would like to offer an important caveat. Although we believe that by clearly differentiating each of these three paradigms from the others, we make it easier for you to understand them, the reality is a bit more complex and fluid. Many communication scholars' work does not fit neatly and precisely into just

paradigm
belief system that represents a particular worldview

theory
a set of statements that explains a particular phenomenon

methods
the specific ways that scholars collect and analyze data which they then use to prove or disprove their theories

If you were a communication scholar, which paradigm would you subscribe to? That is, which of the paradigms or approaches best fits your view of reality?

Did You Know?

Major Debates in Communication

The debates about the best way to approach the study of communication are nothing new! You might wonder how these debates got started and where contemporary communication scholars get their ideas about the varying approaches. Below is a brief description of the origin of the debates between social scientists and interpretivists. This history shows that the disagreements today are just a continuation of a discussion that started many, many years ago (Dues & Brown, 2004).

5th century B.C. in Athens, Greece: The first interpretivists were the **rhetoricians** who, like contemporary rhetoricians, believed that the best way to understand humans is to interpret *individual* behavior. Thus, they studied the public-speaking skills of famous speakers in order to determine the most effective public-speaking strategies for specific contexts. They emphasized the creative, artistic aspects of human nature and represented the major study of human behavior for centuries.

Fast forward to 1800s: In order to understand general (universal) patterns of behavior that are likely to be effective, behaviorists believed that researchers should avoid simple interpretation and critique of speakers' skills and rather study speakers' externally observable behavior as well as audience responses. In the behaviorist view, human behavior is deterministic, meaning that individuals react in predictable ways to others and their environment. Therefore, behaviorists systematically observe (and collect) data with the goal of identifying universal laws that govern human behavior. The fields of psychology, sociology, and political science influenced this behavioral approach.

The behaviorist group included the **elocutionists** who promoted the study of the mechanics of public speaking, including proper pronunciation, grammar, and gestures. Anyone who wanted to function effectively in polite society studied elocution, either in a college course or with a private instructor.

The 20th century: The field of communication became a formal discipline in the early 1920s as the debates over paradigms, theories, and methods continued. Professors of rhetoric in the humanist tradition wanted to focus on speech as the art of public address. Professors of elocution, influenced by behaviorist tradition, wanted to study human behavior of speaking as a social science (Bormann, 1980; Cohen, 1994).

As you can see, today's debates over the best approach to study communication have their roots in long-standing differences among these traditions, their preferred methods, and their assumptions about human nature, the best way to pursue knowledge, and even the nature of reality.

---

one of the research paradigms; nor does it follow a single set of research methods. And although these paradigms may have been more clearly differentiated from one another in the early stages of their development, they have evolved over time. Scholars have borrowed from one another, their understanding of the research process has changed, and the differences among the paradigms have become less clearly defined. Some of the paradigms have more internal variations today than when they were originated. To highlight the underlying principles of these three paradigms in our discussion, let's look now at what each approach might have to offer Ben and Nadia.

TEST YOUR KNOWLEDGE

- What are three contemporary approaches to studying communication?
- What is a theory?
- What is a research paradigm?
- Why don't communication scholars agree on the best way to study communication?

rhetoricians
scholars who study the art of public speaking and the art of persuasion

elocutionists
scholars in the 19th century who promoted the study of the mechanics of public speaking, including proper pronunciation, grammar, and gestures

THE SOCIAL SCIENCE APPROACH

The **social science approach** in communication originally focused on the individual or, less frequently, the dyad (a pair of people, like Nadia and Ben, who interact with each other). Because the social science approach grew out of the fields of psychology and sociology, communication scholars typically relied on some of the same research methods used by these social scientists.

Assumptions

Early social science researchers were oriented to **behaviorism**, a branch of psychology that focuses on observable behavior. They believed that the aim of communication research was to describe, predict, and explain human behavior with the ultimate goal of discovering universal laws that apply across situations and contexts. They believed predictions were possible because they saw reality as both observable and describable. So in Nadia's case, the behaviorist view would involve making observations and then formulating predictions for why Ben seems to withdraw. There are a number of social science theories that might explain their conflict patterns. Let's see how this works.

Theories and Methods

Social science researchers generally focus on causality. Thus they seek to determine what factors influence communication behavior. They first make predictions (hypotheses) that came from theories, and then they test these predictions by gathering data through various methods. Common methods include observing subjects in either a laboratory or a **naturalistic** setting (that is, in everyday, real-life situations, such as a classroom, café, or shopping mall), using surveys, and conducting focused interviews.

Once social science researchers collect their data, they use it to confirm or disconfirm their hypotheses about human communication behavior, most frequently through **quantitative methods**. These methods can be used to answer questions such as "how many?" and "what proportion?" That is, researchers convert their data into numerical indicators, and then analyze these numbers using statistics to establish relationships among the concepts.

One area of research that might help explain Nadia and Ben's conflict communication pattern is the **demand-withdrawal** interaction pattern, which has been investigated by communication researchers for more than 50 years. This pattern occurs when one partner criticizes or tries to change the other partner, who responds by becoming defensive and then disengaging—either psychologically or physically (Christensen, 1987; Eldridge & Christensen, 2002).

Communication scholars have conducted many studies that attempted to explain, and predict, how and why this pattern occurs. Whereas most of the research has focused on dyads composed of heterosexual romantic couples, the pattern seems to extend to many different relationships and contexts, and it seems that, as with Nadia and Ben, women are statistically more likely to be the "demanders" who request change from their male partners, while men are more likely than women to withdraw (Christensen, 1987; Christensen & Heavey, 1990; Eldridge, Sevier, Jones, Atkins, & Christensen, 2007).

A variety of explanations have been offered for the observed sex differences in demanding and withdrawing behaviors in relationship conflict, including differences in how men and women are socialized (Christensen, 1987, 1988). However, some scholars disagree and speculate that it's not a question of sex difference, but rather a function of who wants the other person to change. The person who asks for change will be the "demander," which sometimes influences the other person to withdraw.

John Caughlin and Anita Vangelisti (1999) are among a number of communication scholars who have tested this hypothesis. In their study, they asked 57 married couples to discuss some common topics. In previous studies, the conflicts were

social science approach
contemporary term for the behaviorist approach

behaviorism
the focus on the study of behavior as a science

naturalistic
relating to everyday, real-life situations, such as a classroom, café, or shopping mall

quantitative methods
methods that convert data to numerical indicators, and then analyze these numbers using statistics to establish relationships among the concepts

demand-withdrawal
an interaction pattern in which one partner criticizes or tries to change the other partner, who responds by becoming defensive and then disengaging—either psychologically or physically

not naturally occurring, as the couples were often asked to simply recall or specu-late how they *might* react in a conflict. To ensure that the interactions in their study were as natural as possible, Caughlin and Vangelisti observed conversations that took place in each couple's home. The topics of conversation were common con-flict issues: criticism of the other spouse's lifestyle or beliefs, the amount and type of affection in their marriage, disagreements about spending money, how to spend leisure time together, and so on. For each topic, each spouse was asked to indicate how much they would like their partner to change.

The researchers measured the demand/withdrawal behaviors of each spouse in two ways. First, they observed the couple and rated their demands or pressure to change (blaming, demands, nags) and their avoidance/withdrawal behaviors (hesitating, changing topics, diverting attention, and so on) and then converted their observations into numerical data. Second, they asked each spouse to rate their own and their partner's communication on a numerical scale using the same dimensions (demands and pressure to change; avoidance and withdrawal). Third, participants completed a "Communication Patterns Questionnaire" that asked them to make an overall (numerical) assessment of how often they engaged in demand/withdrawal behavior, and how often their spouse did so. Finally, the researchers conducted a sta-tistical analysis on the numerical data and found that gender was not an important factor in the demand/blame interaction pattern. Rather, whoever (male or female) desired the change on a particular topic was also the one blaming and pressuring the other to change; in response, the other spouse would sometimes withdraw.

More recently, other researchers decided to test the same hypothesis using dif-ferent methods aimed at a more comprehensive view of the problem. This team of researchers asked 116 couples to keep "conflict diaries," recording each instance of marital conflict over a period of two weeks and then returning the diary to the researchers at the end of that time (Papp, Kouros, & Cummings, 2009). The participants were trained to record in great detail exactly what occurred in each conflict episode, with respect to demanding, blaming, and withdrawal behaviors. In addition, they also completed several questionnaires measuring their overall conflict resolution level and their sense of well-being in the relationship. After gathering and coding all the information, converting into numerical data, and conducting statistical analyses, these researchers found results similar to those in the earlier study: when one partner raised a conflict issue, made a demand, or cast blame, this resulted in the other partner withdrawing. The results also indicated that this type of communication pattern (demand-withdrawal) is particularly problematic in close relationships—it seems to go hand in hand with negative emotions and destructive tactics that can eventually lead "to a cycle of increas-ingly negative and hostile conflicts" (p. 298). Additional research even suggests that these negative communication patterns have larger societal implications in the form of higher divorce rates (see *Communication in Society: Can Communication Styles Predict Divorce?*).

Other communication theories can help Nadia and Ben understand their con-flict patterns. For example, some communication experts believe there is a relation-ship between the type of **attachment** infants have with their caregivers and their communication patterns later in life. The idea here is that as children interact with their caregivers (parents and others who care for them), they develop expectations for future interactions in relationships in general. Through these initial interac-tions, they come to see themselves as worthy (or unworthy) of love and affections from others (Bartholomew, 1990; Bowlby, 1982; Rholes et al., 2007). In a recent study, communication scholars Craig Fowler and Megan R. Dillow (2011) pre-dicted that individuals who engage in specific types of conflict communication in close romantic relationships—criticism, defensiveness, contempt and stonewalling (withdrawal)—would also have a history of "avoidant attachment." In order to test this prediction, they gave survey questionnaires to 170 individuals who were in

attachment
an emotional tie, such as the close-ness young children develop with their caregivers

COMMUNICATION IN SOCIETY
Can Communication Styles Predict Divorce?

According to a national research project called "The Early Years of Marriage Study," the patterns spouses use to communicate when a conflict arises may have a bearing not only on the quality of their relationship, but on whether the couple ends up divorcing early in the marriage.

A particularly toxic pattern [occurs] when one spouse deals with conflict constructively, by calmly discussing the situation, listening to their partner's point of view, or trying hard to find out what their partner is feeling, for example—and the other spouse withdraws.

"This pattern seems to have a damaging effect on the longevity of marriage," said [University of Michigan] researcher Kira Birditt, first author of a study on marital conflict behaviors and implications for divorce published in the current issue (October 2010) of the *Journal of Marriage and Family*. "Spouses who deal with conflicts constructively may view their partners' habit of withdrawing as a lack of investment in the relationship rather than an attempt to cool down."

The data are from the Early Years of Marriage Study, supported by funding from the National Institute of Aging and the National Institute of Child Health and Human Development. It is one of the largest and longest research projects to look at patterns of marital conflict, with 373 couples interviewed four times over a 16-year period, starting the first year of their marriages. The study is also one of just a few to include a high enough proportion of Black couples that researchers can assess racial differences in conflict strategies and their effects.

Overall, husbands reported using more constructive behaviors and fewer destructive behaviors than wives. But over time, wives were less likely to use destructive strategies or withdraw, while husbands' use of these behaviors stayed the same through the years.

"The problems that cause wives to withdraw or use destructive behaviors early in a marriage may be resolved over time," Birditt said. "Or, relationships and the quality of relationships may be more central to women's lives than they are to men. As a result, over the course of marriage, women may be more likely to recognize that withdrawing from conflict or using destructive strategies is neither effective nor beneficial to the overall well-being and stability of their marriages."

"We hope this study will lead to additional research on the complex dynamics of conflict between husbands and wives, and the potential explanations for changes versus stability in conflict behaviors over time," Birditt said.

SOURCE: Provided by University of Michigan (news : web:) Retrieved March 10, 2011, from http://www.physorg.com/news204909834.html

romantic relationships, measuring their orientations toward anxiety and avoidance and also their criticalness, defensiveness, contemptuousness, and stonewalling.

Their hypotheses were confirmed; the researchers concluded that individuals whose attachment history includes fears of abandonment and rejection also tend to engage in ineffective conflict behaviors with their loved ones that actually increase the chances of their fears of abandonment becoming reality.

There are many other communication studies that could help Nadia and Ben understand their communication patterns. For example, Guerrero, Farinelli, and McEwan (2009) predicted that satisfaction in relationships would be related to partners' particular attachment style and their emotional communication. They gave questionnaires to 581 couples asking about their attachment style, their relationship satisfaction, and how they expressed emotion in the relationship. They found, as predicted, that individuals were most satisfied in relationships with a partner whose attachment style was "secure" and who also tended toward positive emotional communication. Conversely, participants were less satisfied in relationships with partners who had "dismissive" or "preoccupied" attachment styles and who also expressed destructive negative emotions or detached emotional communication,

Is stonewalling or withdrawal in romantic relationships related to a generally avoidant attachment style?

Communication researchers interact with those being researched during the research process.

respectively. It is possible, then, that Nadia and Ben might explore or reflect on their attachment pattern history or how they express emotions in their relationship to understand their communication during conflict situations.

Jess Alberts (1988) studied the effect of couples' relationship satisfaction on their complaint behavior. In her study, she analyzed the types of complaints that happy and unhappy couples made to each other, such as complaints about behavior and complaints about personal characteristics. She then counted how many of each complaint type happy couples used and how many unhappy couples used. Finally, she applied statistical analyses to the resulting numbers to determine which couple type was more likely to use which complaint type. She discovered that happy couples made more complaints about behavior and their partners often responded in agreement, whereas unhappy couples made more personal complaints and their partners tended to respond with countercomplaints. Perhaps Nadia and Ben could examine their own complaint behavior to see if the type of complaints they make lead to conflict or influence their own satisfaction (or dissatisfaction).

As you can see, researchers in the social science approach to understanding communication often use quantitative analysis of surveys and observation; they may also use experiments and focused interviews to gather data. However, they also sometimes use qualitative methods such as conversation analysis, where they examine naturally occurring conversation to understand better the sequences and functions of everyday talk. Here, they do not use statistical analysis or count the number of times a conversational element occurs (as in Jess Alberts' study); rather they are interested in identifying patterns and providing examples of these patterns.

Ethical Issues

Researchers in all three approaches are concerned about the ethical issues involved in conducting communication research—although they may disagree on which issues are the most important (Martin & Butler, 2001). For example, communication researchers in the social science paradigm often follow the long-standing, very specific ethical guidelines of the American Psychological Association—which in turn are based in ethical guidelines established by the medical profession. This code of ethics emphasizes that no harm should be done to research participants. Specifically, *all* participants must be informed about *all* aspects of the research process, including the expected duration of the research, the exact procedures, the right to decline, and all foreseeable consequences of declining, any potential risks, discomfort, or adverse effects of participating in the research, and any potential research benefit. They must also be informed that their privacy and confidentiality will be maintained; they must be told of any limits of confidentiality, if there are any incentives for participation, and who they can contact for additional information or clarification (http://www.apa.org/ethics/code/index.aspx).

For the most part, these guidelines are followed without any problems; however, there are some areas of communication research that involve challenges to these guidelines. For example, some communication researchers study deception in interpersonal relationships—why people choose to deceive their partners and the potential consequences for that deception. Imagine how difficult it is to study deception without deceiving participants involved in the study—something that is explicitly forbidden by the research code of ethics!

Strengths and Limitations

You can see that social science research can be useful in identifying and explaining communication patterns and predicting their effects. However, the social science approach has its limits (as do the other approaches we will discuss). As you probably

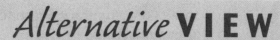

Alternative **VIEW**

Public Deception and Research

Do you think it is ethical for researchers to temporarily deceive participants as part of their research? If not, how do you think researchers should conduct studies that require participants to be unaware of the nature of the study? Do you think it is ethical for reality television to deceive participants in their shows? How are the two contexts similar and different in terms of their uses of deception?

The rape and murder of Kitty Genovese, in which the victim allegedly screamed for 30 minutes while she was brutally raped and stabbed to death, raised questions about why no bystanders or neighbors intervened. In response, Piliavin and Piliavin (1969), realizing that a laboratory experiment with informed consent would not produce accurate enough results, designed an experiment where they would measure "Good Samaritan" behavior upon unsuspecting members of the public traveling in a New York subway train.

A model, either apparently drunk or carrying a cane, would collapse, and the amount of helpful interventions by members of the public would be determined. The results of the experiment determined that people were generally very helpful, although a little more reluctant to help a drunk.

In terms of the ethical code governing deception and research, it could be argued that the experiment could be performed in no other way, as previous attempts showed that if the participants possessed pre-information, and knew that they were being watched, they would be more likely to help as bystanders. The usefulness of the results is also undoubted and unquestionable.

The problem with the experiment is that there was no pre-experimental consent, and the experiment could have emotionally distressed people, either because they thought that somebody was hurt or due to guilt from their failure to help. The fact that there was no psychological evaluation after the experiment, because the participants were unknown, means that this would not be allowed today.

There are some TV shows trying to perform similar experiments, with similar issues of consent, but the producers of these shows are always at least careful to debrief the unwitting participants after the event. Many psychologists consider that these "reality" shows stray across the line governing deception and research.

ADAPTED FROM: Public deception and research. http://www.experiment-resources.com/deception-and-research.html. Retrieved May 13, 2011. Read more: http://www.experiment-resources.com/deception-and-research.html#ixzz1MHtRv67C

---

have realized, human communication is not always predictable, and in particular, predictions based on laboratory research may not hold true outside the lab. Although surveys can provide insight into individuals, beliefs, and attitudes, survey questions cannot fully assess individuals' thoughts and feelings, which are based on a multiplicity of factors and influences, as we described in Chapter 1. In addition, answers to survey questions may be inadequate, particularly for complex issues, because people often provide only short, superficial responses to predetermined questions. One might also argue that when surveys provide a set of answers from which respondents can choose, they are even less likely to tap into their true behaviors, beliefs, and emotions. Critics argue that researchers cannot obtain a full picture if they only measure behavior or if they assess thoughts and feelings only through survey questions.

The social science approach typically has focused on individual forces and their impact on communication without regard for societal forces. For example, social science research can provide useful information about effective strategies for communicating interpersonally, as shown by Ali's observations after attending a workshop on

It Happened to Me: *Ali*

Since I started learning about interpersonal communication, I have become a more assertive and effective communicator. I especially appreciate learning how to use better conflict skills. I know that I can change problems in my life and in other peoples' lives through better listening, which can lead to expressions of care and forgiveness. I think healthy and positive communication can have a huge influence on our day-to-day lives as individuals and as a community.

VISUAL SUMMARY 2.1   Three Contemporary Approaches to the Study of Communication

	SOCIAL SCIENCE (Behaviorism)	INTERPRETIVE (Humanism)	CRITICAL
■ Goal of Research	To describe, predict, and explain behavior	To describe, explain, and understand behavior in context	To describe, explain, and understand society in order to affect change
■ View of Reality	External and describable	Subjective	Subjective and material
■ View of Human Behavior	Complex but predictable	Creative and voluntary	Resistive
■ Primary Methods	Quantitative analysis of surveys, **observation**, experiments, focused interviews	Qualitative analysis of rhetorical texts and ethnographic data (such as **participant observation**, observation, interviews)	Textual analysis, **media analysis**
■ Contributions	Identifies communication patterns and associations among variables	Emphasizes in-depth study of communication	Emphasizes power relations in communication interactions; recognizes societal impacts on communication
■ Limitations	Does not focus on the influence of power or societal forces	Limited number of participants; does not focus on power or societal forces	Does not focus on face-to-face communication

Dealing with Interpersonal Conflict at our university (see *It Happened to Me: Ali*). However, critics say that the social science approach tends to ignore the bigger picture, such as whether relational issues (like interpersonal conflict) are related to particular contexts or are influenced by large societal issues, like structural inequalities (racism, sexism), socioeconomic issues, cultural differences, and forces of globalization, like immigration. Essential elements of the social science approach are shown in *Visual Summary 2.1: Three Contemporary Approaches to the Study of Communication*.

TEST YOUR KNOWLEDGE

- What are the underlying assumptions of the social science approach?
- Identify at least two social science theories that address interpersonal conflict.
- What is the overall guideline for ethical research, according to social science scholars?
- What are the strengths and limitations of the social science approach?

THE INTERPRETIVE APPROACH

Scholars who developed the **interpretive approach** were influenced by the ancient Greek tradition of **rhetoric**, or the art of persuasion, and by **humanism**, a branch of philosophy that celebrates human nature and its potential. Like the social science approach, the interpretive approach focuses on the individual, but interpretive communication researchers have goals and assumptions that differ from those who use the social science paradigm.

Assumptions

The goal of interpretive researchers is to understand and describe individual human communication behavior in specific situations, from the perspective of the communicator. As described in Table 2.1, originating with the ancient Greek rhetoricians, and then the humanists, the interpretive approach has emphasized the creativity, instead of the predictability, of human behavior. Interpretive researchers assume that humans construct their own reality and that researchers must tap into these constructions for a full understanding of human communication.

Theories and Methods

Interpretive researchers generally use qualitative methods for analysis. Rather than reducing data to numbers as quantitative researchers do, interpretivists use qualitative

interpretive approach
contemporary term for humanistic (rhetorical) study

rhetoric
communication that is used to influence the attitudes or behaviors of others; the art of persuasion

humanism
a system of thought that celebrates human nature and its potential

TABLE 2.1	Major Contributions to the Study of Communication
Rhetorical Tradition	
Ancient Greeks	**The power of persuasion**
	Guidelines for effective public speaking
Middle Ages	**Rhetoric established as liberal art**
Renaissance	**Humanism and Enlightenment: foundations of behaviorism**
Behaviorist Tradition	
Nineteenth Century	**Elocution movement: study of proper public speaking**
Twentieth Century	**Rise of behaviorism**
	Establishment of the discipline of communication
	Humanism vs. behaviorism debate

qualitative methods
methods in which researchers study naturally occurring communication rather than assembling data and converting it to numbers

content analysis
approach to understanding communication that focuses on specific aspects of the content of a text or group of texts

data and/or tests to understand how communicators and receivers understand a communication event (Denzin & Lincoln, 2005; Lindlof & Taylor, 2002). These methods—which can answer questions like "what is it like?" and "how does it feel?"—are called **qualitative methods**, as they assess the quality of communication interactions. And rather than manipulating the research situation as one might do in a lab, they tend to study naturally occurring communication.

What type of interpretive studies might help Nadia and Ben understand their communication patterns better? One recent study investigated the nature of defensive communication in romantic relationships. As we will describe in Chapter 5 (Verbal Communication), defensive communication occurs when an individual perceives a threat from another person perhaps due to feelings of inadequacy; the person who feels threatened then may lash out, criticize, and blame the other. In general, defensive communication is unproductive, as it can lead to a cycle of conflict that results in very unsatisfying personal relationships. In order to better understand defensive communication in romantic relationships, communication scholars Jennifer Becker, Barbara Ellevold, and Glen Stamp (2008) conducted in-depth interviews with 50 participants, asking them to recall a conversation with their romantic partner in which they became defensive. The researchers conducted individual interviews with each partner as well as joint interviews with both partners.

In order to analyze the information, they transcribed all the interviews, which totaled 108 single-spaced pages! Unlike researchers in the social science paradigm who categorize the conversational elements and conduct statistical analyses to confirm (or disconfirm) their hypotheses, Becker and her colleagues searched for recurring themes and categories in the interviews in an effort to build a theory of defensive communication that would reflect the reality of the participants' everyday communication. This effort to build a theory based directly on participants' experiences and words is often used by interpretivists; it is called a grounded theory approach (Glaser & Strauss, 1967; Strauss & Corbin, 1998).

This grounded theory approach is a type of **content analysis**—a technique for objectively and systematically identifying specified characteristics of communication messages. For Becker and her colleagues, it involved carefully reading and listening to the interviews over and over again, then developing a framework of categories that grouped, labeled, and summarized particular acts of communication in the data. The researchers systematically compared and contrasted the categories, continually refining them, always with the goal of capturing the actual experiences and views of the participants. Eventually, they developed a theory that outlined the components of defensive communication, as well as what contributes to, and resulted from, defensive communication, and the context of defensive communication.

One of the most useful aspects of the Becker theory for Ben and Nadia (and anyone in close relationships) is a set of four suggestions for how to repair the potential damage caused by defensive communication. These strategies can be used uniquely or in combination.

1. Metacommunication: partners engage in supportive communication by indicating that they understand the other's perspective, relating common experiences, forgiving each other, and engaging in intimacy and behaviors or humor.

2. Apologetic communication: the offending partner apologizes and admits wrongdoing after seeing the damage to the other partner.

3. Partner-centered preventive communication: focuses on preventing future defensive communication—in contrast to metacommunication that involves discussion of a past defensive communication.

4. Avoidance: partners have a brief period of physical or verbal withdrawal to give the couple some time to regain their composure and clarify their thoughts.

Here it is easy to see how theories are not just abstract notions, but also sources of useful insights for improving everyday communication in important relationships.

Ethnographic, or field study, methods are common in interpretive research. In an ethnographic study, researchers actively engage with participants; methods include participant observation, observations, and ethnographic interviewing. During participant observations, the researcher joins the group or community under study. These methods are often used by researchers who are investigating cultures different from their own. For example, communication expert Sheryl Lindsley (1999) spent a year and half in several *maquiladoras* (manufacturing businesses on the Mexican-U.S. border) investigating intercultural interaction and conflicts between Mexican workers and managers and U.S. American managers in the organizations. She spent many hours in the factories, observed the interactions of managers and workers, and conducted in-depth interviews. Her data, then, included her notes and transcriptions, which she analyzed (using content analysis) to discover the themes and categories that characterized the employee interactions. She found that many of the misunderstandings and conflicts were due to cultural differences.

Studying communication can help to identify and understand employee-manager interactions.

In contrast, during purely observational research as in some the studies described earlier, the researcher maintains distance, simply observing participants (for example, couples in conflict) without actually spending a lot of time with the couples.

Communication scholar Donal Carbaugh has conducted a number of interpretive studies in which he describes the communication patterns of Finnish people, Blackfeet Indians, and U.S. residents in varying contexts. For example, using in-depth analyses of ethnographic observations and interviews, he describes the role of silence and listening in Blackfeet communication, the tendency of Finns to be reserved in communication, and the emphasis many in the United States place on speaking for themselves. More importantly, he shows how these communication patterns are inextricably tied to cultural identities in each community (Carbaugh, 1990; 1999; Carbaugh & Berry, 2001). We'll see more examples of these types of cross cultural studies in Chapter 8 (Communication across Cultures).

An important interpretive method is **rhetorical analysis,** in which researchers examine and analyze texts or public speeches as they occur in society. The earliest rhetorical scholars were interested in understanding how a speech affected audiences. These researchers sought to determine the best ways for speakers to construct and deliver speeches so they could affect their audiences in particular ways. Modern researchers also focus on interpreting what texts mean in the settings in which they occur. What do we mean by "the settings in which they occur"? We mean the physical space (e.g., classroom or place of worship) as well as broader environments (e.g., educational versus social; historical versus contemporary) in which the speech or text is delivered.

Researchers who do rhetorical analysis typically do not interact with the speakers or authors of the texts they study, and therefore face different ethical concerns than do ethnographic researchers. Rhetoricians must be especially attentive to accuracy in their depictions of the text and the historical period in which the text occurred.

While rhetoricians typically do not study interpersonal communication, there are some rhetorical studies that relate to gender issues—rhetorical studies that analyze women's contributions through public communication, many of which were unnoticed at the time they were delivered (Borda, 2002; Campbell, 1994; Zaeske, 2002). There are other rhetorical studies related to the issues of interpersonal conflict. One such study was conducted by Jeremy Engels (2009), who focused on the role of "uncivil speech" (invective) and how it functions, then and today, in a democratic society. Engels begins by analyzing a famous speech given by Robert Owen, a well-known philanthropist, on July 4, 1826—the 50th anniversary of the fledgling United States. In this speech, Owen railed against many social institutions, including religion, slavery, and marriage—arguing that all three were a cover for a system of oppression. His speech, "The Declaration of Mental Independence," created so much antagonism and outrage that it is only in retrospect that rhetorical scholars recognized its contribution to society. Owen stated that marriage enslaved women

ethnographic
relating to studies in which researchers actively engage with participants

rhetorical analysis
used by researchers to examine texts or public speeches as they occur in society with the aim of interpreting textual meaning

by making them private property of men; he even championed divorce—utterly unheard of at the time. He was denounced and reviled, called a foreigner and an atheist. However, rhetoric scholar Engels points out that his speech in fact served an important function, as citizens were already anxious about slavery and women's rights and the speech allowed them to transform their guilt into blame on Owen. The "uncivil speech" also provided a common bond, uniting citizens and ultimately affirming a national identity.

Engels goes on to argue that "uncivil speech," which is often used by politicians and commentators on both the conservative and liberal ends of the political spectrum, is central to democracy throughout U.S. history and even today. It fulfills a democratic purpose because it is open to anyone and everyone, and it serves as a way of managing cultural anxiety by making it difficult for people to focus their rage on the real systemic problems in society.

Ethical Issues

For interpretive researchers, particularly those doing ethnographic research, ethical issues go beyond the concern for not harming research participants. Ethnographic researchers strive for equality and reciprocity, a mutual respect in their relationships with participants. Some researchers suggest that an ethical relationship with participants involves being friendly but at the same time maintaining sufficient scholarly distance and disengaging appropriately from participants after the research is completed. Others acknowledge that researchers and participants may become friends during the course of a study and that this relationship then involves a special set of "relational ethics"—a challenge to "act in a "humane, nonexploitative way, while being mindful of our role as researchers" (Ellis, 2007, p. 5).

Another important ethical concern is presenting findings in a way that accurately reflects the views of the participants (González, 2000; Tanno, 1997). To ensure this, researchers often share their interpretations and conclusions with the study participants, a procedure called member-checking (Miller & Crabtree, 2005; Lindlof & Taylor, 2002). Some include their participants in various stages of the research and describe them as co-researchers, rather than subjects or participants (Tanno, 1997).

Strengths and Limitations

The strengths of the interpretive approach include the in-depth understanding it provides of communication in specific situations and the insight it offers into the purposes of those messages. The limitation is that it usually involves few research participants—or none—as is the case in rhetorical analyses of texts. From a social science perspective, its utility is limited because researchers cannot generalize conclusions from such small samples. Thus, it does not help us discover broader laws about human behavior. A second limitation is that the researchers often are outsiders to the communities they study, which means that they may not accurately interpret the communication patterns they see. For example, some studies have concluded that the Amish avoid dealing with conflict, whereas an Amish person might explain that they do deal with conflict, but in a different way—by actively strengthening relationships so that they do not reach the point of open conflict (Kraybill, 2001; Kraybill, Nolt, & Weaver-Zercher, 2010). Essential elements of the interpretive approach are presented in *Visual Summary 2.1* on page 000.

TEST YOUR KNOWLEDGE
- What are the underlying assumptions of the interpretive approach?
- Identify and describe at least two interpretive research methods.
- What is the overall guideline for ethical concerns of interpretive researchers?
- What are the strengths and limitations of the interpretive approach?

THE CRITICAL APPROACH

Both the social science approach and interpretive approach focus on individual behavior, whereas the **critical approach** is much more concerned with how societal forces influence and interact with individual forces—with the ultimate goal of changing society.

Assumptions

In order to reach the ultimate goal of changing society, critical researchers believe that one must understand the societal forces that shape how people come into contact and communicate. The roles that power and hierarchy play in these exchanges must be understood as well. For example, a critical scholar might consider the power differences that exist in everyday interactions between the school custodian and the principal, the refugee and the Red Cross worker, the student and the professor. Critical scholars believe that by examining such interactions and writing about how power functions in them, people gain the awareness they need to resist societal forces of power and oppression.

The critical approach examines power differences such as those between refugees and aid workers.

Cultural studies is one research approach that arises from the critical paradigm. This approach attempts to reveal the complexities of culture and the ways that people actively participate in their culture and resist its powerful influences. Cultural studies scholars believe such resistance might be expressed in a number of ways. For example, factory workers can resist the authority structure of management in many ways, some subtle (e.g., work slowdowns, extending their autonomy) and some more obvious (e.g., whistleblowing) (Mumby, 2005). Communication scholar Angela Trethewey (1997) conducted a critical ethnographic study of a social service organization and found that clients resisted the confining authority structure of the organization in a number of ways, including breaking some of the rules, bitching, and re-visioning, or re-framing, client-social worker relationships. In all these ways of resisting, people find ways to meet their needs and struggle to make relationships and contexts more equitable.

For one of our students, the critical perspective and its focus on uncovering power relations in communication are particularly appealing, as you'll see in *It Happened to Me: Kenneth.*

Like interpretivists, critical scholars believe that reality is subjective, or that we each construct our own reality. However, they also stress that these realities have corresponding material, or physical, consequences—meaning that they have real consequences in people's lives. For example, in the United States we socially construct a reality in which professional athletes are accorded high salaries and power while schoolteachers are not. These social constructions result in real differences in how each group is treated, what each group can buy, and what sacrifices each group must make.

It Happened to Me: *Kenneth*

I had never heard of the critical approach, but I find it kind of interesting. I knew that people weren't treated equally, but it hadn't occurred to me that differences in, say, wealth, education, or attractiveness also can create inequalities and impact communication between people. This is something I intend to pay more attention to.

Theories and Methods

Critical scholars generally use qualitative methods in their research, including both field observation, which we have discussed earlier, and **textual analysis**, a method of analyzing cultural "products" such as media (TV, movies, journalistic essays) and

critical approach
an approach used not only to understand human behavior but ultimately to change society

textual analysis
similar to rhetorical analysis; used to analyze cultural "products," such as media and public speeches

public speeches (in which case they may be called *critical rhetoricians*). Some critical researchers use ethnographic methods, as in the case of the study by Trethewey described above. With these analyses critical scholars seek to understand the influence of societal forces such as the economic, government, and cultural institutions that produce, circulate, and profit from these cultural products. In addition, they may use ethnograhic methods (observation, interviews) to understand how power and privilege affect people's lives. For example, one research project features collaboration between scholars and community members to raise awareness and find solutions to health disparities in minority communities (see *Did You Know? Engaging Through Art and Performance*).

How would critical scholars study interpersonal gender conflict? They would take a broad societal perspective (Litwin & Hallstein, 2007) and might suggest that a female-demand/male-withdrawal pattern is expected in heterosexual romantic relationships because men have traditionally occupied a more privileged position in society and in marriage relationships and therefore would be less likely than women to want to change (Noller, 1993). Conversely, women benefit less from marriage

Did You Know?

Engaging Through Art and Performance

Communication scholar Olga Idriss Davis is part of a research team that works through partnership with community leaders and members with the goal of decreasing health disparities in minority communities in Arizona. Her responsibility is to engage the community in raising awareness and finding ways to promote better health.

Davis, who is trained in rhetoric and theatrical performance, saw an opportunity to combine her two fields of study into one educational and engaging event addressing the weighty issues of "cultural processes in risk and resilience" in minority groups. She put together an event that blended artists and performers (dancers, drummers, singers) with local healthcare professionals using visual and performance art. As she describes it, "The expression of public art is sometimes a better, or alternative, way of educating. Performance art has a way of dispelling boundaries of race, gender, sexuality, class…It's a way of universally connecting humans to humans."

Davis worked closely with some of the artists who performed at this event, helping them to better understand both this concept and the interrelation of art and health. "I had them reflect on the social, political, and cultural issue of health disparities," she said. "Many of them connected through story. They're communicating their life experiences, their relationships, through their visual and performance talents."

In another research project, Davis showed how barbers in African American neighborhoods can serve as information and even intervention centers in the efforts to reduce high blood pressure and heart disease, which are often prevalent in minority communities. The Barbershop Hypertension Screening Program is designed to increase health literacy and knowledge of Black males through high blood pressure screening and referrals.

These projects are both good examples of how scholars, comingling knowledge and action, can work for social change at the grass-roots level.

SOURCES: Engaging through Art and Performance. Retrieved April 20, 2011, from http://community. uui.asu.edu/features/art.asp

Davis, O. I., & Marsiglia, F. F. (2011, June). Cultural catalysts for community dialogues: Black barbers as interventionists in cardiovascular health of African American men. Poster presented at the annual meeting of the Society for Prevention Research, Washington, D.C.

and so are more likely to be the ones to ask for change (more help with household chores, child care, and so on) (Jacobson, 1989, 1990). In one critical study, Elizabeth Suter (2004) explored why, given U.S. women's historical struggle to gain legal and social acceptance, the overwhelming majority of women continue to follow tradition and adopt their husbands' names. In a similar vein, critical scholars Bernadette Calafell and Fernando Delgado (2004) examined the messages that are communicated about Latino identity in *Americanos*, a published collection of photographs of Latina/Latino life in the United States. We will return to a discussion of this study in Chapter 13.

Many critical scholars look to popular texts like films and television to understand male and female roles in society. For example, some Disney characters (the princesses) have been criticized for depicting women in passive roles. On the other hand, Lisa Lazard (2009) analyzes the female characters in horror movies and makes the argument that women in this film genre are often strong.

Some critical scholars have traced the changing roles of men in contemporary U.S. society by analyzing popular movies and books, showing how these movements are responses to societal forces and "crises in masculinities." For example, there was the backlash against the women's movement exemplified by some Michael Douglas films (e.g., *Falling Down*, 1993; *Disclosure*, 1994). Wendy Sommerson (2004) analyzes John Sayles's (1996) film *Lone Star* to explore how a new positive white male type was developing in the 1990s, and notes how this type was represented by Bill Clinton who functioned as the father figure-leader during his presidency. She argues that Clinton's masculinity, open to cultural, national, and racial differences in a positive way, mirrored the political and social realities of the time, as the country was changing to a more transnational multicultural position.

More recently, Helen Shugart (2008) explores the cultural trend of metrosexuality represented by *Queer Eye for the Straight Guy* and the book *The Metrosexual Guide to Style: A Handbook for the Modern Man*—showing that this trend performed a specific, important role in "redressing anxieties inherent in commercial masculinity" as men came to grips with increasing gay social presence, increasing power of women, and decreasing acceptances of traditional macho masculinity.

Another recent critical study examined gender roles portrayed on one of the most popular types of television, the reality show. Asking "how real is reality TV?" critical scholar Dana Cloud (2010) examines male/female role portrayal on one season of *The Bachelor*—where bachelor Brad refused to choose a love interest at the end, which disappointed and irritated a lot of viewers. Cloud shows how this show both reinforces very traditional, retro images of women and men (even the commercials show men as active, women just "there" as objects) and, at the same time, invites the audience to not really take it seriously—as aspects of the show are campy and humorous.

Cloud, like many critical scholars, is not interested in predicting communication or describing communication behavior. Rather, she hopes to educate and illuminate communicators so that, ultimately, they might understand the larger societal impacts (like media) on communicators' attitudes and practices and transform communication to become more just and equitable—a lofty goal for a scholar. Critical scholars look at the larger picture, attempting to see communication in the context of social, political, religious, and historical contexts

Dana Cloud has researched the gender power relationships that are seen in reality TV shows.

(Hill, 2010). To do this, they use a variety of methods, but they often look to media texts. Unlike an interpretivist, who might focus on the specific communication patterns of men and women in various types of relationships and settings, or a social scientist, who might survey large groups of men and women as part of theoretical predictions, a critical scholar always explores the communication in the larger societal contexts.

What insights would these studies contribute to Nadia and Ben's dilemma? How could they help Nadia and Ben understand their relationship better? All these studies attempt to show the relationship between cultural gender roles as represented in popular culture and the political realities—focusing on the intersections of the individual and society. Perhaps Nadia and Ben might gain insights by stepping back and exploring how their own relationship is influenced by societal and cultural gender role expectations and pressures.

Ethical Issues

In analyzing popular texts, critical researchers may have a rather distant relationship to the objects of their study, but they are especially concerned about the way in which they and other scholars present the worldview of others. A key ethical question for them is whether they have the right to study, analyze, and represent other people's views, particularly when crossing racial/ethnic and class boundaries. They point out that many cultural groups—such as Native Americans and the poor—have been exploited and misrepresented by researchers who stood to gain academic rewards by portraying them in certain ways. In the meantime, the communities being researched gained little from their participation (Alcoff, 1991/1992).

Strengths and Limitations

The strength of the critical approach is its emphasis on the importance of economic, political, and historical forces in communication. These factors are largely ignored by the social science and interpretive approaches. A second strength inherent in the critical approach is its acknowledgment of the role of power in communication encounters.

However, a limitation of this approach is the lack of attention to face-to-face interaction by critical researchers who focus primarily on public and media communication such as film, TV, music videos, magazine advertisements, and speeches. So, although critical textual research may help us understand the historical and contemporary roots of sex roles and how contemporary gender images perpetuate stereotypes and may contribute to gender discrimination, it may not help us communicate better in our interpersonal relationships.

Like the interpretive approach, the critical approach relies on qualitative research methods and does not tend to generate generalizable conclusions. For example, in the popular cultural analyses described above, the researchers did not measure viewers' reactions to the various movies and then generalize about all viewers' attitudes toward gender roles. Rather, their essays present *their* analysis of the images and portrayals on the screen, and the validity of their conclusions is based only on the strength of their arguments. The essential elements of the critical approach are presented in *Visual Summary 2.1* on page 000.

Which of the three research approaches we've discussed—the social scientific, the interpretive, and the critical—do you believe is most likely to provide answers to the questions about communication you most would like to have answered? Why? Which do you believe would be least useful for answering your questions? Why?

TEST YOUR KNOWLEDGE
- What are the underlying assumptions of the critical approach?
- Identify at least two critical methods that address conflict.
- What are two ethical concerns of critical researchers?
- What are the strengths and limitations of the critical approach?

A MULTIFACETED APPROACH

We hope that this review of the three major contemporary approaches gives you an idea of the varied viewpoints you will encounter within the field of communication studies. Rather than emphasizing one of the three in this text, we draw from all of them. As shown in *Visual Summary 2.1* on page 40, each approach offers a unique way to view communication, even though those views may sometimes conflict with or contradict each other. This is our position: If you only view a sculpture from one perspective, you can never fully appreciate the work. The same goes for the field of communication studies.

Three Perspectives on Communication

If you want to be able to view the communication process, like a sculpture, from various perspectives, you need to understand and be able to recall the essential contributions each research approach offers. Here is a brief explanation of each approach:

- The social science approach seeks snapshots of certain communication phenomena and from them attempts to find universal laws that explain human communication.

- The interpretive approach uses content analysis, ethnographic field studies, and rhetorical analysis to take a more individualized, specific look at human communication.

- The critical approach seeks to uncover the element of power that exists in every interaction and to use communication analysis to effect social change.

FIGURE 2.1 The Synergetic Model

According to the Synergetic Model of Communication, what are some of the specific influences in the communication situation depicted here? In your answer, consider factors such as societal forces, culture, field of experience, relationship, context, and noise.

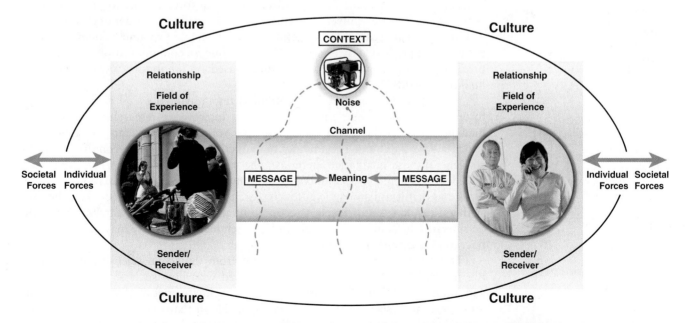

This review of the research paradigms illustrates the way that these three approaches have guided communication research. Our understanding of the communication process flows from all three research approaches, and from this we have formulated the synergetic model of communication, which we presented in Chapter 1. The synergetic model's focus on societal factors evolved from the critical approach, whereas its inclusion of individual forces reflects the influence of the social science and interpretive approaches.

Despite differences in the various communication models and research approaches, individual communicators play a key role in all of them. Therefore, like Nadia and Ben, in order to have a complete understanding of communication, communicators need to understand how individuals' identities influence and are influenced by communication. They also need to understand how individual and societal forces act together to affect identity development. Each communicator is unique because of the ways in which individual and social forces together create individual identities. In turn, these identities influence how individuals communicate and how others communicate with them. We explore the question of identity and communication in Chapter 3.

TEST YOUR KNOWLEDGE

- Why is it important to draw from all three research approaches in studying communication?
- What does each research approach contribute to the synergetic model of communication?

SUMMARY

Currently there are three research paradigms (belief systems) in communication research today. Each approach or paradigm carries with it a set of assumptions about knowledge, the nature of reality, and human nature, and these assumptions guide research methods and theory development. Theory is a set of statements that explains a particular phenomenon. Methods describe the specific ways in which scholars collect and analyze data, the results of which are used to test their theories. The social science approach emphasizes individual forces, seeks to predict human behavior, emphasizes universal theories, and generally uses quantitative research methods. This approach can be useful in identifying and explaining communication patterns and predicting their effects. However, human communication is not always predictable, and in particular, predictions based on laboratory research may not hold true outside the lab.

The interpretive approach also emphasizes individual social forces but seeks to understand, not predict, human behavior. Interpretive researchers assume that humans construct their own reality and that researchers must tap into these constructions for a full understanding of human communication. Interpretive researchers generally use qualitative methods. The strengths of the interpretive approach include the in-depth understanding of communication in specific situations, but it is limited in that it usually involves few research participants—or none—as is the case in rhetorical analyses of texts. A second limitation is that the researchers often are outsiders to the communities they study, which means that they may not accurately interpret the communication patterns they see.

The critical approach is very different from the social science and interpretive perspectives as it is much more concerned with how societal forces influence and interact with individual forces—with the ultimate goal of changing society. In order to change society, critical researchers believe that one must understand the societal forces that shape how people come into contact and communicate. The role that power and hierarchy play in these exchanges must be understood as well. The strength of the critical approach is its emphasis on the importance of economic, political, and historical forces in communication and its acknowledgment of the role of power in communication encounters.

Critical scholars generally use qualitative methods, often conducting textual analysis in which they analyze cultural "products" such as media (TV, movies, journalistic essays) and even speeches (in which case they may be called *critical rhetoricians*). In addition, they may use observations or ethnographic methods to better understand how power and privilege affect people's lives. A limitation of this approach is the lack of attention to face-to-face interaction by critical researchers who focus primarily on public and media communication; as such it may not help us communicate better in our interpersonal relationships.

These three approaches combine to form the foundation for our synergetic model of communication. The synergetic model's focus on societal factors evolved from the critical approach, whereas its inclusion of individual forces reflects the influence of the social science and interpretive approaches.

HUMAN COMMUNICATION IN SOCIETY ONLINE

To review this chapter, use the MyCommicationLab Web site to test your understanding of the following key terms, record your answers to the chapter review questions, and complete the suggested activities. Expand your learning and understanding of chapter concepts by completing additional activities and exercises online. Access code required. Go to www.mycommunicationlab.com for more information or to purchase standalone access.

KEY TERMS

paradigm 33	behaviorism 35	humanism 41
theory 33	naturalistic 35	qualitative methods 42
methods 33	quantitative methods 35	content analysis 42
rhetoricians 34	demand-withdrawal 35	ethnographic 43
elocutionist 34	attachment 36	rhetorical analysis 43
social science	interpretive approach 41	critical approach 45
approach 35	rhetoric 41	textual analysis 45

APPLY WHAT YOU KNOW

1. Find five examples of the word *communication* in popular magazines and newspapers. How is the word being used in those forms? What are some of the different meanings for communication?

2. Identify a common communication topic (e.g., deception, teamwork, intimacy, credibility). How would researchers from the three different paradigms investigate this topic? What would be the general goal of each researcher? What would each emphasize in the investigation? What type of research methods might each use to conduct her or his investigation? What might be the ethical concerns of each? (Hint: Use the information presented in *Visual Summary 2.1: Three Contemporary Approaches to the Study of Communication*.)

3. Locate a journal article and an article in a popular magazine that report on the same communication issue from a social science perspective. How was the issue presented in each? What are the strengths and weaknesses of each article? What are the strengths and weaknesses of a social science approach to this topic? (Hint: Use the information presented in *Visual Summary 2.1: Three Contemporary Approaches to the Study of Communication*.)

3
Communicating Identities

When I'm talking with Americans and ask about their nationality, the answer is usually about ethnicity: "I'm Swedish" or "I'm Polynesian and French." Rarely does anyone answer, "I'm American." In my many travels around the world, I have noticed that the U.S. is the only country whose people fail to understand that their national identity is, in fact, U.S. American. I am nationally an American, and ethnically I am Chinese, Syrian, and Ukrainian. As an Asian American who grew up in New Jersey, I feel culturally tied to my national identity, whereas I merely feel influenced by my ethnic cultural identities.

—Mike

When you think about identity, you may be pondering who you "really" are and how you got to be that way. Do you feel, like Mike, that your national identity is a major determinant of who you are? Or do you feel that your ethnic identities are also a strong influence? What about your gender, religious, and social class identities? Mike notes that he is an "Asian American"; it's true that China, Syria, and Ukraine are all in Asia, but do you think of those ethnicities when you think of Asian Americans? Mike also says he is from New Jersey. How do our regional identities influence who we "really" are? Can you choose to be whomever you want, or do your background and social environment determine who you are? In this chapter we address these identity questions as well as the important role communication plays in them.

As we discussed in Chapter 1, communication is a deeply cultural process. In this chapter we explore how individual characteristics, such as gender and age and the societal meanings associated with them, interact to create cultural identities—and the important role communication plays in that development. Within cultures, communication patterns, habits, values, and practices develop around specific individual characteristics such as race, gender, sexuality, age, social class, and religion. For example, in the United States, people commonly understand that it is not acceptable to tell racist or sexist jokes, particularly in the workplace, at job interviews, and in other formal settings. This understanding exists because people are aware of the impact of this type of communication on people's identities. We all possess many cultural identities, as we identify with genders, races, ethnicities, religions, organizational affiliations, schools, and so on. Some of these identities affect our communication experiences more than others. In this chapter we explain which identities are most influential and why. We also examine how societal forces influence identity and discuss ethical issues associated with communication and identities. We conclude by looking at some skills for communicating about identities.

Once you have read this chapter, you will be able to:

■ Identify five reasons identity is important to communication.

■ Define *identity*.

■ Clarify how reflected appraisals, social comparisons, self-fulfilling prophecies, and self-concept contribute to identity development.

■ Describe how social forces influence the communication of identity.

■ Identify examples of racial, national, ethnic, gender, sexual, age, social class, disability, and religious identities.

■ Discuss three ethical considerations for communicating in a sensitive manner to and about others' identities.

■ Explain three ways to communicate more effectively about identities.

THE IMPORTANCE OF IDENTITY

Identity has a tremendous impact on the communication process in a number of ways. How we communicate, as well as how our communication is received by others, can be shaped by our identities and the identities of others. Let's look at some of the ways that identity influences communication. First, because individuals bring their self-images or identities to each communicative encounter, every communication interaction is affected by their identities. For example, when elderly people converse with teenagers, both groups may have to accommodate for differences in their experiences and language use.

Second, communication interactions create and shape identities (Hecht, 1993). If older adults treat teenagers with respect and admiration during their conversations, these young people may view themselves as more mature and more valuable than they did previously. Conversely, communication can also be used to denigrate other identities and create tension between groups. It is always important to think about the impact of communication on various identity groups.

Third, identity plays an important role in intercultural communication, something that has become increasingly common in our global, technology-based world. As more and more businesses have international branches and subsidiaries, workers are increasingly likely to have contact with people from other cultures. The more familiar they are with the values related to identity in these cultures, the better prepared they will be to succeed in today's society.

Fourth, understanding identity is useful because so much of U.S. life is organized around and geared toward specific identities (Allen, 2004). In the United States we have television stations such as *Black Entertainment Television* and *Telemundo* and magazines like *Ebony* and *More*, which are targeted to groups based on their race, age, and/or sex. We also have entertainment venues such as Disneyland and Club Med that are developed specifically for families, romantic couples, and singles. In this identity-based climate, individuals often communicate primarily with others who share their identities. Consequently, learning how to communicate effectively with individuals whose identities vary from yours may require considerable thought and effort.

Finally, identity is a key site where individual and societal forces come together to shape communication experiences. Although we each possess identity characteristics such as social class or nationality, the society where our communication takes place will define the meanings of those characteristics. For example, depending on whether you are in the United States or visiting a country where anti-American sentiment is common, what it means to be an "American" can have different nuances. Moreover, we cannot separate our identities—as individuals or as members of society—from our communication experiences. Identity is vital to how meaning is created in communication (Hecht, 1993). We explain this interaction more fully throughout this chapter.

TEST YOUR KNOWLEDGE

• List five advantages to understanding the relationship between communication and identity.

WHAT IS IDENTITY?

When you enrolled in college, you were most likely required to provide a piece of identification, such as a birth certificate, passport, or driver's license. Identity is tied closely to identification; it refers to who you are and the specific characteristics that make you different from other individuals. In communication studies, *identity* includes not only who you are but also the social categories you identify yourself with and the categories that others identify with you. Society creates social categories such as *middle aged* or *college student*, but they only become part of one's identity when one identifies with them or others identify you in these categories. For example, you may think of yourself as short, but others may classify you as being of average height. Many young people in their late teens and early twenties identify with the category *college student*, but a growing number of people in their thirties, forties, and even older are also returning to school and identifying with this category. The many social categories that exist can be divided into two types; *primary* and *secondary identities* (Loden & Rosener, 1991; Ting-Toomey, 1999). Primary identities are those that have the most consistent and enduring impact on our lives, such as race, gender, and nationality. Secondary identities, such as college major, occupation, and marital status, are more fluid and more dependent on situation.

> **identity**
> who a person is; composed of individual and social categories a person identifies with, as well as the categories that others identify with that person

To help define the term **identity**, let's examine its essential characteristics. The first characteristic is that identities exist at the individual and the societal levels. Jake Harwood (2006) explains this concept: "At the individual (personal identity) level, we are concerned with our difference from other individuals, and the things that make us unique as people. At the collective (social identity) level, we are concerned with our group's differences from other groups, and the things that make our group unique" (pp. 84–85). For example, if you are an athlete, and you are thinking about how you are different and unique from others who are not athletic, then you are focusing on part of your individual identity. If you are focusing on how your sports team is different and unique from other sports teams, then you are focusing on your social identity.

We should note that identities are not necessarily only individual or social; they can be both, depending on the situation. How is this contradiction possible? Let's look at an example. Many readers of this text are U.S. Americans, and their national identity is part of their social identity. Because they are surrounded by others from the United States, they may not be conscious of this as being part of their individual identity. But if they travel abroad, their national identity becomes part of their individual identity because this significant characteristic will differentiate them from others.

A second important aspect of identity is that it is both fixed and dynamic. Again, this seems like a contradiction. If you think about it, however, you will realize that certain aspects of our identities, although stable to some extent, actually do change over time. For instance, a person may be born male, but as he grows from an infant to a boy to a teenager to a young man to a middle-aged man and then to an old man, the meanings of his male identity change. He is still a male and still identifies as a male, but what it means to be male alters as he ages, and social expectations change regarding what a boy or a man should be (Kimmel, 2005).

A third characteristic of identity is that individual and social identities are created through interaction with others. The relationships, experiences, and communication interactions we share with others shape how we see ourselves. For example, people who travel abroad and then return home may experience stress, but they also experience growth and change—and communication with those they meet as they travel plays a key role in both (Martin & Harrell, 1996). As another example, in the 1960s and '70s, many American women became more aware of, and dissatisfied with, their social identity as wives and mothers. This prompted them to become involved in a larger social movement known as feminism, in which women organized and attended "consciousness raising" groups designed to alter how they

Our relationships with others help us understand who we are and how others perceive us.

perceived and performed their identities as females. Women in these groups were encouraged to think of themselves not primarily as wives and mothers but as the professional and social equivalents of men. This type of mobilization of women also occurred earlier in history, when they organized to gain the right to vote. It also happened for others—both women and men—who organized to protest against racial discrimination. In these instances a common social identity brought people together into communities, and these communities in turn acted to improve the position of the particular social identity in society.

A fourth consideration is that identities need to be understood in relation to historical, social, and cultural environments. The meaning of any identity is tied to how it has been viewed historically and how people with that identity are situated in a given culture and society (Hecht, Jackson, & Ribeau, 2003; Johnson, 2001). For instance, throughout history, we have had varied notions of what it means to be female (Bock, 1989).

Although Cleopatra was an Egyptian Pharaoh and Joan of Arc led the French army into battle in the fifteenth century, these individual women were significant exceptions to the rule. In their times and for much of history, women have been perceived as intellectually inferior, physically delicate, and/or morally weak when compared to men. Because of these beliefs, in many cultures women were denied voting and property rights and even custody of their children in the event of divorce. For example, until 1881, upon marriage, English women's legal identities were subsumed by their husbands such that all of their property and wealth transferred to their spouses as well as their right to enter into any contracts (Erickson, 1993). In the United States, women didn't win the right to vote until 1920—and, more recently, Supreme Court Justice Antonin Scalia has argued that the U.S. Constitution "does not, in fact, bar sex discrimination" (Cohen, 2010).

Contemporary U.S. American women have all of the legal rights of men, yet historical conceptions of women still affect how they are positioned in society today. For example, on average women earn 82.8 percent of men's median weekly pay (Cauchon, 2010). While this gap is closing because the recent recession has had a greater impact on men's jobs than on women's, the gap reflects the lower value traditionally placed on women's work. Moreover, a number of religions still remain opposed to women serving as ministers and priests. The situation for women in other cultures can be even more challenging. In Saudi Arabia, although women make up 70 percent of those enrolled in universities, they compose just 5 percent of the workforce; their testimony in court is treated as presumption rather than fact; and they live mostly segregated lives (Azuri, 2006). Thus, a hierarchy exists across cultures in which one identity (male) is preferentially treated over another (female). You can probably think of other examples in which preferential treatment was given—or denied—based on race, sexuality, religion, social class, or age (Allen, 2004).

In sum, identity is key to understanding communication, and communication is key to understanding identity. As Abrams, O'Connor, and Giles have stated, "identity and communication are mutually reinforcing" (2002, p. 237).

TEST YOUR KNOWLEDGE

- How do individual and societal forces influence our understanding of identity?

THE INDIVIDUAL AND IDENTITY

Although it can be tempting to boil a person's identity down to one word—say, *nerd, jock,* or *sorority girl*—in reality, everyone is more complex than that. If you had to pick only one word to describe yourself and you had to use it in every situation—personal and professional—what word would you choose? For most people this task is impossible, for we all see ourselves as multidimensional, complex, and

Alternative **V I E W**

Census in India Includes a Third Gender Choice

As the official record of a nation's population, what information should any census seek? What categories should the census use?

The United States is just one of many countries that conduct a census at regular intervals. Census forms typically ask for basic personal data like age, race, and gender. In 2000, the U.S. census made history by allowing respondents to check multiple race/ethnicity categories. In the 2010 census, the form was designed to "give the nation's more than 308 million people the opportunity to define their racial makeup as one race or more" (El Nasser, 2010).

The 2011 census in India also made history, as its new census form gave respondents the option of answering the question about their gender identity with either "Male," "Female," or "Other." In India, individuals who are biologically male and adopt female gender identity are considered a third gender known as *hijra*; they face severe discrimination in mainstream Indian society (Venkat, 2008). The 2011 census will "give India a firm count for its 'third-gender' hijra community—the origins of which go back millennia to a time when transsexuals, eunuchs and gays held a special place in society backed by Hindu myths of their power to grant fertility" (Daigle, 2011).

To view a copy of the 2011 census form for India, see: **http://www.censusindia.gov.in/2011-Schedule/Shedules/ English_Household_schedule.pdf**

To view a copy of the 2010 census form for the United States, see: **http://2010.census.gov/2010census/about/ interactive-form.php**

---

unique. People in the United States, especially, are invested in the notion that they are unique. Twins often go to great lengths to assure people that they are *not* the same. Perhaps the most famous example of this is the Olsen twins, Mary-Kate and Ashley. Mary-Kate dyed her hair dark so she would look less like her sister, and when the sisters received a star on Hollywood's Walk of Fame, they requested that they be given separate stars (a request that was denied). Like almost everyone, they recognize and value their uniqueness—and they would like others to do so as well (see *Did You Know? Famous Twins Just Want to Be Individuals*).

Did You Know?

Famous Twins Just Want to Be Individuals

Are you a twin, or do you know any twins? When you communicate with twins, are you careful to differentiate them and their identities? Do you think parents, teachers, and other adults should treat twins differently from non-twins during their formative years?

Mary-Kate: "As you get older, you create your own identity;"
Ashley: "It's not like we're forcing our own identities. It's who we are; our own styles are coming through, and other people are just realizing we're two separate people" (Arnold, 2004).
Mary-Kate and Ashley: "If you can respect us as businesswomen, and powerful young ladies, respect us also as individuals" (Crane, 2004).

Most twins strive to differentiate themselves from one another (Sprainsack & Spector, 2006), whether that means dressing differently or pursuing disparate hobbies and careers. However for famous twins, developing separate identities is a greater challenge than for most. Celebrity twins Mary-Kate and Ashley Olsen, James and Oliver Phelps (who play the

Twins often go to great lengths to assure people they are *not* the same.

(continued)

Did You Know?   *(continued)*

Weasley twins in the *Harry Potter* movies), and Dylan and Cole Sprouse (of Disney's *The Suite Life of Zack and Cody*) all became famous either playing twins or playing the same character on television and in movies. Because their professional identities are so closely connected, people often forget that they have the same needs as "singletons" to be seen as unique and individual. Consequently, they have to remind us—and remind us again—that they are.

Sources: Arnold, T. K. (2004, April 28). Just call them the Olsen "individuals." *USA Today*, 8.

Crane, R. (2004, April 30). Interview: Mary-Kate and Ashley from "New York Minute." *Cinema Confidential*. Retrieved from www.cinecon.com/news.php?id=0404301

Sprainsack, B. & Spector, T. D. (2006). Twins: A cloning experience. *Social Science and Medicine*, 63, 2739–2752.

How is it possible that people who are as much alike as twins can still have distinct identities? It is possible because of the ways in which identities are created and how these identities are "performed" in daily life—the topics we take up in the next section.

Identity Development Through Communication

In communication, our understanding of identity development arises out of a theory called symbolic interactionism (Blumer, 1969; Mead, 1934). According to this theory, individuals' meanings for the objects, actions, and people around them arise out of social, or symbolic, interaction with others. What you define as beautiful, ethical, and even edible is based on what you have heard and experienced during your interactions with others. You likely learned through observing and communicating with others that eating lobster is a luxury but that eating bugs is disgusting. We develop and reveal identities through communication interactions in much the same way. In this section we describe three communication processes involved in identity development—*reflected appraisals*, *social comparison*, and *self-fulfilling prophecies*—and explore how they shape one's sense of self, or self-concept.

Reflected Appraisals A primary influence on identity development is a communication process called **reflected appraisals** (Sullivan, 1953). The term describes the idea that people's self-images arise primarily from the ways that others view them and from the many messages they have received from others about who they are. This concept is also often referred to as the **looking-glass self** (Cooley, 1902; Edwards, 1990), a term that highlights the idea that your self-image results from the images others reflect back to you.

The process of identity development begins at birth. Although newborns do not at first have a sense of self (Manczak, 1999; Rosenblith, 1992), as they interact with others, their identities develop. How others act toward and respond to them influences how infants build their identities. For example, as infants assert their personalities or temperaments, others respond to those characteristics. Parents of a calm and cheerful baby are strongly drawn to hold and play with the infant, and they describe the child to others as a "wonderful" baby. On the other hand, parents who have a tense and irritable baby may feel frustrated if they cannot calm their child and might respond more negatively to the infant. They may engage in fewer positive interactions with their baby and describe the child as "difficult." These interactions shape the baby's identity for him or herself and for the parents, as well as for others who have contact with the family (Papalia, Olds, & Feldman, 2002).

A study of shy and reticent male toddlers explored the influence that parents can have on their sons' interactions (Phelps, Belsky, & Crnic, 1998). The researchers found that parents who encouraged their sons to interact with others and to take social risks became less reserved over time; when parents did not encourage their sons in this way, however, the children maintained their shy and reticent nature. As this

reflected appraisals
the idea that people's self-images arise primarily from the ways that others view them and from the many messages they have received from others about who they are

looking-glass self
the idea that self-image results from the images others reflect back to an individual

study shows, parental communication influences how children behave and ultimately how they, as well as others, view them.

The reflected appraisal process is repeated with family, friends, teachers, acquaintances, and strangers as the individual grows. If as a child you heard your parents tell their friends that you were gifted, your teachers praised your classroom performance, and acquaintances commented on how verbal you were, you probably came to see yourself those ways. However, if family, friends, and acquaintances commented on how you couldn't "carry a tune in a bucket" and held their ears when you sang, then over time you likely came to view yourself as someone who couldn't sing. Through numerous interactions with other people about your appearance, your abilities, your personality, and your character, you developed your identities as a student, friend, male or female, or singer, among others. To read about one student's experiences with reflected appraisals, see *It Happened to Me: Bianca.*

Interaction with two types of "others" influences this process of identity development. George Herbert Mead (1934) described them as *particular others* and the *generalized other*. **Particular others** are the important people in your life whose opinions and behavior influence the various aspects of your identity. Parents, caregivers, siblings, and close friends are obvious particular others who influence your identity. Some particular others may strongly influence just one of your identities or one aspect of an identity. If you perceive that your soccer coach believes you have no talent, then you may see yourself as a poor soccer player even if friends and family tell you otherwise.

Your sense of yourself is also influenced, however, by your understanding of the **generalized other,** or the collection of roles, rules, norms, beliefs, and attitudes endorsed by the community in which you live. You come to understand what is valued and important in your community via your interactions with significant others, strangers, acquaintances, various media such as movies, books, and television, and the social institutions that surround you. For example, if you notice that your family, friends, and even strangers comment on people's appearances, that the media focus on people's attractiveness, that certain characteristics consistently are associated with attractiveness, and that people who look a certain way seem to get lighter sentences in criminal proceedings, get more attention at school, and are hired for the best jobs, then you develop an internalized view of what the generalized other values and rewards with regard to appearance. You then will compare yourself to others within your community to see if you fulfill the norms for attractiveness, which then affects how this aspect of your identity develops.

Gradually, you begin to see yourself in specific ways, which in turn influences your communication behavior, which further shapes others' views of you, and so on. Thus, individual identities are created and re-created by communication interactions throughout one's life. (See *Communication in Society: Reflected Appraisals Affect All of Us—Even the Rich and Famous.*)

However, reflected appraisals aren't the only type of communication interaction that shapes identity. Each of us also engages in a process called *social comparison*, which influences how we see and value our identities.

It Happened to Me: *Bianca*

I really relate to the concept of reflected appraisals. I was born in Brazil with an Italian mother and a Brazilian father. When I attended an all-girls private school in Cleveland, Ohio, I had a very difficult time blending in. After spending so much time with these other students, however, I gradually began feeling like one of them. I was speaking English all the time, even at home with my parents (whose first language is not English). I felt like I was an American. People communicated to me as an American. In my junior year, I moved back to Brazil. Being Brazilian and speaking Portuguese fluently, their reflections of me made me feel completely Brazilian and I began to lose my sense of American identity. Even today, at a U.S. college, I feel confused about my selfhood because of the different ways I am reflected off of people depending on which nationality group I am hanging out with.

Children's self-images are affected by their teachers' reflected appraisals.

particular others
the important people in an individual's life whose opinions and behavior influence the various aspects of identity

generalized other
the collection of roles, rules, norms, beliefs, and attitudes endorsed by the community in which a person lives

COMMUNICATION IN SOCIETY

Reflected Appraisals Affect All of Us—Even the Rich and Famous

How does the looking-glass self explain successful people's low self-esteem and poor self-concepts? Why do you think their significant success does not change how they feel about themselves? How do the concepts significant other *and* generalized other *apply in the examples discussed in the article below?*

Though it may seem unlikely, many famous, beautiful and/or talented people suffer from negative self-concepts. Kate Winslet has admitted that before going off to a movie shoot, she sometimes thinks, "I'm a fraud, and they're going to fire me... I'm fat; I'm ugly..." (Eby, 2009). Michael Jackson spoke often in interviews about his poor self-concept, and many people have attributed his multiple plastic surgeries to his poor self-concept. Perhaps no famous person has spoken more openly about his low self-esteem than Mike Myers. He once told an interviewer that when he sees himself on the big

screen, he sees "a guy with a really thick Canadian accent and acne scars—that's about it" (Rottenberg, 2008).

What accounts for the negative self-concepts of these talented and attractive people? Although Winslet has never spoken about the causes of her feelings, she has remarked on the fact that magazines and reporters at times have commented unfavorably on her body size and weight. Both Myers and Jackson revealed that their parents and other family members made fun of and denigrated them. Jackson revealed that his brothers made fun of his appearance, particularly his nose, and he claimed his father treated him harshly. Famously, Myers told an interviewer, "My mom would say... 'Everyone in the house step forward who's funny. Not so fast, Michael' " (Rottenberg, 2008).

As these examples suggest, success, wealth and fame are no guarantee that individuals will feel happy and satisfied with who they are.

SOURCES: Eby, D. (2009, April 6). Actors and self-esteem-boosting self confidence. Retrieved from ezinearticles.com/?id=2199637
Rottenberg (2008, June 20). Karma chameleon. *Entertainment Weekly, 998*, 38–43.

Social Comparisons Not only do we see ourselves as possessing specific characteristics, we also evaluate how desirable those characteristics are. As we discussed, the generalized other becomes the basis for our understanding of which characteristics are valued. For example, Amish children learn through their interactions with family, friends, the church, and their community that aggression is a negative trait that one should minimize or eliminate (Kraybill, 1989). In contrast, in gangs, aggression is valued and encouraged, and community members learn this as well (Sanders, 1994).

Once we understand what characteristics are valued (or disdained) in our communities, we assess whether we individually possess more, or less, of them than do others in our communities. We compare ourselves to others to determine how we measure up, and through this social comparison, we evaluate ourselves. In this way the groups we compare ourselves to—our reference groups—play an important role in shaping how we view ourselves.

We compare ourselves to others in our identity group and decide how we rate. A woman might say, "I look good for my age," comparing herself to others in her reference group, which in this case is other women her age. Similarly, classmates often want to know each other's test scores and grades so that they can decide how to view their own performances. For example, how would you feel if you earned a 78 on an exam and your grade was the highest in the class? What if 78 were the lowest grade in the class? Thus, your evaluation of yourself and your abilities is shaped not only by a specific trait but also by how it compares to the traits of others in your reference group. However, your self-evaluation can vary depending on what you use as a reference group. If you compare your appearance to that of your friends, colleagues, and classmates, you may feel pretty good. However, if you use the idealized images of actors and models in magazines and movies, you may not feel as positively about your attractiveness.

We compare ourselves with others in our reference group and decide how we measure up.

Self-Fulfilling Prophecy Communication interactions can also influence one's identity through a process known as the **self-fulfilling prophecy**, meaning that when an individual expects something to occur, the expectation increases the likelihood that it will. For example, if you believe you can perform well on an exam, you are likely to study and prepare for the exam, which typically results in your doing well. Others also have expectations for you that can influence your behavior. For example, if your sales manager believes you are a poor salesperson, she may assign you to a territory where you won't have access to big accounts, and she may refuse to send you to sales conferences where your skills could be honed. If you still succeed, she may believe that you just got lucky. However, because you have a poor territory, don't have the opportunity to enhance your sales skills, and receive no rewards for your successes, you probably will not be a very good salesperson.

Thus, the belief in a particular outcome influences people to act and communicate in ways that will make the outcome more likely; in turn, the outcome influences how we perceive ourselves. For example, parents often unwittingly influence how their children perform in math and how their children perceive themselves as mathematicians. If a child hears her mother complain about her own poor math skills and how unlikely it is that her child will do better, the child is unlikely to succeed in math classes. When the child encounters difficulty with math, the messages she heard from her mother may increase the likelihood that she will give up and say, "Well, I'm just not good at math." On the other hand, if a child hears messages that she is good at math, she is more likely to keep trying and work harder when faced with a difficult math problem. This, in turn, will influence her to see herself as a competent mathematician.

Self-fulfilling prophecies can have a powerful effect on an individual's performance, especially when they are grounded in stereotypes of one's identity. For example, stereotypes exist that Asian students excel at math, that African American students are less verbally competent than white students, and that females are worse at math and spatial reasoning than males. Studies have shown that even subtly or implicitly reminding individuals of these stereotypical expectations can impact their performance, a concept called **stereotype threat.**

In one study, African Americans who were simply reminded of race performed significantly worse on a verbal exam than when the issue of race was not mentioned (Steele & Aronson, 1995); and in another study, Asian American students performed better on a math test when reminded of their race (Shih, Pittinsky & Ambady, 1999). In a similar study, females who were cued to think about gender performed worse on math and spatial ability tests than when the issue of gender was not raised (McGlone & Aronson, 2006). Yet another study found that white male engineering students solved significantly fewer problems when told that they were part of a study to examine why Asian Americans perform better in math than when told it was simply a timed test (Smith & White, 2002).

These studies reveal that individuals' performances can be enhanced or hampered when they are reminded, even implicitly, of expectations related to important identities. This is true not only of sex and gender but also has been shown to be true of socioeconomic status (Croizet & Claire, 1998) and age. These findings remind us that we need to be careful about creating self-fulfilling prophecies for others and allowing others' expectations to become self-fulfilling prophecies for us.

Through repeated communication interactions such as reflected appraisals, social comparisons, and self-fulfilling prophecies, we come to have a sense of who we are. This sense of who we are is referred to as one's *self-concept*.

Self-Concept As we have suggested, identity generally continues to evolve; at the same time, individuals also have some fairly stable perceptions about themselves. These stable perceptions are referred to as self-concept. **Self-concept** includes your understanding about your unique characteristics as well as your similarities to, and

self-fulfilling prophecy
when an individual expects something to occur, the expectation increases the likelihood that it will

stereotype threat
process in which reminding individuals of stereotypical expectations regarding important identities can impact their performance

self-concept
the understanding of one's unique characteristics as well as the similarities to, and differences from, others

differences from, others. Your self-concept is based on your reflected appraisals and social comparisons. However, reflected appraisals only go so far. When someone describes you in a way that you reject, they have violated your self-concept. For example, if you think of yourself as open and outgoing, but a friend calls you "a very private person," you are likely to think the friend doesn't know you very well. Thus, your self-concept is an internal image you hold of yourself. It affects the external image you project to others, and in turn, your self-concept influences your communication behavior. If you think of yourself as ethical, you may correct others or assert your views when they behave in ways you believe are unethical.

Self-esteem is part of an individual's self-concept. It describes how you evaluate yourself overall. It arises out of how you perceive and interpret reflected appraisals and social comparisons. Like identity, self-esteem can alter over time. It functions as a lens through which we interpret reflected appraisals and social comparisons, which may make it hard to change. For example, if you have relatively high self-esteem, you may discount negative reflected appraisals and overgeneralize positive ones. So, if a student with high self-esteem fails an exam, he may attribute the failure to external factors (e.g., the test was unfair) rather than to himself. On the other hand, a person with low self-esteem may see negative reflected appraisals where none exist and may consistently compare herself to unrealistic reference groups. In addition, this person is more likely to attribute a failure to the self (I'm not smart enough) than to external factors.

Because self-esteem is such a powerful lens through which you see the world, your self-concept may not be entirely consistent with how others see you. Several additional factors can create a mismatch between how you see yourself and how others do. First, your self-image and the feedback you receive may be out of synch because others don't want to hurt your feelings or because you respond negatively when faced with information that contradicts your self-image. Few people tell their friends and loved ones that they are not as attractive, talented, smart, or popular as they themselves think they are. Why? They don't want make others feel bad and/or they don't want to deal with the recipient's feelings of anger or sadness.

Second, if you hold onto an image of yourself that is no longer accurate, you may have a distorted self-image—or one that doesn't match how others see you. For example, if you were chubby in grade school, you may still think of yourself as overweight, even if you are now very slim. Similarly, if you were one of the brightest students in your high school, you may continue to see yourself as among the brightest students at your college, even if your GPA slips.

Finally, people may not recognize or accept their positive qualities because of modesty or because they value self-effacement. If your social or cultural group discourages people from viewing themselves as better than others, you may feel uncomfortable hearing praise. In such cases, the individual may only compare himself to exceptionally attractive or talented people or may refuse to acknowledge his

strengths in public settings. In Japanese culture the appearance of modesty (*kenkyo*) is highly valued (Davies & Ikeno, 2002). A similar trait of "yieldedness to others" (*glassenheit*) leads the Amish to downplay their accomplishments (Kraybill, 1989). As you can see, both culture and identity are deeply embedded in our communication.

Yet another aspect of self-concept is self-respect. While self-esteem generally refers to feeling good about one's self, **self-respect** describes a person who treats others—and expects themselves to be treated—with respect (Rawls, 1995). Self-respect demands that individuals protest the violation of their rights and that they do so within the boundaries of dignity and respect for others. However, people with high self-esteem may not necessarily have self-respect (Roland & Foxx, 2003). For example, some people with high self-esteem may not treat others with respect or respond to violations of the self with dignity. Many atrocities, such as those committed by Saddam Hussein against his people, have been waged by those who, because of their sense of superiority, thought they had the right to dominate and harm others.

Communication plays an important role in how we develop our self-concept.

Throughout this discussion of identity development we have focused on four separate constructs: reflected appraisals, social comparison, self-fulfilling prophecy, and self-concept. However, identity development is a circular process in which these constructs are interrelated. For example, reflected appraisals influence your self-concept, which affects your communication behavior, which in turn shapes how others see you and, ultimately, what they reflect back to you. Then the process starts all over again. To view an illustration of this process, see *Visual Summary 3.1: Identity Development Through Communication*. The issue of identity goes beyond this complex process of development, however. In everyday life we enact or "perform" these identities. Let's see how this process works.

self-respect
treating others, and expecting to be treated, with respect and dignity

performance of identity
the process or means by which we show the world who we think we are

Performance of Individual Identity

The **performance of identity** refers to the process or means by which we show the world who we think we are. For example, many Green Bay Packers fans express their identity by wearing team colors, calling themselves Cheeseheads, and wearing plastic cheese wedges on their heads. In contrast, Pittsburgh Steelers fans often wave "the terrible towel" to cheer on their team. People also perform their identities in more subtle ways every day—with the type of clothing or jewelry (including wedding rings) that they choose to wear or the name they use. Some celebrities have taken stage names that the public is more familiar with than their legal, birth names. For example, Larry King was born Larry Zieger. Charlie Sheen's name is Carlos Estevez. Lady Gaga's real name is Steffani Germanotta. What do these different names communicate to the public? How do these names help these celebrities perform their public identities?

Communication style is another way people perform, or enact, their identities. For example, do you speak to your mother in the same way that you speak with your friends? If you bring a friend home, do you feel like a different person as he watches you communicate with your family? If so, you're not alone. Most people adapt their communication to the identity they wish to perform in a given context.

We show the world who we think we are through the performance of identity—in this case, identity as Green Bay Packers fans.

In fact, the branch of communication studies called performance studies focuses on the ways people perform, or communicate, their various roles. In other words,

VISUAL SUMMARY 3.1   **Identity Development Through Communication**

Reflected Appraisal (The Looking-Glass Self)

Social Comparisons

Self-Fulfilling Prophecies

How I see myself is developed through communication with others . . .

- Interactions with parents and others shape our early identity and sense of self.
- The process is repeated with family, friends, teachers, acquaintances, and strangers.
- **Particular others** are important people in our lives who influence aspects of our identity.
- **Generalized others** are the collection of roles, rules, norms, beliefs, and attitudes endorsed by our community.

and how I compare myself to others . . .

- Through our interactions with others, we learn what characteristics are valued (or disdained) by others.
- Then, we assess whether we have more or fewer of those characteristics to determine how we measure up to others in our **identity group**.

each of which affects my evaluation of myself.

Self-Concept

affects how I communicate with them and they with me . . .

- When we expect something to occur, that expectation increases the likelihood that it will.
- A belief in a particular outcome influences people to act and communicate in ways that make the outcome more likely.
- Others can also cause their prophecies about us to come true by communicating with us as though they will come true.

Self-Concept

- Self-concept is composed of the fairly stable perceptions we have of ourselves.
- It includes our understanding of similarities and differences between ourselves and others.
- It is an internal image we have of ourselves and affects the external image we project to others.

- It influences our communication behavior.
- **Self-esteem** is the part of self-concept that is the internal valuation of what we see in the looking glass.
- **Self-respect** the extent to which one feels entitled to regard and respect from self and others.

people **enact identities** by performing scripts that are proper for those identities. In his analysis of how tourists tell stories about their trips, Chaim Noy of the Hebrew University of Jerusalem identifies the ways that tourists perform their identities. As a part of this performance of identity, tourists emphasize the ways that their travels have changed their identities and how they view the world. While tourists are often viewed as consuming or watching other cultural identities on performance, Noy underscores the ways "that tourists are in effect acting protagonists who perform on the stages of tourism" (2004, p. 116). For example, in his study, Noy tells the story of a backpacker who tells others of his adventures and performs a form of tourism: "I told everyone of my adventures and so I was a kind of an attraction. It was nice" (qtd. in Noy, p. 130). Through the use of narrative in his communication, this backpacker is able to perform an identity of a tourist who has seen and experienced something special.

Nadene Vevea (2008) analyzed how people use tattoos and body piercing to perform their identities. In her interviews, she found that people use body art for many different reasons, to communicate many different feelings. For example, "some of the fraternity brothers who responded to my survey all got matching tattoos to signify their membership but use body art as a positive connection between friends to show loyalty to one another" (p. 22).

Sometimes we enact family roles; other times we enact occupational roles. The enactment of identity is closely tied to one's movements into and out of different cultural communities and one's expectations regarding particular roles. Police officers, physicians, and teachers also enact particular roles in performing their occupations. If one of these professionals—say, a teacher—steps out of the appropriate role and tries to be the best friend of her students, problems can arise. In Minnesota, a physician "has been reprimanded for allegedly touching 21 female patients inappropriately during what were described as 'unconventional' medical exams" (Lerner, 2008). In this case, "Dr. Jed E. Downs, 51, reportedly would close his eyes and make 'unusual sounds or facial expressions' while examining female patients, according to an investigation by the Minnesota Board of Medical Practice" (Lerner, 2008). In this case, we expect physicians to communicate—verbally and nonverbally—in professionally appropriate ways. When the physician does not do this, problems can arise.

Thus, we perform various roles and communicate with others based on **role expectations.** If you are pulled over for a traffic violation, you expect the police officer to perform in a particular way. In turn, you communicate with the officer based on a prescribed script. If you do not enact the expected role or if the police officer does not enact the prescribed role, then confusion—or worse—can occur. Everyone carries many scripts with them into all kinds of interactions. For example, the authors of this book are all pet owners. When we speak to our pets, we sometimes repeat communication patterns that our parents used with us when we were children. Pets are not children, yet we often communicate to them as if they were because the script is familiar to us.

As we noted earlier, identities are **mutable,** or subject to change. When people change identities, they also change the way they perform them. For example, as people age, if they perform the "grown-up" role appropriately, they hope others will treat them more like adults. If they don't change the way they behave, then they might be told to "stop acting like a child."

Because identities are not fixed, sometimes you see mismatches between the performance of identity and any one identity category. Sometimes the difference between identity performance and identity category can be rather benign. For example, if we say that someone is young at heart, we are saying that we perceive that person's identity performance to resemble that of someone much younger in years. Thus, two people may be the same chronological age, but one may listen to contemporary music, watch current films and television shows, and dress according to the latest fashion trends. The other may listen to oldies radio stations and dress as she did years ago.

enacting identities
performing scripts deemed proper for particular identities

role expectations
the expectation that one will perform in a particular way because of the social role occupied

mutable
subject to change

Sometimes this disconnect is viewed much more negatively. When people enact a gender identity at odds with the cultural identity category, such as when males perform identity scripts that are typically female, they may be ridiculed, ostracized, or worse. Still, how do particular identity categories, or ways of performing them, acquire meaning? How do you know what a particular category is supposed to "look like" or how it is to be performed? The answer has to do with societal forces, the subject we take up next.

TEST YOUR KNOWLEDGE

- What are the key concepts in identity development?
- How is identity performed?

THE INDIVIDUAL, IDENTITY, AND SOCIETY

The development of individual identities is influenced by societal forces. Therefore, you cannot understand yourself or others without understanding how society constructs or defines characteristics such as gender, sexuality, race, religion, social class, and nationality. For example, as a child, you were probably told (some of) the differences between boys and girls. Some messages came from your parents, such as how boys' and girls' clothing differs or how girls should behave as compared with boys. Other messages came from your schoolmates, who may have told you that "they" (either boys or girls) had "cooties." You may also have picked up messages about gender differences, or about any of the identity categories mentioned, from television or other media. By combining messages from these various sources you began to construct images of what is considered normal for each identity category.

Many parents choose clothes that communicate the gender of their babies.

Communication scholars are particularly interested in how identities are communicated, and created, through communication. For example, in his work focusing on communication interactions, Donal Carbaugh (2007) is particularly interested in studying intercultural encounters, and he focuses on how communication interaction reveals insights into cultural identities.

When people enact identities that are contrary to social expectations, they may be pressured to change their performance. Thus, boys and girls who do not perform their gender identities in ways prescribed by society can be called "sissies" or "tomboys." People who do not perform their racial identities in ways that are expected are sometimes called "oreos," "apples," "coconuts," "bananas," or "race traitors." Although the Church of Jesus Christ of Latter Day Saints has banned the use of alcohol, those Mormons who do drink are sometimes called "Jack Mormons." Similarly, a person who does not perform heterosexuality as expected might be seen as gay or lesbian. Chaz Bono, son of Cher and Sonny Bono, has spoken publicly about his decision to transition from female to male starting in 2009. In 2011, the film, *Becoming Chaz,* and the book, *Transitions,* both were released and tell Chaz's story of gender change from Chastity Bono.

Those who do not conform to expected social communication or performance patterns may become victims of threats, name-calling, violence, and even murder (Sloop, 2004). These aggressive responses are meant to ensure that everyone behaves in ways that clearly communicate appropriate identity categories. For example, after a lengthy lawsuit, Shannon Faulkner became the first woman to enroll at the Citadel, South Carolina's formerly all-male military college. During the time she attended the school, she received death threats and had to be accompanied by

Did You Know?

Performing Identity: Chaz Bono

What difference does it make who you think you are and who others think you are? How much of your identity is a feeling that you have about who you are?

In his own words, Chaz Bono describes the difficult journey of transitioning from female to male. Communication plays a key role in this transition.

I always felt like the male from the time I was a child. There wasn't much feminine about me. I believe that gender is something between your ears not between your legs. That is something I discovered in the early 90s. It was just a long process of being comfortable enough to do something about it. I was turning 40 and I thought it's now or never. I want to still feel vibrant and be able to enjoy my life in a male body and not wait until I am an old man....I will be changing for about four to five years in total but I'll be on testosterone for the rest of my life....The nice thing about this process is it is slow. I am literally going through puberty....The most important thing about this for me is that my outsides are finally starting to match my insides. I feel like I'm living in my body for the first time and it feels really good (Chaz Bono opens up, 2009).

federal marshals (Bennett-Haigney, 1995). Thus, some groups in society have strong feelings regarding how identities should be performed, and they may act to ensure that identities are performed according to societal expectations.

In this section of the chapter we will look at a range of primary identity categories. (See *Visual Summary 3.2: Dimensions of Self* to review the most salient identity categories for most people.) Note that each is a product of both individual and societal forces. Thus, whatever you think your individual identity might be, you have to negotiate that identity within the larger society and the meanings society ascribes to it.

Racial Identity

Despite its frequent use, the term *race* is difficult to define. Historically, races were distinguished predominantly by physical aspects of appearance that are generally hereditary. A race was defined as a group with gene frequencies differing from those of other groups. However, many physical anthropologists and other scholars now argue that because there is as much genetic variation among the members of any given race as between racial groups, the concept of race has lost its usefulness (Hirschman, 2003). For more on this contemporary view of race, based on the new tools of DNA analysis, refer to *Alternative View: DNA and Racial Identity*.

Despite the difficulty in accurately delineating the various races, race is still a relevant concept in most societies, and individuals still align themselves with specific racial groups, which we discuss next.

Racial identity, the identification with a particular racial group, develops as a result of societal forces—because society defines what a race is and what it is called. This means that racial categories are not necessarily the same from country to country. For example, unlike the United States, the United Kingdom does not include people of Chinese origin in the category it calls Asian. For those in the United Kingdom, only those of Indian, Pakistani, and Bangladeshi origin are considered to be Asian. The Office for National Statistics has established racial categories for England and Wales and posted them on its Web site at www.ons.gov.uk/about-statistics/classifications/archived/ethnic-interim/presenting-data/index.html.

racial identity
identification with a particular racial group

VISUAL SUMMARY 3.2   **Dimensions of Self**

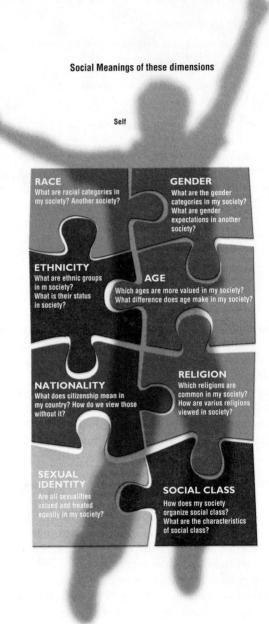

Social Meanings of these dimensions

Self

RACE
What are racial categories in my society? Another society?

GENDER
What are the gender categories in my society? What are gender expectations in another society?

ETHNICITY
What are ethnic groups in m society? What is their status in society?

AGE
Which ages are more valued in my society? What difference does age make in my society?

NATIONALITY
What does citizenship mean in my country? How do we view those without it?

RELIGION
Which religions are common in my society? How are varius religions viewed in society?

SEXUAL IDENTITY
Are all sexualities valued and treated equally in my society?

SOCIAL CLASS
How does my society organize social class? What are the characteristics of social class?

Even within the United States the categorization of racial groups has varied over time. The category *Hispanic* first appeared on the U.S. census form as a racial category in 1980. In the 2000 census, however, Hispanic was categorized as an ethnicity, which one could select in addition to selecting a racial identity. Therefore, one could be both *Asian* (a race) and *Hispanic* (an ethnicity), or one could be both *white* (a race) and *Hispanic* (again, an ethnicity). Similarly, as Susan Koshy (2004) has noted, people from India were once labeled "non-white Caucasians," but today are categorized with

Alternative **VIEW**
DNA and Racial Identity

Would you want to have DNA testing to find out more about your racial heritage? How might it change how you see yourself? Would it change your identity?

"Every year," I once overheard my father say jokingly to a friend, "thousands of Negroes disappear." I remember my 8-year-old imagination going into overdrive, picturing people zapped from their homes in the middle of the night. It was only as I grew older that I realized that the people my father was talking about were *choosing* to disappear, running away from their families, not being taken from them. They were light-skinned blacks who could move into the white world undetected, denying their blackness and the exclusion they suffered in a white-dominated America.

I've been thinking of my father's joke a lot recently. It came back to me last month when scientists reported the discovery of a genetic mutation that led to the first appearance of white skin in humans. Reading about it, I wondered how it is that a minor mutation—just one letter of DNA code out of 3.1 billion letters in the human genome—is so highly prized that it has led scores of people to turn their backs on their families and has served to divide people for generations. Discovery of this mutation, combined with recent findings that all people are more than 99.9 percent genetically identical, has reinforced my belief that race is almost entirely a social demarcation, not a biological one.

Just a month earlier, I'd also recalled my father's joke as I listened to a group of students in a race relations class at Penn State University discuss the results of DNA testing that revealed the complicated strands of their racial backgrounds. Most were surprised by what they learned. African American students expected to find some European ancestry in their DNA, but were surprised at the extent of it. White students, on the other hand, were startled that they had either traces or significant amounts of DNA in common with their African American classmates. According to Mark Shriver, professor of genetics and anthropology at the university, DNA testing reveals that 5 percent of white Americans have some African ancestry and 60 percent of black Americans have white bloodlines.

This type of DNA analysis is becoming increasingly popular among people who do genealogical research, particularly blacks who want to identify their tribal roots in Africa. But I have to wonder: Is it just another manifestation of America's obsession with race? Or can it be used to help us move beyond that obsession?

SOURCE: "DNA Is Only One Way to Spell Identity," by W. Ralph Eubanks, as appeared in *The Washington Post*, January 1, 2006. Reprinted by permission of the author.

Asian Americans on the U.S. census. These categorizations are important because historically they have affected the way people are treated. While discrimination based on race is no longer legal, we continue to live with its consequences. For example, although slavery ended almost 150 years ago in the United States, many churches, schools, and other social institutions remain racially segregated (Hacker, 2003).

Although people often think of racial categories as scientifically or biologically based, the ways they have changed over time and differ across cultures highlight their cultural rather than their biological basis. How cultures describe and define specific races affect who is considered to belong to a given race and, consequently, how those individuals are treated. As anthropologist Gloria Marshall explains: "Comparative studies of these popular racial typologies show them to vary from place to place; studies of these popular racial classifications also show them to vary from one historical period to another" (1993, p 117). Moreover, communication is a strong factor in furthering, affecting, or altering racial categories and identities to serve different social needs. For example, Guzman and Valdivia (2004) studied the media images of three Latinas—Salma Hayek, Frida Kahlo, and Jennifer Lopez—to see how gender and Latinidad are reinforced through the media (see Chapter 11). Face-to-face communication also influences peoples' ideas about racial identities. If individuals have little contact with people of a different racial group, it is especially likely that one or two encounters may lead them to draw conclusions about the entire group.

multiracial identity
one who self-identifies as having more than one racial identity

national identity
a person's citizenship

ethnic identity
identification with a particular group with which one shares some or all of these characteristics: national or tribal affiliation, religious beliefs, language, and/or cultural and traditional origins and background

Beginning with the 2000 census, the U.S. government has allowed people to claim a **multiracial identity** (Jones & Smith, 2001). This category recognizes that some people self-identify as having more than one racial identity. So, how should we categorize Barack Obama? While "there is much to celebrate in seeing Obama's victory as a victory for African Americans," writer Marie Arana (2008) also thinks that "Obama's ascent to the presidency is more than a triumph for blacks." She feels that "Barack Obama is not our first black president. He is our first biracial, bicultural president." What difference does it make if we see Obama as our first African American president or as our first biracial president? As you think through this issue, you can see the complexities of race and racial politics within a culture.

National Identity

Racial identity can often be confused and conflated with **national identity.** We often misuse the notion of nationality when we ask someone "What's your nationality?" but what we really want to know is their ancestry or ethnic background. *Nationality* or national identity refers to a person's citizenship. In other words, Madonna's nationality is not Italian, but U.S. American, as she holds U.S. citizenship. John F. Kennedy's nationality was not Irish; he was a U.S. citizen. Many U.S. Americans did not actively choose their national identity; they simply acquired it by being born in the United States. Although many of us have not actively chosen our national identity, most of us are content with—or even proud—of it.

Like our other identities, the importance placed on national identity can vary, depending on many factors. In their study of national identity, John Hutcheson et al. (2004) found that U.S. Americans communicated a much stronger sense of national identity after September 11, 2001. Do you remember seeing many U.S. flags flying in your neighborhood after September 11? This resurgence of national identity was reflected in the media as well.

Because the ability to travel has made the world seem so much smaller and borders seem more permeable, old ideas of national identity may no longer apply. For example, what does it mean to be Irish? In one study, Vera Sheridan (2004) traced the journey of Vietnamese refugees who moved to Ireland to become Irish citizens. Although they may not meet our expectations of what Irish people look like, their nationality is now Irish.

However, as communication scholars Laura Lengel and John T. Warren (2005, p. 5) remind us, "nation does not equal culture or cultural identity; it is merely one facet." Thus, identifying someone's nationality provides a glimpse of only one aspect of their cultural identity, which is both communicated to them, communicated by them, and communicated about them.

Ethnic Identity

Although race and ethnicity are related concepts, the concept of ethnicity is based on the idea of social (rather than genetic) groups. Ethnic groups typically share a national or tribal affiliation, religious beliefs, language, and/or cultural and traditional origins and background. A person's **ethnic identity** comes from identification with a particular group with which they share some or all of these characteristics. Thus, some U.S. citizens say that they are Irish because they feel a close relationship with Irish heritage and custom, even though they are no longer Irish citizens—or perhaps never were. Likewise, in the United States many U.S. Americans think of themselves as Italian, Greek, German, Japanese, Chinese, or Swedish even though they do not hold passports from those countries. Nonetheless, they feel a strong affinity for these places because of their ancestry. Unlike national identity, ethnic identity does not require that some nation's government recognizes you as a member of its country. It is also unlike racial identity, in that any racial group may contain a number of ethnic identities. For example, people who are categorized racially as white identify with a range of ethnic groups, including Swedish, Polish, Dutch, French, Italian, and Greek.

In other parts of the world, ethnic identities are some-times called tribal identities. For example, "in Kenya, there are 50 tribes, or ethnic groups, with members sharing simi-lar physical traits and cultural traditions, as well as roughly the same language and economic class" (Wax, 2005, p. 18). Tribal identities are important not only across Africa, but also in many nations around the world, including Afghanistan (Lagarde, 2005). In some societies, tribal or ethnic identity can determine who is elected to office, who is hired for particular jobs, and who is likely to marry whom. In Malaysia the three major ethnic groups are Malay, Indian, and Chinese. Since the Malay are in power and make decisions that influence all three groups, being Malay gives one an important advantage. In the United States, however, the ethnic identities of many white Americans are primarily symbolic, as they have minimal influence in everyday life (Waters, 1990). Even if ethnic identity does not play an important role in your life, it can carry great significance in other parts of the world.

When people enact a gender identity at odds with the cultural identity category, they may be ridiculed, ostracized, or worse.

Gender Identity

Similar to race, gender is a concept constructed through communication. *Gender* refers to the cultural differences between masculinity and femininity, while *sex* refers to the biological differences between males and females. Gender describes the set of expectations cultures develop regarding how men and women are expected to look, behave, communicate, and live. For example, in U.S. culture women (who are bio-logically female) are expected to perform femininity (a cultural construction) through activities such as nurturing, crossing their legs and not taking up too much room when sitting, speaking with vocal variety and expressivity, and wearing makeup. How do people respond to women who cut their hair in a flattop, sit sprawled across the couch, speak in an aggressive manner, and refuse to wear makeup? Often, they call them names or ridicule them; occasionally they even mistake them for males because these behaviors are so culturally attached to notions of masculinity.

gender identity
how and to what extent one identifies with the social construction of mascu-linity and femininity

Gender identity refers to how and to what extent one identifies with the social construction of masculinity and femininity. Gender roles and expectations have changed enormously over the centuries, and cultural groups around the world differ in their gender expectations. How do we develop our notions of gender, or what it means to be masculine or feminine? We learn through communica-tion: through the ways that people talk about gender, through the media images we see, and through observing the ways people communicate to males and females. For example, while crying is acceptable for girls, young boys receive many messages that they are not supposed to cry.

A leading scholar on gender, Judith Butler (1990, 1993) was one of the first to argue that gender identity is not biological but based on performances. She asserted that people's identities flow from the ways they have seen them performed in the past. In other words, a man's per-formance of male identity rests on previous performances of masculinity. Because the performances of traditional masculinity have been repeated for so long, individuals come to believe that masculine identity and behaviors are natural. However, some people choose to enact their iden-tity in nontraditional ways, and their performances will be interpreted against the backdrop of what is considered acceptable and appropriate.

In many families in the United States, gender roles follow a cultural rule about inside versus outside activities or chores.

In many families in the United States, gender roles follow a cultural rule about inside versus outside activities or chores. Those activities that take place inside the house are widely viewed as feminine and, therefore, should be performed by a female.

TABLE 3.1 Statistics on Intersex Births, 2000	
People whose chromosomal pattern is neither XX nor XY	1 in 1,666 births
People whose bodies differ from standard male or female	1 in 100 births
People receiving surgery to "normalize" genital appearance	1 or 2 in 1,000 births

Source: Intersex Society of North America (2005). How common is intersex? Retrieved June 12, 2006, from www. isna.org/faq/frequency

Activities that take place outside are seen as masculine and are expected to be performed by a male.

The case of South African runner Caster Semenya underscores the complexity of gender. After Semenya achieved some very fast running times, accusations about her gender arose. If she was not a woman, then she could not compete in women's track events. The IAAF (International Association of Athletics Federations), the governing body of track and field events, decided to test her gender through a series of tests. While the "details of the medical testing that Semenya underwent will remain confidential" (Zinzer, 2010), the difficulty in knowing Semenya's gender highlights the complexity of categorizing people. After 11 months in limbo, the IAAF finally cleared her to compete in women's track events again. The issue of identifying males and females can be problematic (see Table 3.1 for the relative numbers of people who are intersex).

Sexual Identity

Sexual identity refers to which of the various categories of sexuality one identifies with. Because our culture is dynamic, it has no set number of sexual identity categories, but perhaps the most prominent are heterosexual, gay or lesbian, and bisexual. Although most people in our culture recognize these categories today, they have not always been acknowledged or viewed in the same ways. In his *History of Sexuality*, French historian and theorist Michel Foucault (1988) notes that over the course of history, notions of sexuality and sexual identities changed. In certain eras and cultures, when children were born with both male and female sexual organs, a condition referred to as *intersexuality*, they were not necessarily operated on or forced to be either male or female.

Many people think of sexuality or sexual identity as private, but it frequently makes its way into the public arena. In everyday life, we often encounter people who will personally introduce us to their husbands or wives, a gesture that shares a particular aspect of their sexual identity. However, our society often exposes an individual's sexual identity to public scrutiny. For example, in 2006, U.S. Representative Mark Foley resigned from Congress amid questions that he sent inappropriate text messages and instant messages to male teenagers who had been congressional pages. The scandal led him to publicly disclose that he was gay (Candiotti et al., 2006). Senator Larry Craig's arrest for solicitation of sex in a men's restroom at the St. Paul–Minneapolis Airport became national news in 2007. Media coverage drew attention to that particular restroom—although by the end of 2008 it began to lose its appeal as a tourist destination (Sen. Craig restroom, 2008). In contrast to Representative Foley, Senator Craig insisted, "Let me be clear: I am not gay. I never have been gay" (Milbank, 2007). Because identity categories are social constructions, there is not always agreement about what they mean. Clearly, in the public arena, people manipulate these identity categories to help retrieve their reputations when their sexual activities become public.

In daily life, a person's sexual identity plays a role in such mundane matters as selecting which magazines to read and which television shows and movies to watch, as well as choosing places to socialize, people to associate with, and types of

sexual identity
which of the various categories of sexuality one identifies with

products to purchase. Television shows, magazines, books, Internet sites, and other cultural products are targeted toward particular sexual identities, or they assume a certain level of public knowledge about sexual identities and groups. For example, *Gary Unmarried, Millionaire Matchmaker,* and *Real Housewives of Orange County* presume an understanding of U.S. heterosexual culture. In contrast, Logo cable channel is specifically geared to gay and lesbian viewers. *Modern Family* and *Brothers and Sisters*, in contrast, include gay characters. These communication texts can reinforce, confirm, or challenge our notions of various categories of sexual identity.

Age Identity

Age, when thought of strictly as the number of years you've been alive, is an important identity for everyone. But your **age identity** is a combination of how you feel about your age as well as what others understand that age to mean. How old is "old"? How young is "young"? Have you noticed how your own notions of age have changed over the years? When you were in first grade, did high school students seem old to you? While *age* is a relative term, so are the categories we use for age groups. Today, for example, we use the terms *teenager, senior citizen, adult,* and *minor,* but these terms have meaning only within our social and legal system. For example, the voting age is 18, but people have to wait until they are 21 to buy liquor. Someone who commits a heinous crime can be charged as an adult, even if he or she is not yet 18. Still, whether a person feels like an adult goes beyond what the law decrees and comes from some set of factors that is far more complex.

Other age-related concepts are culturally determined as well. For example, the notion of "teenager" has come into use only relatively recently in the United States, and it is certainly not a universal category (Palladino, 1996). The notion that people have "midlife" crises is not a universal cultural phenomenon, either. Moreover, these age categories are relatively fluid, meaning that there are no strict guidelines about where they begin and end, even though they do influence how we think about ourselves (Trethewey, 2001). For example, because people today generally live longer, the span of years thought of as middle age comes later in our lives. These changes all illustrate the dynamic nature of age identity and the categories we have for it.

You probably feel your age identity when you shop for clothes. How do you decide what is "too young" for you? Or what is "too old"? Do you consciously consider the messages your clothing communicates about your age? As you reflect on your shopping experiences, think about the tensions between what you like (the individual forces) and what others might think (societal forces). Here you see the tension that drives all social identities, including age.

Social Class Identity

Social class identity refers to an informal ranking of people in a culture based on their income, occupation, education, dwelling, child-rearing habits, and other factors (Online Glossary, 2005). Examples of social classes in this country include working class, middle class, upper middle class, and upper class. Most people in the United States identify themselves as middle class (Baker, 2003). However, there is no single agreed-upon definition for each of the classes. For example, the Census Bureau describes the middle class as being composed of the 20 percent of the population who earn between $40,000 and $95,000 (Baker, 2003), while the Drum Major Institute for Public Policy (2005) reports that the middle class conventionally has come to include families with incomes between $25,000 and $100,000. However, even 16.8 percent of those with incomes over $110,000 self-identify as middle class (Baker, 2003).

In his work on social class, French sociologist Pierre Bourdieu (1984) found that people of the same social class tended to view the world similarly: They defined art in similar ways, and they enjoyed similar sports and other aspects of everyday

age identity
a combination of self-perception of age along with what others understand that age to mean

social class identity
an informal ranking of people in a culture based on their income, occupation, education, dwelling, child-rearing habits, and other factors

Social class identity is an important influence in the ways that people socialize and engage in leisure activities.

How does your own speech reveal your social class background and identity? Can you identify aspects of your family's home, yard, interior decorating, and clothing that reveal social class identity?

life. Moreover, based on his study of social class, Paul Fussell (1992) noted that U.S. Americans communicate their social class in a wide variety of ways, some verbal and some nonverbal. For example, middle-class people tend to say "tuxedo," while upper-class people are more apt to say "dinner jacket." In the category of nonverbal elements that express social class identity, he included the clothes we wear, the way we decorate our homes, the magazines we read, the kinds of drinks we imbibe, and the ways we decorate our automobiles. We will discuss more about class and verbal and nonverbal communication in the next two chapters.

Those in occupations such as nursing, teaching, and policing soon may no longer be considered middle class. What other occupations have fallen or might fall from middle-class status? In their study *The Fragile Middle Class*, Teresa Sullivan and her colleagues noted the increasing numbers of bankruptcy filings (2001), especially among those in occupations that we consider securely middle class, such as teachers, dentists, accountants, and computer engineers. In the wake of the recent recession, there has been increasing public discussion about income inequality and its toll on the middle class. The recession has drawn attention to the very wealthy and the increasing wealth they are amassing while unemployment remains stubbornly high. These discussions may portend a new focus on social class identity.

One reason people in the United States avoid discussing social class is because they tend to believe that their country is based on *meritocracy,* meaning that people succeed or fail based on their own merit. This idea leads to claims such as "anyone can grow up to be president." However, this has not proven to be true. For example, until the election of Barack Obama in 2008, every president in the United States has been white, male, and, in all cases but one, Protestant. Social identity and class have a powerful impact on one's life, as they can determine where you go to school (and what quality of education you receive), where you shop (and what quality of resources you have access to), which leisure activities you participate in (on a scale from constructive and enriching to destructive and self-defeating), and who you are most likely to meet and with whom you are mostly likely to socialize. In this way, social class identity tends to reproduce itself; the social class one is born into is often the same as the social class one dies in. People who are working class tend to live around other working-class people, make friends with working-class people (who influence their expectations and behavior), and attend schools that reinforce working-class values. In an early study that showed how communication was used to perform social class identity in conjunction with gender and race, Gerry Philipsen (1992) noted that men tended to speak much less than women and rarely socialized outside their working-class community, which he called "Teamsterville." More recently, Kristen Lucas (2011) studied how family is an important site for communication messages that "both encourage and discourage social mobility" (p. 95). By examining how families reproduce their working-class identity, we can see how there are contradictory messages sent to the children about social class and moving toward white-collar occupations.

In our earlier example of the 2011 census in India, the census form does not ask people about their caste. In that cultural context, "census officials worried the sensitive subject of caste in multicultural

It Happened to Me: *Melinda*

My parents went through a divorce when I was two, and my mother has worked hard so we could have a comfortable life. Throughout my life, I've gone to private schools and universities with other students whose families had much more money than mine. I've always tried to fit in with the other students. Recently my mother has gone into debt, and I am having trouble adjusting to this change. I haven't told any of my upper class friends because I am afraid they won't understand my situation. It can be a struggle to be honest with people you don't think will understand your situation, but it is a struggle that I have to overcome. People should accept each other for who they are, not what social class they fit into.

Did You Know?

Social Class ID Check

U.S. Americans often do not think much about their social class. Many U.S. Americans identify as "middle class," and many others don't really think about their social class. The questions below are meant to help you think through your social class and how it has shaped you and your communication experiences.

1. What is your social class?
2. How important is your social class to you?
3. What and who have been the primary sources of socialization for you about your social class? Name specific persons. If relevant, identify the organizations or types of organization with which they were affiliated.
4. How, if at all, do you express your social class—through language, communication style, dress, accessories, music?
5. Does your awareness of your social class ever facilitate your communication with others? Explain.
6. Does your awareness of your social class ever hinder your communication with others? Explain.
7. What situations, if any, do you avoid because of apprehensions related to your social class?
8. What situations, if any, do you seek because of your social class?
9. What advantages, if any, do you enjoy based on your social class?
10. Do you know of any stereotypes about your social class? If so, list them.
11. Are you ever aware of stereotypes about your social class as you interact with others? Explain.
12. How do the media tend to depict your social class? Do media depictions correspond with your sense of your social class? Explain.

SOURCE: Reprinted by permission of Waveland Press, Inc., from Brenda J. Allen, *Difference Matters: Communicating Social Identity* (Long Grove, IL: Waveland Press, Inc., 2004). All rights reserved.

and secular India could upset the results of the population count" (Daigle, 2011). Social class can be a very sensitive topic in many cultures. To better understand your own social class identity, see *Did You Know? Social Class ID Check*.

Disability Identity

People can identify with or be identified as disabled for many different reasons. **Disability identity** is often defined as having an impairment of some kind. Some people experience differences in hearing, sight, and/or mobility. Not all disabilities are visible or evident to others. In 1990, the United States passed the Americans with Disabilities Act, which recognized disability as an important identity that needed federal protection from discrimination. This act also defines "disability" in Section 12102:

The term "disability" means, with respect to an individual

(A). a physical or mental impairment that substantially limits one or more major life activities of such individual;

(B). a record of such an impairment; or

(C). being regarded as having such an impairment (Americans with Disabilities Act, 1990, 2008).

disability identity
identification with physical or mental impairment that substantially impact everyday life

While this legal definition may be helpful to some, it does not tell us what this identity means and how it is performed by those who identify as disabled, nor does it tell us how disability is viewed by others.

It is through communication that "disability" as an identity gains its meaning in our society. As Deanna Fassett and Dana L. Morella explain,

> while someone might have a medical or physical condition that structures her/his experience, it is in her/his interactions with others that that condition takes on meaning and becomes what our collective social environment would consider disability, with all the punishments and privilege that entails. We build this social environment in our own mundane communication, in classrooms and faculty meetings; we learn and reiterate, often unknowingly, as institutional members, what is normal and what is not and what that means (p. 144).

If we are swimming in a sea of communication, the many meanings that we generate in everyday communication give meaning to "disability."

Like other identities, disability is performed; it is "always in the process of becoming, then disability is something we do, rather than something we are" (Henderson and Ostrander, 2008, p. 2). For example, in his study on disabled athletes who play wheelchair rugby, Kurt Lindemann found that "performances of disability, especially in a sport context, can subvert the stigma associated with physical disability in surprisingly effective ways" (2008, p. 113). By focusing on athletic activities, disabled people attempt to challenge stereotypical views of those with disabilities

People who are not disabled can become disabled and then develop this new identity as a part of their larger configuration of identities. For example, many people, as they grow older, may experience increasing hearing loss, reduced visual acuity, or other physical or mental impairments that can render them disabled. But disability, of course, is not limited to older people. How we talk about disability, see it in media images, and experience it in everyday life are all part of how we communicate about and construct the meanings of disability as an identity. In her study on autobiographical narratives of those growing up with chronic illness or disability, Linda Wheeler Cardillo found that "communication at all levels has a powerful impact on these persons and their experiences of difference. A deeper understanding of this experience and how it is shaped by communication can lead to more sensitive, respectful, affirming, and empowering communication on the part of health-care providers, parents, teachers, and others" (2010, p. 539).

Religious Identity

In the United States today, **religious identity** is becoming increasingly important. Religious identity is defined by one's spiritual beliefs. For example, although Jim hasn't been to a Catholic church in decades, he still identifies himself as Catholic due to his upbringing and the impact the religion has had on his outlook. Most researchers and writers agree that "religion is certainly one of the most complex and powerful cultural discourses in contemporary society, and religion continues to be a source of conflict between nations, among communities, within families, and...within one's self" (Corey, 2004, p. 189). While you may believe that your religious identity is part of your private life and irrelevant outside your family, this is not true. For example, in the aftermath of the 2001 September 11 attacks, Muslim identity has been viewed with particular suspicion. A 2004 study done by researchers in the Department of Communication at Cornell University found the following attitudes about Muslim Americans:

religious identity
aspect of identity defined by one's spiritual beliefs

Alternative V I E W
Respecting Religious Differences

Should Americans care about the religious identity of their elected leaders, or is someone's religion a private matter? Should elected leaders be guided by their religious beliefs to a greater or lesser extent than ordinary citizens? Explain your answers.

When any society has multiple religions, difficult issues can arise. As we look back upon the media coverage of the 2008 U.S. presidential election, "much of the coverage related to false yet persistent rumors that Obama is a Muslim" (Pew Forum on Religion and Public Life, 2008). Concerns about John F. Kennedy's religion (Catholicism) also circulated when he ran for the presidency. In a society that values religious freedom, what difference does it make what religion (if any) a political candidate follows?

How should we deal with these claims in a society that wants to respect and tolerate different religious beliefs? In response to the claims that Obama is a Muslim, former Secretary of State Colin Powell stated:

Well, the correct answer is, he is not a Muslim, he's a Christian. He's always been a Christian. But the really right answer is, what if he is? Is there something wrong with being a Muslim in this country? The answer's no, that's not America. Is there something wrong with some 7-year-old Muslim American kid believing that he or she could be president? Yet I have heard senior members of my own party drop the suggestion. 'He's a Muslim and might be associated with terrorists.' This is not the way we should be doing it in America.

SOURCE: Robinson, E. (2007, August 29). The power of Powell's rebuke, *Washington Post*, p. A17. Retrieved December 31, 2000, from **www.washingtonpost.com/wp-dyn/content/article/2008/10/20/AR2008102002393.html**

About 27 percent of respondents said that all Muslim Americans should be required to register their location with the federal government, and 26 percent said they think that mosques should be closely monitored by U.S. law enforcement agencies. Twenty-nine percent agreed that undercover law enforcement agents should infiltrate Muslim civic and volunteer organizations in order to keep tabs on their activities and fund-raising. About 22 percent said the federal government should profile citizens as potential threats based on the fact that they are Muslim or have Middle Eastern heritage. In all, about 44 percent said they believe that some curtailment of civil liberties is necessary for Muslim Americans (Cornell University, 2004).

Religious identity also takes on public significance because it correlates with various political views and attitudes (Corey & Nakayama, 2004). For example, the 2004 Cornell study found that Christians who actively attend church were much more likely to support differential treatment of Muslim Americans. In contrast, the nonreligious, or those less active in their churches, were less likely to support restrictions on civil liberties of Muslim Americans.

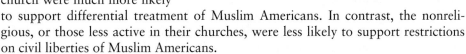

It Happened to Me: *Elizabeth*

If I meet someone in a college class, I don't tell them that I'm involved in a church or that I'm a Christian unless they bring it up or it's obvious they are, too. I do not want to appear to be a religious nut waiting to shove my belief system down their throat. My belief in Christ is really at the core of who I am, though. When I meet people through work who are in churches, I am open with them about my work, my life, and even my challenges. This is because they are my brothers/sisters in Christ, and that's the culture of what we do—care for, and about, one another.

How would you describe your religious identity? How do you communicate it to others? Do you ever conceal it? If so, when and why?

However one responds to other people's religious beliefs, most U.S. Americans feel a very strong need to embrace and enact personal religious identities (Corey & Nakayama, 2004). In 2000, for example, 46 percent of U.S. Americans belonged to religious groups, and approximately 40 percent of U.S. Americans claimed to attend religious services regularly (Taylor, 2005). Thus, in their article on "Religion and Performance," Frederick Corey and Thomas Nakayama (2004) write that individuals feel a "tremendous need to embody religious identities and reinforce those identities through spirited, vernacular performances" (p. 211). To understand how one student's religious identity affects her life, read *It Happened to Me: Elizabeth*.

We've shown throughout this chapter that aspects of our personal identity such as race, nationality, ethnicity, gender, age, social class, and religion develop through the tension between individual and societal forces. While we may assert a particular identity or view of ourselves, these views must be negotiated within the larger society and the meanings that the larger society communicates about that identity. See *Alternative View: Respecting Religious Differences* for an example of how one individual's religious identity became a public issue whose meaning was discussed and negotiated within the larger society. In the next section, we discuss the role of ethics in communication about identity.

TEST YOUR KNOWLEDGE

- What are the primary identity categories? Define each.
- Give an example of how identity might be performed for each primary identity category.

ETHICS AND IDENTITY

As you are probably aware, a person's sense of identity is central to how he or she functions in the world. Moreover, because identities derive their meanings from society, every identity comes with values attached to it. The ways we communicate may reflect these values. If you wish to be sensitive to other people's identities, you should be aware of at least three key ethical issues that can impact your communication with others.

One issue you might consider is how you communicate with people whose identities are more, or less, valued. What do we mean by more or less valued? You probably already know. In the United States, for example, which of the following identities is more highly valued: White or multiracial? Male or female? Lawyer or school bus driver? Still, these rankings are not necessarily consistent across cultures. In Denmark, for example, work identities do not follow the same hierarchical pattern as those in the United States (Mikkelsen & Einarsen, 2001). Thus, Danes are more likely to view street sweepers and doctors as social equals because they don't place as high a value on the medical profession nor as low a value on service jobs as many U.S. Americans do. In the United States, in contrast, many service workers complain that most of the people they serve either ignore them or treat them rudely—even with contempt. Consequently, you might ask yourself, "Do I communicate more politely and respectfully with high- versus low-status people?" If you find yourself exhibiting more respect when you communicate with your boss than you do with the employees you manage, then you might want to consider the impact of your communication on your subordinates' identities.

The second ethical point to reflect on involves language that denigrates or puts down others based on their identities. Such language debases their humanity and shuts down open communication. Examples of unethical communication and behavior related to identity occur if men yell sexual slurs at women on the street, or straight people harass individuals they believe are gay, or when White people are disrespectful to people of color. Although you probably don't engage in such obvious insults to people's identities, do you denigrate them in other, more subtle ways? For example, have you ever referred to someone as "just a homemaker" or "only a dental assistant"?

Third, think about whether you tend to reduce others to a single identity category. As we pointed out earlier, each of us is composed of multiple identities, and even within a specific identity group, individuals may differ widely from one another. Thus, individuals may be offended when others respond to them based on only one of their identities, especially one that is not relevant to the situation at hand. For example, managers in some organizations will not promote mothers of small children to highly demanding positions. They justify this by claiming the women won't be able to fulfill both their family and their professional roles competently. Although these women may be mothers, their identities as mothers likely are not relevant to their workplace identities and performances—just as men's identities as fathers are rarely seen as relevant to their jobs. Each person is a complex of identities, and each person desires others to recognize his or her multiple identities. You are more likely to communicate ethically if you keep this fact in mind.

TEST YOUR KNOWLEDGE
- What are three key ethical concerns related to identity?

SKILLS FOR COMMUNICATING ABOUT IDENTITIES

Related to our discussion about ethical issues, we offer three guidelines for communicating more effectively about identities. The first guideline concerns the self-fulfilling prophecy we discussed earlier: How you communicate *to* someone and *about* someone can influence how they perform their identity or how it develops. If a parent continually communicates with the child as if she were irresponsible, then the child is likely to act irresponsibly. To communicate effectively, be aware of the ways you create self-fulfilling prophecies through your own communication.

Second, there are many ways to perform a particular identity. You can improve your ability to communicate if you are tolerant of the many variations. For example, even if you believe that "real men" should act in certain ways, you are likely to communicate more effectively if you do not impose your beliefs on others. For example, you should not assume that because someone is male, he enjoys watching football, baseball, and other sports; wants to get married and have children; or eats only meat and potatoes. If you do, you are likely to communicate with some men in ways they will find less interesting than you intend.

Third, remember that people change over time. If you have been out of touch with friends for a period of time, when you encounter them again you may find that they have embraced new identities. Sometimes people change religious identities, or sometimes they change occupations. You can increase your communication effectiveness if you recognize that people change and that their new identities may be unfamiliar to you.

TEST YOUR KNOWLEDGE
- What are three strategies you can use to communicate more effectively with regard to identities?

SUMMARY

Learning about identities and communication is important for at least five reasons: (1) we bring our identities to each communication interaction, (2) communication interactions create and shape identities, (3) identity plays a key role in intercultural communication, (4) much of our life is organized around specific identities, and (5) identity is a key site in which individual and societal forces come together.

Identities are defined social categories, and each of us is made up of many of them. They may be primary or secondary. Primary identities (race, ethnicity, age) are the focus in this chapter and have the most consistent and enduring impact on our lives; secondary identities, such as occupation and marital status, are more changeable over the life span and from situation to situation. Our identities exist at both the individual and social level, are both fixed and dynamic, and are created through interaction. Furthermore, identities must be understood within larger historical, social, and cultural environments. Important communication processes that influence personal identity development include reflected appraisals, self-concept, and self-fulfilling prophecies.

The primary identity categories—race, nationality, ethnicity, gender, sexuality, age, social class, disability, and religion—are constructed between individual and social forces and what society communicates about those identities. Individuals perform their identities, and these performances are subject to social commentary. Straying too far from social expectations in these performances can lead to disciplinary action.

Ethical concerns center on how people are treated based on their identities. Guidelines to ethical communication include learning to value and respect people within all identity groups, to avoid using denigrating language or reducing people to a single identity category. Guidelines for more effective communication about identities involve being aware of the ways you create self-fulfilling prophecies through your communication and being tolerant of different ways of enacting various identities.

HUMAN COMMUNICATION IN SOCIETY ONLINE

To review this chapter, use the MyCommunicationLab Web site to test your understanding of the following key terms, record your answers to the chapter review questions, and complete the suggested activities. Expand your learning and understanding of chapter concepts by completing additional activities and exercises online. Access code required. Go to www.mycommunicationlab.com for more information or to purchase standalone access.

KEY TERMS

identity 55
reflected appraisals 58
looking-glass self 58
particular others 59
generalized other 59
self-fulfilling prophecy 61
stereotype threat 61
self-concept 61

self-esteem 62
self-respect 63
performance of identity 63
enacting identities 65
role expectations 65
mutable 65
racial identity 67
multiracial identity 70

national identity 70
ethnic identity 70
gender identity 70
sexual identity 72
age identity 73
social class identity 73
disability identity 75
religious identity 76

APPLY WHAT YOU KNOW

1. List the identities that are most important to you. Some of these identities may not have been discussed in this chapter. Note some situations in which the identities not discussed in the chapter become most relevant and some situations where other identities dominate.

2. Which of your identities are shared by a majority of people in society? What are some of the stereotypes of those identities? To answer this question, you may need to ask people who do not share that identity.

3. Interview someone who is at least twenty years older than you. Ask the person how her or his identities have changed over the years and what those changes entailed. Then reflect on changes in your own identity as you have grown up. How many of these changes were motivated by individual forces and how many might have been due to social forces?

4

Communicating, Perceiving, and Understanding

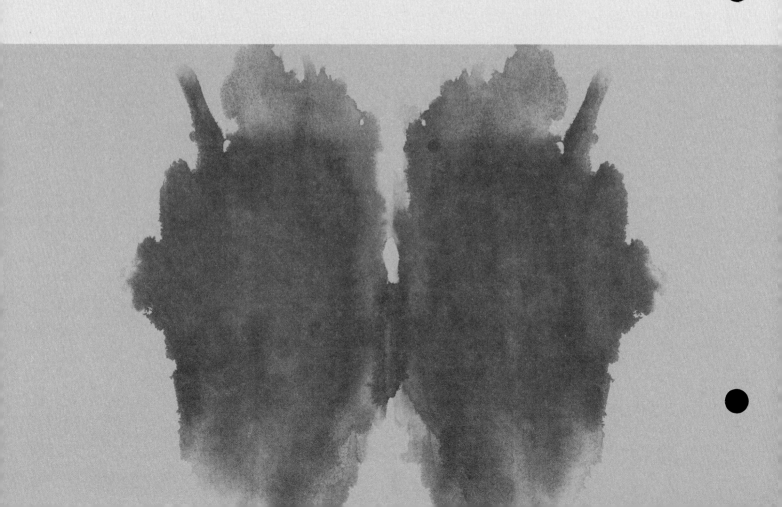

After the first hall meeting in their dorm, Travis and Samantha went out for coffee to discuss their experiences. They soon found themselves sharing their impressions of Bo, the dorm Resident Assistant (R.A.).

TRAVIS: What did you think of Bo?

SAMANTHA: I suppose he's okay. He seemed a little, I don't know, bossy. He was funny, but I don't know if I am going to like having him as my dorm resident; he seems like he might be hard to talk to.

TRAVIS: Really? I liked him a lot. I thought Bo was cool and would be really easy to talk to. He is someone I think I could hang out with.

SAMANTHA: He seemed kind of distant to me. I guess we'll have plenty of chances to find out what he is really like during the semester.

As the conversation between Travis and Samantha illustrates, our perceptions of others strongly influence how we respond to and communicate about them. If we perceive people as friendly, fun, and similar to ourselves, we tend to be drawn toward them and want to communicate with them. If we view individuals as distant, controlling, and quite unlike ourselves, we may try to minimize contact. However, not everyone perceives and responds to people and events the same way. Our perceptions are affected by individual factors, such as age, gender, genetics, and experience, as well as by societal forces including culture, historical events, and social roles.

For instance, on average females experience pain more intensely than do males (Hurley & Adams, 2008), so a touch that feels uncomfortable to a man may feel painful to a woman. (It can be helpful to remember this difference when we are shaking hands with others.) But how can societal forces affect perception? Among other things, societies teach us what foods and beverages are tasty and how they should be served. One example of this is the difference in how soft drinks are served in the United Kingdom versus how they are served in the United States. In most parts of the United Kingdom, cold beverages include a few pieces of ice, while in the United States a glass of soda may be half ice. Because of this, people in the two cultures have very different perceptions of what a "good" cold drink should taste like.

In this chapter we will first explore the importance of perception and the perception process. Next we'll examine how individuals' attributes and experiences affect their perceptions, and we will consider societal influences on perception. We also will discuss how people can evaluate their perceptions through an ethical lens. Finally, we will end the chapter with suggestions for sharpening your perception skills.

Once you have read this chapter, you will be able to:

- ■ Explain why understanding perception is important.
- ■ Define what we mean by perception.
- ■ Name three individual factors that affect one's perceptual processes.

- Understand how power, culture, and historical time period influence perception.
- Explain why ethics is a relevant consideration for one's perceptions.
- Offer three ways to improve one's perception skills.

THE IMPORTANCE OF PERCEPTION

How individuals respond to people, objects, and environments depends largely on the perceptions they have about them. For example, when we perceive people as being polite, we are more likely to agree to their requests (Kellerman, 2004). When we communicate, we don't just respond to others' words; we respond to our perceptions of the way they look, sound, smell—and sometimes how they feel. For example, considerable research has established that when people perceive others as attractive, they treat them better than those viewed as less attractive (Chaiken, 1986; Wilson & Nias, 1999). This may explain the popularity of makeover shows like *The Biggest Loser* and *What Not to Wear*.

In addition, some research suggests that sexual attraction is influenced by the body odor of a potential partner (McCoy & Pitino, 2002; Singh & Bronstad, 2001). So, the next time someone breaks off a relationship by saying, "It's not you; it's me," they may be telling the truth. You just may not smell right to that person! Interestingly, women may be more likely to make this statement than are men since on average they have a keener sense of smell than do men (Estroff, 2004; Herz & Inzlicht, 2002). Overall, women may be more positively influenced by smells they find attractive and negatively by smells they dislike. For more information on the influence of smell on perception, see *Communication in Society: Sex Difference in Smell*.

Research reveals that when people perceive others as attractive, they treat them better than those viewed as less attractive.

As we noted in Chapter 3, identities play an important role in communication. They also influence and are influenced by perception. Thus, just as our perceptions of others impact how we communicate with them, our perceptions and communication impact how they see themselves. Let's take our scenario above as a case in point. How might Travis's or Samantha's perceptions affect Bo's perception of himself? If most people perceive Bo as Travis does—as amusing and open—and, therefore, respond to him by laughing and including him in activities, then Bo probably sees himself positively. On the other hand, if most people respond as Samantha did, and consequently choose to have little contact with him, Bo may perceive himself more negatively.

As you might expect, then, perception and identity are powerfully intertwined. On the one hand, Samantha's perceptions of Bo affect his identity. At the same time, how Bo views himself and others impacts how he perceives and responds to the world around him. If he has a positive self-image, Bo may perceive that others like him, he might be more optimistic and see the positive aspects of a situation more readily, and he could be less aware of others' negative reactions to him.

As you read this chapter, you are receiving considerable sensory input. An air conditioner or heater might be running, cars and people may be moving past you, and the temperature where you sit likely fluctuates over time. In addition, you may feel hungry or tired, you might detect the scent of cleaning products, and the chair you are sitting on could be uncomfortable. How are you able to manage all the information your senses bring to you so that you can focus on your reading? How are you able to make sense of all this sensory input? The answer is that you continuously engage in a variety of processes that limit and structure everything you perceive (Kanizsa, 1979; Morgan, 1977). Let's look at how this works.

TEST YOUR KNOWLEDGE

- Why is perception important to the communication process?

COMMUNICATION IN SOCIETY
Sex Differences in Smell

Have you noticed a difference in sense of smell between the sexes?

Why do you think women typically have a keener sense of smell?

A variety of studies suggest that, on average, women are better at identifying odors than are men. Some researchers have found that women of all ages and in a variety of cultures are better than men of the same age and culture at identifying and remembering smells. However, other researchers claim that this sex difference is most pronounced during the period when women are fertile, especially during ovulation, and that their superior smelling ability fades with age. These scholars believe that women's higher levels of estrogen are likely responsible for this sex difference.

Experiments that have examined men's and women's scent ability reveal that both sexes are able to recognize others from their body odor alone. In an experiment at Hebrew University, Jerusalem, childless women held an unrelated baby in their arms for an hour. When tested later to see if they could recognize the baby they had held by scent, most of them were successful. This study did not test men, so it isn't clear if men possess similar smell recognition ability for unfamiliar others. However, other tests have determined that men and women both can recognize their own children or spouses by their scent. Typically in these studies, participants' children or spouses wore a T-shirt for several days, then the participants were asked to use scent to recognize the T-shirt belonging to their family member.

SOURCES: Doty, R. L., Applebaum, S., Zusho, H., & Settle, R. G. (1985). Sex differences in odor identification ability: A cross cultural analysis. *Neuropsychologia, 23*(5), 667–72.

Doty, R. L. (1984). Smell identification ability: Changes with age. *Science, 226*(4681), 1441–1443.

Maccaby, E. E., & Jacklin, C. N. *The psychology of sex differences*. Palo Alto, CA: Stanford University Press.

WHAT IS PERCEPTION?

Perception refers to the processes of **selection, organization,** and **interpretation** of the information we collect through our senses: what we see, hear, taste, smell, and touch. The sensory data we select, the ways we organize them, and the interpretations we assign to them affect the ways we communicate (Manusov & Spitzberg, 2008). Although these processes tend to happen concurrently and unconsciously, researchers separate them to better explain how they function.

Selection

Because people experience more sensory information than they can process, they selectively focus on and remember only part of it. In every interaction, each communicator has a field of perception. In this field some objects, symbols, or words are at the center, while others are on the periphery, and still others are outside the field altogether. Consciously or unconsciously we attend to just a narrow range of the full array of sensory information available and ignore the remainder. This process is called **selective attention.**

Suppose your friend is telling you a very interesting story about a mutual acquaintance while the two of you are seated in a crowded cafeteria. Most likely, your friend will have your full attention. Peripherally you may notice the sights and sounds of the other people in the room, the smells of food, and the glare of sunlight coming through the window; however, none of this will distract your focus. You probably will not even notice who is sitting at the table next to you, the color of the walls, the type of flooring, or the storm clouds gathering in the sky. Your attention will be devoted to the center of your field: your friend.

selection
the process of choosing which sensory information to focus on

organization
the process by which one recognizes what sensory input represents

interpretation
the act of assigning meaning to sensory information

selective attention
consciously or unconsciously attending to just a narrow range of the full array of sensory information available

cognitive representation
the ability to form mental models
of the world

Take a moment to remember the nicest comment anyone has made to you in the past 24 hours. Next, recall the unkindest remark anyone has made to you in that time period. Which remark did you find easiest to remember? Was your most memorable comment positive or negative? Did your most memorable comment violate your expectations? What were you doing when you heard the comment? To what extent does your experience fulfill or violate the claim that people are more likely to remember negative than positive comments?

The sensory input we select, however, is not random (Greenough, Black, & Wallace, 1987). When a range of sensory experiences accost you, various factors affect your selection, including your identity, features of the person or object you have encountered, and your experiences and values. For example, at large social events you are likely to attend to only one or a few people because you cannot focus on everyone at once. Who captures your focus depends on:

- aspects of your identity (e.g., if you are Native American, you may find your attention drawn more to participants who also are Native American)

- features of the person (e.g., someone dressed differently from everyone else will likely attract your attention)

- your goals (e.g., if you would like to meet a potential romantic partner, you may pay special attention to attractive men or women in your age range)

Researchers have also found that people are most likely to pay attention to and remember comments that are negative, violate their expectations, and are made in situations that are important to them (Siu & Finnegan, 2004). For example, a comment like "What on earth did you do to your hair?" is more likely to remain prominent in your mind than "Nice haircut." Similarly, when an instructor says, "This will be on the test," students usually pay close attention to what the instructor says next. Comments that violate our expectations also become more salient and gain more attention. Suppose you meet someone new and ask "How are you?" Instead of the expected, "Fine, thanks," the person explains in detail all the misfortunes that have befallen him or her in the past year. You not only will be surprised, you will remember the event. You may even decide that this new person is highly negative, or strange, and that you should avoid future interactions with him or her.

Organization

After selecting the sensory input we will attend to, we need to be able to recognize *what* it represents. To do this, we must organize the information into a recognizable picture that has meaning. If you are awakened in the middle of the night by a loud noise, you will certainly attend to that noise and little else. However, you also must be able to make sense of the sound in order to respond. Is it a mechanical sound or an animal one? Is it human? You can make judgments like these because you possess organizational structures or templates that tell you what information belongs together and how to "read" or understand what you perceive (Kanizsa, 1979). How does this work? In this section we examine two primary cognitive principles—cognitive representation and categorization—which help people organize and respond to their perceptions.

Cognitive Representation   The term **cognitive representation** describes the human ability to form mental models, or cognitive maps, of the world we live in (Levinthal & Gavetti, 2000; Weick, 1995). We create these maps and then refer to them later when circumstances call for them. For example, people know that a fire alarm communicates danger; furthermore, they know how to respond to a fire alarm because they have a cognitive map for alarms. Schools and workplaces have fire drills, in fact, to help people create cognitive maps that are familiar and enable them to act appropriately in an emergency.

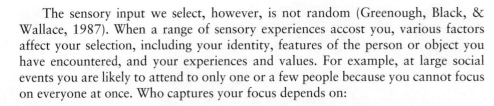

Schools and workplaces have fire drills to help people create cognitive maps that are familiar and enable them to act appropriately in an emergency.

People also develop and use cognitive maps when they communicate. As we grow up, we learn cognitive maps or models for engaging in many types of communication acts, such as complaining, apologizing, and asking for a favor. Many people learn quite early that it is useful to be nice to someone before asking them for a favor, and this information becomes part of the map for requesting favors. Remember that maps are *representations* of things, not the things themselves. Thus cognitive maps consist of general outlines; they are not fixed sets of utterances that are memorized.

Two specific types of cognitive representations, or maps, that individuals use to organize their perceptions about people and communication are called prototypes and interpersonal scripts.

Communication behavior is strongly influenced by idealized **schemas** called prototypes. A **prototype** is the most typical or representative example of a person or concept. For example, many people's prototypical idea of a professor is a person who is male, has white hair (and perhaps a beard), and wears a tweed jacket with leather patches. Although a few professors fulfill this prototype, many more do not. (Just look around your campus.) Nonetheless, this prototype persists, in part because of how media depict college professors.

Prototypes are important because people compare specific individuals to their prototype and then communicate with them based on the degree to which they perceive that the individual conforms to that prototype. This often happens when it comes to the issue of gender. People have prototypical ideas of what a "man" or a "woman" is. These prototypes represent idealized versions of masculinity and femininity. The more an individual resembles one's prototype, the more likely one is to communicate with that person in a stereotypical (or prototypical) manner. For example, men who are muscular and tall and have facial hair are often perceived to be very masculine. Consequently, people tend to communicate with them as if these men embody typical masculine characteristics, such as having an interest in sports, a heterosexual sexual orientation, and a lack of interest in topics such as fashion, interior design, or personal relationships. Similarly, a man who possesses none of those characteristics may be viewed as not masculine and be communicated with accordingly.

How does the script for obtaining food in a fast-food restaurant differ from scripts for obtaining food in other situations?

An interpersonal **script** is a relatively fixed sequence of events expected to occur; it functions as a guide or template for how to act in particular situations (Burgoon, Berger, & Waldron, 2000; Pearce, 1994). We develop scripts for activities we engage in frequently. Most people have a script for how to meet a new person. For example, when you first encounter a student you'd like to get to know, you probably introduce yourself, tell the person a basic fact about yourself such as "I live across the hall from you," and then ask a question such as "How do you like living on campus?" "What is your major?" or "Where is your home town?" Thus, you follow a routine of sorts (Douglas, 1990).

We enact scripts because we find them comfortable, they are efficient, and they keep us from making too many social mistakes. Although many of the scripts we use will be familiar to others, we also tailor them to fit our own expectations for a situation. Our choice of script or the way we alter a script depends on our perceptions of others. We may use a different script to initiate a conversation with someone we perceive as friendly, attractive, and fun than with someone we perceive as shy, quiet, and withdrawn.

As this discussion suggests, cognitive representations help people navigate through the physical and social world. These maps provide guidelines that shape how we communicate with others through the prototypes and interpersonal scripts we develop as we grow up and mature.

Categorization
Another type of cognitive process we use to organize information is **categorization**. Categorization is inherent to all languages. The linguistic symbols (or words) we use represent the groupings we see around us. Because it is

schemas
cognitive structures that represent an individual's understanding of a concept or person

prototype
an idealized schema

script
a relatively fixed sequence of events that functions as a guide or template for communication or behavior

categorization
a cognitive process used to organize information by placing it into larger groupings of information

label
a name assigned to a category based on one's perception of the category

stereotyping
creating schemas that overgeneralize attributes of a specific group

How do you perceive these two males? Do any stereotypes come to mind?

impossible to remember everything, we use groupings that represent larger categories of information or objects (Lakoff, 1987).

For example, we lump a lot of information under the category of *restaurant*. What did you think of when you read the word *restaurant*? You probably envisioned a subcategory, such as a café or a pancake house. However, the concept of *restaurant* has certain features that apply to all subcategories, so that you know what is meant and what to expect when you go to one. You understand that *restaurant* refers to a place to eat and not a place to worship or attend classes. Forming and using categories allows us to understand and store information and makes us more efficient communicators.

Although grouping is a natural cognitive and perceptual process, it also can lead to misperceptions. Categorizing can cause one to reduce complex individuals to a single category or to expect them to behave in ways consistent with the category, regardless of the circumstance. For instance, you might categorize an individual based on your perception that the person is responsible and serious, or silly and fun. Once you reduce people to a category, you may communicate with them as if they possess no other characteristics. For example, if you categorize the students in your biology class as serious, you may never joke around with them or allow them to be silly or fun.

When people categorize others, they typically also assign them a **label**. The two activities tend to go hand in hand. Thus, groups of people and the individuals within those groups may be labeled or described as jocks, sorority girls, emo, or goth. Although labeling others can function as a useful shortcut, it also can lead to negative outcomes (Link & Phelan, 2001). When we label people, we run the risk of viewing them only through the lens of the label. The label also influences our expectations, evaluations, and responses to them. Labeling can cause problems even when the labels are positive, as was the case in *It Happened to Me: Lin Sue*.

When you were growing up, did your family have a label they used to describe you? Were you the smart one or the well-behaved one or the goof-up? If you were labeled the goof-up, you may not have been given many opportunities to disprove the label, and your ideas may have been discounted even when they were valid. Because of such a label, you may have come to discount the value of your own ideas. This effect can be magnified when entire groups of people are labeled in ways that create problems, such as the labeling of British people as snobbish or Muslims as terrorists.

As you may have guessed, labeling is related to stereotyping. **Stereotyping** occurs when schemas overgeneralize attributes of a group to which others belong (Fiske & Taylor, 1991). A stereotype is an assumption that every member of the group possesses certain characteristics. For example, you may assume that most females enjoy talking about fashion trends, so, you initiate a conversation with an unfamiliar woman by discussing the *Style Network*. But not every member of a group fits the stereotype—if you use the fashion opener with every woman you meet, you may encounter some women who give you a blank stare in response.

While grouping individuals makes it easy to remember information about them, it often leads to inaccurate beliefs and assumptions. Overgeneralizing a group's attributes makes it difficult to see the individuality of the people we encounter. Thus, a reliance on stereotypes can get those who use them into trouble.

It Happened to Me: *Lin Sue*

Because I am Chinese American, people often assume that I am some kind of whiz kid in academics. Well, I'm not. I was hit by a car when I was little, and I have residual brain impairment because of it. I have to study hard just to make passing grades. I get both angry and embarrassed when people assume I am this great student and imply that I will surely go to graduate school. I will feel fortunate if I just get out of undergraduate school. I really wish people wouldn't do this to me. They think they are being nice and complimentary, but they are still stereotyping me.

Interpretation

After we perceive and organize sensory information, we assign meaning to it (Bruner, 1958, 1991). Returning to our earlier example, imagine that you are awakened late at night. You hear a loud noise, which you determine is caused by a banging on your bedroom window. You now have to interpret what this means. Is it a tree branch? A loose shutter? Is it someone trying to break in?

We all assign meaning to the information we perceive, but we do not all necessarily assign the same meaning to similar information. One of the factors that influences how we interpret information is the frame through which we view it.

Frames Structures that shape how people interpret their perceptions are called **frames.** An individual's understanding of an event depends on the frame used to interpret it (Dillard, Solomon, & Samp, 1996). For example, if you are someone who frames the world as a dangerous place rife with criminals, you are likely to interpret that banging on your window as an indication of someone trying to break in. In essence, individuals view the world through interpretive frames that then guide how they make sense of events (Dijk, 1977; Fisher, 1997).

Individuals' frames develop over time, based on experience, interaction with others, and innate personality (Neale & Bazerman, 1991; Putnam & Holmer, 1992). Since we cannot perceive every aspect of an experience, frames also direct our attention toward some features of an episode and away from others. A bad mood, for example, directs attention to the negative aspects of an event. Usually, people don't become aware of frames until something happens to force them to replace one frame with another. If a friend points out that you are focusing only on the negative, you will become more aware of how your mood is framing, or focusing, your perceptions and interpretations. Your frame can change, then, as new information is introduced.

How should you use this information about framing? Now that you are aware that interpretations of people, events, and objects are influenced by an individual's specific frames, you should be more critical of your own interpretations. It is helpful to recognize that your interpretations (as well as others') do not necessarily represent the "truth"—but simply represent a particular way of viewing the world.

Frames are important elements of interpretation because they function as lenses that shape how observers understand people and events. But bear in mind that interpretation involves more than just framing; when individuals interpret events, they also offer explanations for them. When we develop explanations for our own and others' behaviors, we are engaged in making attributions. Let's see how this process works.

Attribution How often do you wonder "why did she (or he) do that?" As we observe and interact with others, we spend considerable energy attempting to determine the causes of their behavior. For example, if your friend ignores you before class, you try to figure out why. At heart, most of us are amateur psychologists who search for the reasons people behave as they do.

Attribution theory explains the cognitive and verbal processes we use to judge our own and others' behavior (Manusov & Spitzberg, 2008). Fritz Heider (1958), a psychologist and professor, said that attribution is the process of drawing inferences. When individuals observe others, they immediately draw conclusions that go beyond mere sensory information. When someone cuts you off in traffic, what conclusion do you usually draw? What attribution would you make if you called your romantic partner at 3 A.M. and he or she wasn't home? Although we're constantly being told we shouldn't judge others, attribution theory says we can't help it (Griffin, 1994).

frame
a structure that shapes how people interpret their perceptions

attribution theory
explanation of the processes we use to judge our own and others' behavior

One attribution we often make is whether the cause of an individual's behavior is internal or external. An *internal* cause would be a personality characteristic, while an *external* cause would be situational.

We are particularly likely to make internal attributions when the behavior is unexpected—that is, when it is something that most other people would not do (Kelley, 1973). For instance, if someone laughs during a sad scene in a movie, people are more likely to attribute this unexpected reaction to a personality trait—for example, rudeness or insensitivity. But when the behavior fits our expectations, we are likely to attribute it to external causes. Therefore, if someone cries during a sad movie scene, people are likely to attribute the behavior to the movie.

Besides expectations, attributions may also depend on whether we are the actor or observer of the behavior. We are more likely to attribute our own negative behavior to external causes and our positive actions to internal states (Jong, Koomen, & Mellenbergh, 1988). This is referred to as an **attributional bias.** If you are polite, it is because you have good manners; if you are rude, it is because others mistreated you. These attributions are examples of a **self-serving bias.** Operating under this bias, we tend to give ourselves more credit than is due when good things happen, and we accept too little responsibility for those things that go wrong.

You are likely to attribute an internal cause to unexpected behavior—such as laughter during a sad movie.

Most individuals are harsher judges of other people's behavior than they are of their own. We tend to attribute others' negative behavior to *internal* causes (such as their personality) and their positive behavior to *external* causes (such as the situation). This tendency is referred to as the **fundamental attribution error** (Ross, 1977). For example, when you are driving during rush hour traffic and someone cuts in front of you abruptly as two lanes merge, what attribution do you make about the other driver? According to fundamental attribution error, people are more likely to attribute the behavior to some trait internal to the other driver ("That driver is a jerk and is deliberately trying to get ahead of me") rather than to something external ("That driver is distracted by a child in the car and doesn't realize the lane is merging"). But if the other driver slows down to let you enter the merged lane first, most people might assume the driver was simply following the rules of the road rather than deliberately attempting to be thoughtful.

Attributional biases have implications for the way people communicate and conduct relationships. For example, the types of attributions spouses make are linked to their feelings of marital satisfaction (Sillars, Roberts, Leonard, & Dun, 2000; 2002). Those in unhappy relationships tend to assume the spouse's negative behaviors are internal, or personality-based, and difficult to change. Unfortunately, they also tend to view their spouse's positive behaviors as situational and temporary (Bradbury & Fincham, 1988). Thus, unhappy spouses often feel helpless to change their partner's negative characteristics. This pessimistic outlook can then increase negative communication within the relationship.

Interestingly, when people make attributions about others, they tend to trust the negative information they hear more than the positive information (Lupfer, Weeks, & Dupuis, 2000). If you hear both positive and negative information about a classmate, you tend to remember and rely on the negative rather than the positive information to formulate your attributions. However, you are not confined to these faulty attributional processes; you can work to overcome them.

attributional bias
the tendency to attribute one's own negative behavior to external causes and one's positive actions to internal states

self-serving bias
the tendency to give one's self more credit than is due when good things happen and to accept too little responsibility for those things that go wrong

fundamental attribution error
the tendency to attribute others' negative behavior to internal causes and their positive behaviors to external causes

First, remember that none of us is a mind reader and that the attributions we make are not always accurate. Remain aware that attributions are really just guesses (even if they are educated guesses). It also helps if one remains aware of the self-serving bias and works to minimize it. Recognize that we all have a tendency to attribute our own positive actions to ourselves and others' negative actions to themselves. Look for alternative explanations for your own and others' behavior. Last, avoid overemphasizing the negative. People have a tendency to remember and to highlight the negative, so try to avoid the negative in your own comments and balance the positive against the negative in your evaluations of others. For an example of a mistaken attribution, see *It Happened to Me: Danika.*

It Happened to Me: *Danika*

I was at a party recently when I went up to this attractive guy and stood next to him. When he didn't seem to notice me, I introduced myself and tried talking to him. But he completely ignored me! I was so put off that I stomped away and started complaining to my friend Amira. I told her that the guy might be good looking, but he sure was a snob. She looked puzzled. "Oh, were you standing on his left side?" she asked. When I told her yeah, she explained that he was deaf in his left ear and probably hadn't heard me. I felt bad that I had jumped to a negative attribution so quickly. Later, I approached him on his right side and talked to him; I found out he was a really nice guy.

TEST YOUR KNOWLEDGE

- How important is the role of interpretation in the perception process? What factors most influence how individuals interpret events?

- What two cognitive processes help us organize what we perceive?

- Why is stereotyping "normal"? When is it helpful? When is it harmful?

PERCEPTION AND THE INDIVIDUAL

Thus far we have explained how perceptions are formed: Individuals engage in selective attention, use a variety of organizational processes, and assign meaning to their perceptions. Thus, if you hear a loud noise in the street, you will turn your attention to the street; and if you see a car stopped and a person lying in the road with her motorcycle, you will categorize the event as an accident. Finally, you likely will decide (interpret) that the car hit the motorcycle rider. However, a variety of individual factors influence people's perceptual processes and affect their selection, organization, and interpretation of sensory input. For example, those who often ride motorcycles may attribute fault for the accident to the car driver (since they have frequently experienced inattentive auto drivers) while people who only drive cars my attribute blame to the motorcyclist (because they observed cyclists driving between lanes of cars on the road). The individual factors that influence our perceptual processes generally fall into three categories: physical, cognitive, and personality characteristics. Let's begin with the physical factors.

Physical Differences

Each person's unique physical capabilities affect what they perceive and how they understand it. Some people have more acute hearing than others, as you will see in *Did You Know? The Ringtone Adults Cannot Hear.* Others have more acute sight or taste than others do. For example, professional wine tasters have a very highly developed sense of taste, pilots are required to have 40/40 vision, and musicians must possess the ability to identify various pitches and notes. As mentioned earlier, age can influence perception, and an individual's sex can affect the sensory input they notice.

Synesthesia is another individual physical difference that affects perception, which has only recently been recognized and studied. Synesthesia is a rare cognitive and

Did You Know?

The Ringtone Adults Cannot Hear

Are you familiar with Mosquito Ringtones? What are the implications of the Mosquito Teen Repellent and Mosquito Ringtone for communicating, perceiving, and understanding?

The Mosquito Ringtone is based on technology created by Britain Howard Stapleton, who developed a device described as the Mosquito Teen Repellent. The device emitted a high-pitched frequency tone that adults could not hear but that teenagers found annoying. It was used by shopkeepers to disperse teenagers from public spaces where they congregated.

Later, inventive students converted the same technology into a ringtone that adults could not hear. This allowed them to receive phone calls and text messages while in class without their teachers being aware of it—that is, provided their teachers were old enough.

To test your ability to hear Mosquito Ringtones at different frequency levels, go to http://www.freemosquitoringtone.org.

physical trait that influences people's perception and, to some extent, their communication. To learn what synesthesia is (and whether you have it!), refer to *Alternative View: Hearing Colors, Tasting Shapes.*

Cognitive Complexity

As we discussed earlier, the process of categorization helps us to organize information. Scientists refer to the categories we form as **constructs. Cognitive complexity** refers to how detailed, involved, or numerous a person's constructs are (Burleson & Caplan, 1998). But how does cognitive complexity affect perception?

First, people tend to be more cognitively complex about—and have more constructs for—those things that interest them or with which they have had experience. If you like music, you have a wide range of constructs, such as rap, hip hop, alternative, progressive, and neocountry, and these are constructs that others may not possess at all. This high number of constructs affects your perceptions of music. As you listen, you can distinguish between multiple forms of music, and you recognize when an artist is employing a specific form or fusing two or more. In addition to these sets of personal constructs that help you interpret the world, you also possess *interpersonal constructs* that you use to make decisions and inferences about other people (Deutsch, Sullivan, Sage, & Basile, 1991).

From an early age, everyone possesses simple constructs that help them explain their perceptions of others. These constructs tend to be bipolar, or based on opposing categories of characteristics, such as funny or serious, warm or cold, and responsible or careless. One's age, intellectual ability, and experiences influence how complex or detailed such constructs are. For example, very young children typically describe others with only a few constructs, such as nice or mean; most adults, however, have a much more involved set of constructs that allows them to describe others in more varied and specific ways.

In addition, when you have cognitively complex construct systems, you tend to have many ways of explaining and understanding interpersonal interactions. Suppose, for example, that your friend Laura was almost an hour late meeting you for a dinner date. If you are cognitively complex, you might come up with a number of reasons to explain this behavior: Laura (a) was in a traffic accident, (b) forgot about the date, (c) was detained by an unforeseen event, (d) decided not to keep the date, and so on. These are all plausible explanations; without further

constructs
categories people develop to help them organize information

cognitive complexity
the degree to which a person's constructs are detailed, involved, or numerous

Alternative VIEW
Hearing Colors, Tasting Shapes

People with synesthesia—those whose senses blend together—provide valuable clues to understanding the organization and functions of the human brain.

What does synesthesia reveal about how the brain affects perception? How can these differences in perceptual abilities affect how individuals interact with one another?

When Matthew Blakeslee shapes hamburger patties with his hands, he experiences a vivid bitter taste in his mouth. Esmerelda Jones (a pseudonym) sees blue when she listens to the note C sharp played on the piano; other notes evoke different hues—so much so that the piano keys are actually color-coded, making it easier for her to remember and play musical scales. And when Jeff Coleman looks at printed black numbers, he sees them in color, each a different hue. Blakeslee, Jones, and Coleman are among a handful of otherwise normal people who have synesthesia; they are part of the estimated 1 percent of people worldwide who are synesthetic. They experience the ordinary world in extraordinary ways and seem to inhabit a mysterious no-man's-land between fantasy and reality. For them the senses—touch, taste, hearing, vision, and smell—get mixed up instead of remaining separate.

Modern scientists have known about synesthesia since 1880, when Francis Galton, a cousin of Charles Darwin, published a paper in *Nature* on the phenomenon. But most have brushed it aside as fakery, an artifact of drug use (LSD and mescaline can produce similar effects), or a mere curiosity. About four years ago, however, we and others began to uncover brain processes that could account for synesthesia. Along the way, we also found new clues to some of the most mysterious aspects of the human mind, such as the emergence of abstract thought, metaphor, and perhaps even language.

Overview/Synesthesia

- Synesthesia (from the Greek roots *syn*, meaning "together," and *aisthesis*, or "perception") is a condition in which otherwise normal people experience the blending of two or more senses.

- For decades, the phenomenon was often written off as fakery or simply memories, but it has recently been shown to be real. Perhaps it occurs because of cross activation, in which two normally separate areas of the brain elicit activity in each other.

- As scientists explore the mechanisms involved in synesthesia, they are also learning about how the brain in general processes sensory information and uses it to make abstract connections between seemingly unrelated inputs.

information you will not know which one is correct. The point is that cognitively complex individuals can develop a large set of alternative explanations.

In turn, your degree of cognitive complexity influences your perceptions and thus your communication behavior. For example, if you can only explain Laura's lateness by deciding that she is thoughtless, you will likely perceive her negatively and use a hostile communication style when you meet. Individuals' levels of complexity influence a broad range of communicative issues, such as how many persuasive messages they can generate (Applegate, 1982) and how well they can comfort others (Samter & Burleson, 1984).

Personality and Individual Characteristics

Each person's unique mix of personality, temperament, and experience influences how they interpret and respond to sensory information. Elements that make up this mix include emotional state, outlook, and knowledge.

Cognitively complex individuals can develop a large number of explanations for the late arrival of a dinner date.

Emotional State If you are feeling happy or optimistic, you will tend to interpret and respond to sensory input differently than if you are feeling depressed, angry, or sad (Planalp, 1993). For instance, if you feel angry, you may perceive music, other people's voices, or background noise as irritating. On the other hand, if you are in a positive mood, you may behave more helpfully toward others. In one experiment, researchers tested 800 passersby (Gueguen & De Gail, 2003). In half the cases, researchers smiled at the passerby, and in half they did not. A few seconds after this interaction, the passersby had the opportunity to help another researcher who dropped his or her belongings on the ground. Those who were exposed to the smile in the first encounter were more likely to be helpful in the second. Thus, even a small impact on your emotional state can influence how you communicate and interact with others.

Outlook One's outlook refers to a tendency to view and interpret the world in consistent ways. Research shows that people tend to have a natural predisposition to either optimism or pessimism, based on genetics and experience (Seligman, 1998). People who are optimistic by nature may expect more positive experiences and make fewer negative attributions. These positive expectations can have an influence on their behavior—but not always for the best. For example, young people with an optimistic bias tend to believe that they are less likely than others to experience negative consequences from health behaviors. Therefore, they may be more likely than others to engage in sexual risk-taking (Chapin, 2001).

Knowledge People frequently interpret what they perceive based on what they know of an event. If you know that your friend has a big exam coming up, you may interpret his or her irritability as due to nervousness. Our knowledge of specific topics also influences our perceptions, communication, and decision making. For instance, a study on organ donation revealed that members of families that discussed the subject were twice as likely to donate their organs as were members of other families (Smith, Kopfman, Lindsey, Massi, & Morrison, 2004). The researchers concluded that once people communicate and know more about the topic of organ donation, they perceive it in a more positive light.

Your perceptions strongly shape your communication and your actions. If you strike up a conversation with someone new who looks physically attractive but whose voice reminds you of someone you dislike, you may choose to end the conversation and move on. However, if you meet someone who reminds you of someone you like, you might invest energy in getting to know that person. If you interpret a new friend's teasing as a sign of affection, you may decide to increase your involvement with her. In these ways, your perceptual processes influence your interactions and relationships. In addition, broader societal factors also play a role in what you perceive, how you organize it, and the meanings you attach to it, as shown in *Visual Summary 4.1: Perception and the Individual*. We discuss these societal influences next.

TEST YOUR KNOWLEDGE
- How do physical differences influence the perception process?
- What is cognitive complexity, and how does it influence the perception process?

THE INDIVIDUAL, PERCEPTION, AND SOCIETY

How do societal factors affect perception? As we will explain in this section, the position individuals hold in society and the cultures in which they live affect what they perceive and how they interpret these perceptions. As you read this section, we encourage you to consider the societal forces that affect your perceptions as well as how they might affect the perceptions of others.

VISUAL SUMMARY 4.1 — Perception and the Individual

Which perception factors affect their ability to comunicate with each other?

Individual Perception Factors

PHYSICAL	COGNITIVE	INTERPRETATION
Differences in:	**Complexity of constructs based on:**	**Elements:**
■ Visual acuity	■ Interests	■ Emotional state
■ Sense of taste	■ Intellectual ability	■ Outlook
■ Sense of smell	■ Experiences	■ Knowledge
■ Hearing acuity		
■ Touch sensitivity		

The Role of Power

Every society has a hierarchy, and in a hierarchy some people have more power than others. Your relative position of power or lack of power influences how others perceive you, how you perceive others, and how you interpret events in the world. Moreover, those in power largely determine a society's understandings of reality. For example, in the United States, the dominant perception is that everyone can move up in society through hard work and education ("Middle of the Class," 2005). However, individuals who are born poor and who live in deprived areas with few resources can find it very difficult, no matter how hard they try to follow the path to "success" as defined by mainstream U.S. culture. Thus the perceptual

Power differences affect people's perceptions of how easy or difficult it is to attain financial success.

reality of these people is likely to differ from that of those higher in the power hierarchy. Nonetheless, a specific view of reality dominates U.S. culture because it is communicated both explicitly and implicitly through media messages, public speeches, schools, and other social institutions.

One's individual experiences within that hierarchy may lead one to accept or reject that dominant perception. For example, middle-class people may believe that if they work hard they will get ahead in society, whereas poor people may perceive that it takes a lot more than hard work and education (Ehrenreich, 2001). Similarly, if a you grew up relatively wealthy, you may believe that your admission to a highly selective college is largely due to your intelligence, hard work, and skills, whereas someone who grew up relatively poor may believe that social connections and family money better explain this achievement (Douthat, 2005).

Your position in the racial hierarchy also influences your perceptions about the reality of racial bias. It is well documented that White Americans and African Americans have very different perceptions regarding the role of race in the United States (Hacker, 2003). A study conducted after Hurricane Katrina devastated the Gulf Coast revealed a broad divergence in perceptions: When asked whether racial inequality remains a major problem, 71 percent of African Americans replied yes, compared to only 32 percent of Whites (Pew Research Center for the People and the Press, 2005).

The Role of Culture

Culture strongly influences individual perception. One way it does so is through its *sensory model*. Every culture has its own sensory model, which means that each culture emphasizes a few of the five senses (Classen, 1990). Moreover, what a culture emphasizes affects what its members pay attention to and prefer. People in the United States, for example, tend to give primacy to the visual; thus, we have sayings such as "seeing is believing," and students almost demand that professors use PowerPoint slides in the classroom. On the other hand, people living in the Andes Mountains of South America tend to place more emphasis on what they hear than on what they see. In their culture, important ideas are transmitted through characters in stories and narratives (Classen, 1990). Knowing this, how do you think students in the Andes prefer to learn? You might imagine that they would prefer elaborate stories rather than a list of brief terms and concepts on PowerPoint slides.

A culture is composed of a set of shared practices, norms, values, and beliefs (Brislin, 2000; Shore, 1996), which in turn helps shape individuals' thoughts, feelings, perceptions, and behaviors. For example, individuals in East Asian cultures often are highly interdependent and emphasize the group over the individual. Consequently, they don't approve of bragging and encourage greater self-criticism than some other cultures. By encouraging self-criticism (and then working on self-improvement), the thinking goes, they are contributing to the overall strength of the group (Heine & Lehman, 2004; Markus, Mullally, & Kitayama, 1997). In the United States, however, the emphasis is often on the individual, and most people are encouraged to distinguish themselves from others. For example, current books on dating and work success teach U.S. Americans how to "brand" themselves like a product. The dominant culture in the United States also encourages people to talk about their success and to refrain from self-criticism. As a result, someone from East Asia may see U.S. Americans as braggarts, while a person from the United States may see East Asians as overly modest (Kim, 2002).

Cultural background also influences how people expect to talk to one another (Scollon & Wong-Scollon, 1990). In some Native American cultures, for example, individuals perceive strangers as potentially unpredictable, so they may talk little—if at all—until they have established familiarity and trust with the newcomer (Braithwaite, 1990). This approach differs considerably from the customs of some European American cultures, in which people view strangers as potential friends and strike up conversations to become acquainted with them (Krivonos & Knapp, 1975).

Now imagine a Native American and a European American from these different communication cultures meeting for the first time. How is each likely to behave? The Native American may remain relatively quiet while observing the new person. The European American will most likely try to engage in a lively conversation and may ask a number of questions to draw the other person out. As a result, the Native American may view the European American as nosy, pushy, and overly familiar, while the European American may see the Native American as unfriendly or shy (Braithwaite, 1990). Each perceives or evaluates the other based on expectations that were shaped by his or her own cultural perceptions, values, and the meanings typical for his or her own culture (Scollon & Wong-Scollon, 1990).

Some travelers become upset when their cultural expectations about what is "food" are not fulfilled.

Cultural norms, values, and expectations provide a backdrop of familiarity. When we travel or when we meet people from other cultures close to home, we can learn from exposure to our differences. However, sometimes these differences are upsetting, frustrating, or baffling. For example, one of our students, Simone, was taken aback when she was offered *chapulines* (fried grasshoppers) during her trip to Oaxaca, Mexico. Interestingly, most of us not only value the ways of our own culture, we often feel that others' cultural norms are less desirable—or even wrong—an issue we discuss next.

The Role of Social Comparison

As we discussed earlier, categorizing groups of objects, information, or people is a basic quality of perception. *Social* categorization—or categorizing people—leads us to specific expectations about how others should or should not behave. These social categories and the expectations associated with them typically arise out of our culture and where we are positioned in the culture. For example, in the United States, middle- and upper-middle-class people often perceive individuals who receive government subsidies for food or housing as people who do not want to work hard, and they may therefore categorize them as lazy or dependent. However, people who are in the working class or among the working poor may have a different perception, asserting that those who rely on these government subsidies work hard but are underemployed or have to live on a salary that is not a living wage ("Middle of the Class," 2005; Ehrenreich, 2001). As you can see, the perceptions and categories that we develop tend to be tied to stereotypes and prejudice, which both flow from ethnocentrism, the perceptual concept at the core of social comparison.

Ethnocentrism Most people view their own group as the standard against which they evaluate others. Thus, one's own ethnic, regional, or class group is the one that seems right, correct, or normal. This tendency to view one's own group as the standard against which all others are judged is described as **ethnocentrism.** It comes from the Greek words *ethnos*, which means nation, and *kentron*, which refers to the center of a circle (Ting-Toomey, 1999). People behave ethnocentrically when they view their own values, norms, or modes of belief and behavior as better than those of other groups.

While it is normal to be proud of one's national, cultural, racial, or ethnic group, one becomes ethnocentric when he or she engages in polarized thinking and

ethnocentrism
the tendency to view one's own group as the standard against which all other groups are judged

behavior. This occurs when people believe that if "we" are right, correct, normal, and even superior, then "they" must be wrong, incorrect, abnormal, and inferior. Such thinking can seriously interfere with our ability to communicate effectively with those outside our group.

Stereotypes   Earlier in the chapter, we described stereotypes as broad generalizations about an entire class of objects or people, based on some knowledge of some aspects of some members of the class (Brislin, 2000; Stephan & Stephan, 1992). When you stereotype computer programmers as smart but socially inept, you likely are basing your beliefs on your interactions with a few programmers—or perhaps on no interactions at all. Stereotypes may be based on what you have read, images in the media, or information you have obtained from others, as you'll see was the case with one college student in *It Happened to Me: Damien.*

If you develop a stereotype, it tends to influence what you expect from the stereotyped group. If you believe that someone is a lesbian, you may also believe she engages in specific types of communication behavior, dress, or interests. When you hold these types of beliefs and expectations, they tend to erase the stereotyped person's individual characteristics. In addition, you are likely to communicate with her as if your stereotypes were accurate rather than basing your messages on her actual interests and behavior (Snyder, 1998).

Stereotyping is an understandable and natural cognitive activity; in fact, stereotypes can serve as useful shorthand to help us understand the world. If you are interviewing for a job in the Southern United States, it may be helpful for you to know that many Southerners prefer to engage in social interaction before getting down to business (though this is certainly not always true). However, when stereotyping leads to polarized understandings of the world as "between me and you, us and them, females and males, Blacks and Whites," then it can cause problems (Ting-Toomey, 1999, p. 149). In turn, polarized thinking frequently leads to a rigid, intolerant view of certain behavior as correct or incorrect (Ting-Toomey, 1999). For example, do you believe it is more appropriate for adult children to live on their own than with their parents before they marry? People with polarized thinking assume that their own cultural beliefs regarding this issue are right or correct instead of recognizing that cultures differ in what is considered appropriate.

Prejudice   Stereotypes and feelings of ethnocentrism often lead to prejudice. **Prejudice** occurs when people experience aversive or negative feelings toward a group as a whole or toward an individual because she or he belongs to a group (Rothenberg, 1992). People can experience prejudice against a person or group because of his or her physical characteristics, perceived ethnicity, age, national origin, religious practices, and a number of other identity categories.

Given the negative associations most people have with the concept of prejudice, you may wonder why it persists. Researchers believe that prejudice is common and

---

It Happened to Me: *Damien*

Shortly after school started, I decided to join a fraternity and began going to parties on the weekends. Often when people heard me mention that I was a part-time computer programmer, they would first look shocked and then crack some kind of joke about it, like, "Bill Gates, Jr., eh?" I guess it surprises people that I don't have glasses, that I venture out into the sunlight once in a while, and that I engage in some social activities! I realize that their preconceived notions about "techies" have come from somewhere, but, since at least half of my fellow "computer geeks" are far from the nerdy stereotype, it would be nice if people would recognize that we aren't all pale, glasses-wearing, socially awkward nerds!

---

prejudice
experiencing aversive or negative feelings toward a group as a whole or toward an individual because she or he belongs to a group

pervasive because it serves specific functions, the two most important of which are *ego-defensive functions* and *value-expressive functions* (Brislin, 2000). Let's explore these concepts.

The **ego-defensive function** of prejudice describes the role it plays in protecting individuals' sense of self-worth. For example, an individual who is not financially successful and whose group members tend not to be financially successful may attribute blame to other groups for hoarding resources and preventing him or her from becoming successful. The less financially successful individual may also look down on groups that are even less financially successful as a way to protect his or her own ego. These attitudes may make people feel better, but they also prevent them from analyzing reasons for their own failure. Moreover, they negatively affect the ways people talk to and about the targeted groups. People who look down on groups that are less financially successful may describe them and talk to them as if they were lazy, incompetent, or not very bright.

Prejudice serves its **value-expressive function** by allowing people to view their own values, norms, and cultural practices as appropriate and correct. By devaluing other groups' behavior and beliefs, these people maintain a solid sense that they are right. Unfortunately, this same function causes group members to denigrate the cultural practices of others. You may have seen many examples of the value-expressive function of prejudice, as when individuals engage in uncivil arguments and personal attacks over issues such as men's and women's roles, abortion, and politics.

The Role of Historical Time Period

In addition to a person's place in the power hierarchy, their culture, and their awareness of social comparison, the historical period in which one grows up and lives influences perception and communication (U.S. National Research Council, 1989). For example, this author is writing this chapter on September 11, 2010. Anyone living in the United States who was older than five or six on September 11, 2001, likely has had their perceptions altered by events of that day. They may feel less safe, perceive air travel as riskier, and feel more patriotic than they did before the terrorist attacks on that day. These perceptions may in turn influence how they talk about the United States; or how they communicate, for example, with individuals who are Muslim.

Other historical events have affected the perceptions of individuals who lived through them. For instance, people who lived through the Great Depression may perceive resources as being scarcer than others do; those who were young during the Vietnam War likely believe that collective action can influence political policy; and those who grew up watching *The Real World* and other reality TV programs probably view privacy differently than do prior generations. As you might expect, these perceptions influence how, and about what, the various generations communicate, a process called the **cohort effect.** Thus those who came of age after 2000 may feel comfortable discussing a wide range of topics previously considered taboo, such as sexual conduct or family dysfunction. Similarly, women who grew up when sexual discrimination was more prevalent might object to the use of "girls" when referring to women.

Social Roles

The roles one plays socially also influence one's perception and, consequently, communication. **Social role** refers to the specific position or positions an individual holds in a society. Social roles include job positions, familial roles (such as mother or father), and positions in society. For example, Teri holds a variety of roles, including mother, religious leader, soccer coach, and community activist. The fact that she holds these social roles affects how people perceive and communicate with her in several ways. First, society defines specific expectations for her various social

ego-defensive function
the role prejudice plays in protecting individuals' sense of self-worth

value-expressive function
the role played by prejudice in allowing people to view their own values, norms, and cultural practices as appropriate and correct

cohort effect
the process by which historical events influence the perceptions of people who grew up in a given generation and time period

social role
the specific position or positions one holds in a society

roles (Kirouac & Hess, 1999). Many people, for example, expect that religious leaders will be especially moral, selfless, and well intentioned. In turn, these expectations affect the ways that religious leaders interact with others. If you expect Teri, as a religious leader, to be highly moral, she may work to communicate with you in ways that fulfill your expectations.

Second, the education, training, and socialization Teri undergoes for her social roles influence her perceptions. In much of U.S. culture it is expected that women will become mothers and that they will behave in specific ways as they fulfill that role. As they grow up, girls are socialized and taught, by both word and example, how mothers are supposed to communicate. Because Teri is a parent, she may perceive different issues as important. For example, she may be more concerned with the quality of schools, the safety of her neighborhood, and access to health care than a nonparent might. Similarly, when individuals receive education and training, their perceptions of the world around them are affected. A person trained as a police officer, for example, may perceive the world as populated with more criminals than the average person does; whereas a person trained as a nurse may be more aware of how to prevent illnesses and injuries.

Each individual's perceptions are unique, based on his or her own roles and characteristics. However, individuals also share certain perceptual realities with others in their power position in society's hierarchy as well as with others in their cultures and social role groups. Because of these differing realities and power positions, your perceptions may lead you into prejudicial and intolerant thinking and communication. In the concluding section of this chapter, we suggest strategies for improving your perception processes and communication.

TEST YOUR KNOWLEDGE

- What is social comparison? How is it related to ethnocentrism and prejudice?

ETHICS AND PERCEPTION

As we've discussed throughout this chapter, the ways people communicate to and about others are connected to their perceptions and cognitions about them. That is, what we select to attend to, what categories we put people in, and the attributions we make about them all strongly influence what we believe, say, and do. For example, Sharina was driving home late one night and stopped at a traffic light when she notice a young man of color in the car next to hers. She reached over and locked her door. As she looked up, she saw the man smile slightly then lean over and lock *his* door. In this case, Sharina was responding based on stereotypical perceptions and cognitions, and the other driver was gently reminding her of that fact.

A common example of a time when perception, ethics, and communication intersect occurs when speakers perceive and label other groups of people negatively and then use derogatory terms to refer to them. Unfortunately, using such terms can reinforce and even intensify one's own as well as others' negative responses to these groups. In addition, if what individuals attend to and perceive about people first is their skin color, their sex, or their relative affluence, they may find themselves communicating with those people stereotypically and failing to recognize other roles they fulfill. Doing so may lead one to assume and communicate as if all adult women are mothers (or there is something wrong with them if they are not) or to refer to a physician as nurse because she happens to be female. Each of these behaviors is problematic in that it denies others their right to legitimate identities. Consequently such behaviors are ones that are usefully examined through an ethical lens. That is, when tempted to create stereotypes of others and to communicate with them based on that stereotype, it helps to ask yourself if doing so fits within your own ethical framework.

Although social factors such as power and position can impact many aspects of your life, you do have control of, and responsibility for, your perceptions and cognitions. Even though your social circle and your family may engage in problematic perceptual, cognitive, and communicative processes, once you become an adult you are responsible for how you interpret the world. To help you think about your perceptions and cognitive processes through an ethical lens, below we discuss some guidelines to assist you in this process.

TEST YOUR KNOWLEDGE

• How is ethics relevant to the perception process?

IMPROVING YOUR PERCEPTION SKILLS

You probably realize now that perceptions are subject to variance and error because of the variety of steps one goes through in forming them (selection, organization, and interpretation) and the range of factors that influence the perception process (individual characteristics, cognitive complexity, power, culture, historical time period, and social roles). However, certain cognitive and communication behaviors can improve one's ability to perceive and understand the world.

First, one can engage in *mindfulness* to improve perception and understanding. Mindfulness refers to a clear focus on the activity one is engaged in, with attention to as many specifics of the event as possible (Langer, 1978). People tend to be most mindful when they are engaged in a new or unusual activity. Once an activity becomes habitual, they are likely to overlook its details. Mindfulness requires that one bring the same level of attention and involvement to routine activities as one does to novel ones.

In addition, before assuming your perceptions are accurate, you might ask yourself a few questions to help you check those perceptions:

■ Have you focused too narrowly and missed relevant information due to selective attention? For example, did you focus on what the person was wearing rather than what he or she was saying?

■ What type of organizational pattern did you use? For example, just because two people are standing next to one another does not mean they are together.

■ To what extent have you considered all possible interpretations for the information you perceived, using the full range of your cognitive complexity? For example, if you did poorly on a test, was it due to poor test construction, your lack of sleep, the teacher's failure to prepare you, or your own failure to study sufficiently?

■ How might your physical condition have influenced your perceptions? For example, are you tired, hungry, or frightened?

■ How has your cultural background influenced your perceptions? For example, are you perceiving politeness as deception?

One communication act that can improve your perception skills is checking with others to see if their perceptions of others are similar to yours.

■ How has your social role influenced your perception? For example, have you begun to perceive all elderly people as infirm because you work in a nursing home?

■ How has your social position influenced your perception? For example, have you considered how others with different positions might perceive the same issue?

Another way to improve one's perception and understanding is to clearly separate *facts* from *inferences*. Facts are truths that are verifiable based on observation. Inferences are conclusions that we draw or interpretations we make based on the facts. Thus, it may be a fact that Southerners speak more slowly than do people from other regions of the United States, but it is an inference if you conclude that their slow speech indicates slow thought processes.

Finally, one communication act in particular will greatly improve anyone's perception skills: perception checking. That is, checking with others to determine if their perceptions match your own. If they do not, you may need to alter your perceptions. For example, Rosario once had an extremely negative reaction to a job candidate who interviewed at her company. She perceived him as arrogant and sexist. However, when she talked with her colleagues she discovered that no one else had a similarly strong negative response to the candidate. She decided that her perceptions must have been influenced by something in her own background; for example, he may have reminded her of someone she had once known who did display those negative traits. In revising her opinion of the candidate, Rosario demonstrated a well-developed sensitivity to the perception side of communication. All of us can benefit from greater awareness of the assumptions and attributions we make.

TEST YOUR KNOWLEDGE
- What one skill could you develop that would most improve your perception processes? Why does it help?

SUMMARY

Perception plays an important role in everyday communication. People use three perceptual processes to manage the vast array of sensory data in their environments: selection, organization, and interpretation. From all the sounds, sights, smells, tastes, and textures available, people choose only a few to focus on. Once we attend to particular sensory information, we organize it to make sense of it. Two of the cognitive processes we use to organize information are cognitive representations and categorization. Finally, after we perceive and organize sensory information, we assign meaning to it using frames and attributions.

In addition, the sensory data we select to attend to, how we organize it, and the interpretations we assign are all influenced by our individual characteristics, such as physical abilities and differences, cognitive complexity, and any personality and individual differences. In addition, perception processes are affected by one's position in the power hierarchy, culture, historical events during one's lifetime, and social roles.

Because people vary so much in their perceptions, no one should assume that what he or she perceives is the same as what others perceive. Instead, we all must carefully check our perceptions on a regular basis and expend energy to overcome errors in processing as well as any attributional biases.

HUMAN COMMUNICATION IN SOCIETY ONLINE

To review this chapter, use the MyCommunicationLab Web site to test your understanding of the following key terms, record your answers to the chapter review questions, and complete the suggested activities. Expand your learning and understanding of chapter concepts by completing additional activities and exercises online. Access code required. Go to www.mycommunicationlab.com for more information or to purchase standalone access.

KEY TERMS

selection 85
organization 85
interpretation 85
selective attention 85
cognitive representation 86
schemas 87
prototype 87
script 87

categorization 87
label 88
stereotyping 88
frame 89
attribution theory 89
attributional bias 90
self-serving bias 90
fundamental attribution error 90

constructs 91
cognitive complexity 91
ethnocentrism 97
prejudice 98
ego-defensive function 99
value-expressive function 99
cohort effect 99
social role 99

APPLY WHAT YOU KNOW

1. **Examining Stereotypes** For each of the words below, write down your beliefs about the group represented. In other words, provide a list of specific characteristics you believe are typically displayed by members of these groups.

   a. fraternity members
   b. politicians
   c. models
   d. rap stars
   e. body builders
   f. religious leaders

   After you have done so, compare your list to the lists created by other members of your class. What characteristics for each group did you have in common? What characteristics differed? Can you think of at least one person from each group who does not display the characteristics you listed? What information and perceptions helped shaped your stereotypes? How valid do you think your stereotypes are?

2. **Attributional Biases** As this chapter explains, people have a tendency to attribute their own positive behavior to internal traits and their negative behavior to external factors. However, they are also more likely to attribute others' positive behavior to external conditions and others' negative behavior to internal traits. In this exercise we want you to indicate how the attributional bias would cause you to describe each of the following behaviors, depending on who had performed it.

Example: Forgetting to make a phone call
   I'm busy. You're thoughtless.
Example: Earning a good grade
   I'm intelligent. You were lucky.

Do the exercise for each of the following behaviors/events:

   a. Receiving a raise
   b. Breaking a vase
   c. Arriving late
   d. Winning an award
   e. Burning a meal
   f. Making a group laugh

Compare your responses with those of others in your class. What terms were used to describe one's own experiences? What terms were used to describe others' experiences? What is it about the perception process that makes attribution bias so common?

   Although this is just an exercise, remember that the attributional bias is quite common. Pay attention to your own thoughts and comments the next time something bad happens to you or others.

3. **Ethics and Perception** The authors argue that ethics is relevant to our perceptual processes. To what extent do you agree or disagree with this statement? Provide three arguments for each position. Now that you have considered arguments for both positions, is your opinion the same as it was before or has it altered?

EXPLORE

1. Go to a website that features perception exercises and information, such as the Hanover College Sensation and Perception Tutorials or the Encyclopedia of Psychology's Sensation and Perception tutorial. After experiencing at least two of the tutorials, write a paragraph in which you explain what you have learned about perception.

2. Go to a website such as Gestalt Laws or Perceptual Grouping and read the information regarding the Gestalts laws of grouping. In a brief paper, provide an explanation of the Gestalt laws then describe how these laws might influence how we view and communicate with others.

3. Go to a website such as Harvard University's Interpersonal Perception Communication Lab or Tufts University's Interpersonal Perception and Communication page and read a description of at least one interpersonal perception and communication research project. Write a paragraph summarizing what the project you reviewed explains about the relationship between perception and communication.

Part

DEVELOPING EFFECTIVE
HUMAN COMMUNICATION SKILLS

5 Verbal
Communication

6 Nonverbal
Communication

7 Listening
and Responding

*H*ow do verbal and nonverbal communication influence the communication process? What role does listening play in communication effectiveness?

5
Verbal Communication

chapter outline

When I took a trip to Britain, I thought people would speak with a "British accent." I didn't realize that there are many different accents and the differences are not just pronunciation, but also vocabulary. In order to get my message across, I learned to avoid using slang words as much as I could. I didn't realize how much American slang I use in my everyday speech! Despite the many different ways of speaking English across the UK, I felt the way that I speak English made me stick out as an American.

When we think of "communication," we tend to think about the verbal elements of communication: the words people choose, the accents they speak with, and the meanings they convey through language. We frequently don't consider the ways in which verbal communication assists or hinders relationship development, as illustrated in the opening example, or its effect on the creation of identities.

In this chapter we will explore the verbal elements of communication and how people use verbal communication to accomplish various goals. First we discuss the importance of verbal communication and its value as a topic of study. We then describe how individuals use verbal communication, including the functions it serves and the components of language that make it possible. Next we explore individual characteristics such as gender, age, regionality, ethnicity and race, and education and occupation that influence verbal communication. We investigate the societal forces that influence verbal communication by examining the relationships among language, perception, and power. Finally, we provide suggestions for communicating more ethically and more effectively.

Once you have read this chapter, you will be able to:

- Identify three reasons for learning about verbal communication.
- Describe the functions and components of language.
- Identify and give examples of several major influences on verbal communication.
- Describe the relationships between language, perception, and power.
- Identify and give examples of confirming communication, disconfirming communication, and hate speech.
- Discuss ethical issues in verbal communication.
- Discuss ways to improve your own verbal communication skills.

THE IMPORTANCE OF VERBAL COMMUNICATION

Although the nonverbal aspects of communication are important, the verbal elements of communication are the foundation on which meaning is created. If you doubt that this is the case, try this simple test. Using only nonverbal communication, convey this message to a friend or roommate: "I failed my exam because I locked my keys in my car and couldn't get my textbook until well after midnight." How well was your nonverbal message understood? If you have ever traveled in a country where you didn't speak the language, no doubt you already knew before trying this experiment that nonverbal communication can only get you so far. We will touch on the importance of nonverbal communication here and discuss it in depth in Chapter 6. In this section we propose that to be a highly effective communicator you need to understand the verbal elements of communication.

Verbal communication is also important because of the role it plays in identity and relationship development. As you might remember from our discussion in Chapter 3, individuals develop a sense of self through communication with others. More specifically, the labels used to describe individuals can influence their self-concepts and increase or decrease their self-esteem. People's verbal communication practices also can impede or improve their relationships, a topic we will discuss further in Chapter 9. Research by four psychology professors at Emory University supports our claims about the relationship between verbal communication and an individual's identity development and relationship skills. These scholars found that families that converse and eat meals together on a regular basis have children who not only are more familiar with their family histories but also tend to have higher self-esteem, interact better with their peers, and be better able to recover from tragedy and negative events (Duke et al., 2003).

Children from families who converse and eat meals together on a regular basis have higher self-esteem and interact better with their peers.

In addition, the very language people speak is tied to their identities. Studies of bilingual and multilingual speakers show that their perceptions, behaviors, and even personalities alter when they change languages (Ramírez-Esparza, Gosling, Benet-Martínez, Potter, & Pennebaker, 2006). Why does this occur? The answer is that every language is embedded in a specific cultural context, and when people learn a language, they also learn the beliefs, values, and norms of its culture (Edwards, 2004). So speaking a language evokes its culture as well as a sense of who we are within that culture. Thus the language you use to communicate verbally shapes who you are, as you will see in *It Happened to Me: Cristina*.

WHAT IS VERBAL COMMUNICATION?

Verbal communication generally refers to the written or oral words we exchange; however, as our opening example shows, verbal communication has to do with more than just the words people speak. It includes pronunciation or accent, the meanings of the words used, and a range of variations in the way people speak a language, which depend on their regional backgrounds and other factors.

Language, of course, plays a central role in communication. Some argue that it is our use of language that makes us human. Unlike other mammals, humans use symbols that they can string together to create new words and with which they can form infinite sets of never-before-heard, -thought,

It Happened to Me: *Cristina*

I was teaching an adult education class composed primarily of Mexican immigrants when I first noticed that the language people speak affects how they behave. I'm bilingual, so even though we normally spoke English in my class, sometimes we switched to Spanish. Over time, I noticed that several male students were respectful and deferential when we spoke English; however, when we switched to Spanish, they became more flirtatious and seemed less willing to treat me as an authority figure. Now I understand that these differences probably were related to how men and women interact in the two cultures.

or -read sentences. This ability allows people to be creative and expressive, such as when they coin terms like "Googleganger"—nominated by the American Dialect Society as one of the most creative words for 2007—meaning a person with your name who shows up when you google yourself. This is a play on words with the German word "Doppelgänger," which refers to a double of someone (especially a ghostly double). Even small children who are unschooled in grammar create their own rules of language by using innate linguistic ability together with linguistic information they glean from the people around them. For example, young children often say "mouses" instead of "mice" because they first learn, and apply broadly, the most common rule for pluralizing—adding an *s*.

To help you better understand the role of language in the communication process, the next section explores seven communicative functions of language as well as four components of language use.

Functions of Language

We all use language so automatically that we usually don't think about the many roles it plays. However, language helps us do everything from ordering lunch to giving directions to writing love poems. Moreover, a single utterance can function in a variety of ways. For example, a simple "thank you" not only expresses gratitude, it also can increase feelings of intimacy and liking. Consequently, understanding the ways language functions can help you communicate more effectively. As we discuss next, language can serve at least seven functions: instrumental, regulatory, informative, heuristic, interactional, personal, and imaginative.

- The most basic function of language is **instrumental**. This means we can use it to obtain what we need or desire. For instance, when you invite friends to dinner, the invitation is instrumental in that you want your friends to come to dinner and the invitation helps make that happen.

- A second (and closely related) language function is **regulatory**, meaning that we can use it to control or regulate the behaviors of others. In your invitation, you may ask your friends to bring a bottle of wine or a dessert, as a way of regulating their behavior.

- Another basic function of language is to **inform**—to communicate information or report facts. When you invite your friends to dinner, you usually include the date and time to inform them of when you want them to come.

- We also use language to acquire knowledge and understanding, which is referred to as a **heuristic** use. When you want to invite friends to dinner, you may ask them if they are available at that date and time to learn if your dinner is going to occur as scheduled or if you need to change the date.

- When language is used in an **interactional** fashion, it establishes and defines social relationships in both interpersonal and group settings. Thus, when you invite your friends to dinner, you engage in a behavior that helps maintain your relationship with them as friends.

- **Personal language** expresses individuality and personality and is more common in private than in public settings. When you invite your friends to dinner you might jokingly say, "Don't bring that cheap bottle of wine, like you did last time." In this way, you use language to express your sense of humor.

- A final way you can use language is **imaginatively**. Imaginative language is used to express oneself artistically or creatively, as in drama, poetry, or stories. Thus, if on the cover of your invitation to dinner you wrote "A loaf of bread, a jug of wine, and thou," you would be using the imaginative function of language. For another example of the imaginative use of language, see *Did You Know? A Little Poem Regarding Computer Spell Checkers*.

instrumental
use of language to obtain what you need or desire

regulatory
use of language to control or regulate the behaviors of others

informative
use of language to communicate information or report facts

heuristic
use of language to acquire knowledge and understanding

interactional
use of language to establish and define social relationships

personal language
use of language to express individuality and personality

imaginative
use of language to express oneself artistically or creatively

Did You Know?

Candidate for a Pullet Surprise

I have a spelling checker,
It came with my PC.
It plane lee marks four my revue
Miss steaks aye can knot sea.

Eye ran this poem threw it,
Your sure reel glad two no.
Its vary polished in it's weigh.
My checker tolled me sew.

A checker is a bless sing,
It freeze yew lodes of thyme.
It helps me right awl stiles two reed,
And aides me when eye rime.

Each frays come posed up on my screen
Eye trussed too bee a joule.
The checker pours or every word
Too cheque sum spelling rule.

Bee fore a veiling checker's
Hour spelling mite decline,

And if we're lacks oar have a laps,
We wood bee maid too wine.

Butt now bee cause my spelling
Is checked with such grate flare,
Their are know fault's with in my cite,
Of nun eye am a wear.

Now spelling does knot phase me,
It does knot bring a tier.
My pay purrs awl due glad den
With wrapped word's fare as hear.

Too rite with care is quite a feet
Of witch won should bee proud,
And wee mussed dew the best wee can,
Sew flaw's are knot aloud.

Sow ewe can sea why aye dew prays
Such soft wear four pea seas,
And why eye brake in two averse
Buy righting want too pleas.

SOURCE: Retrieved March 11, 2009, from http://www.latech.edu/tech/liberal-arts/geography/courses/spellchecker.htm

---

As a student, which functions of language do you use most frequently? Which do you use most often in your professional life? If you use different functions in each of these roles, why do you think this is true?

As our discussion thus far indicates, language has seven basic functions, and speakers use them to accomplish specific goals or tasks. Note that these functions overlap and that one utterance can accomplish more than one function at the same time. For example, when inviting your friends to dinner, if you jokingly said, "James, our butler, will be serving dinner promptly at eight, so don't be late!" your utterance would both be imaginative (unless you actually have a butler named James) and regulatory. That is, you would be using language creatively while also attempting to regulate your guests' behavior to ensure they arrived on time.

Now that we have summarized the essential functions that language can serve, let's examine the basic components that allow us to use language as a flexible and creative tool of communication.

Components of Language

Scholars describe language use as being made up of four components: *phonology* (sounds), *syntax* (structure or rules), *semantics* (meaning), and *pragmatics* (use), as shown in *Visual Summary 5.1: Components of Language*. Every language has its own rules of **grammar**—the structural rules that govern the generation of meaning in that language. In this section, we examine the role each plays in the communication process.

Phonology: Sounds **Phonology** is the study of the sounds that compose individual languages and how those sounds communicate meaning. Basic sound units are called phonemes. They include vowels, consonants, and diphthongs (pairs of letters that operate as one, such as *th*). Different languages can use different phonemes. For example, French does not have the *th* sound. As a result, many native French speakers find it difficult to pronounce "this" or "that." Similarly, in Japanese, a phoneme that is between *r* and *l* is the closest equivalent to the English *r* sound. For

grammar
the structural rules that govern the generation of meaning in a language

phonology
the study of the sounds that compose individual languages and how those sounds communicate meaning

VISUAL SUMMARY 5.1

Components of Language: Phonology, Syntax, Pragmatics, Semantics

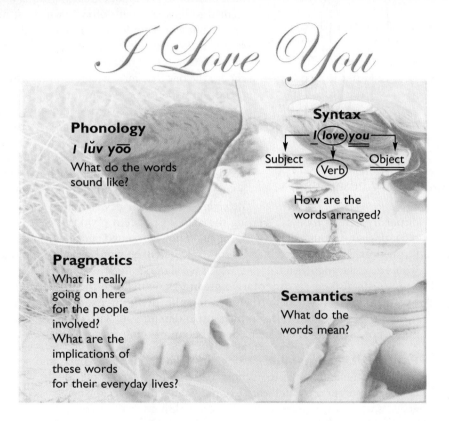

I Love You

Phonology

I lŭv yōō

What do the words sound like?

Syntax

I love you

Subject — Verb — Object

How are the words arranged?

Pragmatics

What is really going on here for the people involved? What are the implications of these words for their everyday lives?

Semantics

What do the words mean?

more information about phonology, see www.langsci.ucl.ac.uk/ipa/, the home page of the International Phonetic Association.

Syntax: Rules Syntax refers to the rules that govern word order. Due to the English rules of syntax, the sentences "The young boy hit the old man" and "The old man hit the young boy" have very different meanings, even though they contain identical words. Syntax also governs how words of various categories (nouns, adjectives, verbs) are combined into clauses, which in turn combine into sentences. Whether or not we are conscious of them, most of us regularly follow certain rules about combining words—for example, that the verb and subject in a sentence have to agree, so people say "the pencil *is* on the table," not "the pencil *are* on the table." Because of these rules, people combine words consistently in ways that make sense and make communication possible.

Semantics: Meaning Semantics is the study of meaning, which is an important component of communication. To illustrate the effect of syntax compared with the effect of meaning, Noam Chomsky (1957), an important scholar in the field of linguistics, devised this famous sentence: "Colorless green ideas sleep furiously" (p. 15). This sentence is acceptable in terms of English grammar, but on the semantic level it is nonsensical: Ideas logically cannot be either colorless or green (and certainly not both!), ideas don't sleep, and nothing sleeps furiously (does it?).

As you remember from Chapter 1, a central part of our definition of communication is the creation of shared meaning. For any given message, a number of factors contribute

syntax
the rules that govern word order

semantics
the study of meaning

'On no! The dog's eaten the Thesaurus!'

to the creation of its meaning. Perhaps most important are the words the speaker chooses. For example, did you have a friend in high school who always gave the right answer in class, got excellent grades, and always seemed to have a wealth of information at his fingertips? What word would you use to describe this friend: *smart, intelligent, clever, wise,* or *brilliant*? Because each word has a slightly different meaning, you try to choose the one that most accurately characterizes your friend. However, in choosing the "right" words, you have to consider the two types of meaning that words convey: *denotative* and *connotative*—terms that we also discussed in Chapter 1.

The **denotative meaning** refers to the dictionary, or literal, meaning of a word and is usually the agreed-upon meaning for most speakers of the language. Referring back to our description of your friend: The dictionary defines *wise* as "Having the ability to discern or judge what is true, right, or lasting; sagacious" and *intelligent* as "Showing sound judgment and rationality" ("American Heritage Dictionary," 2000). Does either word exactly capture how you would describe your friend? If not, which word does?

Words also carry **connotative meanings**, which are the affective or interpretive meanings attached to them. Using the previous example, the connotative meaning of the word *wise* implies an older person with long experience, so it might not be the best choice to describe your young friend.

Pragmatics: Language in Use Just like phonology, syntax, and semantics, the field of **pragmatics** seeks to identify patterns or rules people follow when they use language appropriately. In the case of pragmatics, however, the emphasis is on how language is used in specific situations to accomplish goals (Nofsinger, 1999). For example, scholars who study pragmatics might seek to understand the rules for communicating appropriately in a sorority, a faculty meeting, or an evangelical church. They would do this by examining communication that is successful and unsuccessful in each setting. The three units of study for scholars of pragmatics are *speech acts, conversational rules,* and *contextual rules.* Let's examine what each contributes to communication.

Speech Acts One branch of pragmatics, **speech act theory**, looks closely at the seven language functions described previously and suggests that when people communicate, they do not just say things, they also *do* things with their words. For example, speech act theorists argue that when you say, "I bet you ten dollars the Yankees win the World Series," you aren't just saying something, you actually are doing something. That something you are doing is making a bet, or entering into an agreement that will result in an exchange of money.

denotative meaning
the dictionary, or literal, meaning of a word

connotative meaning
the affective or interpretive meanings attached to a word

pragmatics
field of study that emphasizes how language is used in specific situations to accomplish goals

speech act theory
branch of pragmatics that suggests that when people communicate, they do not just say things, they also *do* things with their words

One common speech act is the request. A recent study examined one type of request that occurs primarily in U.S. family contexts—the common practice of "nagging" (Boxer, 2002). Nagging (repeated requests by one family member to another) often concerns household chores and is usually a source of conflict. The researcher found that nagging requires several sequential acts. First, there is an initial request, which is usually given in the form of a command ("Please take out the garbage") or a hedged request ("Do you think you can take out the garbage this evening?"). If the request is not granted, it is repeated as a reminder (after some lapse of time), which often includes an allusion to the first request. ("Did you hear me? Can you please take out the garbage?") When a reminder is repeated (the third stage), it becomes nagging and usually involves a scolding or a threat, depending on the relationship, for example, whether the exchange is between parent/child ("This is the last time I'm going to ask you, take out the garbage!") or between relational partners ("Never mind, I'll do it myself!").

Nagging is one common type of speech act that occurs in U.S. family contexts.

The researcher found that men were rarely involved in nagging, and she suggests that this is because men are perceived as having more power and are therefore able to successfully request and gain compliance from another family member without resorting to nagging. She also notes that children can have power (if they refuse to comply with a request despite their lack of status) and a parent can lack power despite having status. The researcher also found that nagging mostly occurs in our intimate relationships. She concludes that, by nagging, we lose power—but without power, we are forced into nagging; thus it seems to be a vicious cycle! The study shows that what we *do* with words affects our relationships.

Understanding the meaning of various speech acts often requires understanding context and culture (Austin, 1975; Sbisa, 2002). For this reason, people may agree on what is *said* but disagree on what is *meant*. For example, the other day Katy said to her roommate Hiroshi, "I have been so busy I haven't even had time to do the dishes." He replied, "Well, I'm sorry, but I have been busy, too." What did he think Katy was "doing" with her utterance? When they discussed this interaction, Katy explained that she was making an excuse, while Hiroshi said he heard a criticism—that because *she* hadn't had time to do the dishes, *he* should have. Thus, messages may have different meanings or "do" different things, from different persons' viewpoints. This difference lies in the sender's and receiver's interpretations of the statement. Most misunderstandings arise not around what was said—but around what was done or meant.

As we have seen, speech acts may be direct or indirect. That is, speech acts such as requests can be framed more (or less) clearly and directly. Let's suppose that you want your partner to feed the dog. You may directly ask: "Would you feed the dog?" Or you could state an order: "Feed the dog!" On the other hand, you may communicate the same information indirectly: "Do you know if the dog was fed?" or "I wonder if the dog was fed." Finally, you may make your request very indirectly: "It would be nice if someone fed the dog," or "Do you think the dog looks hungry?"

Which do you think is better—to communicate directly or indirectly? This is actually a trick question. The answer is: It depends—on the situation and the cultural context. Although direct requests and questions may be clearer, they also can be less polite. Ordering someone to feed the dog makes one's desire clearly and unequivocally known, but at the same time, it can be seen as rude and domineering.

Recent research shows that U.S. Americans tend to be more indirect in their requests, when compared to Mexicans (Pinto & Raschio, 2007), but probably not as indirect as many Asians (Kim, 2002). However, when expressing disagreement, most U.S. Americans tend to be more direct than most Asians. A recent study investigated how Malaysians handled disagreements in business negotiation and concluded that the Malays' opposition was never direct or on record, but always indirect and implied. Despite their disagreements with the other party, they honored the other, always balancing power with politeness (Paramasivam, 2007). A pragmatic approach reminds us that how language is used always depends on the situation and cultural context. We'll discuss more cross-cultural differences in communication practices further in Chapter 8.

Conversational rules—such as turn-taking—govern the way we communicate and vary somewhat from context to context.

Conversational Rules Conversational rules govern the ways in which communicators organize conversation. For example, one rule of conversation in U.S. English is that if someone asks you a question, you should provide an answer. If you do not know the answer, others expect you to at least reply, "I don't know" or "Let me think about it." However, in some cultures and languages, answers to questions are not obligatory. For example, in some Native American cultures, such as that of the Warm Spring Indians of Oregon, questions may be answered at a later time (with little reference to the previous conversation) or not answered at all (Philips, 1990).

Perhaps the most researched conversational rules involve turn-taking. The most basic rule for English language speakers, and many others, is that only one person speaks at a time. People may tolerate some overlap between their talk and another's, but typically they expect to be able to have their say without too much interruption (Schegloff, 2000). Still, as a refinement of this point, Susanna Kohonen (2004) found in her cross-cultural study of turn-taking that conversationalists were more tolerant of overlaps in social settings, such as at parties or when hanging out with friends, than in more formal settings. Thus, sometimes the context influences conversational rules. We discuss contextual rules next.

Other rules for turn-taking determine who is allowed to speak (Sacks, Schegloff, & Jefferson, 1978). For example, if you "have the floor" you can generally continue to speak. When you are finished, you can select someone else. You can do this either by asking a question, "So Sue, what is your opinion?" or by looking at another person as you finish talking. If you don't have the floor but wish to speak, you can begin speaking just as the current speaker completes a turn.

The turn-allocation system works amazingly well most of the time. Occasionally, however, people do not follow these implicit rules. For example, the current speaker could select the next speaker by directing a question to her, but someone else could interrupt and "steal" the floor. Also, some speakers are quicker to grab the talk turn, which allows them more opportunities to speak. Then, speakers who are slower to begin a turn or take the floor have fewer opportunities to contribute to the conversation. They may feel left out or resent the other speakers for monopolizing the conversation.

Contextual Rules No matter what language or dialect you speak, your use of language varies depending on the communication situation (Mey, 2001). For example,

Pragmatics involves understanding the implicit communication rules that apply in one setting or another.

you probably wouldn't discuss the same topics in the same way at a funeral as you would in a meeting at your workplace, in a courtroom, or at a party. What would happen if you did? For example, telling jokes and laughing at a party is typically acceptable, whereas those same jokes and laughing might be interpreted very negatively in a courtroom or at a funeral. One challenge for pragmatics scholars, then, is uncovering the implicit communication rules that govern different settings. As noted earlier, communication pragmatics also vary by culture. For example, in some houses of worship, appropriate verbal behavior involves talking very quietly or not all, acting subdued, and listening without responding—but in others, people applaud, sing exuberantly, and respond loudly with exclamations like "Amen!" Neither set of communication rules is "right"; each is appropriate to its own setting and cultural context.

As you can see, verbal language is far more than the words people use; it also includes the sounds and meanings of those words, and the rules individuals use for arranging words and for communicating in particular settings. Moreover, speakers differ in the ways they use language to communicate. They also differ in the ways they enunciate their words and how they present their ideas. For example, Southerners "drawl" their vowels while New Englanders drop the *r* after theirs; some speakers are extremely direct, while others are not. What accounts for these differences? We explore the answers in the next section.

TEST YOUR KNOWLEDGE

- What are the seven functions of language? Give an example that illustrates how each works.
- What is phonology? Syntax? Semantics? How do they work together to facilitate effective communication?
- What do pragmatics scholars study? How do they determine pragmatics in specific communication contexts?
- What is the difference between connotative and denotative meaning?

INFLUENCES ON VERBAL COMMUNICATION

As we saw in Chapter 3, our communication is influenced by our identities and the various cultures to which we belong. In turn, our communication helps shape these identities. When identities influence several aspects of language, we say that speakers have a distinct **dialect**, a variation of a language distinguished by its **lexical choice** (vocabulary), grammar, and pronunciation. In other instances, the influence of identity is less dramatic, and speakers vary only in some pronunciations or word choices. In this section we examine how identities related to gender, age, regionality, ethnicity and race, and education and occupation shape language use.

Gender

Growing up male or female may influence the way you communicate in some situations, because men and women are socialized to communicate in specific ways. In fact—as exemplified in the popularity of books like *Men Are from Mars, Women Are from Venus* (Gray, 1992)—many people believe that English-speaking men and women in the United States speak different dialects. These beliefs are reinforced by media depictions that tend to present stereotypical depictions of men and women in magazines, on television, and in movies (Wood & Dindia, 1998). For example, one team of researchers reviewed how journal articles talked about gender differences in the past fifty years and found that because people are more interested in hearing about differences than similarities, shows and books that emphasize these differences tend to sell better and receive wider recognition (Sagrestano, Heavey, & Christensen, 1998).

Televisions shows, like *The Real Housewives of Orange County,* tend to present stereotypical depictions of men and women.

Even scholarly research tends to focus on, and sometimes exaggerate, the importance of sex differences; some researchers have reported that women's verbal style is often described as supportive, egalitarian, personal, and disclosive, while men's is characterized as instrumental, competitive, and assertive (Mulac, Bradac, & Gibbons, 2001; Wood, 2002). But although these and other studies suggest that men and women do use different language and communication styles, other research refutes this claim. A recent review of studies comparing males and females on a large array of psychological and communication differences, including self-disclosure and interruptions, revealed very few significant differences (Hyde, 2006). In fact, the differences in men's and women's communication patterns are estimated to be as small as 1 percent, or even less (Canary & Hause, 1993).

How can these contradictory findings be explained? To begin, many studies of gender differences ask participants to report on their perceptions or ask them to recall men's and women's conversational styles (e.g., Aylor & Dainton, 2004). This approach can be problematic because people's perceptions are not always accurate.

For example, Nancy Burrell and her colleagues (1988) argue that persistent, stereotypical, gender-based expectations likely influence people's perceptions that men and women behave or communicate differently even when few behavioral differences exist. More recently, Heilman, Caleo, and Halim (2010) found that gender stereotypes were invoked even more strongly when workers were told they would communicate using computer-mediated communication rather than face to face.

How do these faulty perceptions arise about communication differences between men and women? Two important contributors are a person's perceptions of his or her own gendered communication and media representations of men's and women's communication. Knott and Natalle (1997) and Margaret Baker (1991) explain that individuals who see themselves as being very feminine or masculine tend to view others in the same light, and they tend to have rigid views of the sexes and their communication behavior (Canary & Emmers-Sommer, 1997).

Carol Rose (1995) asserts forcefully that such gender-based perceptions are hard to change, whether or not the perceptions are true. For example, the negative stereotype of the talkative woman is very persistent. In one recent study, students were shown a videotaped conflict between a man and a woman and were asked to rate the two on likability and competence. In different versions of the video, the researchers varied how much the man and woman each talked. As the researchers expected, viewers rated the couple as less likable when they saw the woman doing more of the talking. And the man who talked more was rated as most competent (Sellers, Woolsey, & Swann, 2007). Even though this negative stereotype persists, many studies have shown that not only do women generally *not* talk more than men, actually the opposite is true—men tend to be more talkative in many situations (Leaper & Ayres, 2007; Wiest, Abernathy, Obenchain, & Major, 2006). In addition, the stereotype persists that women are more "kind, helpful, sympathetic, and concerned about others" while men are seen as "aggressive, forceful, independent, and decisive" (Heilman, 2001, p. 658). Furthermore, these gender stereotypes can create differential treatment in the workplace.

Laurie Coltri (2004) also claims that the gender of the communicator heavily influences people's perceptions of her or his communication behavior. In her study of gender stereotypes in mediation, or informal dispute resolution, she manipulated transcripts of mediations so that half the time Person A was identified as male and Person B as female, and half the time the reverse occurred. In each case, the person labeled as female was rated more negatively than when that same person was labeled as male. Considering the influence of perception and gender stereotypes, you can see how difficult it can be to objectively evaluate communication differences between the sexes.

Another factor that makes it difficult to pinpoint the impact of gender differences in communication is that researchers sometimes overlook the influence of situation and relationship on individuals' language use and communication styles. For example, imagine that a researcher observes communication in two situations: (1) groups of men talking among themselves and (2) groups of women talking among themselves. After coding the communication behaviors observed in the two types of groups, the researcher concludes that men and women communicate differently. What is wrong with this conclusion? It ignores the possibility that these same men and women might communicate in much more similar ways when they are talking in mixed-gender groups (Aries, 1996). The researcher has failed to consider that they may adapt their communication style to their audience.

When people adapt to a specific audience, they are often adjusting to the communication style of the more powerful members of that audience. Thus, if powerful members of the audience use more direct or task-focused language, so might the speaker. In addition to adapting their communication style, people also often use more deferential or tentative language when communicating with more powerful people. Both men and women adapt to these power differences; thus both groups are more likely to use tentative language with their bosses than with their siblings. Women use language that is more tentative overall because generally they have lower status, and people with lower status are not typically expected to make strong, assertive statements (Reid, Keerie, & Palomares, 2003). Similarly, women tend to use more "filler words" (such as *like* or *well*) and more conditional words (*would*, *should*, *could*) (Mehl & Pennebaker, 2003).

Researchers have wondered whether gender differences in conversations are a consequence of interacting with a partner who uses a particular style of communication. For example, if you encourage another person to talk by nodding your head in agreement, asking questions, or giving supportive linguistic cues (such as "uh-huh," or "yes …"), you are using a facilitative style of communication. To explore this question, social psychologists Annette Hannah and Tamar Murachver assigned male and female partners who were strangers to each other to meet and talk several times. After the first conversation, their communication styles were judged by outside observers to be either facilitative or nonfacilitative; and the researchers found that, regardless of gender, participants responded to each other in ways that mirrored their partner's style (Hannah & Murachver, 2007).

Over time, however, in subsequent conversations, the women and men shifted their speech toward more stereotypically gendered patterns; that is, the men talked more, for longer times, while women increased their use of minimal responses, reduced the amount they spoke, and asked more questions. In other words, the women increased their facilitative style of speech while the men decreased theirs. Discussing their findings, the researchers pose several questions: Why are women more facilitative in their speech? Why do they talk less when talking with men? Do they feel threatened or insecure? Are they less comfortable in talking more than men? Perhaps women feel that dominating conversations with men has negative social consequences and, therefore, they encourage men to do the talking—an explanation that would be confirmed by the earlier study we mentioned, where students negatively evaluated couples in which the women talked more than the men. The researchers provide no definitive explanation, but note, as do we, that gender differences are complicated (Hannah & Murachver, 2007).

In conclusion, women and men do show differences in their communication styles, and much of this difference likely is attributable to differences in power, status, and expectations in communication situations.

Age

You may not think of age as affecting language use, but it does, particularly when it comes to word choice. For example, you might have talked about "the cooties" when you were a child, but you probably don't now. Moreover, children have a whole vocabulary to describe "naughty topics," especially related to bodily functions. Yet, most adults do not use those words. Adolescents also develop vocabulary that they use throughout their teenage years and then drop during early adulthood. Adolescents have described highly valued people and things as "cool," "righteous," "bad," "hot," and "phat," depending on the generation and context. This distinct vocabulary helps teenagers feel connected to their peers and separate from their parents and other adults. For other examples of teen slang terms, see *Did You Know? Contemporary Slang*.

The era in which you grew up also influences your vocabulary. As you age, you continue to use certain words that were common when you were growing up, even if they have fallen out of use. This is called the **cohort effect** and refers to common denominators of a group that was born and reared in the same general period. For example, your grandparents and their contemporaries may refer to dancing as "cutting a rug," while younger speakers rarely use this term. However, recent research suggests that young girls may be becoming the trendsetters in language use both for their own and other cohorts. Some linguists argue that girls in southern

cohort effect
the influence of shared characteristics of a group that was born and reared in the same general period

Did You Know?

Contemporary Slang

Here are some examples of contemporary slang used by various groups in the United States. Which do you recognize or use?

Bama: someone who is unstylish; not fashion forward.

> **Example:** That *Bama* looks like he bought his clothes when he was blindfolded.

Beer goggles: after drinking, someone may be attracted to another person that she or he would not normally be attracted.

> **Example:** He must have had *beer goggles* on last night. He wanted to go home with anyone when the bar was closing.

Hella: "very" or "really."

> **Example:** San Francisco is *hella* expensive place to live.

Pittsburgh left: turning left as soon as the light turns green before the oncoming traffic moves through the intersection.

> **Example:** That freak wouldn't let me do a *Pittsburgh left*!

Packie: liquor store.

> **Example:** He had to go to the *packie* to get ready for the Patriots game.

Recyclopath: someone who is overzealous about recycling.

> **Example:** She is such a *recyclopath* that she takes other people's cans out of the trash and puts them in the recycling bin.

Swamp Yankee: New England low-income white person, typically from Southern New England.

> **Example:** That *swamp Yankee* needs to go back to her trailer park!

Tebowing: the act of getting down on one knee and praying.

> **Example:** Mark was *tebowing* after getting an A on his exam; he's a very religious guy.

Wicked: "very" or "really."

> **Example:** It's *wicked* cold today

California are influencing young men's—and even older women's—language use; they call it the "California vowel shift." For example, "Like, what dew you mean, tha-yt I ha-yve an accent?" At a recent meeting of a high school club in southern California called Girls for a Change, teen girls gathered to discuss ways to fix cultural ills; they talked about social action as "something important to *dew*." Among different approaches, they considered "*tew*-toring." There is evidence that young men and some older women are beginning to adopt some of the sounds started by teenage girls. As new ways of saying things find their way in the general language, a regional—or even statewide—dialect emerges (Krieger, 2004).

People's communication skills and the meanings they attribute to concepts also vary due to their age. Why? Older people are more cognitively developed and have had more experiences; therefore they tend to view concepts differently than do younger people, especially children (Pennebaker & Stone, 2003). For example, children typically engage in egocentric speech patterns (Piaget, 1952). This means that they cannot adapt their communication to their conversational partners nor understand that others may feel or view the world differently. Children lack the number of constructs adults have. For example, very young children have little concept of future or past time, so understanding what might happen next week or month is difficult for them. Consequently, parents usually adapt their communication when trying to help children understand some event in the future.

Regionality

Geographical location also strongly influences people's language use. The most common influence is on pronunciation. For example, how do you pronounce the word "oil"? In parts of New York it is pronounced somewhat like "earl," while in areas of the South it is pronounced more like "awl," and in the West it is often pronounced "oyl" as in "Olive Oyl." Sometimes regionality affects more than just accent, leading to regional dialects. Why do these differences arise?

Historically, verbal differences developed wherever people were separated by a geographical boundary—whether it was mountains, lakes, rivers, deserts, oceans—or some social boundary, such as race, class, or religion (Fromkin & Rodman, 1983). Moreover, people tended to speak similarly to those around them. For example, in the eighteenth century, residents of Australia, North America, and England had relatively little contact with one another; consequently, they developed recognizably different dialects even though they all spoke the same language. Typically, the more isolated a group, the more distinctive their dialect.

In the United States, dialectical differences in English originally arose because two groups of English colonists settled along the East Coast. The colonists who settled in the South, near present-day Virginia, primarily came from Somerset and Gloucestershire—both western counties in England—and they brought with them an accent with strongly voiced *s* sounds and with the *r* strongly pronounced after vowels. In contrast, the colonists who settled in the north, what we now call New England, came from midland counties such as Essex, Kent, and London, where people spoke a dialect that did not pronounce the *r* after vowels, a feature still common to many New England dialects (Crystal, 2003). See Figure 5.1 for an interesting outgrowth of U.S. local dialects.

Other waves of immigration have occurred over the past four hundred years, increasing dialectical diversity in the United States. Each group of immigrants brings a

FIGURE 5.1 The terms we use to refer to soft drinks also vary by region in the United States.

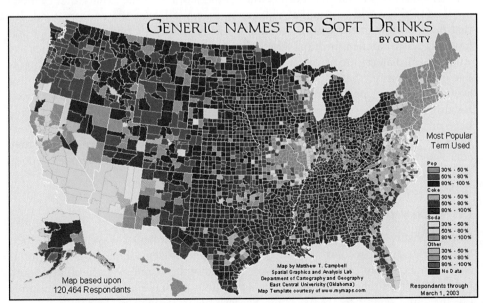

Alternative **VIEW**
The Northern Cities Vowel Shift

Conventional wisdom says that dialects should be disappearing, due to increasingly transient populations, immigration from other countries, and the influence of pervasive mass media. However, University of Pennsylvania linguist William Labov and his colleagues published a phonological atlas (2005) showing that across the country, regional dialects are stronger than ever. In a radio interview, he described some these specific changes.

In what ways do you think regional accents influence communication between people from different areas of the United States? Do you see regional accents as a positive or negative influence on American society?

The most important differences have developed in this huge area around the Great Lakes region which we call the Inland North, extending westward from Syracuse through Buffalo, Cleveland, Detroit, Chicago, and Milwaukee. Those great cities occupied by about 35 million people are all moving in a very different linguistic direction from the rest of the United States.

Now what happens here is that the short-*a* becomes "ai" [like in "yeah"] in every single word, so that people have, say, "theaht" and "feahct." In the meantime, the short words spelled with short-*o* like "socks" or "block" or "cot" move into the position that was formerly occupied by "ah." So the man's name [John becomes] "Jahn"—that's man's name, "Jahn." And the girl's name [Jan] becomes "Jain"... This example of a sound change in the United States called the "Northern Cities Shift."

SOURCES: Adapted from Voice of America (VOA) radio interview with William Labov on January 12, 2005. Retrieved June 2, 2008, from http://www.voanews.com/specialenglish/archive/2005-01/a-2005-01-11-5-1.cfm. And from Labov, W. (Ed.). (2005). *Atlas of North American English*. New York: Walter De Gruyter, Inc.

distinctive way of speaking and culture-specific communication rules. Some groups, especially those who have remained somewhat isolated since their arrival, maintain much of their original dialect; an example is the inhabitants of Tangier Island in the Chesapeake Bay (Crystal, 2003). Other groups' dialects have assimilated with the dialects of their neighbors to form new dialects. Thus, the seventeenth-century "western" English dialect of Virginia has become the southern drawl of the twenty-first century.

Today the world is a global village, so people all over the country (and, for that matter, all over the world) are able to speak frequently with one another and have access to similar media. Nonetheless, according to a recent comprehensive study, local dialects are stronger than ever (Labov, 2005; Preston, 2003). This is due in large part to the fact that people tend to talk similarly to the people they live around and hear speak every day. Thus, dialectic differences originally occurred because of patterns of isolation, but they persist because of exposure. As people have increasing contact and access to a range of language models, dialectic differences may become less pronounced, but it will be a long time—if ever—before they completely disappear. For an example of an increasingly distinct regional dialect, see *Alternative View: The Great American Vowel Shift.*

Ethnicity and Race

One's ethnicity can influence one's verbal style in a number of ways. In the United States, English is a second or colanguage for many citizens. This, of course, influences syntax, accent, and word choice. For example, if one is Latino/Latina and learns Spanish either before or at the same time as one learns English, one may use the same syntax for both. Thus, Spanish speakers may place adjectives after nouns (*the house little*) when they are speaking English because that is the rule for

Spanish. The reverse can also occur: When English speakers speak Spanish, they have a tendency to place adjectives before nouns (*la pequeña casa*), which is the rule for English but not for Spanish.

Speakers' ethnicity can also influence their general verbal style. For example, Jewish Americans may engage in a style of talking about problems that non-Jews perceive as complaining (Bowen, 2003); some Native American tribes use teasing as a form of public rebuke (Shutiva, 2004); and some Chinese Americans who live in the southern United States are particularly likely to let other speakers choose conversational topics (Gong, 2004). When two ethnic or racial groups speak the same language but use different syntax, lexical items, or verbal style, one or both of the groups may view the other's verbal style as incorrect, as a failed attempt at proper speech rather than as a dialect with its own rules (Ellis & Beattie, 1986).

These views can have important real-life implications—political and monetary. Take the controversy about **Ebonics**—a version of English that has its roots in West African, Caribbean, and U.S. slave languages. There is no agreed-upon definition of Ebonics; some linguists emphasize the international nature of the language (as a linguistic consequence of the African slave trade); others stress that it is a variety of English (e.g., the equivalent of Black English) or as different from English and viewed as an independent language. Yet we should also keep in mind that "there is no single and correct way to be 'African American.' These identities are negotiated in context and situationally emergent" (Hecht et al., 2003, p. 2). The controversy over definition has had important real-life consequences. A few years ago the Oakland, California, school board passed a resolution that recognized Ebonics as a separate language, not just a dialect. The resolution instructed teachers to "respect and embrace the language richness of Ebonics." But more important, they required schools to provide English as a second language instruction to students who spoke Ebonics as their first "language." A number of teachers and policymakers viewed Ebonics as simply substandard English, not even a dialect, and were not willing to recognize it as a legitimate language nor provide funds for English language instruction (Wolfram, Adger, & Christian, 1999). This language controversy had far-reaching implications—involving not only teachers and parents, but also linguists and policymakers.

Ebonics
a version of English that has its roots in West African, Caribbean, and U.S. slave languages

jargon
the specialized terms that develop in many professions

Education and Occupation

We will discuss education and occupation together because they are often mutually influencing. For example, medical doctors speak a similar language because they share a profession, but also because they were educated similarly. Typically, the more educated people are, the more similarly they speak (Hudson, 1983). Thus, larger dialect differences occur between easterners and midwesterners if they have not been to college than if they have doctoral degrees. This does not mean that all lawyers talk the same or that all professors speak similarly; rather, it suggests that differences become less pronounced as people receive more education.

Education affects dialect in part because any given university or college attracts people from different parts of the country. Therefore, college students have contact with a variety of dialects. At the same time, as students attend college they develop similar vocabularies from their shared experiences and learn similar terms in their classes. For example, you may never have used the term *dyad* to refer to two people before you went to college, but this is a term you might encounter in a range of courses, including psychology, sociology, anthropology, and communication.

Your occupation also influences the specialized terms you use to communicate. The specialized terms that develop in many professions are called **jargon**. Professors routinely speak of *tenure*, *refereed journals*, and *student credit*

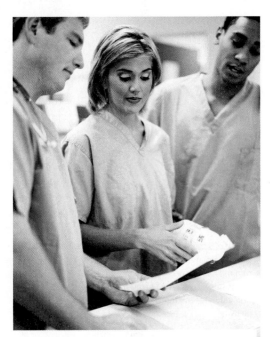

Physicians, like members of other professions, develop specialized terms called jargon.

hours. Physicians speak of *contusions* (bruises), *sequelae* (results), and *hemorrhagic stroke* (a stroke where a blood vessel bursts). In fact, most occupations have their own jargon. In addition to influencing your lexical choices, your occupation may also influence your overall communication style—including tone of voice and some nonverbal behaviors. For example, nursery school teachers are often recognizable not only by their vocabulary but also by the rhythm, volume, and expressivity of their communication style.

To sum up, then, various features of language—phonology, syntax, semantics, and pragmatics—contribute to the development of meaning in verbal communication. These features combine with individual influences in language use, such as gender, age, and level of education, to create one's specific communication style. However, we have not yet covered every aspect of verbal communication. We now turn to the influence of societal forces on verbal communication.

TEST YOUR KNOWLEDGE

- How do regional dialects develop?
- How do our gender, age, ethnicity and race, and education and occupation influence the way we speak?

THE INDIVIDUAL, VERBAL COMMUNICATION, AND SOCIETY

How do societal forces influence verbal communication? Culture and power are two of the most important influences. Culture impacts verbal communication primarily through its influence on language and perception. As we saw in Chapter 4, perception plays a key role in communication. Power is connected to verbal communication because within society, some language styles are viewed as more powerful, with consequences for both the powerful and the powerless.

Language and Perception

Scholars have long argued about the influence of language and culture on perception. The central issue they have debated is whether the words a culture has available to it influence how its members see and perceive the world around them. For example, the English language expresses action in the past, present, and future. Thus, English speakers may say "Alan went to the library" (past), "Alan is at the library" (present), or "Alan will be going to the library" (future). In contrast, Japanese makes no distinction between the present and future. Although the verb for "went" is *ikimashita*, the verb used for both "is" and "will be going" is the same, *ikimasu*. Because English and Japanese have two different verb structures, scholars have questioned whether English speakers and Japanese speakers think about present and future actions in different ways. Scholars who have debated this relationship between language and perception generally fall into two camps: the *nominalists* and the *relativists*.

Nominalists claim that any idea can be expressed in any language and that the structure and vocabulary of the language do not influence the speaker's perception of the world. According to nominalists, English and Japanese may express present and future in different ways, but English speakers and Japanese speakers still understand the distinction.

In contrast, the **relativists** argue that language serves not only as a way for us to voice our ideas but that, in addition, it "is itself the shaper of ideas, the guide for the individual's mental activity" (Hoijer, 1994, p. 194). This idea is the basis for the **Sapir-Whorf hypothesis**. The Sapir-Whorf hypothesis argues that the language people speak determines the way they see the world. Adherents to this hypothesis

nominalists
those who argue that any idea can be expressed in any language and that the structure and vocabulary of the language do not influence the speaker's perception of the world

relativists
those who argue that language serves not only as a way for us to voice our ideas but "is itself the shaper of ideas, the guide for the individual's mental activity"

Sapir-Whorf hypothesis
idea that the language people speak determines the way they see the world (a relativist perspective)

believe language is like a prison, as it constrains the ways individuals can perceive the world (Koerner, 2000). According to this hypothesis, the distinction between the present and the future is not as clear-cut for Japanese speakers as it is for English speakers. As another example, surfers have many more words for the types of waves in the ocean than do nonsurfers (Scheibel, 1995); the Sapir-Whorf hypothesis argues that, because of this, surfers perceive more types of waves than others.

Surfers have many more words for the types of waves in the ocean than do nonsurfers.

So how much does language influence perception? The Sapir-Whorf hypothesis position has been challenged by a number of scholars who investigate the connection between language and how we think (Kenneally, 2008). They represent a modified relativist position on the relationship between language and perception. For example, Steven Pinker (2007), a renowned cognitive scientist, cautions against assuming a simplistic connection between language and thought, and rejects the Sapir-Whorf assumption that the particular language we speak compels us to perceive the world in a particular way or prevents us from thinking in different ways. He uses the example of applesauce and pebbles to argue that we naturally categorize (and therefore label) these two substances differently (as "hunk" and "goo"). By looking at language from the perspective of our thoughts, Pinker shows that what may seem like arbitrary aspects of speech (the hunk–goo distinction) aren't arbitrary at all, but rather that they are by-products of our evolved mental machinery. In sum, all languages have the formal and expressive power to communicate the ideas, beliefs, and desires of their users. From this vast range of possibilities, human communities select what they want to say and how they want to say it (Li & Gleitman, 2002, p. 291). This view allows for more freedom than indicated by the Sapir-Whorf hypothesis.

Which viewpoint makes more sense to you— nominalist or relativist? Why?

Language and Power

In many ways, language and power are inextricably connected. People in power get to define what languages and communication styles are appropriate. In addition, people who use language and communication according to the rules of the powerful may be able to increase their own power. This view of the relationship between language and power is explained by *cocultural theory*. **Cocultural theory** explores the role of power in daily interactions using the five following assumptions:

1. In each society, a hierarchy exists that privileges certain groups of people; in the United States, these groups include men, European Americans, heterosexuals, the able-bodied, and middle- and upper-class people.

2. Part of the privilege these groups enjoy, often subconsciously, is being able to set norms for what types of communication are acceptable or not acceptable (Orbe, 1998). Consequently, communication patterns of the dominant groups (in the United States, rich, male, White, educated, straight) tend to be more highly valued. For example, the preferred communication practice in many large corporations is that used by White males—direct, to the point, task oriented, and unemotional (Kikoski & Kikoski, 1999).

3. Language maintains and reinforces the power of these dominant groups, again, mostly subconsciously. Thus, people whose speech does not conform to what is valued in society may be excluded and/or negatively stereotyped. As we noted earlier, commentators sometimes characterize women's speech as

cocultural theory
explores the role of power in daily interactions

sounding more tentative than male speech. Because society values male speech styles at work, women aspiring to corporate leadership positions may undertake a special effort to make their speech direct or tough enough, or to avoid being too cooperative or nurturing in their communication practices.

4. In the relationship realm, society tends to value a more female communication style, and men may be criticized for failing to communicate appropriately with their intimates. Remember that none of these language variations is inherently good or bad, powerful or powerless; it is the societal hierarchies that teach us how to view particular communication practices. Of course, not every White male is direct, to the point, and task oriented, nor does every woman speak tentatively at work. Nor is every woman supportive and self-disclosive and every man distant and terse in close relationships. These generalizations can help explain communication practices, but they should not solidify into stereotypes.

5. These dominant communication structures impede the progress of persons whose communication practices do not conform to the norms. For example, what are the consequences for women who do not conform to "male" communication norms in a corporation? Or for African Americans who do not conform to "White" communication norms of the organizations in which they work? Or for students who do not conform to the "middle-class" communication norms at a university? They may risk being labeled negatively ("not serious enough," "soft," "doesn't have what it takes") and marginalized.

We explore these ideas further in Chapter 8. Now, let's look at how these societal hierarchies affect attitudes toward words, accents, and dialects, and how they impact identity labels.

Power and Words

Attitudes about power can be built into language by certain roots or by the very structure of the language. Consider words like *chairman*, *fireman*, or the generic use of "he" and "man" to refer to people. In the past it was widely believed that it didn't matter whether we used masculine words to mean *human*, but in recent decades researchers discovered that people didn't think *human* when someone mentioned the word *man*—they thought about a man. Similarly, awareness of the inequality inherent in terms such as *Mr.* (not designating marital status) and *Mrs.* (which does) has resulted in the use of new, more equal terms like *Ms.* and *he/she*.

While some languages, such as Japanese or Korean, are strongly gendered (meaning that traditionally, men and women used almost a separate language), English is somewhat gendered, or androcentric. *Androcentrism* is the pairing of maleness with humanity and the consequent attribution of gender difference to females—often to women's disadvantage. Scholars recently reviewed fifty years of psychology articles for androcentric bias. While they found few uses of "he" for *human*, information was still portrayed in a way that emphasized male as the norm. Male data was placed first in tables, and gender differences were often described as female—subconsciously assuming that male is the norm and female is different. Researchers point out that being different is not necessarily harmful but probably reflects some of the underlying stereotypes (and societal hierarchies) we have discussed earlier (Hegarty & Buechel, 2006).

What are the implications for students? We argue that it's not about freedom of speech or being overly politically correct, but rather about audience and awareness. Gender-neutral language has gained support from most major textbook publishers, and from professional and academic groups, as well as major newspapers and law journals. As an English professor suggested, "You need to be able to express yourself according to their guidelines, and if you wish to write or speak convincingly to people who are influenced by the conventions of these contexts, you need to be conscious of their expectations."

Specific suggestions for avoiding this kind of built-in bias are presented in *Did You Know? Avoiding Bias in Language*.

Did You Know?

Avoiding Bias in Language

The American Psychological Association (APA) provides suggestions for avoiding gender and heterosexual bias in writing. Which view of language is represented here, nominalist or relative? What are the reasons for or against following these suggestions? Which groups of people do you think would be more in favor of these changes—those with or without power in U.S. society? What do you think of the "further alternatives"? Would you use them?

Using Gender-Neutral Language

- **Use "they" as a singular.** Most people, when writing and speaking informally, rely on singular "they" as a matter of course: "If you love somebody, set them free" (Sting). If you pay attention to your own speech, you'll probably catch yourself using the same construction yourself. Some people are annoyed by the incorrect grammar that this solution necessitates, but this construction is used more and more frequently.

- **Use "he or she."** Despite the charge of clumsiness, double-pronoun constructions have made a comeback: "To be black in this country is simply too pervasive an experience for any writer to omit from her or his work," wrote Samuel R. Delany. Overuse of this solution can be awkward, however.

- **Use pluralizing.** A writer can often recast material in the plural. For instance, instead of "As he advances in his program, the medical student has increasing opportunities for clinical work," try "As they advance in their programs, medical students have increasing opportunities for clinical work."

- **Eliminate pronouns.** Avoid having to use pronouns at all; instead of "a first grader can feed and dress himself," you could write, "a first grader can eat and get dressed without assistance."

- **Further alternatives.** "He/she" or "s/he," using "one" instead of he, or using a new generic pronoun (thon, co, E, tey, hesh, hir).

Avoiding Heterosexual Bias in Language

- **Use "sexual orientation" rather than "sexual preference."** The word "preference" suggests a degree of voluntary choice that is not necessarily reported by lesbians and gay men and that has not been demonstrated in psychological research.

- **Use "lesbian" and "gay male"** rather than "homosexual" when used as an adjective referring to specific persons or groups, and lesbians and gay men. The word "homosexual" perpetuates negative stereotypes with its history of pathology and criminal behavior.

- **Such terms as "gay male" are preferable** to "homosexuality" or "male homosexuality" and so are grammatical reconstructions (e.g., "his colleagues knew he was gay" rather than "his colleagues knew about his homosexuality"). The same is true for "lesbian" over "female homosexual," "female homosexuality," or "lesbianism."

(continued)

Did You Know? *(continued)*

- **Bisexual women and men, "bisexual persons," or "bisexual"** as an adjective refer to people who relate sexually and affectionally to women and men. These terms are often omitted in discussions of sexual orientation and thus give the erroneous impression that all people relate exclusively to one gender or another.
- **Use "gender" instead of "sex."** The terms "sex" and "gender" are often used interchangeably. Nevertheless, the term "sex" is often confused with sexual behavior, and this is particularly troublesome when differentiating between sexual orientation and gender.

SOURCES: Adapted from "Some notes on gender-neutral language." Retrieved May 23, 2008, from http://www.english.upenn.edu/~cjacobso/gender.html. And from "Avoiding heterosexual bias in language." Retrieved May 23, 2008, from http://www.apastyle.org/sexuality.html

Power and Accent

Where did people learn that an English accent sounds upper crust and educated? Or that English as spoken with an Asian Indian accent is hard to understand? Why do communicators often stereotype Black English as sounding uneducated? While these associations come from many sources, they certainly are prevalent in the media. People have become so accustomed to seeing and hearing these associations that they probably don't even question them. In fact, William Labov, a noted sociolinguist, refers to the practice of associating a dialect with the cultural attitudes toward it as "a borrowed prestige model." For example, until the 1950s, most Americans thought that British English was the correct way to speak English (Labov, 1980); even today, people continue to think that an English accent sounds very refined and educated. On the other hand, Southern drawls and Black English have become stigmatized so that today, people who speak them are often perceived negatively. For similar reasons, people often find the English accent of people from India (where English often is a first language) difficult to understand—as reported by our student in *It Happened to Me: Bart*.

It Happened to Me: *Bart*

I recently had a course taught by an Asian Indian professor, and it took me some time to understand his accent and form of speaking. Sometimes I thought he was mumbling, and sometimes his speech sounded so fast that I couldn't understand it. After a couple of classes, my hearing disciplined itself to understand him better. In the end, I realized he was a fine teacher.

Such language stereotypes can be "set off" in one's head before a person even speaks, when one *thinks*, generally because of the person's appearance, that she or he will not speak Standard English (Ruben, 2003). This is probably what happened to our student, Bart. Once he adjusted to the Indian English accent, he found he could understand his Indian professor just fine. (For examples of accents from many different language backgrounds, go to classweb.gmu.edu/accent/.)

How does language cause one group to become elevated and another denigrated? The answer lies partly in understanding the social forces of history and politics. The positive and negative associations about African American, White, and British English developed during the nineteenth and twentieth centuries when European Americans were establishing themselves as the powerful majority in the United States, while passing legislation that subjugated African Americans and other minority groups. Thus it is not surprising that the languages of these groups were viewed so differently. Similarly, the English spoken by people from India was negatively stereotyped as the aberrant language of the colonized, since England was the colonial power in India until the mid-twentieth century. Similar attitudes can be seen toward immigrant groups today; their accented English is often stigmatized, sometimes leading to language discrimination and lawsuits, as illustrated in *Did You Know? Language Discrimination.*

Power and Identity Labels

The language labels that refer to particular identities also communicate important messages about power relations. Members of more powerful groups frequently invoke labels for members of other groups without input from those group members. For example, straight people label gays but rarely refer to themselves as straight.

Did You Know?

Language Discrimination

Should language discrimination be illegal? Are there jobs where speaking English with an accent would impair someone's ability to do the job? Does language discrimination happen outside of employment as well?

Language discrimination includes inter-language discrimination and intra-language discrimination. Inter-language discrimination happens when people are treated differently because of the languages that they speak. In countries with an official language, discrimination can occur against those who do not speak the official language(s). Intra-language discrimination happens when people are treated differently because they speak in a way that is not considered "proper" or the dominant language. In the U.S., for example, someone who speaks Hawaiian pidgin, or Ebonics, may be treated differently than someone who speaks standard American English. Both kinds of discrimination can happen in job situations where someone is not hired or promoted because of an accent, or is treated differently from other employees. Language discrimination can also happen in schools when students are forbidden to speak certain languages. In the U.S., for example, some schools require students to speak English, not only in class but also outside of class. Language discrimination can also happen in social settings when someone is rebuffed because of the way they speak.

In contrast, some accents are preferred. For example, some U.S. Americans find a British or French accent to be attractive. Others like the Irish accent or accents from Australia or New Zealand. Some people like or dislike Southern accents, New England accents, and other varieties of English. Do you find yourself treating others with different accents in different ways?

Attempts to impose languages on others can be a legacy of colonialism. English, French, and Spanish are widely spoken around the world, largely due to a history of colonialism. Does requiring people to speak a particular language raise a human rights issue? Some languages that used to be more widely spoken are now marginalized, such as Irish; and some others have become extinct, such as Susquehannock (spoken by the Native Americans along the Susquehanna River). When we discriminate against people who speak in certain ways or speak certain languages, we are discriminating against the individuals, not just the accents or languages.

Think about labels and terms we have for males and females. Why do you think so many more negative terms exist for females than for males?

White people use ethnic and racial labels to refer to others (*people of color, African American*, or *Black*) but rarely refer to themselves as *White*. This power to label seems "normal," so most people don't think twice about specifying that a physician is a "woman doctor" while never describing one as a "male doctor." Or they might identify someone as a gay teacher but not a White teacher (even if this teacher is both). People usually don't think about the assumptions that reflect societal power relations; in sum, individuals feel the need to mark minority differences, but they tend not to identify majority group membership.

Not only do the more powerful get to label the less powerful—they may also use language labels to stigmatize them. However, the stigma comes from the power relations, not from the words themselves. For example, in the Polish language, the word *Polack* simply means "a man from Poland," but the stigma associated with the term comes from the severe discrimination practiced against Eastern Europeans in the early twentieth century, which led to jokes and stereotypes that exist to this day. The term *Oriental* originated when Western countries were attempting to colonize, and were at war with, Asian countries—and the connotative meaning was *exotic* and *foreign*. Today, many Asians and Asian Americans resent this label. Read about one of our student's opinions on the topic in *It Happened to Me: Hiroko*.

It Happened to Me: *Hiroko*

I get really tired of people referring to me as "Oriental." It makes me sound like a rug or a cuisine. I refer to myself as Asian American or Japanese American. I know people probably don't mean anything negative when they use it, but it makes me uncomfortable. If it's somebody I know well, I might ask them not to use that word, but usually I just don't say anything.

This resentment can make communication more difficult for Hiroko and those who use this term to refer to her. As this example reveals, understanding the dictionary meanings of words does not always reveal the impact of identity labels. Members of minority communities are the best informants on the communicative power of specific labels.

Not everyone in an identity group has the same denotative meaning for a particular label. For example, some young women do not like to be called "girl"; they find it demeaning. Others are comfortable with this term. Some people view these calls for sensitivity in language as nothing more then unnecessary political correctness, as seen in *Alternative View:* Swine Flu *Tops Politically Incorrect Phrases for 2009*.

Moreover, the power of labels can change over time. In an earlier age, many viewed the term *WASP* (White, Anglo-Saxon, Protestant) as a descriptor or even a positive label; now, however, it is seen as rather negative (Martin, Krizek, Nakayama, & Bradford, 1999). The shift probably reflects the changing attitudes of Whites, who are now more aware of their ethnicity and the fact that they are not always the majority. Similarly, the term *Paddy* as in "paddy wagon" (a term for a police wagon) originally was a derogatory term; some older Irish Americans may still find it offensive. It reflected a stereotype, widely held one hundred years ago, of Irish men as drunks who had to be carted off to jail. Now that discrimination (and stereotyping) against the Irish has all but disappeared, this term has lost much of its impact.

In summary, language, power, and societal forces are closely linked. The societal environment profoundly influences the way people perceive the world and the language choices available to them. Those in power set the language and communication norms, often determining what verbal communication style is deemed appropriate or inappropriate, elegant or uneducated. They frequently get to choose and use identity labels for those who are less powerful. Those whose language does not fit the standard, or who are the recipients of negative

Alternative **V I E W**
Swine Flu Tops Politically Incorrect Phrases for 2009

Swine Flu, Flush Toilet, Green Revolution, Minority, and Saint have been named the top politically (in) Correct words and phrases of the past year according to The Global Language Monitor in its sixth annual survey of the English Language. Rounding out the top ten were the term Politically Correct, Oriental, Founding Fathers, Black Sheep, and Senior Citizen. "Once again, we are seeing that the attempt to remove all bias from language is itself creating biases of their own," said Paul JJ Payack, president and chief word analyst of The Global Language Monitor. "At this point, it is becoming increasingly difficult to engage in any form of public dialogue without offending someone's sensitivities, whether right, left or center."

What makes the phrases on this list politically incorrect? If you were to join the Language Police, what phrases might you nominate for next year's list? Should we have language police?

The Top Politically Correct Words and Phrases for 2009 include:

1. **Swine Flu**—Though hundreds of millions know of the current pandemic as Swine Flu, various governments and agencies for political motives ranging from protecting pork producers to religious sensitivity have chosen to address the virus by its formal name, influenza A(H1N1).

2. **Flush Toilet**—Flush toilets, toilet paper and toilet use in general are now coming under the watchful eyes of the green movement.

3. **Green Revolution**—In the 1960s the scientific consensus was the world was on the brink of

a 'Malthusian' collapse. The Green Revolution changed all that, but now there are those who believe that the world has paid a "stiff price in environmental degradation."

4. **Minority**—Talking about minorities is considered insensitive to minorities since this can make them feel, well, like minorities.

5. **Saint**—In addition to the word 'saint,' Oxford University Press has removed words such as 'bishop,' 'chapel,' and 'Pentecost' from the *Junior Dictionary.*

6. **Politically Correct**—The term politically correct has, itself, now become politically correct. Be careful how you use it.

7. **Oriental**—In the U.S., considered offensive to Asians because the term is based on the geographic relationship of Asia from a Western perspective. In Europe (and in most Asian nations), however, Oriental is acceptable.

8. **Founding Fathers**—Though all the Signers of the American Declaration of Independence were men, this is considered sexists in some quarters. Founders, please.

9. **Black Sheep**—Though originally referring to the rare birth of a lamb with black fur, now considered ethnically insensitive; the same is true for **Black Day**, Conversely, terms like **White Collar** and **Whiter than White** all can be used to encourage a hierarchical value of skin tone.

10. **Senior Citizen**—In the name of 'inclusiveness,' the UK's Loughborough University's suggests replacing senior citizen with 'older person.'

FROM: "Swine Flu, Flush Toilet, Green Revolution, Minority, and Saint named top politically (in)Correct words and phrases of 2009," *The Global Language Monitor*, October 2, 2009. Retrieved September 6, 2011 from: www.languagemonitor.com/politics/politically_correct/

labels, may feel marginalized and resentful, leading to difficult communication interactions.

TEST YOUR KNOWLEDGE

- What is the difference between the nominalist and relativist perspectives on the relationship between language and perception?
- How does power influence language, words, accent, and labels?
- Can you give examples of the role of power in language, words, accent, and labels?

ETHICS AND VERBAL COMMUNICATION

We have already discussed a number of ethical issues related to verbal communication in this book. In Chapter 1, we argued that ethical communicators consider the benefit and/or harm associated with their messages. In this section, we examine one specific type of language whose use may harm individuals or relationships.

Hate Speech

In the United States, we place a high value on freedom of speech. We have codified this value into our legal system, beginning with the First Amendment to the Constitution. However, freedom of speech is always balanced by competing societal interests. As the familiar saying goes, freedom of speech does not include the right to shout "fire!" in a crowded theater. But what about the right to express negative opinions about others? In the 1980s and '90s, as American society became more aware of the ethics of minority rights, the term *hate speech* began to be used (ACLU, 1994). **Hate speech,** or the use of verbal communication to attack others based upon some social category such as race, ethnicity, religion, or sexuality, is seen as threatening an entire group and/or inciting violence against members of these groups. In the U.S., the first-amendment guarantee of free speech is generally used to protect against laws that would make hate speech illegal (Liptak, 2008). However, many argue that even if hate speech is legal, it is unethical.

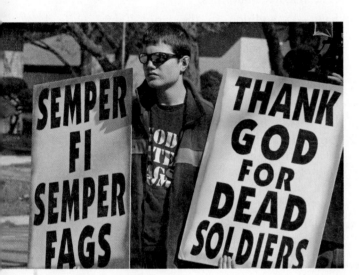

Hate speech is legal in the United States, but many argue that it is unethical.

As ethical communicators, where should we draw the line between free speech and unethical verbal communication?

Many countries view the use of verbal communication to attack, demean, and degrade other groups of people as not only unethical, but also illegal. Canada's criminal code, for example, forbids speech, writing, and Internet postings that advocate genocide or that publicly incite hatred (Media Awareness Network, n.d.). As another example, in some European countries it is illegal to deny that the Holocaust occurred. In 2008, a Belgian court sentenced two people to prison for denying the Holocaust in print (Prison ferme, 2008).

Whether illegal or unethical, the use of verbal communication to attack others based on their group membership is often seen as an attack on the whole group, not just the person who is the receiver of such messages.

Confirming and Disconfirming Communication

While hate speech may be obviously unethical, there are other, less obvious types of communication that can be unethical because of the harm they can cause. One of these is *disconfirming communication*. **Disconfirming communication** occurs when people make comments that reject or invalidate a self-image, positive or negative, of their conversational partners (Dance & Larson, 1976). Consider the following conversation:

> **Tracey:** Guess what? I earned an A on my midterm.
>
> **Lou:** Gee, it must have been an easy test.

Lou's response is an example of disconfirming communication, because it suggests that Tracey could not have earned her A because of competence or ability.

hate speech
use of verbal communication to attack others based upon some social category

disconfirming communication
comments that reject or invalidate a positive or negative self-image of our conversational partners

Consequently, his message disconfirms Tracey's image of herself. You can disconfirm people either explicitly ("I've never really thought of you as being smart") or implicitly (as Lou did).

How can messages such as these cause harm? Imagine that you received numerous disconfirming messages from people who are important to you. How might it affect you? Such messages not only can negatively influence your self-image, but they also can impair your relationships with the people who disconfirm you. For instance, Harry Weger, Jr. (2005) and John Caughlin (2002) have found that when couples engage in disconfirming behavior, their marital dissatisfaction increases. Disconfirming messages can harm both individuals and relationships and may be considered unethical as well as ineffective because they focus on the person.

If you want to avoid sending disconfirming messages, what should you do instead? You can provide others with confirming messages. Confirming messages validate positive self-images of others, as in the following example of **confirming communication**.

> **Tracey:** Guess what? I earned an A on my midterm.
>
> **Lou:** That's great. I know it's a tough class; you deserve to be proud.
>
> **Or Lou might say:** Congratulations! I know you were studying very hard and you deserve that grade.

Confirming messages are not only more ethical, they are usually more effective. Most people enjoy communicating with those who encourage them to feel good about themselves. Although engaging in confirming communication will not guarantee that you will be instantly popular, if you are sincere, it will increase the effectiveness of your communication and ensure that you are communicating ethically. If using confirming communication does not come naturally to you, you can practice until it does.

You might be wondering how you can provide negative feedback to people without being disconfirming. We discuss how to do this in the next section.

IMPROVING YOUR VERBAL COMMUNICATION SKILLS

When considering the ethics of language use, you should think about the effectiveness of your verbal choices. What are some guidelines for engaging in more effective verbal communication? We describe two ways in which you might improve: You can work on using "I" statements and also become more aware of the power of language.

"I" Statements

One type of disconfirming message involves making negative generalizations about others. Although you recognize that people are complex and variable, have you nevertheless found yourself making negative generalizations such as those listed here?

> "You are so thoughtless."
>
> "You are never on time."

As you can see, negative generalizations (which also are called "you" statements) are typically disconfirming. But, in the real world everyone lives in, some people *are* thoughtless, and some *are* consistently late. So is there an ethical and effective way to make your dissatisfaction known? Yes. You can use a type of message called an "I" statement. "I" statements allow you to express your feelings (even negative ones) by focusing on your own experiences rather than making negative generalizations (or "you" statements) about others.

confirming communication comments that validate positive self-images of others

"I" statements are conveyed through a three-part message that describes

1. the other person's behavior,
2. your feelings about that behavior, and
3. the consequences the other's behavior has for you.

Taking the examples just given and rewriting them as "I" statements, you could come up with:

> "When you criticize my appearance (behavior), I feel unloved (feeling), and I respond by withdrawing from you (consequence)."
>
> "I think I must be unimportant to you (feeling) when you arrive late for dinner (behavior), so I don't feel like cooking for you (consequence)."

"You" statements often lead recipients to feel defensive and/or angry because of the negative evaluation contained in the message and because the listener resents the speaker's position of passing judgment. "I" statements can lead to more constructive resolution of conflicts because they arouse less defensiveness. They also are more effective than "you" statements because the receiver is more likely to listen and respond to them (Kubany, Bauer, Muraoka, Richard, & Read, 1995). In addition, in order to make "I" statements, speakers have to explore exactly what they are dissatisfied with, how it makes them feel, and what the consequences of the other person's behavior are. "I" statements prevent speakers from attacking others in order to vent their feelings.

While many communication scholars believe in the value of "I" statements, a recent study found that people reacted similarly to *both* "I" and "you" statements involving negative emotions. However, the authors point out that their study involved written hypothetical conflict situations. They admit that their results might have been different if they had studied real-life conflict situations (Bippus & Young, 2005).

Although "I" statements can be very effective in a variety of contexts, this does not mean they are *always* appropriate. Situations may arise where others' behavior so violates what you believe is decent or appropriate that you wish to state your opinions strongly. Thus, if your friend abuses alcohol or takes illicit drugs, you may need to say, "You should not drive a car tonight" or "You need to get help for your addiction." The effectiveness of one's verbal communication must always be evaluated in the context of the situation, the relationships one has with others, and one's goal.

Become Aware of the Power of Language

As we noted in Chapter 1, language is a powerful force that has consequences and ethical implications. Wars have been started, relationships have been ruined, and much anger and unhappiness has resulted from intentional and unintentional verbal messages. The old adage "Sticks and stones can break my bones, but words will never hurt me" is not always true. Words *can* hurt, as shown *Communication in Society: Mind Your (Terror) Language* describing language offensive to many Arabs and Muslims.

When a speaker refers to others by negative or offensive identity terms, the speaker not only causes harm, he or she also denies those labeled individuals their identities—even if it isn't intentional. For example, one of our students, Cynthia, told us how bad she felt when she realized that some of her gay coworkers were offended by her use of the term "homosexual" (instead of gay). They explained that "homosexual" was used as a description of a psychiatric disease by the American Psychiatric Association's list of mental disorders until 1973, and has a connotation of this sexual orientation as a cold, clinical "condition." Using her embarrassment

COMMUNICATION IN SOCIETY
Mind Your (Terror) Language

Words like "terrorist," "terrorism," and "war on terror" are frequently used, but how often do we think about what they actually mean?

It is often said that one group's "terrorist" is another group's "freedom fighter"—the difference depends on whether the person in question is perceived as being on the side of "us" or "them." Similarly, whether a leader in a foreign culture is described as a "warlord" or a "tribal elder" often depends on whose side we believe the individual supports.

In the 21st century, Muslims and Arabs are particularly sensitive to such language. Referring to someone as a "moderate Muslim" implies that the norm is extremism, not moderation. Equating the term *fatwa* with a threat to someone's life gives the word an inaccurately extreme meaning; it actually refers to a legal pronouncement or judgment to settle a question not covered by Islamic law. The Islamic term *jihad* translates as "striving" or "struggle," not "holy war" as some non-Muslims have rendered it.

When a violent incident occurs in which many people who were going about their business in a public place are injured or killed, it is easy to rush to judgment and use words like "terrorist," "suicide bomber," and "extremist." As a thoughtful communicator, choose to use language that describes what happened—a bomb exploded, several people were shot, or a truck ran through a checkpoint—and refrain from language that characterizes who is responsible and what their motives are before an incident can be investigated.

as a learning experience, she initiated an enlightening discussion with her coworkers. She learned that often the best way to discover what someone "wants to be called" is to ask. However, a conversation of this nature can only occur in the context of a mutually respectful relationship—one reason to have a diverse group of friends and acquaintances.

SUMMARY

Verbal communication plays a significant role in people's lives, assisting in relationship development, creating identities, and accomplishing everyday tasks. Language is the foundation of verbal processes and it functions in at least seven ways: instrumental, regulatory, informative, heuristic, interactional, personal, and imaginative. The four components of language study are phonology, the study of sounds; syntax, the grammar and rules for arranging units of meaning; semantics, the meaning of words; and pragmatics, the rules for appropriate use of language.

Individual influences on language include speakers' memberships in various identity groups (gender, age, regionality, ethnicity and race, education and occupation). When identities influence several aspects of language (vocabulary, grammar, and pronunciation), these speakers have distinct dialects. In other instances identity groups' language variations may be minor, involving only some pronunciation or word choices.

Societal forces affect verbal processes because they shape our perceptions and the power relationships that surround us. The language used in a given society influences its members' perceptions of social reality, while power relationships affect how its members' verbal patterns are evaluated.

Communicating more ethically involves avoiding hate speech and using confirming rather than disconfirming language. To improve your verbal communication skills, learn to use "I" statements when expressing dissatisfaction, and recognize the power of language.

HUMAN COMMUNICATION IN SOCIETY ONLINE

To review this chapter, use the MyCommunicationLab Web site to test your understanding of the following key terms, record your answers to the chapter review questions, and complete the suggested activities. Expand your learning and understanding of chapter concepts by completing additional activities and exercises online. Access code required. Go to www.mycommunicationlab.com for more information or to purchase standalone access.

KEY TERMS

instrumental 109	syntax 111	Ebonics 121
regulatory 109	semantics 111	jargon 121
informative 109	denotative meaning 112	nominalists 122
heuristic 109	connotative meaning 112	relativists 122
interactional 109	pragmatics 112	Sapir-Whorf hypothesis 122
personal language 109	speech act theory 112	cocultural theory 123
imaginative 109	dialect 115	hate speech 130
grammar 110	lexical choice 115	disconfirming communication 130
phonology 110	cohort effect 117	confirming communication 131

APPLY WHAT YOU KNOW

1. For each scenario, write a paragraph describing a typical communication exchange. For each, think about the various elements of verbal communication: sounds, grammar, meaning (word choice), conversational rules, and contextual rules.

   ■ an informal family outing

   ■ a meeting with your advisor

   ■ a bar, where you are trying to impress potential partners

   Hint: Working in a small group, see whether you and your classmates can come up with some shared contextual rules for communication in these various situations. Give some reasons why you can or cannot come up with shared rules.

2. Take three sheets of paper and write one of the following words on each sheet: *garbage, milk, mother.* Take the first piece of paper and crumple it up and then stomp on it. Do the same with the second and third pieces. How did you feel crumpling up and stomping on the first piece of paper? The second? The third? What does this say perhaps about the difference between denotative and connotative meanings?

3. Think about two accents or dialects you've heard, either in a personal encounter or on radio or television. For each one, answer the following questions:

   ■ Do you have a negative or positive association for this dialect/accent?

   ■ Where did these associations (negative or positive) come from?

   ■ How might these associations (negative or positive) influence the way you communicate with a person who uses this accent or dialect?

Share your answers with your classmates. Do you have similar reactions and associations for the same accent or dialect? What does this say about the power of society in influencing perceptions about communication and language use?

4. For each of the examples that follow, create an "I" statement that expresses your feelings about the situation:

- Once again your roommate has borrowed some of your clothes without asking and has returned them dirty and/or damaged.

- For the third time this semester, your instructor has changed the date of an exam.

- Your good friend has developed a habit of canceling plans at the last moment.

- Your romantic partner embarrasses you by teasing you about personal habits in front of friends.

Form a group with two or three of your classmates. Take turns reading your "I" statement for each situation. Discuss the strengths and weaknesses of each statement. As a group, develop an "I" statement for each situation above that best expresses the group's feelings without encouraging defensiveness in the receiver.

5. Locate five people who either grew up in different parts of the United States or who grew up in different countries. Try to include both men and women and people of different ages in your sample. Ask each person to answer the following questions:

- What do you call a carbonated beverage?

- How do you pronounce "roof"?

- What expressions do you use that some other people have had trouble understanding?

- What does the term *feminist* mean?

- Who do you think talks "different"?

6

Nonverbal Communication

Recently a colleague took her four-year-old daughter with her to a business meeting. After observing the interaction for a few minutes, her daughter Anna whispered, "When it's your turn to talk, you have to make your mad face."

Even though Anna is only four years old, she is sensitive to the nonverbal behavior of others. She readily reads others' facial expressions and assigns meaning to them. From a very early age, all children learn the basics of nonverbal communication (Boone & Cunningham, 1998); in fact, infants from an early age imitate others' nonverbal behavior. For example, when newborns observe caregivers sticking out their tongues, they imitate them and do the same (Als, 1977; Meltzoff & Prinz, 2002).

In this chapter, we take a close look at the intricacies of nonverbal communication and the many factors that shape nonverbal messages and their interpretation. First, we describe the importance of nonverbal communication, provide a definition, and explore how it differs from nonverbal behavior. We then give you an overview of the various types of nonverbal codes, and we examine the functions that nonverbal messages serve. We next explore how societal forces intersect with individuals' nonverbal communication. We conclude the chapter by discussing ethical issues in nonverbal communication and providing you with suggestions for improving your nonverbal communication skills.

Once you have read this chapter, you will be able to:

■ Explain the important role of nonverbal communication in social interaction.

■ Identify four factors that influence the meaning of nonverbal communication.

■ Define five nonverbal codes and discuss the five functions of nonverbal messages.

■ Articulate the role of power in nonverbal communication.

■ Understand how nonverbal communication can trigger, and express, prejudice and discrimination.

■ Discuss six guidelines for ethical nonverbal communication.

■ Name five ways to improve your ability to interpret nonverbal behavior.

THE IMPORTANCE OF NONVERBAL COMMUNICATION

Nonverbal communication plays an important role in social interaction. It helps us express and interpret the verbal aspects of communication—such as when a person:

■ smiles to *reinforce* an expression of thanks;

■ uses the "OK" sign to *substitute* for saying "I am all right";

■ laughs flirtatiously to *contradict* the words, "I hate you";

■ puts his fingers close together to *illustrate* how thin his new computer is.

Even young children understand and use nonverbal communication.

Nonverbal communication also influences how individuals interpret messages, especially those related to feelings, moods, and attitudes. Nonverbal cues are important to the expression of emotion because communicators are often more comfortable expressing their feelings nonverbally (such as by smiling or glaring) than they are stating them more explicitly through words (Mehrabian, 2007). For example, how often do you flatly tell a friend or colleague, "I am mad at you"? If you are like most people, this is a relatively rare event; instead, you probably rely on some type of nonverbal cue to indicate your dissatisfaction.

However, nonverbal communication can be complex and ambiguous—both for senders of messages to convey and for receivers of messages to interpret. Even though we begin learning nonverbal communication as children, we often have difficulty interpreting others' nonverbal communication. Why is this so? One reason is the fact that humans express a wide array of nonverbal behaviors, many of which can be quite subtle. Consequently, understanding nonverbal communication requires knowledge and skill.

However, beware of books, Web sites, and magazine articles that promise to teach you to "read a person like a book": there is no such thing as a key to decoding or interpreting every **nonverbal behavior** in every context. Why not? Because understanding nonverbal communication requires interpreting behavior and assigning meaning to it, and we don't always have the information we need to do that. If you are sitting in the library and notice a stranger staring at you, what does the stare mean? Does the person think he knows you? Is he interested in meeting you? Is he being aggressive? Or is the person simply lost in thought and only *appearing* to be gazing at you? As this example illustrates, nonverbal cues can be ambiguous. Because the meaning of nonverbal behavior is determined by a variety of factors, including context, culture, and even intentionality, it can be tricky to interpret a specific behavior.

In addition, nonverbal cues are continuous, meaning that people exhibit nonverbal behaviors virtually all the time they are conscious, and multiple behaviors act in concert to create a given message—or different messages, even unrelated ones. For example, imagine that Joan is talking to her husband about their need to spend time together to strengthen their marriage. Just as her husband asks, "What do you want to do about our marriage?" Joan happens to look over his shoulder at her computer screen and sees it displaying an error message. In frustration, she throws up her hands and sighs heavily. Joan was responding to her computer failure, but her husband thought she was responding to his question. He became very upset, assuming she was expressing a wish to give up on their marriage.

Nonverbal communication also can be difficult to interpret because nonverbal cues are multi-channeled; that is, they can be transmitted in a variety of ways simultaneously. Speakers can convey nonverbal messages through their facial expressions, voice qualities, eye gaze, posture, and gestures and by other channels we will discuss throughout this chapter. Moreover, because a variety of cues may occur at the same time, it can be difficult and confusing to keep up with everything (Schwartz, Foa, & Foa, 1983). If, for example, you are focusing on someone's face, you may miss important messages conveyed by the body.

"Pop psychology" treatments of nonverbal communication typically assume that each behavior has one meaning regardless of the context or who is performing it. Such explanations don't distinguish between nonverbal behavior and nonverbal communication; nor do they consider context, culture, individual variations in behavior, or the relationship that exists between the people being observed. All these factors, and more, can influence the meaning of a nonverbal behavior in a specific instance. So don't believe that just because someone has her arms crossed over her body, it means she is closed off to you. It may simply mean she needs a sweater.

nonverbal communication
nonverbal behavior that has symbolic meaning

nonverbal behavior
all the nonverbal actions people perform

Nonverbal messages are not only complex and ambiguous—they are also key components of communication. Understanding nonverbal communication can make you a better *verbal* communicator. In addition, nonverbal communication can help you navigate everyday life. For example, humans rely on nonverbal cues to determine whether other humans are a threat. In the television show *Going Tribal,* journalist Bruce Parry visited the remote Suri tribe in Ethiopia. As he approached the first tribal member, Parry carefully observed the tribesman thrust his bow and arrow at him and pace quickly back and forth while averting his eye gaze. Although many of the Suri's nonverbal behaviors communicated belligerence, the fact that he did not stare aggressively influenced Bruce to approach him slowly with a gift—which was accepted.

Public policy seeks to regulate nonverbal expression, such as what type of clothing people can wear.

Similarly, on a daily basis people need to be able to read subtle nonverbal behaviors in order to assess how friendly or hostile others may be. This is especially true for individuals whose identities are less valued culturally or whose societal position makes them more vulnerable. Because of this vulnerability, such individuals tend to become quite adept at reading and interpreting nonverbal communication. For example, if Gary's boss walks into the office frowning and shaking her head, Gary may interpret this as meaning that she is in a bad mood; consequently, he may try to be especially helpful and avoid doing anything to provoke her. In a study that compared African Americans' and White Americans' ability to read the nonverbal behaviors of Whites, researchers found that African Americans were far better at detecting prejudicial attitudes as expressed in subtle nonverbal behavior than Whites (Richeson & Shelton, 2005). Similarly, a study of heterosexual and gay men found that gay men were better able to identify the sexual orientation of unfamiliar men when watching videos of them (Shelp, 2002).

Nonverbal communication also is important because it can affect public policy decisions. For example, after several years of allowing students to wear just about anything they wished to school, many public schools now institute dress codes. Although some schools primarily regulate clothing that they see as "inappropriate" or too revealing, others require school uniforms. The supporters of this latter policy argue that school uniforms "help erase cultural and economic differences among students" (Isaacson, 1998) and improve student performance and attendance. Regulating school dress rests on the assumption that one form of nonverbal communication, attire, should be regulated because it can be distracting or even disruptive. Other examples of public policy attempts to regulate nonverbal expression include efforts to ban flag burning and to forbid the wearing of Muslim headscarves. Countries would not engage in efforts to control nonverbal expression if it were not so important.

TEST YOUR KNOWLEDGE
- Why is it impossible to "read a person like a book"?
- What features of nonverbal communication make it challenging for us to interpret it easily?

WHAT IS NONVERBAL COMMUNICATION?

The nonverbal components of communication include all the messages that people transmit through means other than words. More specifically, communication scholar Valerie Manusov and psychologist Miles Patterson define nonverbal communication as "encompassing the sending and receiving of information through appearance, objects, the environment and behavior in social settings" (Manusov & Patterson, 2006, p. xi). Thus, they argue that we communicate nonverbally when we

These sorority members signal their group membership nonverbally through their clothing and gestures.

Which of these two positions regarding nonverbal communication/nonverbal behavior seems more reasonable to you, and why? What evidence or reasoning influenced your decision? Finally, what difference does this distinction make?

blow a kiss, scratch our arm, or wear clothing that signals our group membership. Even more frequently, nonverbal and verbal aspects of communication combine to convey messages, as when we indicate anger by turning our backs and saying "I don't want to talk with you right now."

However, not every scholar believes that all nonverbal behavior is communicative. These researchers argue that nonverbal communication occurs only when nonverbal behavior has symbolic meaning and is communicated intentionally (Burgoon, Buller, & Woodall, 1996). That is, they believe nonverbal communication stands for something, while nonverbal behavior may not. For example, from this perspective, scratching one's arm usually isn't intended by the scratcher, nor understood by the observer, to convey a particular message. Although it may provide information (that one's arm itches), it doesn't necessarily signal an *intentional* message. Rather, it would be considered an involuntary bodily "output." However, these scholars would argue that in baseball when a manager scratches his arm to signal that a runner on base should steal home, scratching the arm is symbolic and, therefore, an instance of nonverbal communication.

Nonetheless, these scholars acknowledge that some nonverbal communication does lack the element of intentionality. For example, a smile may be understood as an expression of pleasure even if the smiler is unaware that he is smiling. Thus, if a behavior typically is used communicatively, then that behavior is understood to be part of our nonverbal "vocabulary" and will be interpreted as such, regardless of one's own conscious use of it (Burgoon, Buller, & Woodall, 1996).

However, scholars who prefer a broader definition of nonverbal communication argue that many actions one might consider just a "bodily output" can still convey messages nonverbally. For example, people usually cough because of a scratchy throat or yawn because they are tired, and when they engage in these behaviors others interpret their meaning. Of course, they also believe that when a person coughs as a signal to capture someone's attention or yawns to indicate he is bored, he is engaging in nonverbal communication.

As our discussion thus far suggests, most nonverbal behaviors have a variety of meanings—just as scratching one's arm can have multiple meanings. Therefore neither we, nor anyone else, can provide you with interpretations for specific nonverbal actions. Perhaps in part because of this difficulty, we cannot accurately estimate the amount of meaning that nonverbal communication contributes to the overall meaning in an interaction. This inability is revealed in *Did You Know? How Much Does Nonverbal Communication Contribute to Meaning?* where you can see why it can be difficult to estimate how much meaning nonverbal components convey in any message.

TEST YOUR KNOWLEDGE

- What is nonverbal communication?
- How do some scholars differentiate nonverbal behavior from nonverbal communication?

NONVERBAL COMMUNICATION AND THE INDIVIDUAL

If a smile is viewed as communicating pleasure even when the smiler doesn't intend to do so, then why don't all behaviors that are part of our nonverbal vocabulary always convey the same meaning? The answer is that assigning one simple meaning to a nonverbal behavior ignores the multiple meanings that may exist, depending on the context in which the behavior occurs. For example, you will read in this chapter that

Did You Know?

How Much Does Nonverbal Communication Contribute to Meaning?

How much of the meaning of a message do you think is conveyed by its nonverbal components? Fifty percent? Seventy-five percent? One of the most common beliefs about communication is that over 90 percent of the meaning of a message is transmitted by its nonverbal elements. However, in truth, we do not know! So where did this belief originate?

In 1967, psychologist Albert Mehrabian(along with Morton Wiener) wrote that 93 percent of the meaning of the utterances he examined was conveyed through the nonverbal aspects of communication. Specifically, he argued that 38 percent of meaning in his study was derived from paralinguistic cues (tone of voice, etc.) and 55 percent from facial expressions, leaving only 7 percent of meaning to be provided by the verbal message. After he published his findings, other people, researchers and non-researchers alike, began to generalize his claims about his one study to all communicative interactions.

However, a variety of scholars have contradicted this claim, either arguing for a different percentage (Birdwhistell, 1985) or suggesting that one cannot accurately determine how much words, context, nonverbal messages, and other factors actually contribute to the meaning of an utterance. Those who critique Mehrabian's analysis argue that his study exhibited several problems. First, it examined how people interepreted the meaning of single tape-recorded words, which is not how we naturally communicate. Second, he combined the results of two studies that most scholars believe should not be combined. Further, he did not consider the contributions to meaning made by gestures and posture. Also, he tried to estimate the contribution of particular nonverbal behaviors—for example, gesture versus facial expression. In practice, however, no one behavior is particularly useful in determining meaning. In other words, inferences made about the meaning of any given action are not all that reliable, nor are estimates of what percentage of the total message a single nonverbal cue communicates.

when a person leans toward another (called a *forward body lean*), this is often a sign of interest or involvement. Does that mean that the forward body lean always indicates interest? Absolutely not! A person might lean forward for a variety of reasons: her stomach hurts, the back of her chair is hot, or her lower back needs to be stretched.

To understand the meaning of a nonverbal behavior you have to consider the entire behavioral context, including what the person might be communicating verbally (Jones & LeBaron, 2002). Therefore, interpreting others' nonverbal behavior requires that you consider a variety of factors that can influence meaning. To interpret nonverbal communication, you also need to know the codes, or symbols and rules, that signal various messages. Finally, you will benefit from a familiarity with the variety of ways that nonverbal messages function. These are topics we take up next.

Influences on Nonverbal Communication

Culture is one of the more important factors that influence the meaning of nonverbal communication. This is not to say that many nonverbal cues and signals aren't shared; in fact, research shows that gaze is used to communicate aggression, dominance, and power as well as connection and nurturance across cultures (and even species) (Matsumoto, 2006); however, the specific manner in which gaze is used to communicate these messages can vary. For example, in many Arabic cultures, eye gaze during social interaction is more direct than is typical in the United

This gesture of support for the University of Texas Longhorns might be misinterpreted in Norway, where it is a sign of Satan.

States (Watson & Graves, 1966); thus, eye gaze that might be interpreted as friendly and involved in an Arabic culture could be perceived as somewhat aggressive by a U.S. American. Similarly, within the United States, gaze and visual behavior differ across sexes and ethnic groups, with women tending to gaze more than men (Briton & Hall, 1995) and African Americans often using more continuous eye gaze while talking and less while listening than many Whites (Samovar & Porter, 2004).

Some nonverbal cues are used widely across cultures, such as nodding to mean yes—though this is not true in every culture. However, many nonverbal gestures have vastly different meanings in different cultures. In the United States, for instance, the "thumbs up" signals success and the "hitchhiker's thumb" asks for a ride, but these nonverbal signs carry potentially vulgar meanings in several other cultures. In East Africa, instead of pointing with fingers, people often point with their lips—a gesture that is completely unfamiliar to most people in the United States. Differences in gestures also occur across ethnic groups in the United States. For example, historically Korean Americans tended to reserve smiling, shaking hands, and saying hello for friends and family; however, many immigrants changed this pattern of behavior once they recognized its meaning and importance in the United States (Young, 1999). Thus, the meaning of any nonverbal behavior is defined by the cultures of those interacting (Axtell, 1993; Segerstrale & Molnár, 1997).

In addition to culture, the relationship between the people interacting affects the meaning of nonverbal behaviors (Manusov, 1995). If a husband takes his wife's arm as they are crossing the street, the meaning likely is some mixture of care and affection; if a police officer were to do so, one probably would interpret it as an aggressive or controlling gesture. However, if a boss were to do the same with a subordinate, the meaning is more complex and potentially confusing or troubling. One might wonder whether she is being friendly, controlling, affectionate—or maybe too affectionate? How we interpret others' nonverbal behavior, then, is highly dependent on the type of relationship we have with them.

Third, the meaning we attribute to someone's nonverbal behavior varies based on how well we know the communicator. For example, if a stranger smiles at you, you might interpret it as a gesture of friendliness, since that is the meaning most often associated with this facial expression. However, if you know your best friend tends to smile when she is angry, then you will be more accurate at interpreting that her smile is a sign of her displeasure than would someone who did not know her well. Once we know people, then, we can usually read their nonverbal behavior and interpret its associated messages with more accuracy, as Abbad explains in *It Happened to Me: Abbad.*

Finally, we tend to interpret individuals' nonverbal behavior based on their sex. For example, when women toss

It Happened to Me: *Abbad*

I am from the Middle East, and I arrived in the United States in 2000 with a couple of my friends. On a school break, we decided to travel to Washington, D.C. On the road, we stopped at a McDonald's to eat and to pray. As Muslims, we have to pray five times a day, and during the prayer we cannot talk at all. While in the middle of our prayer, a McDonald's employee approached and asked what we were doing. Since we could not talk, one of my friends used a hand gesture that in our culture means "wait for a minute." This hand gesture is expressed by holding one's fingers together like a pyramid. For some reason, the employee understood the gesture as an invitation for a fight. I guess this is what it means in some parts of the United States. That's when the employee called 911. By the time the police officer arrived, we were done with our prayer. We explained we were new to this country and that the hand gesture we used means something else in our culture. We apologized to the employee for the misunderstanding and continued on our trip.

their hair, the behavior often is read as flirtatious—and therefore communicative. However, if a man does the same, we are more likely to believe he is just trying to get his hair out of his eyes—a nonverbal behavior that is not necessarily communicative. As we discuss throughout this book, sex differences in nonverbal and verbal communication are due to biological as well as social and cultural influences.

Nonverbal Codes

Nonverbal codes or signals are distinct, organized means of expression that consist of both symbols and rules for their use (Cicca, Step, & Turkstra, 2003). Although we describe a range of such codes in this section, we do not mean to imply that any one code occurs in isolation. Generally, a set of behaviors and codes together determines the meaning or significance of an action. For our purposes, we isolate a specific kind of behavior for analysis; in the real world, without knowing the context, interpretations about any behavior may be questionable or even wrong (Patterson, 1983). In this section, we'll look at the five aspects of nonverbal codes—*kinesics, paralinguistics, time and space, haptics,* and *appearance and artifacts*—to see how this system of nonverbal codes works.

Kinesics **Kinesics** is the term used to describe a system of studying nonverbal communication sent by the body, including gestures, posture, movement, facial expressions, and eye behavior. For clarity we group kinesic communication into two general categories, those behaviors involving the body and those involving the face.

The Body Our bodies convey many nonverbal messages. For example, we use **gestures** such as pointing, waving, and holding up our hands to direct people's attention, signal hello, and indicate that we want to be recognized. Communicators use four types of nonverbal gestures: *illustrators, emblems, adaptors,* and *regulators.* **Illustrators** are signals that accompany speech to clarify or emphasize the verbal messages. Thus when people come back from a fishing trip they hold their hands far apart to indicate the size of the fish that got away. **Emblems** are gestures that stand for a specific verbal meaning; for example, raising one's hand in class indicates that one wishes to speak. **Adaptors** are gestures we use to manage our emotions. Many adaptors are nervous gestures such as tapping a pencil, jiggling a leg, or twirling one's hair. Finally, people use **regulators** to control conversation; for example, if you want to prevent someone from interrupting you, you might hold up your hand to indicate that the other person should wait. In contrast, if you wish to interrupt and take the floor, you might raise a finger to signal your desire.

Gestures contribute a lot to our communication efforts; even their frequency can signal meaning. For instance, how much gesturing we do while speaking can indicate how involved we are in a conversation. Typically, people who are excited indicate their involvement by using many and varied gestures; those who have little involvement may indicate their lack of interest by their failure to gesture.

We also use our bodies to convey meaning through our posture and our movement. In general, posture is evaluated in two ways: by how *immediate* it is and by how relaxed it appears (Mehrabian, 1971; Richards, Rollerson, & Phillips, 1991). **Immediacy** refers to how close or involved people appear to be with each other. For example, when people like someone they tend to orient their bodies in the other person's direction, lean toward them, and look at them directly when they speak. How do people act when they wish to avoid someone? Typically, they engage in the opposite behavior. They turn their backs or refuse to look at them, and if they are forced to stand or sit near the person they dislike, they lean away from them. To understand this, imagine how you would behave if you were attempting to reject an unwanted amorous advance.

Relaxation refers to the degree of tension one's body displays. When you are at home watching TV, for instance, you probably display a relaxed posture: lounging

nonverbal codes
distinct, organized means of expression that consists of symbols and rules for their use

kinesics
nonverbal communication sent by the body, including gestures, posture, movement, facial expressions, and eye behavior

gestures
nonverbal communication made with part of the body, including actions such as pointing, waving, or holding up a hand to direct people's attention

illustrators
signals that accompany speech to clarify or emphasize the verbal messages

emblems
gestures that stand for a specific verbal meaning

adaptors
gestures used to manage emotions

regulators
gestures used to control conversation

immediacy
how close or involved people appear to be with each other

relaxation
the degree of tension displayed by one's body

What nonverbal messages might be understood from this photo? Remember that a nonverbal behavior can have multiple meanings.

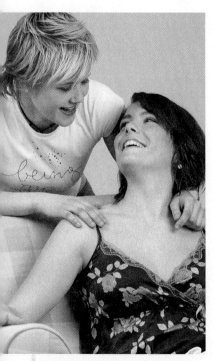

The face and the eyes are particularly important for conveying emotion.

in a chair with your legs stretched out in front of you and your arms resting loosely on the chair's arms. However, if you are waiting at the dentist's office, you may sit hunched forward, your legs pressed tightly together, and your hands tightly grasping the chair arms.

The way you walk or move also can communicate messages to others, particularly about your mood or emotional state. Sometimes you use movement deliberately to communicate a message—such as when you stomp around the apartment to indicate your anger. At other times, your movement is simply a nonverbal behavior—that is, you move naturally and unconsciously without any clear intentionality. Even when your movement is not intentional, observers can and do make judgments about you. One study found that observers could identify when pedestrians were sad, angry, happy, or proud, just from the way they walked (Montepare, Goldstein, & Clausen, 1987). However, some emotional states (anger) were easier to identify than others (pride), and some individuals were easier to classify than others. So although people consciously communicate a great deal with their body movements and gestures and observers interpret others' movements, some messages are more clearly transmitted than others. It should also be noted that many of the same factors discussed earlier, such as culture, context, background knowledge, and gender, can affect the ability to interpret kinesic behavior.

The Face Facial expressions communicate more than perhaps any other nonverbal behavior. They are the primary channels for transmitting emotion, and the eyes, in particular, convey important messages regarding attraction and attention. Some research suggests that facial expressions of happiness, sadness, anger, surprise, fear, and disgust are the same across cultures and, in fact, are innate (Ekman & Friesen, 1969, 1986), although not all scholars agree. Through observations of deaf, blind, and brain-damaged children, researchers have concluded that commonality of facial expressions among humans is not due to observation and learning but rather to genetic programming (Eibl-Eibesfeld, 1972; Ekman, 2003). (To better understand the role of facial expressions in the communication of emotion, go to http://www.persuasive.net/blog/it-is-written-all-over-your-face-understanding-facial-expressions/)

The ability to accurately recognize others' emotions gives individuals an edge in their interpersonal actions. For example, people with greater emotional recognition accuracy are effective in negotiations and are able to create more value for all parties and to achieve more favorable outcomes (Elfenbein, Maw, White, Tan, & Aik, 2007). If you are not very adept at recognizing others' emotions, however, you can improve your ability to do so. A variety of studies show that individuals who are trained in emotion recognition and then receive feedback on their performance can improve their ability to recognize others' emotional expressions, especially if their targets are from different cultures than their own (Elfenbein, 2006).

Of course, people don't display every emotion they feel. Individuals learn through experience and observation to manage their facial expressions, and they learn which expressions are appropriate to reveal in what circumstances. In many cultures expectations of appropriateness differ for men and women. For example, in the United States, males are often discouraged from showing sadness, while females are frequently criticized for showing anger. In addition, women are routinely expected to smile, no matter how they feel, while relatively few men receive the same message. Whether or not they are conscious of such cultural expectations, men and women generally learn to manage their facial expressions so as not to reveal emotions that they believe they shouldn't feel or that they don't want others to see.

Eye behavior is especially important in conveying messages for humans as well as animals. For example, both humans and dogs use prolonged eye gaze (a stare) to communicate aggression, and they avert their gaze when they want to avoid contact. Furthermore, eye behavior interacts with facial expressions to convey meaning. Thus, most people believe a smile is genuine only when the eyes "smile" as well as the lips. Actors such as Julia Roberts and Tom Cruise are particularly gifted at this; they can, at will, express what appears to be a genuine smile.

Like other types of nonverbal communication, context and culture shape the meanings people attach to eye behavior. For example, cultures differ significantly in how long one is supposed to engage in eye contact and how frequently. Many Native Americans such as Cherokee, Navajo, and Hopi engage in minimal eye contact compared to most White U.S. Americans (Chiang, 1993). Swedes tend to gaze infrequently but for longer periods of time, while southern Europeans gaze frequently and extensively (Knapp & Hall, 1992, 2001). Your relationship with others affects how you interpret their eye behavior. Thus, you may find it very appealing when a romantic partner gazes into your eyes but find the same behavior threatening when exhibited by a stranger. For an example of how differences in eye contact and facial expression can affect communication, see *Communication in Society: When You Smile on the Job.*

Paralinguistics The vocal aspects of nonverbal communication are referred to as **paralinguistics**, which include rate, volume, pitch, and stress, among others. Paralinguistics are those aspects of language that are *oral* but not *verbal*. That is, paralinguistics describe all aspects of spoken language except the words themselves. For example, typically you recognize other speakers' voices in large part through their paralinguistics, or how they sound, rather than the specific words they say. Thus, when you call a close friend or relative, you may expect them to recognize you just from hearing your voice on the telephone. If someone close to you has ever failed to recognize your voice on the phone, you may have felt hurt or offended, and the simple phone call may have turned into an anxiety-producing quiz. Paralinguistics are composed of two types of vocal behavior—*voice qualities* and *vocalizations*.

Voice Qualities Voice qualities include speed, pitch, rhythm, vocal range, and articulation; these qualities make up the "music" of the human voice. We all know people whose voice qualities are widely recognized. For example, President Barack

paralinguistics
all aspects of spoken language except the words themselves; includes rate, volume, pitch, stress

voice qualities
qualities such as speed, pitch, rhythm, vocal range, and articulation that make up the "music" of the human voice

COMMUNICATION IN SOCIETY
When You Smile on the Job

Do you think it is reasonable for a retail store to require women cashiers to smile and make eye contact with all customers? Why or why not? Why do you think the female Safeway employees believed their smiles were the cause of the men's attention?

Have you noticed the smiles and greetings you receive when you shop at major grocery store chains such as Walmart and Safeway? Grocery stores weren't always such welcoming places. This friendly behavior, often called the "supermarket mandatory smile" began in the U. S. in the late 1990s. Although many stores encouraged this behavior, Safeway actually required its employees to greet customers with a smile and direct eye contact. However, some female employees lodged complaints over this policy because they argued that male customers repeatedly propositioned them and asked them out on dates when they acted so friendly. Although Safeway denied that their policy was the cause of the men's behavior, they did eventually end it. If the organization had consulted nonverbal research on flirting, they might never have instituted the policy in the first place. One of the most common behaviors women use to signal their interest in men is a smile combined with eye contact and a slight tilt of the head (Trost & Alberts, 2009).

Obama's vocal qualities are frequently remarked upon. One critic (Dié, 2008) described it as resembling that used by preachers, arguing that if you listen only to how the President speaks (rather than what he says), you would feel as if you were sitting in a small church in any black neighborhood in the U. S. He uses the same "ebb and flow" or rhythms and intonations that are common to ministers' rhetorical style. To compare the vocal qualities of various presidents, go to www.presidentsusa.net/audiovideo.html and listen to audio and video recordings of many presidents.

Speakers whose voices vary in pitch and rhythm seem more expressive than those whose voices do not. For example, actor Keanu Reeves is criticized by some as boring and inexpressive because they perceive his delivery as monotonous. (This worked to his advantage, however, during his role as Klaatu in *The Day the Earth Stood Still*.) Speakers also vary in how they articulate sounds, some pronouncing each word distinctly and others blurring their words and sounds. We tend not to notice this paralinguistic feature unless someone articulates very precisely or very imprecisely. If you have difficulty understanding a speaker, usually the fault lies not with how fast the person talks but with how clearly he or she articulates. When combined, the qualities of pitch and rhythm make your voice distinctive and recognizable to those who know you.

Vocalizations Vocalizations are the sounds we utter that do not have the structure of language. Tarzan's yell is one famous example. Vocalizations include vocal cues such as laughing, crying, whining, and moaning, as well as the intensity or volume of one's speech. Also included are sounds that aren't actual words but that serve as fillers, such as "uh-huh," "uh," "ah," and "er."

The paralinguistic aspects of speech serve a variety of communicative purposes. They reveal mood and emotion; they also allow us to emphasize or stress a word or idea, create a distinctive identity, and (along with gestures) regulate conversation.

Time and Space How people use time and space is so important to communication that researchers have studied their use and developed specialized terms to describe them. **Chronemics**, from the Greek word *chronos,* meaning "time," is the study of the way people use time as a message. It includes issues such as punctuality and the amount of time people spend with each other. **Proxemics** refers to the study of how people use spatial cues, including interpersonal distance, territoriality, and other space relationships. Let's see how these factors influence communication and relationships.

Chronemics People often interpret others' use of time as conveying a message, which removes it from the realm of behavior and places it in the realm of communication. For example, if your friend consistently arrives more than an hour late, how do you interpret her behavior? Culture strongly influences how most people answer this question (Hall & Hall, 1987). In the United States, time typically is valued highly; we even have an expression that "time is money." Because of this, most people own numerous clocks and watches. Events are scheduled at specific times and typically begin on time. Therefore, in the United States, lateness can communicate thoughtlessness, irresponsibility, or selfishness. A more positive or tolerant view might be that the perpetually late person is carefree.

Not all cultures value time in the same way, however. In some Latin American and Arab cultures, if one arrives thirty minutes or even an hour after an event is scheduled to begin, one is "on time." When people come together from cultures that value time differently, it can lead to conflict and a sense of displacement. This happened when one of our colleagues taught a class in Mexico. On the first class day, she showed up at the school shortly before the class was scheduled to begin. She found the building locked and no one around. And even though she knew that people in Mexico respond to time differently than she did, during her stay she never was comfortable arriving "late," and routinely had to wait outside the building until someone showed up to let her in.

Think back to the last time you encountered someone you could tell was truly happy to see you. How could you tell? What nonverbal behaviors communicated the other person's happiness to you?

vocalizations
uttered sounds that do not have the structure of language

chronemics
the study of the way people use time as a message

proxemics
the study of how people use spatial cues, including interpersonal distance, territoriality, and other space relationships, to communicate

Did You Know?

Expectancy Violations

Think of a time when someone violated your expectations for nonverbal behavior. How did you interpret the behavior? Did you see it as a positive or negative violation? Why? How did you respond? How can a person use expectancy violation theory to increase liking?

Our expectations are one factor that influences our interpretations of others' nonverbal behavior. *Expectancy violation theory* states that when people violate our expectations, we tend to notice, become aroused, and attribute meaning to the violation, resulting in increased scrutiny and appraisal of the violator's behavior. For example, if you expect a stranger to shake your hand upon being introduced, you likely will search for an explanation if she or he hugs you instead.

However, we don't necessarily interpret and respond to these violations negatively. Judee Burgoon and her colleagues repeatedly have shown that responses to another's violation of our expectations are influenced by how we perceive the violator. In other words, we judge a violation as positive or negative depending largely on whether we view the violator as someone with whom we'd like to interact. Thus, if the stranger who hugs you is very attractive and you are single, you may evaluate this violation positively. This judgment shapes your response to the violation; in this case, if you interpret the hug positively, you may respond by hugging back (Burgoon & Hale, 1988; Burgoon & LePoire, 1993).

The timing and sequencing of events convey a variety of messages. For example, being invited to lunch carries a different meaning than being invited to dinner, and being asked to dinner on a Monday conveys a different message than being asked to dinner on a Saturday. Events also tend to unfold in a particular order; so we expect first dates to precede first kisses and small talk to precede task talk. When these expectations are violated, we often attribute meaning to the violations, as shown in *Did You Know? Expectancy Violations*.

In addition, some people use time **monochronically**, while others use it **polychronically**, and the differences can be perceived as transmitting a message (Hall, 1983; Wolburg, 2001). Individuals who use time monochronically engage in one task or behavior at time—one reads *or* participates in a conversation *or* watches a movie. If you engage in multiple activities at the same time, you are using time polychronically. Historically in the United States, people have used time monochronically; however, now that technology is so pervasive, more people are using time polychronically as they listen to their iPods, talk on cell phones, and cruise the Web while they interact with others. Unfortunately, people who use time monochronically may be insulted by those who use it polychronically, leading to comments such as "Put down that iPhone and pay attention to me when I talk to you!"

Whenever an individual's use of time differs from that of others, miscommunication is possible. If you tend to value punctuality more than others do, you may arrive at events earlier than expected and irritate your host, or you may be perceived as too eager. Similarly, if you don't value punctuality, you may discover that others won't schedule activities with you or are frequently annoyed with you for disrupting their plans. Relationships and communication benefit when the people involved understand how the others value and use time.

Proxemics As we mentioned earlier, proxemics is the study of how one uses space and how this use of space can serve a communicative function. Thus, the distance people stand or sit from one another often symbolizes physical and/or psychological

monochronically
engaging in one task or behavior at a time

polychronically
engaging in multiple activities simultaneously

closeness. If a longtime friend or partner chose not to sit next to you at a movie the-atre, you probably would be perplexed, perhaps even hurt or angry. Research by Edward T. Hall, a well-known anthropologist, has delineated four spheres or catego-ries of space that humans use (Hall, 1966). Let's take a look at each.

Intimate distance (0 to 18 inches) tends to be reserved for those whom one knows very well. Typically, this distance is used for displaying physical and psy-chological intimacy, such as lovemaking, cuddling children, comforting someone, or telling secrets. **Personal distance** (18 inches to 4 feet) describes the space we use when interacting with friends and acquaintances. People in the United States often use the nearer distance for friends and the farther one for acquaintances, but cultures and personal preference strongly influence this choice. When others pre-fer closer distances than you do, you may find their close-ness psychologically distress-ing; comedian Jerry Seinfeld has referred to these people as "close talkers." One of our students details her encoun-ters with such a person in *It Happened to Me: Katarina.*

It Happened to Me: *Katarina*

I have a friend whom I like very much but who makes me really uncomfortable some-times. She tends to lean in very close when she talks, especially if she has been drinking. One night, we were sitting together at a party. I sat in the corner of a couch while she leaned in to talk with me; I kept trying to pull my face away from hers while she talked until I was almost leaning over the back of the couch.

Social distance (4 to 12 feet) is the distance most U.S. Americans use when they interact with unfamiliar others. Impersonal business with grocery clerks, sales clerks, and coworkers occurs at about 4 to 7 feet, while the greatest distance is used in formal situations such as job interviews. **Public distance** (12 to 25 feet) is most appropriate for public ceremonies such as lectures and performances, though an even greater distance may be maintained between public figures (such as politicians and celebrities) and their audiences. (See *Visual Summary 6.1: Proxemics.*)

One's culture, gender, relationship to others, and personality all influence whether one feels most comfortable at the near or far range of each of these spheres. In the United States, two unacquainted women typically sit or stand closer to each other than do two unacquainted men, while many men are more comfortable sit-ting or standing closer to unknown women than they are even to men they know (Burgoon & Guerrero, 1994). However, people in other cultures may prefer the closer ranges. Cultural disparities can result in a comedic cross-cultural "dance," where one person tries to get closer to the other and that person, made uncomfort-able by the closeness, moves away.

What does the space between interactants in a given culture reveal? It can com-municate intimacy or the lack of it; it also can communicate power and dominance. If person A feels free to enter person B's space without permission but refuses to allow B the same privilege, this lack of reciprocity communicates that A is dominant in the relationship. This situation is common between supervisors and subordinates and may exist in some parent–child relationships as well.

All humans, as well as animals, have strong feelings of territoriality. We exhibit territorial behavior when we attempt to claim control over a particular area. A primary way we attempt to claim and maintain control of a space is through personalization or marking, especially by use of artifacts. Thus we alter spaces to make them distinctly our own through activities such as placing a fence around a residence or displaying family photos in an office. These markers are a form of nonverbal communication that specifies territorial ownership or legiti-mate occupancy (Becker, 1973). Markers function mainly to keep people away, thereby preventing confrontational social encounters. An unexpected manifesta-tion of territoriality is described in *Did You Know? Territoriality: Maintaining Private and Public Spaces.*

intimate distance
(0 to 18 inches) the space used when interacting with those with whom one is very close

personal distance
(18 inches to 4 feet) the space used when interacting with friends and acquaintances

social distance
(4 to 12 feet) the distance most U.S. Americans use when they interact with unfamiliar others

public distance
(12 to 25 feet) the distance used for public ceremonies such as lectures and performances

VISUAL SUMMARY 6.1   **Proxemics**

Intimate Distance (0–18 inches)

Personal Distance (18 inches–4 feet)

Social Distance (4–12 feet)

Public Distance (12–25 feet)

Primary territories (areas under private control, such as houses and the bedrooms within them) serve as extensions of the owner's sense of identity, so that markers there often include personally meaningful symbols reflecting the owner's style and taste (name plates, art objects, flower gardens). Public territories are less central to our self-concepts and, therefore, we tend to mark them with objects that are less personalized and/or that represent explicit claims to the space (for example, "reserved parking" signs). When someone violates a public territory, we tend to react with verbal retaliation, for example, asking the violator to leave. In contrast, we are likely to react strongly when someone violates our primary territory, for example, by seeking physical retaliation and legal sanctions (Abu-Ghazzeh, 2000).

Haptics Although researchers in communication know that touch, or **haptics**, is important, it is among the least studied forms of nonverbal communication. Nonetheless, research does indicate that infants and children need to be touched

haptics
the study of the communicative function of touch

Did You Know?

Territoriality: Maintaining Private and Public Spaces

Do you have bumper stickers or decals on your car? If so, do you think the research findings below describe you? Do they describe people you know? How do you mark your other personal and public territories? What do you think your markers say about you?

Watch out for cars with bumper stickers.

That's the surprising conclusion of a recent study by social psychologist William Szlemko. Drivers of cars with bumper stickers, window decals, personalized license plates, and other "territorial markers" not only get mad when someone cuts in their lane or is slow to respond to a changed traffic light, but they are far more likely than those who do not personalize their cars to use their vehicles to express rage—by honking, tailgating, and other aggressive behavior.

It does not seem to matter whether the messages on the stickers are about peace and love—"Visualize World Peace," "My Kid Is an Honor Student"—or angry and in your face—"Don't Mess With Texas," "My Kid Beat Up Your Honor Student."

Szlemko and his colleagues found that people who personalize their cars acknowledge that they are aggressive drivers, but usually do not realize that they are reporting much higher levels of aggression than people whose cars do not have visible markers on their vehicles.

"The more markers a car has, the more aggressively the person tends to drive when provoked," Szlemko said. "Just the presence of territory markers predicts the tendency to be an aggressive driver."

The key to the phenomenon apparently lies in the idea of territoriality. Drivers with road rage tend to think of public streets and highways as "my street" and "my lane"—in other words, they think they "own the road." Why would bumper stickers predict which people are likely to view public roadways as private property?

Social scientists such as Szlemko say that people carry around three kinds of territorial spaces in their heads. One is personal territory—like a home, or a bedroom. The second kind involves space that is temporarily yours—an office cubicle or a gym locker. The third kind is public territory: park benches, walking trails—and roads.

Drivers who individualize their cars using bumper stickers, window decals, and personalized license plates, the researchers hypothesized, see their cars in the same way as they see their homes and bedrooms—as deeply personal space, or primary territory.

"If you are in a vehicle that you identify as a primary territory, you would defend that against other people whom you perceive as being disrespectful of your space," Bell added. "What you ignore is that you are on a public roadway—you lose sight of the fact you are in a public area and you don't own the road."

FROM: Vendantam, S. (2008, June 16). Looking to avoid aggressive drivers? Check those bumpers. *The Washington Post*. © 2008 The Washington Post. Reprinted with permission.

professional touch
type of touch used by certain workers, such as dentists, hairstylists, and hospice workers, as part of their livelihood; also known as *functional touch*

functional touch
the least intimate type of touch; used by certain workers such as dentists, hairstylists, and hospice workers, as part of their livelihood; also known as *professional touch*

in order to be physically and psychologically healthy (Field, 2002). Also, although people vary considerably in how much or what type of touch they prefer, most enjoy being touched by those they care about. To understand how differences in preferences for touch affect relationships, see *It Happened to Me: Beth*.

Touch can be categorized into several general types (Givens, 2005), but people rarely notice the types unless a discrepancy occurs between their expectations and their experience. **Professional**, or **functional, touch** is the least intimate; people who must touch others as part of their livelihood, such as medical and dental caregivers, hairstylists, and tailors, use this type of touch. Because touch often conveys intimacy, people who must use professional touch have to be careful of their interaction style; for example, they may adopt a formal or distant verbal communication style to counteract the intimacy of their touch. **Social-polite touch** is part of daily interaction. In the United States, this form of touch is more intimate than professional touch but is still impersonal. For example, many U.S. Americans shake hands when greeting acquaintances and casual friends, though in many European countries, such as France and Italy, hugging and kissing are appropriate forms of social touch. Even within the United States, people have different ideas about what types of touch are appropriate socially.

Friendship touch is more intimate than social touch and usually conveys warmth, closeness, and caring. Although considerable variation in touch may exist among friends, people typically use touch that is more intimate with close friends than with acquaintances or strangers. Examples include brief hugs, a hand on the shoulder, or putting one's

> **It Happened to Me:** *Beth*
>
> I grew up in upper Michigan, where people rarely touch unless they know each other very well. Then I started working with a guy from the South. From the beginning, he touched me whenever we talked; he touched my arm, put his hand on my shoulder, or even put his arm on the back of my chair. This infuriated me! I thought he was being condescending and too familiar. Later, I realized that he does this with everybody. I understand he doesn't mean anything by it, but I still don't like it.

arm loosely around another's waist or shoulders. **Love-intimate touch** most often is used with one's romantic partners and family. Examples are the long kisses and extended hugging and cuddling we tend to reserve for those with whom we are closest.

As is true of other forms of nonverbal communication, sex, culture, and power strongly influence patterns of touch. In the United States, heterosexual males are more likely to reserve hand-holding for their romantic partners and small children, while females touch other women more frequently and hold hands with older children, their close female relatives, and even female friends. In general, women tend to touch other women more frequently than men touch other men, and in cross-sex interactions, men are more likely to initiate touch than do women (Hall & Hall, 1990). However, in cross-sex interactions, the nature of the relationship influences touch behavior more than does the sex of the participants. Across all stages of heterosexual romantic relationships, partners reciprocate touch, so they do not differ in amount of touch (Guerrero & Andersen, 1991). However, men respond more positively to their partners' touch than do women (Hanzal, Segrin, & Dorros, 2008). In addition, men initiate touch more in casual romantic relationships, while women do so more often in married relationships (Guerrero & Andersen, 1994).

Each form of touch we have discussed thus far has a "positive" quality; but, of course, people also use touch to convey negative messages. For example, one study revealed that individuals (especially parents) use aggressive touch and withdrawal of affectionate touch with children to signal their displeasure (Guerrero & Ebesu, 1993). Aggressive touch can include grabbing, hitting, and pinching, while withdrawal of affection involves rejecting the touch attempts of others, as when one pushes another's arm away or refuses to hold hands. Both children and adults use aggressive touch with their peers as well, though in none of these instances is aggressive touch considered an appropriate or competent way to communicate.

Another type of touch that can be perceived negatively is **demand touching**, a type of touch used to establish dominance and power. Demand touching increases in hierarchical settings, such as at work. One significant characteristic of demand touching is that touchers typically have higher status and have more control over encounters than do receivers; this allows them more freedom of movement and more visual contact. An everyday example of demand touch occurs when a supervisor stands behind a subordinate and leans over to provide directions, placing his

social-polite touch
touch that is part of daily interaction in the United States; it is more intimate than professional touch but is still impersonal

friendship touch
touch that is more intimate than social touch and usually conveys warmth, closeness, and caring

love-intimate touch
the touch most often used with one's romantic partners and family

demand touching
a type of touch used to establish dominance and power

Demand touching is often used to establish dominance and power.

Ideals of what constitutes beauty differ according to time period, culture, class, and other factors.

or her hand on the subordinate's shoulder. The subordinate can't move easily or look directly at the supervisor, and the subordinate may feel both physically and psychologically constrained (Kemmer, 1992).

Appearance and Artifacts In all cultures, individuals' appearance matters, as do their **artifacts**, or the clothing and other accessories they choose. Let's first consider appearance and how it operates as a nonverbal code.

In general, people's looks are believed to communicate something about them, and people develop expectations based on how others look. Hairstyle, skin color, height, weight, clothing, accessories such as jewelry, and other aspects of appearance all influence how we are perceived and how we perceive others. And in the United States, appearance is seen as especially important (Newport, 1999).

What is considered attractive, however, is influenced by one's culture and the time period in which one lives (Grammer, Fink, Joller, & Thornhill, 2003). Many people find it hard to believe that the Mona Lisa was considered a great beauty in her day, and even more people wonder who could ever have liked the clothes and hairstyles their own parents wore when they were young. Although the global village we live in now means the media transmit images that can be seen all over the world, cultures still vary in what they consider most attractive. The current ideal body type for women in the United States, as portrayed in the media, for example, is considered too thin and unfeminine by many African Americans (Duke, 2002). While some American women get collagen injections to achieve full lips, our Japanese students tell us that such thick lips are not considered attractive in Japan. Some Europeans also dislike the defined musculature favored for males in magazines and television ads in the United States.

In the United States, people invest considerable time, money, and energy adapting their appearance to cultural ideals of attractiveness. They diet, color and style their hair, frequent gyms and tanning booths, and even undergo extreme makeovers to be more attractive. People engage in all these efforts because the U.S. culture generally equates beauty with happiness, success, goodness, and desirability.

While people face certain limits in reshaping their bodies and other physical attributes, they also have great flexibility in using clothing and other artifacts to convey important messages about themselves. In most business contexts, a suit is perceived to be authoritative and an indication of status. This is especially true of men; evaluations of their status often are based on their appearance and clothing (Mast & Hall, 2004). People also use artifacts to signal their occupations and identities. Nurses, flight attendants, and police officers wear uniforms to help others identify them and to send specific messages about their jobs (Gundersen, 1990). Thus, police officers wear paramilitary uniforms not only to allow us to easily identify them but also to reinforce their role in maintaining social order.

Individuals also choose their accessories and artifacts, such as purses, watches, jewelry, sunglasses, and even cars, to communicate specific messages about status, personality, success, and/or group membership. A student who carries a leather briefcase on campus creates a different image than one who carries a canvas backpack. On a typical college campus, it is fairly easy to differentiate the communication professors from the business professors and the engineering students from the theater majors based on their dress and artifacts. We might argue that in the United States, where it is not considered polite to announce one's status or success, people often use artifacts to make those announcements for them (Fussell, 1992).

As you can see from the preceding discussion, multiple categories of nonverbal behavior influence communication; these include kinesics, paralinguistics, chronemics

artifacts
clothing and other accessories

and proxemics, haptics, and appearance and artifacts. These categories are, in turn, influenced by multiple individual and cultural factors. In the next section we explore how these categories work together to influence how we send and interpret messages.

The Functions of Nonverbal Messages

As mentioned earlier, when people interpret nonverbal behaviors they don't isolate kinesics from haptics or proxemics from appearance; rather, they observe an integrated set of behaviors, consider the context and the individual, and then attribute meaning. If you see two people standing closely together in a public place, you wouldn't necessarily assume they were being intimate. Rather, you would examine how relaxed or tense their bodies appeared, evaluate their facial expressions and eye gaze, and consider the appropriateness of intimate displays in this public space (for example, a bar versus a church). Only then might you make an attribution about the meaning or function of the couple's behavior.

In general, scholars have determined that nonverbal behaviors serve five functions during interaction (Patterson, 1982, 2003). Those five functions are communicating information, regulating interaction, expressing and managing intimacy, establishing social control, and signaling service-task functions. The most basic function is to communicate information, and this is the one we examine first.

Communicating Information Most fundamentally, nonverbal message are used to **communicate information**. From the receiver's point of view, much of a sender's behavior is potentially informative. For example, when you meet someone for the first time you evaluate the pattern of the sender's behavior to assess a variety of factors. First, you might evaluate the sender's general disposition to determine if it is warm and friendly or cool and distant. You likely will also assess her more fleeting nonverbal reactions to help you decide if she seems pleased to meet you or is just being polite. Finally, of course, you evaluate the person's verbal message. For example, does the speaker say, "I've really been looking forward to meeting you," or does she say, "I'd love to chat, but I've got to run"? You then combine all these pieces of information to ascribe meaning to the encounter.

Nonverbal communication helps individuals convey and interpret verbal messages. They can do this in five ways:

1. By repeating a message (winking while saying "I'm just kidding");
2. By highlighting or emphasizing a message (pointing at the door while saying "Get out!");
3. By complementing or reinforcing a message (whispering while telling a secret);
4. By contradicting a message (saying "I love your haircut" while speaking in a hostile tone and rolling one's eyes);
5. By substituting for a message (shaking one's head to indicate disagreement).

As these examples illustrate, using nonverbal communication effectively can make you a better *verbal* communicator.

Regulating Interaction Nonverbal communication also is used to **regulate interaction**. That is, people use nonverbal behaviors to manage turn-taking during conversation. Thus, if you want to start talking, you might lean forward, look at the current speaker, and even raise one finger. To reveal that you are finished with your turn, you may drop your volume and pitch, lean back, and look away from and then back toward the person you are "giving" your turn to. The regulating function tends to be the most automatic of the five, and most of us rarely think about it. The behaviors you use in this way include the more stable ones such as interpersonal distance, body orientation, and posture, as well as more fluid behaviors like gaze,

What artifacts are important to you in terms of communicating your identity or status? If you had only one means of communicating high status, would you drive an expensive car, wear designer clothes, or live in an upscale neighborhood? What do you think your choice reflects about you?

communicating information
using nonverbal behaviors to help clarify verbal messages and reveal attitudes and moods

regulating interaction
using nonverbal behaviors to help manage conversational interaction

Various nonverbal behaviors regulate the interaction that occurs in a conversation.

facial expression, volume, and pitch, which are important in the smooth sequencing of conversational turns (Capella, 1985).

Expressing and Managing Intimacy A third function of nonverbal communication, and the most studied, involves **expressing and managing intimacy**. The degree of your nonverbal involvement with another usually reflects the level of intimacy you desire with that person. If you are on a date and notice your partner is leaning toward you, gazing into your eyes, nodding his head, and providing many paralinguistic cues such as "uh huh" as you talk, your date is revealing a high degree of nonverbal involvement, which often signals attraction and interest. Of course, people can manipulate these behaviors to suggest attraction and involvement even if they are not experiencing these feelings. For example, in the workplace when subordinates talk with their supervisors, they often display fairly high levels of nonverbal involvement, regardless of their true feelings for their bosses.

Establishing Social Control People also use nonverbal communication to exert or **establish social control**, or to exercise influence over other people. Individuals engage in the social control function when they smile at someone they want to do them a favor or when they glare at noisy patrons in a theater to encourage them to be quiet. You can use either positive or negative behaviors (or both) in your efforts to control others. People who are "charming" or very persuasive typically are extremely gifted at using nonverbal behavior to influence others.

Sports coaches, tailors, and other professionals use nonverbal communication that has a service-task function.

When expressing and managing intimacy people tend to respond in similar, or reciprocal, ways to one another's nonverbal behavior. On the other hand, when engaging in social control, people tend to respond in complementary ways to one another's nonverbal behavior. To better understand the role of these responses in nonverbal interactions, see *Alternative View: Nonverbal Reciprocity or Nonverbal Complementarity?*

Signaling Service-Task Functions Finally, nonverbal communication has a **service-task function**. Behaviors of this kind typically signal close involvement between people in impersonal relationships and contexts. For example, golf pros often stand with their arms around a novice golfer to help her with her golf swing and massage therapists engage in very intimate touch as part of their profession. In each of these cases, the behavior is appropriate, necessary, and a means to a (professional) end.

Accurately interpreting nonverbal messages is a complex endeavor, requiring awareness of a number of elements—factors that influence individuals' communication patterns, nonverbal communication codes and signals, and the communicative functions that nonverbal messages fulfill. However, in some senses, we have only shown you one piece of the picture, as we have thus far focused primarily on nonverbal communication as performed by individuals. In the next section, we expand the frame to explore how societal forces influence both the performance and interpretation of nonverbal messages and behavior.

expressing and managing intimacy
using nonverbal behaviors to help convey attraction and closeness

establishing social control
using nonverbal behavior to exercise influence over other people

service-task functions
using nonverbal behavior to signal close involvement between people in impersonal relationships and contexts

TEST YOUR KNOWLEDGE
- What is a nonverbal code?
- What five functions does nonverbal communication serve?

Alternative **V I E W**
Nonverbal Reciprocity or Nonverbal Complementarity?

Which of the following explanations seems more accurate to you? In what situations do you believe people are more likely to engage in nonverbal reciprocity? In nonverbal complementarity?

Nonverbal Reciprocity

Numerous studies provide evidence that many people unconsciously mimic their partner's postures, gestures, and other movements in social settings. Furthermore, this mimicry, or reciprocity, seems to increase liking and rapport between speakers. In turn, increased liking and rapport lead to more frequent mimicry. However, status or dominance affects who is likely to mimic whom. Lower status individuals are more likely to reciprocate the behaviors of higher status people, which may be unconsciously designed to increase liking and rapport (Chartrand & Bargh, 1999; Dijksterhuis & Smith, 2005).

Nonverbal Complementarity

A set of studies found that people respond to another's nonverbal power moves with complementary responses;

that is, they respond to dominant behaviors with submissive ones and submissive behaviors with dominant ones (Tiedens & Fragale, 2003). Thus, if one person stares aggressively at another (a dominant behavior), the recipient of the stare is likely to look away (a submissive behavior). Furthermore, participants reported feeling comfortable with complementarity.

These studies specifically examined how people negotiate status in relationships with no prior hierarchy. Thus in groups and relationships in which everyone is on equal footing, the first dominant or submissive display by an individual may result from a random movement or a tactical strategy. Whatever the cause of the display, a hierarchical relationship can then result if an observer responds in a complementary fashion. Moreover, since people prefer to complement dominance with submissiveness, and vice versa, they are likely to promote that differentiation. Thus, nonverbal complementarity and the comfort associated with it may encourage hierarchical relationships and help maintain them. This phenomenon, then, may be one reason why hierarchies are so common and widespread.

THE INDIVIDUAL, NONVERBAL COMMUNICATION, AND SOCIETY

Nonverbal communication, like all communication, is heavily influenced by societal forces and occurs within a hierarchical system of meanings. One's status and position within the societal hierarchy, as well as one's identity, are all expressed nonverbally. However, the more powerful elements in society often regulate these expressions. In addition, nonverbal communication can trigger and express prejudice and discrimination. Let's see how this operates.

Nonverbal Communication and Power

Nonverbal communication and power are intricately related—especially via the nonverbal codes of appearance and artifacts. In the United States, power is primarily based on an individual's access to economic resources and the freedom to make decisions that affect others. Economic resources are typically revealed or expressed through nonverbal codes. People display wealth through the clothing and accessories they wear, the quality of their haircuts, and the value of their homes and cars. Whether one can afford to buy the latest designer fashions, or only to shop in discount stores, communicates clearly one's social class and power. English professor Paul Fussell (1992) provides an extensive description of how nonverbal messages communicated in our everyday lives reveal class standing. Consider, for example, the messages communicated by one's home. Fussell notes that the longer the driveway, the less obvious the garage, and the more manicured the grounds, the higher is one's socioeconomic class.

People use nonverbal cues to communicate their own status and identities, and to evaluate and interpret others' status and identities. Based on these interpretations, people—consciously and unconsciously—include and exclude others, and approve or disapprove of others. For example, in wealthy communities, people who don't look affluent may be stopped and questioned about their presence or even be asked to leave. More overtly, gated communities offer clear nonverbal messages about who belongs and who does not belong to a community. Of course, it isn't just the wealthy who use artifacts to convey their identity and belonging. Gang members, NASCAR fans, football fans, and many others also use attire as well as gestures to signal their individual and group identities.

The use of nonverbal cues to communicate social class extends beyond the use of appearance and artifacts. For example, psychology professors Michael Kraus and Dach Keltner (2009) examined individuals' use of nonverbal communication while interacting with a stranger. In these interactions they found that people with high socioeconomic status were more likely to display nonverbal signs of disengagement, such as doodling, and fewer signs of engagement, such as smiling and nodding, than people with lower socioeconomic status. In addition, people who observed these interactions could correctly guess the participants' social class from their nonverbal behavior. Thus, nonverbal communication reproduces—or re-creates—the society and social classes in which we live.

Although all groups use nonverbal communication to convey identity, more powerful segments of society typically define what is allowed. For example, many corporations have dress codes designed to communicate a particular professional image to the public. For the same reason, they may also have rules that regulate nonverbal expression of men's facial hair. The military and many police organizations have policies on tattoos as well (Zezima, 2005). Because these organizations are hierarchical, the decisions made by those in power in the organization must be followed by those who wish employment there.

In 2005, the National Basketball Association issued rules governing the off-court dress of NBA players: They are to dress in "business casual" whenever engaged in team or league business, and they are specifically excluded from wearing sleeveless shirts, shorts, T-shirts, headgear of any kind, chains, pendants, and sunglasses while indoors. See http://worklaw.jotwell.com/does-the-nbas-dress.code-violate-title-vii/ for more information on this topic. Through these dictums, the organization is attempting to regulate not only the players' clothing, but their expression of their identities as well. Of course, not all players support these regulations (Wise, 2005). Some NBA players feel that the ban on chains and other jewelry was racially motivated. In short, this new policy "called attention to a generational chasm between modern professional athletes, many of whom are Black, and their mostly White paying customers" (Wise, 2005, p. A-1).

The number and range of dress codes and regulations on appearance underscore the powerful impact that nonverbal cues can have. The more powerful segments of society also define what is most desirable and attractive in our culture. For example, cosmetic corporations spend $231 billion annually on the development of beauty products and advertising to persuade consumers to buy them. The largest cosmetic companies have recently expanded to China where the nation's 451 million women are of great interest to the cosmetic market—which has doubled in the past five years to $8 billion (Carvajal, 2006). The media broadly communicate to us the definitions of beauty. This is why many U.S. Americans believe that blonde hair is better than brown, thin is better than fat, large breasts are better than small, and young is better than old—beliefs that are not shared universally. Messages promoting a specific type of youth and beauty might seem rather harmless, until one considers the consequences for those who are not thin and blonde, especially those

The NBA issued rules governing NBA players' off-court dress to help shape the images they present to the public.

who have no possibility of meeting the dominant standards of beauty. How does this hierarchy of attractiveness affect their communication with others? Do people respond to them negatively because of their appearance? Might they feel marginalized and resentful—even before they interact with others who more clearly meet the dominant standards?

Nonverbal expressions also are an important part of cultural rituals involving societal expectations. For example, in U.S. culture it is traditionally considered unacceptable to wear white to a wedding unless one is the bride, while black or other dark colors are considered appropriate to wear to funerals. Aspects of dress are very important in the United States at other cultural events, particularly for women. The outfits worn to the Academy Awards and other "show business" honor ceremonies are reviewed and evaluated and are a topic of great interest for many people. Similarly, what the President's wife wears on Inauguration Day and at subsequent parties is a subject of conversation; in fact, the First Lady's wardrobe is discussed and critiqued every day on TV, in blogs, and in magazines. The interest (and evaluation) of these nonverbal expressions, like clothing, is driven by societal forces. In all of these cases, women know that their nonverbal messages will be carefully scrutinized and evaluated.

Nonverbal Communication, Prejudice, and Discrimination

At the intersection of societal forces and nonverbal communication are prejudice and discrimination. Both can be triggered by nonverbal behavior and are also expressed through nonverbal behavior. Let's look at how this works. First, one's race and ethnicity, body shape, age, or style of dress—all of which are communicated nonverbally—can prompt prejudgment or negative stereotypes. How often do people make a snap judgment or generalization based on appearance? Second, prejudice and discrimination are expressed nonverbally. In some extreme cases, nonverbal signals have even triggered and perpetrated hate crimes. For example, one night in Phoenix, Arizona, Avtar (Singh) Chiera, a small-business owner and a Sikh, waited outside his business for his son to pick him up. Two White men pulled up in a small red pickup truck, yelled at him, and then opened fire on him. Because of anger over the events of 9/11, the two men likely targeted him as an Arab because of his turban and beard, even though Sikhs are neither Arab nor Muslim (Parasuram, 2003). In this encounter, nonverbal messages were the most important; the words spoken (if any) were of minimal impact.

This antigroping sign from Japan illustrates a common problem in many parts of the world. What are the ethical issues in this nonverbal behavior?

Although the example of the shooting of Mr. Chiera is extreme, there are many other more subtle ways that prejudice can be communicated nonverbally—for instance, averting one's gaze or failing to reciprocate a smile. It can be as subtle as shifting your gaze, leaning your body away, or editing your speech. Sociologist A. G. Johnson (2001, pp. 58–59) gives a list of specific nonverbal behaviors that can be interpreted as prejudicial. These are mostly noticed only by the person experiencing them and often happen unconsciously and unintentionally:

- Not looking at people when we talk with them;
- Not smiling at people when they walk into the room, or staring as if to say, "What are you doing here?," or stopping the conversation with a hush they have to wade through to be included in the smallest way;
- Not acknowledging people's presence or making them wait as if they weren't there;
- Not touching their skin when we give them something;
- Watching them closely to see what they're up to;
- Avoiding someone walking down the street, giving them wide berth, or even crossing to the other side.

Given the potential consequences of nonverbal communication, you may find it helpful to consider how your nonverbal communication reflects your own ethical stance. To guide you in making appropriate and ethical choices, in the next section we explore the ethics of nonverbal communication.

TEST YOUR KNOWLEDGE
- How does power influence nonverbal communication norms?
- How does status influence one's nonverbal communication?

ETHICS AND NONVERBAL COMMUNICATION

The ethics of nonverbal communication are actually quite similar to the ethics of communication in general. When people engage in behavior such as deceiving or threatening others or name-calling, their nonverbal behavior typically plays a central role in their messages. For instance, liars use nonverbal behavior to avoid "leaking" the deception, and they may also use it to convey the deceptive message. Moreover, deceivers may feel that lying nonverbally—for example, by remaining silent—is less "wrong" than lying with words. In the Old Testament, Joseph's brothers were very jealous of their father's affection for him, so they sold Joseph into slavery. When they returned without him, however, they didn't "tell" their father what happened; instead they gave him Joseph's bloody coat and let their father draw the conclusion that wild animals had killed Joseph. In this way, they deceived their father without actually speaking a lie. What do you think? Is it better, or less unethical, to lie nonverbally than it is to do so verbally?

When communicators use nonverbal cues that ridicule, derogate, or otherwise demean others, they run the risk of their behavior being viewed by others as unethical. For example, if someone speaks in a patronizing vocal tone, screams at the less powerful, or touches others inappropriately, would you view this behavior as unethical? What if people respond to others' communication in a way that misrepresents how they actually feel? For instance, if they laugh at a racist or sexist joke even though they dislike it, would you see that behavior as unethical?

Since these are the types of decisions you have to make routinely throughout your life, here are some guidelines for ethical nonverbal communication to help you make those decisions. Consider whether:

- your nonverbal behaviors reflect your real attitudes, beliefs, and feelings;
- your nonverbal behaviors contradict the verbal message you are sending;

- your nonverbal behaviors insult, ridicule, or demean others;
- you are using your nonverbal behavior to intimidate, coerce, or silence someone;
- you would want anyone to observe your nonverbal behavior;
- you would want this nonverbal behavior directed to you or a loved one.

Although there is no litmus test for evaluating the ethics of every nonverbal message in every situation, if you keep these guidelines in mind, they will help you make better, more informed decisions.

TEST YOUR KNOWLEDGE
- Describe some ways in which it is possible for people to engage in unethical nonverbal communication.

IMPROVING YOUR NONVERBAL COMMUNICATION SKILLS

By now you may be wondering how to decide what a set of behaviors means. How do you decide, for example, if your sports coach's touch is appropriately intimate (service-task) or just intimate? In the workplace, how can you determine whether your subordinate genuinely likes you and your ideas (nonverbal involvement) or is merely trying to flatter you (social control)?

One way you can assess your own and others' nonverbal communication is to examine how it interacts with verbal messages (Jones & LeBaron, 2002). That is, how congruent (similar) are the two sets of messages? When the two types of messages are **congruent**, they are often genuine (and/or we assume them to be so). For example, a positive verbal message ("I like you") combined with a positive nonverbal message (smile, forward body lean, relaxed posture) usually conveys a convincing positive message. However, it is also possible that people who are very good at deception are able to offer congruent messages while lying, and those who are less adept at communicating may unintentionally offer contradictory messages when telling the truth. Given all of this, what other factors could you rely on to help you decide whether a congruent message is truthful?

Of course, verbal and nonverbal messages can also purposely **contradict** one another. When using sarcasm, people intentionally combine a positive verbal message ("what a nice pair of shoes") with a contradictory or negative nonverbal message (a hostile tone). However, at other times people offer contradictory messages unintentionally or carelessly. Caretakers often confuse children (and encourage misbehavior) by telling a child to stop a particular behavior while smiling or laughing. How does a child interpret this message? Most children will accept the nonverbal aspect of the message and ignore the verbal (Eskritt & Lee, 2003.)

In addition to assessing the congruence of the verbal and nonverbal components of a message, you improve your comprehension of nonverbal messages by analyzing the context, your knowledge of the other person, and your own experiences. For example, if you are playing basketball and a teammate slaps you on the rear and says "good going," the message may be clear. Given the context, you may read it as a compliment and perhaps a sign of affection or intimacy. But what if the slap on the rear occurs at work after an effective presentation? Given that such behavior is generally inappropriate in a business context, you probably will (and should) more closely assess its meaning. You might ask yourself whether this person simply lacks social skills and frequently engages in inappropriate behavior. If so, the message may be inappropriate but still be meant in a positive fashion. In contrast, if the person knows better and has touched you inappropriately at other times, the behavior may be intentionally designed to express inappropriate intimacy or social control.

congruent
verbal and nonverbal messages that express the same meaning

contradicting
verbal and nonverbal messages that send conflicting messages

The meaning of this nonverbal behavior is strongly affected by the context.

Here are a few more suggestions to keep in mind:

- Recognize that others' nonverbal messages don't always mean the same as yours.
- Be aware of individual, contextual, and cultural factors that influence meaning.
- Ask for additional information if you don't understand a nonverbal message or if you perceive a contradiction between the verbal and nonverbal messages.
- Remember that not every nonverbal behavior is intended to be communicative.
- Don't place too much emphasis on fleeting nonverbal behaviors such as facial expression or vocal tone; rather, examine the entire set of nonverbal behaviors.

TEST YOUR KNOWLEDGE

- What are some specific strategies you can use to improve your ability to communicate nonverbally?

SUMMARY

Nonverbal messages are an important component of communication. They help you interpret and understand verbal messages and, in doing so, help you more effectively navigate your everyday life. Studying nonverbal communication is particularly important because they are complex and ambiguous.

Nonverbal communication is defined as all the messages that people transmit through means other than words. To understand the meaning of a nonverbal messages, you have to consider the entire behavioral context, including culture, relationship type, background knowledge, and gender. Nonverbal communication occurs through five codes or types of signals: kinesics, paralinguistics (vocal qualities), chronemics and proxemics (time and space), haptics (touch), and appearance and artifacts. These codes can combine to serve one of five functions, such as communicating information, regulating interaction, expressing and managing intimacy, exerting social control, and performing service-task functions.

Power relationships as well as societal norms and rules influence the range of nonverbal behaviors we are allowed to perform and how those behaviors are interpreted. In addition, everyone needs to be aware that nonverbal communication can trigger and express prejudice and discrimination. Thus, nonverbal communication has ethical aspects one must consider when composing one's messages.

You can become more effective in interpreting others' nonverbal communication by assessing the congruence of the verbal and nonverbal components of a message; analyzing the context, your knowledge of the other person, and your own experiences; recognizing that others' nonverbal messages don't always mean the same as yours do; asking for additional information if you don't understand a nonverbal message; and remembering that not every nonverbal behavior is intended to be communicative.

HUMAN COMMUNICATION IN SOCIETY ONLINE

To review this chapter, use the MyCommunicationLab Web site to test your understanding of the following key terms, record your answers to the chapter review questions, and complete the suggested activities. Expand your learning and understanding of chapter concepts by completing the exercises and activities available online. Access code required. Go to www.mycommunicationlab.com for more information or to purchase standalone access.

KEY TERMS

nonverbal communication 138	vocalizations 146	friendship touch 151
nonverbal behavior 138	chronemics 146	love-intimate touch 151
nonverbal codes 143	proxemics 146	demand touching 151
kinesics 143	monochronically 147	artifacts 152
gestures 143	polychronically 147	communicating information 153
illustrators 143	intimate distance 148	regulating interaction 153
emblems 143	personal distance 148	expressing and managing
adaptors 143	social distance 148	intimacy 154
regulators 143	public distance 148	establishing social
immediacy 143	haptics 149	control 154
relaxation 143	professional touch 150	service-task functions 154
paralinguistics 145	functional touch 150	congruent 159
voice qualities 145	social-polite touch 151	contradicting 159

APPLY WHAT YOU KNOW

1. **Waiting Times** How long is the "appropriate" amount of time you should wait in each of the following situations? Specifically, after how long a period would you begin to feel angry or put out?

   Estimate waiting times for:

   a. your dentist
   b. a checkout line in a department store
   c. a movie line
   d. a friend at lunch
   e. a friend at dinner
   f. being on hold on the telephone
   g. your professor to arrive at class
   h. a stop light
   i. your romantic partner at a bar
   j. your professor during office hours.

   Do you see any patterns in your expectations for waiting times? What influences your expectations most—your relationship with the other party? The comfort of the waiting area? Your ability to control events? Compare your waiting times with others' to see how similar or different they are.

2. **Violating Norms for Proximity** For this exercise we would like you to violate some of the norms for spacing in your culture. Try standing slightly closer to a friend or family member than you normally would, then note how they react. If you have a romantic partner or very close friend, sit much farther from them than you normally would. For example, in a theater, sit one seat away from him or her, or sit at the opposite end of the couch if you would typically sit closer. Pay attention to the reactions you elicit. Finally, when talking with an acquaintance, increase the distance between you each time the other person tries to decrease it and see how the other person responds. What do these responses to your space violations reveal to you regarding the importance of spacing norms in the United States?

   NOTE: Be careful in your selection of people with whom you violate norms of space, and be prepared to explain why you are behaving so oddly.

3. **Cultural Differences in Nonverbal Communication** Go to a search engine such as Google, and look for a Web site that explains the rules for nonverbal communication and behavior in a culture outside the United States with which you are not familiar. What rules surprised you? What rules were similar to the ones you use? What do you think would happen if you used your "normal" rules for nonverbal behavior in this culture?

EXPLORE

1. Go to a website such as Michigan State University's Presidential Audio Recordings or Archer Audio Archives and compare the vocal qualities of four presidents–two presidents who served before the widespread use of television and two who have served since. What role do you think vocal versus visual cues played in the popularity of each president? Are there presidents whose appearance you find more appealing than their vocal qualities? Are there presidents whose vocal qualities you find more appealing than their appearance?

2. The study of facial expressions of emotion is complex and ongoing. Recently, researchers have begun studying the effect of Botox (which paralyzes facial muscles) on facial expressions and emotional response. Go to a website such as PsychCentral's *Facial Expressions Control Emotions* or WebMD's *Botox May Affect Ability to Feel Emotions* and read the articles. Based on what you read, write a brief paper in which you hypothesize how the use of Botox could affect interpersonal interaction.

7
Listening and Responding

In my family, we enjoy arguing about things like politics and religion, so I was surprised when people did not respond well to my comments in my first college classes. I felt like people weren't listening to what I said, and sometimes they looked away and wouldn't respond. After taking a class in communication and learning about bad listening habits and effective strategies, I realized that many of my fellow students didn't have very good listening skills. I also realized that I often don't listen to what others are saying because I'm busy thinking of the next thing I'm going to say. It was hard, and it took conscious effort, but I've been trying to listen to what others say and acknowledge their thoughts before I respond. I think it's helped me a lot because now I find the discussions in my classes more productive and interesting.

Listening may be the single most important skill in the communication process, but most of us, like our student Iasha, don't really think about it very much. Why is this? Perhaps because listening seems like a passive skill, unlike speaking or writing. Or perhaps we think that listening can't be taught or learned. After all, very few college courses teach listening theory and practice. However, as we'll discover in this chapter, a great deal of academic research focuses on the listening process, which includes not only hearing what others say but also critically evaluating messages and responding. Communication experts have shown that by being aware of the dynamics of listening and working on being better listeners, we can become better communicators overall.

In this chapter, we will first identify six important reasons for improving listening and responding skills. We will then describe the process of listening as well as some of the influences and barriers to effective listening. Finally, we'll discuss the role of societal forces in listening, ethical issues related to listening, and suggestions for becoming a more effective listener.

Once you have read this chapter, you will be able to:

- ■ Identify reasons for learning about listening and responding.
- ■ Describe the listening process, including listening styles and skills.
- ■ Describe the influences on listening and barriers to effective listening.
- ■ Understand the role of societal forces (power and privilege) in listening.
- ■ Describe ethical challenges in listening.
- ■ Discuss three ways to improve your own listening behavior.

THE IMPORTANCE OF LISTENING

You might not understand why it is important to learn about listening. After all, it seems rather automatic, something we don't think about very often. As this section shows, however, improving our listening skills can lead to many personal and professional benefits.

Students spend about half of
their listening time in media
listening.

The most important reason for learning more about listening is that we spend so much time doing it! Listening is the primary communication activity for college students (Janusik & Wolvin, 2009), and experts estimate that they spend 55 percent of their total average communication day listening. About half that time is spent in interpersonal listening (class, face to face conversations, phone, listening to voice messages) and the other half in media listening. The rest of students' communication time is distributed in the following way: 16 percent speaking, 17 percent reading, and 11 percent writing (Emanuel et al., 2008). In addition to the pervasiveness of listening in our daily communication, there are five other important reasons for learning about listening: Better listening skills can lead to improved cognition, improved academic performance, enhanced personal relationships, enhanced professional performance, and even better health. Let's look at each of these in turn.

First, having better listening skills can improve your memory, give you a broader knowledge base, and increase your attention span (Diamond, 2007). The brain is like any other muscle; you have to use it to improve it. The more you exercise it, the better you'll be able to process and remember information. The first step in exercising the brain is to pay better attention when others are speaking. You can't remember something if you never learned it, and you can't learn something—that is, encode it into your brain—if you don't pay enough attention to it.

A second, related reason to learn more about listening is that good listening skills can enhance academic performance. Not surprisingly, a number of research studies have shown that college students who have good listening skills are better students than those who are less effective listeners (Cooper & Buchanan, 2010). For example, in one study, college students were given a listening test after their first year of college. The results showed that almost half the students (49 percent) who scored low on the listening test were on academic probation, while only 4 percent of those who scored high were in that situation. Conversely, 69 percent of those who scored high on the listening test were in the honors program, while only 4 percent of the low scorers had achieved academic honors status (Bommelje, Houston, & Smither, 2003). With these figures in mind, you may wonder whether someone can learn to be a good listener. The most recent research shows that one of the most important outcomes of classes on listening is that students become more aware of what constitutes good listening (Beall, Gill-Rosier, Tate, & Matten, 2008). Although this indicates that a college course can help you identify the skills needed to be a good listener, you may need a lot of practice and attention to skill building on your own to become an effective listener. This is what Iasha, the student in the opening vignette, realized.

Better listening is also linked to enhanced personal relationships—a third reason to learn more about listening. In earlier chapters, we have discussed how effective communication skills can lead to enhanced personal relationships. This is also true for listening skills. It's easy to understand how better listening can lead to fewer misunderstandings, which in turn can lead to greater satisfaction, happiness, and a sense of well-being for us and those we care about (Diamond, 2007).

Business professionals have long emphasized that effective listening is a highly desirable workplace skill; in fact, the *Harvard Business Review*, one of the most respected business journals, has published 43 articles containing "listen" as a key word in the past 50 years (Flynn, Valikoski, & Grau, 2008). Effective listening in the workplace starts in the hiring process. Employers place high importance on oral communication skills (including listening) and look for listening skills when hiring potential employees. Once on the job, listening skills are

Learning to be a better listener
can boost academic performance.

an important part of effective work performance; studies show that for many professionals—including information technology professionals, safety managers, manufacturing agents, business coaches, and change managers, to name a few—effective work performance is positively related to listening ability (Flynn, Valikoski, & Grau, 2008). Poor listening skills can be costly: the consequences include wasted meeting time; inaccurate orders/shipments; lost sales; inadequately informed, misinformed, confused, or angry staff and customers; unmet deadlines; unsolved problems; wrong decisions; lawsuits; and poor employee morale (Battell, 2006). Listening skills are particularly important in medical contexts (Holmes, 2007). Physicians with good listening skills have more satisfied patients, and better listening skills can even have monetary value, as doctors with better listening skills have fewer malpractice lawsuits (Davis, Foley, Crigger, & Brannigan, 2008).

Listening skills are particularly important in medical contexts.

What makes listening so important in professional contexts? Part of the answer may lie in that fact that (as with personal relationships) better listening at work means fewer misunderstandings, less time lost on the job, and greater productivity (Diamond, 2007). Listening seems to play an interesting role in career advancement as well. One study showed that as workers move into senior-level management, listening skills become more important (Brownell, 1994). This may be because managers spend more time listening than other employees, and in addition, they need to not only listen for information but also demonstrate empathy in their listening (Kotter, 1982; Nichols, 2009; Sypher, 1984). As shown in the *Communication in Society* box, managers with effective listening skills probably

COMMUNICATION IN SOCIETY
Effective Listening Skills of Managers

In the article summarized below, journalist Martin Kornacki describes the results of recent research emphasizing the importance of line (factory) managers' communication skills. Do you think these findings can be generalized to other work contexts—for example, supervisors in fast-food restaurants or department supervisors in white-collar professions? Why or why not?

According to new research findings, line managers' communication skills—especially listening and responding skills—are particularly important during periods of economic downturn.

In a recent news article, journalist Martin Kornacki describes a research study that found that employees who believe that their managers listen to them and answer questions honestly have greater confidence in their organization's future, which then translates into commitment to the organization and greater productivity—even if the economic outlook is uncertain.

The key seems to be good relationships between managers and workers—fostered by listening skills. Kornacki also interviewed clinical psychologist Dr. Amy Silver, who has worked with organizations in turbulent situations. She emphasizes the role of active listening in establishing solid trusting relationships between line managers and line workers. According to Dr. Silver, the best relationships—characterized by genuineness, empathy, and rapport—are built from "active listening by both parties, with slightly more emphasis on the more powerful party to do so." She goes on to say that it's called active listening "because it is easy to listen, but not so easy to truly listen." She also points to many research studies that demonstrate that the quality of the relationship is crucial in determining productivity in business contexts.

Kornacki concludes that companies who do not invest in improving managers' communication skills are generally less productive and these differences between good and poor business practices are highlighted during economic recessions.

SOURCE: Kornacki, M. (2009, April 20). Managers' communication skills put under scrutiny by new research. *TJ online.* Retrieved March 28, 2011, from **http://www.trainingjournal.com/news/2009-04-20-managers-communication-skills-put-under-scrutiny-by-new-research/**

develop good relationships with their employees, which can actually lead to more productivity—particularly important during economic downturns.

Finally, you may not know that good listening can actually lead to improved health—our final reason for learning how to be a better listener. Some studies show that when we listen attentively, heart rate and oxygen consumption are reduced, which leads to increased blood and oxygen to the brain—a healthy cardiovascular condition (Diamond, 2007). Health psychologist James J. Lynch conducted pioneering research showing that human interaction (or the lack of it) can dramatically affect cardiovascular systems. Lynch (1985) described an experiment in which patients with hypertension (high blood pressure) conversed with the experimenter while connected to a computerized blood-pressure-monitoring system. When the patients talked about their own problems, their blood pressure increased to high levels. However, when the experimenter distracted the patients by telling them a nonthreatening personal story or reading a passage from a book, the patients' blood pressure dropped to much lower levels. Lynch explains that these drops in blood pressure occurred because the patients momentarily focused on something outside themselves—listening to and interacting with the experimenter (cited by Shafir, 2000, p. 241). These results suggest that listening—an important aspect of personal connectedness—can improve human health.

Now that we've discussed the importance of learning about listening, the next section describes the process of listening, showing that listening is much more than just hearing what others are saying.

TEST YOUR KNOWLEDGE

- What are six reasons for learning about listening and responding?
- Why are good listening and responding skills so important in professional contexts?

WHAT IS LISTENING?

The first step in striving to improve listening skills is to understand exactly what we mean when we talk about listening. Thus, we first provide a definition and then describe the process of listening.

While there are various definitions for **listening,** the one we'll use is provided by the International Listening Association. Listening is "the process of receiving, constructing meaning from, and responding to spoken and/or nonverbal messages" (ILA, 1995, p. 4). As you can see, this definition includes the concept described in Chapter 1 as the decoding phase of the communication process. It involves four stages: *sensing, understanding, evaluating,* and *responding* (Rosenfeld & Berko, 1990). (See *Visual Summary 7.1: Stages of Listening.*)

Let's see how this might work. **Sensing** is the stage most people refer to as "hearing"; it occurs when listeners pick up the sound waves directed toward them. Suppose you're sitting in your apartment at the computer deep into Facebook and you hear sounds in the kitchen; it's your roommate, Josie, returning from her job as a server in a restaurant near campus. She yells out, "Guess what happened at work today?" For communication to occur, you must first become aware that information is being directed at you. In other words, you have to hear the sounds. But of course, sensing or hearing something is not the same as understanding or evaluating the information—the next steps. This means that hearing is not the same as listening. Hearing is really only the first step.

Once you sense that sounds are occurring, you have to interpret the messages associated with the sounds—that is, you have to **understand** what the sounds mean. The meaning you assign affects how you will respond—both physiologically and communicatively. In the example of your roommate, Josie, you understand her words—she's asking you to guess what happened at her work that day.

listening
the process of receiving, constructing meaning from, and responding to spoken and/or nonverbal messages

sensing
the stage of listening most people refer to as "hearing"; when listeners pick up the sound waves directed toward them

understanding
interpreting the messages associated with sounds or what the sounds mean

VISUAL SUMMARY 7.1   **Stages of Listening**

STIMULUS

STAGE 1
Sensing
"Michelle is calling."

STAGE 2
Understanding
"She's asking me out."

STAGE 3
Evaluating
"I think I like that idea."

STAGE 4
Responding
"I'd love to!"

evaluating
assessing your reaction to a message

responding
showing others how you regard their message

Think of a recent conflict you had, and describe how listening behaviors might have influenced the outcome. How might it have been different if those involved had spent more time listening instead of talking?

After you understand (or at least believe you understand) the message you have received, you **evaluate** the information. When you evaluate a message, you assess your reaction to it. For example, what do you think Josie is really asking you? Did something incredibly important happen to her at work? Or does she ask you this every time she returns from work, so that you know it doesn't matter what you answer because she is going to tell you some long, drawn-out story about people she works with whom you don't know? Or is she trying to engage you in conversation because you have both been busy and haven't seen each other much lately? As you can see, critical thinking skills are important in evaluating what you have heard—what are the possible interpretations of the message sent? What are the logical interpretations?

Finally, you **respond** to messages. Maybe you decide that you really want to hear what Josie's going to tell you or at least want to have a conversation with her and you tell her so—"no, I can't imagine what happened at work today, tell me!" Your response provides the most significant evidence to others that you are listening. Responding means that you show others how you regard their messages. For example, you could have responded to Josie in a sarcastic tone, letting her know that you'll listen but you're not really interested; or you could have just said "hmmm," telling her you don't even want to engage in a conversation. Even failing to respond is a type of response! You can respond in numerous ways; however, your response will be influenced by *how* you listen.

Now that you understand the process of listening, the next section shows how an individual's personal characteristics influence listening and responding. We also describe how different situations require different types of listening skills.

TEST YOUR KNOWLEDGE
- What is a definition of listening?
- What are the four stages of listening?
- What is the role of critical thinking in the process of listening?

LISTENING AND THE INDIVIDUAL

Do you have any friends who are especially good listeners? Any who are not so good? Do you yourself find it easier to listen in some situations than in others?

While some studies have identified general listening skills (see *Did You Know? The "Big Five" of Listening Competency*), there are many factors that influence whether listening in any particular situation is easier or more difficult. In this section, we describe some of these factors, including individual listening styles and individual

Did You Know?
. . . .

The "Big Five" of Listening Competency
A recent study asked 1,319 students to describe, in an online questionnaire, what it means to be an effective listener. The results revealed the following top or "Big Five" dimensions of effective listening.
Notice how each of these dimensions is associated with the phases of listening (hearing, sensing, and so on). Are there other skills that you would add?

1. Openness or willingness to listen
2. Ability to read nonverbal cues

(continued)

Did You Know?   *(continued)*

3. Ability to understand verbal cues
4. Ability to respond appropriately
5. Ability to remember relevant details

   While these skills are important and confirm findings from earlier studies, the authors of the study note that other factors, like age, maturity, and personal experiences, influence an individual's listening competence. In addition, they note that the study design did not address the influence of context or interpersonal relationship.

Source: Cooper, L. O., & Buchanan, T. (2010). Listening competency on campus: A psychometric analysis of student listening. *International Journal of Listening, 24*(3), 141–163.

characteristics like gender, age, and nationality. Finally, we discuss physical and psychological barriers to listening.

Influences on Listening

Not everyone listens in the same way; our personal listening habits may be influenced by gender, age, ethnicity, or even certain idiosyncratic patterns. These influences can then affect how we respond to others. Let's look first at the various listening styles and then turn to other characteristics that may influence how we listen and respond.

Listening Styles According to experts, a **listening style** is a set of "attitudes, beliefs, and predispositions about the how, where, when, who, and what of the information reception and encoding process" (Watson, Barker, & Weaver, 1995, p. 2). To put it more simply, it is "the way people prefer to receive oral information" (Watson et al., 1995, p. 9). Researchers have identified four listening styles used in various situations (Bodie & Worthington, 2010; Watson et al., 1995; Barker & Watson, 2000) and find that a given individual will tend to prefer to use just one or two of these styles (Barker & Watson, 2000).

   Each listening style emphasizes a particular set of skills that are useful for responding to others in particular situations. The point of this is not that you should strive to develop a particular style or that having a particular style ensures you will be a good listener, but that your listening style should vary somewhat by context or situation. And, indeed, studies have shown that most people do vary their listening style from situation to situation (Imhof, 2004).

Action-Oriented Listening Style The **action-oriented** listening style reflects a preference for error-free and well-organized speaking, with an emphasis on active responding. People using this style focus more on the content of the message than on the person delivering it, and they want to not only hear the message, but to do something with it. They may get impatient if a speaker is not direct or concise enough.

   The action-oriented style requires **informational listening** skills, useful in situations requiring attention to content. For example, at work you probably listen primarily for content, to make sure you understand the instructions of your boss, supervisor, or coworkers. Informational listening skills are also useful at school, during course lectures, or when professors give detailed instructions about assignments. How can you improve your informational listening skills? Here are some suggestions:

1. Attend to what the speaker is saying: Maintain eye contact; face the person, and lean toward him or her. Show the speaker that you *want* to understand what he or she is saying.

2. Don't judge the speaker prematurely: Making mental judgments can prevent you from understanding the content of the speaker's message.

listening style
a set of attitudes, beliefs, and predispositions about the how, where, when, who, and what of the information receiving and encoding process

action-oriented
listening style that reflects a preference for error-free and well-organized speaking

informational listening
listening skills that are useful in situations requiring attention to content

3. Paraphrase: Reflect the speaker's words back to make sure you understand and let the speaker know you are listening—for example, if your professor is describing instructions for an assignment, you might say, "You're saying that the five-page paper needs to cite at least ten different research sources."

4. Clarify: Ask questions to clear up any confusion or seek more information. For example, if you don't completely understand your professor's instructions, you might ask, "How should we submit the paper? Can we email it to you or do you want us to hand it to you in class?"

5. Review and summarize: Periodically review and summarize to make sure you understand the information. Summarizing captures the overall meaning of what has been said and puts it into a logical and coherent order, but summaries should not add any new information. After your summary, you might also ask, "Is that correct?" so that the speaker still has control. For example, you might say, "So we hand in a five-page research paper to you in class Thursday on the topics we discussed today? Is this correct?"

content-oriented
a listening style that reflects an interest in detailed and complex information, simply for the content itself

critical listening
listening skills that are useful in a wide variety of situations—particularly those involving persuasive speaking

people-oriented
a listening style that is associated with friendly, open communication and an interest in establishing ties with others

supportive listening
listening skills focused not only on understanding information but also "listening" to others' feelings

Content-Oriented Listening Style The **content-oriented** listening style reflects an interest in detailed and complex information, simply for the content itself. People using this style prefer debate or argument content over simpler speech; they attend to details and are interested in the quality of the speech. Critical thinking skills are particularly important in this style.

This style involves the informational listening skills detailed above and an additional set of **critical listening** skills (Mooney, 1996), which go hand in hand with critical thinking skills. These skills are useful in a wide variety of situations, particularly those involving persuasive speaking—for example, when you are listening to a political speech or a sales pitch—or even in more informal settings, such as when friends or acquaintances try to persuade you to see their point of view about an issue or activity. Here are some suggestions for developing critical listening skills:

1. Consider the speaker's credibility. Is this speaker qualified to make these arguments? Is this speaker trustworthy?

2. Listen between the lines. Are the words and the body language consistent? Are the content and the emotion in harmony?

3. Evaluate the messages being sent and their implications. Ask yourself, "What conclusions can be drawn from what is being said? Where is this leading?"

4. Weigh the evidence. Does what is being said make sense? Are the speaker's opinions logical? Are they supported by fact?

5. Periodically review and summarize. As with informational listening, you need to periodically check to make sure you understand the message. Ask yourself, "Do I have it straight? Do I understand the speakers' arguments and main points?"

People-Oriented Listening Style People using this style are interested in hearing about others' experiences, thoughts, and feelings and finding areas of common interest. The **people-oriented** listening style is often associated with friendly, open communication and an interest in establishing ties with others rather than in controlling them (Villaume & Bodie, 2007). The people-oriented style is particularly useful in informal personal situations, as when we are listening to friends, family, and relational partners.

People-oriented listening involves **supportive listening** skills, focused not only on understanding information but also "listening" to others' feelings—which they may communicate nonverbally, as we've seen in Chapter 6. Consider the following suggestions for effective supportive listening

People-oriented listening involves listening not only to words but also to others' feelings.

(Fowler, 2005; Salem, 2003). Notice also how many of them involve nonverbal behaviors on the listener's part, and also the overlap with informational listening skills:

time-oriented
a listening style that prefers brief, concise speech

1. Put the other person at ease. Give space and time and "permission to speak." Do this by showing that you *want* to hear the speaker. Look at him or her. Nod when you can agree. Encourage the speaker to talk.

2. Remove distractions. Be willing to turn off the TV, close a door, stop texting on your cell phone or reading your mail. Let the speaker know he or she has your full attention.

3. Empathize with the other person, especially if he or she is telling you something personal or painful; take a moment to stand in the other person's shoes, to look at the situation from his or her point of view. Empathy can be expressed by (a) being a sounding board, which means allowing the person to talk while maintaining a nonjudgmental, non-critical manner; (b) resisting the impulse to discount the person's feelings with stock phrases like "it's not really that bad" or "you'll feel better tomorrow"; and (c) paraphrasing what you think the person really means or feels. This can help the person clarify his or her thoughts and feelings—for example, "It sounds like you're saying you feel overwhelmed by the new project"—and communicates that you understand the emotions and feelings involved.

4. Be patient. Some people take longer to find the right word, make a point, or clarify an issue.

5. Be aware of your own emotions. As we'll discuss later in the chapter, emotions can be a barrier to effective listening.

Time-Oriented Listening Style The **time-oriented** listening style prefers brief, concise speech. Time-oriented listeners don't want to waste time on complex details; they just want the aural equivalent of bullet points. They may check their watches when they think someone is taking too long to get to the point. They may also state how much time they have for an interaction in order to keep the interaction concise and to the point. No specific set of skills accompanies this style; in fact, this style seems to involve rather ineffective listening behavior, except in cases where time is of the essence and concise information is imperative (e.g., emergency situations). If you find yourself using this style in many situations, you may want to consider which of the other three styles may be more effective.

In conclusion, to become a more effective listener in a variety of personal and professional contexts, identify your preferred style(s) and then work on developing the skill sets that accompany the other styles. For example, if you tend to be a people-oriented listener, you might improve your informational and critical listening skills. On the other hand, if you tend to prefer the content-oriented style, you might work to develop your supportive listening skills.

Time-oriented listening can be effective in emergencies when information must be communicated quickly and concisely.

Individual Identity Characteristics Now let's turn to other individual influences on listening behaviors. How do individual identity characteristics such as gender, age, and ethnicity affect listening behaviors? Do males and females tend to listen differently? Do older people listen in a different way than do younger people? And a related set of questions: Should we adapt our listening behaviors depending on who we are listening to? For example, should we listen to children differently from adults? Let's look at how the experts weigh in on answers to these questions.

Consider the various listening styles and think about which style(s) you tend to use. Which are you less likely to use? Which sets of skills might you need to work on to become a more effective listener?

Gender Some scholars think that in general men and women not only differ in their listening styles, but that women tend to be better listeners than men. Other researchers have found no gender differences in listening behavior (Pearce, Johnson, & Barker, 2003; Imhof, 2004). Before looking at the research on this topic, let's discuss the issue of gender stereotypes—the common perceptions people have concerning gender and listening.

Two communication scholars have identified common gender-based listening stereotypes: Men, they say, are supposedly logical, judgmental, interrupting, inattentive, self-centered, and impatient; whereas women are stereotyped as emotional, noninterrupting, attentive, empathetic, other-centered, responsive, and patient (Barker & Watson, 2000). Just by reading these stereotypes, you may think that women are better listeners than men, and many people do seem to hold this belief (Brownell, 1994; Pearce, Johnson, & Barker, 2003). Contrary to the stereotypes, however, researchers have only documented three areas of gender differences in listening behavior: Women are more accommodating and focused on the speaker, men focus on facts and handle distractions better, and men interrupt more than women.

Apparently, some of these differences have roots in biological characteristics of males and females. Take the findings that women tend to be more other-oriented, empathetic, and responsive listeners (focused on relationships and people) and men focus on facts when listening (Johnston, Weaver, Watson, & Barker, 2000; Silverman, 1970; Villaume & Bodie, 2007). Let's look at an example of how these differences might apply to an everyday conversation. Gustavo, Susan, and Natalie are coworkers and good friends. Natalie returns from lunch and she and Gustavo have the following conversation:

G: Your friend Susan stopped in a few minutes ago while you were out for lunch. She was looking for you.
N: Oh, did she leave a message? Was it anything important?
G: I don't think so. I think she said maybe you could give her a call sometime, something about her work schedule.

Later, Natalie calls Susan and the next day Natalie explains to Gustavo:

N: I really wish you had given me Susan's message yesterday. She said she specifically told you to ask me if I could give her a ride to work tomorrow. Her cousin's been having trouble with his girlfriend and the girlfriend's moving out, so now he can't use her car, so he borrowed Susan's for a few days. Susan's supervisor changed her work schedule and she and I have the same schedule. She wondered if I was driving to work tomorrow or whether my husband was dropping me off—like he does sometimes. So why didn't you explain this to me?

Do these conversations sound typical? They seem to demonstrate the conventional notions that females listen for relational details, and males recall general ideas and pay little attention to details—particularly in a relational context. As we've discussed in earlier chapters, most behavioral scientists believe that while some innate gender differences may exist, most behavioral differences between men and women are influenced more by cultural norms than biology. In many cultures, women are socialized to be more considerate, cooperative, helpful and sympathetic, as Natalie may be demonstrating in the examples above. With this in mind, it is easy to see why women are often regarded as more effective listeners.

To sum it up, there do seem to be a few gender differences in listening behaviors, but both men and women can demonstrate feminine *and* masculine listening behaviors.

Remember, too, that gender differences are not fixed and given; people of both genders can learn to be effective listeners (Barker & Watson, 2000; Nichols, 2009).

Age Do you listen differently to your parents than to your younger siblings? The fact is that people have different communication capacities and skill levels during various life stages, which means that we often adapt our listening behaviors depending on the age of the speaker (Nichols, 2009). We can and should adapt our listening behaviors for children (Clark, 2005). For example, since young children are in the process of developing their communication skills, they struggle sometimes to interpret the meanings of others and to follow adult conversational norms—that is, to listen when others are speaking, not interrupt, and respond to instructions. In fact, when children don't understand what is being discussed, they then may not be able to communicate what they don't know and can become withdrawn or act out in socially inappropriate ways (Jalongo, 2010). Be patient when they are struggling to say something; children have more to say than they can express. You can demonstrate patience and involvement by maintaining eye contact when they're speaking and asking questions; in other words, be a good listening role model. As one communication expert says, "as children experience the joy of someone else's undivided attention, they learn to value listening and acquire the disposition to listen thoughtfully to others" (Jalongo, 2010, p. 5). And be aware of the impact your feedback and responses have. Children tend to think literally, so if you tell them that a big bad witch is going to come and take them away if they misbehave, they may fear that this will actually happen.

Teenagers may also require some special listening behaviors. In many cultures, including the United States, teenagers are in a crucial stage of learning to be independent. Part of this process may involve closing off channels of communication or being critical of parents and other adults (Nichols, 2009). As with children, listening effectively to teenagers involves patience and restraint—not asking too many questions or giving too much criticism, being available to listen when the teen wants to talk, and acknowledging when the teenager acts responsibly (Barker & Watson, 2000; Nichols, 2009).

Our potential for effective listening seems to increase as we grow into adulthood; for example, college seniors are better listeners than college freshmen (Aurand, Ridnour, Timm, & Kaminski, 2000). But these capacities may also diminish as we grow even older. At least one study found that younger managers (under age 45) were better listeners than older managers (Brownell, 200). And as we get older, listening may become more difficult if hearing ability is an issue (we'll discuss hearing disability in the next section, under barriers to listening). However, not everyone who is old is deaf. Assuming that they are—that is, yelling or treating listeners like children—can be hurtful and insulting.

Listening to children involves adjusting one's listening style and being tolerant of children's "breaking" conversational rules.

Nationality Do people in other countries listen and respond differently? If so, one difference may lie in what people consider appropriate nonverbal expressions of listening and responding (Pearce, Johnson, & Barker, 2003; Thomlison, 1996). In most western cultures, good listening is demonstrated by eye contact, head nods, and some back-channeling vocalizations such as "hmmm" and "oh." However, in some countries, like Vietnam and Thailand, good listening behavior (listening respectfully) involves avoiding eve contact. In other countries, like Japan, good listening may involve responding with lots of head nods, back-channeling, and even saying "yes, yes," which actually means, "I hear you," not "I agree with you" (Fujii, 2008). We'll explore more cross-cultural differences in communication patterns in the following chapter.

Here, however, to summarize, factors that can influence an individual's listening behavior include gender, age, ethnicity, and nationality, as well as one's own listening style preferences and the particular situation. Still, one cannot assume that an individual will listen in a particular way just because she or he belongs to a certain gender, age, or nationality group. Listening is a complex behavior, and numerous factors beyond these kinds of identity characteristics can serve as barriers, the topic we turn to next.

Barriers to Listening

Like the student Iasha in the opening vignette, people have many reasons for not listening to others. Some typical ones include physical and physiological barriers, psychological barriers, conflicting objectives, and poor listening habits (Robertson, 2005). Let's explore in more detail how these factors can interfere with effective listening.

Physical and Physiological Barriers Physical barriers to listening include a noisy environment or physical discomforts that make it difficult to concentrate. We have all had the experience of trying to listen to someone in a noisy bar or in a room with a loud television, or while standing outside with traffic whizzing by on a busy highway. Physical barriers are the most elemental; if we can't hear because of the noise around us, it doesn't matter how refined our listening skills are.

Another physical barrier is fatigue. Whether a listener is tired from lack of sleep or from high stress, it can be a barrier to good listening. For example, it's difficult for students to listen effectively in class when they are exhausted; and it's difficult for parents to listen to children when they are stressed out from working hard and managing their many responsibilities. As we hope you understand by now, listening well takes effort and requires alertness and focus—both of which may be absent when one is tired.

Fatigue is a common barrier to listening.

Another type of listening barrier is physiological—for example, a hearing disability. Good listening is a skill, but it is also strongly affected by a person's physical ability to hear. The American Speech and Hearing Association estimates that more than 30 million people in the United States have a hearing loss that could be treated and, in fact, an increasing number of younger people have hearing problems associated with Personal Media Players (PMP) (McCormick & Matusitz, 2010). (See *Alternative View: Statistically Speaking, How Many People Are Deaf or Hard of Hearing?*) Unfortunately, many people with hearing loss do not treat it—whether because of vanity (not wanting to wear a hearing aid), lack of funds, or lack of knowledge about the disability. Getting over this barrier may mean recognizing and treating the disability or, in the case of mild impairment, asking people to enunciate more clearly and use adequate speech volume.

Psychological Barriers Common psychological barriers that prevent us from listening effectively are boredom and preoccupation. The human mind can process information at a rate of about 600 words per minute, about three times faster than the typical speaker can talk (Battell, 2006). Consequently, your mind has plenty of time to wander, and you can easily become distracted or bored, which will certainly undermine the amount that you listen to and retain.

Preoccupation, or distracted listening, is a related psychological barrier. During an interaction, people often think of other things and, thus, do not listen to what is being said. Preoccupation can be caused by having an extensive to-do list and feeling stress about getting it all done. Two other common sources of preoccupation include having a personal agenda in a conversation (Shafir, 2000, p. 62) and being emotional.

How can having a personal agenda in a conversation lead to preoccupation and inattentive listening? As one example, let's say you've just met someone in a social setting who is the head of a corporation where you would like to work.

Alternative VIEW

Statistically, How Many People Are Deaf or Hard of Hearing?

How often do you assume that the person listening to you has good hearing? How might this assumption influence how you respond and, ultimately, the outcomes of your communication encounters? How might you modify your way of speaking if you knew you were speaking to someone with a hearing loss?

Deafness guide Jamie Berke was born deaf but has been able to hear using various technologies, including a cochlear implant. In this article, she addresses the question of how many people are deaf and hearing impaired.

Statistically, how many people are deaf or hard of hearing? No one really knows. There are some demographic statistics available, but they are either outdated or unreliable because some people may not wish to identify themselves as having a hearing loss, or the question forms may not ask directly if a person has a hearing loss. The estimated demographic figure has ranged from 22 million deaf and hard of hearing to as high as 36 million deaf and hard of hearing. Of these, only a few million are considered "deaf" and the remainder are hard of hearing. Further muddy-

ing statistics is the fact that some "deaf" people may actually be hard of hearing, and some "hard of hearing" people may actually be deaf. There are certainly enough of us with hearing losses that companies recognize the potential purchasing power of such a large segment of society…

While most people with hearing loss are older folks who have lost hearing with age, approximately 12 out of every 1,000 persons with hearing impairment is under 18 years of age, based on the most recently available NCHS statistics. That means that the chances are excellent that at least one student in your child's school will have a hearing loss.

The Census Bureau offers demographical statistics on disability and employment, taken from a Survey of Income and Program Participation (participation in public assistance programs). That data has numbers only in the thousands, rather than the millions. One interesting pattern that emerges from this statistical data set is that people with less severe hearing loss are more likely to be employed than those with more severe hearing impairments.

SOURCE: Berke, J. (2010, September 6). Hearing Loss—Demographics—Deafness Statistics. Retrieved March 28, 2011, from http://deafness.about.com/cs/earbasics/a/demographics.htm

During your conversation, you do your best to impress her as she talks about her professional activities and ideas; you smile, nod enthusiastically, and try to act in a professional manner. However, when you finally get to speak, you repeat ideas that she has just expressed or ask questions that she has already answered. Why? Because you weren't listening; you were too preoccupied with your own agenda to hear what she was saying. In this case, you probably failed to do the one thing you wanted to do—impress her. These kinds of listening failures can lead to frustration and maybe even feelings of low self-worth. What is the lesson, then? Listeners do better to put their own goals aside during a conversation and focus on the priorities and concerns of their conversational partner.

A second source of preoccupation comes from strong emotions. Anger or fear or even joy, for example, can make a person too preoccupied to listen and can also influence how he or she understands and reacts to messages (Nichols, 2009). If you are frustrated or irritable, you are more likely to interpret casual comments as criticism. On the other hand, if something wonderful has just happened to you, you may be concentrating on your good news and how you are going to celebrate, rather than focusing on the speaker. Thus, a wide variety of emotions can distract you and influence how you listen and respond in communicative interactions.

Strong emotions can interfere with listening by making people defensive, overly sensitive, or hostile.

Emotions can also make people defensive and thus impair their listening abilities. Defensive listening occurs when someone perceives, anticipates, or experiences a threat (Nichols, 2009). In such cases, the listener often puts up a "wall" for protection. These walls can distort incoming messages, leading to misinterpretation. For example, one of our colleagues described how her emotional reactions to her father hindered her ability to listen to him: "We had such a rotten relationship that every time he even opened his mouth to speak, I was so defensive, so sure he was going to criticize me or yell at me that I never even heard a word he said." Some people are more defensive than others; their personalities and experiences have influenced them to respond defensively to many messages. However, certain types of messages are more likely to elicit defensive listening. As we discussed in Chapter 5, messages that are evaluative, controlling, superior, or dogmatic tend to prompt a defensive reaction.

Preconceived ideas about issues or participants can also trigger strong emotions. For example, sometimes we allow negative past experience with a person to interfere; that is, if you expect your sibling (or father) to be angry at you, you will likely interpret any comment as hostile—as was the case with our colleague and her father. For another example, if you are usually sarcastic, then others are likely to hear even your compliments as insults. Unfortunately, people often find it difficult to acknowledge their own preconceptions, let alone recognize those of others. Good advice here is to use your past experience to help you learn about the world, but do not rely on it as your only source for evaluating a present situation.

The psychological barriers discussed here can act as "filters that allow only selected words and ideas into our consciousness… [they can also] screen out the less comfortable and uncomfortable messages, [so that] only pieces of message are received—the comfortable pieces" (Shafir, 2000, p. 47). The end result is that these barriers can stifle the potential for developing meaningful relationships and new ideas.

Conflicting Objectives A third barrier to listening involves conflicting objectives. How people understand and react to others' communicative attempts depends in part on their objective(s) for the conversation. For example, how do you listen to a lecture when your instructor announces, "This will be on the midterm"? How do you listen when told the material will *not* be on a test? Your different objectives for these situations are likely to influence how well you listen.

Sometimes participants to a conversation differ in their objectives for an interaction. For example, during a business meeting Hank's objective was to explain a new procedure for evaluating employees, while Roberta's objective was to get a raise. Consequently, the two focused on different aspects of their conversation, assigned different meanings to what occurred, and remembered different aspects of their meeting. Of course, people may have multiple objectives for an interaction, each of which will influence how they listen and respond.

Poor Listening Habits As it turns out, people can more easily define poor listening than effective listening. Similarly, people can more easily identify the listening habits and flaws of others than they can their own. In our opening story, Iasha saw other students' poor listening behaviors before she recognized her own.

Here are five common ineffective listening behaviors, which result in not really getting the speaker's message.

1. Wandering: Probably the most common. The listener's mind wanders from time to time, not really focused on what the speaker is saying. The words go in one ear and out the other.

2. Rejecting: The listener "tunes out" the speaker at the very beginning of the message, often because of a lack of respect or dislike for the speaker.

3. Judging: The listener focuses on what the speaker says, but makes a hasty evaluation of the speaker's message, ignoring the remainder of the message.

4. Predicting: So common—the listener gets ahead of the speaker and finishes her thoughts; again, missing at least some of the speaker's message.

5. Rehearsing: The listener is thinking about what she is going to say next.

Are there other annoying habits you would like to add to this top-ten list? Are you guilty of any of these? Most of us are. Perhaps the most important way to avoid these bad habits is to first become more aware of our own listening behavior and to really focus on the speaker rather than on our own thoughts, feelings, and what *we're* going to say next. As we've mentioned, however, societal factors can have an important impact on one's ability to listen effectively, and this is the subject we turn to next.

TEST YOUR KNOWLEDGE

- What are the four primary listening styles, and in what contexts are each of them most appropriate?
- How do gender, age, and nationality influence listening and responding behaviors?
- What are four common barriers to effective listening and responding?
- What are common sources of preoccupation that prevent us from listening?

THE INDIVIDUAL, LISTENING, AND SOCIETY

As emphasized throughout this textbook, communication behaviors do not exist solely on the individual level but are a complex interaction of individual and societal factors, reflected in our synergetic model of communication. Let's examine listening as it's affected by three levels of societal forces: social hierarchy, context, and community.

Social Hierarchy

Societal norms and social hierarchy influence much of our communication behaviors, and listening is no exception (Dillon & McKenzie, 1998). Let's look more closely at how this works. Every society transmits messages about who is most powerful and important, and these are the people who set the communication norms. How do these messages affect our listening and responding?

Each time we meet someone for the first time, we immediately evaluate whether that person is worth listening to. We mentally go through our personal (influenced by society's) criteria. If the person doesn't meet the criteria, the person's words "become fainter and fainter until only our thoughts fill our attention" (Shafir, 2000, p. 58). Some of the most crucial information to be gained as listeners—like people's names—gets lost while we process acceptability checklists. Three important "filters" are social status, physical appearance, and vocal cues.

Social Status One criterion on many people's acceptability checklist is social status. We ask ourselves: Is this person worthy of my time and attention? Most of us are more attentive and listen more closely to those we consider equal to us or higher in society's hierarchy. For example, we listen closely to the words of physicians,

It is easier to identify poor listening habits in others than in ourselves.

Review the listening barriers described in the chapter. Which do you think are the most common in your own life? Which do you think are the most difficult to overcome? What is the evidence for your answers to these questions?

teachers, successful business people, and celebrities. Rebecca Z. Shafir (2000), a renowned speech pathologist and listening expert, recounts the story of a manager of a large department who, as part of his power trip, ordered his staff to follow him down the hall as they asked questions or presented ideas (like the scheming boss, Wilhelmina, in the TV sitcom *Ugly Betty*):

> He rarely made eye contact with his subordinates and walked past them as they spoke. Yet, when conversing with his peers or those higher on the administrative ladder, a dramatic change in his voice and body language took place. He looked them in the eye and smiled, nodding his head at any comment or suggestion. He laughed uproariously at their jokes and thanked them profusely for their unique insights. (p. 53)

It Happened to Me: *Danny*

Being in college, I'm a part of a culture that's very different from the culture where I grew up. In college, people value talking about ideas, learning new information, and working toward becoming more "educated." When I go home, however, I have to remember that not everyone in my family, and not all of my friends, went to college. They don't understand a lot of the jargon I use, and they don't know about the things I've studied. I try to be mindful of this when I visit; I don't want to sound condescending. I also try to remember that their opinions are equally valid and that I need to listen as attentively to them as I do to my college friends.

Shafir goes on to say that this manager's attention to status overrode his ability to gain the voluntary cooperation of his staff and resulted in ineffective management, low staff morale, and high turnover. Regardless of the positions we hold, most of us are similarly influenced by systems of hierarchy, and these systems are sometimes tinged with prejudice. For example, do we listen with as much attention to people who have less education? Perhaps not, as Danny found out in *It Happened to Me*.

Physical Appearance One of the most common obstacles to listening relates to physical appearance. Societal forces set the norms for physical attractiveness, which include being physically able-bodied, having symmetrical features, and embodying certain weight and height norms. This means that many people hold stereotypes about people with disabilities or physical challenges (e.g., people who are extremely overweight or small), and they often find it difficult to listen to them, avoiding eye contact or ignoring the person entirely. One of our colleagues, Tanya, had a stroke as a young adult and uses a walker or wheelchair. She describes a common situation she encounters:

> It really irritates me sometimes when I'm in public and people avoid looking at me, look at my husband instead and ask him what I want. Why can't they listen to what *I'm saying* and respond to *me*?

In sum, social hierarchies can act as a filter that, in turn, influences people's listening behaviors.

Vocal Cues In addition to social status and appearance, vocal cues (the *way* a person talks) can also be a filter that influences how people listen to others. Sometimes these judgments are factually accurate. For example, people can often tell by hearing someone's voice whether the speaker is male or female, young or old. However, a recent study showed that people make other judgments about a person, in addition to gender and age, based on the pitch and sound of their voice (Imhof, 2010). In this study, the researchers found that people with higher pitched voices were judged by others to be more outgoing and open, but less conscientious and less emotionally stable. The judgments stem from societal cues and assumptions that link people's vocal cues to personality. The important

Physical appearance has a strong effect on listening. How well do you listen when the speaker has a disability or other characteristic that makes you feel uncomfortable?

question is, how do we listen to people we consider "less conscientious" or "less emotionally stable"? Something to keep in mind is whether we are making unwarranted judgments that then influence how we listen.

The point here is that these "filters," based on social hierarchy, can prevent us from listening to others with openness and in a nonjudgmental manner that is usually thought of as part of effective listening. However, several experts have pointed out that it is probably not really possible to "set aside prejudices" and "consider all people as equal," so that setting these goals as a necessary and sufficient condition for effective listening means almost certain failure. Rather, they suggest that we see them as ideals—goals to strive *toward*. In so doing, certainly becoming aware of our "filters" is a first step (Bodie, 2010; Floyd, 2010).

Listening in Context

As discussed earlier, different contexts may call for different listening styles and behaviors. For example, in professional contexts we generally focus on content or action listening, whereas in social contexts we generally focus more on people and relationship affirmation. With friends, we are often called on to listen sympathetically and with little judgment, establishing empathy and communicating a recognizable "*feeling* of being heard" (Shotter, 2009, p. 21).

In professional contexts, too, whether one is working on an assembly line or as a manager, listening with empathy is important because it enables people to understand each other and get the job done (Battell, 2006; Imhof, 2001). At the same time, employees must be cautious about letting their work relationships get too personal. For example, when Donna's new boss, Lena, spoke freely to her about her divorce and problems with her children, Donna felt pleased that her boss would choose to confide in her. However, she soon found that Lena's confidences were taking lots of time and keeping her from getting work done. In addition, she discovered that her coworkers were critical of her for being unable to keep things on a professional level. The lesson, then, is that colleagues need to balance task and relational listening skills (Nichols, 2009).

Societal forces may affect listening behavior in any context. For example, some individuals are the victims of prejudice, discrimination, or even bullying in social or workplace contexts due to gender, age, race, ethnicity, or sexual orientation. When this happens, they may not be able to easily adapt their listening behavior. Others' bullying or discriminatory reactions to them may completely undermine their attempts to demonstrate good communication skills. A disabled person, for instance, may display good listening skills in a conversation by making eye contact, leaning forward, and paying close attention, but these good communication skills can be undermined if the speaker expresses prejudice toward the disabled person by *avoiding* eye contact. We'll address the role of prejudice and discrimination in communication further in Chapter 8.

Listening and Community

Communication scholar David Beard (2009) reminds us that in addition to all the voices in various hierarchies and contexts we listen to every day, we also listen to **soundscapes**—the everyday sounds in our environments. Together these sounds establish a community identity. For example, in many small towns, church bells—or in some countries, the imam calling Muslims to prayer five times daily—help define the boundaries of regional or religious communities and shape a community identity.

Community-specific soundscapes can also vary with generational differences. Contrast the technological soundscapes of your parents' and grandparents' generation—the hiss of the needle on a record player, the sound of rotary phone dialing (and perhaps even a live operator's voice), the chimes of the NBC logo, the screech of dial-up Internet access—with your own soundscapes. What were

soundscape
the everyday sounds in our environments

the soundscapes of the neighborhood where you grew up? What sounds do you hear every day that may represent your generational identity and communities? Perhaps more importantly, how do these affect you? Are they comforting? irritating? Are there some that you tune out? Perhaps they are so much a part of the sound "background" that we don't consider their effect on us.

Although, as you've seen, the quality of one's listening is subject to powerful social forces as well as individual factors such as listening style, gender, and age, we do have some latitude for making choices about our own behavior. In other words, we do make ethical decisions about listening—the topic we turn to next.

TEST YOUR KNOWLEDGE

- What are two "filters" of social hierarchy that influence how we listen and respond to others?
- How do contexts affect how we listen and respond to others?
- What are "soundscapes," and how do they influence our listening?

ETHICS AND LISTENING

People have several ethical decisions to make about listening. These decisions include choosing what you will listen to and when, as well as how you will respond when listening to other people or to the soundscapes that surround you.

To begin, choosing to listen or not is an ethical decision (Beard, 2009; Stoltz, 2010). Just because someone wants to tell you something doesn't mean you have to listen. And sometimes the very act of listening—or refusing to—means taking a moral stand. For example, let's say a friend of yours is passing along a vicious rumor about another person or telling a racist joke. You have an ethical decision to make. Are you going to listen? How are you going to respond?

You also have an ethical choice about offering feedback. You can tell your friend you don't want to listen or even gently explain why you don't want to. Or you can say nothing, sacrificing honesty to avoid making yourself (and others) feel uncomfortable. In certain situations (e.g., a business meeting or a formal social gathering), offering negative feedback may cause great embarrassment, and you may decide to wait and deliver your feedback in private. What are the consequences of each of these decisions? If you listen to something offensive, you are in effect agreeing with the remark. It may be awkward to tell your friend (either at the moment or later) that you don't want to listen to such remarks, but the friend may think twice before making similar comments in the future. Obviously, there are no easy answers; you need to consider the consequences and possible outcomes in each situation as you make these ethical decisions.

Mediated communication contexts also can pose ethical issues with regard to listening. The more you use computers, PDAs, cell phones, and other communication technologies, the more likely you are to have access to personal information (e.g., through email and voice and text messages) that may not be intended for you. When you have access to messages not intended for you, you choose what messages to listen to and also what to do with the information. Many of these choices hold consequences for yourself and others and, as such, constitute ethical decisions (Brownell, 2002).

What are some guidelines for dealing with information that is not intended for you? As we suggested in Chapter 1, you might first consider the expectations of the individual who sent the message. Perhaps this person has made it clear that he or she wants this information kept private. Or you might consider that if you were in this person's position, you would want the information to be kept private. Or perhaps you know that the sender does not mind if the information is shared more widely—but what about the person to whom the message is addressed? You need to consider his or her wishes, too. Depending on the privacy expectation, the ethical decision might be to listen to/read the message—or not. Would the sender or addressee feel harmed? Would any benefit result from your listening to the message? The answer to these questions probably depends a great deal on your relationships with the sender and addressee. A very close friend may not mind your listening in on messages; someone you don't know very well may object strenuously.

Say you accidentally got a text message that your friend just got engaged and you told this to another friend who happened to be having lunch with you when you got the text. The newly engaged friend might be furious if friends found out through the grapevine. For a variety of reasons, brides- and grooms-to-be usually want to choose when and how to announce the news of their engagements. They may be very upset if casual friends learn of their news before they have had a chance to invite family and close friends to be in the wedding party. Their parents may be offended at not having been personally notified before it was made public. Or the couple may want to plan a party to make the announcement; by spreading the news without their consent you would spoil the surprise.

What other kinds of choices do we make, as listeners, to become more or less ethical beings? Here are some you might not have considered:

1. The choice to cut ourselves off from listening to our immediate environments: We can choose to listen alone (putting on the headset/earphones), which sometimes might be a positive, self-constructive act. At other times, however (e.g., in a work situation or at home when our relational partner wants to talk), doing so can be isolating and damaging to relationships.

2. The choice to listen selectively: For example, we can choose to listen to media "candy" or to media that enhance and inspire us as people. We can choose to listen to a friend's choice of media, so we can discuss it together, or we can listen only to our own choices.

3. The choice not to listen: For example, in the public arena, we can decide to listen (or not listen) to a political speaker who espouses ideas we oppose. Our choice has a potential impact on us and our thinking, as listening implies the possibility of change in attitudes and behavior. Listening to a political speaker (or even a friend) promoting ideas and beliefs that we disagree with may open us up to ideas previously unexplored or may reinforce our own beliefs. Choosing never to listen to opposing views ensures that we won't alter our beliefs or learn to defend them in a logical and constructive way.

4. The choice to listen together: For example, when we attend a music concert or a political rally, we open ourselves to being part of a community of music fans or political sympathizers (Beard, 2009). The consequences of the decision to listen with a particular community may open up opportunities for new experiences that may alter our future thinking and/or behavior.

The point is that all these choices are just that—choices. While we don't usually consider these types of choices when we think of listening, the decisions we make regarding them do influence our communication life—influencing our communication identity and relationships with those important to us.

Ethical listening involves knowing how to handle confidentiality if you receive a message not intended for you.

TEST YOUR KNOWLEDGE

- What are some contexts where choosing to listen (or not listen) is an ethical decision?
- What are some ethical choices related to listening and responding?

IMPROVING YOUR LISTENING SKILLS

As we have shown in this chapter, listening (including responding appropriately) is an important communication skill. As is the case with all communication skills, however, there are no surefire, easy recipes for becoming a more effective listener. Still, three guidelines might help you improve.

Become Aware

Most of us think of ourselves as better listeners than we really are. In fact, we don't think much about our personal listening behaviors until something bad happens as a result of poor listening—for example, we show up at the wrong location for an important meeting, we forget to return an important call, or we miss an important social event. Then friends or colleagues might draw attention to our poor listening habits. Our first reaction might be to get defensive or make excuses. Perhaps a better response would be to take inventory of our listening behaviors; only then can we identify any poor listening habits.

Identify Poor Habits

As noted, most people have some poor listening habits, particularly in our close and intimate relationships, where partners often develop irritating practices such as finishing the other person's sentences, interrupting, and "tuning out" the other person. These irritating behaviors crop up especially if you are an action- or time-oriented listener. Ask yourself, then: What keeps you from really listening? Which filters block your ability to hear and understand what others are saying? Overcoming listening barriers—especially those that are reinforced by social hierarchies—can be very challenging.

Perhaps one way to overcome those societal messages is through awareness that our listening behaviors play an important role in the outcome of communication encounters. A number of research studies have shown that when people listen attentively to one another, the speaker is more likely to speak coherently. On the other hand, when listeners do not pay careful attention, speakers tend to be less coherent. Put another way, regardless of who they are or their social location, when speakers feel they are listened to with respect and attentiveness, they become better communicators and vice versa.

Interrupting or completing other people's sentences are barriers to listening that we can all learn to overcome if we try.

Strive for Mindful Listening

Applying the concept of mindful listening, described by renowned listening expert Rebecca Z. Shafir (2000), can help. We defined mindfulness in Chapter 4. Mindful listening, a specific kind of mindfulness, is based on Eastern philosophy and Zen Buddhism; it is defined by focus, concentration, and compassion, and it can bring health, peace, and productivity to our everyday lives. This very holistic approach requires that we listen with the heart, body, and mind, and for most of us, that means a major change in attitude. Mindful listening focuses on the *process* of listening versus the *payoff*.

Shafir suggests that in order to be a better listener to each of our friends, family, and acquaintances, we need to understand their "movie." What does that mean? Shafir compares listening to movies with listening to people. Most of us don't have trouble focusing on and paying attention while watching a movie; we get caught up in the plot, the emotion, and the characters. Why, she asks, should listening to people be any different? To continue the comparison, if we approach a listening opportunity with the same self-abandonment as we do a movie, think how much more we might gain from those encounters (Shafir, 2000, p. 95).

Being a mindful listener requires three elements:

1. the desire to get the whole message,

2. the ability to eliminate the noisy barriers discussed earlier, and

3. the willingness to place your agenda lower on the priority list than the speaker's.

Mindful listening is based upon empathy—the ability to identify with and understand someone else's feelings. As listening expert Michael Nichols states it, listening is not just taking in information; it is also "bearing witness" to, validating, and affirming another's expression. The core of listening, he says, is "to pay attention, take an interest in, care about, validate, acknowledge, be moved... appreciate" (2009, p. 14).

SUMMARY

Listening is considered to be one of the most important communication skills, partly because we spend so much time doing it! In addition, better listening skills can lead to improved cognition, improved academic performance, enhanced personal relationships, enhanced professional performance, and even better health.

Listening is defined as "the process of receiving, constructing meaning from, and responding to spoken and/or nonverbal messages" and occurs in four stages: sensing, understanding, evaluating, and responding. Not everyone listens in the same way; our personal listening habits may be influenced by our gender, age, ethnicity, or even our own predominant listening style, which can be people-, action-, content-, or time-oriented. Action-oriented style involves informational listening skills; content-oriented style involves informational and critical listening skills; people-oriented style involves supportive listening skills. People have many reasons for not listening to others, but some typical ones include physical or physiological barriers, psychological barriers, conflicting objectives, and poor listening habits.

Finally, listening habits and preferences are influenced by societal forces: contexts and hierarchies. Ethical considerations also come into play with respect to listening behavior. Ethical decisions include choosing what to listen to and when, how to respond when listening to other people or to the soundscapes around us, including media. While we can offer no surefire, easy recipes for becoming a more effective listener, three guidelines might help: Become aware of your personal listening patterns, identify your poor listening habits or barriers, and practice mindful listening.

HUMAN COMMUNICATION IN SOCIETY ONLINE

To review this chapter, use the MyCommunicationLab Web site to test your understanding of the following key terms, record your answers to the chapter review questions, and complete the suggested activities. Expand your learning and understanding of chapter concepts by completing additional exercises and activities online. Access code required. Go to www.mycommunicationlab.com for more information or to purchase standalone access.

KEY TERMS

listening 166
sensing 166
understanding 166
evaluating 168
responding 188

listening style 169
action-oriented 169
informational listening 169
content-oriented 170
critical listening 170

people-oriented 170
supportive listening 170
time-oriented 171
soundscape 179

APPLY WHAT YOU KNOW

1. When you are in class or in a large group, notice how people listen to each other and respond. Reflect on what you think is more or less effective about others' listening skills. Then apply what you observed to your own listening skills.

2. Ask someone to observe your listening skills over a period of time. This person can be a parent, friend, teacher, or romantic partner. Ask the observer to give you constructive feedback on how you can improve your listening skills. Try to implement those suggestions.

Part

COMMUNICATING IN CONTEXT

8 Communicating Across Cultures

9 Communicating in Close Relationships

10 Small Group Communication

11 Communicating in Organizations

12 Rhetorical Communication

13 Mass Media and Communication

14 Communication and New Technologies

*I*s communication that is effective in one context also effective in other contexts? Do the same principles apply to mediated communication as to face-to-face communication?

8
Communication Across Cultures

In my first semester in the United States, I lived in the dorm and made many friends from different countries. One day I was eating lunch when my Korean and Turkish friends started arguing loudly. The issue was the value of our school. The Turkish girl didn't like our school and was thinking of transferring. The Korean student defended our school vehemently.

The Korean and Turkish students wouldn't talk to each other after the argument, and the conflict created a very uncomfortable climate. I was concerned about both of them because we were all friends. So I asked some of my American friends what they thought about the issue. They said, "It's not your problem, Kaori. It's their problem. Stay away from it." I was shocked that my American friends didn't seem to care about the conflict and its negative influence, and it took me a while to understand what the phrase "it's their problem" actually means in this highly individualistic American society. I've been in the States seven years, and now I use the phrase myself. Do I think it's good? I don't know. At least, I know I am adapting better to American culture. Do I like it? I don't know. It's just how it is here. But I know that I would never ever say that to my family or friends in Japan.

Kaori's story illustrates several points about intercultural communication. First, intercultural contact is a fact of life in today's world; and second, although intercultural contact can be enriching, it can also bring conflict and misunderstanding. In Kaori's case, the clash between her American friends' individualistic belief and her more collectivistic orientation led her to believe that Americans did not care about friendships as much as she did. Finally, Kaori is an example of someone living "on the border"—between two cultures—having to negotiate conflicting sets of cultural values.

In today's world, we typically have many opportunities to meet people from different cultures. You may sit in class with students who are culturally different from you in many ways—in nationality, ethnicity, race, gender, age, religion, and sexual orientation. In addition, today's widespread access to communication technologies and foreign travel provide many opportunities for intercultural encounters beyond the classroom. But the many political and ethnic conflicts around the globe may inspire doubt about the ability of people from different cultures to coexist peacefully. Interethnic violence in Sudan and other African nations, in the former Yugoslavia, and in the Middle East; clashes between Buddhists and Hindus in India; and tension in the United States between African Americans and Whites may lead people to believe that cultural differences necessarily lead to insurmountable problems. However, we believe that increased awareness of intercultural communication can help prevent or reduce the severity of problems that arise due to cultural differences.

In this chapter, we'll first explore the importance of *intercultural communication* and define what we mean when we use this term. Next, we will describe the increasingly common experience of individuals who must negotiate different cultural realities in their everyday lives. Then we'll examine how culture influences our communication and present a dialectical perspective on intercultural communication. Finally, we'll discuss how society affects communication outcomes in intercultural interactions and provide suggestions for how one can become a more ethical and effective intercultural communicator.

Once you have read this chapter, you will be able to:

■ Identify four reasons for learning about intercultural communication.

■ Define *intercultural communication*.

■ Identify six cultural values that influence communication.

■ Describe the dialectical approach to intercultural communication.

■ Understand the role of power and privilege in communication between people from different cultural backgrounds.

■ Give three guidelines for communicating more ethically with people whose cultural backgrounds differ from your own.

■ Discuss three ways to improve your own intercultural communication skills.

THE IMPORTANCE OF INTERCULTURAL COMMUNICATION

How many reasons for studying intercultural communication can you think of? If you are like many students, entering college has given you more opportunities than ever before for intercultural contact, both domestically and internationally. You will communicate better in these situations if you have a good understanding of intercultural communication. In addition, increased knowledge and skill in intercultural communication can improve your career effectiveness, intergroup relations, and self-awareness. Let's look at each of these reasons more closely.

Increased Opportunities for Intercultural Contact

Experts estimate that twenty-five people cross national borders every second—1 billion journeys per year ("Numbers," 2008). People leave their countries for many reasons, including national revolutions and civil wars (Afghanistan, Yugoslavia, Congo, Sudan) and natural disasters (floods in Pakistan, earthquake in Haiti). Experts estimate there are currently 36 million displaced persons (United Nations High Commissioner for Refugees, 2009). Sometimes, in a process called **diaspora**, whole groups of people are displaced to new countries as they flee genocide or other untenable conditions or are taken forcefully against their will. Disaporic groups often attempt to settle together in communities in the new location while maintaining a strong ethnic identity and a desire to return home. Historically, diasporic groups include slaves taken from Africa in the 1700s and 1800s, Jews persecuted throughout centuries and relocating around the world, Chinese fleeing famine and wars in the 19th and 20th centuries, and Armenians escaping Turkish genocide in early 1900s (Pendery, 2008; Waterston, 2005). More recent diasporas include Cubans fleeing their homes during the revolution in 1959; Afghans fleeing the Soviet invasion and Iranians leaving when the Shah was deposed, both in 1979; and in the 1990s, Eritreans from Ethiopia, Albanians from Kosovo, and Chechnyans from Russia (Bernal, 2005; Koinova, 2010). Some experts refer to the current Latino diaspora (increasing numbers of Latin Americans who settle outside their homelands) or the Katrina diaspora (the thousands of Hurricane Katrina survivors who are still unable to return home) (Anderson, 2010). You can trace some of these diasporas and explore the global effects of these international migrations by visiting Stalker's Guide to International Migration (see Figure 8.1).

diaspora
group of immigrants, sojourners, slaves, or strangers living in new lands while retaining strong attachments to their homelands

FIGURE 8.1 Stalker's Guide to International Migration (diaspora migration map)

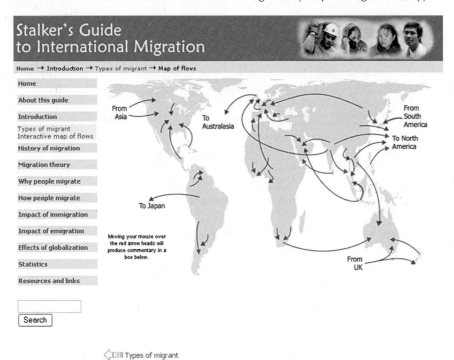

On this Web page (www.pstalker.com/migration/mg.map.htm), you can explore some of the global migration patterns of humans and some of the reasons why people move from their homelands.

Increasing numbers of people travel for pleasure, some 880 million in 2010 ("Tourism Highlights," 2010). Many people, like the student Kaori in the opening story, also travel for study. According to the Institute of International Education, approximately 700,000 international students study in the United States each year and approximately 250,000 U.S. students study overseas (IIE, 2010a, 2010b). Many students study abroad because of the exciting opportunities that exist for intercultural encounters, as exchange student Allison describes in *Did You Know? Meeting Other Travelers Adds Depth to Argentina Visit*.

Did You Know?

Meeting Other Travelers Adds Depth to Argentina Visit

Have you had experiences with people from other cultures that changed how you saw the world and/or the United States? If so, what was it about those interactions that changed your views? If you could change other countries' views of the United States, what would you want to tell them?

Allison, from the United States, is an exchange student in Argentina. Here's an excerpt from her travel blog:

We went to the North West last week; four of us stayed in a youth hostel there. I felt like I had discovered a secret that had been hidden from me all my life. I IMMEDIATELY felt at home. It was just a bunch of kids all traveling from all parts of the world just hanging

(continued)

Did You Know?   *(continued)*

out and meeting people and sharing all their stories. Our first friends we met were two Canadian kids who had been backpacking through South America the past two months. We spent a lot of time with them drinking mate (the traditional Argentine tea) and chatting about all their experiences in South America. There was a Venezuelan girl and a Japanese girl. It was a pleasure sharing a room with them. In talking to everyone I became even more aware of how misinformed about international news we are in America and how uncommon it is for us to actually be interested enough to really be concerned about what's going on in the rest of the world.

I had a really intriguing conversation with an Israeli soldier who had been traveling through South America during his time off. Hearing his stories was absolutely heartbreaking… all that he was forced to see and to do was absolutely awful! No one of any age should have to endure those things, and he's been doing it since he was 18. I guess that's how it is for people that live in countries where that's just their reality. They become accustomed to falling asleep with gun shots outside their window and getting up to go to work not having any idea what their day will hold and whether or not they'll die. It's awful and such a foreign concept to us; maybe we should make it more of a reality.…

SOURCE: Allison Nafziger Travel Blog. Reprinted by permission of Allison Nafziger.

Another source of increased opportunity for intercultural contact exists because of the increasing cultural diversity in the United States. Preliminary information from the 2010 census shows continuing dramatic increases in ethnic and racial diversity (Yen, 2011). As shown in Figure 8.2, the Hispanic population will triple in size and constitute approximately 30 percent of the population by 2050; in the same time period, the Asian American population will double in size and will constitute about 10 percent of the total population. African Americans will remain approximately the same in numbers and compose 13 percent of the population; Whites will continue to be a smaller majority as minority populations increase in number. The nation's elderly population will more than double in size from 2005 through 2050,

FIGURE 8.2 Population by Race and Ethnicity, Actual and Projected: 1960, 2005, and 2050 (percentage of total)

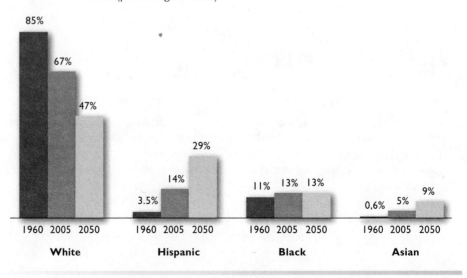

as the baby-boom generation enters the traditional retirement years. The number of working-age Americans and children will grow more slowly than the elderly population, and will shrink as a share of the total population (Passel & Cohn, 2008).

Of course, the Internet also provides increased opportunity for intercultural encounters. You could play chess with an opponent in Russia on a game site, debate rock climbing techniques with climbers from Norway to New Zealand on a sports discussion forum, or collaborate with students from around the country for a virtual team project in one of your classes. In the next sections of this chapter, we will discuss the opportunities that these types of contacts offer—and the benefits to be had from learning more about the intricacies of intercultural communication.

How multicultural is your circle of friends? How many of your friends differ from you in nationality, religion, class, gender, age, sexual orientation, or physical ability?

Enhanced Business Effectiveness

Studying intercultural communication can lead to greater success in both domestic and international business contexts. In the domestic context, the U.S. workforce is becoming increasingly diverse as the general population does the same. Furthermore, businesses are becoming more multinational as virtual communication makes it faster and cheaper to collaborate with vendors and customers around the globe. Many industries are also outsourcing services overseas to countries where wages are lower (e.g., Latin and South America, China, Vietnam) and sometimes to former colonies where the colonizer's language is already firmly established. For example, British and U.S. businesses have outsourced services to Ireland and India, and French businesses have sent jobs to Tunisia and Morocco (Bertrand, 2011).

Even though the trend toward globalization is no longer a new phenomenon, a primary cause for international business failures is still lack of attention to cultural factors. For example, when Disney Corporation established its Euro Disney outside Paris, the venture almost failed, in part because Disney executives mistakenly assumed they could transfer their U.S. cultural practices lock, stock, and barrel to the French context. French workers rebelled at the Disney dress code that mandated their hair and fingernail length; they also rebelled at being told they had to smile and act enthusiastic (also part of Disney code), and eventually they took their displeasure to court (Schneider & Barsoux, 2003).

What cultural differences prompted this displeasure? According to intercultural communication experts, the Disney policies went against French people's fundamental distrust of conformity and disrespect for mandated procedure (Hall & Hall, 1990, p. 106). Also, the notion of smiling constantly at work offended the French—contrary to the U.S. service industry's expectation for workers. The company seemed to learn from these cross-cultural challenges; it relaxed its rules on personal grooming for cast members and park employees, not only in France but in other countries. The most recent Disney venture in Hong Kong takes Chinese culture into consideration: green hats are not sold (green is associated with marital infidelity) and there are few clocks (the phrase for giving a clock sounds similar to that of attending the recipient's funeral) (Tai & Lau, 2009).

Improved Intergroup Relations

While we cannot blame all the world's political problems on ineffective intercultural communication, the need for better communication and understanding between countries and ethnic groups is clear. A case that is particularly important to U.S. citizens is improving relationships with people in the Middle East. Many experts think that to facilitate better relationships in this region the United States should establish meaningful contact with average citizens in the Muslim world, something that cannot be accomplished through military force or traditional diplomacy. One way to do this is to acquire intercultural knowledge and skills through learning the language, culture, and history of a country or region and being able to listen (Finn, 2003). U.S.-sponsored programs such as the Peace Corps and the

mediation
peaceful third-party intervention

Fulbright scholarship were designed with this kind of intercultural exchange and understanding in mind.

Intercultural communication expertise also can facilitate interethnic relations, which have frequently involved conflict. Consider the ethnic struggles in Bosnia and the former Soviet Union; the war between Hutus and Tutsis in Rwanda (Africa); the continued unrest in the Middle East; and the racial and ethnic struggles and tensions in neighborhoods of many U.S. cities. These conflicts often call for sophisticated skills of intercultural communication and **mediation**, or peaceful third-party intervention (Bercovitch & Derouen, 2004). For example, communication scholar Benjamin Broome (2004) has successfully facilitated interethnic relations on the island of Cyprus, one of the most heavily fortified regions in the world. Through his efforts, small groups of Greek and Turkish Cypriots have worked together to identify communication barriers and propose suggestions for improved relations between their two groups. It should be acknowledged, however, that even with mediation, miscommunication and intercultural conflicts can persist: witness the long-standing conflicts in the Middle East, where mediation has long been part of the attempts at resolution.

Improved communication and understanding between countries and ethnic groups may help in solving many of the world's political problems.

In some cases, people are not motivated to resolve intergroup conflict. Although we must admit that there is no easy cure-all for intercultural tensions and misunderstandings, intercultural communication skills are certainly valuable in this area.

Enhanced Self-Awareness

The final reason for studying intercultural communication is to increase self-awareness. This may seem like a contradiction, but it is not. Psychologist Peter Adler (1975) says that intercultural exploration begins as a journey into the cultures of others but often results in increased self-knowledge and understanding. People often learn more about themselves and their own cultural background and identities by coming into contact with people whose cultural backgrounds differ from their own, as our student discovered during her stay in South Africa (see *It Happened to Me: Susan*).

What you learn about intercultural communication may depend on your social and economic position. For example, individuals from minority racial and ethnic groups in the United States may learn to be a bit wary of intercultural interactions and expect some subtle slights—like a Chinese American colleague who is sometimes approached at professional meetings by White communication professors who assume she is a waitress and ask her to take their drink order!

On the other hand, White and middle-class individuals may find that intercultural learning includes an enhanced awareness of privilege—like a White colleague who tells of feeling uncomfortable staying at a Caribbean resort, where he was served by Blacks whose ancestors were brought there as slaves by Europeans colonizers. While he realized that it was his relative privilege

It Happened to Me: *Susan*

I rarely ever thought about being White or an American until my family and I spent a year in South Africa. Then, I thought about both every day, especially about my being White. The official language of South Africa is English, but even though we technically spoke the same language as the South Africans, my family and I had problems. It started when we were to be picked up from the airport in a *combie*, but I didn't know what that was. It turned out to be a van! Small pick-up trucks were *bakkies*, traffic signals were *robots*, and friends wanted to collect my *contact details*, which meant that they simply wanted the number of my *mobile*, better known as a cell phone, and our address. I felt that every time I opened my mouth, everyone *knew* I was American. The Black/White thing was even more pronounced. When we went down to the flea market or to the Zulu mass at the church we attended, we stood out like "five white golf balls on a black fairway" as my husband liked to say. I wondered if the self-consciousness I felt being White was the same as an African American has walking down the street in America.

that allows him to travel and experience new cultures and places, he also wondered whether this type of travel simply reproduces those same historical post-colonial economic patterns.

With these reasons for studying intercultural communication in mind, we need to define precisely what we mean by intercultural communication and culture, which is the subject we turn to next.

TEST YOUR KNOWLEDGE

- What are four reasons for studying intercultural communication?
- Of the reasons given, which do you think are most important? Can you think of other reasons?

WHAT IS INTERCULTURAL COMMUNICATION?

Generally speaking, **intercultural communication** refers to communication that occurs in interactions between people who are culturally different. This contrasts with most communication studies, which focus on communicators in the same culture. Still, in practice, intercultural communication occurs on a continuum, with communication between people who are relatively similar in cultural backgrounds on one end and people who are extremely different culturally on the other. For example, your conversations with your parents would represent a low degree of "interculturalness" because while you and your parents belong to two different cultural (age) groups, you probably have much in common—nationality, religion, and language. On the other hand, an interaction with a foreign teaching assistant who has a different nationality, language, religion, age, socioeconomic status, and gender would represent a high degree of interculturalness. While these two examples represent different ends on the continuum, they are both intercultural interactions. So you can see that many, if not most, of your daily interactions are intercultural in nature.

The two essential components of intercultural communication are, of course, culture and communication. Having read this far in your text, you should have a good understanding of communication. However, we think it is worthwhile to review our definition of **culture**. In Chapter 1, we defined culture as *learned patterns of perceptions, values, and behaviors shared by a group of people.* As we also mentioned, culture is dynamic (it changes), **heterogeneous** (diverse), and operates within societal power structures (Martin & Nakayama, 2008, p. 28). Next we explore how these features of culture impact individuals' intercultural interactions.

TEST YOUR KNOWLEDGE

- What is a definition of intercultural communication?
- What is meant by the phrase "culture is dynamic, heterogeneous, and operates within societal power structures"?

INTERCULTURAL COMMUNICATION AND THE INDIVIDUAL

However, not all cultural differences have equal impact on one's interactions. For example, while your parents may sometimes seem to come from a very different culture, age differences generally have a less dramatic effect on people's interactions than do ethnic and national differences. Here we will examine some of the cultural differences that affect individuals' interactions with one another. We begin by exploring three types of intercultural interactions that can occur when individuals from different cultures coexist. We then explore specific cultural values that shape individuals' communication experiences, and we conclude this section by examining the ways that individuals within a culture can be both similar to and different from one another.

intercultural communication
communication that occurs in interactions between people who are culturally different

culture
learned patterns of perceptions, values, and behaviors shared by a group of people

heterogeneous
diverse

Intercultural Communication on the Borders

Because of increased opportunities for cultural contact, more people find themselves living a multicultural life. Travelers, racial and ethnic groups that live in proximity, immigrants, and people whose intimate partners come from other cultural backgrounds are only some of the groups that live between cultures, or as **border dwellers**. Here we refer to people who live on cultural borders as border dwellers because they often experience contradictory cultural patterns; thus, they may have to move between ethnicities, races, religions, languages, socioeconomic classes, or sexual orientations. One can become a border dweller in one of three ways: through travel, through socialization (cocultural groups), and through participation in an intercultural relationship. Let's look at each in turn.

Border Dwellers Through Travel Individuals travel between cultures both voluntarily and involuntarily, and for both long and short periods. **Voluntary short-term travelers** include study-abroad students, corporate personnel, missionaries, and military people. **Voluntary long-term travelers** include immigrants who settle in other locations, usually seeking what they perceive is a better life, as is the case for many immigrants who come to the United States. **Involuntary short-term travelers** include refugees forced into cultural migration because of war, famine, or unbearable economic hardship. For example, many people fled Iraq during the first Gulf War and then returned when it was safe to do so (UNHCR, 2009). **Involuntary long-term travelers** are those who are forced to permanently migrate to a new location, including the many diasporic groups referred to earlier. For an illustration, see *Visual Summary 8.1: Border Dwellers Through Travel*.

When people think of traveling or living in a new culture, they tend to think that learning the language is key to effective intercultural interaction; however, intercultural communication involves much more than language issues. Most sojourners find there are two types of challenges: (1) dealing with the psychological stress of being in an unfamiliar environment (feeling somewhat uncertain and anxious) and (2) learning how to behave appropriately in the new culture, both verbally (e.g., learning a new language) and nonverbally (e.g., bowing instead of shaking hands in Japan) (Kim, 2005).

The first of these two challenges is often called *culture shock*. **Culture shock** is a feeling of disorientation and discomfort due to the unfamiliarity of surroundings and the lack of familiar cues in the environment. When travelers return home to their own country, they may experience similar feelings, known as **reverse culture shock** or **reentry shock**—a sort of culture shock in one's own country. After being gone for a significant amount of time, aspects of one's own culture may seem somewhat foreign, as the student Maham discovered on his return home to Pakistan after living in the United States for four years (see *It Happened to Me: Maham*).

Most travelers eventually adapt to the foreign culture to some extent if they stay long enough and if the hosts are welcoming. This is often the case for northern Europeans who visit or settle in the United States. Sometimes people even experience culture shock when they move from one region of the United States to another, such as someone who moves from Boston to Birmingham or from Honolulu to Minneapolis. The evacuation of tens of thousands of African American southerners from New Orleans after Hurricane Katrina highlighted this experience. Some of the evacuees were sent to stay in

It Happened to Me: *Maham*

I would say that I experienced culture (reentry) shock when I visited Pakistan after moving away from there four years ago. In those four years, I had basically forgotten the language and became very unfamiliar with the culture back home. Even though I enjoyed my visit to Pakistan a lot, I had problems adjusting to some of the ways of life. I was not familiar with the bargaining system… where people can go to the store and bargain for prices. I felt very out of place…. As I spent more time there, I got adjusted and used to how people did things there.

VISUAL SUMMARY 8.1   Border Dwellers Through Travel

	Voluntary	Involuntary

Voluntary

Involuntary

Short Term

Tourists, Missionaries,
Study Abroad Students

Temporay Refugees from War, Famine,
or Economic Hardship

Long Term

Immigrants

Permanent Refugees from War, Famine,
or Economic Hardship

the mostly White state of Utah; a number of them said that Utah was so different from what they were used to that the experience seemed unreal.

There are many reasons why an individual may be more, or less, successful at adapting to a new culture. Younger people who have had some previous traveling experience seem to be more successful than older people and first-time travelers. On the other hand, if the environment is hostile or the move is involuntary, adaptation may be especially difficult and the culture shock especially intense. For example, many evacuees from Hurricane Katrina were forced to relocate. In some instances, they were greeted with great sympathy and hospitality in the new locations; in other instances they were subjected to considerable racism ("Rabbi: My radio," 2005). Asian, African, and Latino students in the United States tend to have a more difficult adaptation due to experiences of discrimination and

Alternative **V I E W**
Immigrants

Why do you think people continue to have negative feelings toward recent immigrants, despite past, successful adaptations of earlier immigrant groups? What could we do to help people feel more comfortable with and accepting of new immigrants?

Some people in the United States think that compared to earlier immigrants, today's immigrants do not try hard enough to assimilate and learn English. Ivonne Figueroa, an immigrant herself, the editor of a monthly cultural and bilingual publication, and a student of business management and history, points out that this is not entirely true. She describes how patterns of immigrant assimilation (and anti-immigrant attitudes) have not changed all that much in the past 200 years. For example, she explains that the idea that earlier, non-Hispanic immigrants in the U. S. learned English quickly and easily adapted to their new country is really a myth. She says that, according to historical accounts, they mostly spoke their native language at home and even encouraged their children to do the same and to not assimilate too easily to the American culture. They also received some financial assistance from the U. S. government (similar to today's

welfare) to facilitate their settling in to their new country. Similar to today's immigrants, their children did learn English. By the third generation, the grandchildren of the original immigrants spoke only English.

Ms. Figueroa also describes how anti-immigrant attitudes were alive and well then, just like today. In fact, at the turn of the 20th century (about 100 years ago), immigration from Southern and Eastern Europe was restricted, and immigration from Asia was totally prohibited due to the Oriental Exclusion Act of 1882. She also notes that even as recently as the mid-20th century, strong anti-Catholic attitudes were common. And throughout American history, immigrant groups have been blamed for various national problems. Italians were blamed for the 1916 polio epidemic in New York City, and Jewish immigrants were accused of "diluting the nation's pioneer stock."

She concludes that, overall, recent immigrants have many things in common with earlier immigrants: most are here legally, most were poor in their country and struggle to survive here economically, most try to hold onto their cultural traditions, and most are feared by those who harbor anti-immigrant sentiments.

SOURCE: Figueroa, I. (n.d.). Immigrants. El Boricua: A monthly bilingual, cultural publication for Puerto Ricans, http://www.elboricua.com/index.html. Retrieved February 17, 2011 from http://www.elboricua.com/immigrants.html

hostility based on their race/ethnicity (Jung, Hecht, & Wadsworth, 2007; Lee & Rice, 2007). While we may think that anti-immigrant attitudes are a recent phenomenon in the United States because of the number of immigrants or where they come from, one writer suggests that today's immigrants have much in common with earlier immigrants—including anti-immigrant attitudes (see *Alternative View: Immigrants*).

For diasporic groups, whether relocated within their own country or in a foreign country, the culture shock and disorientation can be complicated and even extended due to their strong desire to return home and feeling of rootlessness. Alisse Waterston (2005) recounts the story of her Jewish father's struggles: as a young boy in the 1920s, he narrowly escaped being killed in the horrific massacre of Jews in the small town of Jedwabne, Poland; he resettled in Cuba, then fled again to the United States after the Cuban revolution in the 1960s. Although he achieved economic and professional success, his daughter observes that he never got over:

...the feelings of isolation and loneliness that come from being cast out, from forced absence. I can barely stand all the tears...so often describes himself and his family in the process of running, suffering and barely surviving. My father hasn't ever stopped running, remains confused and still lost....having traveled through the twentieth century, my father remains burdened by the defining events of the century. (p. 56)

One thing that can ease culture shock and make cultural adaptation easier is having a social support network. This can come from organizations like an international student office or a tourist bureau that can assist with housing, transportation, and so forth. Close relationships with other travelers or host-country acquaintances can also provide support in the form of a sympathetic ear; through these relationships sojourners can relieve stress, discuss, problem-solve, acquire new knowledge, or just have fun (Kashima & Loh, 2006; Lin, 2006).

The role of social support is even more crucial for long-term travelers, such as immigrants. Diasporic individuals often maintain strong relationships with other members of their group, providing for each this much needed social support, sometimes through cyber communities or in face-to-face interaction (Bernal, 2005; Pendery, 2008). If there is little social support or the receiving environment is hostile, immigrants may choose to separate from the majority or host culture, or they may be forced into separation (Berry, 2005).

Another option for immigrants is to adapt in *some* ways to the new culture, which means accepting some aspects, such as dress and outward behavior, while retaining aspects of the old culture. For many recent immigrants to the United States, this has been a preferred option and seems to lead to less stress. For example, Asian Indians constitute one of the largest immigrant groups in the United States. Many have successfully adapted to U.S. life both professionally and socially. Still many retain viable aspects of their Indian culture in their personal and family lives—continuing to celebrate ethnic or religious holidays and adhering to traditional values and beliefs (Hegde, 2000). However, this integration of two cultures is not always easy, as we'll see in the next section. Families can be divided on the issues of how much to adapt, with children often wanting to be more "American" and parents wanting to hold on to their native language and cultural practices (Ward, 2008).

Border Dwellers Through Socialization The second group of border dwellers is composed of people who grow up living on the borders between cultural groups. Examples include ethnic groups, such as Latinos, Asian Americans, and African Americans, who live in the predominantly White United States, as well as people who grow up negotiating multiple sexual orientations or religions. In addition to those who must negotiate the two cultures they live within, the United States has increasing numbers of multiracial people who often grow up negotiating *multiple* cultural realities. The 2000 Census form was the first that allowed people to designate more than two races—and since then, the group of people who choose to categorize themselves as multiracial has grown faster than any other (Yen, 2011).

Probably the best known multiracial U.S. American today is President Barack Obama—his father was an exchange student from Kenya and his mother a U.S. American student. Other famous multiracial U.S. Americans include Vin Diesel, who is Black and Italian American; Dwayne Johnson (also known as the "Rock"), who is Black and Samoan; and Tiger Woods, who is African American, European American, and Thai. Genetic experts point out that many of these multiracial individuals could only have been born in the twentieth century. Their complex web of ancestors, originating from distant world regions, could have encountered each other in the United States only within the past 100 years (Wells, 2002).

Typically, cultural minorities are socialized to the norms and values of both the dominant culture and their own; nonetheless, they

Border dwellers through socialization include many multiracial individuals and families. How might the concept of border dwellers change as these many children grow up?

often prefer to enact those of their own. They may be pressured to assimilate to the dominant culture and embrace its values, yet those in the dominant culture may still be reluctant to accept them as they try to do so (Berry, 2005). For example, a German woman whose family came from Turkey encountered teachers in Germany who perceived her to be part of a Turkish minority and thus had low expectations for her performance (Ewing, 2004). And members of minority groups sometimes find themselves in a kind of cultural limbo—not "gay" enough for gay friends, not "straight" enough for the majority; not Black enough or White enough.

All of the multiracial U.S. Americans we discuss above have had to respond, at some point, to criticism that they did not sufficiently align themselves with one or another of their racial groups. During the 2008 presidential campaign, President Obama was criticized for being "too white." Vin Diesel has been criticized for refusing to discuss his Black racial heritage while Dwayne Johnson originally was condemned for not recognizing his Black heritage but later was praised for attending the Black Entertainment Television awards.

Border Dwellers Through Relationships Finally, many people live on cultural borders because they have intimate partners whose cultural background differs from their own. Within the United States increasing numbers of people cross borders of nationality, race, and ethnicity in this way, creating a "quiet revolution" (Root, 2001). Overall, partners in interethnic and interracial romantic relationships have faced greater challenges than those establishing relationships across religions, nationalities, and class groups.

Did you know that until June 12, 1967, it was illegal in Virginia (and 13 other states) for Whites and Blacks to marry? This ban against miscegenation (interracial sexual relationships) was challenged in Virginia by Mildred and Richard Loving, who had been married in 1958 in Washington, D.C. (where interracial marriages were permitted). In 1967, the Supreme Court declared Virginia's anti-miscegenation ban unconstitutional, thereby ending all race-based legal restrictions on marriage in the United States. Attitudes toward intercultural relationships have changed significantly in the ensuing decades, particularly attitudes toward interracial relations (Taylor, Funk, & Craighill, 2006). For example, in recent surveys, 77 percent of respondents said it's all right for Blacks and Whites to date each other—up from 48 percent who felt this way in 1987. The young are the most accepting; 91 percent of respondents born after 1976 said that interracial dating is acceptable—compared with 50 percent of the oldest generation (Kreager, 2008; Levin, Taylor, & Caudle, 2007).

However, such relationships are not without their challenges, as described in *Did You Know? Sobering Advice for Anyone Contemplating a Cross-Cultural Marriage.* The most common challenges involve negotiating how to live on the border between two religions, ethnicities, races, languages, and, sometimes, value systems. A recent study of intercultural marriages, some based on religious and some on racial and ethnic differences, found that communication played an important role in the success of these relationships. That is, open communication about the differences helped promote relationship growth. If partners were able to understand, appreciate, and integrate each other's similarities and differences, they would be able to use these in an enriching manner (Reiter & Gee, 2009).

The balancing act between cultures can be especially challenging when friends, family, and society disapprove (Fiebert, Nugent, Hershberger, & Kasdan, 2004). A Jewish professor who married a Muslim woman reflects on how people would react if he decided to convert to Islam:

What a scandalous action! My family would be outraged and my friends startled. What would they say? How would I be treated? What would colleagues at the university do if I brought a prayer rug to the office and, say, during a committee meeting, or at a reception for a visiting scholar, insisted on taking a break to do my ritual prayers? (Rosenstone, 2005, p. 235)

Did You Know?

Sobering Advice for Anyone Contemplating a Cross-Cultural Marriage

How useful do you think this advice would be for people entering cross-cultural marriages and romantic partnerships? How helpful do you think it would be for people who are forming romantic partnerships with someone from their own culture?

This hard-won advice is intended only for those couples who are truly considering entering into a cross-cultural marital situation. Simply marrying someone whose ancestry is different from your own is not quite the same thing.

My personal experience centers around the relationship between a Japanese female and an American male, although I'd like to think that the basic ideas could be applied to any cross-cultural situation.

Rule #1: *Don't assume that your interest in your partner's culture will last, or that it will somehow prevent conflicts from occurring.* Never underestimate the depth of the roots of your own upbringing. Your beliefs, your emotions, your priorities, in short, your whole approach to life, are shaped by the culture in which you were brought up.

Rule #2: *Don't assume that the other person will change significantly just because of the relationship or because of your charming influence.* The best thing you can do for each other is to acknowledge the fact that conflicts will occur and will often occur for the simplest and most unexpected reasons.

Rule #3: *Don't assume anything. Make sure you discuss with your partner every aspect of your future life together.* Also, don't assume that when your partner says something is unimportant that it does not have to be discussed. Those areas are often the *most* important things to discuss.

Rule #4: *Make it a point to talk about some tough topics (like money, raising children, where to live, etc.) before making those wedding arrangements.* Start an argument or two. Find out what it's like to fight by your partner's rules. You might as well know whether you will be able to work together toward a solution when the inevitable crisis comes up.

Rule #5: *Make sure that between the two of you, there is at least one language in which you are both fluent.* As a test, try taking some very subtle feeling or belief and explain it to your potential mate. Have him or her explain it back. If there is not a substantial understanding of what you explained, wait a while until one or the other of you is able to achieve a good degree of fluency in the other's language.

Rule #6: *Examine your own motives.* Is this someone you would hook up with even if you were safe and happy in your own country? If you are the partner who is trying to live in another culture, remember this: Culture shock can do funny things to a normally rational mind. First get yourself comfortable with your surroundings. Disarm the "convenience" in the relationship and then see what you think. Learn more about the subtle parts of your partner's culture and then decide if you can tolerate, work with, and actually love that person because they are different and not *despite* those differences.

Rule #7: *Don't underestimate the importance of keeping good relations with your partner's parents.* This is especially true if your partner is the one from Japan (or some other non-Western culture). It seems that we in the U.S. (and I can hardly speak for any other Western cultures) have developed a great deal of independence from our families. However, the same is not true in Japan. There is still a great deal of synergy between parent and offspring, even well after they have left the nest and formed families of their own. If you can't get their active support, then at least settle for passive acceptance. Anything less should be a sign of trouble ahead.

(continued)

These challenges can be even more pronounced for women, since parents often play an important role in whom they date and marry. A recent study found that women were much more likely than men to mention pressure from family members as a reason that interethnic dating would be difficult (Clark-Ibanez & Felmlee, 2004).

Negotiating Cultural Tensions on the Borders How do people negotiate the tensions between often-contradictory systems of values, language, and nonverbal behavior of two or more cultures? The answer depends on many factors, such as one's reason for being on the border, length of stay or involvement, receptivity of the dominant culture, and personality characteristics of the individuals (Kim, 2005).

In most cases, people in such situations can feel caught between two systems; this experience has been described as feeling as if one were swinging on a trapeze, a metaphor that captures the immigrant's experience of vacillating between the cultural patterns of the homeland and the new country (Hegde, 1998). Writer Gloria Anzaldúa (1999), who is Chicana, gay, and female, stresses that living successfully on the border requires significant flexibility and an active approach to negotiating multiple cultural backgrounds. She struggles to balance her Indian and Spanish heritage, as well as her patriarchal Catholic upbringing, with her spiritual and sexual identity. The result, she says, is the *mestiza*—a person who has actively confronted and managed the negative aspects of living on the border.

Americans have become much more accepting of Black-White marriages and dating relationships over the past few decades.

Similarly, communication scholar Lisa Flores (1996) shows how Chicana feminist writers and artists acknowledge negative stereotypes of Mexican and Mexican American women—illiterate Spanglish-speaking laborers, passive sex objects, servants of men and children—and transform them into images of strength. In their descriptions and images, Chicana artists are strong, clever bilinguals, reveling in their dual Anglo-Mexican heritage. In so doing, they create a kind of positive identity "home" where they are the center. In addition, they gain strength by reaching out to other women (women of color and immigrant women), and together strive to achieve more justice and recognition for women who live "in the middle" between cultural worlds.

Managing these tensions while living on the border and being multicultural can be both rewarding and challenging. Based on data from interviews she conducted, Janet Bennett (1998) described two types of border dwellers or, as she labeled them, "marginal individuals": *encapsulated marginal people* and *constructive marginal people.*

encapsulated marginal people people who feel disintegrated by having to shift cultures

Encapsulated marginal people feel disintegrated by having to shift cultures. They have difficulty making decisions and feel extreme pressure from both groups. They try to assimilate but never feel comfortable or at home.

constructive marginal people people who thrive in a border-dweller life, while recognizing its tremendous challenges

In contrast, **constructive marginal people** thrive in their "border" life and, at the same time, recognize its tremendous challenges, as Gloria Anzaldúa described.

They see themselves as choice makers. They recognize the significance of being "in between," and they continuously negotiate and explore this identity.

To summarize, people can find themselves living on cultural borders for many reasons: travel, socialization, or involvement in an intercultural relationship. While border dwelling can be challenging and frustrating, it also can lead to cultural insights and agility in navigating intercultural encounters.

TEST YOUR KNOWLEDGE
- How do individuals come to live on cultural borders?
- What are some benefits and challenges to border dwelling?

The Influence of Cultural Values on Communication

In Chapters 5 and 6, we described how culture influences verbal and nonverbal communication. You might think that these differences would be key to understanding intercultural communication. Just as important is understanding **cultural values,** which are the beliefs that are so central to a cultural group that they are never questioned. Cultural values prescribe what *should* be. Understanding cultural values is essential because they so powerfully influence people's behavior, including their communication. Intercultural interaction often involves confronting and responding to an entirely different set of cultural values. Let's see how this works.

About fifty years ago, anthropologists Florence Kluckhohn and Fred Strodtbeck (1961) conducted a study that identified the contrasting values of three cultural groups in the United States: Latinos, Anglos, and American Indians. Later, social psychologist Geert Hofstede (1997, 1998, 2001) and his colleagues extended this analysis in a massive study, collecting 116,000 surveys about people's value preferences in approximately eighty countries around the world. Psychologist Michael Bond and his colleagues conducted a similar, though smaller, study in Asia ("Chinese Culture Connection," 1987). Together, these studies identified cultural values preferred by people in a number of countries, six of which are listed in *Visual Summary 8.2: Cultural Values and Communication* and discussed in the following sections. While these value preferences may apply most directly to national cultural groups, they can also apply to ethnic/racial groups, socioeconomic class groups, and gender groups.

As you read about these cultural value orientations, please keep three points in mind. These guidelines reflect a common dilemma for intercultural communication scholars—the desire to describe and understand communication and behavior patterns within a cultural group and the fear of making rigid categories that can lead to stereotyping:

1. The following discussion describes the *predominant* values preferred by various cultural groups, not the values held by *every person* in the cultural group. Think of cultural values as occurring on a bell curve: Most people may be in the middle, holding a particular value orientation, but many people can be found on each end of the curve; these are the people who *do not go along* with the majority.

2. The following discussion refers to values on the cultural level, not on the individual level. Thus, if you read that most Chinese tend to prefer an indirect way of speaking, you cannot assume that every Chinese person you meet will speak in an indirect way in every situation.

3. The only way to understand what a particular individual believes is to get to know the person. You can't predict how any one person will communicate. The real challenge is to understand the full range of cultural values and then learn to communicate effectively with others who hold differing value orientations, regardless of their cultural background.

Now that you understand the basic ground rules, let's look at six key aspects of cultural values.

cultural values
beliefs that are so central to a cultural group that they are never questioned

VISUAL SUMMARY 8.2   **Cultural Values and Communication**

Individualistic/Collectivistic

Highly
Individualistic ←——————————————————————————————→ Highly
                                                  Collectivistic

- North American
- Northern European

- South American
- Asian
- Hispanic and Asian Americans
  in the United States

Preferred Personality

More Important
"to Do" ←——————————————————————————————→ More Important
                                          "to Be"

- European Americans
- Asian Americans
- African Americans

- African Americans
- Latinos

View of Human Nature

Humans Are
Fundamentally Evil ←——————————————————————————→ Humans Are
                                                 Fundamentally Good

- United States

- Middle East
- United States

Human–Nature Value

Humans Intended   Harmony   Nature Intended
to Rule Nature ←——————————————————————————————→ to Rule Humans

- United States

- American
  Indians
- Asians

- Middle East
- United States

Power Distribution

Equal Distribution
of Power ←——————————————————————————————→ Unequal Distribution
                                           of Power

- Denmark
- Israel
- New Zealand

- Mexico
- Philippines
- India

Long-Term Versus Short-Term Orientation

Short-Term
Orientation ←——————————————————————————————→ Long-Term
                                              Orientation

- Judaism
- Christianity
- Islam
- (monotheistic religions)

- Confucianism
- Hinduism
- Buddhism
- Shintoism
- (polytheistic religions)

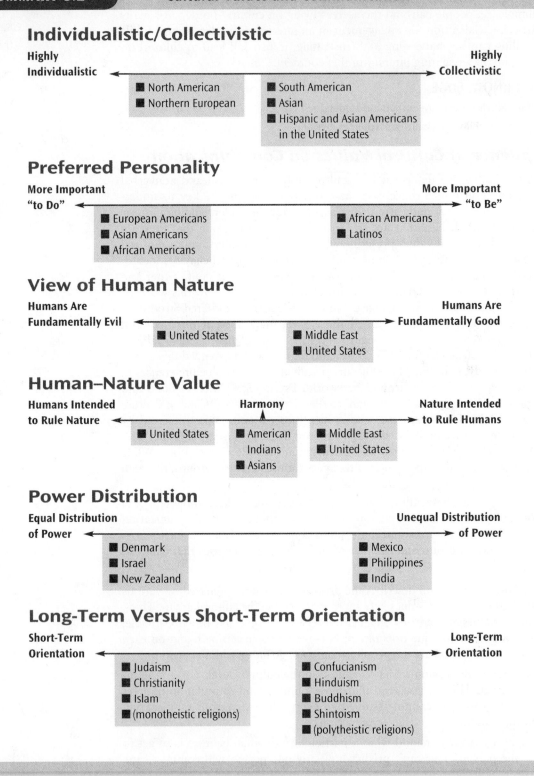

Individualism and Collectivism One of the most central value orientations identified in this research addresses whether a culture emphasizes the rights and needs of the individual or that of the group. For example, many North American and northern European cultural groups, particularly U.S. Whites, value individualism and independence, believing that one's primary responsibility is to one's self (Bellah, Madsen, Sullivan, Swidler, & Tipton, 1996; Hofstede, 2001; Kikoski & Kikoski, 1999). In relationships, as Kaori discovered in our opening vignette, those with this **individualist orientation** respect autonomy and independence, and they do not meddle in another's problems unless invited. For example, in cultures where individualism prevails, many children are raised to be autonomous and to live on their own by late adolescence (although they may return home for short periods after this). Their parents are expected to take care of themselves and not "be a burden" on their children when they age (Triandis, 1995).

In individualistic cultures, children are raised to be autonomous and to live on their own by late adolescence, while parents are expected to not "be a burden" on their children when they age.

As you were growing up, in what ways were you reared to be individualistic? Collectivistic? Which orientation was the predominant cultural value of your family?

In contrast, many cultures in South America and Asia hold a more **collectivistic orientation** that stresses the needs of the group (Hofstede, 2001; Triandis, 1995), as do some Hispanic and Asian Americans in the United States (Ho, 1987). Some argue that working-class people tend to be more collectivistic than those in the middle or upper class (Dunbar, 1997). For collectivists, the primary responsibility is to relationships with others; interdependence in family, work, and personal relationships is viewed positively. Collectivists value working toward relationship and group harmony over remaining independent and self-sufficient. For example, giving money to a needy cousin, uncle, or aunt might be preferable to spending it on oneself. In many collectivist cultures, too, children often defer to parents when making important decisions (McGoldrick, Giordano, & Pearce, 1996). A U.S. American software consultant who has done extensive employment interviewing with software professionals in India has observed that the cultural tradition of respecting one's parents is very prevalent in India. He is particularly struck by how often adult professionals consult with their parents before deciding whether to accept a job (Budelman, 2006).

As noted earlier, however, not all Japanese or all Indians are collectivistic. In fact, generational differences may exist within countries where collectivism is strong. For example, some Japanese college students show a strong preference for individualism while their parents hold a more collectivistic orientation—which sometimes leads to intercultural conflict (Matsumoto, 2002). Young people in many Asian countries (Korea, Vietnam) are increasingly influenced by Western capitalism and individualism and are now making their own decisions regarding marriage and career, rather than following their family's wishes—a practice unheard of fifty years ago (Shim, Kim, & Martin, 2008). In addition, not all cultures are as individualistic as U.S. culture or as collectivistic as Japanese culture. Rather, cultures can be arranged along an individualism–collectivism continuum (Gudykunst & Lee, 2002) based on their specific orientations to the needs of the individual and the group.

Preferred Personality In addition to differing on the individualism–collectivism spectrum, cultural groups may differ over the idea of the **preferred personality,** or whether it is more important to "do" or to "be" (Kluckhohn & Strodtbeck, 1961). In the United States, researchers have found that *doing* is the preferred value for many people (Stewart & Bennett, 1991), including European Americans, Asian Americans, and African Americans (Ting-Toomey, 1999). In general, the "doing mode" means working hard to achieve material gain, even if it means sacrificing time with family and friends (Kohls, 2001). Other cultural groups, for example, many Latinos, prefer the *being* mode—which emphasizes the importance of experiencing life and the people around them fully and "working to live" rather than "living to work" (Hecht, Sedano, & Ribeau, 1993).

individualist orientation
a value orientation that respects the autonomy and independence of individuals

collectivistic orientation
a value orientation that stresses the needs of the group

preferred personality
a value orientation that expresses whether it is more important for a person to "do" or to "be"

In many collectivist cultures, adult children often defer to parents when making important decisions.

Some scholars suggest that many African Americans express both a doing mode (fighting actively against racism through social activity for the good of the community) and a being mode (valuing a sense of vitality and open expression of feeling) (Hecht, Jackson, & Ribeau, 2002). Cultural differences in this value orientation can lead to communication challenges. For example, many Latinos believe that Anglos place too much emphasis on accomplishing tasks and earning money and not enough emphasis on spending time with friends and family or enjoying the moment (Kikoski & Kikoski, 1999).

A third value difference concerns the **view of human nature**—in particular, whether humans are considered fundamentally good, evil, or a mixture. The United States, for example, was founded by the Puritans who believed that human nature was fundamentally evil (Hulse, 1996). In the years since the founding of the country, a shift occurred in this view, as evidenced in the U.S. legal and justice systems. It emphasizes rehabilitation, suggesting a view of humans as potentially good. In addition, the fact that the U.S. justice system assumes people are innocent until proven guilty indicates that people are viewed as basically good (Kohls, 2001).

In contrast, cultural groups that view humans as essentially evil, such as some fundamentalist religions, emphasize punishment over rehabilitation. Some evidence indicates that U.S. Americans in general are moving again toward this view of human nature. For example, recent laws such as the "three strikes rule" emphasize punishment over rehabilitation by automatically sending to prison anyone who is convicted three times. Also, incarceration rates in the United States have increased by more than 500 percent since the early 1970s, and among developed countries, the United States now has the highest percentage of incarcerated individuals (Shelden, 2004). As you might imagine, people who differ on the question of human nature can have serious disagreements on public policies concerning crime and justice.

What kinds of communication problems might occur when members of a diverse work team hold different value orientations toward being and doing? How might someone who usually uses a being mode view someone with a doing mode, and vice versa?

Human–Nature Value A fourth value that varies from culture to culture is the perceived relationship between humans and nature, or the **human–nature value orientation**. At one end of this value continuum is the view that humans are intended to rule nature. At the other extreme, nature is seen as ruling humans. In a third option, the two exist in harmony. Unsurprisingly, the predominant value in the United States has been one of humans ruling over nature, as evidenced in the proliferation of controlled environments. Phoenix, Arizona, for example, which is in a desert, has more than 200 golf courses—reflecting the fact that Arizonans have changed the natural environment to suit their living and leisure interests. In other parts of the United States, people make snow for skiing, seed clouds when rain is needed, dam and reroute rivers, and use fertilizer to enhance agricultural production. Such interventions generally reflect a belief in human control over nature (Trompenaars & Hampden-Turner, 1997).

In contrast, many in the Middle East view nature as having predominance over humans. This belief that one's fate is held by nature is reflected in the common Arabic saying *"Enchallah"* ("Allah willing"), suggesting that nature will (and should) determine, for example, how crops will grow. A comparable Christian saying is "God willing," reflecting perhaps a similar fatalistic tendency in Christianity. Interestingly, many Spanish-speaking Christians express the same sentiment with the word *"Ojalá,"* which is rooted in *"Enchallah"* and originates from the centuries when southern Spain was a Muslim province.

Many American Indians and Asians value harmony with nature. People who hold this cultural orientation believe that humans and nature are one and that nature enriches human life. For many traditional American Indians, certain animals such as

view of human nature
a value orientation that expresses whether humans are fundamentally good, evil, or a mixture

human–nature value orientation
the perceived relationship between humans and nature

buffalo and eagles are important presences in human activity (Porter, 2002). For example, a yearly "Good Buffalo Festival" is held in Kyle, South Dakota, to educate young Indians about the importance of the buffalo in Lakota culture (Melmer, 2004). Many native cultures believe eagles carry messages to the Creator, and they use eagle feathers in many solemn, sacred ceremonies. The use of feathers can be an important part of the sundance, a religious ceremony practiced by many different American Indian groups. In this ceremony the eagle is viewed as the link between humans and creator. When people see an eagle in the sky during a ceremony, they are especially thankful, since the eagle flies highest of all birds and the moment it disappears into the skies, people's prayers are heard. These traditions show high regard and utmost respect for these animals and reflect a belief in the close and important relationship between humans and nature ("Zuni eagle aviary is a beautiful sign," 2002).

Reverence for nature plays an important role in many American Indian ceremonies.

In the United States, differences arise between real estate developers, who believe that humans take precedence over nature, and environmentalists and many Native American groups, who believe that nature is as important as humans. This conflict has surfaced in many disagreements; for example, in controversies over water rights in Oregon (Hemmingsen, 2002) and over the proposed eight-million-acre habitat for the endangered spotted owl in the southwestern United States (McKinnon, 2004).

Power Distance Power distance, the fifth value orientation, refers to the extent to which less powerful members of institutions and organizations within a culture expect and accept an unequal distribution of power (Hofstede, 2001). In Denmark, Israel, and New Zealand many people value small power distances. Thus, most people in those countries believe that inequality, while inevitable, should be minimized, and that the best leaders emphasize equality and informality in interactions with subordinates. In many situations, subordinates are expected to speak up and contribute.

Societies that value large power distance—for example, Mexico, the Philippines, and India—are structured more around a hierarchy in which each person has a rightful place, and interactions between supervisors and subordinates are more formal (Hofstede, 2001). Seniority, age, rank, and titles are emphasized more in these societies than in small power distance societies.

People who are used to large power distances may be uncomfortable in settings where hierarchy is unclear or ambiguous. For example, international students who come from countries where a large power distance value predominates may initially be very uncomfortable in U.S. college classrooms, where relations between students and teachers are informal and characterized by equality, a situation described in *It Happened to Me: Nagesh.*

In contrast, U.S. Americans abroad often offend locals when they treat subordinates at work or home too informally—calling them by their first names, treating them as if they were friends.

It Happened to Me: *Nagesh*

I was amazed when I first saw American classrooms. The students seemed very disrespectful toward the teacher. They had their feet on the desks and interrupted the teacher while he was talking if they didn't understand something. In my country (India), students would never behave this way toward a teacher. I found it difficult to speak up in this kind of classroom situation.

For example, when former President Bush visited Europe, he referred to the Belgian Prime Minister by his first name, Guy. This surprised and amused many Belgians, who are accustomed to more formality.

Note that value orientations often represent a cultural ideal rather than a reality. While many Americans say they desire small power distance, the truth is that rigid social and economic hierarchies exist in the United States. Most Americans are born into and live within the same socioeconomic class for their whole lives (Herbert, 2005).

power distance
a value orientation that refers to the extent to which less powerful members of institutions and organizations within a culture expect and accept an unequal distribution of power

Long-Term Versus Short-Term Orientation The research identifying the five values we've described has been criticized for its predominately western European bias. In response to this criticism, a group of Chinese researchers developed and administered a similar, but more Asian-oriented, questionnaire to people in twenty-two countries around the world ("Chinese Culture Connection," 1987). They then compared their findings to previous research on value orientations and found considerable overlap, especially on the dimensions of individualism versus collectivism and power distance. These researchers did identify one additional value dimension that earlier researchers hadn't seen—**long-term versus short-term orientation**.

This dimension reflects a society's attitude toward virtue or truth. A **short-term orientation** characterizes cultures in which people are concerned with possessing one fundamental truth, as reflected in the **monotheistic** (belief in one god) religions of Judaism, Christianity, and Islam. Other qualities identified in the research and associated with a short-term orientation include an emphasis on quick results, individualism, and personal security and safety (Hofstede, 1997).

In contrast, a **long-term orientation** tends to respect the demands of virtue, reflected in Eastern religions such as Confucianism, Hinduism, Buddhism, and Shintoism, which are all **polytheistic** religions (belief in more than one god). Other qualities associated with a long-term orientation include thrift, perseverance and tenacity in whatever one attempts, and a willingness to subordinate oneself for a purpose (Bond, 1991, 1996).

While knowing about these value differences can help you identify and understand problems that arise in intercultural interactions, you might be concerned that this approach to the study of intercultural communication leads to generalizing and stereotyping. The next section presents an approach that helps counteract this tendency to think in simplistic terms about intercultural communication.

A Dialectic Approach

Dialectics has long existed as a concept in philosophical thought and logic. In this book we introduce it as a way to emphasize simultaneous contradictory truths. Thus, a **dialectic approach** helps people respond to the complexities of intercultural communication and to override any tendencies to stereotype people based on cultural patterns. This concept may be difficult to understand because it is contrary to most formal education in the United States, which often emphasizes **dichotomous thinking,** in which things are "either/or"—good or bad, big or small, right or wrong. However, a dialectic approach recognizes that things may be "both/and." For example, a palm tree may be weak *and* strong. Its branches look fragile and weak, and yet in a hurricane it remains strong because the "weak" fronds can bend without breaking. Similar dialectics exist in intercultural communication; for example, Didier may be a Frenchman who shares many cultural characteristics of other French people, but he also is an individual who possesses characteristics that make him unique. So, he is both similar to and different from other French people. A dialectic approach emphasizes the fluid, complex, and contradictory nature of intercultural interactions. Dialectics exist in other communication contexts such as relationships, which we explore in Chapter 9. Six dialectics that can assist you in communicating more effectively in intercultural interactions are discussed next.

Cultural–Individual This dialectic emphasizes that some behaviors, such as ways of relating to others, are determined by our culture, while others are simply idiosyncratic, or particular to us as individuals. For example, Robin twists her hair while she talks. This idiosyncratic personal preference should not be mistaken for a cultural norm. She doesn't do it because she is female, or young, or Protestant, or African American. Although it isn't always easy to tell whether a behavior is culturally or individually based, taking a dialectic approach means that one does not immediately assume that someone's behavior is culturally based.

Personal–Contextual This dialectic focuses on the importance of context or situation in intercultural communication. In any intercultural encounter, both the

---

long-term versus short-term orientation
the dimension of a society's value orientation that reflects its attitude toward virtue or truth

short-term orientation
a value orientation that stresses the importance of possessing one fundamental truth

monotheistic
belief in one god

long-term orientation
a value orientation in which people stress the importance of virtue

polytheistic
belief in more than one god

dialectic approach
recognizes that things need not be perceived as "either/or," but may be seen as "both/and"

dichotomous thinking
thinking in which things are perceived as "either/or"—for example, "good or bad," "big or small," "right or wrong"

individual and the situation are simultaneously important. Let's take the example of a French and an American student striking up a conversation in a bar. The immediate situation has an important impact on their communication, so their conversation would probably differ dramatically if it occurred at a synagogue, mosque, or church. The larger situation, including political and historical forces, also plays a role. In the build-up to the Iraq War of 2003, for example, some French students encountered anti-French sentiment in the United States. At the same time, the characteristics of the specific individuals also affect the exchange. Some students would ignore the immediate or larger situation and reject the anti-French sentiment—especially if they were opposed to the war themselves. Others would attach great importance to the larger context and view the French students negatively. The point is that reducing an interaction to a mere meeting of two individuals means viewing intercultural communication too simplistically.

Differences–Similarities Real, important differences exist between cultural groups; we've identified some of these in this chapter. However, important commonalities exist as well. One of our students summed up this point nicely in *It Happened to Me: Angelina*.

Static–Dynamic While some cultural patterns remain relatively stable and static for years, they also can undergo dynamic change. For example, many people form impressions about Indians from popular films like *Smoke Signals*—or

> ### It Happened to Me: *Angelina*
>
> In my first year of college, I had the most memorable friendship with a person from the Middle East. Through this friendship I learned a lot about the way people from the Middle East communicate with friends, family, and authority. My new friend and I differed in many ways—in religion, culture, nationality, race, and language. However, we were both female college students, the same age, and we shared many interests. She dressed like I did and styled her hair similarly, and we shared many ideas about the future and concerns about the world.

even children's movies like *Pocahontas* or *The Indian in the Cupboard*, which portray Indians living the rural life they lived centuries ago—even though the majority of Indians in the U.S. today live in urban areas (Alexie, 2003). A static–dynamic dialectic requires that you recognize both traditional and contemporary realities of a culture.

History/Past–Present/Future An additional dialectic in intercultural communication focuses on the present and the past. For example, one cannot fully understand contemporary relations between Arabs and Jews, Muslims and Christians, or Catholics and Protestants without knowing something of their history. At the same time, people cannot ignore current events. For example, the conflict over where Yasser Arafat was to be buried in the autumn of 2004 flowed from a complex of historical and contemporary relations. His family had resided for generations in Jerusalem and wanted him laid to rest there. Israel, having current control of Jerusalem and viewing Arafat as a terrorist leader of attacks against Israel, refused.

While being White involves cultural advantages, being poor involves disadvantages.

Privilege–Disadvantage In intercultural interactions, people can be simultaneously privileged and disadvantaged (Johnson, 2006). This can become quite clear when one travels to developing countries. While U.S. Americans may be privileged in having more money and the luxury of travel, they can also feel vulnerable in foreign countries if they are ignorant of the local languages and customs. Poor Whites in the United States can be simultaneously privileged because they are White and disadvantaged due to their economic plight. As a student, you may feel privileged (compared to others) in that you are acquiring a high level of education, but you may also feel economically disadvantaged because of the high cost of education.

This dialectic approach helps us resist making quick, stereotypical judgments about others and their communication behavior. A single person can have individualistic and collectivistic tendencies, can be both culturally similar and different from us, and can be culturally privileged in some situations and culturally disadvantaged in others. All these elements affect communication in both business and personal relationships.

TEST YOUR KNOWLEDGE

* Identify six common core values that differentiate various cultural groups.
* How might these values influence intercultural communication?
* How does adopting a dialectical perspective help us avoid stereotyping and prejudice?

THE INDIVIDUAL, INTERCULTURAL COMMUNICATION, AND SOCIETY

As you have probably gathered by now, intercultural communication never occurs in a vacuum but must be understood in the context of larger societal forces. In this section we first focus on social, political, and historical forces; second, we turn our attention to the role of power in intercultural communication.

Political and Historical Forces

That societal forces can affect intercultural encounters is exemplified by the varying reactions toward some immigrant groups after the attacks of September 11, 2001. Scholar Sunil Bhatia (2008) found, through interviews with Asian Indian-Americans, that these immigrants experienced reactions from others that caused them to question their "American" identity. Before 9/11, they considered themselves well-adapted to American culture. However, after 9/11, people treated them differently. Their neighbors, who knew them well, were much friendlier and sympathetic. However, some strangers were more hostile to them (sometimes mistaking them for Muslims). Thus, they were reminded that they were different; they were not completely accepted as Americans by the American majority. One of our students recounts how the events of 9/11 influenced her relationship with a college friend from Jordan in *It Happened to Me: Monica*.

It Happened to Me: *Monica*

I had a roommate in college from Jordan. We shared many interests. I even planned on taking a trip to visit her in Jordan, but after 9/11 she didn't mention the trip again. Also, for a month or two after 9/11, when others asked where her accent was from, she lied and replied "Turkey" to protect herself from people perhaps blaming her for the attacks. These events really put a strain on our relationship.

Historical forces also can influence contemporary intercultural interaction, as we noted earlier in our discussion of dialectics. For example, while slavery is long gone in the United States, one could not understand contemporary Black–White relations in this country without acknowledging its effect. Author James Loewen (1995) describes the twin legacies of slavery that are still with us: (1) social and economic inferiority for Blacks brought on by specific economic and political policies from 1885 to 1965 that led to inferior educational institutions and exclusion from labor unions, voting rights, and the advantage of government mortgages; (2) cultural racism instilled in Whites. The election of Barack Obama as the first African American U.S. president demonstrates significant progress in interracial relations and has presented new opportunities for cross-racial dialogue (Chisholm, 2008; Dyson, 2009). However, the intense political and social conversations that have occurred since the election, often centering around race, might also demonstrate that the historical legacies of racism impact interracial encounters even today (Martin, Trego, & Nakayama, 2010; Simpson, 2008).

As a society, which institutions or contexts now promote the best opportunities for interracial contact? Neighborhoods? Educational institutions? Churches, synagogues, and other places of worship? The workplace? Neighborhoods and workplaces do not seem to provide opportunities for the *type* of contact (intimate, friendly, equal-status interaction) that facilitates intercultural relationships (Johnson & Jacobson, 2005). On the other hand, it appears that *integrated* religious institutions and educational institutions provide the best opportunities for intercultural friendships and the best environment to improve interracial attitudes (Johnson & Jacobson, 2005). For example, a study of six California State University campuses found that the students on these campuses interacted equally, in interracial and intraracial encounters (Cowan, 2005). These campuses are very diverse; no single ethnic or racial group is a majority. However, a more recent study cautions that sometimes students in multicultural campus assume that they have intercultural relationships just by virtue of being surrounded by cultural diversity and may not make the effort to actually pursue intercultural friendships (Halualani, 2008).

Intercultural Communication and Power

As we noted in Chapter 5, the more powerful groups in society establish the rules for communication, and others usually follow these rules or violate them at their peril (Orbe, 1998). A number of factors influence who is considered powerful in a culture. For example, being White in the United States has more privilege attached to it than being Latino (Bahk & Jandt, 2004). While most Whites do not notice this privilege and dominance, most minority group members do (Bahk & Jandt, 2004). Being male also has historically been more valued than being female (Johnson, 2006), and being wealthy is more valued than being poor. Further, being able-bodied is traditionally more valued than being physically disabled (Allen, 2003; Johnson, 2006). Every society, regardless of power distance values, has these kinds of traditional hierarchies of power. While the hierarchy is never entirely fixed, it does constrain and influence communication among cultural groups.

How do power differences affect intercultural interaction? They do so primarily by determining whose cultural values will be respected and followed. For example, faculty, staff, and students in most U.S. universities adhere to the values and communication norms set by the White, male-dominant groups. These values and communication norms emphasize individualism (Kikoski & Kikoski, 1999). Thus, while group work is common in many courses, professors usually try to figure out how to give individual grades for it, and most students are encouraged to be responsible for their own work. Moreover, the university is run on monochronic time (see Chapter 6), with great emphasis placed on keeping schedules and meeting deadlines—and these deadlines sometimes take precedence over family and other personal responsibilities (Blair, Brown, & Baxter, 1994). The communication style most valued in this culture also is very individual-oriented, direct and to the point, and extremely task-oriented, as is the case in many organizations in the United States (Kikoski & Kikoski, 1999).

What is the impact for those who come from other cultural backgrounds and do not fit into this mold—say, for those who have collectivistic backgrounds and value personal relationships over tasks and homework assignments? Or for those whose preferred communication style is more indirect? They may experience culture shock; they also may be sanctioned or marginalized—for example, with bad grades for not participating more in class, for not completing tasks on time, or for getting too much help from others on assignments.

To more fully consider these problems we need to introduce the concept of the **cocultural group,** meaning significant minority groups within a dominant majority

cocultural group
a significant minority group within a dominant majority that does not share dominant group values or communication patterns

that do not share dominant group values or communication patterns. Examples include some Native American, Mexican American, and Asian American individuals who choose not to assimilate to the dominant, White U.S. culture. Researcher Mark Orbe (1998) suggests that cocultural group members have several choices as to how they can relate to the dominant culture: They can assimilate, they can accommodate, or they can remain separate. He cautions that each strategy has benefits and limitations. For example, when women try to assimilate and "act like men" in a male-oriented organization, they may score points for being professional, but they also may be criticized for being too masculine. When African Americans try to accommodate in a largely White management, they may satisfy White colleagues and bosses, but earn the label "oreo" from other African Americans. In contrast, resisting assimilation or remaining apart may result in isolation, marginalization, and exclusion from the discussions where important decisions are made. These strategies can sometimes be seen, in all places, in reality TV (Deggans, 2004), as when an outspoken African American confronted his White counterparts about racial issues on the first season of *Big Brother* (see *Communication in Society: The Greater Reality of Minorities on TV*).

COMMUNICATION IN SOCIETY
The Greater Reality of Minorities on TV

In this essay, the author makes the point that problematic relations among racial (and other) groups in the United States makes for interesting television and may ultimately help to diversify the television industry. However, do they really help improve race relations overall? Do they encourage others to seek better intercultural relationships? How do you think these encounters impact the participants themselves?

Despite decades of public pressure on the major networks to diversify, the lead characters in all but a few of prime-time scripted shows this season are still white—and usually young and affluent. In contrast, reality programs consistently feature a much broader range of people when it comes to race, age, class and sexual orientation.

For example, CBS' "The Amazing Race" includes an Asian American brother-and-sister team and two African American sisters in its 14th season, which premiered Sunday. Three African Americans are in the current cast of CBS' "Survivor." Four African Americans and two Tongan Americans have been featured on the current season of NBC's "The Biggest Loser."… That's no accident, according to reality TV producers and creators.

"We're looking to create shows that everyday people can relate to, and for that you really need a true representation of the population," said Dave Broome, executive producer of NBC's "The Biggest Loser."

The culture mix is driven by more than just political correctness. Although reality shows aren't directly in the business of bringing racial and ethnic enlightenment to America, they are in business. For shows that thrive on conflict and drama, a collection of cast members from varied backgrounds often serves that goal. Unresolved issues surrounding race, class and sexual orientation can either quietly fuel tension on programs or generate outright emotional explosions.…

Though the issue of race is often secondary to unscripted series' story lines, it does at times directly fuel the drama. William "Mega" Collins, an outspoken African American houseguest on the first edition of CBS' "Big Brother," was the first evicted from the show after he angrily confronted his predominantly white fellow participants about race. CBS' "Survivor" in 2006 sparked a furor when the series initially divided tribes along racial and ethnic lines.

Vic Bulluck, executive director of the NAACP's Hollywood office, noted: "The marketplace has changed, and the producers of reality shows are obviously more sensitive or conscious of that change than the producers of scripted shows. It really comes down to relevance."…

Network executives say that comparing the two genres is unfair and that scripted shows are governed by creative restrictions that don't apply to reality TV.…

Still, critics like Kristal Brent Zook, author of "I See Black People: Interviews With African American Owners of Radio and Television," argue that diversity behind the camera in scripted programming will increase it in front of it. "It all comes down to what goes on in the writing room," Zook said. "It's a reflection on their imagination, or lack thereof. It's going to remain this way until you bring in people with wider experience."

From: Deggans, E. (2004, October 24). TV reality not often spoken of: Race. *St. Petersburg Times.* Reprinted by permission of St. Petersburg Times. See also articles.latimes.com/print/2009/feb/17/entertainment/et-realitytv17

ETHICS AND INTERCULTURAL COMMUNICATION

How can you communicate more ethically across cultures? Unfortunately, no easy answers exist, but a few guidelines may be helpful.

First, remember that everyone, including you, is enmeshed in a culture and thus communicating through a cultural lens. Recognizing your own cultural attitudes, values, and beliefs will make you more sensitive to others' cultures and less likely to impose your own cultural attitudes on their communication patterns. While you may feel most comfortable living in your own culture and following its communication patterns, you should not conclude that your culture and communication style are best or should be the standard for all other cultures. Such a position is called ethnocentrism, which you learned about in Chapter 4. Of course, appreciating and respecting other cultures does not mean you don't still appreciate and respect your own.

Second, as you learn about other cultural groups, be aware of their humanity and avoid the temptation to view them as an exotic "other." Communication scholar Bradford Hall (1997) has cautioned about this tendency, which is called the "zoo approach."

When using such an approach, we view the study of culture as if we were walking through a zoo admiring, gasping, and chuckling at the various exotic animals we observe. One may discover amazing, interesting, and valuable information by using such a perspective and even develop a real fondness of these exotic people, but miss the point that we are as culturally "caged" as others and that they are culturally as "free" as we are (Hall, 1997, p. 14). From an ethical perspective, the "zoo approach" denies the humanity of other cultural groups. For example, the view of African cultures as primitive and incapable led Whites to justify colonizing Africa and exploiting its rich resources in the nineteenth century.

Third, you will be more ethical in your intercultural interactions if you are open to other ways of viewing the world. The ways that you were taught about the world and history may not be the same as what others were taught. People cannot engage in meaningful communication if they are unwilling to suspend or reexamine their assumptions about the world. For example, some Europeans believe that the United States became involved in the Middle East so it could control its oil interests, while many U.S. Americans believe that concern over weapons of mass destruction and human rights was the motivation. If neither group will consider the opinion of the other, they will be unlikely to sustain a mutually satisfying conversation.

It is difficult to engage in meaningful communication if people are unwilling to suspend or reexamine their assumptions about the world.

TEST YOUR KNOWLEDGE
• What three strategies can you use to help you respond ethically during intercultural interactions?

IMPROVING YOUR INTERCULTURAL COMMUNICATION SKILLS

How can you communicate more effectively across cultures? As with ethics, no magic formula exists, but here are several suggestions.

Increase Motivation

Perhaps the most important component is *motivation*. Without the motivation to be an effective communicator, no other skills will be relevant. Part of the problem in long-standing interethnic or interreligious conflicts—for example, between the Israelis and the Palestinians—is the lack of interest, on both sides, in communicating more effectively. Some parties on both sides may even have an interest in prolonging conflict. Therefore, a strong desire to improve one's skills is necessary.

Increase Your Knowledge of Self and Others

In addition to being motivated, you become a more effective intercultural communicator if you educate yourself about intercultural communication. Having some knowledge about the history, background, and values of people from other cultures can help you communicate better. When you demonstrate this type of knowledge to people from other cultures, you communicate that you're interested in them and you affirm their sense of identity. Obviously, no one can know everything about all cultures; nonetheless, some general information can be helpful, as can an awareness of the importance of context and a dialectical perspective.

Self-knowledge also is very important. If you were socialized to be very individualistic you may initially have a hard time understanding collectivistic tendencies. Once you become aware of these differences, however, you can more easily communicate with someone who holds a different perspective. Growing up in a middle-class family may also influence your perceptions. Many middle-class people assume that anyone can become middle class through hard work. But this view overlooks the discrimination faced by people of color and gays and lesbians. How can you increase your cultural self-awareness? Perhaps the best way is to cultivate intercultural encounters and relationships.

Developing facility in intercultural communication occurs through a cyclical process. The more one interacts across cultures, the more one learns about oneself, and then the more prepared one is to interact interculturally, and so on. However, increased exposure and understanding do not happen automatically. Being aware of the influence of culture on oneself and others is essential to increasing one's intercultural experience and competence (Ting-Toomey, 1999).

Where should you start? You can begin by examining your current friendships and reach out from there. Research shows that individuals generally become friends with people with whom they live, work, and worship. So your opportunities for intercultural interaction and self-awareness are largely determined by the type of people and contexts you encounter in your daily routine.

Avoid Stereotypes

Cultural differences may lead to stereotyping and prejudices. As we discussed in Chapter 4, normal cognitive patterns of generalizing make our world more manageable. However, when these generalizations become rigid, they lead to stereotyping and prejudices. Furthermore, stereotyping can become self-fulfilling (Snyder, 2001). That is, if you stereotype people

Wahoo, the Cleveland Indians mascot, is a controversial figure. To some, Wahoo represents an offensive stereotype; to others, an expression of pride in the team. How might we respond to a similar caricature of African Americans or White Americans?

and treat them in a prejudiced or negative manner, they may react in ways that reinforce your stereotype.

On the other hand, we must note, overreacting by being very "sweet" can be equally off-putting. African Americans sometimes complain about being "niced" to death by White people (Yamato, 2001). The guideline here is to be mindful that you might be stereotyping. For example, if you are White, do you only notice bad behavior when exhibited by a person of color? Communicating effectively across cultural boundaries is a challenge—but one we hope you will take up.

TEST YOUR KNOWLEDGE

- What are three suggestions for communicating more effectively across cultures?

- Which do you think is the most important? Why?

SUMMARY

Four reasons for learning about intercultural communication are increased opportunity, increased business effectiveness, improved intergroup relations, and enhanced self-awareness. Intercultural communication is defined as communication between people from different cultural backgrounds, and culture is defined as learned patterns of perceptions, values, and behaviors shared by a group of people. Culture is dynamic and heterogeneous, and it operates largely out of our awareness within power structures. Increasing numbers of individuals today live on cultural borders—through travel, socialization, or relationships. Being a "border dweller" involves both benefits and challenges.

Six core cultural values differentiate various cultural groups, and these value differences have implications for intercultural communication. A dialectical approach to intercultural communication can help individuals avoid quick generalizations and stereotyping. There are at least six intercultural communication dialectics: cultural–individual, personal–contextual, differences–similarities, static–dynamic, history/past–present/future, and privilege–disadvantage.

Society plays an important role in intercultural communication because intercultural encounters never occur in a vacuum. Societal forces, including political and historical structures, always influence communication. Power is often an important element in that those who hold more powerful positions in society set the rules and norms for communication. Those individuals who do not conform to the rules because of differing cultural backgrounds and preferences may be marginalized. To ensure that you are communicating ethically during intercultural interactions, attend to the following: avoid ethnocentric thinking, recognize the humanity of others, and remain open to other ways of understanding the world. Finally, you can become a more effective intercultural communicator in at least three ways: by increasing your motivation, acquiring knowledge about self and others, and avoiding stereotyping.

HUMAN COMMUNICATION IN SOCIETY ONLINE

To review this chapter, use the MyCommunicationLab Web site to test your understanding of the following key terms, record your answers to the chapter review questions, and complete the suggested activities. Expand your learning and understanding of chapter concepts by completing additional exercises and activities online. Access code required. Go to www.mycommunicationlab.com for more information or to purchase standalone access.

KEY TERMS

diaspora 188
mediation 192
intercultural communication 193
culture 193
heterogeneous 193
border dwellers 194
voluntary short-term travelers 194
voluntary long-term travelers 194
involuntary short-term travelers 194
involuntary long-term travelers 194
culture shock 194

reverse culture shock/reentry
   shock 194
encapsulated marginal people 200
constructive marginal people 200
cultural values 201
individualist orientation 203
collectivistic orientation 203
preferred personality 203
view of human nature 204
human–nature value orientation 204
power distance 205

long-term versus short-term
   orientation 206
short-term orientation 206
monotheistic 206
long-term orientation 206
polytheistic 206
dialectic approach 206
dichotomous thinking 206
cocultural group 209

APPLY WHAT YOU KNOW

1. **Cultural Profile** List all the cultural groups you belong to. Which groups are most important to you when you're at college? When you're at home? Which groups would be easiest to leave? Why?

2. **Intercultural Conflict Analysis** Identify a current intercultural conflict in the media. It can be conflict between nations, ethnic groups, or gender. Read at least three sources that give background and information about the conflict. Conduct an analysis of this conflict, answering the following questions:

   - What do you think are the sources of the conflict?
   - Are there value differences?
   - Power differences?
   - What role do you think various contexts (historical, social, political) play in the conflict?

3. **Intercultural Relationship Exercise** Make a list of people you consider to be your close friends. For each,

identify ways that they are culturally similar to and different from you. Then form groups of four to six students and answer the following questions. Select a recorder for your discussion so you can share your answers with the rest of the class.

- Do people generally have more friends who are culturally similar or different from themselves?
- What are some of the benefits of forming intercultural friendships?
- In what ways are intercultural friendships different or similar to friendship with people from the same cultures?
- What are some reasons people might have for not forming intercultural friendships?

9
Communicating in Close Relationships

chapter outline

Julia and her friend Cristina were at a club one weekend when Julia spotted a man who had "hit" on her earlier in the evening. As he walked toward the two women, Julia leaned over to Cristina and said, "There's that jerk I was telling you about." Eighteen months later, Cristina and the "jerk" were married.

How is it that one person's jerk is another person's ideal mate? On more than one occasion, you may have wondered why your friends pick the romantic partners they do. Or perhaps you even have questioned your own choices. Though relationship researchers haven't unraveled all the mysteries of love and friendship, they have made considerable progress in explaining how and why relationships develop, are maintained, and sometimes fail—and the role communication plays at each stage.

To help you understand communication in close relationships, we begin by describing the importance of these relationships and providing a definition for them. Next, we address the role of the individual in close relationships and explore the factors that increase the likelihood that you will become involved with another person. We then examine five theories and two models that explain how communication influences relationship development between friends and romantic partners. We conclude our focus on individuals in relationships by discussing problems that can occur in friendship and romance, such as aversive communication, jealousy, aggression, and sexual coercion. Finally, we explore the societal forces that influence relationships and the communication within them and present you with guidelines for communicating more ethically and effectively in your own relationships.

Once you have read this chapter, you will be able to:

- Explicate the importance of close relationships.
- Explain five communication theories of relationship development.
- Describe two models of relationship development.
- Identify a wide range of tactics for initiating, maintaining, and terminating friendships and romantic relationships.
- Discuss how aversive communication behaviors, deception, jealousy, interpersonal violence, and sexual coercion arise—and describe their impact on relationships and the communication skills you can use to respond to them.
- Understand the role that society plays in the formation and maintenance of interpersonal relationships.
- Describe the role of authentic communication in ethical interpersonal communication.

THE IMPORTANCE OF COMMUNICATION IN CLOSE RELATIONSHIPS

Friends play an important role in people's lives. Close relationships are a source of much happiness (and some distress) and serve as a significant context within which a person's interactions take place (Donaghue & Fallon, 2003). As is illustrated in *It Happened to Me: Olivia*, friends can come to the rescue in a crisis by providing both emotional and physical support. Relationships with friends, lovers, and family members also offer a sense of belonging, help alleviate loneliness, and are central to psychological and physical health.

Researchers have found that loneliness, or a lack of close relationships, is associated with psychological disorders such as depression and anxiety (Miller, 2002). People with even a few close relationships experience greater well-being than those who are lonely (Gierveld & Tilburg, 1995). People with satisfying relationships also experience better physical health. For example, an examination of 148 studies found that the quantity and quality of individuals' social relationships were linked both to their mental health and to their longevity. The authors found that high quality social relationships were associated with a 50 percent increased likelihood of living longer (Holt-Lundstad, Smith, & Layton, 2010).

Similarly, studies of marital relationships reveal that people in happy marriages are less likely to experience high blood pressure and serious heart episodes (Holt-Lunstad, Birmingham, & Jones, 2008). Thus, close relationships can improve not only our satisfaction with life, but also our health.

The relationships we develop with friends, family, and romantic partners are qualitatively different from other types of interpersonal relationships, such as those people have with their mail carriers or dry-cleaner attendants (LaFollette, 1996). Close relationships are distinguished by their frequency, intensity, and diversity of contact (Kelley et al., 1983) as well as their level of intimacy, importance, and satisfaction (Berg & Piner, 1990).

People in close relationships see each other as unique and irreplaceable. They are more open in their communications with each other than with other people, and they tend to disclose more personal details (Janz, 2000). In addition, the communication in these relationships is influenced more by individual factors (as opposed to social factors) than is usually true of casual relationships. That is, people in close relationship know each better and share more experiences, so they are better able to adapt their own communication and more effectively interpret their partner's communication. This can lead to greater ease in communicating as well as increased understanding and intimacy. For these reasons, people in close relationships expect their relationships to endure over time because they are committed to them (Wright, 1999).

Casual relationships, in contrast, involve little disclosure or affection, and are perceived as interchangeable because they are usually role-based, as between a salesperson and a customer (Janz, 2000). For example, although you might like your mail carrier and would miss seeing her if she quit her job, you probably would be perfectly content to receive your mail from someone new. But if your fiancé or best friend terminated your relationship, it's unlikely that you would be content with a substitute. Because these relationships are not based on the participants' knowledge of each other as individuals, the communication that occurs within them

It Happened to Me: *Olivia*

I was at a friend's house, eating junk food and watching TV, when someone knocked on the door. Standing there in the rain, with tears running down her face and sobbing, was one of our friends. She told us that her mom had hit her and thrown her things out her bedroom window. We sat with her for ages until she calmed down; then, we asked her to stay the night. Without us, she would have had nowhere to go and no one to talk to.

tends to be influenced more by social norms for interacting and, therefore, less personal and more superficial.

TEST YOUR KNOWLEDGE

- What are the benefits of having close interpersonal relationships?
- How does the communication in close relationships differ from communication in casual relationships?

CLOSE RELATIONSHIPS AND THE INDIVIDUAL

Because relationship development is an important aspect of life and because the process sometimes goes awry—for example, one-third of first marriages end in divorce or separation within ten years (Bramlett & Mosher, 2002)—scholars have devoted considerable effort toward creating theories and models to explain it. Although no theory can completely explain or model exactly represent how human relationships evolve, the following approaches offer insight into how relationships develop and change over time as people communicate with one another.

Close relationships can be a source of happiness, comfort, even distress.

Theories of Relationship Development

Do you ever question why you form friendships and romantic relationships with some people but not others? Many social science scholars have, so they studied close relationships extensively and, based on those studies, they have developed a variety of theories to explain why we choose whom we choose. Here are several communication theories that help explain why and how we develop relationships with others.

Attraction Theory For any romantic or platonic relationship to develop, you must first notice that a particular person exists and be interested enough to initiate contact. Sara still remembers meeting her husband, Luis, fifteen years ago when she was a doctoral student. A mutual friend introduced them, and she became very interested when she saw him (tall, good looking, and muscular!) and learned that he was finishing his doctorate. She spent most of the evening talking to him, even though thirty other people were at the party.

Attraction theory explains the three primary forces that draw people together to form relationships. These three forces—*proximity, interpersonal attractiveness*, and *similarity*—were all operating the evening Sara and Luis met. They were students at the same university, they found each other attractive, and they discovered that they had similar career goals.

Of course, proximity, attractiveness, and similarity don't guarantee a lasting friendship or romance, but they do set the stage for relationships to develop. Let's see how these three factors influence relational development and the role that communication plays in each.

Proximity Most people are not aware of it, but **proximity**—how close you are to others—plays an important role in relationship development. Historically, proximity referred to physical closeness between people. Thus, people typically became friends with or dated those who lived in their apartment complexes, neighborhoods, or dorms; those who were in their classes; or those with whom they worked (Sias & Cahill, 1998; Sprecher, 1998). Now, however, technologies such as email, text messaging, and cell phones have made it easier for people to create the feeling of proximity even with individuals who are not physically nearby.

attraction theory
A theory that explains the primary forces that draw people together

proximity
how physically close one is to others

Proximity has a strong impact on individuals' interactions and relationships. One of the ways proximity affects relationship development is that it facilitates informal, relatively unplanned communication that provides the opportunity for people to notice others' attractive qualities, learn about their similarities, and develop a relationship (Berscheid & Reis, 1998). Usually, then, the easier it is to interact with someone, the easier it will be to develop and sustain a relationship. A slang term exists for people who are not physically proximate and therefore harder to sustain a relationship with—*GUD*, or geographically undesirable. Of course, some people do develop and maintain long-distance relationships, but they may need to make more effort to sustain their relationships than those in more proximate relationships (Rindfuss & Stephen, 1990). They can do this by creating more mediated opportunities for informal interaction through texts, phone calls, emails, and Skyping. If you are in a long-distance relationship and want ideas for maintaining it, go to www.sblake.com/index.phtml for some suggestions.

Attractiveness Obviously, proximity is not enough to launch a relationship. Most of us have daily contact with dozens of people. How is it that you form relationships with some and not others? One of the more obvious answers is **attractiveness**. While most of us are attracted to those we find physically appealing (Buss, Shackelford, Kirkpatrick, & Larsen, 2001), we also tend to develop relationships with people who are approximately as attractive as we are. This tendency is called the **matching hypothesis**. Interestingly, researchers have found that the matching hypothesis applies to friendships (Cash & Derlega, 1978), romantic relationships (White, 1980), marriage (Hinsz, 1989), and even roommates (Kurt & Sherker, 2003).

Fortunately, attractiveness is a broad concept. It is composed of physical attractiveness, social attractiveness, and task attractiveness (McCroskey, McCroskey & Richmond, 2006). Social attractiveness refers to how friendly, outgoing, warm, and sociable one is perceived to be while task attractiveness refers to how desirable people are as work coworkers or task partners (Burgoon & Bacue, 2003). People are attracted to others not only because of their physical appearance but also for their contributions to mutual tasks, wonderful personalities, and/or charming ways. Most of these qualities are revealed through communication—therefore, individuals with good communication skills are often perceived as more attractive than they might be otherwise (Burleson & Samter, 1996). Consequently, improving your communication skills can increase others' desire to form relationships with you.

Similarity It may be equally obvious that most people are attracted by **similarity**— they like people who are like them, who enjoy the things they enjoy, who value what they value, and with whom they share a similar background (Byrne, 1997). In many cases opposites *do* attract, but when it comes to background, values, and attitudes, "birds of a feather [more often] flock together." For example, Buss (1985) found that the more similar the participants in his study were, the more likely they were to report increased levels of attraction. This makes sense. If you like to socialize, enjoy the outdoors, and are involved in a religious community, you may find it difficult to develop a relationship with someone who is introverted, prefers to stay home to

attractiveness
the appeal one person has for another, based on physical appearance, personalities, and/or behavior

matching hypothesis
the tendency to develop relationships with people who are approximately as attractive as we are

similarity
degree to which people share the same values, interests, and background

read and listen to music, and avoids organized religion. However open-minded you are, you probably view your orientation to the world as preferable, especially concerning values such as religion, politics, and morals.

You may wonder how individuals determine whether they are similar in values, attitudes, and background. Generally, they discover this during the early stages of conversational interaction (Berger & Calabrese, 1975; Berger & Kellerman, 1994). Researchers also have found that individuals are attracted to people, especially friends, whose communication skills are similar to their own (Burleson & Samter, 2006). This is true whether one possesses low or high levels of communication skills. It's important to note that friendship pairs who have low levels of communication skills are just as satisfied with their friendships as are those who have high levels of skills. In sum, similarity in communication competence as well as similarity in the attitudes and values that are revealed through communication influence individuals' attraction to one another. You can see, then, why communication is considered the foundation on which all relationships are built. Next, we look at four theories that expand upon this idea.

Social Penetration Theory Social penetration theory (Altman & Taylor, 1973, 1987) is based on the premise that communication, specifically self-disclosure, is the key to relationship development. According to this theory, people gradually increase their self-disclosure as they get to know one another and, through a process of reciprocal disclosure, strangers become friends or lovers. The authors propose that self-disclosure occurs across three dimensions: breadth, depth, and frequency.

Breadth describes the number of different topics dyads willingly discuss. For example, you probably discuss only a few general topics with strangers, such as movies, what you do for a living, or hobbies; however, as you become more intimate with others you likely discuss a wider range of topics, including how you feel about the people in your life or dreams you have for the future. At the same time, the depth of your conversations also increases as the two of you learn more about each other. *Depth* refers to how deep or personal communication exchanges are; people tend to provide superficial disclosures to strangers (e.g., I like Thai food) and reserve more personal revelations for their intimates (e.g., I am disgusted if the different foods on my plate touch each other). *Frequency* is how often self-disclosure occurs; individuals usually share more disclosures with people with whom they are close.

Altman and Taylor propose that through increases in communication breadth, depth, and frequency people become more familiar with and trusting of one another, and as they become closer, they feel comfortable revealing more of themselves. Through this circular process, relationships of increasing intimacy are developed. However, not all dyads engage in increasingly intimate disclosure and closeness. Some, such as romantic couples who repeatedly break up and reconcile, move back and forth between stages of increasing and decreasing disclosure and intimacy.

Uncertainty Reduction Theory One communication theory of relationship development that builds on social penetration principles is uncertainty reduction theory. According to **uncertainty reduction theory** (Berger & Calabrese, 1975), much of the interaction when we first meet someone is dedicated to reducing uncertainty and determining whether we wish to interact with them again. This theory argues that relationship development is facilitated or derailed by participants' efforts to reduce their uncertainty about each other. It assumes that people are uncomfortable with uncertainty about others and seek to reduce it in order to decide if the other person is safe, interesting, and desirable—or dangerous, boring, and undesirable.

Uncertainty reduction theory explains much of the behavior we engage in when we first meet people. For example, if you are introduced to someone new at a party, what do you do? If you are like most people, you probably provide a bit of information about yourself and/or ask questions about the other person. You might ask how your new acquaintance knows the host, what he or she does for a living, or whether he or she likes the music that is playing. If you like the other person based

social penetration theory
a theory that proposes relationships develop through increases in self-disclosure

uncertainty reduction theory
a theory that argues relationship development is facilitated or derailed by participants' efforts to reduce their uncertainty about each other

on this relatively superficial interaction, you will probably continue to talk with him or her. If, however, you find the person strange or uninteresting, you're likely to excuse yourself and find someone new with whom to talk.

If we find others desirable based on our early attempts to reduce uncertainty and continue to have opportunities to interact, we tend to increase our levels of disclosure and to solicit more personal disclosure from the other person. This process continues until the two participants either form a relationship or cease to have opportunities to interact. An important assumption of uncertainty reduction theory, however, is that as we reduce our uncertainty about someone, we like the person more because we dislike uncertainty.

Predicted Outcome Value Theory Have you ever liked someone initially but over time, as you learned more about the person, you discovered you didn't like the person after all? How can this be explained by uncertainty reduction theory? According to communication researcher Michael Sunnafrank, it can't. Consequently, he developed **predicted outcome theory** (1986), an adaption of uncertainty reduction theory that attempts to explain how reducing uncertainty can lead to attraction *or* repulsion. Sunnafrank argues that during initial conversations with others we attempt to determine whether continuing to interact with another person is of value, that is, whether it is worth our time and energy. If we predict that future interactions will be valuable, we continue to talk with the person, and if we continue to predict positive outcomes, we will form a relationship. However, if at any point we begin to predict negative outcomes for our interactions, then we will de-escalate or end the relationship.

What does it mean to predict positive or negative outcomes for a conversation? Think back to the last time you met someone new. Did you enjoy the interaction and want to see the person again or did the conversation take so much work that you decided it wasn't worth trying to talk to the person, so you avoided her or him? This is exactly how predicted outcome value theory explains relationship development—we form relationships with people based on consistent predictions that future interactions will be positive and valuable. Like uncertainty reduction theory, predicted outcome theory suggests that uncertainty reduction is a good thing and something that we strive for. However, is it ever valuable to have a lack of certainty in a relationship? This is something discussed in our next theory, relational dialectics.

Relational Dialectic Theory Communication professor Leslie Baxter and her colleagues have examined relationship dialectics to explain how relationships develop. As you may remember from Chapter 8, dialectic is a term that is used in many areas of study, such as philosophy, psychology, and communication (Altman, Vinsel, & Brown, 1981; Baxter, 1988). It refers to the tension people experience when they have two seemingly contradictory but connected needs. As you will see, developing close relationships is associated with the ability to manage these contradictory but connected desires.

Have you experienced any of the following: You feel lonely when you are separated from your romantic partner, but you sometimes feel suffocated when you're together? You want to be able to tell your best friend anything, but sometimes you feel the need for privacy? You want your friends to be predictable—but not so predictable that they're boring? These types of feelings arise when you experience a dialectical tension, and they are common in all types of relationships. How you respond to and manage these tensions impacts how successfully you can develop and maintain relationships.

Three primary dialectical tensions exist in relationships: autonomy/connection, expressiveness/privacy, and change/predictability (Baxter, 1988). Autonomy/connection refers to one's need to connect with others and the simultaneous need to feel independent or autonomous. For example, early in relationships people typically have a high need to feel connected to their romantic partners and can barely tolerate being separated from them. But as the relationship develops, most people need time away from their partners so they don't feel stifled or

predicted outcome theory
a theory that attempts to explain how reducing uncertainty can lead to attraction or repulsion

overwhelmed. Once this occurs, they are faced with managing the autonomy/ connection dialectic both as individuals and as members of a dyad. The autonomy/ connection tension is more prevalent during the initial stages of relationship development, and the extent to which dyads can effectively manage this tension influences their ability to successfully develop a relationship. If they insist on too much autonomy, the relationship may cease; if they have too much connection, one person may feel overwhelmed and withdraw from the relationship. An example of the dialectical tension between autonomy and connection can be found in *It Happened to Me: Laurel*.

The second tension, expressiveness/privacy, describes the need to be open and to self-disclose while also maintaining some sense of privacy. For example, while Warren may reveal his feelings about his romantic partner to his closest friend, he may not disclose that he was fired from his first job. To maintain their relationships, dyads need to manage this tension effectively. If you reveal too much

It Happened to Me: *Laurel*

I started seeing this guy a few weeks ago, and finally I understand why I've been feeling the way I do. Although I enjoy being with him, I have started to feel smothered. He wants to talk on the phone several times a day, he texts me constantly when we are apart, and he wants to spend more evenings together than I do. I enjoy hanging out with my friends and being alone; he wants to be with me all the time. I was beginning to think there was something wrong with him, then I read Baxter's article on relationship dialectics. Now I think we just have different needs for autonomy. However, I don't know if we will be able to manage this so that we'll both be happy.

information too early, others may find your communication behavior inappropriate and may shy away from you. On the other hand, if you fail to open up and express yourself, others may perceive you as aloof or cold and may not continue the relationship. Thus, this dialectical tension is important to relationships in the initiating stage of development as well as during the development and maintenance stages.

Finally, the change/predictability tension delineates the human desire for events that are new, spontaneous, and unplanned while simultaneously needing some aspects of life to be stable and predictable. For example, you probably want your partner's affection for you to be stable and predictable, but you might like your partner to surprise you occasionally with a new activity or self-disclosure. This tension exists at all stages of relationship development but may be most prevalent during the maintenance phase. Relationships that are completely predictable (that is, certain) may become boring, but those that are totally spontaneous are unsettling; either extreme may render the relationship difficult to sustain.

Dialectics are constantly in process. Each day, couples and friends manage their individual and relationship needs for autonomy/connection, expressiveness/ privacy, and change/predictability; the manner in which they manage these tensions influences the continuance of their relationships. Understanding dialectical tensions is useful because it can help you respond to the competing feelings you may experience in relationships. (For a more controversial, and biological, take on romantic relationship development, see *Alternative View: An Evolutionary Theory of Relationship Development*.)

Models of Relationship Development

Thus far, we have discussed five theories that attempt to explain why and how voluntary relationships such as romantic relationships and friendships develop. Because they are theories, these explanations tend to be somewhat general and do not focus on the particular types of interactions that occur during relationship development. Therefore, several scholars have developed models of relationship development that seek to explain more specifically the ways that communication promotes or inhibits relationship development and maintenance.

Alternative **VIEW**
An Evolutionary Theory of Relationship Development

What courtship behaviors does the evolutionary model of relationships explain well? What courtship behaviors does it fail to explain? How would an evolutionary model explain the phenomenon of "hooking up"—or could it?

Evolutionary theories of relationship development come to us from studies in anthropology and social psychology. These theories assume that the primary (though unconscious) motivating factor for most species, including humans, is to reproduce—and that this need influences how and why people form what is typically referred to as a romantic relationship. Psychologist Davis Buss, an important scholar in the field of evolutionary psychology, argues that heterosexual relationship development or mating is not, in fact, a romantic or particularly civilized process; rather, he claims that even among humans mate selection and retention involves competitive, conflictual, and even manipulative processes.

Evolutionary theory posits that since males and females make different contributions to reproduction, they behave differently during relationship development (Buss, 2003; Kenrick & Trost, 1996). More specifically, Buss suggests that females and males communicate and behave during relationship development in ways designed to aid them in achieving their goals and maxi-

mizing their outcomes. The female's goal is generally to attract a mate who is reliable, trustworthy, and committed to the relationship since she will need help rearing her children. The male's goal may be to have a number of relationships (since his parental investment is less) or to find one mate he can trust, because he does not want to invest time and energy in a child who is not his own.

This model of relationship development also suggests that because we can always be certain who a child's mother is, while fatherhood is not certain in the same way, men and women behave differently in relationships. For example, this view is used to explain men's greater promiscuity, expressions of jealousy, and lesser willingness to forgive acts of infidelity as adaptive mechanisms that help men achieve their reproductive potential (Buss, 2003).

To better understand this theory, consider the amount of time and energy each parent invests in his or her offspring. The mother's investment is inherently greater than the father's. Women generally need to invest at least two years (nine months of pregnancy and the remainder of the time to nurture an infant), while men must invest only a short time—theoretically, only a few minutes—to father a child. The evolutionary model argues that these differences explain why men may try to have sex earlier in a relationship and require less commitment than women typically do (Buss, 2003; Trost & Kenrick, 1993).

Knapp's stage model
model of relationship development that views relationships as occurring in "stages" and that focuses on how people communicate as relationships develop and decline

initiating
stage of romantic relational development in which both people behave so as to appear pleasant and likeable

experimenting
stage of romantic relational development in which both people seek to learn about each other

intensifying
stage of romantic relational development in which both people seek to increase intimacy and connectedness

integrating
stage of romantic relational development in which both people portray themselves as a couple

Stage Models of Relationship Development The best-known stage model was developed in 1978 by Mark Knapp, a communication scholar (Knapp, 1978; Knapp & Vangelisti, 1997). **Knapp's stage model** conceptualizes relationship development as a staircase. The staircase depicts relationship development as being composed of five steps that lead upward toward commitment: **initiating, experimenting, intensifying, integrating,** and **bonding.** It also portrays relationship dissolution as occurring in five steps that lead downward: **differentiating, circumscribing, stagnating, avoiding,** and **terminating.** In this model, couples at the relationship maintenance level of development move up and down the staircase as they move toward and away from commitment due to the fluctuation of their relationships.

Knapp's stage model is a *communication* model because it explores how individuals' communication practices affect relationship development and decline. For example, *circumscribing* is identified by the fact that couples' conversations focus mostly on "safe" topics, such as household tasks, while *experimenting* is defined by couples' communication efforts to learn more about one another. This stage model assumes one can determine what stage a couple is in by observing what the two people say and do. For example, if couples spend most of their communication interactions discussing the ways in which they are different, they are at the *differentiating* stage. As Table 9.1 reveals, each stage is based on the types of communication couples perform within it.

TABLE 9.1 Knapp's Stages of Romantic Relational Development

Stage	Goal	Example
Initiating	Appear pleasant, likeable	"Hi! I sure like your car."
Experimenting	Learn about each other	"Do you like to travel?"
Intensifying	Increase intimacy, connectedness	"I can't imagine being with anyone else."
Integrating	Establish dyad as a couple	"I love you. I feel like you are a part of me."
Bonding	Public commitment	"Will you marry me?"
Differentiating	Increase interpersonal distance	"I'm going; you can come if you want to."
Circumscribing	Discuss safe topics	"Did you pick up the dry cleaning?"
Stagnating	Prevent change	"Let's not talk about it right now, okay?"
Avoiding	Decline to interact with partner	"I'm too busy now. I'll get back to you later."
Terminating	Ending the relationship	"It's over."

SOURCE: Knapp, M. L., & Vangelisti, A. L., *Interpersonal Communication and Human Relationships*, 2/e. Published by Allyn and Bacon/Merrill Education, Boston, MA. Copyright © 1992 by Pearson Education. Adapted by permission of the publisher.

As you might have noticed, Knapp's model includes a *termination* stage. This does not suggest that all relationships end, but it does recognize that many relationships do (Weber, 1998). Relationships that end are often treated as "failures," and the people who experience them often feel that they have done something wrong. But, in fact, as people grow and mature, it is not unusual for them to change their social networks (Dainton, Zelley, & Langan, 2004). This is not to suggest that you won't have long-lasting or permanent relationships, but not every relationship termination should be viewed as a mistake.

Knapp's stage model helps us organize events so that we can better understand how relationships develop; however, stage models tend to be linear. They assume that people move from one stage to another in a fairly orderly progression. Knapp has responded to this critique by arguing that dyads can skip stages but that they have to go back at some point and move through the skipped stages. For example, when two people "hook up," they may move from initiation to integration in a matter of hours. However, if they go on to form a relationship and stay together they will have to go back and experience the experimenting and intensifying stages. Knapp also argues that over the course of a relationship, dyads move up and down the staircase as people and events change.

As you read about Knapp's stage model of relationship development, you may have thought that this model doesn't describe your own experiences very well. If so, you are not alone. A number of researchers questioned whether all dyads follow sequentially organized stages. Instead, they believed that relationships can follow a number of paths: Some may be fairly straight like a sidewalk, while others may be like winding mountain paths. **Relational trajectory models** view relationship development as more variable than previously thought (Baxter & Bullis, 1986; Surra, 1987).

Turning Point Model of Relationship Development The most popular model that emerged from research on relational trajectory research is the **turning point model** (Baxter & Bullis, 1986). It is a nonlinear model that best captures the fact that relationship development can be bidirectional—that is, that couples move both toward and away from commitment over the course of their relationship. The original model proposed that romantic couples engage in approximately fourteen types of "turning points" that influence the direction of their relationship trajectory (see Table 9.2). For example, the turning point "passion" (first kiss or saying "I love you") tends to be an event that increases couples' commitment to their relationship, while the turning point "external competition" (such as a rival lover) decreases commitment to the relationship.

bonding
stage of romantic relational development characterized by public commitment

differentiating
stage of romantic relational dissolution in which couples increase their interpersonal distance

circumscribing
stage of romantic relational dissolution in which couples discuss safe topics

stagnating
stage of romantic relational dissolution in which couples try to prevent change

avoiding
stage of romantic relational dissolution in which couples try not to interact with each other

terminating
stage of romantic relational dissolution in which couples end the relationship

relational trajectory models
relationship development models that view relationship development as more variable than do stage models

turning point model
a model of relationship development in which couples move both toward and away from commitment over the course of their relationship

TABLE 9.2 Turning Points in Developing Relationships

Turning Point	Description	Effect on Relationship
Get-to-know time	Events and time spent together learning about one another	Increases commitment
Quality time	Special occasions for appreciating the other and/or the relationship	Increases commitment
Physical separation	Time apart due to school breaks, etc.	Little effect on commitment
External competition	Competing for partner's time/attention due to others or events	Decreases commitment
Reunion	Coming back together after physical separation	Increases commitment
Passion	Physical/emotional expression of affection	Increases commitment
Disengagement	Ending the relationship	Decreases commitment
Positive psychic change	Acquiring a more positive outlook on partner/relationship	Increases commitment
Exclusivity	Decision to date only each other	Increases commitment
Negative psychic change	Acquiring a more negative outlook on partner/relationship	Decreases commitment
Making up	Getting back together after a breakup	Increases commitment
Serious commitment	Moving in with one's partner or getting married	Increases commitment
Sacrifice	Providing support or gifts to one's partner	Increases commitment

SOURCE: Baxter, L. A., & Bullis, C. (1986). Turning points in developing romantic relationships. *Human Communication Research,* 12, 469–493.

A turning point model of friendship also has been developed, with turning points different from those in the romance-based model (Baxter & Bullis, 1986; Becker et al., 2009). For example, turning points most often associated with increased closeness between friends include participating in activities together, taking a trip together, sharing living quarters, self-disclosing, hanging out with mutual friends, and sharing common interests. Decreased closeness most often occurred when friends stopped living together, had conflicts, experienced interference from one person's romantic partner, moved so that they no longer lived near one another, or underwent change (Johnson, Wittenberg, Haigh, & Wigley, 2004).

While we know more about heterosexual relationships than we do about gay and lesbian relationships, what we do know suggests that these two types of relationships may follow different relational development paths. In heterosexual relationships, friendship and romantic sexual involvement traditionally have been mutually exclusive; therefore, the termination of romantic intimacy usually meant the end of the friendship as well (Nardi, 1992, 2007). In contrast, gay friendships often start with sexual attraction and involvement but evolve into friendship with no sexual/romantic involvement, or vice versa (Nardi, 1992, 2007). However, this difference appears to be less true than it once was, as more heterosexual young people appear to be combining the categories of friendship and sexual involvement.

Visual Summary 9.1 Models of Relationship Development summarizes the major models we have discussed. In the next section, we will examine the specific communication processes that individuals use to develop, maintain, and terminate their relationships.

TEST YOUR KNOWLEDGE

- What are the five theories of relationship development discussed in this chapter?
- How are the five theories alike? How are they different?
- What is the primary claim of the evolutionary theory of relationship development?
- What is the primary difference between stage models and relational trajectory models of relationship development?

The Knapp and Vangelisti Stages of Relational Development
Stage models conceptualize relationship development as occurring in a stair-step fashion, with some stages leading toward commitment and other stages leading toward dissolution.

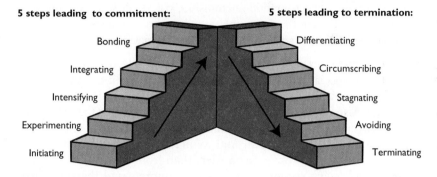

5 steps leading to commitment:

Bonding

Integrating

Intensifying

Experimenting

Initiating

5 steps leading to termination:

Differentiating

Circumscribing

Stagnating

Avoiding

Terminating

The last stage in this model is relationship dissolution or termination.

The Baxter and Bullis Turning Point Model
The best-known example of a relational trajectory model, this model captures the fact that relationship development can be bidirectional—that is, that couples move both toward and away from commitment over the course of their relationship.

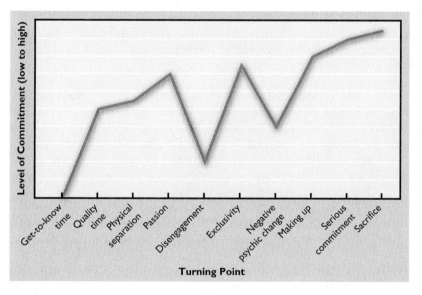

Level of Commitment (low to high)

Get-to-know time · Quality time · Physical separation · Passion · Disengagement · Exclusivity · Negative psychic change · Making up · Serious commitment · Sacrifice

Turning Point

Becoming engaged represents a turning point in one's level of commitment.

COMMUNICATING IN FRIENDSHIPS AND ROMANTIC RELATIONSHIPS

People tend to see friendship as being a very different type of relationship than a romance. If that is true, how do you think communication differs between friendship pairs and romantic couples?

In the following, Jeff describes how he sees the difference between friendship and romantic relationships:

> You're more likely to let your friends see you warts and all. There's no fear of rejection, for me anyway.... In a romantic relationship, you don't want them to see you at your worst.... You want them to think you're very well adjusted. And your friends know that's a total crock so there's no use even pretending. (Reeder, 1996)

As Jeff's description illustrates, friendships can differ markedly from romances in how much we reveal, especially in the early stages. But other differences exist as well. For example, we typically expect exclusivity from our romantic partners, but not from our friends. Also, people often have higher expectations for their romantic partners, especially with regard to physical attractiveness, social status, and a pleasing personality (Sprecher & Regan, 2002). And we may require greater expressions of commitment and caring from romantic partners than from friends (Goodwin & Tang, 1991). In the following sections, we explore in more detail the similarities and differences between friendships and romances.

Initiating Relationships

An individual's ability to begin a conversation is essential to the development of any relationship. While many people disparage small talk, there can be no "big talk" if small talk does not precede it. But even before you engage in small talk, you need to be able to signal your interest to others.

Initiating Romantic Relationships Meeting romantic partners and establishing relationships can be a problem for many people. Dating anxiety is pervasive among adolescents and young adults (Essau, Conradt, & Petermann, 1999) and even among adults who have previously been married (Segrin & Givertz, 2003). Recent research suggests that for young adults, finding sexual partners may be easier than initiating and developing long-term relationships (Mongeau, Ramirez, & Vorell, 2003).

Although men in heterosexual relationships traditionally initiate romantic relationships, waiting for a man to make the first move does not seem to be an effective strategy for women. When men were asked if they would pursue a relationship with a woman who didn't at least hint at her interest and availability, most said no (Muehlenhard & McFalls, 1981; Muehlenhard & Miller, 1988). Thus, in order for men to initiate interaction, they need women to send cues that they are interested and available. How does a woman do this? Frequently, potential romantic partners "test the waters" by flirting. Considerable research has been conducted on flirting in heterosexual relationships, both because of its crucial role in the initiation of romantic relationships and because of its ambiguity. Unfortunately, we know much less about flirting during gay and lesbian courtship, so the discussion that follows refers primarily to heterosexual relationships. Much flirting (though not all) is nonverbal, because nonverbal communication entails less risk: if the other person does not respond, you can pretend you weren't flirting after all.

When initiating a potential romantic/sexual relationship, women are typically more active than men; they use more eye contact, smiles, brief touches, and grooming behavior to signal interest and attraction.

Most flirting, though not all, is nonverbal.

Although men do use gazing, smiling, and grooming behaviors, the only behavior they engage in more than women do is intimate touching (hugging, hand holding). Thus, women engage in more flirtation at the onset of the interaction; then, men tend to escalate the relationship through touch (McCormick & Jones, 1989). Visit the Web site for the Social Issues Research Centre at www.sirc.org/publik/flirt.html if you would like to learn more about the "science of flirting."

Once couples successfully convey their interest and initiate a conversation, if their interest continues they may begin dating. Or do they? Some scholars, journalists, and college students suggest that dating no longer exists. They argue that traditional dating has been replaced by group dates, hook-ups, friends with benefits, and celibacy. To explore this idea further, see *Communication in Society: Is Dating Dead?*

Initiating romantic and dating relationships is not always easy. People often lack confidence in their social and communication skills (Essau, Conradt, & Petermann, 1999). Many people aren't sure how or where to approach others, and they worry about being rejected.

In general, successful relationship development appears to be related to effective communication skills. For example, individuals who self-disclose a little as they

Think back to the last time you were aware that someone was interested in you romantically. How did you know? What verbal and nonverbal behaviors suggested that romance was a possibility?

COMMUNICATION IN SOCIETY
Is Dating Dead?

Do you think dating as it traditionally has been practiced is dead? What evidence supports your belief? What do the studies discussed below suggest about the state of traditional dating?

Over the past ten years, a number of media stories have argued that dating—at least in the sense of a man meets and asks a woman out, organizes the date, and picks her up for the evening—has ceased to exist. Some commentators claim that dating is on the decline because the age at which young people marry has been steadily rising, so adolescents and college students are less invested in dating to locate a long-term romantic partner. In addition, they argue that young people are busy with friends, going to school, and developing their careers so they don't have time for serious romantic relationships (Wolcott, 2004). Many anecdotal stories have been offered to support this claim, but few studies have been conducted.

One of the earliest studies to examine the prevalence of dating versus hooking up was a 2001 study of more than 1,000 college women. The researchers found that the vast majority (83 percent) of respondents hoped to marry and preferred to meet their marital partners in college; however, many believed their relationships with men involved either too little or too much commitment. They felt they couldn't date around to find a suitable partner before falling into an exclusive relationship with one man (Glen & Marquardt, 2001).

Unexpectedly, respondents articulated several different definitions or uses of the term "dating." In addition to the traditional meaning of "dating," some referred to dating as occurring when a couple developed a fast-moving, exclusive, and sexual relationship but did not go out on "dates" per se; this was the type of relationship the respondents often characterized as "too committed." Dating was also used to describe a couple who spent time together hanging out but didn't make their interest explicit; respondents saw this type of relationship as demonstrating too little commitment. Participants also indicated that a couple who had been hanging around and then hooked up were dating as well. However, they argued that the phenomenon of just hooking up (without hanging out), though it exerted a strong influence on campus, was actually engaged in by a relative minority of students.

More recently, a 2010 study of college students determined that men still initiate more first dates than do women, but that for both men and women the number of hook-ups was almost double the number of first dates (Bradshaw, Kahn, & Saville, 2010). Nonetheless, both sexes preferred traditional dating over hooking up, with women twice as likely as men to express a *strong* preference for traditional dating. However, when considering the possibility of developing a long-term relationship, both women and men preferred traditional dating.

initiate relationships are more successful than those who disclose a lot or none at all. Competent daters know that one should disclose primarily positive information early in relationships. They also act interested in what others have to say, help others out, and are polite and positive. Finally, those who successfully initiate relationships are more able to plan and ask for dates.

Unfortunately, many individuals haven't learned the skills needed to initiate romantic relationships (Essau, Conradt, & Petermann, 1999; Galassi & Galassi, 1979). Some people even display conversational behaviors that have been found to be *unsuccessful* in dating situations. These behaviors include trying too hard to make an impression, disclosing too much information too soon, being passive (waiting for the other person to initiate conversation and activities), and acting too self-effacing (or modest) (Young, 1981).

At times, initiating a romantic relationship may seem like a rather complicated dance. Each person has a part, but the dance steps vary from one couple to the next. Fortunately, initiating friendship can seem a bit more straightforward.

Initiating Friendships Initiating a conversation is perhaps the most crucial communication skill in developing friendships. However, saying hello and initiating conversation can be difficult. Why? Just as in courtship situations, people may fear rejection. In fact, many people assume that the other person's failure to initiate a conversation is due to lack of interest (Vorauer & Ratner, 1996). If everyone felt this way, however, no relationship would ever begin! Therefore, you may need to begin the conversation if you wish to meet new people.

What is the best way to approach a new person? A nonthreatening comment such as "This sure is an interesting class" usually works, as does a question expressing interest in the other person, such as "Are you a communication major?" If the other person is receptive, you will feel more comfortable continuing the conversation. And if the person doesn't respond in a way that furthers the conversation, you can easily move on.

Once you begin the conversation, you can keep it going by asking a broad, open-ended question. For example, you could ask, "Why did you choose this university?" or "What do you enjoy doing when you're not working?" The idea is to ask questions that can't be answered with a yes or no or with only a brief response. Your goal is to get the other person talking and to learn more about him or her.

Maintaining Relationships

Effective communication is, of course, essential to developing and maintaining relationships. In fact, a strong association exists between peoples' communication skills and their satisfaction with their relationships, particularly romantic ones (Emmers-Sommers, 2004; Noller & Fitzpatrick, 1990). As romantic relationships become more intimate and move toward greater commitment, couples' ratings of their communication satisfaction increase. In contrast, as dating relationships move toward dissolution, couples' satisfaction with their communication decreases (Guerrero, Eloy, & Wabnik, 1993). It appears that effective communication and relationship satisfaction operate in a circular process in which effective communication increases couples' happiness with their relationships, and satisfaction with the relationship leads to more effective communication. Communication also is essential to developing friendships. Most of the important functions that friends serve—providing companionship and a sense of belonging, offering emotional and physical support as well as reassurance, and giving feedback on self-disclosures—are communication-based (Duck, 1991).

Though initiating friendships and romances can be anxiety-producing, it can also be exhilarating and fun. When relationships are new, we tend to focus on their more positive aspects. However, as relationships endure, we have a harder time ignoring their shortcomings. Consequently, maintaining relationships over time can be challenging.

A strong association exists between people's communication skills and their satisfaction with their relationships.

Maintaining Romantic Relationships Through Communication Only in the past twenty years have communication scholars really begun to focus on how romantic couples maintain their relationships communicatively. Communication researchers Dan Canary and Laura Stafford conducted some of the earliest studies of how couples keep their relationships satisfying. Based on their research, they created a typology of **relational maintenance** behaviors that heterosexual, gay, and lesbian couples use (Canary & Stafford, 1994; Haas & Stafford, 1998) (see Table 9.3).

More recently, scholars have examined the nonstrategic, routine behaviors couples perform that help maintain their relationships. Alberts, Yoshimura, Rabby, and Loschiavo (2005) studied heterosexual and gay couples to see what types of communication they engaged in day to day. They determined that couples use twelve types of conversational behaviors as they live their lives together, including humor/joking, self-report (or self-disclosure), positivity (attempts to make interactions pleasant), and talking about television. Moreover, they found that couples tend to engage in more conflict, humor, household task talk, and planning on weekends than during the work week.

Couples maintain their relationships through routine as well as strategic behaviors.

In general, studies of relationship maintenance indicate that specific communication patterns such as joking, spending time talking about one's day, encouraging self-disclosure, and expressing commitment to the relationship may help couples maintain their relationships.

Maintaining Friendships Through Communication Conversation plays an important role in friendship as well. One study determined that many conversations with friends last only about three minutes and that these conversations were mostly small talk. Nonetheless, people rated these conversations as highly significant (Duck, 1991). Thus, intimate disclosures may be important, but so are daily, routine interactions, which connect friends and reaffirm or maintain their relationships.

Interestingly, scholars have found that friends are most satisfied with each other when they possess similar levels of communication skills (Burleson & Samter, 1996). It is not how skillful friends are overall that predicts their satisfaction with each other, but whether they possess "similar or different degrees of communication skill (or lack of skill)" (Dainton et al., 2003, p. 85).

relational maintenance
behaviors that couples perform that help maintain their relationships

TABLE 9.3   Couples' Maintenance Behaviors

Behavior	Examples
Positivity	Act nice and cheerful; make interactions enjoyable
Openness	Encourage partner to disclose thoughts and feelings; discuss relationship
Assurances	Stress commitment to partner; imply relationship has a future
Social networks	Spend time with the other's friends; focus on common friends; show willingness to spend time with the other's friends and family
Sharing tasks	Help equally with tasks; perform household tasks
Joint activities	Spend time hanging out; engage in activities together
Mediated communication	Write letters; use email or phone to keep in touch
Avoidance/antisocial	Be less than completely honest; avoid the other; act badly
Humor	Tease; be sarcastic in a funny way; use funny nicknames

SOURCE: *Maintaining Relationships Through Communication: Relational, Contextual, and Cultural Variations* by D. Canary & M. Dainton. Copyright 2002 by Taylor & Francis Group LLC–Books. Reproduced with permission of Taylor & Francis Group LLC–Books in the format Textbook and Other Book via Copyright Clearance Center.

Communication is key to
maintaining friendships.

Scholars also have studied the maintenance behaviors friends use to keep their relationships alive. For example, Canary, Stafford, Hause, and Wallace (1993) found that friends use assurances (indicating the importance of the friendship), positivity, open discussion, and listening, though less often than do romantic partners. Several researchers have found that simply spending time together is an important maintenance strategy for friends (Fehr, 2000; Messman, Canary, & Hause, 2000). More specifically, they discovered that shared activities and ongoing interaction are necessary to sustain a relationship and that absence of interaction is often given as the reason for a friendship ending (Dainton et al., 2003). Other communication researchers argue that good conflict management skills are vital for enduring friendships (Burleson & Samter, 1996), and several point out that the use of telephone calls and email is essential to long-distance ones (Johnson, 2000).

As you can see, communication is essential to both friendship and romantic relationship maintenance. However, sometimes we find ourselves unable, or unwilling, to invest energy in maintaining previously valued friendships or romances.

Ending Relationships

Not all relationships endure. When couples consistently engage in behaviors that are not satisfying, one or both partners likely will exit the relationship. Some courtship relationships end after the first date, while others end after months or years. Friendships end as well. Relatively few people retain all the friends they make over the course of their lives (Rawlins, 1992). Despite this, relationship termination can be an awkward stage—both to experience and to study.

People generally are much more willing to answer questionnaires and speak with researchers about developing or maintaining a relationship than about ending one. Studying this process is also difficult because relationship de-escalation and termination typically occur over an extended period, with no easy way to say when exactly the process began. Some relationships do end abruptly and decisively, however. The two basic trajectories for ending romantic relationships as well as friendships are called *sudden death* and **passing away** (Duck, 1982; Hays, 1988).

Sudden death refers to relationships that end without prior warning (at least for one participant). Some people are shocked to discover their partners are leaving. Though unexpected for the one partner, the other may have been thinking about his or her departure for some time. Regardless of who has been thinking what, and for how long, occasionally an event occurs, such as infidelity or betrayal, that so damages the relationship that the partners terminate the relationship relatively quickly.

More typically, relationships **pass away,** or decline over time, and the partners are aware that problems remain unresolved. During this period, the partners may vacillate between attempts to improve the relationship and efforts to de-escalate it. Over months or even years, romantic couples may seek counseling, take trips together, or try other methods to improve the relationship, while friends may sporadically try to renew their friendship. At the same time, they may develop outside interests or friends as they withdraw from the relationship. It can be a difficult period, especially for romantic couples.

To help you understand this often-confusing stage of relationship development, we next explore the reasons that relationships end and the communication strategies people use to terminate them.

passing away
the process by which relationships decline over time

sudden death
the process by which relationships end without prior warning for at least one participant

Reasons for Courtship Dissolution When asked why their relationship terminated, gay and heterosexual couples provide very similar reasons (Baxter, 1991; Kurdek, 1991). The most frequent explanations were lack of autonomy, lack of similarity/compatibility, lack of supportiveness, and infidelity. Heterosexual couples also indicated that insufficient shared time, inequity, and the absence of romance contributed to the demise of their relationships.

People also terminate relationships because characteristics they thought they liked in a partner become less appealing over time. One study determined that in almost one-third of the courtship relationships examined, the qualities individuals initially found attractive became the qualities that led to the end of the relationship (Felmlee, 1995), a concept called *fatal attractions*. For example, one woman liked her relational partner because he had a "don't-care" attitude and liked to have fun, but later she found him irresponsible (Felmlee, 1995).

When relationships end, everyone looks for explanations. People blame themselves, they blame the other person, they may even blame people outside the relationship. Sometimes no one is to blame (Duck, 1991). For example, relationships may end because the partners live too far apart or the timing is wrong. You might meet Ms. or Mr. Right, but if you meet immediately following a painful breakup or just as you are beginning a new and demanding job, you won't have the emotional stability or time needed to develop a successful relationship.

In sum, relationship termination is normal, though it can be difficult. If you would like more information on how to terminate a romance, or how to recover from one that has ended, you can find a directory of sites at www.43searchengines. com/?dir=/Top/Society/Relationships/Dating/Advice that offer advice on ending romantic relationships.

Romance Termination Strategies Researchers have identified five general categories of disengagement strategies for dissolving romantic relationships (Cody, 1982). Surprisingly (or perhaps not), the most frequent strategy romantic couples use to end their relationships is negative identity management, which means communicating in ways that arouse negative emotions in order to make the other person upset enough to agree to break off the relationship. When using this communication strategy, one might criticize one's romantic partner or convey indifference to his or her feelings and desires.

De-escalation strategies were used next most often. De-escalation covers a broad range of strategies, from promising some continued closeness ("we can still be friends") to suggesting that the couple might reconcile in the future. De-escalation strategies are characterized by conversations that attempt to reframe or change the definition of the relationship.

Justification strategies occurred third most frequently. As the label implies, justification strategies attempt to provide a reason or excuse for why the relationship has failed and should end. In this case, one partner might explain the positive consequences of ending the relationship ("we can devote more time to our careers") or the negative consequences of not ending the relationship ("we will come to hate each other"). Positive tone strategies, on the other hand, address the feelings and concerns of the partner and try to make her or him feel better; for example, a partner might say, "I care for you, but you deserve someone who can commit to you."

Behavioral de-escalation strategies occurred least frequently. These strategies involved avoiding the partner. Behavioral de-escalation strategies likely are the least common because it is difficult to avoid a person with whom you have a romantic relationship. If Richard doesn't return Jamie's phone calls or avoids the classes they have together, Jamie most likely will track him down to find out why.

Reasons for Friendship Dissolution Why do friendships end? Friendships are particularly vulnerable to termination because few societal pressures encourage their continuance (Blieszner & Adams, 1992) and because friends may not expect to have consistent contact. Some friendships decline without either person being aware of it. Once the friends recognize the decline, it may no longer be possible for the relationship to recover (Rose, 1984). Thus friendships, unlike romantic relationships, can end without either person being dissatisfied with the relationship.

Friendships end for a range of reasons, based on how close the friendship was. Casual friends are more likely to report that their relationships ended due to lack of proximity, while close and best friends more often state that their relationships terminated because of decreased affection. In addition, best and close friends report that their friendships dissolved due to interference from other relationships, such as one person's romantic partner (Johnson et al., 2004).

Scholars have identified five specific factors that can contribute to the termination of a friendship: lack of communication skills, rule-breaking, deception, boredom, and other reasons (Duck, 1988). With regard to the first factor, if you wish to maintain relationships you must display appropriate communication skills. We know that poor conversationalists tend to be lonely (Duck, 1988) and that lonely people are not perceived to be competent communicators (Canary & Spitzberg, 1985).

Friendships also end because one or both members violate fundamental, often unspoken rules of the relationship that have been established over the course of the friendship (Argyle & Henderson, 1984; Bowker, 2004). For example, most friends believe that good friends don't gossip about each other, flirt with each other's romantic partners, or lie to each other. Successful relationship partners discern the rules of the relationship and adhere to them.

Friends' Termination Strategies
Because friendships are generally less formal than romantic relationships, their endings may be more subtle and less obvious (Hays, 1988). For example, a friend's permission is not required to end a friendship, and one can simply stop contacting a friend, which happens only rarely in romantic relationships.

When friends desire relationship dissolution, they are likely to use one or more of the following disengagement strategies: withdrawal/avoidance, Machiavellian tactics, positive tone, and openness (Baxter, 1982). As with behavioral de-escalation among romantic couples, when friends engage in **withdrawal/avoidance** they spend less time together, don't return phone calls, and avoid places where they are likely to see the other. **Machiavellian tactics** involve a different type of avoidance; they use a third party to communicate one's unhappiness about the relationship and one's desire to de-escalate or end it. Positive tone strategies, like those used by romantic couples, communicate concern for the rejected friend and try to make the person feel better. Thus, you might tell a friend that you wish to end your friendship because school and work take up too much time, rather than admitting you do not enjoy his company any more. Finally, openness means that one straightforwardly explain to one's friend why the relationship is ending.

Although this section has focused on how and why friendships and romances end, relationship termination isn't the only difficulty friends and romantic partners face. Individuals face relationship problems at all stages. In the next section, we discuss some of the communication challenges that can occur in close relationships.

Aversive Communication Behaviors in Relationships

Although relationships can provide love, companionship, and joy, they also can be the source of some of our greatest suffering. Once we open ourselves to intimacy and commitment, we also open ourselves to the possibility of hurt and betrayal. Not all communication behaviors are associated with successful or satisfying relationships; some have negative effects on relationships, the topic we discuss next.

Close relationships are often marked by the presence of aversive, or negative, behaviors. According to Miller (1997), 44 percent of us are likely to be annoyed by a relational partner on any given day, and young adults have 8.7 annoying experiences with their romantic partners weekly. In the context of our close relationships, we "criticize, nag, betray, lie, disappoint, ostracize, embarrass, and tease one another, to name just a few behaviors" (Kowalski, Valentine, Wilkinson, Queen, & Sharpe, 2003, p. 473). Whatever the intention of the perpetrator, these

What rules do you have for close friendships? That is, what could a friend do that would be such a significant violation of your expectations that you would terminate your friendship?

withdrawal/avoidance
a friendship termination strategy in which friends spend less time together, don't return phone calls, and avoid places where they are likely to see each other

Machiavellian tactics
having a third party convey one's unhappiness about a relationship

negative actions are likely to hurt their victims. In turn, victims often respond with even more negative behaviors, which can lead to a cycle of blame and criticism (Kowalski et al., 2003). Fortunately, close relationships tend to be resilient and most of them bounce back from these interactions. However, if these behaviors occur too frequently or the cycle escalates, they can devastate close relationships.

Deception Some types of **deception** can impair relationships, though not all. For example, a person may withhold information because it is too private to share or because it might cause pain. ("Dinner was wonderful; it didn't taste burned at all.") The importance of the information lied about best predicts the effect the deception will have on the relationship. Individuals who discover they've been deceived about an important issue become resentful, disappointed, and suspicious (Bok, 1978; Sagarin, Rhoads, & Cialdini, 1998).

While relationship partners consider deception to be a rare occurrence, research indicates that concealment and distortion of information are integral to many conversations (Turner, Edgley, & Olmstead, 1975). One study revealed that 85.7 percent of respondents had deceived their dating partners within the previous two weeks (Tolhuizen, 1990), while in another, 92 percent of individuals admitted having lied to their romantic partners (Knox, Schacht, Holt, & Turner, 1993). The most frequent issue individuals deceived their partners about was competing relationships.

The findings about deception in dating relationships are especially interesting for two reasons: First, research has established that people are not very good at detecting deception (Burgoon, Buller, Ebesu, & Rockwell, 1994); and second, most people assume that those they love tell the truth (Buller & Burgoon, 1996). This tendency to not suspect our intimates is called the **truth bias,** and it is especially strong in romantic relationships. For example, research shows that people generally do not look for cues that a partner is deceiving them (McCornack & Parks, 1986). However, other research suggests that once suspicion has been introduced, romantic partners' deception detection improves (Stiff, Kim, & Ramesh, 1989). Thus, you probably have a fairly good chance of deceiving your partner *unless* she or he is suspicious; in that case, you are more likely to get caught.

Lying can be just as devastating between friends as between romantic partners. College students have reported being as distressed by a friend's betrayal of their confidences as by a romantic partner's infidelity (Cauffman, Feldman, Jensen, & Arnett, 2000). Some people expect their friends to be even more honest and open with them than are their romantic partners, and, as we previously mentioned, deception is one of the primary reasons friends give for terminating their friendships.

Jealousy Given the findings about deception, it is not surprising that one of the more problematic types of communication for dating couples is the expression of jealousy. **Jealousy** is a complex and often painful emotion that frequently leads to ineffective communication. The feeling combines anger, sadness, worry, embarrassment, and disappointment (Guerrero & Andersen, 1998). Jealousy occurs when a person perceives a threat to an existing relationship. Of course, one can perceive a threat to a relationship and not feel jealous. Jealousy seems to flow from feelings of insecurity about the relationship and/or the ability to cope with a change in it (Cano & O'Leary, 1997).

Men and women often differ in the ways they express and manage jealousy. Men are more likely to consider leaving the relationship and to become involved with other women in an attempt to repair their self-esteem; women are more likely to focus on repairing the relationship (Buss, 1988; White & Mullen, 1989).

One problematic aspect of jealousy concerns the manner in which couples communicate about their jealous feelings (Guerrero & Afifi, 1999). Communication researchers have discovered that how couples deal with and communicate about jealousy has a stronger impact on the relationship than the jealous feelings themselves (Andersen, Eloy, Guerrero, & Spitzberg, 1995). Paradoxically, jealous people tend to seek proof to justify their feelings. In some relationships, an individual can

deception
concealment, distortion, or lying in communication

truth bias
the tendency to not suspect one's intimates of deception

jealousy
a complex and often painful emotion that occurs when a person perceives a threat to an existing relationship

dispel the partner's fears, but this requires trust. Unfortunately, jealousy often arises because one partner has little trust in the relationship. Thus, jealous people may reject all assurances and even escalate their accusations (White & Mullen, 1989).

Regrettably, some communication interactions about jealousy lead to physical violence (Cano & O'Leary, 1997). A study of 138 jealous subjects determined that almost 80 percent had acted aggressively because of their jealousy, and more than 50 percent had actually assaulted their partners (Mullen & Maack, 1985). What types of communication are more likely to escalate interactions about jealousy to these dangerous levels?

Overt rejection or the expression of disdain by an accused partner during an argument can precipitate relationship violence (Psarska, 1970). For example, a part-

Jealousy often arises because one partner has little trust in the relationship.

ner accused of infidelity may angrily reply, "I've never been involved with anyone else, but who knows why, since you are such a lousy partner." The feelings of jealousy themselves give rise to strong passions, but the hostile response of the loved one may influence expressions of jealousy to explode into violence (White & Mullen, 1989).

Although jealousy may be more common in romantic relationships, it does exist within friendships (Aune & Comstock, 1991). For example, if a person is becoming close to a second friend and fails to include his first friend in their joint activities, the first may feel the relationship is threatened and experience jealousy.

Individuals are often jealous of their friends' romantic partners as well. When people fall in love, they often focus intently on their romantic partners, to the detriment of their friendships (Roth & Parker, 2001). However, the friend who communicates those feelings of insecurity and jealousy poorly can damage the friendship. Criticizing the third party, engaging in aggression toward the third party, or complaining repeatedly to the friend can lead to increased conflict and rejection (Grotpeter & Crick, 1996).

Interpersonal Violence Interpersonal violence—physical violence against a partner or child—is a serious problem in the United States. By the most conservative estimate, 1 million women suffer nonfatal violence by an intimate each year (Bureau of Justice Statistics, 1995); by other estimates, 4 million American women experience a serious assault by an intimate partner during an average twelve-month period (American Psychological Association, 1996). The statistics on violence against men are less consistent and may be underreported, due to men's reluctance to admit being battered by their partners. Current estimates suggest that relational aggression against men constitutes 8 to 18 percent of all interpersonal violence (Rennison & Welchans, 2000).

Two types of interpersonal aggression can occur in romantic relationships: battering and situational couple violence. *Battering* describes relationships in which one individual uses violence as a way to control and dominate his or her partner (though most batterers are male). The factors that contribute to battering syndrome are many and complex; therefore, just improving one's communication skills is not believed to be effective in redressing the situation, and creating change can be challenging.

Situational couple violence is characterized by less intense forms of violence and tends to be more mutual in its performance, although women usually suffer more serious injuries than do men. Ineffective communication patterns are common with these couples, so improving communication skills may reduce interpersonal violence in their relationships.

Research reveals that couples who engage in situational couple violence lack fundamental communication and problem-solving skills. Unfortunately, they also tend to engage in more conflict discussions. They appear unable to let even small

interpersonal violence
physical violence against a partner or child

matters slide (Lloyd, 1990), and when they do discuss their differences they are unable to present and defend their positions on issues without becoming hostile (Infante, Chandler, & Rudd, 1989; Lloyd, 1999).

During conflict, these couples are more likely than non-abusive couples to attack each other's character, curse, and threaten their partners (Sabourin, 1996). They also make few attempts to de-escalate the conflict or facilitate their conversations calmly (Cordova, Jacobsen, Gottman, Rushe, & Cox, 1993). In addition, husbands in aggressive relationships attribute hostile intent to their wives' communication and behavior and respond negatively when their wives attempt to influence them (Anglin & Holtzworth-Munroe, 1997). Thus, the communication of couples who engage in situational violence appears to contribute significantly to their hostility and abuse.

Situational violence is also present in friendship and peer relationships, although this is a topic that has not received much research attention. Aggressive behavior among friends can be demonstrated in different forms: physical aggression, verbal aggression, and indirect aggression. Physical aggression includes such behaviors as pushing, shoving, or hitting. Verbal aggression includes threatening and intimidating others as well as engaging in malicious teasing, taunting, and name-calling. Indirect aggression includes behaviors such as gossiping, spreading cruel rumors, and encouraging others to reject or exclude someone. More than one in three high school students say they have been in a physical fight in the past year (Centers for Disease Control and Prevention, 2002); however, it is not clear how many of these violent conflicts involve friends specifically. What information is available suggests that aggression among friends tends to be more verbal and indirect than physical.

Sexual Coercion Sexual coercion is another type of negative, possibly violent, interaction in which the participants' communication is of central importance (Willan & Pollard, 2003). People often find it difficult to discuss sexual coercion. Part of the problem arises from lack of clarity on what it is. **Sexual coercion** is most effectively defined as "the act of using pressure, alcohol or drugs, or force to have sexual contact with someone against his or her will ... (including) persistent attempts to have sexual contact with someone who has already refused" (Struckman-Johnson, Struckman-Johnson, & Anderson, 2003, p. 76). Some people believe that a person who "gives in" to such pressure is equally to blame; however, sometimes people engage in unwanted sex because of concern for the relationship, difficulty with resisting pressure, and/or real concern for personal safety (Spitzberg, 1998).

One contributing factor to unwanted sex is the fact that men and women experience cross-sex interaction differently. Behaviors that women call friendly, men are more likely to label *sexy*, and men are more likely than women to believe that women's behavior communicates sexual interest and intent (Abbey, 1987; Muehlenhard, 1989). This difference in perception can lead to differing expectations about sexual contact and misunderstandings regarding sexual consent (Lim & Roloff, 1999). Some research suggests that such misperceptions can contribute to the likelihood of date rape (Abbey, 1991). Some female college students admit to using *token resistance* (saying no; then giving in) (Muehlenhard & Hollabough, 1988), while some males acknowledge that they have discounted their partners' refusals, and persisted in making unwanted sexual advances (Lloyd & Emery, 2000). These patterns can make communicating and interpreting sexual consent more difficult or even constitute illegal or unethical conduct. And if these communication behaviors occur when one or both parties are drinking, as is frequently the case (Muehlenhard & Linton, 1987), ambiguity and miscommunication are even more likely.

How can you tell if you are being coerced? If your partner makes comments such as "If you value me and our relationship, you'll have sex with me" or "We've had sex before, so you can't say no" or attempts to make you feel that you "owe" him or her sex because of money your partner has spent, then you are probably experiencing sexual coercion (McCoy & Oelschlager, n.d.). For advice on how to

sexual coercion
physically nonviolent pressure to engage in unwanted sex

Did You Know?

Preventing Sexual Coercion

How widespread do you think sexual coercion is? What are some factors that contribute to sexual coercion? What could be done to make sexual coercion less common?

Based on the research concerning sexual coercion, we recommend that you:

1. Don't drink on a date or in a group unless you are already involved in a positive sexual relationship with your partner. You will not be as effective in communicating your wishes and desires, nor in understanding your partner's, if you are under the influence of alcohol.
2. Do not assume you know what your partner desires. Instead, ask! Reading another's verbal and nonverbal cues can be difficult, especially if you do not have experience with each other in this area.
3. *Always* assume a no is a real no.
4. A corollary of number three: Do not use token resistance. If you do, how can your partner differentiate a "token" no from a real one?
5. Communicate your desires and expectations clearly. If you don't want to engage in sexual activity, say so firmly, clearly, and unequivocally. Sometimes in trying to be polite, people end up being indirect and unclear about what they want.

Here are some specific ways to respond to sexual pressure (McCoy & Oelschlager, n.d.):

■ "I really like you. I'm just not ready to have sex."

■ "If you really care about me, you'll respect my decision."

■ "I said no. I don't owe you an explanation."

Have you ever engaged in physical intimacy when you really didn't want to? Why? Can you think of communication strategies you could have used to change the outcome?

minimize the likelihood that you will become involved in coercive sexual contact, see *Did You Know? Preventing Sexual Coercion.* If you would like additional information, the health clinics and security departments of most colleges and universities can provide pamphlets, books, and other resources.

The effectiveness of individuals' communication plays an important role in how enduring and rewarding their relationships are. Thus, individuals are at the center of relationships, and what they say and do affects their relationships at every stage. However, societal norms and pressures shape relationships as well. In the next section, we examine relationships within this broader frame.

TEST YOUR KNOWLEDGE

● What strategies do women use to initiate a relationship through flirting? How do men and women compare in their understanding and interpretation of women's flirting communication?

● What strategies do romantic partners use to terminate their relationships? Which strategies do friends also use to end their relationships?

● What are aversive communication behaviors? What are the most common aversive behaviors that occur in close relationships?

THE INDIVIDUAL, RELATIONSHIP COMMUNICATION, AND SOCIETY

Many people think that relationships are an individual matter, that our decision to befriend or become intimate with another person is a matter of choice, and that how we communicate and behave within relationships is strictly a matter of preference. However, society wields strong influences on our choices and behavior. Sometimes these influences are explicit and a matter of law, as in restrictions against marriage between underage teenagers. Other societal influences are more subtle. For example, why is it that 95 percent of all marriages are racially homogeneous (U.S. Bureau of the Census, 1998)? Similarly, why do most couples who marry have a wedding ceremony, and why are people expected to tell their romantic partners, "I love you"? The reasons lie in powerful, sometimes unrecognized societal norms. These laws and norms determine to a large extent whom we find desirable as romantic partners and friends and how we communicate with them.

Society, Power, Courtship, and Marriage

Most heterosexuals are unaware of the effect of cultural norms on their romance choices (O'Brien & Foley, 1999) or on how they express affection and commitment in them. Until fifty years ago, partners of different races could not legally have intimate relationships in the United States; until the year 2000, Alabama still had a law against interracial marriages (Root, 2001; Sollors, 2000). Not surprisingly, the vast majority of marriages in the United States are still racially homogeneous. Moreover, they occur primarily between people of similar religious backgrounds (Shehan, Bock, & Lee, 1990), economic status (Kalmijin, 1994), age (Atkinson & Glass, 1985), education (Mare, 1991), weight (Schafer & Keith, 1990), and appearance (Chambers, Christiansen, & Kunz, 1983). Such a high degree of similarity, or **homogeneity,** suggests individual preference is not the only factor influencing our choices.

Commonly held stereotypes also influence choices about whom one should or should not date and marry. In intercultural couples, certain combinations are more common than others. In 75 percent of Black–White marriages, the husband is Black, and in 75 percent of White–Asian couples, the husband is White (Sailer, 2003). The frequency of these pairings reflects strong societal norms about who is attractive (and who is not) as well as common stereotypes about what type of woman makes a good wife.

Just as societies have norms for mate selection and behavior, they also have norms for communication in the context of romantic relationships. For example, who do you think should say "I love you" first? Who should be the one to propose marriage? Many people believe males in heterosexual relationships should take the lead (Owen, 1987). In some cultures, romantic couples rarely express their feelings or only express them in private. In Japan, couples rarely touch or express emotion in public. Although young Japanese couples may hold hands, spouses virtually never kiss in public (Times Square Travels, 2004). Other cultures prohibit public expressions of affection, as in Indonesia, where it is illegal to kiss in public (MSNBC News, 2004), or in Kuwait, where homosexuality is illegal, as is any public display of affection between men and women (World Travels, 2004). Thus every relationship is situated within a set of societal and cultural norms and expectations, and what occurs within that relationship is likely to be affected by those norms.

Because of the national debate concerning gay and lesbian marriage, most people recognize that through laws, society in most parts of the United States limits the sex of the person one can choose to marry. However, many heterosexuals fail to consider how strongly social norms and laws affect the ways in which gays and lesbians can communicate with and about their romantic partners. Regardless of one's position on the desirability of gay and lesbian romances and marriage, the impact of legal and normative restrictions on gay relationships merits consideration. Gay people often can't express affection in public without fear of negative, even violent, responses. In many instances, they don't even feel safe recognizing their partners

homogeneity
a high degree of similarity

or referring to them. For this reason they may refer to their lovers as "friends" or "roommates" or attempt to conceal their romantic partner's sex by never using pronouns such as *him* or *her*.

Having to alter one's verbal and nonverbal behavior to conform to society's norms may seem a small matter if you are heterosexual. But imagine what life would be like if in many contexts you could never acknowledge your partner, you had to pretend that you were "just friends," and you had to be continuously on guard to avoid revealing this "secret"? Not only would this be exhausting, it would significantly inhibit your ability to be close to others. Unfortunately, this is the life that many gays and lesbians live. Visit the Web site www.glbtcentral.com to learn more about the experiences of gays and lesbians in U.S. culture.

In addition to the social norms that affect how we develop and communicate within romantic and courtship relationships, the practices of specific institutions impact our communication and relationships. For example, many faiths have long prescribed whom their members should marry, how many spouses they could have, and even if they should date. For example, the Mormon faith once permitted men to have more than one wife (although it no longer does); Muslim men are instructed to marry Muslim women; and Hindus often discourage young people from dating and selecting their own marital partners.

Although over time religions can and do alter their positions on these issues (for example, the Church of Jesus Christ of Latter Day Saints' position on polygamy), they may be slower to change than other social institutions. For example, Penny Edgell (2003) surveyed 125 churches and discovered that 83 percent of them still maintained an organization and theology based on the idea of the nuclear family in which the father works, the mother stays at home, and the couple has children. She further points out that a number of churches are not receptive to gay and lesbian couples, who then have difficulty practicing their faith. In these ways, religious institutions influence how we view relationships as well as how we act within them and communicate about our relationships.

Societal institutions such as synagogues influence our communication and relationships.

Similarly, business organizations create policies and practices that affect the types of relationships and communication practices their employees can have. Many organizations prohibit coworkers from establishing "affectional relationships" while others (such as the military) ban fraternization—relationships that cross the organizational hierarchy. Corporations also develop policies to limit nepotism—hiring one's family members—or express their views on same-sex relationships by providing, or not providing, domestic-partner benefits. Organizations often create rules that attempt to control and influence employees' communication, through sexual harassment policies, secrecy clauses, and dictates on what can be communicated to others outside the organization.

In addition to shaping relationships in the ways already discussed, societal factors influence negative aspects of romantic relationships, such as violence and rape. For example, most talk about violence in romantic relationships focuses on the behavior of individual aggressors rather than on the social structures that allow abuse (Lloyd & Emery, 2000). Most people assume that men and women experience equity in their relationships (Ferraro, 1996; Lloyd & Emery, 2000) and that men are not abused by their partners. However, the facts are that women typically earn less money than men, are more responsible for children than men, and often are physically weaker than men. These factors seriously compromise how equal women can be in heterosexual relationships and likely account for the fact that far more women are severely injured and murdered by their partners than vice versa (Ferraro, 1996).

At the same time, little conversation occurs about violence against men; in fact, men who are abused are often ridiculed and stigmatized so that they have few places to turn for help and support (Kimmel, 2002).

In addition, the ways we talk about romance can encourage acceptance of aggression in relationships. For example, U.S. media frequently portray male aggression as normal and acceptable, as in romance novels, where male aggression is often a central, and recurrent, plot point (Kramer & Moore, 2001), and women often interpret that aggression as a sign of love. The popular image that men have urgent and difficult-to-control sexual drives implies that women are responsible for controlling sexual contact. Thus, more attention is paid to how *women* behave during unwanted sexual encounters than how men behave.

Finally, people frequently blame the victim. For example, people often ask "What was she doing out late at night by herself?" When we blame victims, we ask what they could have done to prevent the violence rather than focusing on what we should do as a culture to minimize relational aggression. Lloyd and Emery argue that how we define aggression is important; when we make statements such as "He just slapped her around a bit," we diminish the real emotional and physical trauma associated with assault. Overall, these researchers propose that if we truly wish to reduce the violence in relationships, we must examine and alter the ways we talk about relational aggression.

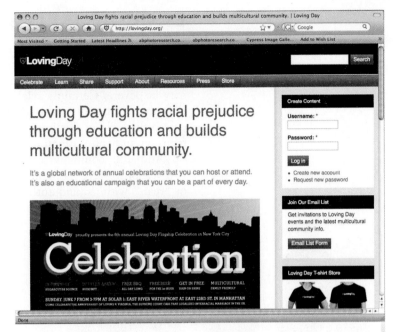

Loving Day is meant to celebrate interracial relationships in remembrance of Loving v. Virginia, the Supreme Court ruling that outlawed bans on interracial marriage.

Society, Power, and Friendship

Unlike marriage, friendships are not governed by laws and institutions. However, social norms still affect our choice of friends or our behavior within friendships. Take a moment to think about your closest friends over the past five years. How similar are they to you? Do you have any friends who are decades older than you? How many of your friends are from a different ethnic group than you are? Clearly some people do have friends who differ from themselves on demographic factors such as race, age, income, and education, but this is more often the exception than the rule (Aboud & Mendelson, 1996). As we discussed in Chapter 8, these multicultural relationships, though potentially very rewarding, sometimes take more "care and feeding" than relationships in which two people are very similar. Intercultural friends may receive pressure from others, particularly from majority group members, to stick with people who are similar to them (Pogrebin, 1992).

Thus, friendship is not only an individual matter; it also is a social event that occurs in contexts that exert a powerful influence on its development (Allan, 1977). In the United States it is understood that friendships play an extremely important role in the lives of adolescents. In this culture, parents are encouraged to understand that their adolescent children will turn away from talking and spending time with them (Rawlins, 1992). On the other hand, married adults are expected to place their romance partners and families before their friends (Dainton et al., 2003).

TEST YOUR KNOWLEDGE
- Describe some ways in which society affects individuals' romantic relationships.
- List some cultural norms that influence individuals' friendships.

ETHICS AND CLOSE RELATIONSHIPS

Although communicating ethically is important in all contexts and relationships, it is nowhere more important than in the context of close relationships. If we communicate unethically with our friends, family, and romantic partners, the consequences may be severe. Certainly relationships have ended due to deception, secrecy, and even the truth, too harshly expressed. All the ethical considerations we have discussed throughout this book are important in close relationships, but here we will focus on authentic communication.

Authentic communication is particularly important in close relationships for two reasons: We expect our closest friends and family members to be authentic, or "real," with us, and authentic communication is connected to intimacy. Why is authenticity in communication an ethical issue? Because inauthentic communication attempts to manipulate the interaction or the other person for one's own goals. It can be considered a type of deception given that during inauthentic communication one hides how one really feels and misrepresents one's feelings and beliefs. In addition, inauthentic communication denies people the information they need to make an informed choice about their relationships with others.

For most people, intimacy is based on the feeling that one knows and is known by another. When we feel intimate with others, we believe that we are connecting with their "true" selves and that we are able to be our truest selves in the relationship. However, when people are not authentic in their communication with those close to them or deny them the right to communicate authentically, it can decrease intimacy and even lead to termination of the relationship. And if we discover that an intimate friend or partner was being inauthentic and manipulative, we may feel not only deceived but betrayed. For example, if you discover that your friend has been pretending to like your romantic partner while making negative remarks about her on the sly, you might feel angry and betrayed. In addition, if you want to continue the relationship, you now have to deal not only with your friend's feelings about your romantic partner but also with your friend's deceit.

To maintain an authentic relationship, you need to confront issues that are important to the relationship.

How can we ensure that our interactions with close others are authentic? We can do so by being open to others' communication efforts, being open in our own communication, taking responsibility for what we say, and respecting the rights of others to speak. In effect, we need to avoid the three "pitfalls" of inauthentic communication: topic avoidance, meaning denial, and disqualification.

To maintain an authentic relationship with another, it is vital to confront issues that are important to the relationship and to the other person. If one or both people in a relationship prohibit the other from discussing issues that are important to either of them, it can be difficult for them to maintain intimacy and commitment. For example, if a good friend wishes to discuss his or her sexual identity and one refuses to do so, she risks damaging the closeness and relationship with the other person by shutting down communication on this topic.

In addition, authentic communication involves taking responsibility for what we say and mean. If one is angry and teases a friend harshly because of it, it is inauthentic to deny that one is angry and trying to be hurtful. Even worse, if one puts the onus on the friend for being "too sensitive," he may be compounding the problem. Repeated interactions such as this can undermine trust and intimacy.

Finally, authentic communicators allow others to speak regardless of their own position or experience. If a single friend attempts to give relationship support and advice, she may feel disqualified if her friend refuses to listen because she isn't married. We also can disqualify a romantic partner by denying him or her the right to speak on a topic because of his or her sex or because we perceive ourselves to be more expert on the topic. If a person finds herself saying, "What could you know about this?" then she may be disqualifying the other party and potentially engaging in inauthentic communication.

Engaging in authentic communication can help people develop and maintain their relationships more effectively. To help you begin the process, we conclude this chapter with suggestions for how you can more effectively engage in an important but difficult type of relationship communication—hurtful messages.

TEST YOUR KNOWLEDGE
- What is authentic communication?
- Why is authenticity considered an ethical issue?
- What communication strategies can you use to ensure you engage in authentic communication?

IMPROVING YOUR RELATIONSHIP COMMUNICATION SKILLS

Of the many communication skills that are important to the development and maintenance of close relationships, perhaps none is more difficult to enact than effectively offering negative feedback to one's friends, family, and romantic partners. The closer people are to one another and the more regularly they interact, the more often they may feel the need to express their dissatisfaction with the other person or the relationship.

Unfortunately, many people (unintentionally, and some perhaps intentionally) wound others when they attempt to express dissatisfaction (Vangelisti, 2007). When we do this, we are conveying hurtful messages. **Hurtful messages** occur when a person criticizes, teases, rejects, or otherwise causes an emotional injury to another (Folkes, 1982). Such messages often critique another person's behavior, appearance, abilities, personality, or identity. In general, they suggest the other party is deficient in some way. These messages are painful because they convey negative feelings and rejection (Vangelisti, 1994). The most upsetting messages tend to be those that convey dissatisfaction or a lack of regard for the relationship. Comments such as "I don't think we have anything in common anymore" or "I think we should start seeing other people" are perceived as the most distressing because they signal a fundamental shift in a partner's feelings.

Hurtful messages can be intentional or unintentional. Intentional messages are those that are perceived as being designed specifically to cause harm to the recipient. When people make hurtful comments to one another when angry, their messages typically are seen as intentional. Hurtful messages also can be unintentional, that is, not intended to hurt the recipient. People can utter unkind comments accidentally, out of thoughtlessness or insensitivity (Myers, Schrodt & Rittenour, 2006). For example, small children are well known for making hurtful comments (e.g., "Why are you so fat?") because they lack awareness and perspective-taking abilities. Although unintentional hurtful messages may be somewhat less painful than those perceived as intentional (Mills, Nazar & Farrell, 2002), both can wound the recipient and the relationship.

Of course, recipients' interpretations aren't based only on their perceptions of the other person's intentions. The way a message is framed also influences how it

hurtful messages
messages that criticize, tease, reject, or otherwise cause an emotional injury to another

affects the recipient. The intensity and hurtfulness of the message impact the degree to which the recipient feels injured. Intensity refers to the degree of emphasis with which a speaker makes his or her claim (McEwen & Greenberg, 1970). For example, "I am miserable in our relationship" is more intense than "I am not as happy as I once was in our relationship." In addition, the harsher or more negative the language ("I can't stand the sight of you"), the more painful the message is likely to be (Tracy, Van Dusen, & Robinson, 1987). On the other hand, when a hurtful message is framed in a humorous manner it is perceived as less harsh, and recipients experience less intense feelings and less hurt than when a message is offered seriously (Young & Bippus, 2001).

Finally, the context in which the message is delivered can impact the recipient's feelings of injury. Hurtful speech that occurs when the dyad is alone may be painful, but if it occurs when others are present, that pain and discomfort often is intensified (Miller & Roloff, 2005). Hurtful comments, by definition, are attacks on the recipient's identity, so the presence of an audience can worsen the feeling of being denigrated plus add feelings of embarrassment.

Despite how painful they can be, at times we need to convey negative messages to our friends and romantic partners. Sometimes friends break rules we see as fundamental to a friendship, and we must address the issue to maintain our closeness. At other times we need to terminate a relationship with our romantic partner. Although it is unlikely that one could find a way to convey these messages painlessly, there are

Did You Know?

Delivering Potentially Hurtful Messages

Think of a time when you needed to tell someone something that might hurt him or her. How did you handle the situation? Are there ways in which you might have handled it better?

Occasionally, almost everyone has to deliver a message that has the potential to cause the recipient emotional pain. Though you might not be able to avoid delivering such messages, you can learn how to minimize others' pain. To help you accomplish this, we offer the following guidelines for how to deliver hurtful messages more effectively:

1. Convey your message in private. Don't offer it in front of other people. Doing so in private will decrease feelings of hurt and embarrassment for the recipient and make it easier for him or her to respond without being defensive.
2. Use less intense and kinder language. You want to avoid: saying "always" and "never;" using harsh words (e.g., "you look ridiculous"), and using extreme language (e.g., "I hate it when you do that"). Instead, mitigate your statements ("Sometimes you …); use softer language (e.g., "I worry that others won't see how wonderful you are"), and select more reasonable word choices (e.g., "I prefer it when …). Overall, be polite.
3. Express your intentions. You should express your concern, caring, and desire to help the other person. Let them know that you are making the comment because you want to help or bring out the best in him or her.
4. Offer fewer rather than more criticisms. Everyone finds friends and partners to be less than ideal. However, instead of offering frequent critiques, save your potentially hurtful comments for when they are most needed.
5. Use humor, if it is appropriate. Do not make fun of the other person, but if offering the comment humorously softens the blow, consider doing so.

better and worse ways to communicate them. If you need to offer negative feedback in a close relationship, it is best to think through what you are going to say and how you are going to say it. Your message is likely to cause some hurt, but you can minimize its degree by following the guidelines in *Did You Know? Delivering Potentially Hurtful Messages.*

If, however, you have accidentally blurted out something, misspoken, or made a teasing remark that was not received well, you should consider attempting to repair the situation. Typically, apologies and/or justifications have some success at repairing a relationship after one makes a hurtful comment (Dunleavy, Goodboy, Booth-Butterfield, &Sidelinger, 2007). You can apologize for speaking without thinking or for attempting a joke that fell flat. You also can justify or explain your intentions and behavior. You can explain that you were trying to be funny, but weren't successful; that what you said didn't express what you meant to say; or that you were angry, stressed, or distracted so you didn't think carefully. Perhaps surprisingly, research suggests that justifications (which often place the blame outside the speaker) are more successful in romantic relationships than in professional ones (Dunleavy et al., 2007).

SUMMARY

Close relationships are worth studying because they affect our health and emotional well-being. Close relationships are those in which the participants see each other as unique and irreplaceable and in which communication is marked by high disclosure and openness. In addition, people in close relationships are committed to their relationships and expect them to endure.

Five communication-based theories help explain how individuals develop close, voluntary relationships: attraction theory, social penetration theory, uncertainty reduction theory, predicted outcome value theory, and relational dialectic theory. Attraction theory explains the influence of three factors—proximity, physical attractiveness, and similarity—in our communication interactions. Once people are attracted to one another, they use communication to develop a relationship. Four theories—social penetration theory, uncertainty reduction theory, predicted outcome theory, and relational dialectic theory—attempt to explain how communication serves to increase or decrease intimacy and commitment in relationships.

We discussed two communication-based models of relationship. Knapp's stage model divides the process of relationship development into phases leading to growth and decline. The turning point model examines the events that lead individuals to move toward and away from commitment.

Communication behaviors are connected with three basic stages of relationship development: initiation, maintenance, and termination. Strategies for initiating relationships include opening with impersonal questions, listening attentively, being polite, expressing approval, and asking open-ended follow-up questions. Relationship maintenance strategies and behaviors include being open, expressing positivity, and offering assurances. Researchers have examined the reasons individuals give for ending relationships and the strategies they use to do so, which include negative identity management, positive tone strategies, justification, and de-escalation strategies.

Problematic communication events can arise even in close relationships. Specifically, aversive communication, deception, relational aggression, jealousy, and sexual coercion all can affect, and potentially damage, relationships.

Finally, societal laws and norms influence the development of friendships and romances and the communication that occurs within them; these societal elements may determine whom we marry and/or befriend, how we communicate with relational partners, and how we communicate with the rest of the world about these relationships.

HUMAN COMMUNICATION IN SOCIETY ONLINE

To review this chapter, use the MyCommunicationLab Web site to test your understanding of the following key terms, record your answers to the chapter review questions, and complete the suggested activities. Expand your learning and understanding of chapter concepts by completing additional exercises and activities online. Access code required. Go to www.mycommunicationlab.com for more information or to purchase standalone access.

KEY TERMS

attraction theory 219
proximity 219
attractiveness 220
matching hypothesis 220
similarity 220
social penetration theory 221
uncertainty reduction theory 221
predicted outcome theory 222
Knapp's stage model 224
initiating 224
experimenting 224

intensifying 224
integrating 224
bonding 224
differentiating 224
circumscribing 224
stagnating 224
avoiding 224
terminating 224
relational trajectory models 225
turning point model 225
relational maintenance 231

passing away 232
sudden death 232
withdrawal/avoidance 234
Machiavellian tactics 234
deception 235
truth bias 235
jealousy 235
interpersonal violence 236
sexual coercion 237
homogeneity 239
hurtful messages 243

APPLY WHAT YOU KNOW

1. **Understanding the Role of New Technologies in Relationship Development**
In this chapter, we discuss the three factors that influence relationship development, including proximity, physical attractiveness, and similarity. Traditionally, proximity referred to how physically close potential friends and romantic partners were to one another. However, with the advent of email, the proliferation of cell phones, and the use of texting, Twitter, and Facebook, proximity has taken on new meanings. Read at least three articles on the impact of new technologies on relationship development and maintenance; then write a one-page summary of your findings.

2. **Maintaining Friendships and Romantic Relationships**
Interview two people and ask them how they maintain their closest friendship. What conscious, deliberate strategies do they use to ensure they will stay close with their good friends? Also, what routine behaviors do they use to maintain closeness (for example, using nicknames, emailing funny stories)? Then interview two people and ask them the same questions about how they maintain their current romantic relationship. Finally, compare the four sets of responses. Do your interviewees use similar or different strategies for maintaining their friendships and their romances?

3. **Societal Influences on Relationships**

Choose six popular magazines from your local grocery store. Be sure to select a wide range of magazines, including those directed toward men and women as well as some focused on political, social, and health issues. Skim through the magazines, first looking at the advertisements. What can you tell about the way friendships and romances are viewed in the United States? As you look through the magazines, ask yourself these questions:

a. To what degree do the people in the ads "match" by ethnicity, age, attractiveness, height and weight, and other factors?

b. How many of the romantic couples are gay or lesbian?

c. How many of the friendship pairs depicted are female? Male?

d. In the ads depicting friends, what are female friends doing? What are male friends doing?

e. How many ads picture people who are "overweight"? Physically unattractive? What products are they advertising?

f. What population of readers does the magazine target?

After answering these questions, look for patterns that exist within magazines by their target audience. What does this reveal about society's views of friendships and romantic relationships?

EXPLORE

1. Go to the *Psychology Today* (or similar website) and locate the page on relationship self-tests and take a jealousy quiz. If possible, choose the quiz that describes your sexual orientation and gender (e.g., gay male, straight female) and complete it. Do your results agree with how you see yourself? What scenarios made you feel most jealous? If you rated in high in jealousy, what can you do to moderate your feelings and/or responses?

2. Go to a reputable marriage research site, such as John Gottman's (Dr. Gottman is the foremost scholar of marital relationships) or LiveSciene's webpage *Six Scientific Tips for a Successful Marriage*. Read through the strategies that the site you choose provides for how to have a successful marriage. Compare this list to the strategies listed in Tables 9.3 and 9.4. How are the lists alike? How are they different? Which of the various strategies and recommendations would you find most helpful? Most realistic? What can you do to maintain your romantic relationship (if you have one) more effectively?

10
Small Group Communication

The quality of a group depends on the contributions of individual members.

My most interesting group experience happened last year in my Business Communication class. One of our assignments involved working in teams with students from another campus. Each team had six students (half from our campus and half from the other campus). As a group, we were assigned to select one team on a TV show (either reality or staged—for example, judges on *American Idol*, teams on *Amazing Race*, family salespeople on *American Chopper* or *Pawn Stars*). Using concepts we learned in class, we evaluated the effectiveness of the group communication on the chosen show. We had to show our analysis in a PowerPoint presentation to be posted on a course Facebook page.

It was fun because we could select a show that most of us were interested in and use creativity in our analysis and presentation. Of course, it was a challenge to work virtually without meeting face to face. But most of us worked well together; we "met" often on Facebook or on the course discussion forum, and many of us actually became friends. We completed our tasks on time, helped each other, and always knew what the other members were doing. However, there was one member who never emailed his work on time, rarely communicated with others, and in general didn't do a good, thoughtful job. He never knew what was going on because he never communicated with us. That part was frustrating even though we tried to work around him.

The group experience described by our student Sophia illustrates many of the issues we will discuss in this chapter. As she describes, group work can be productive and fun when group members are motivated and get along. However, it can be frustrating if one or more group members communicate poorly or, as in Sophia's case, fail to participate altogether. It is easy to imagine that Sophia's group presentation would have been better if the entire group had worked together as assigned.

In this chapter, we begin by discussing reasons for studying small group communication; we explain what a small group is and define small group communication. We then identify the benefits and challenges of small group work, some of which are illustrated by Sophia's experience, and discuss the various communication roles and behaviors that help make groups effective and satisfying for group members. Next, we turn to a discussion of group leadership and describe decision-making processes in a common type of group: problem-solving groups. Finally, we discuss the impact of society on small group communication, addressing the issues of power, cultural diversity, and technology in small group communication. We conclude the chapter with suggestions for how you can communicate more effectively and ethically in small groups.

Once you have read this chapter, you will be able to:

- Identify four reasons for learning about small group communication.
- Define *small group communication*.
- Identify and give an example of task, relational, and individual small group roles.
- Define group leadership and identify two reasons why small group leadership is important.
- Describe five theories of group leadership.
- Identify four characteristics of effective small group communication.
- Describe the five steps in the problem-solving agenda.
- Describe the characteristics of communication that occur during the four phases of small group decision making.
- Discuss how diversity influences small group processes.
- Give four guidelines for communicating more ethically in your small group communication.
- Discuss ways to improve your own small group communication skills.

THE IMPORTANCE OF SMALL GROUP COMMUNICATION

Small groups seem to be an integral part of life. You probably belong to a number of groups—social groups, course project groups, work teams at your job, or perhaps support or interest groups in your community. However, you might be surprised to discover that learning how to communicate better in groups can actually enhance your academic and professional achievements. Let's see why this is so.

Reasons to Study Small Group Communication

There are at least four reasons to study small group communication: small groups are a fact of life, they enhance college performance, they enhance your career success, and they can enhance your personal life.

A Fact of Life If you have mixed feelings about working in small groups, you are not alone. In fact, a term exists, **grouphate**, which describes the distaste and aversion that some people feel toward working in groups (Keyton, Harmon & Frey, 1996). As one of our students told us, "I would rather just do the whole group project myself than try to get together with a group of students I don't know and might not trust to do a good job." A recent study found that students (in a small group communication course) who reported an active dislike for working in groups (grouphate) also reported experiencing less group cohesion, consensus, and relational satisfaction in their group work (Myers & Goodboy, 2005). Thus, it is possible that by actively disliking group work, students are negatively influencing how they experience working with a group.

Regardless of how you feel about working in groups, groups are everywhere. Most of the groups we belong to are either primary or secondary groups (Poole, 1999). **Primary groups** are those that provide us with a sense of belonging and affection, the most common being family and social groups. Social groups fill an important function for many at different phases of life, and there are as many groups as there are interests: social groups for teenage skateboard enthusiasts, young adults who love salsa dancing, older people who play bridge. The purpose of these groups is simply to socialize and enjoy each other's company.

grouphate
the distaste and aversion that people feel toward working in groups

primary groups
groups that provide members with a sense of belonging and affection

Although primary groups fulfill an essential social function in our lives, this chapter's focus is on **secondary groups**: those that meet principally to solve problems or achieve goals, such as support groups or work groups. Secondary groups can involve long-term commitments, as in the case of support groups that meet regularly for months or even years. Support groups, particularly those related to health and wellness issues, have become increasingly popular in the United States in recent years. These groups often "meet" online, instead of or as a supplement to face-to-face meetings (Eysenbach, Powell, Englesakis, Rizo, & Stern, 2004). Their purpose is to bring together people who have a problem in common so that they can provide and receive empathy and sympathy. As one support group expert says, "You're in a good support group when you feel comfortable and safe. You will feel welcome. The group leader will have materials available. It should be structured, but not so structured that you're on a time clock during discussions" ("Support Groups," n.d.). Long-term secondary groups also include standing committees in business and civic organizations. However, probably most common secondary groups are short-term project groups; these include the work groups that students belong to in various classes, as well as work groups in business organizations. Increasingly, most of these groups accomplish their work through technologies such as email, electronic bulletin boards, and chat rooms, which we'll discuss later in the chapter.

Enhanced College Performance Considerable research indicates that college students who study in small groups perform at higher intellectual levels, learn better, and have better attitudes toward subject matter than those who study alone (Allen & Plax, 2002). This is probably because studying with others allows you to encounter different interpretations and ideas. As we'll see in the next section, group work can also lead to higher quality thinking and decision making. Thus, learning how to interact more effectively in groups and seeking out learning groups to participate in can lead to enhanced college performance.

Enhanced Career Success According to a recent *Wall Street Journal* survey, when corporate recruiters rate the most important attributes of job candidates for business jobs, "Topping the list are communication, interpersonal skills and the ability to work well in teams" (Alsop, 2003, p. 11). Whether you are in business or another profession, organizations tend to hire those who have proven they can work well with others (Hansen & Hansen, 2003; Hughes, 2003). Thus your career advancement prospects could very well depend on your success in a collaborative work environment.

Enhanced Personal Life Most people also participate in at least some small groups outside work. For one thing, most people communicate with family and friends on a regular basis. In addition, many people serve on committees in religious or political organizations, as well as in many other kinds of nonprofit and community organizations. Increasing numbers of people join support groups in order to deal with crises, life transitions, or chronic health conditions. So learning how to communicate better in small group settings can serve you personally, academically, and professionally. Despite its prevalence and importance, group work has both advantages and disadvantages, as we will discuss in the next section.

Advantages and Disadvantages of Group Work

Working in small groups brings many advantages in addition to those already described. Research shows that groups often make higher quality decisions than do individuals. This occurs for at least two reasons. First, a group can produce more innovative ideas than can an individual working alone. The small group discussion itself actually stimulates creativity. In fact, a research team at Northwestern University analyzed almost 20 million papers published in the past fifty years and

secondary groups
groups that meet principally to solve problems

social facilitation
the tendency for people to work harder and do better when others are around

confirmed that the most frequently cited research is published by teams, rather than single authors (Brown, 2007; Moore, 2000). This creativity may be due to the **social facilitation** aspect of group work, meaning that "the mere presence of people is arousing and enhances the performance of dominant responses" (Kent, 1994, p. 81). Scholars speculate that the social facilitation response may be innate because, ultimately, we depend on others to survive; or it may result from awareness that others can reward or punish us. In any case, research shows that people often tend to work harder and do better when others are around, particularly if others may be evaluating their performance (Gagné & Zuckerman, 1999).

Second, some evidence indicates that small group work can promote critical thinking, leading to better decisions. A group of people offers more collective information, experience, and expertise than any single person can. For example, if a group member offers an opinion or makes a claim, collectively, other group members may offer evidence that supports or refutes it; they may also contribute alternative opinions or suggestions (Propp, 1999). Because group members have to justify their opinions and judgments to other group members, each opinion is subject to careful scrutiny, which can lead members to recognize the flaws in their own and others' arguments and encourage the group to think more critically (Gokhale, 1995). However, some experts caution that critical thinking and cognitively complex ideas are not automatic consequences of small group discussion. Rather, it may take some leadership to elicit diverse ideas and to then facilitate the type of discussion described above that promotes critical analysis, interpretation, and critiquing (Bensimon & Neumann, 1994).

Of course, group work also has disadvantages. Education scholars Bensimon and Neumann (1994) identify three:

1. Group work can be time consuming. As we will show later in the chapter, effective teams need to establish trust and credibility among members and this takes time. Groups also take more time to make decisions than do individuals.

2. Groups can fall into the trap of too much closeness and too much agreement and then get distracted from the task at hand or jump to premature conclusions and make unwise decisions.

3. Groups can also silence divergent opinions, particularly those of minority group members. Sometimes group members hold to a "mythology of teamwork," believing that the very meaning of team equals consensus of thought and opinion. They then fail to use the critical thinking processes that are so important in effective decision making.

We add a fourth disadvantage: group discussion can be less than satisfying when some group members dominate or withdraw, as happened with Sophia's group in our opening vignette. Such communication behaviors can cause frustration and conflict, preventing members from working productively (Adams & Galanes, 2003) and cohesively. Given, these disadvantages, one can admit that teamwork has limits, as author Richard Reeves cautions in *Alternative View: Enough of the T-Word.*

Given that most of us need to work in small groups from time to time and that learning how to communicate better in small groups can enhance critical thinking as well as lead to academic and professional success, what do you need to know to be a successful group member? In order to answer this question we first must clarify what we mean by *small group communication.*

"To improve our legal team teamwork, only three of the parachutes will open."

Alternative VIEW
Enough of the T-Word

Do you think of yourself as a team player or more of an individual performer? Do you agree with the author that teamwork is often over-emphasized? Why or why not?

Business writer Richard Reeves provides an alternative view on the popular concept of teamwork.

"NATP" is the ultimate contemporary workplace putdown: 'Not A Team Player.' All performance management systems contain a section on 'ability to work in a team.' Team days, team-building and bonding, team ¡dynamics; the T-word is ubiquitous. I team, therefore I am. Businesses are in the grip of a team tyranny. . . . Guff such as 'there's no "I" in team!' surrounds us.

In team sports we expect the hero of the hour—say, David Beckham after a final-minute match-winning free kick—to say: 'It wasn't about me, you know. The lads all worked really hard. It was a team effort.' This is the case even when it is clear that the 'team' has had a terrible game and only the genius of the individual in question saved the day.

Even in literature, by definition one of the most individual art forms, authors now feel the need to spend the first few pages thanking everyone they've ever met, and claiming that the errors are their own. . . . It is enough to make you long for someone to write: 'I wrote this despite the constant nagging of my wife, inane interventions of my editor and obstructionism from certain key people. If it's any good, it is because I am.'

No, no—of course we don't want a world of pompous prima donnas, although it would certainly be more fun than the false modesty that currently besets us. But it is necessary to keep the teamwork bug at bay. One of the reasons we need managers is precisely that envy, suspicion, rivalry and long-standing grudges mean that many 'teams' are constantly on the verge of civil war. . . . It is more helpful to think of teams as short-term groupings of people assembled to work on specific projects than as fixed families within the corporate world.

Part of the historical dynamic behind the reverence for teams comes from the discovery in the 1980s that Japanese manufacturing was outperforming U.S. and European factories by adopting 'quality circles' and involving teams of workers in decision-making. And by comparison to the stultifying philosophy of the production line, the new philosophy was progressive. But most of us work in services now, where the danger is of too much teamness rather than too little. And it is worth noting that Asian societies are significantly more collective in psychological and social orientation than western ones, which have a consistently more individualistic ethos, and so there may be limits to the degree of importation possible.

We have to strike a balance between individual and collective success, and allow ourselves to celebrate both. Marianne Williamson, in her poem "Our Deepest Fear"—made famous by Nelson Mandela—writes: 'There's nothing enlightened about shrinking/so that other people/won't feel insecure around you. . . . And as we let our own light shine/we unconsciously give other people/ permission to do the same.'

P.S.: My section editor had some ideas for this column, but all the best ones were mine.

SOURCE: This is a condensed version of "Enough of the T-word," by Richard Reeves, as first published in *Management Today*, March 2004. Reproduced from *Management Today* magazine with permission of the copyright owner, Haymarket Business Publications Limited.

TEST YOUR KNOWLEDGE
- List four reasons for studying small group communication.
- What are some major advantages and disadvantages of group work?

WHAT IS SMALL GROUP COMMUNICATION?

To acquire a clear idea of what we'll be discussing in this chapter, let's consider two types of groups: (1) a group of people waiting in line for a movie, and (2) a group of students working on a semester-long research project. The first type of group is not the focus of this chapter, while the second is. We will explain why as we articulate our definition of small group communication. We define **small group communication** as "communication among a small number of people who share a common

small group communication communication among a small number of people who share a common purpose or goal, who feel connected to each other, and who coordinate their behavior

purpose or goal, who feel connected to each other, and coordinate their behavior" (Arrow, McGrath, & Berdahl, 2000, p. 34). Let's look more closely at who the small group in this definition is.

A Small Number of People

Most experts agree that three is the fewest number of people that can constitute a small group and that five to seven people is the optimum upper limit for working groups. This general guideline may vary depending on whether the small group is working face to face or in virtual teams. In general, small groups of three (whether working in direct contact or virtually) experience better communication in terms of openness and accuracy than do larger groups of six. As group size increases, people may feel more anonymous, and discussions can become unwieldy and unfocused as members tend to break into smaller groups. However, a recent study found that although group size does decrease the quality of communication in face-to-face groups, it has less impact on groups that are working virtually (Lowry, Roberts, Romano, Cheney, & Hightower, 2006). Under this portion of our definition, people waiting in line for a movie would not likely be considered a small group since any number of people can wait for a movie.

We define small group communication as "communication among a small number of people who share a common purpose or goal, who feel connected to each other, and who coordinate their behavior."

A Common Purpose

While a group of people waiting for a movie fulfills the second requirement of our definition—they share a purpose—that purpose is rather limited. Here we focus on communication in small groups that are working toward a common purpose. Sometimes the purpose may be assigned by an instructor or employer—a semester-long course project, completing a marketing research study for a client, or working together to recommend a candidate for a job. Sometimes groups from many organizations meet to solve a specific problem, such as when a task force is assembled to study the state's disaster preparedness. Having a clear purpose or goal is important and is directly (positively) related to group productivity and increased team performance (Crown, 2007).

A Connection with Each Other

People waiting for the movie don't generally feel any sense of group connection, nor do they need to. In contrast, people in work groups need to experience a group identity and recognize their interdependence because—as we saw in Sophia's experience—when members do not feel a sense of connection, the group won't function as it should. The challenge for the small group is to find ways to create a sense of group identity for all members, and communication is often the key to making this happen.

An Influence on Each Other

Members of small groups need to coordinate their behavior, and, in doing so, they may exert influence on each other. People waiting for a movie do not need to exert influence on each other, but members of a work group do. This influence can be positive or negative, and each group member contributes to the success or failure of the whole group. Most groups aren't successful without the positive contribution of all members. In Sophia's experience, the negative influence of one member detracted from the success of all.

In sum, a collection of people waiting in line for a movie rarely constitutes a "small group" because they typically don't influence one another, they don't feel connected to each other or develop a shared identity, and they share a common purpose only in the most limited way. We should note that "team" is sometimes used interchangeably with "group," but experts distinguish the two in that a work team is a special type of group: a self-managed group that works on specific tasks or projects within an organization (Engleberg & Wynn, 2010, pp. 11–12) and shares responsibility for specific outcomes for the organization (Landy & Conte, 2010, p. 587). With these features of small groups in mind, in the next section we will look at individual communication in small groups.

Think about all the groups you belong to. Which could help you be more success-ful personally? Academically? Professionally?

TEST YOUR KNOWLEDGE

• What is a definition of small group communication?

• How does a small group, as defined in this chapter, differ from a group of individuals waiting in line at a bank?

• What is the difference between primary groups and secondary groups?

SMALL GROUP COMMUNICATION AND THE INDIVIDUAL

The quality of a group depends on the contributions of individual members—so much so that one reason for ineffective groups is the poor communication skills of individual members (Li, 2007; Oetzel, 2005). Lack of communication among group members can even be disastrous. Poor communication has been cited as the primary cause of several deadly airplane crashes, as Malcolm Gladwell explains in his popular book *Outliers*: "The kinds of errors that cause plane crashes are invariably errors of teamwork and communication. One pilot knows something important and somehow doesn't tell the other pilot . . . a tricky situation needs to be resolved through a complex series of steps and somehow the pilots fail to coor-dinate and miss one of them" (2008, p. 184). Fortunately, poor teamwork doesn't usually have such disastrous consequences; nevertheless, communication scholar Lawrence Frey (1994) points out that "communication *is* the lifeblood that flows through the veins of groups" (p. X).

To better understand communication processes in small groups, it is helpful to think of its two primary dimensions: task communication and relational communi-cation. Task communication is the more obvious of the two. It focuses on getting the job done and solving the problem at hand; for example, requesting information or asking for clarification. Relational communication focuses on group maintenance and interpersonal relationships, such as offering encouragement or mediating dis-agreement. These two types of communication are thoroughly mixed during group interaction; in fact, one statement can fill both functions. When a group is getting bogged down in discussion, one member might encourage the group *and* focus on the task by saying something like, "All of these ideas show how creative we are. Which do you think would be the most useful in helping us solve our problem?"

Socializing in a group is not the same as relational communication. While ef-fective relational communication usually facilitates task accomplishment, too much social talk can have a negative impact as it may not only reduce the time that should be used to complete the task, but also distract from the task focus that is critical for group effectiveness (Li, 2007). Effective relational communication (e.g., "It's great to hear about the awesome trips everyone took over spring break, but we should probably get back to our task if we want to finish by the end of the class period") could be key in managing excessive social talk.

To help you understand how individuals can contribute to (or detract from) the performance of task and relationship communication, we next explore the various communication roles that members of small groups perform. We then explore another important ingredient of small groups—leadership; and in so doing, we present several important theories of leadership. Finally, we'll look at principles and processes that can make small groups effective.

Types of Communication Roles

Every group member plays a variety of roles within a group. **Group roles** describe the shared expectations group members have regarding each individual's communication behavior in the group. These roles can involve task communication or relational communication, or both. When you join an established group, you learn these expectations through communication with current members. If all members are new to the group, they rely on their perceptions and beliefs, as well as their group skills and previous group experience, as they work out various role behaviors (Riddle et al., 2000).

For example, our friend Mitchell works for a software company. Although the employees of this company are scattered across the country and primarily work at home, they must work together to design software that meets a client's specific needs. Because Mitchell is the expert at writing software programs, he assumes that role. He is careful not to overstep his role, even if he feels that Giuliana, the designer, is not putting the "buttons" where he would put them or the frames where he thinks they would look best. Similarly, Mitchell and Giuliana make sure to follow the advice of Bob, the market researcher who has studied the client's market needs. In this case, each group member knows his or her roles; they have developed this understanding based on their individual and collective experiences in groups. The owner of Mitchell's company flies everyone out to Los Angeles periodically so they can work together and build relationships. Mitchell flies in from Providence, Rhode Island, while others travel from Minneapolis, Atlanta, Miami, Seattle, Phoenix, and Milwaukee. Others simply drive in from nearby Orange County, Santa Barbara, or San Diego. These face-to-face meetings build work relationships and a sense of cohesion.

Although group roles often evolve as the team works together, sometimes roles are assigned as part of a job description. For example, LaKresha, the chair of her community's Animal Welfare League, always leads the group's discussions, because this is one of her responsibilities as chair. Kristie, as secretary of the organization, always takes notes because that is her role. Effective group members contribute by filling roles that are of interest to them and compatible with their skills, but they also fill roles that the group needs at a particular time. Thus, successful small group work depends on task and relational communication, which in turn depends on individuals' effective performance of task and relational roles (Benne & Sheats, 1948). In addition, small group members may perform a third, less productive type of role, referred to as an individual role. Let's look at these three types of roles and how they contribute to, or detract from, effective group communication.

Task Roles **Task roles** are directly related to the accomplishment of group goals; they include behaviors such as leading the discussion and taking notes. These communication roles often involve seeking, processing, and evaluating information. A list of task roles is provided in Table 10.1.

Let's explore how task roles function within a group using a case study. Lenore and Jaime were part of a campus task force working to improve campus safety. Their small group of seven members met twice a month for several months and discussed the problem and possible solutions. During the discussions, group members filled the various task roles, depending on their particular strengths and interests and the needs of the group, changing roles as needed.

group roles
the shared expectations group members have regarding each individual's communication behavior in the group

task roles
roles that are directly related to the accomplishment of group goals

TABLE 10.1 Small Group Task Roles

Task Role	Description	Example
Initiator–contributor	Proposes new ideas or approaches to group problem solving	"How about if we look at campus safety as issues of personal security *and* protection of private property?"
Information seeker	Asks for information or clarification	"How many instances of theft occur on our campus each year?"
Opinion seeker	Asks for opinions from others	"How do you feel about charging students a fee that would pay for extra police protection?"
Information giver	Provides facts, examples, and other relevant evidence	"My research showed that other campuses have solved similar problems by increasing numbers of campus police and improving lighting."
Opinion giver	Offers beliefs or opinions	"I'm often concerned about my personal safety when I walk to certain campus parking lots at night."
Elaborator	Explains ideas, offers examples to clarify ideas	"If the university had increased security patrols, my bike might not have been stolen last month."
Coordinator	Shows relationships among ideas presented	"Installing new light fixtures might improve personal safety and reduce thefts on campus."
Orienter	Summarizes what has been discussed and keeps group focused	"We've now discussed several aspects of personal safety; maybe it's time to turn our attention to issues of protection of private property."
Evaluator–critic	Judges evidence and conclusions of group	"I think we may be overestimating the problem of theft."
Energizer	Motivates group members to greater productivity	"Wow! We've gotten a lot accomplished this evening, and we have only have a few more points to discuss."
Procedural technician	Performs logistical tasks—distributing paper, arranging seating, etc.	"If all four of us sit on the same side of the table, we'll be able to read the diagrams without having to pass them around."
Recorder	Keeps a record of group activities and progress	"We have 10 more minutes; let's see if we can get through our agenda in time to review any questions."

SOURCE: Benne, K. D., & Sheats, P. (1948). Functional roles of group members. *Journal of Social Issues, 4,* 41–49.

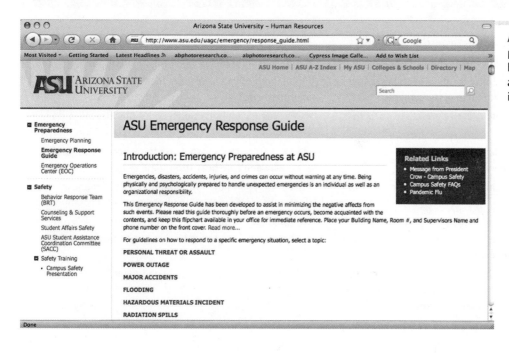

A small group focusing on campus security might be part of a larger program such as this one at Arizona State University focusing on general campus safety.

relational roles
roles that help establish a group's social atmosphere

For example, Karin tended to serve as initiator-contributor, proposing new ideas and suggesting that the group look at several dimensions of the problem, such as personal security and the protection of private property. Information seekers, in particular John and Ralph, often asked for clarification of facts or information. Opinion seekers, such as Eliza and Wen Shu, asked how other group members felt about various proposals—say, the potential expense that would be incurred by implementing suggested solutions. In addition, opinion givers responded by sharing how they felt about the expense.

As information givers, several members provided statistics about the security problem so that the group could know the extent of the problem. They also provided information on how other campuses had solved similar problems—by increasing numbers of campus police, installing better lighting, and having volunteer "security teams" patrol campus. Serving as elaborator, Lenore told about having her bike stolen and suggested that having an increased number of campus police might have prevented the theft. Jaime often served as coordinator and orienter, showing how various ideas related to each other, while other members filled the role of evaluator-critic, carefully evaluating various ideas. The procedural technician made sure that everyone had paper and pens, and a designated recorder took notes so that at the end of each meeting, members knew what they had covered. One member often served as the energizer, infusing interest into the group when attention and focus lagged.

Not every group has members who can fill each of these roles, and certainly not with the same level of skill. But the more effectively these roles are filled, the better the group will function and the more likely it is that goals will be met.

Relational Roles In contrast with task roles, **relational roles** help establish a group's social atmosphere (see Table 10.2). Members who encourage others to talk or mediate disagreements are filling relational roles. Group members can fill both task and relational roles, depending on the needs of the group. For example, in Lenore and Jaime's group, one member sent out emails to get the group organized (task role), and he also sent congratulatory emails after the group did a presentation to the student governing council (relational role).

TABLE 10.2 Small Group Relational Roles

Role	Description	Example
Encourager	Offers praise and acceptance of others' ideas	"That's a great idea; tell us more about it."
Harmonizer	Mediates disagreement among group members	"I think you and Ron are seeing two sides of the same coin."
Compromiser	Attempts to resolve conflicts by trying to find an acceptable solution to disagreements	"I think both of you have great ideas. Let's see how we can combine them."
Gatekeeper	Encourages less talkative group members to participate	"Maria, you haven't said much about this idea. How do you feel about it?"
Expediter	Tries to limit lengthy contributions of other group members	"Martin, you've told us what you think about most of the ideas. Why don't we hear from some of the other members?"
Standard setter	Helps to set standards and goals for the group	"I think our goal should be to submit a comprehensive plan for campus safety to the dean by the end of this semester."
Group observer	Keeps records of the group's process and uses the information that is gathered to evaluate the group's procedures	"We completed a similar report last semester. Let's refer to it before we spend time working on this new one."
Follower	Goes along with the suggestions and ideas of group members; serves as an audience in group discussion and decision making	"I like that idea. That's a really good point."

SOURCE: Benne, K. D., & Sheats, P. (1948). Functional roles of group members. *Journal of Social Issues, 4*, 41–49.

During their discussion of campus safety, some members served as encouragers (praising and accepting others' ideas). Others served as harmonizers (mediating disagreement) or compromisers (attempting to find solutions to disagreements). As communication majors, Lenore and Jaime paid close attention to how the discussion was going and, when necessary, served as gatekeepers, encouraging participation from less talkative members, or as expediters, gently limiting the contributions of more talkative members. One group member served as standard setter, periodically reminding his colleagues of the group's standards, while others served as observers, gathering information that could be used to evaluate group performance. In this group, most members served as followers from time to time, simply listening to others' contributions. Overall, the group met its goal of addressing the problems of campus security partly because members effectively filled both task and relational roles as needed.

How can you apply this information to improve your own skills as a group member? First, try to keep these roles in mind during your own group work, noting who is playing which roles and whether some essential role is missing. Once you've made this assessment you can try to fill in the missing role behaviors. For example, if a group seems "stuck" and keeps rehashing the same ideas, you might try the role of initiator-contributor or information giver. Or if one person in the group is dominating the discussion and talking constantly, you might assume the expediter or gatekeeper role and try to balance out the contributions of the various members. Or if one group member is providing complex information that seems to confuse other group members, you might try the elaborator or coordinator roles to help synthesize and clarify the information.

Individual Roles The **individual role** tends to be dysfunctional to the group process (See Table 10.3). Group members serving in individual roles focus more on their own interests and needs than on those of the group. Thus they tend to be uninvolved, negative, aggressive, or constantly joking. A group member who consistently assumes one or more negative individual roles can undermine the group's commitment to goals and its sense of cohesion—ultimately resulting in decreased

individual roles
roles that focus more on individuals' own interests and needs than on those of the group

TABLE 10.3 Small Group Individual Roles

Role	Description	Example
Aggressor	Attacks other group members, tries to take credit for someone else's contribution	"That's a stupid idea. It would never work."
Blocker	Is generally negative and stubborn for no apparent reason	"This whole task is pointless. I don't see why we have to do it."
Recognition seeker	Calls excessive attention to his/her personal achievements	"This is how we dealt with campus security when I was at Harvard."
Self-confessor	Uses the group as an audience to report non-group-related personal feelings	"I'm so upset at my boyfriend. We had a big fight last night."
Joker	Lacks involvement in the group's process, distracts others by telling stories and jokes	"Hey did you hear the one about. . . ?"
Dominator	Asserts control by manipulating group members or tries to take over group; may use flattery or assertive behavior to dominate the conversation	"I know my plan will work because I was a police officer."
Help seeker	Tries to gain unwarranted sympathy from group; often expresses insecurity or feelings of low self-worth	"You probably won't like this idea, either, but I think we should consider contracting out our campus security."
Special-interest pleader	Works to serve an individual need, rather than focusing on group interests	"Since I only have daycare on Wednesdays, can we meet on Wednesday afternoons?"

SOURCE: Benne, K. D., & Sheats, P. (1948). Functional roles of group members. *Journal of Social Issues, 4*, 41–49.

group performance and productivity. This is why it is so important for other group members to be aware of effective task and relational behaviors and to demonstrate them (Wellen & Neale, 2006).

A common individual role that hinders effectiveness in student projects is the dominator, who insists on doing things his or her way. Another individual role is the blocker, a member who is negative for no apparent reason, as was the case for one of our students (see *It Happened to Me: Tiacko*).

As illustrated by Tiacko's experience, group members can deal with critical group members by assuming a relational communication role, complimenting other group members for their ideas (i.e., encourager role), and counteracting criticism

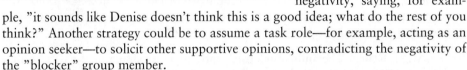

It Happened to Me: *Tiacko*

In one of my classes, we had to complete a group project. One of our members dominated the discussion and was always very critical. No matter what contributions we made to the project, he always found a way to criticize them. Nothing was good enough for him. Fortunately, we also had some very skilled communicators in our group and they limited his impact on the group by always countering his negative remarks with more positive comments.

with positive feedback, such as "I have to say I thought Tanya's idea was really intriguing. Let's look at how we might implement it in our project." A single member's criticism has less force when several members note the high quality of a contribution. A gatekeeper can also deal with negativity, saying, for example, "it sounds like Denise doesn't think this is a good idea; what do the rest of you think?" Another strategy could be to assume a task role—for example, acting as an opinion seeker—to solicit other supportive opinions, contradicting the negativity of the "blocker" group member.

Another common individual role is the joker. When another member contributes, the joker always has to "one up" the comment with a joke or a story, assuming that others will be interested. This member constantly moves the group off-task. Here, a member filling the orienter role can help the group refocus on the task at hand. You may also be familiar with the self-confessor, who uses the group as his or her own personal audience; the help seeker, who seeks sympathy and expresses insecurity or feelings of low self-worth; and the special-interest pleader, who places his or her individual need or biases above the group goal or focus. These individual roles take up a lot of air time in unproductive conversation.

Think about group experiences you've had. Which task communication roles do you tend to fill? Which relational communication roles? Which communication roles would you like to fill? How flexible have you been in your ability to fill various task and relational roles?

How can you deal with these types of roles? Perhaps the best strategies come from those relational roles that help the group refocus on the task: the gatekeeper and expeditor roles. Several task roles may also prove helpful—for example, the initiator-contributor, who may start a new line of conversation, or the orienter, who helps the group see where they are in accomplishing their task.

Any group member may serve in any of these roles at any time. In a successful group, like Jaime and Lenore's task force, members play various roles as needed, with minimal indulgence in the individual roles. Some group members play only to their strengths and consistently serve in one or two particular roles. This is fine as long as all the needed roles are being filled. *Visual Summary 10.1: Roles in Groups* illustrates several roles that may be at work in small groups.

Leadership in Small Groups

As a group member in community, religious, school, or social groups, you have probably noticed that most groups and organizations function better with effective leadership. In fact, a group or organization's success is often directly related to the presence of good leadership. For example, one study showed that the most important influence on worker satisfaction and productivity in organizations is the actions of the immediate supervisor (Bock, 2006). In this section, we explore why leadership is important in small groups and describe exactly what we mean by leadership.

VISUAL SUMMARY 10.1 Roles in Groups

Scene from *The Office* (television sitcom)

Importance of Good Leadership Leadership should be a concern for all of us because it is not just a quality for those with formal subordinates. Rather, leadership occurs in many forms and contexts; as one expert says, leadership can take place "during a sales call, a customer service response, a family decision or a meeting with friends" (Gollent, 2007). As we'll see later, there is often little difference between leaders and followers. We can be both leaders and followers at different times in the same group or organization; in fact, we all share in the responsibility for contributing to smooth and effective functioning of the groups we belong to (Komives, Lucas, & McMahon, 1998).

For the most part, leaders are made, not born. Good-quality leadership doesn't just happen, it involves skills that can be learned and that require practice. As we describe leadership characteristics and theories, think about the ways in which you may play leadership roles in the various groups and organizations in which you a member.

Definition of Leadership What exactly do we mean by "leadership"? Organizational behavior scholar Richard Daft defines it as "an influence relationship among leaders and followers who intend changes and outcomes that reflect their shared purposes" (Daft, 2010, p. 4). Perhaps the most important element in this definition is the idea of an influence relationship (see *Did You Know? Leadership Is an Influence Relationship*). Influence does not just reside in one person, but rather is a process that involves relationships between leaders and followers. In fact, good leaders not only know how to set an example for others, they also know how to follow other people's good examples (Daft, 2010; Northouse, 2010; Rost, 2008).

Did You Know?

Leadership Is an Influence Relationship

Shawn M. Fouts, who works with student leadership training at his university, blogs about his view of leadership as an "influence relationship."

Do you think there can be relationships without leadership, and influence without relationships? Explain your opinion. Fouts asserts that lack of leadership is a widespread problem. What evidence do you find to support or refute this idea?

This leadership thing is consuming me. Not that I have always been the consummate leader, mainly due to a lack of knowledge and modeling. But, as I work with this thing called leadership I have come to a few conclusions:

1. Leadership is a philosophy, not a theory.
2. Leadership philosophy is life philosophy, in my mind the two are one.
3. Leadership is nothing more than Relationships + Influence. How can I influence people in my relationships?

Leadership = Relationships + Influence

Profoundly simple, really. I wonder why we see such a lack of leadership all around us then? I intentionally choose to be a leader (at the least an active participant) in everything I do, everywhere I go, and in every relationship I currently have and make on a daily basis, no matter how big or how small. But, I have to choose to be an influence and I have to choose what kind of influence I will be, either positive or negative. I wonder if influencing one really is influencing many? I think it's worth a try.

SOURCE: Fouts, S. M. (2007, June 4), *The Student Affairs Blog*, West Texas A & M University. Retrieved March 30, 2011, from http://www.thesablog.org/2007/06/leadership_as_a.html

The second element in Daft's definition of leadership also involves the intention to change; this distinguishes it from the concept of management, which is more about order and stability. In addition, Daft refers to outcomes that reflect the shared purposes of leaders and followers. An important aspect of leadership, then, is to influence others to come together around a common vision. For example, Martin Luther King, Jr., built a shared vision of a society in which people would be judged by their character, not their color; he mobilized his followers to act via nonviolent protest in realizing this vision. Similarly, today's ordinary citizens and students can rally others around a strongly held idea of change.

Effective Leadership in Small Groups Most small groups have a leader. Some leaders are designated or appointed, whereas some emerge during group interaction. In either case, a good leader can be the key to successful communication in a small group. We will first examine the importance of communication in leadership and then identify the characteristics of a good leader.

It would be easy to assume that leaders are naturally good communicators, but communication researchers have not confirmed this (Pavitt, 1999). As one leadership expert says, "just because leaders are smart doesn't mean they communicate well. Just because a leader sounds good and has an impressive looking presentation, doesn't mean he or she communicates well. In the end, it's not what you say but what your audience hears—and, we argue, what your audience *does*—that counts" (Matha & Boehm, 2008, p. 8).

Most experts agree that communication is key to being an effective leader, regardless of the particular leadership style or the context in which one provides leadership—whether it's providing guidance on a small group project in a communication course, heading up a fund-raising project for your sorority, or leading a support group for cancer patients. According to Matha and Boehm (2008), "communication is the face of leadership" (p. 20). However, it is easy to take communication for granted and focus on other challenges in the group—a reason that many leaders fail at communication. As one leadership communication consultant puts it, "Communication requires discipline, thought, perseverance and the willingness to do it again and again" (Baldoni, 2004, p. 24).

The role of communication in leadership is not a matter of declaring a vision, giving orders, and ensuring that the vision is implemented. Instead, it depends on building trust and commitment to the vision through communication; it is ultimately about bringing people together for a common cause—in short, building relationships (Uhl-Bien, 2006). Leadership experts Robert and Janet Denhardt (2004) describe the essence of leadership as the capacity to "energize" potential followers by *connecting* with people at a personal, sometimes emotional, level so that they become engaged and active. Think about the communication that occurs in many small groups brought together to solve a problem or complete a task:

> The conversation will swirl around inconclusively for a while (sometimes a long time) until one person makes a suggestion that others pick up on and begin to act upon. People's reactions may be based on the substance of what was said or on the way in which it was presented, or most likely, some combination of both. But, in any case, we would say that where people react with energy and enthusiasm, leadership has been exercised. (Denhardt & Denhardt, 2004, p. 20)

Connecting with potential followers can also be part of a larger strategic communication plan. What is **strategic communication**? According to leadership experts Bob Matha and Macy Boehm (2008), it is communication that is *purpose directed*—it directs everyone's attention toward the leader's vision, values, and desired outcomes and motivates people to take action to help achieve the vision. This means that a leader must first understand what motivates people and appeal to that, giving them the information they need to do their job, listening to them, and then getting out of their way, as exemplified by the story our student tells about her boss in *It Happened to Me: Martha*.

Effective leaders are committed to communicating willingly and consistently. Because followers are individuals with their own differences, and each leadership situation is unique, there is no one "right" way of communicating. The test of successful leadership communication is whether leaders are able to form meaningful relationships, energize their potential followers, and achieve desired results (Baldoni, 2004). As we will see, there is no one way of leading, and just as there is no one "right" way of communicating,

It Happened to Me: *Martha*

I've worked at several different organizations in different sectors, but I have found that the most important thing that leaders, bosses, or supervisors can do is give their subordinates a sense of empowerment. When you're given a task by your boss, you want her to trust that you'll do a good job—you want her to believe in your abilities and give you the space to succeed. I couldn't work for someone who questioned everything I did or watched my every move.

there is no one "right" type of leadership. However, researchers have identified five theories that explain effective leaders: trait theory, functional theory, style theory, transformational leadership theory, and servant leadership theory. Let's examine them one by one.

Trait Theory Probably the oldest theory concerning leadership in the communication field is **trait theory** (Stogdill, 1974). Trait theory suggests that leaders are born. Some of the traits associated with effective leadership are physical and include being male, tall, and good looking. For example, not since 1896 have U.S. citizens elected a president whose height was below average, and even today, people associate height with leadership ability (Judge & Cable, 2004).

strategic communication
communication that is purpose directed

trait theory
leadership theory that suggests that leaders are born

Other studies have examined the relationship of leadership to personality traits. For example, leaders seem to be more extroverted, open to experience, agreeable, and conscientious than nonleaders (Judge, Bono, Ilies, & Gerhardt, 2002; Stogdill, 1974). Moreover, they seem to be smarter than other people as measured by standard IQ tests (Judge, Colbert, & Ilies, 2004).

Despite the correlation between leaders and particular traits, one cannot ignore the role of society in forming our judgments about who we think makes a good leader. For example, early business writings suggested that the function of the business leader was to "fit in" with others in the workplace. Requirements for fitting in were shared "education, experience, age, sex, race, nationality, faith, politics, and such very specific personal traits as manners, speech, personal appearance" (Barnard, 1938, p. 224). Of course, in 1938, fitting in was only possible for White males of a certain background and education. In addition, the trait approach may reinforce the notion that only people born with certain qualities can achieve leadership, ignoring the fact that only those who have the most status and power in the society also possess these qualities.

Many examples challenge the trait approach to leadership. In recent years a number of people have developed leadership qualities out of a tragedy or a deep motivation to make the world a better place. Candy Lightner, who founded MADD (Mothers Against Drunk Driving) when her own child was killed by a drunk driver, is one of these. Judy Shepard, whose son Matthew was attacked, tortured, and left to die because he was gay, became an outspoken leader and advocate for tolerance and justice (Groutage, 1999). Neither woman was a "born leader," but both took on leadership roles when the situation demanded it.

As an undergraduate, Sindhura Citineni started a campus project to combat world hunger and later led a group of students to form Nourish International, a worldwide nonprofit organization.

Perhaps you know of college students who have been motivated to take on similar leadership roles. For instance, undergraduate Sindhura Citineni felt determined to make a difference when confronted by the appalling statistics of world hunger she found while researching on the Internet. Citineni negotiated with her university to sell several simple food items in the cafeteria where part of the revenue went to hunger-relief work—called Hunger Lunch. She then led a group of students who expanded that project into Nourish International, now a nonprofit organization that connects college students from universities around the United States to development projects abroad (http://nourishinternational.org). As you see, while there are some personality characteristics associated with good leadership, most experts now reject the trait theory notion that leaders are born, not made. The four following theories provide more plausible definitions and explanations of effective leadership.

Functional Theory A second approach to analyzing leadership, the **functional (situational) theory**, stands in direct contrast to the trait approach. Unlike trait theory, which assumes leadership is innate, this theory assumes that leadership behaviors can be learned, even by group members who are not "leadership types." Functional theory assumes that whatever the group needs at a particular time can be supplied by a set of behaviors any group member can contribute (Barnlund & Haiman, 1960; Benne & Sheats, 1948; Pavitt, 1999). Thus this theory argues that the leader can change from time to time, depending on the changing needs of the group.

According to functional theory, a group does not need a designated leader; rather, any group member can serve as leader at any particular time by filling the required role. For example, the leader can fill task roles when the group needs direction, then step into relational roles when group members understand the task but need encouragement. Occasionally, no leadership is needed, such as when the short- and long-term purpose is clear and group members are working well independently.

As we noted earlier, group success does not depend on the number of task behaviors or relational behaviors that group members engage in, but rather on whether they exhibit the required role behavior when needed. For example, too much emphasis on task behaviors can be counterproductive if the task is already

functional (situational) theory
a theory that assumes leadership behaviors can be learned

clearly defined and understood by all group members. Too much relational leadership is distracting if members view it as getting in the way of completing the group task (Rauch & Behling, 1984). Thus, if a group has almost completed its task and discussion is going smoothly, constant encourager behavior may be distracting and unnecessary.

A related notion is **shared leadership,** also called *collaborative* or *distributed leadership*. Here the functional leadership approach is extended to an organizational level where team relationships become more of a partnership in an organization (MacNeil & McClanahan, 2005). The requirements for this kind of leadership are a balance of power where:

- all members are equal partners;
- all share a common purpose or goal;
- all share responsibility for the work of the group (take an active role and are accountable for completing their individual contribution); all have respect for the person—and skills and ideas that each brings to the team; and
- all work together in complex, real-world situations.

Style Theory A third approach to analyzing leadership asserts that a leader's manner or **style** of leading a group determines her or his success. Further, this theory describes three common styles of leadership: authoritarian, democratic, and laissez-faire.

An **authoritarian leader** takes charge and has a high level of intellect and expertise (Lewin, Lippit, & White, 1939). The authoritarian leader makes all the decisions and dictates strategies and work tasks. This type of leadership is appropriate in military, sports, or crisis situations. For example, military organizations have a highly authoritarian structure, and the chain of command must be rigorously followed. In battle, there is no time for discussion and little room for trial and error. This is also true of sports-team leadership. For example, when twenty-five seconds are left in a basketball game and the score is tied, only one person—the coach—can tell the team members how to execute the next play.

Authoritarian leadership is also appropriate in crises. Medical teams in an emergency room generally follow authoritarian leadership—one person, the doctor, directs the others in what needs to be done. This style of leadership may also be followed when time for discussion is short or when the stakes are very high (Meade, 1985).

Democratic leadership is the style we are most familiar with, and the one that seems to work best in many group situations. A **democratic leader's** style is characterized by a great deal of input from group members; the qualities of this leader are best summarized by Lao-tse (550 B.C.E.): "A good leader is one who talks little; when his work is done, his aim fulfilled, they will all say 'We did this ourselves'" (cited in Foels, Driskell, Mullen, & Salas, 2000, p. 677).

In this style, group discussion determines all policies, strategies, and division of labor. Members are free to assume a variety of roles, to contribute when appropriate, and to share leadership. Further, research supports the idea that most groups are more satisfied with a democratic leader than an authoritarian one (Foels et al., 2000; Gastil, 1994).

In contrast, some small group situations call for a **laissez-faire** style. This style is characterized by complete freedom for the group in making decisions. The leader participates minimally and may supply materials and information when asked, but she makes no attempt to evaluate or influence the discussion. The laissez-faire style may work well when little is at stake, as in some social groups like book clubs or gourmet clubs (Barge, 1989). As we can see, these three styles each have their strengths, and different situations call for different leadership styles.

Transformational Leadership Theory A relatively new theory, **transformational leadership** theory, emphasizes the importance of relationships in leadership.

shared (collaborative or distributed) leadership
a type of leadership style where functional leadership is extended to an organizational level; all members are equal partners and share responsibility for the work of the group

Rick Pitino is the first coach in NCAA history to lead three different basketball teams to the Final Four (Providence, Kentucky, and Louisville). As a leader, he has to make split-second decisions during basketball games.

style theory
theory that asserts that a leader's manner or style determines his or her success

authoritarian leader
leader who takes charge, makes all the decisions, and dictates strategies and work tasks

democratic leader
leader whose style is characterized by considerable input from group members

laissez-faire
a leadership style characterized by complete freedom for the group in making decisions

transformational leadership
a leadership style that empowers group members to work independently from the leader by encouraging group cohesion

The role of the transformational leader is to empower group members to work independently from the leader by encouraging collaboration between members and group cohesion. Research identifies at least four general characteristics shared by transformational leaders. First, they have high moral and ethical standards that engender high regard and loyalty from followers. Second, they have a strong vision for the future, which stimulates enthusiasm and builds confidence among followers. Third, they challenge the status quo and encourage innovation in an organization; and last, they recognize unique strengths and capabilities of followers and coach and consult with them to help them develop their full potential (Bono & Judge, 2004). While researchers have attempted to identify very specific personality traits, like agreeableness, conscientiousness, or openness, as characteristics of transformational leaders, only one quality seems to be consistent—extraversion—which includes the ability to convey positive emotions and project optimism and enthusiasm (Bono & Judge, 2004).

Transformational leaders are especially effective when they can motivate followers to perform beyond standard expectations, often by inspiring them to put the collective needs of the group above their own individual needs. When this occurs, groups are empowered, cohesive, and effective (Jung & Sosik, 2002).

A recent study of workers in European health-care facilities compared several different types of leadership (authoritarian, laissez-faire, transformational) to discover which, if any, could lead to better employee involvement and better teamwork, all of which have been shown to reduce stress levels in an often stressful work environment, such as a hospital. The study found that transformational leadership was the most effective in inspiring individual employee involvement (Savič & Pagon, 2008).

Transformational leadership is sometimes confused with **charismatic leadership,** a style proposed by scholars in political science and religious studies. Like transformational leaders, charismatic leaders have a strong belief in their vision. They are also extremely self-confident and able to inspire great dedication and loyalty in their followers. Followers of charismatic (and transformational) leaders are often willing to set high (sometimes unrealistic) objectives and often make tremendous sacrifices, ultimately achieving more than was expected or deemed possible (Rowold & Heinitz, 2007).

As you might imagine, strong communication skills are central to both charismatic and transformational leadership. In fact, a recent study confirms this, finding that both verbal and nonverbal competencies are considered essential (Levine, Muenchen & Brooks, 2010). Public speaking skills—ease and comfort when speaking, pleasant and positive vocal style, and the ability to persuade and motivate a group—were mentioned as very important. But such leaders don't succeed only by speaking; listening was also identified as an important communication skill in these leadership styles.

However, as shown in Table 10.4, there are important differences between charismatic and transformational leaders. Specifically, charismatic leaders rely upon their strong personalities and charm to create loyalty to themselves, while transformational leaders build relationships and strive to create loyalty to the group or organization, not to the individual leader. Thus, when a transformational leader exits the group, the organization is more likely to thrive, since member commitment is to the group. When charismatic leaders leave, the group may falter because the individuals' commitment is to the leader, not to one another. And unlike transformational leaders who manage to inspire their followers for a long time, charismatic leadership may be relatively short-lived, since they may also be autocratic and self-serving, and followers may become disillusioned (Daft, 2010; Pavitt, 1999). In fact, charismatic leadership can have disastrous results: Hitler and Mussolini, for example, were charismatic leaders. While such leaders inspire trust, faith, and belief in themselves, there is no guarantee that their vision or mission will be correct, ethical, or successful.

charismatic leadership
a leadership style in which extremely self-confident leaders inspire unusual dedication to themselves by relying upon their strong personalities and charm

TABLE 10.4 Transformational and Charismatic Leaders	
Transformational	**Charismatic**
Strong Vision	Strong Vision
High Expectations for Followers	High Expectations for Followers
Builds Relationships	Relies on Strong Personality
Creates Loyalty to Organization	Creates Loyalty to Self
Enduring Inspiration	Leadership May Be Short-Lived

Servant Leadership Theory The idea of **servant leadership** was introduced to organizations through Robert Greenleaf's 1970 essay, "The Servant as Leader." The concept was further popularized by writers such as Stephen Covey, whose 1989 bestseller *The Seven Habits of Highly Effective People* made a major impact in the business world.

According to Greenleaf, a servant-leader must excel at ten characteristics. As you can see, the first ones are very specific communication skills and the rest broaden to include more general relational skills:

- awareness
- listening
- empathizing
- persuasion
- conceptualization
- foresight
- stewardship
- healing
- commitment to the growth of others
- building community

You will notice that most of these ten characteristics are communication skills. Servant leadership emphasizes collaboration, trust, and the ethical use of power. The theory proposes that at heart, the individual is a servant first and makes a conscious decision to lead in order to better serve others, not to increase his or her own power. The objective is to enhance the growth of individuals in the organization and to increase teamwork and personal involvement (Greenleaf, 1991, 2002).

Effective Small Group Communication

Now that we have described the important role of communication in effective leadership, and various theories of group leadership, we are ready to ask the question: What communication behaviors are necessary for effective small group interaction? The answer seems to be that effective groups maintain a balance of task and relational communication, and the sequence of each appears to be more important than the relative amount of each. For example, after an intense period of task talk, group members might defuse their tension with positive social, or relational, talk and then return to task talk (Pavitt, 1999).

What types of communication lead to effective sequencing of task and relational communication? And how can members best use these skills when the primary goal of a small group is to solve a particular problem? Experts find that the following four communication processes lead to task effectiveness and member satisfaction (relational effectiveness) in small groups in many situations—whether a team project

Consider the definition of leadership provided in this chapter. In which of your relationships and everyday activities do you provide leadership? In which contexts (school, home, extracurricular activities) are you most likely to provide leadership?

servant leadership
a leadership style that seeks to ensure that other people's highest priority needs are being served in order to increase teamwork and personal involvement

in a *Fortune* 500 company, a fundraising committee for a charity organization, or a small group assignment in a communication course (Oetzel, 1998, 2001, 2005).

1. *Equal participation:* All group members contribute at relatively equal levels, taking approximately the same number of turns talking. You might think that it's not important that everyone talks during a group discussion; or perhaps you yourself tend to be quiet and reserved in group meetings. However, the fact is that if everyone participates, the group can consider a wider variety of ideas, attend to more aspects of the topic, and thus make better decisions. Furthermore, group members who do not contribute feel less commitment to the group outcomes and implementation, and may ultimately sabotage the group effort (Lewis, Isbell, & Koschmann, 2010). What can you, as a group member, do to ensure that everyone participates equally? You can monitor the participation of all members, playing the expeditor role to prevent talkative or domineering members from talking too much and the gatekeeper role in drawing out those nonparticipating members. In addition, if you, as a group member, tend to be silent, consider the importance of expressing your views, even if they are primarily expressions of support and agreement.

2. *A consensus decision-making style:* Members participate in and agree with the decisions made by the group. While it is not always possible to have every group member agree with every decision, nonparticipating members and members who disagree with group decisions can have very negative impacts on group outcomes—as described above. Therefore, it is in the best interests of the group to get buy-in from as many members as possible. As a group member, you can facilitate agreement by encouraging participation of all members (described above), by showing how ideas are related (coordinator role), and by encouraging a cooperative conflict style (described below).

3. *A cooperative conflict style:* The group manages conflict by integrating all parties' interests. As we will see later, some conflict is an inevitable part of small group discussion, and when handled well, it can be productive in sharpening issues and getting out various positions. For now, let's just say that effective groups approach conflict in a cooperative rather than a competitive, divisive manner. This means that the goal in a cooperative approach is to try to turn the conflict into a mutual problem that all members can work on to their mutual benefit. A little later in the chapter, we will provide more specific strategies for dealing with group conflict in a cooperative manner.

4. *A respectful communication style:* Group members demonstrate that other members are valued and important. How is this accomplished? Most often, members show respect by communicating a sense of mutual support and acceptance. This means using the verbal and nonverbal strategies that strengthen interpersonal relationships—described in other chapters in this book. For members of a problem-solving group, it includes being specific and softening messages of criticism; and when promoting a position, it means providing evidence focused primarily on the ideas and tasks and separating the ideas from the person who puts them forward.

How can members best use these skills when the primary goal of a small group is to solve a particular problem? One of the great communication challenges for groups is to pinpoint the problem and all its possible solutions. In this section, we'll first describe a five-step agenda that problem-solving groups have found useful. Second, we'll examine how decision making occurs in small groups including a negative group process—*groupthink.* Finally, we'll describe the characteristics of discussions in small groups whose members are separated geographically and, in particular, the role technology can play in them.

Problem-Solving Agenda A danger in problem-solving groups is jumping immediately to a solution. One useful tool for avoiding a premature and incomplete solution is to develop and follow a sequence or agenda. In fact, early research surveying hundreds of small group participants identified lack of strong procedural guidelines as one of the primary barriers to effective problem solving (Broome & Fulbright, 1995). While many agendas exist, perhaps the best known are variations of educator John Dewey's five-step procedure (Cragan & Wright, 1999, p. 97). Two points are central to using an agenda effectively, and at first they may sound contradictory. First, researchers have found that most problem-solving groups have less conflict and a more consistent focus when they follow formal procedures (Klocke, 2007). Second, successful groups do not necessarily solve all problems in strict sequential order; they may take a variety of paths (Schultz, 1999). In general, then, groups benefit from keeping the agenda in mind, but members should realize that they may have to cycle back and forth between phases before reaching a solution.

Earlier in the chapter, we discussed the example of a campus task force working to improve campus safety. Let's return to that example and see how that group might follow the five-step problem-solving agenda and the recommendations for effective communication at each step.

STEP 1. *Define and Delineate the Problem.* The first step in solving a problem is to make sure that everyone in the group understands it in the same way. After all, the problem can't be solved unless group members know what it is (and is not). On the campus security task force case study, the group members were successful in part because they agreed on the definition of the problem. They decided their problem was twofold: (1) the personal security of students in dorms and while walking on campus and (2) the protection of students' personal property. They decided that they would not address the security of classroom and office equipment because they were primarily a student group. This helped them narrow the focus and set limits for the discussion of solutions.

STEP 2. *Analyze the Problem.* In some ways, this is the most important phase of the agenda because it determines the direction of potential solutions (Hirokawa & Salazar, 1999). Group members must look at all sides of the problem. To do so, they answer questions like *Who is affected by the problem? How widespread is it?* In the case of the campus security team, the group had to gather data on the exact nature of security problems—the frequency of burglaries, rapes, assaults, and robberies on campus; where and when these incidents were occurring; and what consequences the incidents had. However, a word of caution is in order. In some cases, too much analysis can result in **analysis paralysis** and prevent a group from moving toward a solution. (Rothwell, 1995). Our campus security group, for example, could continue to gather statistics, interview people about the problem, and discuss the problem—and never move on to possible solutions.

STEP 3. *Identify Alternative Solutions.* One challenge at this stage is to avoid rushing to premature solutions; instead, the group should consider several possible solutions. One way to make sure that many solutions are considered is to **brainstorm**,

If you were a member of this problem-solving group, what communication roles might you use to improve the group's effectiveness?

analysis paralysis
potential pitfall in small group interaction; occurs when excessive analysis prevents a group from moving toward a solution

brainstorm
to generate as many ideas as possible without critiquing them

generating as many ideas as possible without critiquing them. By brainstorming, the campus security group put forth a wide range of possible solutions, including putting up more lighting, increasing the number of campus police, and helping students to register their private property (bikes, computers, stereo equipment, and so on) so that stolen property could be traced. Some solutions were more unusual, including suggestions to eliminate foliage where assailants could hide, to sell wristband tracking devices to students, to place guard dogs in dormitories, and to have 24/7 volunteer security details in the dorms.

STEP 4. *Evaluate Proposed Solutions.* Evaluating proposed solutions involves establishing evaluation criteria. The campus security task force, for example, identified three criteria for its solutions: They had to be economically feasible, logistically feasible, and likely to solve the problem of campus security. With these criteria in mind, the task force had a basis for evaluating each solution. This stage is critical, but it can be difficult. If members are tired or frustrated by all the work they've already done, they may jump to conclusions. However, if they keep to the agenda and carefully consider each alternative, they will quickly reject some solutions and find others attractive. According to one study, a strong positive relationship exists between a group's decision-making performance and members' satisfaction with alternatives chosen (Hirokawa & Salazar, 1999).

STEP 5. *Choose the Best Solution.* While this step may seem redundant, choosing the best solution(s) is not the same as evaluating all proposed solutions. Here it is especially important that everyone participates and buys into the solution, and decision-making procedures are most critical.

The problem-solving agenda is a specific format or set of guidelines that task groups can follow to ensure high-quality solutions. As groups progress through the stages, however, they will need to make multiple decisions. For example, during stage four, the evaluation stage, the group will need to decide what the appropriate criteria are for evaluating proposed solutions, whether they will evaluate all or just some of the proposed solutions, and how they will manage differences of opinion regarding the value of proposed solutions. To help you understand the decision-making process that occurs throughout the problem-solving agenda, in the next section we explore the *process* of decision making.

Decision-Making Phases　How do small groups arrive at good decisions? Are there specific communication processes that can lead to good decisions? What are some warning signs of unproductive decision-making? Is conflict a necessary part of the group decision-making process, or should it be avoided? These are questions we'll tackle in this section. As you can imagine, there is no one recipe for effective decision making. However, there are several phases that seem to represent the communication that occurs in effective problem-solving groups: orientation, conflict, emergence, and reinforcement (Bormann, 1975; Fisher, 1980; Fisher & Ellis, 1993; Wheelan, Davidson, & Tilin, 2003).

Before describing these phases, we should note that most groups do not proceed through them in an orderly, linear fashion. Rather, they may cycle through the first phase twice before moving to the next phase, or they may revert back to the conflict phase after reaching the final, emergence phase (Poole, 1983). With these thoughts in mind, let's look at the four phases individually.

Phase 1. *Orientation.* During this phase of decision making, group members usually orient themselves to the problem and to each other (if they have just met). Uncertainty at this stage is common and is referred to as **primary tension**. For example, as a group member, you might wonder how the group is going to function. You may have questions about the relational aspect of the group processes: Are you going to like the other members? Will you all get along, or will you clash? In *It Happened to Me: Kirstin,* one of our students describes a relational problem that

primary tension
the uncertainty commonly felt in the beginning phase of decision making

emerged at the beginning of her group project and that contributed to the tension the group felt as they began their talk. As you can see, she played an important relational role as a gatekeeper in encouraging the nonparticipating members to communicate and as a harmonizer in helping the group members work through a situation that seemed well on its way to becoming a conflict situation.

During Phase 1, you may also experience uncertainty about the task you are to undertake: Will everyone contribute equally? Will the work get done efficiently and on time?

Communication at this phase is generally polite, tentative, and focused on reducing uncertainty and ambiguity

It Happened to Me: *Kirstin*

Being the only communication major in our group, I immediately noticed some problems. The nonverbal cues from two members contradicted their verbal messages. They rolled their eyes or turned their bodies away from the group when they were asked to do a task. When someone asked what was wrong, those two replied "nothing." I knew this did not bode well for the group, so I shared some of my communication skills and knowledge. I encouraged the two nonparticipating members to contribute and asked them if anything was wrong. They told us they were worried because they'd had a bad experience in an earlier group project. We talked about how we all needed to pull together. I was kind of a cheerleader for the group. So we got through this, and the group arrived at a decision and completed the task without any major conflict.

through clarification and agreement. The importance of the orientation phase is that many relational and task norms are set for the future. Fortunately for Kirstin's group, she realized the importance of group communication and got the group off to a good start.

Regardless of norms that they establish, groups often experience recurring primary tension if they meet over an extended period. For example, at the beginning of each meeting, group members may need to spend time reconnecting and reviewing their views on the task. In response, then, a group member filling the orienter role might summarize what has been accomplished at the most recent meetings, and the recorder could read back minutes or notes from the last meeting.

Phase 2. *Conflict.* The conflict phase in decision making is characterized by **secondary (recurring) tension.** This phase usually occurs after group members become acquainted, after some norms and expectations are set, and when decision alternatives are to be addressed.

As members become more relaxed, this phase of their communication becomes more animated and honest. Members may interrupt each other, talk loudly, and try on group roles. Some may try to dominate, push their own agendas, and form coalitions in an effort to increase their influence; others may engage in side conversations as they lose their focus on the decision at hand. It is especially important at this time to follow the suggestions for effective group communication mentioned earlier: equal participation, consensus decision making, and respectful communication.

Equal participation is especially important in this phase, and the type of information contributed by members is also important. For example, recent research shows that *unique* information is more useful than *shared* information (information known by all members) in reaching high-quality decisions. That is, when group members repeat what they and every other group member knows and fail to share new information with others, they neglect to take advantage of the diverse valuable group resources (Bonito, DeCamp, & Ruppel, 2008). In order to ensure that unique information is shared, experts suggest assigning members explicit roles like "decision-maker advisor," someone who monitors and encourages information-giving (van Swol, 2009).

Of course, all groups experience some conflict, and a certain amount of conflict can be both healthy and functional because it can increase member involvement (Klocke, 2007). One productive way to handle group conflict is through using a cooperative conflict style that integrates all members' interests (Oetzl, 2005; Poole & Garner, 2006). If tensions become very high, the strategies outlined in *Did You Know? Handling Conflicts in Meetings* might help to manage the conflict.

secondary (recurring) tension conflict or tension found in the second or conflict phase of the decision-making process

Did You Know?

Handling Conflicts in Meetings

For each of the principles listed below, can you think of a group conflict situation where the specific principle would be especially useful? Consider conflict situations you have experienced personally (e.g., in your family or with roommates, on class projects or sports teams, or in clubs or other organizations) as well as those you have observed (e.g., in political groups or corporations as reported in the news).

Conflicts in group meetings can be very disruptive, but they can also be helpful. Remember, conflicts are disagreements. If the person who is disagreeing is raising valid questions, the group may benefit by addressing the issues he or she is presenting. In fact, by listening, you may gain valuable insight into what is and is not working within your group. However, if you are the person involved in the conflict, you might not be able to listen well, and the group may need someone else to step in to fill the harmonizer or compromiser role.

When conflict takes precedence over problem solving, here are a few principles to keep in mind:

- Clarify what the conflict is about.
- Affirm the validity of all viewpoints.
- Frame the conflict in terms of a problem to be solved.
- Create space for problem solving to occur.
- Help participants save face.
- Discuss what happens if no agreement is reached.
- Ask if the group can proceed with what they do agree on and hold back on areas of disagreement.

Adapted from: Duncan, M. (2009). *Effective meeting facilitation: The sine qua non of planning.* Retrieved March 30, 2011, from http://www.nea.gov/resources/Lessons/DUNCAN1.HTML

Phase 3. *Emergence.* In the **emergence phase,** the group has worked through the primary and secondary tensions, and members express a cooperative attitude. In successful groups, coalitions dissipate, and group members are less tenacious about holding their positions. Comments become more favorable as members compromise to reach consensus, discuss their problem at length, consider possible alternatives, and eventually generate a group decision (Fisher, 1970, cited in Littlejohn, 2002). This is the longest phase. For various procedures that can help groups reach agreement, see *Did You Know? Procedures That Help Groups Agree.*

Recurring and sustained bouts of secondary tension or conflict can be problematic. In response, members can fill relational roles that promote trust (assuring members that they can rely on each other to put forward their best effort) and cohesion (expressing a desire to remain in the group). Members can also reduce tension by articulating a positive attitude or feeling about their group, the task, or other members and by emphasizing group identity and pride in the group's effort. In short, strong relational bonds within a group promote high-quality decisions and problem solving (Keyton, 1999, 2000), and groups with high trust have fewer relationship conflicts (Peterson & Behfar, 2003).

Phase 4. *Reinforcement.* During the **reinforcement phase,** members reach consensus, the decision solidifies, and members feel a sense of accomplishment and satisfaction. If a small majority makes the decision, they spend phase four convincing other members of its value. In successful groups, members unify and stand behind the solution. Comments are almost uniformly positive.

emergence phase
the third phase of the decision-making process; occurs when group members express a cooperative attitude

reinforcement phase
the final phase of the decision-making process when group members reach consensus, and members feel a sense of accomplishment

Did You Know?

Procedures That Help Groups Agree

List some advantages and disadvantages to each of these procedures. Do some of them promote deeper agreement than others? How so?

- *Voting:* simultaneous (raised hands, vocal), sequential (round robin), or secret (written)
- *Decision rule:* predetermined level of support needed to reach agreement (for example, two-thirds majority, simple majority, or unanimity)
- *Straw poll:* nonbinding voting method that allows the group to get a sense of members' preferences while still allowing them to change preferences
- *Concession:* agreement to eventually agree, in spite of individual preferences
- *Problem-centered leadership:* procedure in which the leader acts as facilitator, guiding group toward agreement
- *Negotiating:* reaching agreement through series of trade-offs

Adapted from: Sunwolf & Seibold, D. R. (1999). The impact of formal procedure on group processes, members, and task outcomes. In L. R. Frey, D. S. Gouran, & M. S. Poole (Eds.), *Handbook of group communication theory and research* (p. 401). Thousand Oaks, CA: Sage.

Groupthink

Coming to a decision easily with lots of group cohesion may seem like the ideal situation, but it may actually reflect a negative group process—**groupthink**. Groupthink occurs when members arrive at a consensus before all alternatives have been realistically assessed. This occurs when group members feel a pressure to conform; they reject new information and may react negatively to individuals outside the group who volunteer information that contradicts the group decisions. In addition, the group members have an illusion of invulnerability and unanimity. These symptoms produce pressure on group members to go along with the favored group position, assuming not only that the group preferences will be successful but also just and right (Henningsen & Henningsen, 2006). This phenomenon can have disastrous consequences. The term was coined in an analysis of several foreign policy fiascoes, such as the Bay of Pigs Invasion in 1961 and the U.S. decision to invade Iraq in 2003.

Another example of the disastrous consequences of groupthink was the *Challenger* space shuttle explosion seventy-three seconds into its launch on January 28, 1986. Within days, President Reagan appointed a commission of experts who discovered that the primary cause of the accident was a mechanical failure in one of the joints of the right solid rocket booster. The commission concluded that the contributing cause was a flawed decision-making process at NASA. Several NASA personnel had warned of potential problems with the launch, and numerous opportunities arose to postpone it. However, on each occasion, one or more of the following influences surfaced and reduced the chances for preventing the disaster:

- the unwillingness of individuals to step outside their roles and question those in authority;
- questionable patterns of reasoning by key managers;
- ambiguous and misleading language that minimized the perception of risk;
- failure to ask important questions relevant to the final decision.

groupthink
a negative, and potentially disastrous, group process characterized by "excessive concurrence thinking"

In deciding to protest a tuition increase, might groupthink lead the group to neglect to consider how the increased revenue might actually benefit students?

GSS software ensures that every group member has an equal chance to participate since any-one can submit a comment at any time.

In this case, poor communication skills and an unwillingness to explore possible problems and to risk disagreement led to an event that ultimately undermined the respect for prior achievements of the space agency (Gouran, Hirokawa, & Martz, 1986).

What causes people to engage in groupthink? One reason may be a high level of cohesiveness. Although group cohesion is usually viewed as a positive thing, too much of it can lead to premature agreement. Other reasons may be insulation—very tight boundaries that prevent a group from being open to relevant new information (Putnam & Stohl, 1996). Leadership can also promote groupthink: either very strong leadership, where one dominating person promotes only one idea; or the opposite—a lack of leadership, leaving the group without direction. Groupthink can also result from a failure to set norms for decision making or from a failure to follow a problem-solving agenda. Finally, extreme homogeneity in the backgrounds of group members may also lead to rushed solutions rather than careful examination of alternatives (Henningsen & Henningsen, 2006).

Groupthink can be prevented in several ways. For example, following an established procedure and making sure adequate time is spent in discussion before reaching a decision are both helpful. Perhaps even more important, group members should be aware of the causes and consequences of groupthink and encourage critical evaluation (at the appropriate time) of ideas to prevent premature decisions.

Technology and Group Communication

Technology is playing an increased role in group work, a topic we will address in more detail in Chapter 14. Some researchers assert that technology enhances positive outcomes in a diverse workforce, as communication technologies reduce the cues that often lead to stereotypes and prejudice. For example, in virtual teams, members cannot see the gender, skin color, or age of their colleagues, which may equalize contributions and facilitate discussion (Scott, 1999).

For example, Marek, one of our students, works for an international pharmaceutical company and often collaborates on projects with group members whom he has never met. Members of his team are scattered around the globe in multiple time zones. Thus he may be online with Luc in Montreal, Caroline in London, Liana in Buenos Aires, Ahmed in Riyadh, Setsuko in Osaka, and Giles in Melbourne. Although he may not have met his group members face to face, their tasks are well defined, and this enables the group to complete their projects with few problems. Moreover, their diverse cultural backgrounds enhance the group's ideas and produce a stronger product.

Teams like these that are separated by time or distance rely on a variety of technologies. Some are immediate and synchronous, like audio and teleconferencing technologies that allow members to see and hear each other from remote locations. Another technology is Group Support Software (GSS), a computer-aided program that supports real-time discussion between members regardless of physical location; with GSS, each participant sits at a computer terminal and the discussion is facilitated by the software program. The best known of these programs is Group Decision Support Software (GDSS) (Broome & Chen, 1992).

An additional trend involves combining several technologies such as live videoconferences, text-based document sharing, audio connections, and shared whiteboards on which participants in one location can write, allowing participants in other locations to see their notes. An increasing number of people are working in virtual (or distributed) work teams; in fact, nearly two-thirds of U.S. employees have participated in virtual work (Connaughton & Shuffler, 2007). A virtual work team is a group of people identified as a team by their organization. The members are responsible for making decisions important to their organization; moreover, it may be culturally diverse, geographically dispersed, and have members who communicate electronically substantially more than they do face to face. Additionally, a new kind of virtual team phenomenon is changing the way people and businesses develop ideas using Internet collaboration. (See *Communication in Society: COINs: The Future of Innovation?*)

Virtual teams face a number of challenges, including distance, geography, and available technology (Poole & Garner, 2006). Some experts say that the communication problems between virtual team members are related to the number of time zones that separate them (Smith, 2001). If only a few time zones away, members can come to work earlier or later and still have overlapping workdays. If members are separated by many time zones, it becomes a much bigger challenge, particularly

COMMUNICATION IN SOCIETY
COINs: The Future of Innovation?

A recent book describes a new kind of virtual team phenomenon that is changing the way people and businesses develop ideas—through collaboration on the Internet. What are the communication challenges of working in these types of virtual teams compared with face-to-face teams?

Peter A. Gloor, a research scientist at Massachusetts Institute of Technology, and his colleagues have been studying a recent Internet phenomenon: Collaborative Innovation Networks, or COINs. Gloor defines a COIN as "a cyberteam of self-motivated people with a collective vision, enabled by the Web to collaborate in achieving a common goal by sharing ideas, information and work" (2006, p. 4). These inspired individuals, working together spontaneously as a virtual team, often at great distances, are not motivated by financial gain. Rather they collaborate because of their shared passion for innovation and a commitment to common goals and/or causes. Gloor describes their collaboration as "swarm creativity." As they spontaneously "swarm" together in cyberspace, they create an envi-

ronment that promotes dynamic and innovative collaborative thinking.

The results of these virtual collaborations have been astounding. As Gloor notes, the Internet itself is an example of a successful COIN. It was started by a group of people working at a physics research lab, then developed and fine-tuned by various groups of students, researchers, and computer scientists, crossing conventional organizational structures and hierarchies. The rest, as they say, is history. Other examples of more recent COIN successes are Linux and other open-source software products, as well as a number of other lesser-known commercial innovations.

Gloor point outs that while COINs existed well before the Internet, the Internet provides instantaneous global accessibility, ensuring a tremendous upsurge in productivity. In addition, Gloor and colleagues stress that for COINs to be successful, the team members not only need to share a passion for the products they're developing but also need a certain level of trust in fellow team members, balanced communication, and a shared code of ethics guiding their collaboration.

SOURCES: Gloor, P. A. (2006). *Swarm creativity: Competitive advantage through collaborative innovative networks.* Oxford: Oxford University Press. Gloor, P. A., Heckman, C., & Makedon, F. (2004, April 14–16) Ethical issues in virtual communities of innovation. Ethicomp 2004, the 7th International Conference on the Social and Ethical Impacts of Information and Communication Technologies, Syros, Greece. Retrieved July 17, 2011 from https://exchange.asu.edu/exchange/mar22/Drafts/documents/COIN4Ethicomp.pdf Gloor, P. A., Paasvaara, M., Schoder, D., & Willems, P. (2007, April). Finding collaborative innovation networks through correlating performance with social network structure. *Journal of Production Research*, Taylor and Francis. Retrieved July 17, 2011 from exchange.asu.edu/exchange/mar22/Drafts/documents/Gloor_JPR_3.pdf

When people work together in virtual teams, periodic face-to-face meetings are important to build trust and cohesion.

on Fridays and Mondays. However, other experts say that distance is not necessarily a big problem, and that teams find a way to work with the geographical distance and time differences (Connaughton & Shuffler, 2007). For example, one company with team members in the United States and Australia (a fifteen–time zone difference) has a policy that members from each country take turns getting up at 2 a.m. once a month for videoconferencing with members from the other country. The rest of the time, they rely on voicemail and email.

How can virtual teams work together most effectively? There seem to be two guidelines. One is to engage in frequent communication, which seems to reduce conflict and build trust, and the second is to choose the most appropriate communication technology for the task at hand (Maznevski & Chudoba, 2000; Schiller & Mandviwalla, 2007). Each technology works best in its niche. Telephone and videoconferences provide high-quality communication in real time, but when dealing with large time differences, email is probably better. Some experts suggest that face-to-face communication, particularly at the beginning of a group project, enhances the effectiveness of virtual teams (Connaughton & Shuffler, 2007).

A recent study compared the effectiveness of face-to-face and virtual student groups all working on the same task—a final class project in which students were presented with a survival scenario and required to work together to decide what they would need to survive after a plane crash in northern Canada (Li, 2007). After the task was completed, the researchers asked the students to assess their group's performance in terms of task and relational procedures (e.g., cohesion, process satisfaction, satisfaction with outcomes) as well as the quality of their communication. How satisfied were they with group cohesion? How satisfied were they with the group's processes? With its outcomes? Who do you think performed better, the virtual groups or the students who were working face to face? Not surprisingly, each type of team was effective in some ways. The virtual teams demonstrated somewhat higher quality task behaviors, but also took more time than did the face-to-face groups to complete the tasks. The face-to-face groups were better at performing relational role behaviors and completed the task more quickly, but—contrary to the researchers' expectations—did not have significantly better group outcomes. Perhaps this is because some of their relational role behaviors (e.g., too much social talk) did not actually facilitate high-quality task completion.

In sum, it seems that virtual teams—whether in business, academic, or social contexts—may be most useful for tasks that do not require quick decisions, but their work can be enhanced by frequent communication and even face-to-face meetings when possible. We'll discuss computer-mediated communication further in Chapter 14.

TEST YOUR KNOWLEDGE

- What is the difference between task and relational role behaviors in small group communication? How are they related to each other?
- What is the definition of group leadership, and why is leadership important in small group communication?
- What are the four elements of effective small group communication?
- What are the five steps in the problem-solving agenda?
- What is groupthink? What are its causes, and what are some strategies for avoiding it?
- What is a virtual team, and in what circumstances are virtual teams most effective?

THE INDIVIDUAL, SMALL GROUP COMMUNICATION, AND SOCIETY

Small group communication, like all communication, is influenced by societal forces. The world outside influences this form of communication in two important respects: (1) the way power is used inside and outside groups, and (2) the role cultural diversity plays.

Power and Group Communication

Small groups function within the influences of the societal forces we have discussed throughout this book: political, economic, and historical. People communicating in small groups bring with them their identities and the hierarchical meanings associated with those identities (see Chapter 3). Those group members who hold the values and follow the communication rules of the dominant group in society may more easily contribute to the group and dominate it, which may cause resentment among those who feel marginalized in society generally (Oetzel, 2005).

Groups also establish a power structure. For example, a group member may be elected or appointed to lead a group, which allows that person to wield *legitimate* power (French & Raven, 1959). Much of an individual's power is derived from her society/social status and standing. For example, when an individual is appointed to lead a group, this usually occurs because of her position within the social hierarchy of the organization.

These power arrangements come with benefits and drawbacks. On the one hand, productive uses of power can facilitate group processes (Sell, Lovaglia, Mannix, Samuelson, & Wilson, 2004). On the other hand, leaders or group members may turn legitimate power into *coercive* power, or threats, to get others to do what they want. For example, they may threaten to withdraw or undermine the process if group members don't do what they want, as experienced by one of our students in *It Happened to Me: Sarah*. In dealing with this dominating member, Sarah's group might have tried some relational roles such as expediter and/or harmonizer to prevent the dominator from derailing the group discussions.

The use of coercive power is usually unproductive because, as you can see in Sarah's experience, group members resent the threats and may reciprocate by using coercive power when they get the chance. Thus, too much power or a struggle for power can lead to resentment and poor decision making (Broome & Fulbright, 1995). In contrast, researchers

It Happened to Me: *Sarah*

We had one girl in our group who was headstrong, but very nice. She wanted to do the project "her way." She insisted that we follow her suggestions. If we didn't, she refused to participate and made comments that undermined the group work. If we did listen to her, then she was sweet and cooperative, and everything went fine. Some members wanted to try to please her; others resented her manipulation, and this situation caused a lot of conflict in the group.

find that groups whose members share power equally exhibit higher quality communication. When everyone participates and contributes to the discussion equally, power will more likely be distributed equally. In contrast, the unequal power of social hierarchies often occurs in the small group situation because members bring their identities and experiences to the group. Thus members' cultural identities, which fall along a power hierarchy, can impact small group work. Let's examine how this happens.

Cultural Diversity and Small Group Communication

Given the changing demographics in the United States and abroad, small groups will increasingly include members whose backgrounds differ. As we discussed in

Chapter 8, cultural backgrounds influence communication patterns, and small group communication is no exception (Broome & Fulbright, 1995; Poole & Garner, 2006). For example, people from countries where a collectivistic orientation dominates may be most concerned with maintaining harmony in the group, whereas members with an individualistic orientation may be more assertive and competitive in groups (Oetzel, 1998). These differences can lead to challenges in accomplishing group goals (Crown, 2007).

How does cultural diversity affect small group processes? Does it result in poor communication, more conflict, lower productivity, and less satisfaction? Or can diverse groups, with their various viewpoints, make better, more effective, and more creative decisions?

Research indicates that even though interactions might be more complex, especially in the early stages of group work, diversity can lead to positive and productive outcomes. Let's look at how diversity influences four aspects of group communication: innovation, efficacy, group processes, and group enjoyment.

Because diverse groups can outperform homogeneous groups, it is often wise to seek out opportunities to work with people who are different from you.

Innovation Several researchers have found that groups with a diverse membership are more innovative than homogeneous groups (King & Anderson, 1990). In one study, ethnically diverse groups produced higher quality ideas in brainstorming tasks (McLeod, Lobel, & Cox, 1996). In a study of *Fortune* 500 teams, racially diverse groups came up with a greater number of innovative ideas than did homogeneous groups (Cady & Valentine, 1999).

This makes sense, because having different perspectives means also having a variety of information sources to apply to a problem or issue (Salazar, 1997). This variety of information broadens people's views and their ability to evaluate. So, ultimately, a diverse workforce operating in a rapidly changing world is better able to monitor, identify, and respond quickly and innovatively to external problems than a homogeneous one (Haslett & Ruebush, 1999). What are the implications for you, as a potential group/team member in professional, academic, or social settings? If the group is a diverse one, know that the potential is there for innovative work. But also remember that for maximum innovation and effectiveness, you and other team members need to encourage equal participation.

Performance (Efficacy) Some research studies report that diverse groups work more effectively (Bowers, Pharmer, & Salas, 2000), while other studies report the opposite (van Knippenberg, De Dreu, & Homan, 2004). This isn't surprising, given the many types of diversity and the fact that each group develops communication and processes that may help or hinder performance. Communication in diverse groups may be more challenging at the onset, so that cultural differences in attitudes and communication styles may lead to early conflict (Poole & Garner, 2006). However, if group members handle these differences well, the outcome may be as good as or better than in homogeneous groups (Larson, 2007; Oetzel, 2005; Poole & Garner, 2006).

There are several ways to accomplish this. One is by focusing the group's attention on the goal of the group, something shared by all, rather than on individual cultural differences (Crown, 2007; Poole & Garner, 2006). A second strategy is to explore commonalities among group members—for example, shared interests, activities, or experiences. In a college course, group members may discover that they are enrolled in other courses together as well or that they participate in the same extracurricular sport or social activity. In a business setting, the team members may find that they have shared professional experiences or hobbies. Some discussion of these commonalities helps solidify relationships, leading to enhanced group cohesion.

It seems that building early group cohesion in diverse groups smoothes the way to managing differences in later discussions (Bantz, 1993; Oetzel, 2005; Polzer,

Milton, & Swann, 2002). As a group member, you can help a diverse group perform more productively by facilitating cohesion early on in the team effort.

Group Processes As we discussed in Chapter 8, one way that individuals differ across cultures is in their preference for individualism or collectivism, and these preferences have an impact on **group processes**. To understand these preferences, one group of researchers used a method quite similar to the study we described above. They randomly assigned students to task groups so that each group had varying degrees of age, gender, and ethnic diversity. Their group task was a course assignment in which they analyzed conversations using various theories presented in class. The students then filled out a questionnaire measuring their communication processes in the group (e.g., participation rate, listening, respect, and conflict management), their own individualistic–collectivist tendencies, and their satisfaction with the group work (Oetzel, 1998).

Interestingly, ethnic, gender, and age diversity in this study had very little effect on the communication process, but those who preferred more interdependent or collectivistic interaction participated more and cooperated more in the group, thus having a more positive impact on group processes. Group members who convey respect and participate in a cooperative manner are also likely to put forth substantial effort toward completing a task and to encourage the contributions of others. Why? Effective communication by some may reduce isolation and encourage effort of all group members. Not surprisingly, those members who participated more were more satisfied with the group outcome.

Like the other studies, this research suggests that groups that are diverse in terms of race, ethnicity, and gender don't necessarily experience more difficult processes. Moreover, because people are diverse and different in so many ways, one can't make assumptions about any collection of individuals based on physical attributes like age, race, or gender.

Another implication is that team leaders can implement team-building exercises to increase interdependence, promote an open communication climate, and help establish group cohesion (Oetzel, 2001). This kind of leadership, as well as effective group member communication, can enhance cooperation, participation, satisfaction, and effort.

Group Enjoyment While diverse groups may be more innovative and effective, are they more enjoyable? To explore this question, another study examined the experience of college students who worked in groups that were composed of either (1) mostly Whites or (2) mostly ethnic minorities (Asians, Asian Americans, African Americans, Hispanics, and others of mixed ethnicity). The researchers found that minorities and White students all preferred minority-dominated teams to White-dominated teams. How can one explain these findings? The researchers suggest that some level of collectivism may have been working in the minority-oriented groups, and whether or not it was, members of these groups were more attentive to relational harmony (Paletz, Peng, Erez, & Maslach, 2004).

What are the implications to be drawn from all these studies that have examined the effect of diversity on group work? First, it seems there are two types of diversity: demographic diversity (age, gender, ethnicity, and race) and deeper cultural differences in attitudes and values (individualism and collectivism preferences) that also play an important role (Crown, 2007). Some research shows that demographic differences may influence group processes early in a group's history, while value differences may have more of an impact later on (Ilgen, Hollenbeck, Johnson, & Jundt, 2005).

Second, culturally diverse groups *may* produce more innovative ideas, *may* be more enjoyable, and *can* be as productive as homogeneous groups. However, enjoyment and productivity do not occur automatically in these groups; they depend

group processes
the methods, including communication, by which a group accomplishes a task

largely on the communication skills of the group members, which do not always come naturally. "Many people believe that good communication skills are 'common sense.' Contrary to expectations, the problem with common sense is that it is not all that common" (Oetzel, 2005, p. 366). Thus, leaders of culturally diverse groups need to focus on helping all team members, including reticent ones, learn to participate fully and to communicate respectfully in a way that promotes collaboration, group cohesion, and consensus building.

These findings suggest that organizations need to develop policies and programs allowing for and valuing the unique characteristics of each group (Cady & Valentine, 1999). Further, with proper education and development, diverse teams have the potential to experience higher levels of satisfaction and lower turnover (Cox, 1994, cited in Cady & Valentine, 1999). Supporting this idea is the finding that groups with high diversity but without proper education in group process are associated with high turnover and more conflict (Poole & Garner, 2006; Sargent & Sue-Chan, 2001).

To summarize, communicating in groups occurs within societal structures—whether the groups are teams working in a small business, task forces in a non-profit organization, or small problem-solving groups in a college course. These social structures establish power relations and status hierarchies that in turn come into play in group interaction. The cultural backgrounds of group members also influence group communication, and if handled well, cultural diversity can enhance group innovation, performance, communication processes, and enjoyment. However, the bottom line is that effective group work flows from effective and ethical communication skills, the topics we turn to next.

TEST YOUR KNOWLEDGE

- What is the difference between legitimate and coercive power in small groups?
- What are some different types of cultural diversity that can be found in groups?
- Under what conditions are diverse groups more productive, innovative, and enjoyable than homogeneous groups?

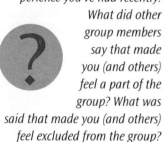

Think about a small group experience you've had recently. What did other group members say that made you (and others) feel a part of the group? What was said that made you (and others) feel excluded from the group?

ETHICS AND SMALL GROUP COMMUNICATION

Ethical communication in small groups is especially important because the success of the group and the task depend on it. One might argue that being in a group carries additional ethical responsibilities because one's individual actions can affect how people think about and react to other members of the group and their ideas. In short, in groups, you are no longer responsible only for yourself but for other members as well. Consider three types of ethical guidelines: (1) those aimed at strengthening group relationships, (2) those dealing with specific communication practices, and (3) those related to group decisions

Relational ethics involve demonstrating commitment to the group. For example, an ethical small group member attends group meetings and participates. As we've discussed, equal participation, buy-in, and establishing trust are all important aspects of group success that cannot be achieved when members are absent from or silent in group discussions. Another relational ethic involves doing your fair share of the group work, as equal participation extends to sharing equally in the responsibilities for completing the tasks. A third ethical guideline to strengthen small group relationships is to maintain open channels of communication (maintaining contact with other group members, contacting others when needed, and responding to others in a timely manner).

In considering ethical communication practices in small groups, it might be helpful to think about the ethical guidelines discussed in Chapter 1 and consider how they might apply to a small group context. First, being truthful in your communication is particularly important, as you are making contributions that affect larger collective decisions (Hargrove, 1998). Truthfulness also includes being accurate and avoiding exaggeration. For example, if you were reporting facts about crime on campus, you would offer statistics, not just say "I found out that crime is really a huge problem." Although you should strive for accuracy and honesty in your language, there may be times when you should not say everything you know—for example, when you should respect the confidentiality of others, including group members. If your friend has been raped and you know this information might be helpful to your group discussion about campus security, you should ask for your friend's permission before divulging this information. Similarly, group members may disclose personal information in the group discussion that they may not wish repeated outside the group.

Secondly, ethical group members also work toward communicating authentically, as discussed in Chapter 1. Why is authentic communication essential? As we noted earlier, group cohesion and trust are important to the performance and success of groups. Authentic communication that is open and free from pretense and language that is inclusive and not hurtful to others go a long way in promoting the kind of group cohesion necessary for group effectiveness. Finally, as a receiver, you must listen with an open mind while also evaluating others' contributions. Doing so will enhance the quality of discussions and help prevent groupthink, in which groups jump to premature conclusions and decisions.

A third area of small group ethics concerns the collective actions of the group members. How to make ethical decisions as a group? How to act ethically as a group? For example, what if you find a project paper on the Internet that closely resembles the project you've been working on? Your group is running out of time at the end of the semester and it would be easy to copy portions of the paper, making only a few minor changes. What ethical guidelines apply here? Perhaps the ethics of fairness and taking responsibility for one's own actions apply. Submitting someone else's work instead of your own is not fair to other students in the course who did their own work, and taking responsibility for poor time management as a group is a more ethical action than using someone else's work.

TEST YOUR KNOWLEDGE
- What are three areas of ethical guidelines for small group work?
- Which guidelines do you think are most important, and why?

IMPROVING YOUR SMALL GROUP COMMUNICATION SKILLS

While no strategies will work in every group communication situation, two strategies can help you be more effective in many of them.

First, cultivate an interdependent or collectivist attitude, a "we" orientation instead of a "me" orientation, and work toward collaborative communication (Lewis, Isbell, & Koschmann, 2010). This means that you must sacrifice some of your personal ambition, needs, and wants in favor of the group's needs and work to ensure buy-in from all group members. People who are extremely individualistic may find this difficult. Yet those with a more collectivist attitude can influence group processes toward more effective communication, more participation, and more satisfaction of all members (Oetzel, 2005).

In addition to cultivating an interdependent attitude, striving for cohesion also is very important in successful small group relationships and task accomplishment. Cohesion occurs when team members trust each other. Further, group success depends on the participation of each member, but members are unlikely to give their best to the group if they can't trust other members to do the same. Trust is particularly important in virtual teams, where members have less face-to-face interaction that might otherwise provide important cues to the intent or attitude of fellow group members. Several strategies build trust and cohesion:

- Focus on the strengths of all group members, and recognize their contributions to group goals. Be sure to acknowledge all group achievements.

- Remind the group of common interests and background experiences. Doing this can help build cohesion, prevent unnecessary conflict, and strengthen group identity.

- Be observant and notice when a member might be feeling unappreciated or uninvolved in the group. Encourage that person to participate. People gain trust and become more trusting as they participate, especially if their participation is encouraged. Fortunately, more trust leads to more cohesion and stronger group identity, which in turn leads to better communication, more satisfaction, and more cohesion.

In sum, the effectiveness of a small group depends in large part on the communication and the relationships established among the members. As a group member, you can promote (or inhibit) the productive communication needed. We believe that using the tools discussed in this chapter will not only make your small group work more effectively but will also make it more enjoyable.

TEST YOUR KNOWLEDGE

- What are two general strategies for improving your small group communication?
- Why is cohesion so important in small group communication?
- What is a collectivist perspective, and how does it enhance small group work?

SUMMARY

Small group communication is a fact of life, and learning to be a better small group communicator can enhance your academic performance, your career achievement, and your personal success.

Small group members share a common purpose, are interdependent, and exert influence on each other. The primary benefit of small groups is that they are more productive and creative than individuals working alone. The disadvantages are that decisions take longer; groups can silence minority opinions, get distracted, and make poor decisions; and relational problems and conflicts can make the experience less than satisfying.

Communication is the "lifeblood that flows through the veins of the small group." Thirteen task and eight relational roles are required for effective group work. In effective groups, individuals fill these roles as needed at any given time during group work. Eight individual roles also exist that group members may fill; these roles, however, tend to be dysfunctional and unproductive. A group's or organization's success is often directly related to the presence of good leadership. Leadership is defined as an influence relationship among leaders and followers who intend changes and outcomes that reflect their shared purposes. Finally, five theories of leadership—trait, style, functional, transformational, and servant—explain leadership effectiveness.

The most common type of small group is the problem-solving group, which often follows a five-stage agenda: (1) defining the problem, (2) analyzing the problem, (3) identifying alternative solutions, (4) evaluating the proposed solutions, and (5) choosing the best solution. Related to the five-stage agenda are the four phases of decision making that most groups complete in every stage of the problem-solving agenda: orientation and primary tension, conflict and secondary tension, emergence, and reinforcement.

Although group cohesion is generally beneficial, too much of it can lead to groupthink.

Technology plays an increasing role in small group work, as we touched on here. We'll discuss it in more depth in Chapter 14.

Societal forces impact small group processes via the role of power in small group work and through cultural diversity. While cultural diversity can present challenges for group processes, it can also produce innovative, efficient, and enjoyable group experiences if handled appropriately. Building cohesion and trust in early stages of group work is particularly important in diverse groups.

There are three types of ethical guidelines that should guide small group work: (1) those aimed at strengthening group relationships, (2) those dealing with specific communication practice, and (3) those related to group decisions.

Skills for achieving effective group communication include cultivating an interdependent attitude and striving for trust and cohesion.

HUMAN COMMUNICATION IN SOCIETY ONLINE

To review this chapter, use the MyCommunicationLab Web site to test your understanding of the following key terms, record your answers to the chapter review questions, and complete the suggested activities. Expand your learning and understanding of chapter concepts by completing additional activities and exercises online. Access code required. Go to www.mycommunicationlab.com for more information or to purchase standalone access.

KEY TERMS

grouphate 250
primary groups 250
secondary groups 251
social facilitation 252
small group communication 253
group roles 256
task roles 256
relational roles 258
individual roles 259
strategic communication 263

trait theory 263
functional (situational) theory 264
shared (collaborative or distributed) leadership 265
style theory 265
authoritarian leader 265
democratic leader 265
laissez-faire 265
transformational leadership 265
charismatic leadership 266

servant leadership 267
analysis paralysis 269
brainstorm 269
primary tension 270
secondary (recurring) tension 271
emergence phase 272
reinforcement phase 272
groupthink 273
group processes 279

APPLY WHAT YOU KNOW

1. **Group Roles Activity**

   Think of a recent group experience you've had. Look at the lists of task, relational, and individual role behaviors in Tables 10.1 through 10.3. Record all behaviors and roles that you filled. Which behaviors (if any) were missing in your group? Which other roles might you have filled?

2. **Group Problem-Solving Activity**

   This activity can be assigned either as an individual or small group exercise. Identify a problem you have encountered recently on your campus. Come up with a viable solution to this problem by following the problem-solving agenda. Which steps of the agenda were relatively easy? Which were more difficult? Why?

3. **Groupthink Exercise**

   Consider experiences you've had in group work. Answer the following questions concerning groupthink. After answering the questions, meet with several classmates and compare answers. Then, as a group, come up with suggestions for ensuring against groupthink.

   - Have you ever felt so secure about a group decision that you ignored all the warning signs that the decision was wrong? Why?

   - Have you ever applied undue pressure to members who disagreed in order to get them to agree with the will of the group?

   - Have you ever participated in a "we-versus-they" feeling—that is, depicting those in the group who are opposed to you in simplistic, stereotyped ways?

   - Have you ever served as a "mind guard"—that is, have you ever attempted to preserve your group's cohesiveness by preventing disturbing outside ideas or opinions from becoming known to other group members?

   - Have you ever assumed that the silence of the other group members implied agreement?

Adapted from: Meade, L. (2003). Small group home page. *The message: A communication website*. Retrieved June 19, 2006, from http://lynn_meade.tripod.com/id62.htm

11
Communicating in Organizations

Lauro's first assignment in his organizational communication class was to list all the organizations he interacted with for one day. As he went through his day, buying a cup of coffee at Starbucks, interviewing for a job, listening to class lectures, ordering lunch at Burger King, and tutoring at a community center, he had a realization. Almost every interaction he had that day either occurred with representatives of organizations or within organizations.

We live in a society of organizations. You may not realize it, but organizations shape your life in many ways. For example, legislative bodies and law enforcement agencies implement formal codes—like traffic laws—that constrain your daily behavior. Educational institutions shape what counts as knowledge, such as when schools determine whether evolutionary theory, intelligent design, or both will be taught in science classes. In addition, religious groups influence popular moral beliefs about issues such as gay marriage or abortion rights.

Business corporations also are major players in shaping our society. Some argue that because they control vast economic resources, huge transnational corporations have become even more powerful than governments, and thus heavily influence government personnel and policy, educational content and practices, and international relations (Deetz, 1992). Corporations also affect our lifestyle desires and choices. For instance, why do consumers want and purchase new, "improved" cell phones, iPads, and computers when their current ones work perfectly well (Deetz, 1992)?

Even though organizations cast a strong influence on individuals, individuals also affect organizations—as consumers, as supporters and participants in religious and civic institutions, and as individuals who work for, or against, specific organizations. Although living in an organizational society generally means you can't escape the influence of organizations, you can have a profound effect on them, just as they do on you. Your ability to have this effect depends on your understanding of organizations and your skills communicating with and within them.

In this chapter we explain what we mean by *organizational communication* and explore the types of communication that commonly occur within organizations. First we look at how individuals communicate within organizations. Then we broaden the discussion to examine the ways society impacts the interactions between individuals and organizations as well as how organizations influence society and individuals. We wrap up this chapter with a discussion of ethical issues associated with communication in and by organizations and offer ways to improve your ability to manage conflict more effectively within organizations.

Once you have read this chapter, you will be able to:

■ Define organizations and explain their structures and communication functions.

■ Discuss three types of communication that are integral to organizations.

- Understand the types of communication that occur among coworkers and explain their functions.
- Discuss the current social influences on organizations and organizational communication.
- Clarify the role of power in organizations and organizational communication.
- Distinguish between individual and communal perspectives on organizational ethics.
- Identify four steps involved in a strategic approach to conflict management.

THE IMPORTANCE OF ORGANIZATIONAL COMMUNICATION

Because you participate in organizations regularly, you will benefit from understanding how to communicate more effectively with and within them. Doing so will enhance your professional success, allow you to ask more informed questions about everyday organizational practices, and help you decide what organizations you wish to frequent and support.

Much of your success within organizations is connected to your communication abilities. For example, if you want an organization to hire you, you must first display good interviewing skills. If you want a promotion, it may be essential to understand your boss's goals and beliefs (Eisenberg, Monge, & Farace, 1984). And if you seek public or civic office, you must have strong public-speaking and social-influence skills to gain support from your political party and endorsements from influential organizations.

In addition to enhancing your professional success, understanding organizational communication will help you ask more informed questions about everyday organizational practices, such as how the corporation you work for determines pay raises, how a nonprofit charity you support can become a United Way organization, or how you can influence legislation in your community. Knowing what questions to ask and how to ask them will improve your ability to accomplish your goals. Finally, given that a wide variety of religious, corporate, and community organizations exist, there is a limit to how many you can support. Understanding how to question organizations and how to interpret their responses and policies can help you make informed choices regarding which ones to embrace. For example, you might decide not to purchase products or services from for-profit organizations that force their employees to work mandatory overtime at the expense of their home lives. Or you might decide that you are better off working for an organization whose goals and beliefs you support strongly, since your agreement with those goals likely will influence your career success.

In sum, organizational communication is central to a person's ability to navigate successfully the myriad legal, educational, religious, corporate, and civic organizations one confronts across a lifetime.

TEST YOUR KNOWLEDGE

- What are the benefits of studying organizational communication?

DEFINING ORGANIZATIONAL COMMUNICATION

Next, we define what we mean when we say *organization*, and we explain the role communication plays in it. As part of this definition, we focus on two aspects common to all organizing efforts: communication functions and structures. We then conclude this section by examining the role of communication in establishing organizational cultures.

Organizations from a Communication Perspective

Scholars from a variety of fields including sociology, economics, psychology, and business management are interested in understanding organizational life. However, communication scholars bring a particular focus to the study of organizations. From their perspective, communication is not just another variable of organizational life. Thus, it is not merely the oil that lubricates other parts of the machine or the glue that binds parts together. Put bluntly, without communication, they argue, there are no "parts"; there is no "machine."

Consider the organization of a college classroom, for instance. Communication scholars argue that it is in the *process of interacting* as student and teacher—giving and listening to lectures, taking and grading exams—that the meaning of these abstract roles becomes real. In this view, then, communication is the process that calls organizations into being. Thus communication scholars argue that *communication constitutes organizations*. It enables or creates them.

Individuals join organizations such as Habitat for Humanity because they can accomplish their goals more effectively if they work with others.

From this perspective, then, **organizations** are defined as the set of interactions that members of groups use to accomplish their individual and common goals (Taylor & Van Every, 1993). Two parts of this definition are important: That organizations are composed of group members' interactions, and that organizational members pursue goals.

In Chapter 9, we explained how a dyad (a pair of individuals) creates and maintains a relationship through communication; this same process occurs within organizations. As individuals in organizations maintain, or alter, their communication practices, they influence the organization itself. For example, if a new store manager is hired who encourages employees to be more courteous in their interactions with each other as well as with customers, the nature of the organization is likely to change. Employee turnover may be reduced, employees may feel more positively about their jobs and therefore work harder, and the more positive interactions with clients could increase sales. Thus, just changing an organization's communication interactions can significantly affect the organization and its members.

In addition to being composed of communication interactions, our definition indicates that organizations are purposeful. Organizations are not random groupings of people; organizational members come together to accomplish individual and collective goals. For example, organizations such as Greenpeace, Doctors without Borders, and Habitat for Humanity exist because their individual members want to make positive changes in the world, and they can do so more effectively if they work together.

Communication Function and Structure

Organizational communication is interaction that organizes purposeful groups, and it generally exhibits several properties—two of which are especially relevant here. The first we will call **function**, by which we mean the goals and effects of communication. Traditionally, scholars recognized three major functions of organizational communication (Daniels, Spiker, & Papa, 1996). **Production** refers to communication that coordinates individuals' activities so they can accomplish tasks. For example, when a manager creates a set of store opening and closing procedures, informs employees of monthly sales goals, or develops a standardized process for assembling products, she allows employees to accomplish various tasks. The **maintenance** function of organizational communication serves to maintain existing aspects of the

organizations
the set of interactions that members of purposeful groups use to accomplish their individual and common goals

function
the goals and effects of communication

production
a function of organizational communication in which activity is coordinated toward accomplishing tasks

maintenance
a function of organizational communication in which the stability of existing systems is preserved

innovation
a function of organizational communication by means of which systems are changed

structure
recurring patterns of interaction among organizational members

downward communication
in a traditional conduit model of communication, communication with subordinates

upward communication
in a traditional conduit model of communication, communication with superiors

horizontal communication
in a traditional conduit model of communication, communication with peers

hierarchy
a power structure in which some members exercise authority over others

formal structure
officially designated channels of communication, reflecting explicit or desired patterns of interaction

informal structure
unspoken but understood channels of communication, reflecting patterns that develop spontaneously

organizational culture
a pattern of shared beliefs, values, and behaviors

organization. Consider, for example, awarding an employee-of-the-month plaque, conducting a performance review, and clarifying a vague set of workflow procedures—all of which enforce the status quo and keep the system running smoothly. A third function is **innovation**, which involves communication that encourages change in the organization. Examples might include suggestion boxes, restructuring and retraining, policy revisions, and the like.

You may have noticed that in most of these examples the three traditional functions overlap considerably. Let's take performance reviews as an illustration. As a manager, you may hope to reinforce the status quo (maintenance) by providing an employee with positive feedback, but you may also hope to instigate change (innovation) in that employee's behavior by offering suggestions for improvement. Also, most performance reviews involve other goals not adequately captured by the three-function model, such as negotiating trust, flexing egos, and so forth. With closer examination, you may see that at least some of these performance-review goals are at odds with one another. In fact, most organizational communication serves multiple, even competing, functions.

The second major property of organizational communication is **structure**. Traditionally, communication structure referred to lines of communication, or a system of pathways through which messages flow. Such a conduit model of communication emphasizes *direction*: **downward communication** (with subordinates), **upward communication** (with superiors), and **horizontal communication** (with peers) (Putnam, Phillips, & Chapman, 1996). Note that direction-based metaphors presume **hierarchy**, a kind of power structure in which some members exercise authority over others. A more contemporary way to define structure is as *recurring patterns of interaction among members*. Rather than treating messages as literal objects moving through conduits, this newer definition points to communication networks that emerge among members. It recognizes that such networks may be hierarchical, though other possibilities exist.

Another important distinction exists between **formal structure** and **informal structure**. Formal structure refers to the officially designated channels of communication, whereas informal structure refers to unspoken but understood channels (Blau & Meyer, 1987; Roy, 1995). As an analogy, think of sidewalks on your campus as the official walkway (formal structure), while footprints worn in the grass represent the shortcuts and detours people take from the path they are given (informal structure). Thus, formal structures are explicit or desired patterns of interaction (that is, what the organization suggests we do). Informal structures are patterns of interaction that develop spontaneously. Most organizational members use both formal and informal structures, for example, following corporate procedures for requesting a leave of absence (formal) and asking a friend in a position of power to recommend their leave request to the boss (informal). *Visual Summary 11.1: Communication Function and Structure in Organizations* illustrates these concepts.

Of the many features of organizational communication we might choose to discuss, we highlight function and structure because they have surfaced continually in scholarly visions of organizational communication.

Organizational Culture

In addition to structure and function, each organization also develops a distinct organizational culture. **Organizational culture** refers to a pattern of shared beliefs, values, and behaviors, or "the system of meanings and behaviors that construct the reality of a social community" (Cheney, Christensen, Zorn, & Ganesh, 2004, p. 76). More informally, organizational culture can be thought of as the "personality" of an organization (McNamara, 2008). As these definitions suggest, organizational cultures are created as people act and interact with one another.

VISUAL SUMMARY 11.1 **Communication Function and Structure in Organizations**

Function: Goals and Effects of Communication Within the Organization

Production: Communication that coordinates activity toward accomplishing a task

When colleagues work together to accomplish tasks, they are engaging in the production function.

Maintenance: Communication that preserves the stability of existing systems

Employee performance reviews are an example of the maintenence function.

Innovation: Communication that facilitates change within the system

Recognizing employees for improving the organization is an example of the innovation function.

Structure—Recurring Patterns of Interaction Among Members

Formal Structure: Officially designated channels of communication

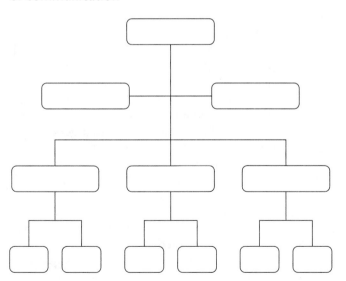

An organizational chart represents formal structure.

Informal Structure: Unspoken but understood channels of communication

Employees often develop informal channels of communication to help them accomplish their goals.

Did You Know?

Comparing Corporate Cultures

What type of organizational culture do you think you would find most compatible? Are you aware of any current organizations whose culture sounds appealing to you? How influential do you think an organization's culture is on employees' job satisfaction?

Two organizations whose culture is discussed widely in business and popular cultural media are Groupon's and Google's. Both are known for being relaxed, innovative, and creative. However, when Google attempted to buy Groupon in 2010, many experts believed the two organizations would not be a good fit for one another because of differences in their organizational cultures. Here one author describes what he sees as the differences in the cultures of Groupon and Google.

"In Groupon's bustling 1,000-person Chicago headquarters, heroes include comedy writers, improv actors, and buzzing rooms of salespeople. There is an office elaborately decorated as a bedroom for an imaginary, deranged tenant. It's hilarious, but also the kind of thing that the brains at Google probably wouldn't find funny, or support.

Why? Because Groupon is primarily a sales and writing organization, built on people-power and smiles. Google, meanwhile, is the master algorithm. Yes, there are lots of people at Google, too, including many sales and support staff. But Google's culture is dominated by engineers—the sort of high-GPA geniuses who can answer all of the brain-teaser Google interview questions—and by the image of being clean and non-evil."

FROM: Frommer, D. (2010, November 24). Here's the problem with Google buying Groupon: A clash of corporate cultures. *Business Insider Online*. Retrieved July 10, 2011, from http://www.businessinsider.com/google-groupon-culture-clash-2010-11#ixzz1RpxNlsJ9

The television show *Mad Men* is engaging, in part, because it depicts the organizational culture of an advertising agency in the 1960s.

Organizational cultures are composed of the languages, habits, rituals, ceremonies, stories, beliefs, attitudes, and artifacts performed by members of that group. For example, universities and colleges usually have specific names for their student unions, nicknames for buildings, rituals that occur around graduation and/or sporting events, and beliefs about what constitutes a good education. As newcomers, students, faculty, and staff become familiar with and integrated into the organization, they learn the specific languages, attitudes, stories, and so on enacted by that organization.

Organizational cultures develop as a result of organizations' attempts to integrate, or assimilate, new members and as they respond to internal and external feedback. Thus, organizational culture is not static but changes over time. The television shows *Mad Men* and *Pan Am*, for example, are engaging, in part, for their depictions of specific organizational cultures that no longer exist—an ad agency and an airline in the 1960s. As these shows reveal through their depictions of male/female work relationships and employee drinking and smoking practices, organizational culture reflects larger cultural values as well as the beliefs, attitudes, and practices of the specific organizations, which can and do change over time.

Edgar Schein (2002), a management professor, argues that to understand an organization's core values or culture, one must examine three aspects (or layers) of the organization: its artifacts, stated beliefs, and underlying assumptions. He suggests that one first examine the organization's artifacts, such as the furniture, the pictures hanging on the walls, and employees' attire as well as the organization's communication style, rituals, and stories. He points out that artifacts can be ambiguous or misleading but do portray the image or culture the organization wishes to display, which tells us something about that culture.

Secondly, he recommends that one identify the values and beliefs espoused by organizational leaders. That is, what do the leaders claim the organization stands for? These beliefs, however, may not be consistent with what the organization truly values. For example, Kenneth Lay and other executives at Enron publicly extolled their company for its strong ethical stance, though it was later proven that many executives had engaged in highly unethical behavior.

The third and final aspect one should analyze to understand an organization's culture is the underlying assumptions or beliefs that influence organizational members' behavior. One way to do this is to evaluate the values and behaviors the organization actually rewards rather than what it claims to value.

For example, a company may say it is "family friendly" and offer work–life policies designed to enhance employees' lives, but at the same time fail to promote people who refuse to work on weekends or who actually use work–life policies on maternity or paternity leave (Kirby & Krone, 2002).

Each organization develops its own culture, though some organizations may share similar cultural characteristics. One cultural characteristic that is common to a variety of organizations is gender. That is, organizational cultures often are classified as masculine or feminine based on the values they embrace. For instance, fire stations, law enforcement groups, and the military all share a "masculine culture" that values risk taking, courage, and bodily strength (Highgate & Upton, 2005; Prokokos & Padavik, 2002; Thurnell & Parker, 2008). On the other hand, "feminine cultures" such as Mary Kay Cosmetics and nursing are described as sharing a value of family-friendly policies, open communication, and participative and egalitarian decision making (Everbach, 2007).

Nonetheless, organizations can be of a similar type or serve a similar function but still have aspects of their culture that differ considerably. Thus, although they are all restaurants, the organizational cultures of McDonald's, Applebee's, and Hooters differ. If you were to assess their cultural differences as Schein suggests, you might think about who the employees are, the type of clothing employees wear, how they interact with patrons and each other, and what type of qualities are rewarded and valued. Even a brief visit to these establishments quickly reveals cultural differences.

In addition to the corporate culture, groups within organizations develop their own subcultures (Martin, 2002). In law firms, for example, support staff, law clerks, and the firm's law team likely each develop their own unique subculture. The lawyers may even develop separate subcultures—for example, one for partners and one for associates. Each group may have its own style of dress, its own values and stories, and its own practices for celebrating birthdays, promotions, or weddings. This illustration also suggests that the subcultures within such an organization likely differ in their power and interests (Howard-Grenville, 2006). Thus, they likely impact the corporate culture to varying degrees, with the more powerful groups having a stronger overall influence.

Now that you have been introduced to the basic features of organizations, in the following section we discuss how individuals become members of organizations and the important role communication serves in supervisor–subordinate and co-worker relationships.

assimilation
the communicative, behavioral, and cognitive processes that influence individuals to join, identify with, become integrated into, and (occasionally) exit an organization

organizational identification
the stage of assimilation that occurs when an employee's values overlap with the organization's values

TEST YOUR KNOWLEDGE

- What is the contemporary definition for organizational structure? How does it differ from the previous description of organizational structure?
- What three aspects of the organization does Edward Schein recommend we analyze in order to understand an organization's culture?

ORGANIZATIONAL COMMUNICATION AND THE INDIVIDUAL

If you wish to influence the organizations you interact with, you need to understand some of the basic types of communication that help create organizations and organizational life. It is important to be familiar with guidelines for how you might perform these types of communication most successfully. Although all the communication skills and abilities we examine in this book will definitely make you a better communicator in organizational contexts, here we focus on three types of communication that are integral to organizations: assimilation, supervisor–subordinate communication, and coworker communication. We also explore three types of organizational dilemmas or tensions that employees must manage.

Assimilation

In the organizational context, **assimilation** refers to the communicative, behavioral, and cognitive processes that influence individuals to join, identify with, become integrated into, and (occasionally) exit an organization (Jablin & Krone, 1987). When you join an organization, you usually don't become an accepted member of the group automatically, nor do you immediately identify with the organization and its members. Instead, over time you go through a process in which you and others begin to see you as an integral and accepted part of the organization. The pledge process for sororities and fraternities is one highly ritualized form of assimilation.

Assimilation is a common experience for individuals who join any type of organization, whether it is a business, a religious group, or a social group. However, you probably most often think of assimilation as occurring when you begin a new job. Assimilation is similar to the process of cultural adaptation experienced when individuals enter a new culture, as we discussed in Chapter 8.

Organizational identification is a stage of assimilation that occurs when an employee's values overlap with the organization's values (Bullis & Tompkins, 1989). For example, Arizona Public Service (a utility company) values community involvement, encourages its employees to volunteer, and even provides time off for workers to do so. Some new hires, however, may not inherently value volunteerism, and others may even resist the corporation's attempt to influence their behavior outside work. However, over time, some of these new hires will begin to identify more strongly with the organization and its values, and their attitudes will change. Those who had not given much thought to volunteering may now see it as a corporate responsibility, and those who were opposed may come to see time off for community service as a benefit.

Of course, not every new employee experiences organizational identification. Some employees never come to accept their organization's values. For instance, if an employee values an environment in which coworkers become friends and socialize frequently, he or she likely will never identify with a highly competitive sales organization in which employees work independently and socialize only rarely.

When these soldiers joined the U.S. Army, they were not immediately integrated. As they learned about the organizational culture and its rules, they became assimilated.

Such employees often leave their jobs, or if they remain, they never come to see themselves as part of the organization.

Over time, most people do identify with the organizations they join, and they become increasingly integrated. If they leave such organizations, they go through a process of decoupling their identities from the organization and move from being seen as insiders to once again being viewed as outsiders. This leaving process can be difficult, especially if one does not have a new identity and organizational affiliation. For example, people who retire often feel sad and disconnected because they have lost an important identity.

The communication process most central to assimilation is information seeking, a reciprocal process in which individuals seek out information that helps them adapt to the organization and the organization attempts to convey information that will assist in this process. Two organizational communication scholars, Vernon Miller and Fred Jablin (1991), developed a typology of the information-seeking tactics that newcomers use to ascertain organizational roles, rules, and norms. These strategies take the same forms as other types of uncertainty-reduction techniques (see Chapter 9) and include active, passive, and interactive strategies (Berger, 1979).

The passive strategies new members use include observation and surveillance. These strategies involve watching others' communication and behavior or interpreting stories about past communication and behavior so that one can infer the rules and norms of the organization. For example, if you wonder what time employees typically arrive for work, you could go to work quite early one day and observe who arrives at what time, or you might attend to stories about people who arrived consistently late to work and what happened to them.

Active strategies include overt questioning, indirect questioning, disguising conversations, and questioning third parties. In these instances, the employee tries to discern organizational expectations by acquiring information from others. For example, a new employee might directly ask a more experienced coworker, "Are we expected to stay after 5 p.m.?" or she might pose the question more indirectly by saying, "How often do most employees stay past 5 p.m.?" Or she could engage in a disguising conversation by complaining about how late she had to stay in her previous job, to see how her colleague responds. In addition, she might ask a third party (a secretary) rather than a primary source (her supervisor) whether employees at her level are expected to stay past five o'clock.

Finally, new employees seek information through the interactive strategy of "testing limits." A newcomer tests limits by seeing how far he or she can push specific boundaries. For instance, an employee might determine whether leaving at 5 p.m. is acceptable by leaving consistently at that time and then noting how people respond. (To see a different perspective on organizational assimilation, see *Alternative View: What Is a "Real Job"*?).

The communication strategies that employees use to assimilate to their workplaces often set the tone for how they will interact with the organization. Another type of communication that influences how employees' interact act at work is supervisor–subordinate communication.

Which assimilation strategies do you think would be the most effective for a new employee to use?

Supervisor–Subordinate Communication

Supervisor–subordinate communication occurs when one person has the formal authority to regulate the behavior of another. In hierarchical organizations, virtually all employees engage in supervisor–subordinate communication, even CEOs—who must report upward to boards of directors (their supervisors) and downward to other organizational members (their subordinates).

When organizational hierarchies exist, subordinates frequently attempt to please their supervisors to keep their jobs, receive raises and promotions, or perhaps even to become supervisors themselves someday. By the same token, successful supervisors

Alternative **VIEW**
What Is a "Real Job"?

How would you define what a "real job" is? What types of jobs do you think of as not being "real jobs"? Where have you heard the term "real job," and who taught you its meaning?

In Robin Clair's work *The Political Nature of a Colloquialism, "A Real Job": Implications for Organizational Assimilation* (1996), she critiques current models of organizational assimilation, such as Miller and Jablin's, for assuming that any work that occurs prior to or aside from working for an organization is not "real" work. To help us understand how individuals become socialized outside the context of organizations and to understand what constitutes work, she studied the popular expression "real job" by asking undergraduate students to write an essay about a time they encountered the term. She did so in order to examine what students mean by the term "real job" as well as to understand who was socializing them into a belief about what a real job looks like.

In their essays, Clair's respondents identified five dominant characteristics of a "real job":

- The money (i.e., one is well paid)
- Utilizes one's education
- Is enjoyable

- Requires 40 hours of work per week/8 hours per day
- Advancement is possible

Specific jobs that were identified as *not* being "real jobs" included serving in volunteer organizations such as the Peace Corps, working in a fast-food restaurant, working for one's family, or not making enough money to provide for a family. Overall, the respondents suggested that people with a college degree do not belong in unskilled labor positions, which for them did not constitute "real jobs."

A number of respondents did acknowledge that the concept of a "real job" was a social construction and some even rejected it. But even those who embraced jobs that others might consider not a "real job" continued to compare their own work to the societal standard and felt the need to justify their choices.

When asked who shaped their perceptions of what constitutes a real job, respondents pointed to family members (particularly fathers), friends, and coworkers. As Clair also points out, however, socialization is not a linear process in which society socializes young people into a particular belief about what constitutes a real job. Instead, she argues, those who are being socialized also serve to socialize themselves and others by the ways they talk about their own and others' employment plans and desires.

SOURCE: Clair, R. (1996). The political nature of a colloquialism, "A real job": Implications for organizational assimilation. *Communication Monographs*, 63, 249–267.

must motivate and manage their subordinates. These sets of needs and goals impact how supervisors and subordinates communicate. At times, a supervisor and subordinate's needs can be such that they communicate in ways that create misunderstandings and problems. An example of this is called semantic-information difference.

Semantic-information distance describes the gap in information and understanding between supervisors and subordinates on specific issues (Dansereau & Markham, 1987). What causes this gap? Behaviors of both subordinates and supervisors contribute, but we'll look at the subordinate side first. See *It Happened to Me: Yoshi* for an employee's view on this communication gap.

When subordinates are hesitant to communicate negative news and present information in a more positive light than is warranted, they engage in a behavior called **upward distortion** (Dansereau & Markham, 1987). Why do subordinates do this? Employees naturally edit the information they send upward because not everything is relevant to their bosses and because they can manage many issues without the supervisor's intervention. However, when workers withhold or alter important information, supervisors may be making decisions based on distorted and inadequate information. This can impair their ability to perform their own jobs successfully. For example, if an employee knows that an important production deadline is looming, he

semantic-information distance
describes the gap in information and understanding between supervisors and subordinates on specific issues

upward distortion
occurs when subordinates are hesitant to communicate negative news and present information to superiors in a more positive light than is warranted

or she may be reluctant to tell the supervisor that the deadline can't be met for fear of reprisals or blame. Fear of negative repercussions is probably the most important reason that employees distort information as they communicate with their supervisors.

Supervisors, too, may communicate a more positive image than they actually perceive. Why? They do so in part because they need to motivate employees and to create and maintain employee satisfaction with the organization. Employee satisfaction is central to the supervisor–subordinate relationship and, ultimately, to the supervisor's ability to influence subordinates and impact their performance. For example, employee satisfaction has been linked to decreased absenteeism and decreased turnover as well as increased productivity (Richmond, McCroskey, & Davis, 1986).

Although the reasons for it make intuitive sense, semantic-information distance can cause problems in supervisor–subordinate relationships. Supervisors need accurate, honest information to perform successfully. Therefore, when

> ## It Happened to Me: *Yoshi*
>
> Upward distortion creates difficulties and makes it impossible to fix a lot of organizational problems. I usually have a conversation with my coworker about problems in our department on a weekly basis. When we talk, he blows off steam and tells me exactly what the problem is and how it can be fixed; however, when he talks to our manager, he tends to simplify the problem and makes it seem like it is due to his own shortcomings instead of the operation's. This in turn makes it almost impossible to really get the problem fixed. I think that one big cause of this upward distortion is the fact that most managers have the attitude that they don't want excuses, they just want results. How can we address a problem with our manager if he doesn't want to hear anything negative?

they become aware that employees have been distorting information, they are unlikely to trust or reward those employees. Of course, supervisors also need to communicate clearly so subordinates have the information they need to perform their jobs competently.

What can supervisors do to minimize semantic-information distance as well as increase employees' (as well as their own) satisfaction and success? As you might imagine, we suggest that they engage in effective communication. Although many communication strategies contribute to supervisor success, we highlight four: openness, supportiveness, motivation, and empowerment.

Openness occurs when communicators are willing to share their ideas and listen to others in a way that avoids conveying negative or disconfirming feedback (Cheney, 1995; Jablin, 1979). When supervisors are open, they create an environment of trust that decreases the likelihood that upward communication will be distorted.

Even though openness is a desirable characteristic, one can engage in *too much* openness. For example, if an employee is on leave to undergo rehabilitation for addiction, a supervisor typically should not share that information directly, or even indirectly, with others, as doing so would be inappropriate. In addition, sometimes supervisors need to shield their employees from information. For example, informing subordinates of a possible layoff before the decision is final could cause unnecessary stress and panic.

Supportive supervisors provide their subordinates with access to information and resources. Thus, supportive supervisors explain roles, responsibilities, and tasks to those they manage; they also take the time to answer employees' questions. Further, managers are supportive when they give their subordinates the tools, skills, education, and time they need to be successful. Overall, supervisors who help their employees solve problems, listen actively, provide feedback, and offer encouragement are not only supportive, they are successful (Whetton & Cameron, 2002).

Productive and successful supervisors are able to motivate their subordinates. Workers experience **motivation** when they feel personally invested in accomplishing a specific activity or goal (Kreps, 1991). Many U.S. American supervisors and organizations focus on creating extrinsic or external motivators, such as pay raises,

Think about supervisors you have had. What was it about their communication strategies that you liked or disliked? Which of the strategies we've mentioned here did they use?

openness
a state in which communicators are willing to share their ideas as well as listen to others in a way that avoids conveying negative or disconfirming feedback

supportiveness
refers to supervisors who provide their subordinates with access to information and resources

motivation
feeling personally invested in accomplishing a specific activity or goal

Positive communication between supervisors and their subordinates is characterized by openness and the empowerment of subordinates.

bonuses, promotions, titles, and benefits. However, supervisors who can instill intrinsic motivation in their subordinates are more successful. Intrinsic motivation occurs when people experience satisfaction in performing their jobs well, find their jobs to be enriching, and are, therefore, dedicated to their organizations or professions (Cheney et al., 2004).

Supervisors can create intrinsic motivation by setting clear and specific goals that are challenging but attainable and by engaging workers in the creation of those goals. In addition, they need to provide frequent and specific feedback, including praise, recognition, and corrections. Positive feedback is especially important because it encourages job satisfaction, organizational identification, and commitment (Larson, 1989). Finally, intrinsic motivation thrives in a positive work environment that stresses camaraderie or social relationships.

Empowerment, the fourth characteristic that improves communication, relates to the supervisor's ability to increase employees' feelings of self-efficacy. He or she does this by instilling the feeling that the subordinate is capable of performing the job and has the authority to decide how to perform it well (Chiles & Zorn, 1995). In general, supervisors who empower their subordinates function more like coaches than traditional managers. They encourage employees to be involved in decision making, to take responsibility for their tasks, and to provide suggestions for improving their own and the organization's performance. Employees who feel empowered are more likely to develop intrinsic motivation and to communicate openly with their supervisors.

Communication is also central to subordinates' success on the job. Subordinates who get along with their supervisors are much more likely to be satisfied and successful. Consequently, subordinates use a variety of means to manage and maintain the quality of their relationships with their supervisors. Studies of subordinate communication tactics determined that employees who use three specific upward communication tactics—ingratiation, assertiveness, and rationality—were most likely to positively affect their manager's perceptions of them (Dockery & Steiner, 1990; Wayne & Ferris, 1990).

Ingratiation refers to behavior and communication designed to increase liking. It includes friendliness and making one's boss feel important. Of course, one can be too ingratiating and come off as being insincere, but genuine respect and rapport can be effective. **Assertive** subordinates who can express their opinions forcefully without offending or challenging their bosses also tend to engender liking and approval. In addition, subordinates who can argue **rationally**—meaning that they communicate with their bosses through reasoning, bargaining, coalition building, and assertiveness—are often adept at managing their supervisors. Finally, employees who understand their bosses' professional and personal goals as well as their strengths and weaknesses, and who can adapt to their preferred communication styles, can create positive working relationships.

Communicating with Coworkers

Along with assimilation and supervisor–subordinate communication, communication with coworkers is fundamental to organizations and their employees. Sometimes the communication that occurs among coworkers or peers is described as *horizontal*, because it is directed neither upward (to superiors) nor downward (to subordinates). No matter how they are described, workplace relationships are distinctive interpersonal relationships that influence both the individuals within them and the organization as a whole (Sias, 2005).

Employees become friends with their colleagues for many of the same reasons they develop other types of interpersonal relationships—proximity, attraction, and

empowerment
employees' feelings of self-efficacy

ingratiation
behavior and communication designed to increase liking

assertiveness
expressing one's opinions forcefully without offending others

rationality
the ability to communicate through reasoning, bargaining, coalition building, and assertiveness

similarity. Some people, especially those who live alone, may spend more time with their colleagues than they do with anyone else. Even people who live with others may spend as much—or more—time with coworkers as they do with their families or housemates. However, unlike other interpersonal relationships, friendship development at work is affected by an additional dimension—how supervisors treat individual employees. If supervisors are perceived to treat some employees more favorably and this treatment is perceived as undeserved, coworkers may dislike and distrust favored employees. On the other hand, if a manager is seen as treating a subordinate more negatively than others and the treatment is perceived as unwarranted, it can increase employee interaction and cohesiveness (Graen & Graen, 2006; Sias & Jablin, 1995).

Coworkers in organizations engage in both formal–professional and informal–personal interactions. The formal–professional category includes communication about tasks, solving problems, making plans, and influencing one another's beliefs and decisions (Kram & Isabella, 1985). In addition, coworkers engage in considerable informal, or personal, interaction. In fact, adults draw many of their friends from the pool of people at work, and approximately 50 percent of employees state that they have engaged in a romance at work (Vault, 2003). Coworkers also can serve as an important source of emotional and social support (Rawlins, 1994).

In the movie *Office Space*, these coworkers engage in considerable informal and personal interactions, including launching a plan to take revenge on the company for its planned layoffs.

The professional and the personal aspects of coworker communication and relationships are not distinct. Rather, professional interactions influence coworkers' personal relationships, and vice versa. Sias and Cahill (1998) found that more talk about more topics among coworkers not only resulted from increased closeness in their relationships but also contributed to it. Thus, coworkers who also are friends tend to communicate more intimately and about more topics, both professionally and personally, than those who are not (Sias, Smith, & Avdeyeva, 2003). They also tend to be both less careful and more open in their communication with each other (Sias & Jablin, 1995). Therefore, they are likely to provide increased and more useful task-related information to each other.

As you might expect, being isolated from employee networks can result in isolation from quality work-related information (in addition to loneliness) and cause one to be at an information disadvantage relative to one's colleagues (Sias, 2005). Research indicates that this information disadvantage has important consequences. Poor coworker communication and lack of access to information have been found to predict lower job satisfaction and commitment.

The presence of friendly relationships among coworkers has positive consequences for individuals and organizations. When employees feel connected to their colleagues, they provide each other with support and assistance that can increase their success. Such relationships also intensify workers' loyalty to the company and increase job satisfaction and organizational identification, which can help minimize job turnover (Kram & Isabella, 1985).

Despite the ease, attractiveness, and advantages of forming close relationships at work, such relationships can require careful navigation. Friendship, by its nature, is egalitarian, but power differences often occur among coworkers. Even employees at the same level in the organization may have different levels of informal power, and the situation can become increasingly problematic if one of them receives a promotion and thereby acquires greater formal power in the organization. In addition, coworkers may find themselves torn between their loyalty to the organization and their loyalty to a friend. For example, how should one respond if a friend engages in unethical behavior at work, decides to become a whistleblower, or quits in protest over a denied promotion? It can be difficult for individuals to decide how to respond in a way that protects their own as well as their friends' interests. Finally, it can be more difficult to be objective with a friend, to withhold confidential information, and to provide honest feedback.

In addition, other employees can develop negative perceptions and interpretations of the friendships and courtship relationships of their colleagues. Coworkers may question the motives of the partners, may believe that the individuals involved are conspiring to affect corporate policy, or may perceive that the relationship partners treat others unfairly in comparison. For instance, if two salespeople become close, their coworkers may perceive that they are sharing information or client lists that permit them to be more successful than those outside the relationship. In addition, because of the potential for trouble and bad feelings, some organizations have explicit policies that discourage "affectional" relationships, which may include friendships but most certainly include romance. For suggestions on how supervisors can encourage good coworker communication, see *Did You Know? Encouraging Effective Coworker Communication*.

Did You Know?
. . . .

Encouraging Effective Coworker Communication

How do you communicate with your coworkers? How effective are you when you communicate with them? Which of the following strategies would help you be more effective?

- **Communicate your vision**. If you're the team leader, your job is really about communicating clearly. By choosing words that connect with different learning styles and personality types, you can paint a picture of the end goal everyone can get excited about.

- **Make sure your expectations are clear**. Team members won't be able to be successful if they don't know what's expected of them. Make sure that everyone knows what they need to do to be successful—this creates a collaborative environment that is more open and trusting and ultimately more supportive and productive.

- **Be definitive about a time frame**. Let others know specifically when you need what you're requesting of them. If the time frame spans a long period, establish checkpoints (one week, two weeks) where you can check in to find out how things are going. This keeps a big project from going horribly wrong when the writers have been holed up in an office for three weeks playing video games and suffering from writers' block.

- **Invite feedback and questions**. The "open door" policy may be a myth in some offices, but listening nondefensively—to questions, concerns, and criticism—is a huge part of building honest communication with others. This shows that everyone has a voice in the success of the project and helps create the openness for creativity and trust to emerge.

- **Encourage and support good communication**. To show others that improving teamwork is important, you might host a series of lunches, invite a speaker in to give an afternoon seminar on communications skills, or hire a consultant to help with team relations. The most important way to encourage good communication is to model it yourself—to make mistakes, to honestly explain what happened, and to try again, all in the name of moving toward better communication with your peers.

FROM: Murray, K. (2005, February).Improve staff communications. Retrieved September 5, 2005, from www.revisionsplus.com/February article.doc. Reprinted by permission of the author.

Organizational Dilemmas

Although organizations can provide many benefits to an individual, including status, money, a sense of belonging, and even a significant part of one's identity, they also can create physical and psychological distress. Thus in addition to being proficient at the three key types of organizational communication, members of organizations may have to communicatively manage and respond to three types of organizational dilemmas: emotion labor, stress and burnout, and work–life conflict.

Emotion Labor As we discussed earlier, employees learn a variety of norms for organizational behavior during assimilation. Some of these norms pertain to emotion display rules (Scott & Myers, 2005). Emotion display rules are the explicit or implicit rules that organizations have for what emotions can be appropriately displayed and how those emotions should be communicated. For example, firefighters learn early in the assimilation process that they should not express strong negative emotions such as fear, disgust, and panic (Scott & Myers, 2005). Instead, they learn to speak in calm tones, to offer verbal assurances, and to suppress any comments that might distress the public. Similarly, the employees at the local grocery store have learned to show cheerfulness and helpfulness toward customers, even if they actually feel irritation, anger, or frustration. Consequently, no matter how their day is going, they greet customers with a friendly hello, offer assistance, and wish customers a good day as they leave the store.

When the organization expects or requires workers to display particular feelings, employees are engaging in emotion labor (Hochschild, 1983). Typically, organizations ask employees to alter their emotional behavior in three ways. First, they may ask employees to heighten or increase their expressions of joy (i.e., cruise ship and other tourism employees), to appear mean or indifferent (debt collectors and law officers, on occasion), or to convey "a vaguely pleasant professional demeanor" (nurses and receptionists) (Cheney et al., 2004, p. 68). (For one student's experience with emotion labor, see *It Happened to Me: Sonya*.)

It Happened to Me: *Sonya*

For a year, I worked on a cruise line as an assistant cruise director. My job was to organize activities and help entertain the passengers. I helped with bingo games, organized costume contests, and participated in various games with the passengers. In addition, I was expected to dance with the passengers in the evening at the nightclub. Unfortunately, I often had to deal with passengers who had had a few drinks and wanted to "get friendly" or invite me back to their rooms. No matter how the passenger behaved, I was expected to be polite, pleasant, and friendly without, of course, ever actually becoming involved with one! It was really difficult sometimes. I would be so angry, upset, or embarrassed at how a passenger behaved, but I could never show it. This is one of the major reasons I did not sign up again after my first year on the ship.

Some scholars believe that performing emotion labor benefits employees. They argue that when workers perform emotions they do not actually feel, they can better cope with stress (Conrad & Witte, 1994), and they are more able to interact in emotionally satisfying ways with their clients (Shuler & Sypher, 2000). These scholars suggest that social workers, emergency medical personnel, and other employees in the social services find their work easier and more meaningful when they perform emotion labor.

Others believe it can be harmful (Tracy, 2000; Waldron, 1994), especially when it is required and when it benefits the organization but not the employee. For example, Sarah Tracy (2005), an organizational communication scholar, studied correctional officers' emotion labor and its consequences. She found that the officers often were expected to manage contradictory emotional displays—for example, showing respect for inmates but not trusting them, or nurturing them while also being tough. She discovered that performing these contradictory emotions led some of the officers to experience withdrawal, paranoia, stress, and burnout. Thus, consistently having to perform emotion labor, especially when the requirements are ambiguous and contradictory, may cause psychological and physical harm to some workers.

Do you believe that performing emotion labor is beneficial or detrimental to employees? Why? Could it be beneficial in some jobs but not others? Why?

burnout
a chronic condition that results from the accumulation of daily stress, which manifests itself in a very specific set of characteristics, including exhaustion, cynicism, and ineffectiveness

Stress and Burnout As you just read, correctional officers often experience stress and burnout. But they are not the only employees who suffer in this way; stress and burnout have become widespread in the American workplace, and the terms have become common in everyday speech. However, **burnout** includes a very specific set of characteristics, including exhaustion, cynicism, and ineffectiveness (Maslach & Leiter, 1997; Maslach, 2003). It is a chronic condition that results from the accumulation of daily stress, where stress is defined as a common response to important and consequential demands, constraints, or opportunities to which one feels unable to respond (McGrath, 1976).

Exhaustion, which is a core characteristic of burnout, can include physical, emotional, or mental exhaustion. It expresses itself as physical fatigue, loss of affect (or emotion), and an aversion to one's job. Employees who are emotionally exhausted may try to reduce the emotional stress of working with others by detaching from them, a behavior called depersonalization, which is related to the second characteristic of burnout—cynicism. Cynicism is manifested as an indifferent attitude toward others. A person with a cynical attitude may view others as objects or numbers and may also express hostility and harsh criticism toward them. Employees might feel ineffective, the third characteristic of burnout, which occurs when workers negatively evaluate their own performance. Ineffectiveness may result in absenteeism, decreased effort, and withdrawal (Richardsen & Martinussen, 2004).

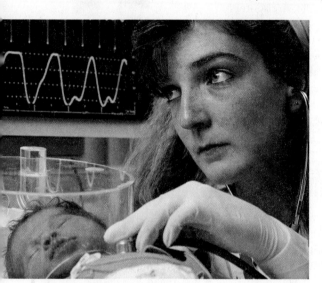

Job stress tends to be high for health care workers because of the highly consequential demands inherent in the job and the fact that, in some cases, even the most highly skilled professionals are unable to save a patient's life.

Burnout arises due to a combination of personality factors (for example, how well one manages ambiguity and stress) and organizational stressors. Organizational stressors are aspects of one's job that create strain. Some of the more significant organizational stressors include work overload; confusion, conflict, and ambiguity related to job roles; being undermined by a supervisor (Westman & Etzion, 2005); and low levels of social support (Koniarek & Dudek, 1996).

Workload refers to the amount of work an individual is expected to perform. Work overload occurs when employees feel they have more work than they can accomplish, and this is a major contributor to feelings of exhaustion. Despite expectations that technology, and especially computer technology, would lessen the burden for workers in the United States, people today are working longer hours and dealing with heavier workloads than before the advent of these technologies. In addition, workers frequently find that now they are never "away" from the job, since they are instantly and constantly available through cell phones, BlackBerries, and pagers. The resulting work pressures are having an increasingly negative effect on individuals, families, and organizations (Glisson & Durick, 1988).

Work overload also is related to our second major organizational stressor—role confusion, conflict, and ambiguity. Role ambiguity occurs when employees do not understand what is expected of them. This is most likely to occur when one begins a new job, but it also occurs when organizations undergo change (Chambers, Moore, & Bachtel, 1998). Because today's workers are faced with continual change due to budget cuts, reorganizations, and new technologies, they frequently experience role ambiguity (Chambers et al., 1998).

To give some perspective on the role ambiguity and confusion play as work stressors, consider this. As recently as twenty years ago, newly hired engineers primarily needed to communicate with other engineers, most of whom were born in the United States and were native speakers of English. Since that time, however, U.S. companies have hired more engineers from other countries and have expanded their operations around the world. Consequently, many engineers now need to communicate with and supervise others who do not share their native culture and background. They have been required to develop intercultural communication skills they never expected would be necessary and to become conversant with cultures outside the United States. Some long-term employees are unsure of their ability to respond appropriately. Employees in many industries face similar challenges as organizations respond to changing market conditions, globalization, and new technology. Unfortunately, uncertainty about one's job duties and one's ability to perform those duties creates considerable stress for workers.

Role conflict arises when employees find it difficult to meet conflicting or incompatible job demands (Igbaria & Guimaraes, 1993). For example, the correctional officers we mentioned in our discussion of emotion labor experienced considerable role conflict. On the one hand, they were expected to act like social workers whose job it was to treat prisoners with respect, to nurture them, and to facilitate their well-being and rehabilitation; on the other hand, they were expected to function as paramilitary agents whose job it was to maintain order and safety, to mistrust the prisoners, and to be tough. Similarly, when managers are told to treat their employees fairly and humanely but also to meet tight production deadlines, they suffer from role conflict. Research indicates that being asked to perform such incompatible tasks on the job gives rise to considerable stress and ill effects (Rizzo, House, & Lirtzman, 1970). For example, role conflict and ambiguity can cycle into burnout, leading workers to experience feelings of ineffectiveness in their jobs.

To complete our discussion of organizational stressors and burnout, we focus squarely on communication issues. When employees feel undermined by their supervisors, whether through having information withheld, being denied the resources they need to do their jobs, or being treated unfairly, they are more likely to experience cynicism and a lack of efficacy (Maslach & Leiter, 1997). They may feel they cannot accomplish their work because they lack the resources to do so, and they may believe that even if they do perform well, they will not be rewarded.

Communication with coworkers can contribute to burnout when one's colleagues are unable to provide the social support one needs to cope with organizational stressors. Feelings of burnout then may spread from one employee to his or her colleagues. This fact, combined with the faster pace of most organizations, can lead to a breakdown of community within the organization and disconnect coworkers from one another (Maslach & Leiter, 1997).

Interestingly, research has established that communication itself can be an important moderator of employee burnout. Findings show that supervisor communication that includes active listening, effective feedback, participative decision making, and supportiveness can decrease the severity of subordinate burnout (Casey, 1998; Golembiewski, Boudreau, Sun, & Luo, 1998). Similarly, communication with coworkers that conveys warmth and support and reaffirms the meaning of one's work can help employees cope with burnout (Casey, 1998).

If you would like to see if you are experiencing burnout, go to www.mindtools .com/pages/article/newTCS_08.htm and take the Burnout Self-Test.

Work–Life Conflict A third type of organizational dilemma that workers face is work–life conflict, defined by the difficulties individuals and families face as they try to balance job and home responsibilities. Since the 1990s, work–family balance has become an issue of concern and another type of role conflict, especially for dual-career couples (Kirby & Krone, 2002). As more women have entered the workforce and more families have become reliant on two incomes, people are finding it difficult to manage their competing demands. The pervasiveness of communication technologies such as email, cell phones, instant messaging, and pagers has made it difficult for some workers to ever get away from work and focus on the other aspects of their lives.

In response to these concerns, organizations began to develop family-friendly policies, such as flextime, family leave, and dependent-care benefits (Morgan & Milliken,

Alternative VIEW
Men Now Have More Work–Life Conflict than Women

Who do you think is more like to experience conflict when trying to manage paid and unpaid work, men or women? Why? If you believe women experience more conflict, why do think that more men than women in this study reported it?

Though it may come as a surprise to stressed-out working moms, a new report says American men now experience more work–life conflict than women. The Families and Work Institute tries to explain why in a study, *The New Male Mystique*, that takes its cue from Betty Friedan.

Much like the conflict women felt when they first entered the workforce in large numbers, the institute says men today feel "the pressure to do it all in order to have it all." That is, be the breadwinner, spend more time with the kids, and wash the dishes after dinner, thank you very much. The report finds a host of factors contributing to this pressure, including "flat earnings, long hours, increasing job demands, blurred boundaries between work and home life, and declining job security."

Perhaps not surprisingly, work–life conflict is most acute for men in demanding jobs, those who work longer hours, and those in dual-earner households. Based on the results of a 2008 national survey of 1,298 men, the institute reports that 60 percent of men in dual-earner couples reported work–family conflicts, up from 35 percent in 1977. Among women, the percentages rose much less, to 47 percent from 41 percent.

But here's a tidbit that would make Friedan worry: fathers actually work 3 hours more per week on average than men the same age without young children at home. Spouses, good luck bringing that up at the dinner table.

What can mitigate male work–life conflict? The study suggests supportive supervisors and a flexible work schedule. That way, men will know they're not alone with their struggle that, at least, now has a name.

SOURCE: Ludden, J. (2011, June 30). Men now have more "work-life conflict" than women, study says. *National Public Radio*. Retrieved July 14, 2011, from http://www.gpb.org/news/2011/06/30/men-now-have-more-work-life-conflict-than-women-study-says

1992). However, studies have shown that many employees do not take advantage of these benefits (Kirby & Krone, 2002; Rapoport & Bailyn, 1996). The reality is researchers have found that some employees are discouraged from taking advantage of these benefits or are not informed about their existence. For example, managers may indirectly communicate that employees should not use the available benefits because it causes problems for them, their departments, and the organization (Rapoport & Bailyn, 1996).

A study of Corning, Xerox, and Tandem Computers determined that employees who used such benefits experienced negative career consequences (Rapoport & Bailyn, 1996). Once employees discovered that their coworkers suffered when they used the company's family leave or flextime benefits, they simply stopped requesting them. Kirby and Krone (2002) conducted another study whose title aptly describes this organizational policy: "The Policy Exists, But You Can't Really Use It." The irony is that some organizations receive credit for being family friendly while not having to actually implement their policies (Jenner, 1994; Solomon, 1994). However, when workers are not able to balance the many demands in their lives, they, their families, and society at large suffer the consequences.

Although both men and women must manage work–life issues, much of the research on work–life conflict has focused on the difficulties working women face as they try to manage paid and unpaid labor. Men are perceived to work as hard or harder at paid work than women, but research indicates that women contribute at least twice as much unpaid labor to their families, resulting in high levels of work–life conflict (Alberts, Tracy, & Trethewey, 2011). To read another perspective on how the experience of work–life conflict differs between women and men, see *Alternative View: Men Now Have More Work–Life Conflict than Women.*

To summarize, communication is central to an individual's life within an organization, and individuals face many communication-related issues as they navigate organizations. Such challenges involve assimilation as well as communication with supervisors, subordinates, and coworkers. Inevitably, conflicts arise, as do a variety of potential organizational dilemmas, including emotion labor, stress and burnout, and work–life conflict. Thus, successful individuals are those who are able to communicate effectively as they negotiate the challenges, conflicts, and dilemmas of organizational life. However, as you've seen throughout this book, if you only consider individual forces or factors, you can't understand the whole picture. Individuals and organizations both are subject to numerous societal forces, the topic we turn to next.

TEST YOUR KNOWLEDGE

- What is organizational identification? How is it related to the process of assimilation?
- What four communication strategies contribute to supervisors' success?
- How are (1) emotion labor, (2) stress and burnout, and (3) work–life conflict related to one another? How do they differ?

THE INDIVIDUAL, ORGANIZATIONAL COMMUNICATION, AND SOCIETY

In this section, we explore how organizations and the societies in which they are located exert influence upon each other and the individuals within them. First we examine two of the most significant societal forces that impact organizational communication—history and globalization. Next, we discuss four of the important recent organizational practices that influence individuals and society, including the development of a new social contract between organizations and employees, the increase in organizations' use of contingent workers, the rise of urgent organizations, and the blurring of boundaries between home and work. Finally, we examine power relations within organizations and their impact on employees. We address these topics to explicate how each has influenced beliefs about organizational communication and its performance.

Societal Influences on Organizations

Organizations are shaped in part by the societies in which they are located. As societies change over time, so do the organizations within them. In addition, as organizations spread their operations into new cultures, they must change and adapt to those cultures to be successful. In the next section, we focus on these two societal influences on organizations: (1) social change and its impact on organizations and the communication within them, and (2) globalization and its effects on organizations and organizational communication.

Historical Forces Prevailing beliefs about work, individuals, and knowledge creation have influenced what people expect of organizations as well as how they are expected to act within them. For example, until the early 1900s, popular talk about organizational techniques took a moral tone. Journalists, novelists, clergy, and other prominent figures often described business owners as men of superior character, which they were obligated to model for the betterment of the lower, working class (Barley & Kunda, 1992). During this time, managers' and owners' opinions and communication were considered important while those of the working classes were not.

By the 1930s, a major change in thinking about organization and communication occurred. Due to cultural changes as well as researchers such as Mary Parker Follett (1942), people began to question the absolute right of managers to command and control employees and began to focus, instead, on the human relations function of organizations. That is, management began to be seen as needing to educate (through teaching and persuading), to interact with employees (by seeking input), and to integrate everyone's input. Thus, for the first time, organizational theorists and managers came to believe that workers needed to have a voice in the organization.

A variety of developments around the 1960s prompted another shift in thinking about organizations and communication (Barley & Kunda, 1992) toward what we might call a *systems mentality*. Military operations research began to find a home in industry, and the rise of computers fostered interest in organizational communication processes. Across many academic disciplines, researchers began a quest for general, even universal, theoretical principles. Biologist Ludwig von Bertalanffy (1968), for instance, developed a highly influential **general systems theory** that, he believed, applied as well to the social sciences as it did to the life and physical sciences. Many organization scholars agreed. They saw organizations as systems not only composed of many subsystems but also embedded in larger systems. Hence, they sought to develop strategies for communication that occur within the units or subsystems of the organization as well for communication that occurs between the organization and its environment.

Today, one of the most important societal factors to impact organizations, and the individuals who work within them, is globalization. **Globalization** refers to the increasing connectedness of the world in economic, political, and cultural realms (Cheney et al., 2004). Although we typically think of globalization in economic terms, it also describes the ways in which political and cultural events affect people around the world. For example, terrorist attacks in Europe and the Middle East influence tourists' travel plans as well as governments' political alliances. From an economic perspective, conflict in the Middle East leads both to fears that oil production will suffer and to higher energy costs in the United States and other countries reliant on this source of oil. Because of globalization, people in the United States are connected intimately to other parts of the world; as a result, decisions and events in far-removed places can affect them.

Although many scholars and experts agree on what globalization *is*, considerable disagreement exists concerning whether globalization, specifically economic globalization, is a positive or negative force in individuals' lives. Proponents believe that globalization leads to decreased trade barriers that result in increased prosperity and economic development across societies (Krugman, 2002). Critics, however, argue that globalization leads to a growing gap between the rich and the poor since transnational organizations can operate without oversight by national and international institutions that protect the interests of individuals (Ganesh, Zoller, & Cheney, 2005). More specifically, these critics maintain that this lack of oversight leads to companies attempting to profit by ignoring worker safety, not providing fair compensation, and exploiting the environment.

What are the communication implications of globalization? First, it means that more people and businesses have intercultural contact and that they need to learn how to communicate more effectively across cultures, as we noted in Chapter 10. Many categories of individuals need to interact with support personnel around the world, even in their nonwork lives, and increasingly workers in multinational organizations must communicate and work with people from diverse cultures. Second, global forces such as market deregulation may have leveling or homogenizing effects on organizational practices all over the world. Learn more about this issue in *Communication in Society: Case Study: Anti-Globalization Protests.*

Influence of Organizations on Individuals and Society

Not only are organizations influenced by society and cultures, they influence them and the individuals who comprise them. In this section, we explore four trends in

COMMUNICATION IN SOCIETY
Case Study: Anti-Globalization Protests

Do you think economic globalization, on the whole, improves individuals' lives in the U.S. and elsewhere? Why or why not? What terms would you use to refer to those in the movement opposing globalization? What do you predict the future of corporations and other organizations will be like with regard to globalization?

Most Americans first became aware of the so-called anti-globalization movement in 1999, when protests erupted in Seattle outside the meeting of the World Trade Organization; hundreds of demonstrators were arrested and thousands were injured. In subsequent years, anti-globalization demonstrations were organized in U.S. and foreign cities outside meetings of the International Monetary Fund (IMF), World Bank, Group of Eight (G8), and other high-level global economic institutions.

Activists in the movement argue that "anti-globalization" is a misnomer, as they are not against globalization as such. Instead, they use terms such as "anti-plutocracy" and "anti-corporate." Many consider themselves proponents of a global justice movement. In 2001, they organized the first World Social Forum in Porto Alegre, Brazil, as a counter-event to the World Economic Forum, which was taking place in Davos, Switzerland at the same time.

The loosely organized global social justice movement includes a wide variety of organizations and individuals, among them Nobel prize-winning economists Amartya Sen and Joseph E. Stiglitz. In general, what they oppose is "corporate personhood" and the unbridled capitalism inherent in "free trade" under agreements such as the North American Free Trade Agreement (NAFTA) and the Association of Southeast Asian Nations Free Trade Area (AFTA). They also oppose what they see as the exploitation of workers in free-trade zones (FTZ) such as the *maquiladora* zone in Mexico along the U.S. border—manufacturing centers, located primarily in developing countries, where raw goods can be imported, manufactured into finished goods, and re-exported without having to pass through normal international trade barriers such as customs inspections.

The anti-globalization movement has been criticized for lacking a coherent set of goals. Critics also point to data indicating that poverty has decreased in developing countries since the early 1990s, when the globalization trend began. They argue that U.S. workers have benefited from increased opportunities to export goods to developing countries.

contemporary organizations and the ways in which they impact society and individuals' lives. These trends include the new social contract, contingent workforces, urgent organizations, and blurred boundaries between work and life.

The New Social Contract Over the past twenty-five years, a fundamental change has occurred in the relationship between individuals and their employers (Chilton & Weidenbaum, 1994; Jablin & Sias, 2001). Until recently, employees expected to spend years, if not their entire working lives, with a single company and to be rewarded for their service and loyalty with job security and good retirement benefits (Eisenberg, Goodall, & Trethewey, 2010). This is no longer the case. Along with globalization, an increase in organizations' willingness to lay off workers during economic downturns and corporate restructuring have led to a **new social contract** between employers and employees. Under this "new social contract," loyalty is not expected by workers or organizations and job security rarely exists (Eisenberg et al., 2010). This means that if it is deemed profitable, companies are quick to sell or merge with other corporations, and employees are willing to jump ship if the right opportunity arises.

A number of individuals have argued that the current financial crisis in the United States and across the world has led to a greater imbalance in the social contract between companies and employees. They argue that organizations have

new social contract
assumes that loyalty is not expected by workers or organizations and that job security is unlikely

used the crisis as an excuse to engage in hiring practices that benefit organizations at great cost to employees. Although not everyone agrees, it is true that during the "Great Recession" approximately 7 million people have lost their jobs (Zuckerman, 2011) and the number of Americans working part-time because full-time work is not available has doubled in the past five years to 9.2 million people (Coy, Conlin & Herbst, 2010).

This change in the employee–employer relationship has resulted in job holders more fearful of or unable to change jobs, so the unemployed now are willing to settle for low wages and/or no benefits. It also has led to an increase in job and career shifting as well as to an increase in the employment of contingent workers— workers who do not have a long-term commitment to their organizations nor their employers to them.

Contingent Workers   **Contingent employees** work in temporary positions, part-time or as subcontractors (Belous, 1989; Jablin & Sias, 2001). Based on this definition, experts estimate that as many as one-third of U.S. employees are contingent workers (U.S. General Accounting Office, 2000).

Proponents of the trend toward the increased use of contingent workers argue that this practice is a productive response to the forces of a global marketplace. They point out that contingent work offers flexibility both to management and to workers. Firms can use contingent arrangements to maximize workforce flexibility in the face of seasonal and cyclical forces and the demands of just-in-time production. This same flexibility, they say, helps some workers balance the demands of family and work (U.S. Department of Labor, 2008). In addition, working in different organizations is believed to help contingent workers develop a wide set of skills that can lead to innovation (Jablin & Sias, 2001). Some commentators claim that these changes have led to the lowest unemployment rate in the United States and have allowed people to obtain better jobs than in the past.

On the other hand, detractors argue that companies often hire contingent workers simply to reduce employee wages, even though these employees perform the same amount and value of work (Conrad & Poole, 2005). They also point out that current tax, labor, and employment laws increase the likelihood of this practice by giving employers incentives to create contingent employment positions merely to sidestep their legal financial obligations to employees and to society. For certain types of contingent workers such as contractors, for example, employers do not have to make contributions to Social Security, unemployment insurance, workers' compensation, and health insurance; they also can save the administrative expense of withholding, and they are relieved of responsibility to the worker under labor and employment laws. At least one study has confirmed that such practices are fairly widespread; a 1989 General Accounting Office (GAO) study found that 38 percent of the employers the GAO examined had misclassified employees as independent contractors (U.S. Department of Labor, 2008).

Although some employees voluntarily choose contingent work to evade their own tax obligations, to provide flexibility, or to supplement retirement income, a large percentage of workers who hold part-time or temporary positions do so involuntarily. Many have been forced into temporary or part-time work due to organizational mergers, layoffs, restructuring, and downsizing (Lipson, 2011) or because they have limited choices. A significant portion of contingent workers is drawn from the most vulnerable sectors of the workforce—the young, female, and/ or Hispanic. To read about one employee's experience as a contingent worker, see *Communication in Society: The Disposable Worker.*

Overall, contingent employees are more likely than traditional full-time workers to have low family incomes and are less likely to receive health insurance and pension benefits through their employers. The expansion of contingent work has contributed to the increasing gap between high- and low-wage workers and to the increasing

contingent employees
individuals who work in temporary positions, part-time or as subcontractors

COMMUNICATION IN SOCIETY
The Disposable Worker

How do you think the shift from permanent jobs to contingent jobs has affected employee communication and relationships? How do you believe it affects families? In what ways can organizations maintain interpersonal contact with their contingent workers who work outside of the office?

On a recent Tuesday morning, single mom Tammy DePew Smith woke up in her tidy Florida townhouse in time to shuttle her oldest daughter, a high school freshman, to the 6:11 A.M. bus. At 6:40 she was at the desk in her bedroom, starting her first shift of the day with LiveOps, a Santa Clara (Calif.) provider of call-center workers for everyone from Eastman Kodak (EK) and Pizza Hut (YUM) to infomercial behemoth Tristar Products. She's paid by the minute—25 cents—but only for the time she's actually on the phone with customers.

By 7:40, Smith had grossed $15. But there wasn't much time to reflect on her early morning productivity; the next child had to be roused from bed, fed, and put onto the school bus. Somehow she managed to squeeze three more shifts into her day, pausing only to homeschool her 7-year-old son, make dinner, and do the bedtime routine. "I tell my kids, unless somebody is bleeding or dying, don't mess with me."

As an independent agent, Smith has no health insurance, no retirement benefits, no sick days, no vacation,

no severance, and no access to unemployment insurance. But in recession-ravaged Ormond Beach, she's considered lucky. She has had more or less steady work since she signed on with LiveOps in October 2006. "LiveOps was a lifesaver for me," she says.

You know American workers are in bad shape when a low-paying, no-benefits job is considered a sweet deal. Their situation isn't likely to improve soon; some economists predict it will be years, not months, before employees regain any semblance of bargaining power. That's because this recession's unusual ferocity has accelerated trends—including offshoring, automation, the decline of labor unions' influence, new management techniques, and regulatory changes—that already had been eroding workers' economic standing.

The forecast for the next five to 10 years: more of the same, with paltry pay gains, worsening working conditions, and little job security. Right on up to the C-suite, more jobs will be freelance and temporary, and even seemingly permanent positions will be at greater risk. "When I hear people talk about temp vs. permanent jobs, I laugh," says Barry Asin, chief analyst at the Los Altos (Calif.) labor-analysis firm Staffing Industry Analysts. "The idea that any job is permanent has been well proven not to be true." As Kelly Services (KELYA) CEO Carl Camden puts it: "We're all temps now."

FROM: Coy, P., Conlin, M., & Herbst, M. (2010, January 7). The disposable worker. *Bloomberg BusinessWeek*. Retrieved September 17, 2011 from http://www.businessweek.com/magazine/content/10_03/b4163032935448.htm.http://www.businessweek.com/magazine/content/10_03/b4163032935448_page_4.htm

sense of insecurity among workers (U.S. Department of Labor, 2008). The rise in the number of contingent workers has raised concerns that the United States is moving toward a two-tiered system in which more highly educated and trained employees are supported by lower paid part-time and temporary workers (Jablin & Sias, 2001). Experts worry that this division of workers may result in a caste system whereby permanent employees look down on and denigrate temporary or part-time workers.

Miller (2009) argues that a "disposable workforce" may not be good for organizations, either. Contingent employees are aware of the organizations' lack of commitment to them—especially during economic downturns, when they are the first to be let go; this decreases their loyalty to the organization and their commitment to its goals. Also, because organizations are less likely to invest time and money in socializing contingent workers and providing them with the support needed to be successful (Jablin & Sias, 2001), such employees are likely to feel disconnected from the organization and less likely to buy into its organizational culture. In turn, employees' lack of identification with the organization likely decreases job satisfaction and increases job turnover.

How do you feel about your job prospects once you leave college? Why? What can you do to make your career opportunities the strongest?

In addition, working alongside a contingent workforce can encourage traditional employees to question the value of organizational commitment and loyalty (Gossett, 2001; Miller, 2009). These traditional employees also may be less likely to form relationships and support networks with employees they see as transitory, which can negatively impact all employees' performance and the organization's productivity.

However, the increased use of a contingent workforce is, in part, a response to the competitive demands that U.S. companies face, the topic we take up next.

Competitiveness and Urgent Organizations Another significant change is the rise of **urgent organizations**. Urgent organizations are companies that attempt to "shorten the time in which they develop new products and respond to customer demands" (Eisenberg, Goodall, & Trethewey, 2010, p. 17). Urgent organizations occur because of the intense time pressures related to global competition and the subsequent consumer demand for innovation and immediate fulfillment of wants and needs. Apple and other technology companies manifest many of the behaviors typical of urgent organizations. For example, the first iPhone was sold to the public in June 2007, and then just ten weeks later its price was dropped $200 in response to customer demand (though doing so infuriated those "early adopters" who bought the phone in June and July). In July 2008, just one year later, the iPhone 3G was released, with the price once again reduced, this time by half. Similarly, Walmart attempts to compete globally by requiring all of its suppliers to abide by a policy that requires every vendor to either lower the price or increase the quality of each product every year (Fishman, 2006).

Google and other technology companies manifest many of the behaviors typical of urgent organizations.

Urgent companies evolve and thrive because they are successful. Speed and quick response time provide them with an edge; companies that release products first tend to attract the most media and consumer attention, and clients and consumers are more likely to patronize companies that respond quickly to their requests for services and products.

Of course, when organizations increase the speed of innovation and delivery of services, it means that the employees of those organizations also are under time pressures to increase productivity and response time. This development has led to the issue we discuss next, the blurring of boundaries between work and home.

Blurred Boundaries Between Home and Work The time pressures associated with urgent organizations have led to a blurring of the boundaries between individuals' work and nonwork lives. These pressures in conjunction with the advent of new communication technologies have increased organizations' ability to intrude into what has traditionally been one's nonwork life. The widespread use of email, cell phones, text messaging, and instant messaging has made it possible, and in some instances mandatory, that employees respond to organizations' demands at almost any hour of the day or night, during weekends as well as weekdays, and even when on vacation. Interestingly, just as the use of contingent workers has had a more profound impact on low-wage earners, the blurring of boundaries has had a stronger effect on high-wage earners, leading to positions that are now described as "extreme jobs" (Hewlitt, 2007; Schor, 1992).

Extreme jobs are those held by well-paid employees who are required to work more than sixty hours per week (often many more) as well as being subjected to

urgent organizations
companies that try to shorten the time it takes to develop new products and respond to customer demands

unpredictable workflow, tight deadlines, responsibilities that amount to more than one job, expectations of work performance outside regular work hours, client availability twenty-four/seven, extensive travel, many direct reports, and/or physical presence at the workplace ten or more hours per day. Jobs with such extreme requirements often negatively affect employees' personal and family lives as well as their ability to contribute to their communities.

Organizations, Communication, and Power

Organizations in the United States historically have been hierarchical, meaning that power, decision-making authority, and control have been held by a relatively small percentage of people within the organization, including managers, vice presidents, presidents, and chief executive officers (CEOs). To a great extent this is still true today. Although a hierarchical structure seems natural and normal to most of us, it can lead to power differences and to communication behavior that negatively affects those workers who hold little or no power. In the discussion that follows, we examine three of the communication problems that can result from large power differences.

The widespread use of technology in many jobs has caused a blurring of the boundaries between work and time off.

Bullying Organizational **bullying** refers to repeated, hostile behaviors that occur in the workplace over an extended period and that are intended, or are perceived as intended, to harm one or more parties who are unable to defend themselves (Lutgen-Sandvik, Tracy, & Alberts, 2005). Although interpersonal conflict is common in organizations, and perhaps necessary, bullying is not necessary. Bullying differs from conflict in that conflict can be constructive and positive. In addition, intent to harm may not be present in typical interpersonal conflict, and the parties in an interpersonal conflict often are relatively equal in power. However, in bullying, the intent to harm is a defining element, and power differences are key. Bully targets lack the ability to defend themselves and have limited strategies with which to respond. During interpersonal conflict, participants both act and are acted upon. In contrast, in bullying interactions, one party (or group) is the actor or perpetrator and one (or more) person(s) is the target.

You may wonder why we bring up the issue of bullying, since it may not seem like a prevalent problem. However, it probably is more common than you think. One study found that 30 percent of more than 400 respondents claimed that they had been bullied at some point in their careers (Lutgen-Sandvik et al., 2005). Eleven percent revealed that they had been bullied in just the past year. These statistics are similar to reports from workers in Great Britain, though somewhat higher than those reported in Scandinavia. In addition, bullying is important because, fundamentally, it is a communication issue (Alberts, Lutgen-Sandvik, & Tracy, 2005). Of the twenty-two behaviors used to enact bullying, seventeen of them involved verbal interaction, such as ridicule, rumors, false allegations, insults, and threats of violence (Alberts et al., 2005).

Because bullying does occur regularly and is related to one's power in the organization, scholars have sought to determine strategies that can help targets respond. However, because targets typically have low power in the organization, their options are limited. For example, a problem-solving approach involves discussing the issue and seeking resolution. It requires that all parties be able to participate openly. This is rarely true for the target of bullying. Similarly, compromising can occur only if one has leverage within the organization, meaning that

bullying
repeated hostile behaviors that are or are perceived to be intended to harm parties who are unable to defend themselves

each party must be able to offer something in return for a change in the other's behavior, which a low-power person may not possess. Obliging, or accommodating to the bully's demands, may be the only strategy if one wishes to remain in the organization. Withdrawing may be an option if one is willing to leave, and targets report that leaving the organization was the most effective, and often only, solution to the problem. Competing typically is not a useful strategy; it only intensifies the bully's abusive behavior. For a student's account of organizational bullying, see *It Happened to Me: Bob*.

It Happened to Me: *Bob*

I still can't believe it happened to me. About a year ago, I was transferred to a new branch of my credit union. Within a few months, my supervisor began to criticize everything I did and make sarcastic and mean comments about me in front of other people. I tried to talk to her about it, but she just told me I was too thin-skinned. I don't know if it was because I was one of only a few males in the office or what. Finally, it got so bad that I asked for a meeting with my supervisor and her supervisor. During our meeting, I became so upset that I started having chest pains. I thought I was having a heart attack and had to go to the hospital by ambulance. It turns out it was a panic attack. When I got back to work a few days later, my supervisor started ridiculing me for having a panic attack. I have asked for a transfer, but I am also looking for another job.

Sexual Harassment Sexual harassment describes unwanted sexual attention that interferes with an individual's ability to do his or her job and/or behavior that ties sexual favors to continued employment or success within the organization (Equal Employment Opportunity Commission, 1980). Federal law recognizes two types of sexual harassment, quid pro quo and hostile work environment (Roberts & Mann, 2000). **Quid pro quo** is the request for sexual favors as a condition of getting or keeping a job or benefit. ("You do what I ask, and I'll help you advance in the organization.") A **hostile work environment** results when a coworker or supervisor engages in unwelcome and inappropriate sexually based behavior and creates an intimidating, hostile, or offensive atmosphere. Indulging in inappropriate verbal and nonverbal behaviors; repeatedly asking someone for a date; calling coworkers or subordinates by affectionate names (e.g., honey, sweetie); touching, patting, and stroking; and displaying posters and objects of a sexual nature can all constitute acts of sexual harassment.

Sexual harassment is primarily a communicative behavior.

Even with this list of criteria, however, people could differ over what constitutes a hostile work environment. As a guideline, the U.S. Court of Appeals (Aeberhard-Hodges, 1996) ruled that sexual harassment should be examined from the perspective of what a "reasonable woman," not a "reasonable person," would find offensive. This led some to this central question: If a reasonable woman standard prevailed, would men, even "reasonable men," ever be sure how to behave? The court's ruling, however, rests on the understanding that women are the most frequent targets of sexual harassment and that their experiences in the workplace and around issues of sexuality often differ markedly from men's.

At this point, you might be wondering how bullying differs from sexual harassment. We see sexual harassment as a specific type of bullying behavior because it contains many of the same elements: It is rooted in power differences, the target typically is unable to defend himself or herself, and the target perceives it as hostile and intentional.

As you can see, sexual harassment primarily is a communicative behavior. Because of this, researchers have typically explored how targets can use communication to respond effectively. The typical strategies recommended include confronting the harasser and stating that the behavior must stop, complaining to one's boss or the human relations department, suing, or leaving the organization (Sigal, Braden-Maguire, Patt, Goodrich, & Perrino, 2003).

However, the majority of female targets of sexual harassment (in fact 95 percent or more) do not respond assertively by confronting the harasser or reporting the harasser to a supervisor or the organization (Gruber & Smith, 1995; Rudman, Borgida, & Robertson, 1995). Why not? Sexual harassment typically occurs between people of unequal power, so confronting the harasser may not be an option. Targets risk losing their jobs, seeing the harassment intensify, or losing out on promotions and raises.

Complaining to a third party does sometimes work, particularly in organizations that have a clearly articulated sexual harassment policy and in which the human resources department has been empowered to handle sexual harassment cases effectively. However, some organizations do not wish to deal with these issues, or do not see them as important, so complaining to a third party does not always result in a benefit. Of course, suing the harasser and the organization that allows harassment is possible, but not every case is settled to the target's satisfaction, and the process can be long, painful, and ultimately unrewarding.

Finally, although leaving the organization does tend to resolve some aspects of the problem, some employees lack the option of leaving or find that leaving takes considerable time and effort. In addition, leaving one's job may resolve the physical/behavioral aspect of the harassment, but it does not help targets manage the long-term physical or psychological effects of harassment, does not address the impact of the harassment on the target's career, and does not result in changes in the perpetrator or the organization.

None of this means that targets should tolerate inappropriate behavior, but it does mean that they should carefully consider their options before committing to a response strategy. Targets should consider what response will be most effective in their specific situations. To do so, targets of sexual harassment (or bullying) might consider the following options. First, a target should consider responding assertively the first time the harassment occurs. This strategy is most likely to be successful when the perpetrator and target have equal power or a relationship of trust. If direct confrontation does not seem to be an option or has not been successful, then the target should consider approaching his or her supervisor, human resources department, or an organizational ombudsperson. Many organizations want to and will respond to such complaints, recognizing that the organization as a whole is harmed by such behavior.

If confrontation and appealing to authorities have not succeeded, targets must assess their needs and options carefully. They might consider seeking social support from family and friends, seeking assistance from a counselor or therapist to help them manage the emotional distress, developing strategies to avoid the perpetrator (if possible), and/or requesting a transfer or another job.

Unfortunately, the most common strategy targets select is to do nothing. This is not a response that, in the long run, benefits the individual *or* the organization. Moreover, doing nothing is especially problematic if the target has not even determined what other options exist. Too often, targets assume their efforts will be unsuccessful before they even make an attempt. If you do become a target, we encourage you not to make this assumption.

quid pro quo
requests for sexual favors as a condition of getting or keeping a job or benefit; one of two types of sexual harassment recognized by federal law

hostile work environment
an intimidating, hostile, or offensive workplace atmosphere created by unwelcome and inappropriate sexually based behavior; one of two types of sexual harassment recognized by federal law

Employee Privacy and Monitoring Monitoring employees electronically and in other ways is a growing part of the way American companies do business (American Management Association, 2005). According to the American Management Association's survey, 76 percent of employers monitor workers' Web connections, while 50 percent store and monitor employees' computer files. Workers are exposed to many other types of privacy-invasive monitoring as well. These include drug testing, closed-circuit video monitoring, email monitoring, instant message monitoring, phone monitoring, location monitoring, personality and psychological testing, and keystroke logging.

Although employers do have an interest in monitoring employees in order to address security risks, sexual harassment, and acceptable performance of work duties, these activities may diminish employee morale and dignity as well as increase worker stress (DiTecco, Cwitco, Arsenault, & Andre, 1992). To better understand the complexities of this issue, read *It Happened to Me: Nichole*. In addition, monitoring may interfere with employee productivity. A study of 134 corporate employees examined the effects of monitoring and found that pro-

It Happened to Me: *Nichole*

The chapter on organizational communication helped me better understand a problem I encountered with Residential Life at my college. It wasn't about drinking or drugs, or letting in strangers, or any of the usual problems that students have with the dorm; it was about my Resident Assistant, who now is my boyfriend.

Just to clarify, there were no rules stated that I could not date my RA, and he was never told he couldn't date his residents. Plus, there is actual love involved, not just random friends-with-benefits hookups and we really feel as though we have met the right person. But, Residential Life has a huge problem with our relationship, and they called us into a meeting. We both felt as though it was a violation of our privacy. We had the meeting, he quit his job, and we are still dating, ten months strong!

Now, though, when I look at the relationship through the eyes of the school, I can see their problems with it. What would have happened if an employee of the college got me pregnant? Also, he lived in my hall and his duty was to keep us in line, but there was huge preferential treatment going on. I mean, would my boyfriend really write me up for anything? So now I see that they had a point. But I don't understand why nothing was ever said about this practice being against the rules.

ductivity diminished when people believed they were being monitored for quality (Stanton & Julian, 2002). Nonetheless, employers and employees can develop policies that meet the needs of both parties. Both sides must have a voice in developing the policies, and the process itself must be transparent (Trethewey & Corman, 2001).

In conclusion, organizations experience significant impact from the society and historical time period in which they exist. Two societal factors currently influencing corporations in the United States are globalization and changing power relations in the workplace. Globalization has meant that many jobs have been transferred from the United States to other countries, and both consumers and employees now must increase their contact with workers around the world. This change has been accompanied by an increased focus on power relationships at work and their impact on employees. This tendency to critique organizational uses of power has also led to more discussion of organizational ethics, which we examine next.

TEST YOUR KNOWLEDGE

- What is globalization? What are the communication implications of globalization?
- How has the "social contract" between individuals and organizations changed over the past twenty-five years?
- In what ways can organizations exert power over individuals?

ETHICS AND ORGANIZATIONAL COMMUNICATION

Due to organizational behavior such as providing bonuses to CEOs who lead failing financial companies and phone hacking by members of the Rupert Murdoch-owned News Corporation, U.S. Americans are paying more attention to business ethics than perhaps ever before (MSNBC.com News Service, 2011) However, observers don't agree on where responsibility for ethical behavior and communication rests within the organization. For example, who should be held accountable for the phone hacking conducted by reporters of News Corp.? Should only the reporters themselves be prosecuted? Should the manager of the newspaper also be accountable? How about Rupert Murdoch himself? Is he responsible for the ethical standards within his company? When attempting to determine the ethical choices and decisions organizations should make, people usually view the process either from the *individual perspective* or the *communal perspective* (Brown, 1989).

Many U.S. Americans take an individualistic perspective, viewing ethical failures as resting on the shoulders of specific individuals within the organization. From this outlook, each person in the corporation is responsible for his or her own behavior. In the case of News Corp., then, only the reporters themselves as well as others who knew about their behavior but did not "blow the whistle" are accountable. In the communal view, however, individuals are considered to be members of community and are all partially responsible for the behavior of its members. The assumption here is that the ethical standards within an organization are created by and should be monitored and reinforced by all of its members. From this perspective, everyone within the News Corp. organization, especially the managers and owners, is responsible, because they had a duty to create and maintain high ethical standards within the company.

When ethics is discussed in organizational contexts, the focus typically is on the rights of the individual—such as the rights to free speech or privacy—and policies and behaviors that infringe on these rights are seen as unethical. However, a communal approach focuses on the "common good," or what is in the best interests of the entire community. Thus, the morality of an action is assessed based on its consequences for the group. In an individualistic approach, the responsibility for phone hacking at *News of the World* lies with the reporters who directly engaged in it. From a communal approach, the reporters' phone hacking is harmful to the organization as well as society, and the people responsible for that harm are the members of the organization collectively, that is, the organization itself.

Problems exist with both approaches. When we view individuals alone as responsible, they alone are punished while the organization is left essentially unchanged. Yet, when we view corporations in a completely communal way and hold them responsible for their unethical practices, no individual may be held accountable or liable. Consequently, those responsible for the decision to engage in unethical and often illegal practices may not suffer any consequences—and may be free to continue these practices.

How should we balance these two approaches? Most likely, we need to hold both the organization and the individuals who lead them responsible for their practices—just as political leaders are tried in war courts for crimes against humanity, even though their subordinates performed the atrocities. At the same time, corporate leaders need to consider the impacts of their decisions on both individuals and society.

How is communication a factor in organizational ethics? Communication figures in organizational ethics in two ways (Cheney et al., 2004). First, many of the ethical issues in organizations revolve around communication. For example, organizations have to decide when to tell employees of impending layoffs, they develop advertising campaigns that communicate the identity of their corporation and its products to consumers, and they must decide how to communicate information regarding their profits and losses to shareholders and Wall Street. Second, the ways in which an organization defines, communicates about, and responds to ethical and unethical behavior shape how individuals within the organization behave. If corporate policy and organizational leaders are vague on the issue of ethics, or worse yet, fail to address it, employees may believe that ethics is not a central concern of the organization and may behave accordingly. For example, in 2005, *Esquire* magazine published an article about the alleged ethical violations of military recruiters. The military personnel interviewed for the article claimed that despite written policies that encouraged ethical behavior, their communication with their superiors revolved only around their success or failure at meeting their recruitment goals and never about *how* they met those goals.

Thus, they concluded that recruiting ethically was a secondary, or perhaps even an unnecessary, consideration.

TEST YOUR KNOWLEDGE

- How do the individual and communal approaches to organizational ethics differ?
- What role does communication play in organizational ethics?

IMPROVING YOUR ORGANIZATIONAL COMMUNICATION SKILLS

Much of the time, if not most, people are only willing to engage in conflict when they are angry and/or emotional. How often have you been involved with, or observed others engaging in, highly emotional conflict at work? As you probably have noted, this style of conflict engagement typically doesn't resolve anything and may cause long-lasting damage to one's relationships with others.

A better way to manage conflict with co-workers is to use a strategic approach to conflict management. People who use a strategic approach prepare for their conflicts and engage in **strategy control** (Canary & Lakey, 2012). When behaving strategically, one assesses the available information and options, which increases one's understanding of the conflict and the other party. In turn, these behaviors help people choose conflict behaviors that are responsive to the partner's as well as their own needs and increase the possibility for cooperation, collaboration, and compromise.

When using a strategic approach, before you even initiate a discussion over an issue in conflict, you should know what you want to occur as a result of the interaction. If you wish to confront your coworker about not doing his fair share of a joint project, you should first decide what your goal is. Do you want your colleague to apologize? To stay late until the report is finished? To complete the project by himself? To take the lead on the next joint project? Or do you desire some combination of these outcomes? You will be far more successful and satisfied with your conflict interactions if you go into them knowing what you want.

Second, decide if the issue is worth confronting—or worth confronting now. You may know what you want, but do you have a reasonable chance of accomplishing your goals? That is, how likely is your coworker to apologize or to successfully take the lead on your next joint project? If the answer truly is "highly unlikely," you may choose not to engage in the conflict or to seek other solutions. For example, you might decide to ask your supervisor to assign someone else to work with you. Alternatively, you may decide you do want to have the conversation, but perhaps not right now, because both of you are hungry and tired.

strategy control
assessing the available information and options in order to increases one's understanding of the conflict and the other party before engaging in conflict communication

If you decide that the conflict is worth confronting, you next want to try to understand the other party's goals, that is, what he or she wants. What, for example, do you think your coworker's goal is? Does he want to receive credit for the work without having to do it? Does he want assistance with parts of the project he doesn't feel competent to complete? Is he busy with other projects and wants more time to finish the project? Depending on your understanding of his goals and interests, you will likely suggest different solutions. Please remember, however, the tendency for each of us to attribute negative motivations to others' behavior. If you are upset, you will be particularly like to believe your colleague's goal is to avoid work but receive the rewards of it. Recognize that your attributions may be incorrect and that you probably will need to talk with your coworker in order to determine what his motivations really are.

You have one more step to complete before you are ready to talk with your colleague; you need to plan the interaction. More specifically, you should think about when and where the conversation should take place and what tactics you believe will be most effective. Typically, you will want to choose a time when neither you nor your coworker is angry, rushed, or stressed. In addition, you should probably have the conversation in private. If others are around, one or both of you may behave more competitively or avoid the interaction entirely because you are embarrassed to be observed by others. Finally, you should think through how you will explain your dissatisfaction with the current state of affairs neutrally and how you will frame your suggested solutions. Once you have done all of this, you are ready to talk with your colleague and discuss calmly what the two of you can do to reduce your feeling that you alone are working on the project.

TEST YOUR KNOWLEDGE

- What is mean by "a strategic approach" to managing conflict?
- What are the four steps to the "strategic approach" to conflict management?

SUMMARY

Organizations have a powerful influence on individuals' lives; consequently, it is important to learn how to communicate effectively in organizational contexts. Doing so can enhance professional success, allow one to ask more informed questions about everyday organizational practices, and help individuals decide which organizations they wish to frequent and support.

Organizations are composed of interactions that members use to accomplish their individual and common goals. The two fundamental properties of organizations are function, or the goals and effects of communication, and structure, or the lines of communication through which messages flow.

Some of the basic types of communication that occur and that affect employee success within the organization include assimilation, supervisor–subordinate communication, and coworker communication. In addition, employees can face three types of organizational dilemmas during their careers: emotion labor, stress and burnout, and work–life conflict.

Three of the most significant societal forces that impact organizational communication are history, globalization, and power; each influences beliefs about organizational communication and its performance. Power differences in organizations can result in three specific communication problems for workers—bullying, sexual harassment, and employee monitoring.

Ethical issues in organizational communication are key for twenty-first-century workers, as is becoming a more effective communicator. When assessing the ethical choices and decisions organizations should make, people usually approach the process from the individual perspective or the communal perspective. Each approach has consequences for the organization, and the most ethical approach combines the two perspectives. Finally, conflict management skills are among the most important organizational communication skills one can develop, and a strategic approach to conflict management can help you significantly improve your ability to manage conflict with your colleagues.

HUMAN COMMUNICATION IN SOCIETY ONLINE

To review this chapter, use the MyCommunicationLab Web site to test your understanding of the following key terms, record your answers to the chapter review questions, and complete the suggested activities. Expand your learning and understanding of chapter concepts by completing additional activities and exercises online. Access code required. Go to www.mycommunicationlab.com for more information or to purchase standalone access.

KEY TERMS

organizations 287
function 287
production 287
maintenance 287
innovation 288
structure 288
downward communication 288
upward communication 288
horizontal communication 288
hierarchy 288
formal structure 288
informal structure 288

organizational culture 288
assimilation 292
organizational identification 292
semantic-information
    distance 294
upward distortion 294
openness 295
supportiveness 295
motivation 295
empowerment 296
ingratiation 296
assertiveness 296

rationality 296
burnout 300
general systems
    theory 304
globalization 304
new social contract 305
contingent employees 306
urgent organizations 308
bullying 309
quid pro quo 311
hostile work environment 311
strategy control 314

APPLY WHAT YOU KNOW

1. **Understanding Emotion Labor** Think of five jobs that require employees to engage in emotion labor and delineate the emotions that these employees are "expected" to display. What emotions are they expected to suppress? What contradictory emotions and behaviors are they expected to perform? Which of the five jobs that you listed appears to have the heaviest emotion labor load?

2. **Understanding Relationships at Work** Form a group with one or more of your classmates. Assume that you are a work group that has been charged with developing a fraternization policy for your job. Develop a policy about the types of relationships that are appropriate in your workplace and how people who have these relationships should communicate and behave while at work.

3. **Improving Your Job Interview Skills** Go to job-interview.net's "Mock Interviews" site at www.job-interview.net/sample/Demosamp.htm and review the information about communicating effectively during job interviews. Engage in one of the mock interviews provided, and then write a brief analysis of your performance. Explain what you did well and what you could have done better.

EXPLORE

1. Go to the *Psychology Today* website and locate the page on workplace Self Tests. Select two self-tests (such as the Entrepreneurial Personality Profile or the Leadership Style test) and complete them. After completing the tests, analyze your score. Does the score you received reflect your understanding of yourself and your work life? Which of you answers surprised you? How can this information help you in your future career?

2. Go to a job interviewing website such as the U.S. Labor's Job Interview Tips or About.com's Job Interview Tips and read the suggestions offered for how to interview for a job effectively. Afterward, develop a short checklist of helpful hints for interviewing that you can keep on hand for future job interview.

3. Locate a website devoted to exploring work-life issues, such as the Center for Work-Life Policy site or the Canadian Center for Occupational Health and Safety's Work/Life page, and read at least one essay on work-life issues. After reading the essay, write a brief summary of it that you could share with your classmates.

12
Rhetorical Communication

chapter outline

> *Rhetoric is essential to a vital democracy.*

I was asked to give the eulogy at my best friend's funeral. I had never given a speech like that, and at first, I wasn't sure what I would say. I decided that I should talk about what a special person he was and tell some stories about the thoughtful things he did and the crazy stunts he pulled. I figured we needed to remember his life as much as we needed to mourn his death.

—Dan

Dan recognized the power of rhetorical communication to honor and commemorate. **Rhetoric** is communication that influences the attitudes or behaviors of others; it is also called the art of persuasion. Dan's eulogy was rhetorical in that it was designed to influence how his listeners viewed his deceased friend; through his speech, he encouraged them to see his friend as unique, fun, and thoughtful. On other occasions, communicators might use rhetoric to influence people to vote a particular way, to recognize Pope John Paul II as a saint, or to participate in a Walk for the Cure for breast cancer.

Dan's speech served important cultural and personal functions, and gaining insight into such functions is, by itself, an important reason to study the art of rhetoric. But people study rhetoric, which comes from the ancient Greek word for speaking, for a variety of other important reasons as well, which we will explore throughout this chapter. Since most of us spend more time as receivers of rhetorical communication, this chapter also focuses on how to be a responsible rhetorical critic.

In this chapter, we explore rhetoric as it informs the study of communication today. We will first consider the definition and functions of rhetoric. We next examine how characteristics of public speakers, or *rhetors*, make them credible, influence what they say, and impact how they relate to their audiences. We then turn our focus to a broader topic—the intersection of society and rhetoric. And, before providing a guide for preparing a rhetorical presentation, we consider the merits of being a rhetorical critic.

Once you have read this chapter, you will be able to:

■ Describe some of the key issues in rhetorical communication.

■ Identify cultural and social influences on the development of rhetoric.

■ Identify and define the three artistic proofs (ethos, pathos, logos).

■ Explain four functions of rhetoric: reaffirming cultural values, increasing democratic participation, securing justice, and promoting social change.

■ Understand the ethical issues facing rhetors and audience members.

■ Identify the basic steps in preparing a speech.

THE IMPORTANCE OF RHETORIC

The rhetorical tradition lies at the heart of communication studies. Since the days of Aristotle in ancient Greece, rhetoric has been considered the art of persuasion. Its practice is contingent upon culture, political arrangements, and social contexts and

rhetoric
communication that is used to
influence the attitudes or behaviors
of others; the art of persuasion

conventions. For example, how might courtroom rhetoric differ among people who believe in magic, witches, and the presumption of guilt from courtroom rhetoric among people who believe in DNA, forensic science, and the presumption of innocence? Or in a political system with a dictator versus one with elected officials? We'll look at the changing notions of rhetoric as cultures and societies have differed. First, let's look at how rhetoric functions in our society.

Rhetoric's Functions in Society

Rhetorical communication serves at least three important social functions. First, as you may have surmised, rhetoric is essential to a vital democracy. For people to make informed decisions (and vote) about a range of issues, they must listen critically and speak with care. By advocating for one's perspective and engaging with the perspectives of others, people can make decisions together regarding the common good. Hence, rhetoric can strengthen democratic society, and speeches or other types of communication to the public can serve important political and social functions.

Second, rhetoric helps people seek justice. Probably one of the most obvious sites of this rhetorical function is the courtroom. Not only lawyers but also jurors need rhetorical skills; they need to listen carefully and critically not only to what is said, but how it is said, and they must be able to persuade other jurors of the proper verdict. Speakers also use rhetoric to persuade others to pursue social justice—for example, to support a moratorium on the death penalty or treat animals more ethically.

Third, rhetoric helps people clarify their own beliefs and actions. For example, after the attacks of September 11, 2001, many people, like our student in *It Happened to Me: Denise*, were not sure what to believe about why the United States was attacked or how they should respond or behave. Therefore, they turned to experts and national leaders, such as the president, to gather information that could help them clarify their beliefs and understanding. In his speech after 9/11, President George W. Bush told the nation and the world that "America was targeted for attack because we're the brightest beacon for freedom and opportunity in the world. And no one will keep that light from shining" (2001). Many people who heard his message felt that it spoke to their own views and helped them articulate how they were feeling. Conversely, others who heard the message realized that it did not reflect their feelings, but in thinking

It Happened to Me: *Denise*

When the president was going to speak about 9/11 for the first time, I was right there listening. Most of the people I knew, including me, were frightened and not sure what to believe or how to understand the attacks. We wanted to know what was really happening and what he was doing to protect the United States.

and talking about their reaction to the speech, they were better able to explain to themselves and others what they *did* believe.

The Advantages of Studying Rhetoric

In addition to serving important functions in society, rhetoric is also an important area of academic inquiry. Studying rhetoric as a field of scholarship is useful for four reasons. First, the study of public communication generates findings that help people understand the range of viewpoints on social issues. For example, if you wanted to understand the reasoning behind the U.S. immigration policy, you could examine the rhetoric of people who are attempting to influence that policy. You might listen to the president's speeches on immigration; you could examine the Catholic Church's views on pending immigration legislation; you could review the public comments of various members of Congress, some of whom are themselves the children or grandchildren of immigrants; and you could listen to interviews and speeches of other people who support various changes to immigration policy. By examining the rhetoric of these individuals and groups, you would be better able to understand how U.S. immigration policies respond to these varied perspectives.

Second, the study of rhetoric helps people better understand culture. Both consciously and unconsciously, through listening to and analyzing public communication, people learn the expectations of their own cultures—what it means to be a good parent, how to present oneself, how to decorate one's home, and much more. People can study and understand other cultures, too, by being attuned to how public communication sustains patterns of social life.

Third, studying rhetoric can help people critically evaluate messages designed to influence them, such as advertising. Other rhetoric tries to persuade people to support particular policies or to vote for or against certain politicians or propositions. As receivers of these persuasive messages, people can learn to listen critically, analyze these messages, and respond appropriately.

Finally, the study of public communication helps us to become better public communicators or to understand what makes specific public communicators effective or ineffective. We can learn much about public speaking by analyzing instances of public speech. In addition, we can determine why some speakers are more successful or persuasive than others by comparing their public communication.

Becoming a Rhetorical Critic The term **rhetorical critic** refers to an informed consumer of rhetorical discourse who is prepared to analyze rhetorical texts. You may think that a critic's job is simply to be negative about whatever is under analysis. However, everyone is a critic in everyday life, and we have an ethical duty to think critically about the rhetorical texts we encounter. Although some people reserve the term *rhetorical critic* for those who work in academia, we see it differently. We consider anyone who pursues sustained and detailed analyses of rhetorical discourse to be a rhetorical critic.

We hope that you and your fellow citizens all become more attuned to the sensitivities of rhetorical discourse and that you become strong analysts of it, as it has tremendous influence on the ways you conduct your everyday life and the way society functions. To give just one example, rhetorical discourse likely shapes your understanding of what it means to be a good parent. Do you think that good parents have to sacrifice everything for their children? Pay for their college educations? Do good parents expect their children to take care of them in their old age? Or should good parents do everything possible to avoid being a burden? Of course, no "right" answer exists for any of these questions. But it's important to be aware that you do have some ideas about what constitutes good parenting. It's also important to be aware that these ideas came from a barrage of rhetorical messages from newspaper reporters, magazine writers, psychologists, religious organizations, and others. Becoming more aware of your opinions and where they come from can make you a more effective rhetorical critic.

Being an informed rhetorical critic can also help one appreciate the artistic aspects of discourse (Darsey, 1994), as well as what makes a particular rhetorical message effective or persuasive. When you read the excerpt from a famous antislavery speech in *Did You Know? Frederick Douglass*, consider what makes it effective. What are the artistic aspects of this speech? Why didn't Douglass simply say, "Slavery is wrong"?

Rhetorical criticism is a method for generating knowledge about rhetoric. Through attentiveness to how rhetoric has functioned and continues to function in various contexts, you can build an understanding of your culture, society, and the ideas that predominated during a given period. Hence, an analysis of any one rhetorical message should be seen as part of a much larger and ongoing dialogue.

A variety of approaches to rhetorical criticism exist. We cannot cover all the major approaches to rhetorical criticism in this introductory course. There are many courses and textbooks that focus on rhetorical criticism. Instead we hope to teach you to listen carefully to how rhetoric functions every day and to analyze

rhetorical critic
an informed consumer of rhetorical discourse who is prepared to analyze rhetorical texts

Did You Know?

Frederick Douglass

When Frederick Douglass began to speak out against slavery, many White Americans did not believe he had really been a slave, or that he was African American. In her biography of Douglass, Sandra Thomas explains: "People gradually began to doubt that Douglass was telling the truth about himself. Reporting on a lecture that he gave in 1844, the Liberator wrote that many people in the audience refused to believe his stories: 'How a man, only six years out of bondage, and who had never gone to school could speak with such eloquence—with such precision of language and power of thought—they were utterly at a loss to devise.'" Unfortunately, this response to minority speakers may not be unusual.

Here is a famous excerpt from a speech Douglass gave about the Fourth of July. How do the artistic proofs used in this speech help to move an audience?

What, to the American slave, is your 4th of July? I answer; a day that reveals to him, more than all other days in the year, the gross injustice and cruelty to which he is the constant victim. To him, your celebration is a sham; your boasted liberty, an unholy license; your national greatness, swelling vanity; your sounds of rejoicing are empty and heartless; your denunciation of tyrants, brass-fronted impudence; your shouts of liberty and equality, hollow mockery; your prayers and hymns, your sermons and thanksgivings, with all your religious parade and solemnity, are, to Him, mere bombast, fraud, deception, impiety, and hypocrisy—a thin veil to cover up crimes which would disgrace a nation of savages. There is not a nation on the earth guilty of practices more shocking and bloody than are the people of the United States, at this very hour.

SOURCES: Douglass, F. (1852, July 5). The meaning of July Fourth for the Negro. Retrieved June 26, 2006, from www.pbs.org/wgbh/aia/part4/4h2927t.html Thomas, S. (n.d.). From slave to abolitionist/editor. Retrieved June 26, 2006, from http://www.history.rochester.edu/class/douglass/part2.html

Frederick Douglass was a powerful rhetor who spoke out against slavery in the United States.

How do you view the sophists' relativistic approach to rhetoric? Have you ever been in a situation in a class or debate where you were required to argue for a position that clashed with your personal values? How did it feel to make the argument?

sophists
the first group to teach persuasive speaking skills in the Greek city-states

what purposes it serves. As you listen to rhetoric from presidents, governors, mayors, church leaders, or others, ask yourself, how does this message reinforce the status quo? How does it argue for change? What ideas are mentioned and what ideas are absent? How and why is it persuasive, and how might it influence the public in making public policy decisions?

Because you can only consume a limited amount of the rhetoric generated, and because the rhetorical environment is always changing, the ways in which you understand and think about the world will always be changing as well. By adopting a critical approach, you can empower yourself to better understand the messages and the issues at hand.

Truth and Rhetoric

Since the fifth century B.C.E., teachers and scholars of rhetoric have argued over its fundamental purpose. Does it help speakers and listeners discern truth—or is it only concerned with what an audience can be persuaded to believe? If persuasion is the goal, then truth plays a smaller, perhaps even nonexistent, role.

The first people to teach persuasive speaking skills in the Greek city-states were called **sophists.** Their approach to rhetoric was practical; they believed rhetoric's purpose was to persuade, especially on matters of urgency. Therefore, they taught speakers to adjust their notions of right or wrong, true or untrue, depending on their speaking situation, their audience, and their goals.

Others disagreed, however. One of the more prominent of these was Plato (429–347 B.C.E.), who strongly opposed this relativistic approach. In his well-known dialogue, *Gorgias,* he disparagingly compared sophistic rhetoric to "cookery," in which a set of elements (or ingredients) were "mixed together" to create the final speech (or dish) for the sake of pleasure and not of the good. Plato believed speakers should use rhetoric to search for universal principles of truth and that these truths should then influence people's behavior for the better. In fact, he thought the best way to search for truth was through oral dialogue, and in the *Phaedrus* he argued for a philosophical rhetoric based on truth (Conley, 1994; Infante, Ranceer, & Womack, 1990).

Not unlike students today, Plato's student Aristotle (384–322 B.C.E.) challenged his teacher's arguments. He did not agree with Plato's insistence on the relationship of absolute truth to rhetoric; instead he believed speakers needed to learn skillful persuasion so they could defend truth and justice. As you might guess, his position was more relativistic than Plato's, but less relativistic than the sophists'.

Aristotle defined rhetoric as "the art of discovering all the available means of persuasion in a given situation" (Aristotle, 350 B.C.E./1991, p. 42). With this perspective in mind, he sought to create general rules of rhetoric that could be applied to a variety of circumstances and occasions. He was so successful that his text *The Rhetoric* has been used as a handbook for public speaking for more than 2,000 years.

When the Romans conquered the Greeks in 146 B.C.E., they incorporated the writings of Greek rhetoricians into Roman education. Cicero (106–43 B.C.E.), a prominent advocate and politician, is often considered the greatest Roman **orator,** or public speaker, and the most influential theorist of ancient rhetoric. Cicero believed speakers should use rhetoric for the public good and that eloquence without wisdom was feeble and even dangerous.

Cicero offered guidelines for organizing speeches and was a master of style; in fact, his speeches are still appreciated today for their rhetorical force. He is known best for identifying the three purposes or goals of public speaking: to instruct, to please, and to win over. Modern public speaking courses require mastery of these three types of speeches, which we now refer to as speeches to inform, to entertain, and to persuade.

As the Roman Empire declined, the Catholic Church replaced secular educational institutions as the leading disseminator of knowledge in the West. Once again the issue of truth's relationship to rhetoric became important. First, since rhetoric had developed from a non-Christian tradition, concerns arose about its relevance and appropriateness to Christianity. The most prominent thinker and writer of this era was Augustine of Hippo (354–430 C.E.), whom you may know as St. Augustine. He was a professor of rhetoric before converting to Christianity, and he struggled to reconcile his rhetorical background with his religious beliefs. Augustine's view of truth was close to Plato's—that truth exists in an absolute way—and he promoted the idea that rhetoric could impart the divine truth (Conley, 1994). From this perspective, ethical decisions were not situation specific; choices were always right or wrong, good or evil.

WHAT IS RHETORIC? A BROADER VIEW

When you think of rhetoric, you may think about overblown statements, exaggerations, or even outright lies and misstatements—as in, "Oh, that's just a bunch of political rhetoric." Unfortunately, this dismissive view of rhetoric is all too common today. However, as we saw in the preceding section, rhetoric has a rich history, and it serves important functions in a democratic society. As you saw in the opening example about giving the eulogy at a friend's funeral, rhetoric in its truest sense refers to communication that is used to influence others. Thus, rhetoricians would not view the president's communication following 9/11 as simply an attempt to provide information, but also as an attempt to guide us to view this topic in a way that suits his particular goals. In both the historical and the contemporary sense,

orator
a public speaker

rhetoric focuses primarily on public communication or messages designed to influence large audiences.

More than forty years ago, communication professor Douglas Ehninger suggested that throughout history people have had different ideas of what rhetoric is and the purposes it serves (1967). Ehninger's thinking sparked interest in connecting rhetoric to the cultural, social, and historical forces that exist in any particular time and in exploring how these forces shape rhetoric. Therefore, scholars began to research the ways that rhetoric serves social needs in societies around the world. For example, they looked at how the uses of rhetoric in a religious state may differ from those in a secular one. In addition, their research showed that the methods and reasons that people speak out in public depend on how such communication is received. While Ehninger focused on the European tradition, his argument stirred interest in understanding how non-Western cultures developed their own rhetorical traditions (Lucaites, Condit, & Caudill, 1999). See *Did You Know? Scholarly Definitions of Rhetoric.*

Did You Know?

Scholarly Definitions of Rhetoric

As you can see from the following list, the term rhetoric has been defined again and again, with many variations. Which definitions are most helpful in thinking about using communication strategically and which ones are least useful? Which ones are most helpful in contemporary society? Why?

Plato: Rhetoric is "the art of winning the soul by discourse."

Aristotle: Rhetoric is "the faculty of discovering in any particular case all of the available means of persuasion."

Quintilian: "Rhetoric is the art of speaking well."

George Campbell: "[Rhetoric] is that art or talent by which discourse is adapted to its end. The four ends of discourse are to enlighten the understanding, please the imagination, move the passion, and influence the will."

I. A. Richards: "Rhetoric is the study of misunderstandings and their remedies."

Kenneth Burke: "The most characteristic concern of rhetoric [is] the manipulation of men's beliefs for political ends … the basic function of rhetoric [is] the use of words by human agents to form attitudes or to induce actions in other human agents."

Lloyd Bitzer: "… rhetoric is a mode of altering reality, not by the direct application of energy to objects, but by the creation of discourse which changes reality through the mediation of thought and action."

Douglas Ehninger: "[Rhetoric is] that discipline which studies all of the ways in which men may influence each other's thinking and behavior through the strategic use of symbols."

Gerard A. Hauser: "Rhetoric is an instrumental use of language. One person engages another person in an exchange of symbols to accomplish some goal. It is not communication for communication's sake. Rhetoric is communication that attempts to coordinate social action. For this reason, rhetorical communication is explicitly pragmatic. Its goal is to influence human choices on specific matters that require immediate attention."

John Locke: "[Rhetoric,] that powerful instrument of error and deceit."

Alfred North Whitehead: "The creation of the world—said Plato—is the victory of persuasion over force. The worth of men consists in their liability to persuasion."

SOURCE: Excerpts taken from: Scholarly definitions of rhetoric. Retrieved June 26, 2006, from http://www.americanrhetoric.com/rhetoricdefinitions.htm. Reprinted by permission.

The European rhetorical tradition is only one of many in the world, and public communication functions in different ways in other places. It can, however, be difficult to research and study rhetoric historically and/or globally because the word *rhetoric* is not used in all cultures to describe that which is called "rhetoric" in the European tradition. The term comes to the English language from the Greek word *rhetor*. A **rhetor** is a person or institution that addresses the public. George Kennedy, a scholar of the ancient world, focuses less on the word and more on the concept itself: "Rhetoric is apparently a form of energy that drives and is imparted to communication.... All communication carries some rhetorical energy" (1998, p. 215). In this sense, rhetoric is not a cultural phenomenon unique to the West (see *Did You Know? Ancient Chinese Rhetoric*), but a facet of communication across cultures—it is the motive for communicating.

rhetor
a person or institution that addresses a large audience; the originator of a communication message but not necessarily the one delivering it

Did You Know?

Ancient Chinese Rhetoric

It is important to remember that the concept of rhetoric was not unique to the Greeks. For example, the ancient Chinese had a well-developed sense of the power and impact of language on their social, political, and individual lives. The Western study of rhetoric is comparable to the Chinese Ming Bian Xue: the study of naming (Ming) and argumentation (Bian).

Why do you think most Westerners are unaware of the Chinese rhetorical tradition? Can you imagine a society that could thrive without rhetoric? What would such a society look like? From the fifth to the third century B.C.E. China had five schools of thought in rhetorical philosophy.

School of *Ming*: These philosophers were interested in the function of language in political settings as well as in rational thinking. They lived in the same time period and shared some similarity in worldview and theoretical perspectives with the Greek sophists. Both recognized the power of language and were intelligent, professional, eloquent speakers who traveled around selling their expertise. But unlike the Greek sophists, the Chinese *Mingjia* used their psychological and rational appeals in mostly private settings.

Confucianism: This philosophy is concerned with morality and three principles—*ren* (benevolence), *li* (rites), and *zhong* (the middle way). Each directly affects rhetorical perspectives. Confucians were primarily interested in speech as an ethical issue, believing that proper use of language keeps society orderly and moral. A person with high moral standards is ethical in speech and action, knows his audience, and can use language appropriately. You can see that ancient Chinese and Greek thinkers have much in common.

School of *Mohism*: This philosophy closely resembles Western logical, religious, and ethical systems. It is deeply concerned with questions about sources of knowledge, uses of names, and methods of inference, but always with a preference for a commonsense attitude. This very practical, utilitarian approach threatened the then-ruling class in China and was considered unethical by the standards of Confucianism. Those associated with *Mohism* became unfairly equated with the *Mingjia* and rejected for their lack of concern for the morals of society.

School of *Daoism*: The three schools of thought we have described thus far all assumed that reality could be represented by language, and language could affect social, political, and moral conditions. In contrast, Daoism is a mystical philosophy that points out the limitation of speech. Instead, it advocates the boundlessness of the mind, the wealth of rhetorical possibilities, and the artfulness of living wisely and freely.

(continued)

Culturally, the social position of the rhetor often determines his or her right to speak or to access civic speaking spaces. In some cultures, it is important that the rhetor is an elder or that he be male or come from a high-status family. In others, everyone is able to speak. These cultural differences influence who has the ability to speak and who needs to study rhetoric to be the most capable communicators.

To understand how these social positions differ across cultures, it is important to seek out the structures of different cultures and societies. In some cultures, people rise to leadership positions by being democratically elected, while in other cultures leaders gain and hold onto power through financial prowess, political intrigue, or military force. Religious leaders sometimes hold the most powerful positions. Some cultures are led by a group instead of a single leader. Relationships to certain families, credentials from certain schools, or even one's physical attractiveness can lead to empowerment (or disempowerment). Yet, how one's rhetoric is received is very much dependent on where one is in society.

As you think about the role of rhetoric around the world, consider how decisions are made in different societies. You might also contemplate how our own culture is changing as we take part in public debates over such far-reaching topics as gay marriage, immigration reform, retirement and pension plans, and more.

Different cultures assign power to people based on different factors.

TEST YOUR KNOWLEDGE

- What are some of the ways that the study of rhetoric has been influenced by its historical context?

THE RHETOR: RHETORIC'S POINT OF ORIGIN

It is conventional to think about a rhetor as a specific public speaker; for example, when the president speaks to the nation, the president is a rhetor. As notions of rhetoric have expanded over time, however, corporations, organizations, and governments have also come to be thought of as rhetors. Thus, a rhetor is the originator of a communication message, not necessarily the person delivering it.

Like other areas of communication studies, the study of rhetoric acknowledges the relationship between individual forces and societal forces. In this segment of the chapter, we look at the individual forces that make for more or less effective rhetors. These forces include the rhetor's artistic proofs, position in society, and relationship to the audience.

Ethos, Pathos, and Logos

In the *Art of Rhetoric*, Aristotle argued that there are three **artistic proofs,** or means through which a rhetor gains the trust of an audience and designs credible messages. They are: ethos, pathos, and logos.

Ethos Aristotle considered **ethos**—usually translated as "character"—the most important of the three artistic proofs. Aristotle emphasized that rhetors create ethos, or a sense of their character, by displaying to their audience good sense, moral character, and goodwill. He also included family background, attractiveness, and athletic ability as valuable assets in persuasion through ethos. Advertising commonly exploits this aspect of ethos, using famous family names, attractive models, and celebrated athletes to promote products.

To communicate a certain aspect of their ethos, a rhetor can create and project a *persona*. **Persona** is related to the notion of identity that we discussed in Chapter 3 it describes the identity one creates through one's public communication efforts. A speaker's public persona may be quite different from his or her private one. In contrast, a speaker's social identities, such as race, ethnicity, age, and nationality, remain unchanged from situation to situation and are not under the speaker's control. The public persona a speaker projects can enhance her ethos if audiences find the persona credible, informed, or intelligent; it can diminish her ethos if audiences perceive the persona to be untrustworthy, deceitful, unintelligent, or misinformed.

Interpretations of ethos are influenced not only by how a speaker presents herself or himself but also by social factors such as stereotypes and assumptions. For example, sometimes people hear accents that increase or decrease their perceptions of the speaker's intelligence. British accents tend to increase credibility in the United States, while southern accents may have the opposite effect, especially in the northern United States.

Pathos **Pathos** refers to the rhetorical use of emotions to affect audience decision making. Speakers often use emotion to influence the audience to identify with a particular perspective. In a court case, the prosecuting lawyer may reenact the crime to help the jury see the case from the victim's point of view. An effective reenactment may influence the jury to emotionally identify and thus side with the prosecution rather than the defense.

There are many different emotional appeals that can be made. Emotional appeals to fear have been used many times throughout history. Fear can get people to support government actions that they otherwise would not, such as the USA PATRIOT Act, TSA screening procedures, and other measures instituted in reaction to fears of terrorism.

Emotional appeals are often more subtle. For example, the athletic and alumni Web sites of many universities incorporate pathos to invite participation in their events and support for their organizations. Some of these emotional appeals may involve feelings of pride by associating with the university, as well as positive memories that alumni may have about their student days. You may have similar feelings some day.

Logos While the word **logos** looks like "logic," it is not as narrowly defined. Rather, logos refers to reasoning or argumentation more generally. As an artistic proof, logos refers to how rhetors construct arguments or present evidence so that audiences reach a particular conclusion. For example, a lawyer may use evidence such as fingerprints to build a case and explain how a crime occurred, or a politician may point to her voting record to establish her credibility as a conservative.

Aristotle felt that combining ethos, pathos, and logos was more effective than relying on only one kind of proof. For example, if a rhetor wanted to address the problem of obesity, it would be important to use ethos appeals to establish goodwill, avoiding mockery or mean-spiritedness. Logos, in turn, could offer the rationale for

artistic proofs
artistic skills of a rhetor that influence effectiveness

ethos
the rhetorical construction of character

persona
the identity one creates through one's public communication efforts

pathos
the rhetorical use of emotions to affect audience decision making

logos
rational appeals; the use of rhetoric to help the audience see the rationale for a particular conclusion

What characteristics do you think are important to a speaker's credibility, or ethos? Which of Aristotle's list apply today? Which characteristics are most important to you?

losing weight. Combining these appeals with the pathos-based approach of television shows like *The Biggest Loser* might enhance the impact on waistlines. The three artistic proofs work best synergistically.

Social Position and Relationship to Audiences

Related to the concept of ethos is the social position from which a rhetor speaks. Aristotle noted that those who came from noble families were better positioned as rhetors. Yet **social position** refers to more than the prestige of one's family. One's social position comes from the way society is structured. Everyone is located in more than one position in the social structure as she or he speaks—as a student, a customer, a friend, a voter, and so on. As a receiver of public communication, you should always consider the position or positions from which the rhetor is speaking.

What aspects of social position might help or hinder a speaker's ability to advocate a point of view? The answer is that it depends on the society and the situation. We expect certain people to speak in certain situations, such as family members at a funeral or the governor after a natural disaster. In these cases, the rhetor's authority comes from a combination of her or his position and the audience members' expectations. Yet these social positions are also hierarchical, meaning that some positions have more power than others. For example, if you, as a student, were to speak out about U.S. immigration policies, you would be less influential than the president when he speaks about the same topic. Even if you spoke well, you could not make up for the difference in social positions between a student and a president. Social positions and positions of power are deeply intertwined, as social positions gain their power from the society that supports the structure. This power structure allows certain rhetors to be more effective than others in promoting a message.

In societies that have strong caste systems, such as India, lower castes have few rhetorical mechanisms for changing the rules that guide their lives. Compared with higher castes, fewer of them have access to the Internet, they are less able to garner media coverage of their issues, and they therefore have fewer opportunities to be heard by those in power. Furthermore, in her study of the use of Native Americans as sports mascots, Janis King (2002) concluded that Native Americans have few opportunities to change the use of these mascots, as "team owners and the majority of the fans are White. And it is these individuals who have the power to eliminate the mascots, clothing and actions" (p. 211).

Social institutions, also considered rhetors according to our definition, have distinct social positions that contribute to the effectiveness or persuasiveness of their public messages. For example, when the U.S. Supreme Court issues a ruling, it sends a public message that—coming from its position of power within our social structure—has tremendous implications for the ways we live. Other social institutions, including those involved in medicine, religion, the military, and education, also exercise their power through rhetoric.

Just as different rhetors wield different amounts of influence, so do audiences differ in terms of cultural, social, and political assumptions and perspectives. For example, in the aftermath of Hurricane Katrina, polls showed that Whites and African Americans had very different views on the role of race in the response to this disaster. A Pew Research Center Survey (2005) found that 66 percent of African Americans felt that the response would have been faster if the victims were White, whereas only 17 percent of Whites felt that way (Pew Research Center for People and the Press, 2005). One common mistake of speakers is to think only of the dominant culture, overlooking minorities who may also be part of the audience. The wide disparity in the ways racial groups viewed the government's response to Katrina serves as an important reminder of the range of opinions that may be represented in any audience.

Who, then, is the rhetorical audience for any particular message? Rhetorical scholar Lloyd Bitzer (1968) argued that only those people who could take the

If this officer were to testify against you in court, how might your different social positions influence how the officer's testimony and your testimony are heard?

social position
place in the social hierarchy, which comes from the way society is structured

appropriate action are part of the **rhetorical audience.** In other words, if a candidate for president of the United States wants to persuade a group of people to vote for her, only those people in the audience who are U.S. citizens and registered voters are part of the rhetorical audience. While citizens of other nations or minors may be physically present for the campaign pitch, because they cannot vote for this candidate, they would not be part of the rhetorical audience. Thinking about the audience in this way may help the speaker design an appropriate, appealing, and potentially persuasive message.

Yet, this perspective on audience is quite narrow. As you may have noticed from following presidential elections, U.S. citizens are not the only people who pay attention to campaign rhetoric. People around the world are also quite interested in who is elected and which policies—economic, military, cultural—this president will pursue. We live in a global environment in which the actions of the United States affect others around the world. Thus, the presidential candidate can use rhetoric to construct the desired rhetorical audience, perhaps including non-U.S. citizens and even people living in other countries.

In addition to being broader than a speaker might initially think, audiences are also fragmented. French theorist Michel Maffesoli (1996) has suggested that society consists of multiple "tribes," or identity groups, with their own ways of seeing the world. These groups are often marked by how they consume products, wear clothing, or participate in certain activities. These tribes might include NASCAR dads, soccer moms, or goths. This tribe theory can help illuminate the complexity of audiences and how rhetoric works in differing contexts with various groups. Much more work needs to be done on the use of specific rhetorical devices among diverse cultural audiences so that we can better understand their complex functions.

In summary, a rhetor's effectiveness depends on a configuration of characteristics such as artistic proofs—ethos, pathos, and logos—as well as social position and relationship to audiences. Many factors contribute to our impression that one speaker is more charismatic and powerful than another. Audience members may not always agree on which speaker is the best, but most can say which one moves them and which leaves them cold—or drowsy! Considering individual rhetor characteristics gives us only a partial view of rhetoric. In the next section, we will broaden our focus to examine the relationship between rhetoric and society and the roles rhetoric plays in giving meaning to major events, fulfilling democratic functions, and bringing about justice and social change.

TEST YOUR KNOWLEDGE
• What are the most important characteristics of individual rhetors?

THE INDIVIDUAL, RHETORIC, AND SOCIETY

Since rhetoric always arises within a specific social context, its functions can vary considerably. Thus the distinct cultural forces that influence a particular society should be considered when studying its rhetoric. In the United States today, rhetoric serves four important democratic functions that form the basis of how we come to decisions and work together collectively. We will look at these four functions next.

Reaffirming Cultural Values

The term **rhetorical event** refers to any event that generates a significant amount of public discourse. Such "explosions" of rhetoric give insight into the ways meaning is constructed and rhetoric and cultural values are affirmed. For example, unusual weather or natural disasters incite a great deal of rhetorical discourse that attempts to explain what has occurred. Some of the discourse usually comes from scientists, who provide scientific explanations about the event. Other discourse may come

rhetorical audience
those people who can take the appropriate action in response to a message

rhetorical event
any event that generates a significant amount of public discourse

from political commentators, who try to connect such natural disasters to a larger political or religious meaning. For example, after the devastating earthquake and tsunami that hit Japan in March 2011, radio commentator Rush Limbaugh snickered that Japan was hit in spite of its environmental consciousness: "Even now, refugees are still recycling, and yet Gaia levels them! Just wipes them out!...What kind of payback is this?" (qtd. in Witt, 2011). Limbaugh used this disaster to criticize environmentally friendly policies and practices.

Part of the function of rhetorical events, then, is to reaffirm cultural values. Every four years, for example, the United States inaugurates a president, and the speeches given, particularly the president's inaugural speech, highlight important national values along with that president's goals. Holidays, sports events, weddings, funerals, retirement parties, campaign speeches, declarations of war, and protest marches are also rhetorical events. Such occasions often include speakers who celebrate cultural values relevant to and that resonate with their respective audiences.

Increasing Democratic Participation

As noted, among the ancient Greeks and Romans, rhetoric was valued for its use in civic life. The belief that advocating for one's ideas is in the best interests of society is a cornerstone of democracy. Not all societies are democracies, of course, and in those nondemocratic societies rhetoric has served very different purposes. For our discussion we will examine aspects of rhetorical communication that influence citizen participation, a key part of the democratic process.

Deliberative rhetoric, the type of rhetoric used to argue what a society should do in the future, is deeply embedded in the democratic process. When legislators argue about raising taxes to pay for new roads or increasing funding for education, they are engaged in deliberative rhetoric. A speaker's ability to advocate effectively drives the open discussion and debate about what society should or should not do.

Also essential to a democracy is citizens' ability to evaluate the many important arguments they hear. In 2003, the United States argued in front of the United Nations Security Council that Saddam Hussein had weapons of mass destruction and that, therefore, military intervention was needed. In hindsight, both government officials and citizens can see the errors made in arguments for the invasion. However, at the time, social position played an important role in the persuasiveness of the argument to go to war. Because Secretary of State Colin Powell was well respected nationally and internationally, he spoke from a position of power and credibility. Donald Rumsfeld, as Secretary of Defense, also spoke in favor of invading Iraq, as did President George W. Bush. In this instance, however, as well as in many others, citizens in a democracy benefit from listening to a variety of arguments and evaluating them based on the evidence available—without the undue influence of social position.

Another important area of inquiry within rhetorical studies as it relates to democracy focuses on the public sphere. The **public sphere** is the arena in which deliberative decision making occurs through the exchange of ideas and arguments. For example, legislative bodies such as Congress are places where decisions are made about a wide range of issues. Protests against the World Trade Organization, underground and alternative magazines and newspapers, and performance art that critiques social issues also constitute types of public sphere rhetoric, but are sometimes referred to as *counter-publics,* as they occur outside the mainstream media and institutions. This type of rhetoric is also central to the functioning of a democratic society because it typically includes the voices of marginalized or less powerful individuals and groups.

Bringing About Justice

As we noted earlier in this chapter, a specific type of rhetoric is used in courts of law to bring about justice. Called **forensic rhetoric,** this form addresses events that

deliberative rhetoric
the type of rhetoric used to argue what a society should do in the future

public sphere
the arena in which deliberative decision making occurs through the exchange of ideas and arguments

forensic rhetoric
rhetoric that addresses events that happened in the past with the goal of setting things right after an injustice has occurred

happened in the past, as in "Where were you on the night of April 24?" The goal of forensic rhetoric is to set things right after an injustice has occurred. Another function of rhetoric in the context of justice is to allow citizens to exchange and negotiate ideas about what constitutes "just" and "unjust." As we look back over U.S. history, we can see how notions of justice have changed. In 1692, people in Salem, Massachusetts, felt that justice was served when they hanged nineteen people and jailed hundreds more for practicing witchcraft. Today, we see those trials as examples of injustice. In 1872, Susan B. Anthony, along with a number of other women, voted in an election in Rochester, New York. Anthony was arrested and convicted of violating laws that prevented women from voting. Today, most people view her actions as not only just but also courageous.

As these examples illustrate, laws and court judgments can only determine what is just and unjust within specific situations at particular moments in history. For example, Dred Scott was a nineteenth-century slave who tried to buy freedom for himself and his wife, but when the owner refused, he sought freedom through the court system. The U.S. Supreme Court ultimately ruled that he was neither a citizen—and therefore could not bring a case in federal court—nor entitled to his freedom, as he was someone's personal property. Today, we would be shocked at this kind of Supreme Court ruling. As a nation, we have decided that slavery is an injustice, but coming to this decision involved considerable public communication, or rhetoric, about slavery. It also involved a bloody civil war. Nevertheless, debates about citizenship and racial restrictions on who was eligible to be a U.S. citizen continued well into the twentieth century.

Hindsight makes it easy to see that slavery or the denial of rights to women or Blacks is unjust. In many cases, however, considerable disagreement exists about what is just. For example, the U.S. military has been grappling with cases of torture, the most notorious being those committed at Abu Ghraib prison in Iraq in 2003. Some of the photographs of tortured prisoners at Abu Ghraib were broadcast on television. What is the just response to this set of events? As the discussion about justice ensues, some will argue that these soldiers were under orders from their superiors and thus not responsible, while others will argue that each person is responsible for her or his own acts. Lawyers are generally at the forefront of these discussions, at least in the courtroom, but the public, the press, and politicians also weigh in.

In the effort to find justice, Ameneh Bahrami, an Iranian woman, has asked that Islamic law be imposed on a man who threw acid on her face, disfiguring and blinding her. This man had wanted to marry Bahrami, but she declined his marriage proposal. Recently, "an Iranian court ordered that five drops of the same chemical be placed in each of her attacker's eyes, acceding to Bahrami's demand that he be punished according to a principle in Islamic jurisprudence that allows a victim to seek retribution for a crime" (Erdbrink, 2008, p. A1). In late July 2011, she pardoned her attacker so that he did not end up being blinded (Dehghan, 2011). While recognizing cultural and religious differences, is this justice? How do we determine what is just and what is unjust, except through public discussion and deliberation? As you contemplate these types of questions you will undoubtedly realize that many different kinds of punishments were (and are) acceptable in different periods and places. Questions of justice are neither easily settled nor universally agreed upon, and they are negotiated rhetorically. Through our public discussions, we try to build a more just society.

Prompting Social Change

As you can see from the Dred Scott case and others, laws do not always ensure justice for all. Thus, people who want to bring about social change and promote their views of justice often use rhetoric to mobilize large numbers of people. If a mobilization succeeds, it can lead to a **social movement,** a mass movement of people motivated

social movement
a large, organized body of people who are attempting to create social change

Led by Janice Dickinson, owner of a modeling agency, fashion models protest against the use of fur. They are using rhetoric to try to change how society views and uses animals.

to create social change. Scholars have studied the public messages of social movements, such as the movement to abolish slavery, the women's suffrage movement, and the anti-Vietnam War movement. Social movement scholars also have tried to understand opposition to such movements and to evaluate the persuasiveness of that opposition.

Other social movements that have received attention from rhetoricians include the Chicano movement (Delgado, 1995), the environmental movement (DeLuca, 1999), and the gay/lesbian movement (Darsey, 1991). In this latter study, Darsey tracked the changing arguments of gay rights activists over time in relation to the changing contexts of sexual liberation, antigay legislation, and AIDS. The goals of his study and other similar ones are to understand the arguments that activists in social movements make, the social and historical context in which they put forth these arguments, the events that spark the emergence of social movement discourse, the resistance to the arguments, and why arguments on both sides are or are not persuasive.

As you can see, public messages are deeply embedded in the culture of their times. In past eras, debates and speeches about slavery, women's suffrage, and U.S. involvement in the Vietnam War permeated the daily life of U.S. Americans. Today, far more rhetoric focuses on terrorism, Iraq, and gay marriage. As people perceive wrongs that need to be corrected, social movements emerge, and people utilize rhetoric to argue for the desired changes. Because a social movement is typically controversial, those who prefer to maintain the status quo will oppose it and also use rhetoric to argue against change. This has been the case in every social movement mentioned.

Today, the uses of rhetoric extend far beyond the traditional medium of public speaking. People who desire to change our society use every available means of communicating. This means that rhetoric is a part of our everyday lives, relayed via advertising, blogs, emails, texts, television programming, and newspapers. Rhetoric is embedded in all manner of communicative media, which are themselves the topic of the next chapter. Various aspects of communication often overlap.

In sum, rhetoric plays an important role in a society. It can provide meaning and shape our thoughts about major events. It can also serve democratic functions in the political life of a society. Furthermore, rhetoric can bring about justice and provide momentum for major social changes, as it has in historical movements and as it continues to do today. (For a summary of these functions, see *Visual Summary 12.1: Functions of Rhetoric.*) But how can you use these ideas about rhetoric to become more ethical? This is the topic of the next section.

TEST YOUR KNOWLEDGE

- Why is rhetoric important in a democratic society?
- How can rhetoric bring about justice and social change?

ETHICS AND RHETORIC

While there are limited and specific instances in which rhetors may be justified in deceiving audiences—such as in cases of immediate national security—outright lying can rarely be considered ethical. But in the context of rhetoric, outright lying is not usually the ethical concern. More commonly, rhetors push against the boundaries of ethical communication by omitting facts or taking information out of context.

Functions of Rhetoric

REAFFIRMING CULTURAL VALUES

Rhetorical events reinforce and sustain our cultural values, as we emphasize the values that are important to us.

INCREASING DEMOCRATIC PARTICIPATION

Democratic institutions depend on rhetoric for the presentation and evaluation of ideas and viewpoints.

BRINGING ABOUT JUSTICE

The legal system relies on rhetoric for persuading judges and juries of the merits of a case.

PROMPTING SOCIAL CHANGE

Rhetoric plays a key role in creating, sustaining, and maintaining social movements that strive for social change.

In addition, some rhetors may demean or disparage a particular social group, either overtly or subtly. And, of course, each rhetor is generally promoting only one among many possible points of view, an aspect of rhetoric that is not unethical but needs to be considered by those in the audience.

Using what you know about rhetoric, then, what can you do to become an ethical receiver of rhetorical communication? Here are some guidelines:

- Be willing to listen to a range of perspectives on a particular topic. While you may not initially agree with a particular rhetor, you should consider her or his perspective (Makau, 1997), including why you do or do not agree.

- Be willing to speak out if you know that a rhetor is giving misinformation or deceiving an audience.

- Don't be silenced by information overload. If a speaker gives too much information, focus on the main points and be critical of this kind of presentation.

- Listen critically to the rhetor; don't accept the arguments presented at face value.

- Be willing to speak out publicly if a rhetor communicates in a way that dehumanizes or demeans others (Johannesen, 1997).

- Listen to and fairly assess what you hear, which may require that you postpone judgment until you hear the entire message.

- Be willing to change your mind as more evidence becomes available.

USING YOUR RHETORICAL SKILLS: SPEAKING IN PUBLIC

Throughout this chapter, we have discussed rhetoric primarily from the viewpoint of the receiver or critic. But we can also be rhetors by writing for an audience, by using other media such as video to reach audiences, and by practicing the art of public speaking. Becoming an effective rhetor is very important, as speaking in public is a cornerstone of our participatory democracy in the United States. Citizens need to become adept public speakers so that they can advocate for what they think is best (Gayle, 2004). Learning to speak up for your interests can also improve your satisfaction from participating in student organizations, as well as in local organizations such as a city council or a volunteer group. Public speaking skills are also important for success in most jobs. Increasingly, businesses want employees who can speak well in meetings and in public settings outside the organization (Osterman, 2005).

In the following sections, we introduce the basic elements of speech preparation. We'll look at the range of communication events where people may be called to speak, the importance of understanding audiences, and the basics of constructing, organizing, and delivering a speech. These elements supply the foundations for effective public speaking.

Understanding the Communication Event: The Synergetic Model

Recall from Chapter 1 that the Synergetic Model of Communication depicts communication as a transactional process that is influenced by individual, societal, and cultural factors. It is easy to see how this model applies to public speaking. Far from being a one-way communication in which the rhetor delivers a speech to the audience, effective public speaking is a transaction between the rhetor and the audience. You as an individual bring yourself to the speech—speaking is self-presentation as well as being the presentation of a message. A good speaker also relates to audience members as individuals, giving each listener the sense that the speaker is "talking to me." Finally, every speech event is influenced by the societal and cultural contexts in which it takes place.

In this section, we will examine the steps in understanding the communication event: identifying your general purpose, understanding your audience, selecting your topic, and identifying a specific purpose for your speech.

Identifying Your General Purpose The great Roman orator Cicero identified three objectives for public speaking: to inform, to persuade, and to entertain. These three types of speeches are still taught in most public speaking courses today (McKerrow, Gronbeck, Ehninger, & Monroe, 2003; O'Hair, Stewart, & Rubenstein, 2004). However, the objective "to entertain" has been broadened to "to evoke feeling," which is a more accurate description of what this type of speech can do. We will refer to this third type as the *evocative speech*.

The *informative speech* explains, instructs, defines, clarifies, demonstrates, or teaches. The *persuasive speech* attempts to influence, convince, motivate, sell, preach, or stimulate action. Finally, the purpose of the *evocative speech* is to entertain, inspire, celebrate, commemorate, or build community (Sprague & Stuart, 2005, p. 65). A common type of evocative speech, including the wedding toast, celebrates aspects of a person or topic. Sometimes evocative speeches are also known as **special-occasion speeches,** and they include speeches given at retirement dinners, award ceremonies, weddings, graduations, and funerals.

Obviously, the three general purposes do not function in isolation. Speakers often persuade others by informing them about something, or they inform audiences by entertaining them. A speech by a politician might primarily aim to persuade voters to adopt a particular point of view, but it might also be informative and evocative. Of the three, the one that is dominant in a given speech is known as the **general purpose** of that speech. Once you identify your general purpose, you are ready to begin the next step of developing your presentation by focusing on your audience.

Understanding Your Audience Because the speaking event is a transactional process between you and your audience, it is important to learn as much as possible about your audience as you develop your speech. In public speaking this is called **audience analysis.** Understanding and relating to your audience are crucial aspects of public speaking because, regardless of purpose or goals, the success of your presentation depends on its appropriateness for your audience.

Audience analysis involves learning as much as you can in response to the following four questions.

1. What does the audience already know about your topic? What do they want to know?

2. What do your listeners know about you? What do they need to know about you?

3. What expectations do your listeners have for the presentation?

4. Who are your audience members in terms of identity characteristics such as age, gender, race and ethnicity, education, socioeconomic status, and group membership? These characteristics are known as audience demographics, and the process of investigating them is known as **demographic analysis.**

special-occasion speeches
evocative speeches intended to entertain, inspire, celebrate, commemorate, or build community

general purpose
whichever of three goals—to inform, persuade, or entertain—dominates a speech

audience analysis
the process of determining what an audience already knows or wants to know about a topic, who they are, what they know or need to know about the speaker, and what their expectations might be for the presentation

demographic analysis
the portion of an audience analysis that considers the ages, races, sexes, sexual orientations, religions, and social class of the audience

Audiences can be complex groups of people who may share some interests but differ on others. Demographic information can be helpful, but avoid playing into stereotypes.

While it may seem difficult to obtain answers to these questions, it is easy to see that if your audience consists of people you have already met—such as fellow students in your class—you may already be able to provide many answers. You can also ask them about various aspects of these audience analysis questions, either in informal conversations or by developing an audience analysis questionnaire. If you are speaking to an unfamiliar group of listeners and do not have an opportunity to meet them before the speech, ask the person who invited you to speak. Like most facets of public speaking, audience analysis is a rich topic in itself, but we hope these essentials will enable you to approach the task effectively.

Selecting Your Topic Selecting a topic can be the most interesting and the most difficult part of any speech presentation. Assuming that the topic is not already determined for you, here are some guidelines to help you choose:

- Consider the communication event. What are the expectations for your presentation? What types of topics would be appropriate to speak about?
- Consider your interests. Take a personal inventory. What are some unusual experiences you've had? What subjects do you know a lot about? What topics do you feel strongly about? What would you like to learn more about?
- Consider your relationship to the communication event. Why are you being asked to speak? Do you have a special relationship to someone—for example, the bride at a wedding or the deceased at a funeral? If so, you may have special insight into topics the audience would consider appropriate and effective. Have you been chosen because you are an expert in a particular area? If so, the audience will expect you to demonstrate that expertise and to answer questions effectively.

If you had to give a speech today to the graduating class of the high school you attended, what topics might you consider for your speech?

We'll return to the development of speech topics below when we guide you through the important process of narrowing a broad topic to an appropriately focused one.

Identifying a Specific Purpose Once you know the general purpose of your speech and have selected your speech topic, you can begin focusing on the specific purpose of your speech. As discussed earlier, your general purpose may be to inform, persuade, or evoke a certain feeling from your audience. Your **specific purpose** focuses on what you would like to inform or persuade your audience about, or what type of feelings you want to evoke. Identifying your specific purpose helps you focus your topic and establish your organizational structure.

The specific purpose of your speech should be a "nutshell" summary of what you want your audience to take away. Here are some examples of specific purposes for informative, persuasive, and evocative speeches.

- My specific purpose is to inform my audience about the cost of private preschools in our local area.
- My specific purpose is to inform my audience about the history of immigration at Ellis Island.
- My specific purpose is to persuade my audience that our public school system should raise taxes to institute a universal preschool program.
- My specific purpose is to persuade my audience to donate money to the Ellis Island Museum.
- My specific purpose is to evoke a humorous mood regarding parents' anxiety over their children's performance in preschool interviews.
- My specific purpose is to evoke nostalgia with the story of my great-grandfather's immigration experience at Ellis Island.

specific purpose
what a speaker wants to inform or persuade an audience about, or the type of feelings the speaker wants to evoke

COMMUNICATION IN SOCIETY
Communication Event Checklist

What other details might you need to know for a particular speaking event?

_____ 1. When will you speak (date and time), and how long is your speech supposed to last?

_____ 2. Where will you speak (address, directions), and what will the size and physical layout of the room be?

_____ 3. What is the general purpose of your speech? The specific purpose?

_____ 4. What do you know about your audience?

_____ 5. Have you arranged for any computer or audiovisual equipment you will need?

_____ 6. Do you have the name and phone number of a person in charge whom you can contact in case a question or emergency arises?

Once you have a specific purpose, you need to research your topic, gather evidence for your claims, and organize your speech. We will turn to those steps next. But first, to make sure you've obtained all the preliminary "nuts and bolts" information you need to prepare your speech, refer to communication in society: communication event checklist.

TEST YOUR KNOWLEDGE
- Identify three general purposes in public speaking. How is the general purpose different from the specific purpose? Provide some examples.

Researching and Organizing Your Presentation

Once you have laid the foundation for developing your speech, you are ready to craft your thesis statement, locate supporting materials, and decide how to organize your message.

Crafting Your Thesis Statement By rephrasing your specific purpose as a **thesis statement**, you create a statement of your topic and your position on it. The thesis statement is important because it is the foundation on which you construct your presentation. For example, if your specific purpose is to argue that voting should be mandatory, you might articulate your thesis statement this way: "Voting should be mandatory in the United States." This is an effective thesis statement because it clearly sets out the proposition to be considered. Each of the main points you want to convey should clearly connect to and develop your thesis statement.

Finding Supporting Materials Some topics require extensive research, particularly those on which you are not an expert. However, all speech preparations should include some research to find **supporting materials** that support your ideas.

Supporting materials are available from at least three sources: electronic, print, and personal. You can start with the electronic card catalog in your library, accessing databases and online journals. You will also want to search the Internet, which is increasingly an excellent and acceptable source for research, even scholarly studies. One caution about Internet sources, however: You must evaluate them carefully, as you should any source. Referring to credible sources is especially important for informative and persuasive speeches.

Print sources include books, magazines, and newspapers. Again, evaluate the source. Newspapers like *The Wall Street Journal* or *The Washington Post* are considered highly reliable on certain topics. Note that some print materials (e.g., *The New American, The Nation, Ms. Magazine*) have a specific point of view. You

thesis statement
a statement of the topic of a speech and the speaker's position on it

supporting materials
information that supports the speaker's ideas

may use such sources to support your point, but you should acknowledge their viewpoint or bias in your speech. You can find magazines that address every topic imaginable—from general news (e.g., *Newsweek*) to specific hobbies (e.g., *Model Railroader, Scrapbooking, Sky and Telescope*). Use Internet databases like EBSCO or NexisLexis® to help you locate print magazine articles that address your speech topic. In addition to newspapers and magazines, there are encyclopedias and other reference works (e.g., *Statistical Abstract of the United States, People's Almanac, Guinness Book of World Records*) that offer a wealth of information on a variety of topics.

A final source of supporting materials can be personal interviews. You might want to interview people who can give you facts, opinions, and background information on your topic. In addition, you can use interviews to find leads to other sources, including the faculty at your college or university. Most professors have a wealth of information in several areas of expertise and enjoy sharing that information, including where you might do further research. Before any interview, be sure to prepare well. Know what kind of information you're looking for, contact potential interviewees in advance to make appointments, and be able to explain why you chose them (this shows you've done some homework).

As you identify and use any of these kinds of sources, take careful notes since you may need to refer to them. Moreover, some instructors require that references be sumitted with a speaking outline.

Once you have a collection of relevant sources, what kinds of material do you look for within them? Statistics, examples, and personal narratives can all be useful in bolstering your points. Visual aids also provide effective support, especially when a topic is complex. Let's look at the uses for each of these types of support materials.

Statistics   Statistics can highlight the size of a problem and help the audience understand a contrast or comparison. However, they can be overwhelming or confusing if they are too complex for the audience to follow. If you are dealing with large numbers, it is often best to round them off. For example, according to the U.S. Census Bureau, 178,014 people in the United States spoke the Navajo language in 2000 (U.S. Census Bureau, 2003). Your audience is more likely to remember this statistic if you round it off and say that there are just over 175,000 Navajo speakers in the United States.

When citing statistics, however, be careful about attributing meaning to them, as the reasons for statistical differences are not always apparent or reported with the statistical data. For example, you may find that the Pew Forum on Religion and Public Life reported in a 2008 survey that nearly two-thirds (65 percent) of U.S. Americans with religious affiliations believe that many religions can lead to eternal life. In contrast, only 29 percent agreed that their religion "is the one, true faith leading to eternal life." The rest did not know or did not answer. While this is interesting information that may be useful in supporting a point you want to make about religion in the United States, it is important to be aware that the Pew survey did not attribute any causes to these percentages. We don't know why the survey respondents answered as they did, so you would not want to mislead your audience by adding attributions of your own unless you clearly state that such attributions are your own opinion.

Examples   A second type of supporting material, examples, can also add power to a presentation. A speaker might give a brief example to illustrate a point in passing or use a more extended example, woven throughout a speech. Examples provide a concrete and realistic way of thinking about a topic and clarifying it. If you were to speak about nonfiction television programming, for example, your audience may better understand your point if you name specific programs, such as *60 Minutes, Nova,* or *Monday Night Football*. Without these examples, some audience members might think you are referring to reality television programs, such as *Survivor, Amazing Race,* and *Big Brother*.

Personal Narratives A third kind of support for your presentation—personal narratives and testimony of others—can give your speech a human touch. For example, if you are speaking about non-English languages in the United States and you describe your own family's struggle to retain its non-English language, your story adds emotional texture to the issue. See *It Happened to Me: Lisa* to read how a personal narrative can influence your audience.

Visual Aids As a student in elementary school, you may have used visual aids in show-and-tell speeches. In these speeches, the visual aid—perhaps a favorite toy, gift, or souvenir—was at the center. As part of your college coursework, your instructors may also require that you use visual aids in speeches. Even if you are not required to do so, you

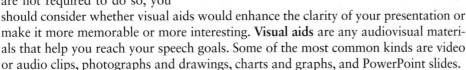

It Happened to Me: *Lisa*

We once had a speaker in class who told us about her family's struggle with diabetes. I had never really thought about diabetes before, and the statistics about diabetes didn't impact me as much as her story. I didn't know that some diabetics had to have their feet amputated, but now that I know, I am much more sensitive to the struggles of diabetics.

should consider whether visual aids would enhance the clarity of your presentation or make it more memorable or more interesting. **Visual aids** are any audiovisual materials that help you reach your speech goals. Some of the most common kinds are video or audio clips, photographs and drawings, charts and graphs, and PowerPoint slides.

Always select and incorporate visual aids carefully, remembering that their purpose is to augment and enhance your presentation, not to detract from your presentation. They are also not a substitute for content, as Edward Tufte instructs in *Alternative View: PowerPoint Is Evil: Power Corrupts. PowerPoint Corrupts Absolutely*.

To determine whether a visual aid is going to augment or detract, ask yourself why you are using it and how it will support your speech goals. Here are some tips for handling visual aids effectively:

1. Prepare visual aids in advance.
2. Make sure your visual aids are easy for all audience members to see.
3. Make sure the equipment you need will be available when you speak.
4. Make sure your speech can stand on its own in case of a technology failure.

In using a visual aid during your speech, follow these three steps: (a) introduce the visual aid to your audience members by explaining what they will see, (b) point to the parts of the visual aid that you want them to focus on, and (c) reaffirm the major point of the visual aid, thus pointing audience members to the conclusion you want them to draw.

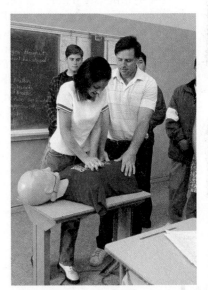

Visual aids can be helpful in explaining ideas and instructions. In this photo, students receive hands-on training in CPR.

Organizing Your Message Once you have gathered enough information and evidence to build your speech, you need to organize the presentation in a clear manner. Organizing an effective presentation means choosing and following a pattern that is compatible with your topic and that will make sense to your audience. It also involves creating an outline that can serve as the framework for your material. To anchor your organizational structure, you will develop an introduction, a conclusion, and transitions.

Organizational Patterns In most cases, a speech should be organized around three to five main points. If you have fewer than three points, you may not yet have sufficiently thought about or researched your topic. Once you have identified your main points, divide them into subpoints. These subpoints should all clearly relate

visual aids
audiovisual materials that help a speaker reach intended speech goals

Alternative **VIEW**

PowerPoint Is Evil: Power Corrupts. PowerPoint Corrupts Absolutely

Have you experienced boring or poor-quality PowerPoint presentations? In creating a PowerPoint presentation, how would you avoid the errors Tufte complains about?

Imagine a widely used and expensive prescription drug that promised to make us beautiful but didn't. Instead the drug had frequent, serious side effects: It induced stupidity, turned everyone into bores, wasted time, and degraded the quality and credibility of communication. These side effects would rightly lead to a worldwide product recall.

Yet several hundred million copies of Microsoft PowerPoint are churning out trillions of slides each year.... The standard PowerPoint presentation elevates format over content, betraying an attitude of commercialism that turns everything into a sales pitch....

In a business setting, a PowerPoint slide typically shows 40 words, which is about eight seconds' worth of silent reading material. With so little information per slide, many, many slides are needed. Audiences consequently endure a relentless sequentiality, one damn slide after another. When information is stacked in time, it is difficult to understand context and evaluate relationships. Visual reasoning usually works more effectively when relevant information is shown side by side. Often, the more intense the detail, the greater the clarity and understanding. This is especially so for statistical data, where the fundamental analytical act is to make comparisons....

Presentations largely stand or fall on the quality, relevance, and integrity of the content. If your numbers are boring, then you've got the wrong numbers. If your words or images are not on point, making them dance in color won't make them relevant. Audience boredom is usually a content failure, not a decoration failure.

At a minimum, a presentation format should do no harm. Yet the PowerPoint style routinely disrupts, dominates, and trivializes content. Thus PowerPoint presentations too often resemble a school play—very loud, very slow, and very simple.

The practical conclusions are clear. PowerPoint is a competent slide manager and projector. But rather than supplementing a presentation, it has become a substitute for it. Such misuse ignores the most important rule of speaking: Respect your audience.

SOURCE: Tufte, E. (2003, September). PowerPoint is evil. *Wired Magazine*, pp. 118–119. Reprinted by permission from Edward R. Tufte, *The Cognitive Style of PowerPoint* (Cheshire, CT: Graphics Press, 2003).

---

chronological pattern
one that follows a timeline

spatial pattern
one that arranges points by location and can be used to describe something small

topical pattern
one that has no innate organization except that imposed by the speaker

problem–solution pattern
one in which the speaker describes various aspects of a problem and then proposes solutions

cause–effect pattern
one used to create understanding and agreement, and sometimes to argue for a specific action

to their corresponding main points. Once you have all your main points and subpoints, you need to consider how to arrange them. Speakers generally follow one of five organizational patterns: chronological, spatial, topical, problem–solution, or cause–effect.

A **chronological pattern** follows a timeline; for example, a speech on the life of a famous person lends itself well to a chronological outline.

A **spatial pattern** arranges points by location and can be used to describe something small (for example, parts of a flower—moving from the edge to its center) or something large (for example, the immigration center buildings at Ellis Island—moving along a central hallway).

A **topical pattern** of organization, the most common, is used when your main points have no innate pattern except the one you impose on them. This situation requires more thinking because the points have no predetermined relationship, and you will need to find the scheme that is most logical and will work best for your audience.

In the **problem–solution pattern,** you describe various aspects of a problem and then propose solutions; it is frequently used in persuasive speeches.

A final approach to organization, the **cause–effect pattern,** is often used to create understanding and agreement, or to argue for a specific action in light of the cause that is associated with a given result.

Outlining Your Speech Once you have selected your pattern, you will have a good idea of the order in which you want to present your points. Thus, you are ready to create your outline. You are probably already familiar with how to outline. In the past, you may have used outlining chiefly to organize your written compositions. However, outlining also is useful in organizing a public-speaking presentation. An outline should be considered a working document, so you shouldn't hesitate to change it again and again. The idea is to create a sound organizational structure and a road map from which you can best build your presentation.

Visual Summary 12.2: Speaking in Public highlights the process of developing your speech.

Introduction, Body, and Conclusion After you have developed your outline, arranging your points and subpoints according to the pattern you have chosen, you will need to develop this skeleton into a full-bodied presentation. In doing so, you will pay special attention to your introduction and conclusion. Audiences usually remember much more about these opening and closing elements than they do about the body of the speech.

From your **introduction**, audience members gain a first impression of your speech's content and of you as the speaker, so both the content and presentation of the introduction are very important. You'll want to start with a bang, not a whimper. To do this, your introduction should: (1) gain audience attention, (2) focus their attention on your topic by relating it to them, (3) give them an overview of your organizational pattern, and (4) help them understand your thesis.

You can gain audience attention with a snappy quotation, a startling fact, a personal example, or a shocking statistic connected to your speech topic. Once you have gotten the audience's attention, you need to focus it on your specific topic. Your next task is to present your thesis statement so the audience understands the point of the speech. In the final part of your introduction, you would preview the overall organization of the presentation.

Moving on to the body of your speech, you will want to insert transitions to help your audience understand your organization as you progress from main point to main point, and from subpoint to subpoint. These transitions, called **signposts**, tell the audience where you are in the overall organization, thus making it easier for them to follow along and stay oriented. Common signposts include phrases such as, "my second point is" or "a second stage of the" or "in addition." These devices are not merely mechanical. You can use them in an artful way to help your words and ideas flow together gracefully.

The transition into your conclusion needs to be marked by a major signpost so that the audience knows you are preparing to end your speech. The **conclusion** should accomplish several goals. First, it should review the three to five main points in the body of your presentation. Second, if you are giving a persuasive speech, during the conclusion, you will challenge the audience to act. Actions may include finding out more about the topic or becoming more involved in the issue—for example, by registering to vote, donating blood, or signing a petition. As you formulate this challenge, or call the audience to action, consider how you want your presentation to impact their lives. Do you want them to vote a particular way? Change their eating habits? Use sunscreen? Finally, the conclusion should leave the audience with a positive view of you and your topic.

Whatever closing technique you choose, remember that public speaking is an art that requires artistic judgment. There is no one right or wrong way to do it, only more effective and less effective ones. See Figure 12.1 for an outline of the basic speech structure that has just been described.

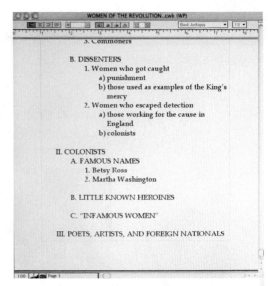

Outlining your speech is a very important part of the public speaking process. Your outline will form the basis of your speaking notes.

introduction
opening material of a speech from which the audience members gain a first impression of the speech's content and of the speaker

signposts
transitions in a speech that help an audience understand the speaker's organization, making it easier for them to follow

conclusion
closing material of a speech where the speaker reviews the main points, may challenge the audience to act, and leaves the audience with a positive view of speaker and topic

Phase I: Understand the Communication Event

Identify your general purpose
Understand your audience
Select your topic
Identify your specific purpose

Developing Your Speech

Phase II: Research and Organize Your Presentation

Identify your thesis statement
Find supporting materials
Consider incorporating visual aids
Select an organizational pattern
Create a speech outline
Develop your introduction, body, conclusion, and transitions

Phase III: Rehearse and Deliver Your Presentation

Be aware of the time
Develop a persona
Rehearse and seek feedback
Overcome anxiety during the presentation

FIGURE 12.1 Basic Speech Structure

I. Introduction
   A. Attention-getting step
   B. Connection to audience
   C. Thesis statement
   D. Preview of main points
   E. Transition to first point
II. First Main Point
   A. Signpost your first point.
   B. Make your point (include supporting material).
   C. Transition to your next point.

III. Second Main Point
   A. Signpost your second point.
   B. Make your point (include supporting material).
   C. Transition to your next point.
IV. Third Main Point
   A. Signpost your third point.
   B. Make your point (include supporting material).
   C. Transition to conclusion.
V. Conclusion
   A. Review main points.
   B. Connect back to audience.
   C. Create a memorable conclusion.

TEST YOUR KNOWLEDGE

- What elements are included in a speech outline?
- What are some benefits and potential drawbacks of using visual aids?
- What elements go into a strong introduction and conclusion?

Rehearsing and Delivering Your Speech

After you have developed, researched, and organized your materials, you are ready to consider the presentation of your speech. Many people think of public speaking as being all about delivery, but delivery is, as we hope you have seen, only one aspect of the entire process. In the context of public speaking, **delivery** refers to the presentation of the speech you have researched, organized, outlined, and practiced. Delivery *is* important, of course, because it is what is most immediate to the audience. In this section, we focus on three important aspects of delivery: being aware of time, developing a speaking persona and, finally, putting your speech into action.

Being Aware of the Time In the United States, we often think about time as absolute, a phenomenon that can be broken down into clearly measurable units: seconds, minutes, and hours. Yet, communication scholars have repeatedly shown that notions of time are relative. Many public speakers experience this relative nature of time, feeling like they have been speaking for a very long time, while their audience may feel that they have heard only a short speech, or vice versa.

Knowing for how long to speak is an important aspect of the art of public speaking. The length of any speech should be guided by audience expectations in a particular context as well as by the content of your message. In some instances, the guidelines are rather loose, such as speeches at weddings and retirements. In other cases, the time limits are very strict, and you may be cut off before you finish. For example, a citizen advocating a position in city council meetings often faces strict time limits. In classroom speech situations, you are often told how long to speak, and your audience will expect you to stay within those limits.

If your speech is significantly longer than expected, your audience may become restless, impatient, or even hostile. On the other hand, if your speech is significantly shorter than the time expected, your audience may leave feeling disappointed or shortchanged, as they may have made a significant effort to attend your presentation. If your speech is part of a larger program, the planners will be depending on you to fill a particular time slot.

delivery
the presentation of a speech before an audience

eye contact
looking directly into the eyes of another

One way to make sure you comply is to time yourself when you practice. Doing this will ensure that you know how long your speech runs and whether you need to adjust it. If you have prepared, practiced, and timed your speech, you should have no problem meeting your time requirement.

Projecting a Persona Developing a persona, or the image a speaker conveys, is one of the most artistic aspects of public speaking. If you have seen Ellen DeGeneres on her talk show, you know that she projects a down-to-earth, almost naïve persona. She dresses casually and jokes with her audience. Her nonverbal communication is very informal and relaxed. She makes direct eye contact with her audience and the television camera; she sometimes slouches in the chair and even does a little dance at the beginning of every show. These elements together contribute to her public persona.

As you create your public persona, consider a few factors that shape it. First, the speed at which you speak will shape your persona and how people perceive you. There is no one ideal speaking rate; it should vary to fit your message. For example, speaking slowly and deliberately can be very effective if you want to highlight the gravity of a situation. At other times, you may wish to speak more quickly, particularly for a light, humorous presentation. You may also vary your speed as you move from point to point, slowing down, perhaps, to emphasize one item in particular.

Eye contact is another important element of creating your persona. Making **eye contact** is one of the most direct ways to show your engagement with your audience, and it can lend credibility to your presentation. If you watch *Law & Order* on television, you may have noticed that the lawyers make direct eye contact with the jury in their closing remarks. Gestures and movement also contribute to one's persona. One of the best ways to ensure that your gestures and movement are smooth and natural-looking is to practice them along with your speech.

Finally, although you may think that your delivery begins when you stand up to speak, you begin to present your persona well before that. In some cases, for example, speakers are part of a panel, seated at a table in front of the audience, or a single speaker is introduced by someone else. In both cases, the speakers are constructing their personas while they wait to speak. Fidgeting, rolling the eyes, yawning, chewing gum, being late, and displaying other unflattering nonverbal behaviors will detract from the persona you want to project. Assume that you are "on stage" from the moment you walk into the room until the moment you leave.

Rehearsing Your Speech One of the best ways to become an effective public speaker is to practice. However, going over the points silently in your head does not count as practice. Practice means giving your speech out loud, standing up and speaking as if you were in front of an audience. In fact, it is ideal to practice in front of an audience—ask one or two of your friends to watch, listen, and give you feedback. To see yourself as others will see you, it is helpful to practice in front of a mirror or to record yourself with audio or video equipment. Do this as many times as necessary to ensure that you are familiar with your speech and feel comfortable delivering it.

Rehearsing will enable you to identify and avoid any distracting nervous mannerisms you may have, and to improve your signposting, your speaking rate, and your eye contact. In other words, you can work on projecting the type of public persona you desire. Each time you practice your speech, you can focus on a different aspect—one time on your gestures, one time on clear enunciation, and so on—until you

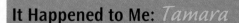
It Happened to Me: *Tamara*

I have had to deliver several speeches this year, and I discovered that I like to practice the beginning of my speech a little bit more than the middle or end. Why? I've learned that if I do well at the beginning, after a few minutes, I feel confident, I get into the rhythm, and I even relax a bit.

feel comfortable with the persona and style you have developed. See *It Happened to Me: Tamara* to learn how one speaker approaches practice.

Although you may practice your speech many times, your goal is not to memorize it. A memorized speech often sounds like a recording rather than a real human being. In addition, if you work strictly from memory and you stumble over a word or phrase, you may lose your place and find it difficult to recover. Instead, during practice, focus on a delivery that is enthusiastic, vibrant, and engaging. Each time you practice, you will come out with different phrasing, different wording, and different movements. When the time comes to give your speech "for real," yet another version may appear, but this time, it will likely be a version that you are comfortable presenting.

With practice, you can develop a delivery style that is enthusiastic, vibrant, and engaging.

Speech Delivery and Overcoming Anxiety When the day comes for you to give your speech, be sure to arrive early enough to check out the room and any audiovisual or computer equipment you have arranged for. Have alternative plans in mind in case anything goes wrong with your equipment.

It's very likely that you will be nervous, but if you have prepared well, you will be able to speak confidently in spite of any apprehension you may feel. In fact, seasoned performers depend on nerves for an extra boost of energy when they are in front of an audience. Remember that your listeners want you to do well. Focus on the faces in the audience who look friendly and who may be smiling or nodding in agreement. The peak anxiety time for most speakers is the first moment of confronting the audience (Behnke & Sawyer, 1999, 2004). Receiving positive reinforcement early on is an excellent way to get over this initial anxiety. Before you know it, your speech will be over and you'll be beaming as the audience applauds.

If you are very troubled by performance anxiety, you may want to try using relaxation techniques just before speaking. While the fear may be in your head, it manifests itself in physiological changes in your body: Your muscles tense, your breathing becomes shallow, and adrenaline pumps through your system (Behnke & Sawyer, 2004). Effective relaxation techniques for such situations include taking several deep, even breaths; yawning once or twice to relax your throat; smiling, shaking hands and talking with attendees; taking sips of water (avoid caffeine); and looking at your notes. Visit the Great Speaking Center's "Stage Fright Strategies" at www.antion.com/articles/stagefright.htm for many more suggestions. While you may feel very nervous, your inner anxiety is not often easy for your audience members to see. Do not assume they see how nervous you feel—and it's best not to mention it. Project confidence, and you will feel more confident as you speak.

Finally, the strategy most public speaking instructors and students use to overcome anxiety is to take the opportunity to give lots of speeches (Levasseur, Dean, & Pfaff, 2004). Public speaking becomes easier and easier with each speech. As one seasoned speaker said, "Learning to become a confident speaker is like learning to swim. You can watch people swim, read about it, listen to people talk about it, but if you don't get into the water, you'll never learn" (Sanow, 2005). Take opportunities to hone your public-speaking skills. Volunteer to give speeches or become a member of Toastmasters International or a local group of public speakers.

The public speaking process involves a lot of preparation and practice. We hope that these guidelines will help you become a more effective rhetor.

SUMMARY

Rhetoric is important in our society for at least three reasons. It is vital to the functioning of a democracy; it plays an important role in finding justice; and it helps us understand our world.

The study of rhetoric is important for four reasons. It allows us to understand the many issues we are facing, reinforce or resist dominant cultural values, critically analyze the many rhetorical messages we encounter, and improve our own rhetorical communication.

Rhetoric is persuasive communication that is typically directed toward a large audience, and its purpose is to influence how an audience sees or understands the world and acts in and upon it. By becoming a rhetorical critic, one can evaluate the rhetorical messages one receives. Rhetoric is tied intimately to the social, cultural, and historical environment in which it functions; it has been defined differently in different societies, cultures, and historical eras.

Characteristics of rhetors play an important role in effective public communication. Such characteristics include a rhetor's: use of ethos, pathos, and logos; position in society; and relationship to the audience. Organizations, institutions, and corporations can also be rhetors. Rhetoric gives meaning and shape to public thinking about major events, and it can serve vital democratic functions. Rhetoric also can bring about justice and provide momentum for major social changes.

To be an ethical receiver of rhetoric, one should be willing to: listen with an open mind, speak out when one disagrees, and change one's mind based on persuasive evidence.

Finally, one can become a more effective rhetor oneself by practicing the art of public speaking. Effective rhetors understand the communication event, have focused their topics and purpose with the audience in mind, have researched and organized their speeches, and have practiced their delivery to be aware of the time, project a persona, and overcome anxiety.

HUMAN COMMUNICATION IN SOCIETY ONLINE

To review this chapter, use the MyCommunicationLab Web site to test your understanding of the following key terms, record your answers to the chapter review questions, and complete the suggested activities. Expand your learning and understanding of chapter concepts by completing additional activities and exercises online. Access code required. Go to www.mycommunicationlab.com for more information or to purchase standalone access.

KEY TERMS

rhetoric 320
rhetorical critic 321
sophists 322
orator 323
rhetor 325
artistic proofs 327
ethos 327
persona 327
pathos 327
logos 327
social position 328
rhetorical audience 329

rhetorical event 329
deliberative rhetoric 330
public sphere 330
forensic rhetoric 330
social movement 331
special-occasion speeches 335
general purpose 335
audience analysis 335
demographic analysis 335
specific purpose 336
thesis statement 337
supporting materials 337

visual aids 339
chronological pattern 340
spatial pattern 340
topical pattern 340
problem–solution
    pattern 340
cause–effect pattern 340
introduction 341
signposts 341
conclusion 341
delivery 343
eye contact 344

APPLY WHAT YOU KNOW

1. **Create a List of Ten Speakers You Have Heard**
   This list might include politicians such as Hillary Clinton, John Edwards, Arnold Schwarzenegger, or Barack Obama, entertainers such as Margaret Cho, Jon Stewart, or Oprah Winfrey, and so on. Put these speakers in order of most to least effective and powerful, and be clear about your reasons for ranking them in this way. Then without revealing your order, exchange lists with a classmate. Rank each other's speakers and see how your rankings compare. If they differ, discuss your reasons. Think about the criteria that you are using.

2. **Research the Characteristics of a Particular Kind of Speech**
   Ask your family and friends what they might expect from a speaker who is giving a eulogy, a graduation speech, or a retirement speech. How long would they expect the presentation to be? What level of formality do they expect? Do the people you ask differ in their opinions? What did you learn from this exercise? Compile your findings in a presentation to your class, following the steps outlined in this chapter.

3. **Learn about Techniques for Dealing with Communication Apprehension**
   Talk to some people who frequently speak in public. Ask them for ideas on dealing with nervousness or fears about speaking. Do some library research to see what communication researchers have found about communication apprehension. Identify some techniques that will help you deal with communication apprehension. List the techniques that you learned from doing this research.

4. **Watch a Videotape of Someone You Consider to Be a Good Speaker**
   Possibilities include Barack Obama, Oprah Winfrey, Ken Burns, Alec Baldwin, Pat Schroeder, or Helen Thomas. Analyze the speech, the style, and the delivery. How do your favorite speakers organize their speeches? Do they project a particular persona or use a particular style? Take notes as you watch them and compile your notes into a report that identifies some public-speaking skills that you would like to incorporate.

5. **Research Some Ways that Public Speaking Functions in Other Cultures.**
   How might culture influence how we speak in public?

13
Mass Media and Communication

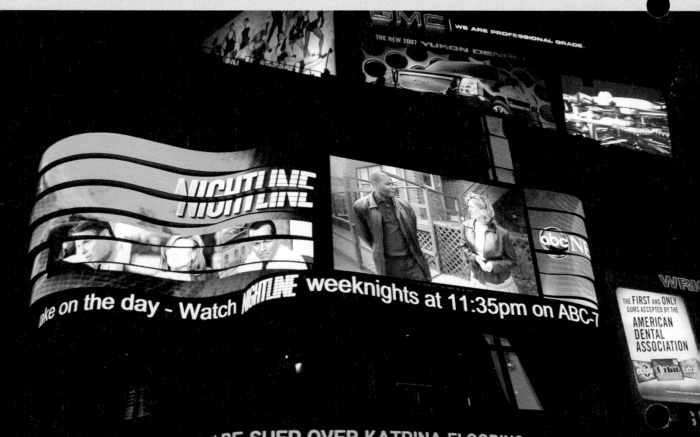

I always record my favorite soap opera so I can watch it when I have time. Sometimes I watch it later the same day, but sometimes I wait until the end of the week and "veg out" on hours of it. My best friend in college got me hooked on this soap opera, and now it's a part of my everyday life.

This student's experience with television is not unique; many television viewers are devoted to a favorite show and don't want to miss a single episode. When you think about this behavior on the individual level, you probably view it as a matter of choice or taste. When communication scholars analyze television viewing on the social level, however, they examine the influence media have on individuals and how media messages exert influence. For example, in August 2001, when the soap opera *The Bold and the Beautiful* ran a segment about HIV, researchers noted that telephone calls to the National STD and AIDS Hotline rose dramatically (Kennedy, O'Leary, Beck, Pollard, & Simpson, 2004). More recently, in 2010, *Law & Order SVU* ran an episode that highlighted the backlog of untested rape kit samples (Rubin, 2010). Rape kits store the evidence collected after a reported rape to help convict suspected rapists. Actress Mariska Hargitay, who plays a detective on that show, testified before a House committee about this issue (Dwyer & Jones, 2010). Although her television character is fictional, Hargitay uses her image to be an advocate. Soap operas and other television programs, like other types of mass media from radio to film, can influence people's lives in important ways.

In this chapter, we first look at the importance of media in everyday life. We then briefly examine the major forms of mass media. Next, we investigate how individuals use media and the influence that media messages have on individuals. Then we consider media usage within the context of the societal framework and explore the influence media have on society overall. Finally, we discuss media activism as a means for individuals to express media ethics, and we introduce guidelines for becoming more effective consumers of media. Although the Internet is also a type of media, we address that topic in Chapter 14, where we will focus on the role of digitally mediated communication.

Once you have read this chapter, you will be able to:

- ■ Be able to identify the main forms of mass media.
- ■ Describe various models of media.
- ■ Understand five issues in media studies: social identities, understanding the world, media events, media violence, and media economics.
- ■ Identify five ethical issues with mass media.
- ■ Describe three ways to be a more effective consumer of media messages

THE IMPORTANCE OF MASS MEDIA

Media hold a very important place in our society. As an indication of their importance to you, consider these questions. If you met someone who did not watch television shows, see or rent movies, or listen to the radio, would you be surprised? What if the same person never heard of Lady Gaga, Stephen Colbert, Oprah Winfrey, A-Rod, or J-Lo? Would knowing this change your interaction with that person? What topics could you and couldn't you discuss? If you concluded that many topics would be off limits, you can see that media messages serve important social functions. For example, they help people bond with others who like or dislike the same shows, movies, advertisements, singers, or actors. Media messages and images also help shape how people view the world and what they understand—and perhaps misunderstand —about events around the globe. Because people are so deeply immersed in this media environment, however, they rarely think about their participation in it. Nevertheless, it is indeed an interaction, as individuals participate in the communication process by selecting certain programs and agreeing or disagreeing with what they hear or see.

Why is media studies important? To begin with, U.S. Americans watch an enormous amount of television, although the exact number of hours is difficult to pin down. In 2005, Nielsen Media Research reported that the average U.S. household watched 8 hours and 11 minutes of television per day, which is the highest level recorded since Nielsen began measuring television viewing in the 1950s. The Washington State Department of Health (n.d.) notes that, on average, African Americans watch about 2 hours per day more than other U.S. Americans. Of all U.S. Americans, children watch the most television and are the center of most concern about television viewing.

People turn to communication media both for information and entertainment. For example, in the aftermath of the Japanese earthquake and tsunami in March 2011, 83 percent of Japanese said they got their news about the natural disaster primarily from television (comScore, 2011). While the Internet has become increasingly important in seeking out information, including information about the Japanese earthquake and tsunami, it is important to recognize that television remains the primary information source. Of course, not all people turned to television. People at work may not have had access to television, but could check frequently for news on the Internet while working at their computers. People traveling by car relied on radio for their information.

Media scholars today recognize that they work during an era of rapid media change and development. For example, communication scholars Jennings Bryant and Dorina Miron (2004) identified six kinds of changes that are currently affecting and being affected by mass communication:

1. new form, content, and substance in mass communication;
2. new kinds of interactive media, such as the Internet;
3. new media ownership patterns in a global economy;
4. new viewing patterns and habits of audiences;
5. new patterns in family life; and
6. new patterns of interactive media use by youth.

Because of the rapid pace of these changes, measuring and studying their influence can be a challenge.

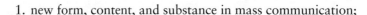

Viewers often record television shows for viewing at their convenience.

While it is difficult to measure the precise power of media messages, these messages surround and influence people every day. The importance of media in our everyday lives and in our society has been rapidly increasing. The rise of the Internet, cell phones, and other "new media" has led to a distinction being made between "mass media" and "new media." In this chapter, we will focus on mass media, and in Chapter 14, we explore new media. To help you understand the term *mass media*, we discuss this topic next.

WHAT ARE MASS MEDIA?

Mediated communication refers to communication that is transmitted through a channel, such as television, film, radio, and print. We often refer to these channels of communication more simply as media.

The word **media** is the plural form of *medium*. Television is one communication medium; others include film, radio, magazines, advertisements, and newspapers. When you pick up the telephone to speak to someone, you are using yet another communication medium. When you write a letter, your communication is mediated by the form of letter writing. Even the voice and the body can be considered media of communication.

For all the complexity and variety of media studies, its focus typically falls on **mass media,** or mediated communication intended for a large audience. Mass-mediated messages are usually produced and distributed by large organizations or industries in the business of mass communication. Mass media businesses are also known as **culture industries** because they produce television shows, made-for-television movies, video games, and other cultural products as an industry. The creation of these cultural products is not driven by individual artists, but by large groups of workers in for-profit (and some nonprofit) organizations.

The study of media is often a moving target, as changes in media continually occur. Part of understanding the influence of media on our everyday lives entails understanding the changes that have occurred and what media were available in other time periods. Historically, communication has been framed by the media available during a given time. Let's now look at some of these industries and the media texts they produce.

One of the first media addressing a large public were newspapers. During the nineteenth century, many newspapers grew in distribution and readership as the cost of mass printing declined. As expansion westward continued in the United States, the newspaper played a critical role in community building. Newspapers flourished during this period in staggering numbers. For example, "Before the end of 1867, at least four newspapers had been published in Cheyenne, a town that still had a population well under 800, in the Wyoming Territory" (Boorstin, 1965, p. 131). These numbers are all the more impressive in view of today's decline in newspaper readership. As you can see, different eras embraced different communication media.

Today, when most people think of newspapers, they first think of large-circulation papers in large metropolitan areas, such as the *New York Times*, *Washington Post*, and *Los Angeles Times*. They might also think about smaller, local papers, including the *Corvallis Gazette-Times*, the *Nome Nugget*, and the *Knoxville News Sentinel*. Because large-circulation newspapers serve different needs from local papers, many readers subscribe to both. Other newspapers target specific demographic groups, such as immigrant communities, ethnic and racial communities, gay and lesbian communities, or retirees. Some are bilingual. Others are referred to as the "alternative" press. These alternative-press newspapers attempt to present perspectives and voices that may not be heard in the mainstream press. Examples of alternative papers include the *Seattle Stranger*, the *San Francisco Bay Guardian*, and New York City's *Village Voice*.

media
the plural form of *medium*, a channel of communication

mass media
mediated communication intended for large audiences

culture industries
large organizations in the business of mass communication that produce, distribute, or show various media texts (cultural products) as an industry

Some magazines offer important forums for political discussions. Others address distinct interests, such as sports, travel, gardening, and more.

Another development that followed the lowered cost of mass printing was the development of the magazine. Magazines are produced weekly, monthly, bimonthly, or quarterly. Some, such as *Newsweek, Harper's, Reader's Digest*, and *Smithsonian*, target broad, general audiences. Other magazines focus on more limited audiences—*Ebony, Latina, Men's Health*, and *Woman's World*, for example—and still others on very specific topics, as shown by the titles *Gourmet Magazine, Hot Rod Magazine*, and *Rhode Island Magazine*. Like newspapers, magazines offer important forums for political discussions, but they also address distinct interests, such as crafts, hobbies, or travel.

Popular books are another medium addressed to a large audience. Sometimes called **mass-market paperbacks**, these books include romance novels, self-help books, and comic books, as well as other genres that are produced in very large numbers and distributed widely. **E-books** (electronic books) constitute a recent development in mass media. E-books are books read on a computer screen instead of a printed page. Currently, it is not clear how important a form of media this will become. Though e-reader devices are becoming increasingly user-friendly, many readers still say they prefer the printed page.

Motion pictures, first shown commercially in the 1890s, flourished throughout the twentieth century. Although today people can make movies relatively cheaply with digital video, high-quality productions that draw large audiences cost millions of dollars to produce, distribute, and advertise. Therefore, movie studios with adequate resources dominate the motion picture industry. While some documentary movies do become popular, such as *March of the Penguins, Fahrenheit 9/11*, and *Supersize Me*, most best-selling movies are purely entertainment-oriented, such as the *Harry Potter* movies, *The Dark Knight, The Chronicles of Narnia*, and *Captain America*. Typically, large-budget films receive the widest distribution and the most publicity, but small-budget films can also reach audiences and sometimes offer alternative views of important social issues.

Like movies, radio technology emerged in the late nineteenth century. At first, it had important applications at sea, but in the 1920s stations sprang up all over the United States. As journalism professor Jane Chapman notes, "Radio's take-off was swift, and public enthusiasm for it peaked during the 'golden age' of the 1930s and 1940s" (2005, p. 147). Radio programming included not only news and commentary but also quiz shows, dramas, and situation comedies. With the rise of television, the Internet, and other competing media, radio broadcasting has become much more specialized, with radio stations serving specific audiences by broadcasting classical music, jazz, country music, news, sports, or other focused content. Audiences for these specialized programs are often targeted based on identities, such as age, socioeconomic class, race and ethnicity, or language. Today, radio is also broadcast over the Internet, via satellite, and through podcasts. And while commercial enterprises dominate radio in the United States, nonprofit radio, such as National Public Radio and Pacifica, also exists.

Popular music, another form of mass media, existed long before radio, and people listened to it live in public and private venues and, later, on gramophones and record players. Popular music now also plays on television and via other communication media, such as CDs, DVDs, and MP3 players. As different trends grew in popularity, a large number of commercial enterprises arose to glean the profits. In turn, many smaller companies have gone out of business or been bought out, so that fewer, but larger, music corporations select, produce, and distribute the music we hear today.

Should consumer-created media such as blogs, Twitter, and video sites like YouTube and Vimeo be considered mass media? Why or why not? In what ways are their functions similar to, or different from, those of mass media created by larger organizations?

mass-market paperbacks
popular books addressed to a large audience and widely distributed

e-books
electronic books read on a computer screen instead of a printed page

Television is among the most familiar forms of communication media. Early in its development, in the mid-twentieth century, networks such as ABC, CBS, and NBC dominated, since they were the only providers of content. The rise of cable television, with its multiple specialized channels, has taken significant market share away from the networks, yet they remain important and continue to draw large audiences. Since its inception, cable television has expanded to include pay channels such as HBO, Showtime, and Cinemax. In addition, satellite television is challenging cable television. Because television programming is expensive, the medium is dominated by commercial enterprises; however, the United States also has nonprofit television stations, many of which belong to the Public Broadcasting network or to the satellite network Deep Dish TV. In addition, cable TV stations are required to provide public, educational, and government access channels.

All told, these many forms of mass media saturate our world and penetrate deeply into our individual consciousness, yet we still have some choices regarding which messages to accept. Let's see how this works.

active agents
seekers of various media messages and resisters of others

TEST YOUR KNOWLEDGE
- What are some of the most common forms of mass media?

THE INDIVIDUAL AND MASS MEDIA

Media scholars are interested in the impact media messages have on individuals, but they are also interested in how individuals decide which media messages to consume or avoid. Marketers and media producers especially want to know how they might predict and characterize individuals' choices so that they can more effectively influence consumer choice. In this section we'll explore both aspects of individual media consumption—how media messages influence us and how we become **active agents,** or active seekers, of various media messages and resisters of others. With the term *active agent*, we stress that even though people inhabit a densely media-rich environment, they need not be passively bombarded by media messages.

How Media Messages Affect the Individual

One approach to studying the influence of media messages relies on the linear model. Recall that in Chapter 1 we described how early models conceived of communication as a linear process involving the transfer of information without feedback from one person to another. Similarly, when it comes to media, there is a traditional linear model that portrays communication as a process that occurs in a linear fashion—for example, on a path from the television to the viewer (see Figure 13.1). In this traditional approach, scholars focus on the sender, the medium, the audience, and the effect of the message. This model views media communication as a process that moves from one source to many receivers. While researchers who use this approach recognize that people are not passive viewers or consumers of media messages, they are interested only in measuring the influence of media messages on the individual, not vice versa.

FIGURE 13.1 The Linear Model
The linear model emphasizes the effect of media messages on the individual. Communication in this model is largely (although not entirely) one-way.

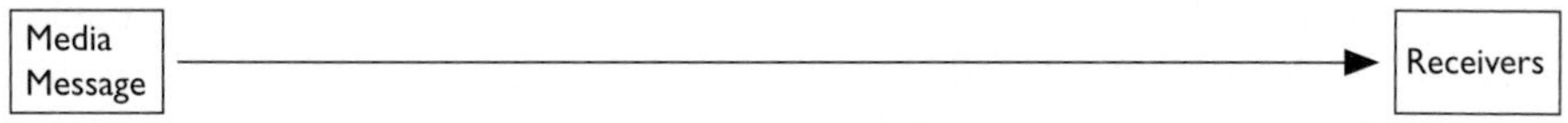

Media Message ⟶ Receivers

STARBUCKS GETS A RADIO STATION

By understanding the effects of media messages, communication scholars in the linear tradition hope to assist public policy debates about media regulation. For example, their research findings might be used in debates about the effects on viewers of violence or sexuality in the media. So, on a societal level, research based on the linear model often influences public policy decision making. On an individual level, this kind of research may help you select the types of television shows you watch or the movies you allow your children to see.

As an analytic tool, the linear model of media analysis has its limits. For example, critics argue that its simplicity cannot account for the multiple ways people respond to media messages (Sproule, 1989). Viewers are not merely passive receivers of messages, these critics say, nor do they necessarily believe or imitate everything they watch or read. Those who watched *Modern Family*, for example, did not necessarily model their family behaviors on the show's characters. Nor did everyone who watched the trial of Casey Anthony, accused of murdering her daughter, Caylee, agree with the jury's verdict (Hightower & Sedensky, 2011).

On the other hand, the linear model does highlight the power and influence of media messages. Some people did try to imitate the antics of Johnny Knoxville on the MTV television show *Jackass*, resulting in very serious injuries despite televised warnings against trying to imitate the stunts. And in a classic example, a mass panic was set off when thousands of listeners to Orson Welles' 1938 Halloween radio broadcast, *War of the Worlds*, believed that Martians were landing in New Jersey.

Scholars who study media influence work in an area called **mass media effects.** The study of mass media effects has undergone significant changes over the years, as researchers have disagreed about how much effect a particular media message has on people's everyday lives (McQuail, 1987). In the 1930s, Paul Lazarsfeld and his colleagues studied radio's effect on listeners and, in particular, its effect on voting behavior. This study, titled *The People's Choice* (Lazarsfeld, Berelson, & Gaudet, 1948), argued that media had limited effects, as they found that radio tended to reinforce preexisting beliefs rather than shape new ones.

Today, the focus on effects remains important in media research. For example, contemporary researchers have examined media images of beautiful bodies and how those images influence people's perceptions of their own bodies and their resultant behavior in response to those images, including dieting, working out, taking diet pills, and undergoing cosmetic surgery. An early influential book, *The Beauty Myth* by Naomi Wolf, argued that these images of beauty are unattainable and are used against women. Originally published in 1991, it has remained a best seller; a new edition was released in 2002. In their study of the effects of entertainment television and sports media, Kimberly Bissell and Peiqin Zhou (2004) found a high correlation between images of thin women's bodies that appear repeatedly in entertainment television and eating disorders among college-age women who watched those shows.

Another area of inquiry among media-effects scholars involves media images of violence. In their study of media usage among middle-school children in ten regions in the United States, Michael Slater and his colleagues found that aggressive young people seek out violent media and that exposure to media violence can predict aggression (Slater, Henry, Swaim, & Anderson, 2003). Thus, they see media violence and aggression as mutually reinforcing and call their model a *downward spiral model* to describe the powerful, negative influence the interaction has on youth. Those youth who are prone to violent behaviors seek out violent media that

mass media effects
the influence that media have on people's everyday lives

reinforce more violent behavior. More recently, Bushman and Gibson (2011) have also found that aggression continues long after engaging with violent video games.

Promoting health through media messages is another significant area of inquiry among scholars seeking to understand media effects. In a recent study on antidrug advertisements for adolescents, Hunyi Cho and Franklin J. Boster (2008) compared antidrug messages framed around the costs of using drugs (loss) versus the benefits of avoiding them (gain). The study found that framing loss rather than gain was more effective among adolescents who had friends who used drugs. There was no difference among adolescents whose friends did not use drugs. In order to engage the most effective communication messages to promote public health, media effects scholars are also trying to better understand how media messages can be more effective.

How Individuals Choose Media Messages

Advertisers, political campaign strategists, and communication scholars all want to understand which groups of people consume which media texts. They want to know who watches *Grey's Anatomy*, who reads the *New York Times*, and who reads *People* magazine. As you might guess, this type of information enables advertisers to target their messages more accurately toward certain consumers. It also enables campaign strategists to focus their message to attract more votes. But why would media scholars be interested in this information?

Media scholars need this information so that they can correctly target their research. For example, if scholars want to study the effect of a particular **media text**—for example, a television show, advertisement, or movie—they need to know which audience group to study. If they want to know how people interpret a particular media text, they need to know the audience of that text. Or if scholars want to know about the economic influence of particular media texts, they need to know which audience groups advertisers target with these messages.

As an individual, you are constantly faced with media choices, and your choices have increased considerably in the past decade due to the increased predominance of online news and blogging as well as instant downloads of movies and TV episodes. Researchers are interested in not only *what* we choose but *how* we choose. See how one of our students considers this in *It Happened to Me: Josh*.

Although Josh doesn't mention it explicitly, both what people choose and how they choose are related to their identities. And, as we noted in Chapter 3, identities are not fixed; they are dynamic across time and situations. With them, media choices change as well. For example, as a child, Josh may have been a fan of Saturday morning cartoons or *Sesame Street*, but as a young

It Happened to Me: *Josh*

I love comedies, but I seem to be the only person who doesn't like Will Ferrell movies. We saw *Stepbrothers* with some friends and I just wasn't impressed. Some of the scenes were verbally and physically exaggerated and every time I looked around and saw others laughing, I wondered why I didn't find it funny. I'd say Ferrell's last funny movie was *Old School*, and I think I like it because Vince Vaughn is more my style of humor. To me, Will Ferrell's type of humor is more slapstick, and I like a more "dry" humor. I always give every movie a chance, but I know that I have my favorite actors.

adult, perhaps he preferred *Monday Night Football* or MTV's *Real World*. Josh's age and the ages of his friends likely influence the movies he selects. But age is only one aspect of identity—and perhaps one of the simplest factors that influence media choices. Other aspects, such as regional identity, might also have an effect, but they are more difficult to correlate with media tastes.

Selective Exposure **Selective exposure** theories help us understand how identity plays a role in media tastes and preferences. These theories are based on the idea that people seek media messages and interpret media texts in ways that confirm their beliefs—and, conversely, that they resist or avoid messages that challenge

COMMUNICATION IN SOCIETY
Watching or Not Watching the British Royal Wedding

What were your most noteworthy reasons for deciding to watch or not watch the broadcast of the British royal wedding? What might have interested those Americans who watched the ceremony? Why might other Americans have ignored or avoided this media event?

When Prince William and Catherine Middleton were married on April 29, 2011, they became the Duke and Duchess of Cambridge. Perhaps curiously, many U.S. Americans were eager and interested to watch the wedding. Indeed, many people worldwide watched the wedding as well.

Prior to the wedding, there were estimates that two billion people would tune in (BBC, 2011). British culture secretary Jeremy Hunt is credited with claiming this high number (Holden, 2011). With the world's population at about 6.9 billion, did over 28 percent of the world watch the royal wedding?

After the wedding, audience estimates fell dramatically. Nielsen Media Research estimated that 22.8 million Americans watched the royal wedding over 11 different U.S. media networks (Schucker, 2011). This represents a little over 7 percent of the total U.S. population of more than 308 million. In other words, the royal wedding "was a snooze for most Americans" (Stelter, 2011). In contrast to the 22.8 million Americans who watched the royal wedding, 111 million Americans watched the 2011 Super Bowl (Powers, 2011).

As you think about which Americans watched the royal wedding and why, you might also want to consider the reasons the British government promoted the event and overestimated the audience for the wedding.

SOURCES: BBC. (2011, April 28). World awaits Britain's royal wedding. Retrieved July 13, 2011, from http://www.bbc.co.uk/news/world-europe-13228153

Holden, M. (2011, April 6). Culture secretary says 2 billion to watch royal wedding. *Reuters*. Retrieved July 19, 2011, from http://uk.reuters.com/article/2011/04/06/uk-britain-wedding-audience-idUKTRE73543V20110406

Powers, L. (2011, February 7). 10 most watched TV shows ever. *The Hollywood Reporter*. Retrieved July 19, 2011, from http://www.hollywoodreporter.com/blogs/live-feed/10-watched-tv-shows-97180

Schucker, L. A. E. (2011, May 2). Wedding ratings: Perchance to dream. *Wall Street Journal*. Retrieved July 13, 2011, from http://online.wsj.com/article/SB10001424052748703703304576297334268253192.html

Stelter, B. (2011, May 1). Mixed TV ratings for the royal wedding. *New York Times*. Retrieved July 19, 2011, from http://artsbeat.blogs.nytimes.com/2011/05/01/mixed-tv-ratings-for-the-royal-wedding/

their beliefs. Depending upon their personal and political beliefs, some people enjoyed watching the royal wedding of Prince William and Kate Middleton. Others chose not to watch the wedding. (See *Communication in Society: Watching or Not Watching the British Royal Wedding.*)

One television show that was studied heavily in terms of selective exposure is *The Cosby Show,* a prime-time situation comedy that ran from 1984 to 1992. According to selective exposure theory, if someone believes racism no longer exists, then she or he is likely to interpret media messages as confirming or reinforcing this perception. In a study of *The Cosby Show*, Sut Jhally and Justin Lewis (1992) set up focus groups. Twenty-six of these focus groups were composed of White viewers of the show, and twenty-three were composed of African American viewers. In analyzing the White focus group responses, Jhally and Lewis found that Whites were more likely to think that *The Cosby Show* proved Black people can succeed; therefore, they said, African Americans who did not succeed were to blame for their own failure. In other words, as the White focus groups saw it, personal failings rather than discrimination or racism were what blocked success. In contrast, Black respondents saw *The Cosby Show* as a "cultural breakthrough" in terms of positive portrayals of Black culture (p. 121). Thus, they expressed far more concern about the pervasive negative images of African Americans in media and the influences of those images

Alternative V I E W

Hostile Media Effect

In what ways do you selectively expose yourself to media messages? Do you generally listen to the same news commentators rather than seeking alternative voices? Do you watch the same shows your friends watch, or do you look for something different?

Selective exposure theories tell us that people tend to consume media that reinforce or support their own views. Yet, some media researchers counter this idea. Why? Researchers have found that people on both sides of an issue can be exposed to the same media coverage, and when asked what they thought of the coverage, both groups say that it was biased against their views. If both sides find the same coverage biased, it may undermine the idea that people only seek messages that confirm their views. Thus, the researchers concluded that while bias in media news stories surely does occur, another kind of bias rests with the viewer—a phenomenon called the "hostile media effect" because it reflects a general hostility toward media.

In their study, Albert C. Gunther and Kathleen Schmitt (2004) used the controversy over genetically modified foods to understand the hostile media effect. In part, their study found that regardless of respondents' position on genetically modified foods, they viewed news media stories as biased against them. However, when respondents saw the same information in a student essay format, the hostility tended to be absent or at least minimal. The researchers conclude, then, that the hostile media effect is created by the perception that a media message has the potential to influence large numbers of people for or against a particular viewpoint.

If the selective exposure theory is correct, and people tend to select media messages that support their own views, then why would they interpret these messages to be biased against them? There is no easy answer, but perhaps questions of bias and media selection need to be thought about in more complicated ways. When charges of bias arise against a media source, how often do we consider that the bias may be our own?

SOURCE: Gunther, A. C., & Schmitt, K. (2004). Mapping boundaries of the hostile media effect. *Journal of Communication, 54,* 55–70.

on viewers. As you can see, while both racial groups were watching the same television show, their interpretations were very different.

Selective exposure theories point to the ways that both groups interpret the show to confirm their own beliefs and views. Those who subscribe to selective exposure theory argue that people rarely inhabit a media environment that challenges their social identities, including their religious and political beliefs, notions about gender, or ideas about race. Not all scholars subscribe to this theory, however: see *Alternative View: Hostile Media Effect.*

Another line of media research, called **uses and gratifications** studies and explores how people use media messages and what types of gratifications they find in some media texts rather than others. Working within this approach, researchers might want to know why viewers watch *The Bachelor* instead of *Dancing with the Stars, Rookie Blue* instead of *Law and Order,* or *Wipeout* instead of *Big Brother.* For example, a researcher might note that a certain type of entertainment is popular—say, violent movies, romance novels, or wrestling—and wish to explore why so many people seek out those kinds of texts and what needs they satisfy. Denis McQuail and his colleagues (1972) suggested four general uses and gratifications that audiences have for media texts:

- information
- personal identity
- integration and social interaction
- entertainment

uses and gratifications
the idea that people use media messages and find various types of gratifications in some media texts rather than in others

According to selective exposure theories, people seek out media that confirm what they already believe. What beliefs might viewers of Fox News and MSNBC disagree on?

The first motivation, information seeking, is straightforward: audiences want to learn from some media presentations, as in the case of a news event. The second motivation, personal identity, refers to the idea that viewers may use media messages to affirm some aspect of their personal identity—for example, as mothers, consumers, or political conservatives. The third motivation, integration and social interaction, underscores the role that media can play in helping people connect with others, as they do when discussing sports or the events on a soap opera. Finally, the entertainment motivation refers to the use of media for pleasure, or the desire simply to be entertained. Of course, these motivations can overlap, so that we can watch a program for information, while at the same time using it as a topic for conversation with others, which would fit within McQuail's third motivation.

Cultural Values in Media Consumption Understanding why some groups choose one program over another highlights the cultural values at work in the consumption of media. In his study of television preferences among Israeli adults, Jonathan Cohen (2002) examined viewing habits and choice. He found that factors influencing media selection included loyalty to particular channels, preferences for certain types of shows, and even the language of the programs, as programming in Israel is available in Hebrew, English, and other languages. His conclusion was that "Most Israeli viewers seem to prefer native programming, whether due to language problems or to cultural resonance" (p. 218). Cohen suggests that Israeli audiences use television not only for entertainment but also to affirm their Israeli identities and as a context for social interaction with other Israelis.

Determining why people seek specific media texts and not other texts is very important from an economic perspective. After all, a media corporation does not want to spend a lot of money on a television show or magazine if it is going to fail. However, it is notoriously difficult to predict which media texts will become popular and which will not. *Desperate Housewives*, for example, was described as "the surprise hit of the television season" (Glaister, 2005). In spite of major investments in market research, there is no completely foolproof way to predict audience response.

Of course, the inability to accurately predict audience response does not mean that media producers have no information on trends. In certain eras, viewers are more interested in Westerns or police dramas, reality shows or evening soap operas than they are during other periods. Today, reality shows are quite popular. Furthermore, advertisers know that some groups prefer to consume certain kinds of media. For example, the advertising that appears during televised football games reveals what advertisers have learned about that audience through careful market research and analysis.

How Individuals Resist Media Messages

While media messages bombard people every day, individuals do not necessarily, or even easily, accept all that they receive. In addition, people actively resist certain media texts. For example, some people sought out and watched *Kill Bill* films, *Restrepo*, *127 Hours*, and similar graphic movies. Others actively avoided them. Why? We resist media texts every day for many reasons, including something as hard to quantify as individual taste and something as personal as what we see as negative portrayals of our political, moral, or religious views; our interests, age, or level of education; or our gender, sexuality, and racial and ethnic identities. Other far less political reasons can create consumer resistance as well, as our student reveals in *It Happened to Me: Jessica.*

Resisting media messages entails much more than simply whether we go to a particular movie or watch a particular video. It is also about how we resist the power of media to shape our identities. For example, in one study, Meenakshi Gigi Durham (2004) interviewed South Asian immigrant teenage girls living in the United States. She explored the question of how these girls dealt with traditional Indian notions of female gender expectations in the context of available media. She found that the only mainstream U.S. show they liked to watch was *Friends,* which they found to be funny, while they disliked *Dawson's Creek*, which they thought was unrealistic. In general, they distanced themselves from mainstream U.S. media. In contrast, they consumed large amounts of media (films, popular music) from India, which they rented from Indian grocery stores and restaurants, borrowed from others, and watched or downloaded from the Internet. They particularly identified with the narratives in *Mississippi Masala, Bend It Like Beckham,* and *American Desi*, three Indian films with narratives involving "taboo relationships between Indian girls and men of different racial/cultural backgrounds" (p. 154).

Durham concludes that these adolescent girls use media to create new identities, and that these identities do not conform to stereotypes of either Asian Indian women or U.S. American women.

A television show produced by Radio Canada from 2004 to 2006, *Les Bougon*, highlighted the interrelatedness of social identities and media consumption and the complexities of consumption and resistance. *Les Bougon* was described in the *New York Times* as "a politically incorrect version of *Father Knows Best*, with twists so wicked and crude that even fans of *The Simpsons* might blush" (Krauss, 2004). The Canadian magazine *Macleans* described the Bougon family as "rough, truculent, beer-soaked urban trash. In their commitment to not working, though, they come out as likeable, funny anarchists" (Aubin, 2004). This representation of a poor family created a controversy in Canada, as well as high ratings. This television show was popular across social class identities in Québec, even if the classes interpreted it differently. For example, poor people may have liked the show because they interpreted it as empowering to their identities, and they saw this family as heroes for using the system to their advantage. In contrast, well-to-do viewers may have appreciated the program as a satire. Others, in any social class, may simply have seen a tight-knit family loving and protecting each other to survive (Cernetig, 2004).

As you have seen through our discussion, communication researchers are interested in all aspects of the relationship between individuals and the media messages that surround them. First, they wonder what effect media messages have on individuals; and second, they explore how individuals choose, resist, and interpret these messages. Research has revealed that the answers to both questions involve complex processes related to individual identity, individual needs, and individual taste. Audiences respond to and interpret

> ### It Happened to Me: *Jessica*
>
> My boyfriend really wanted me to go see *127 Hours*. Although I do like James Franco, I just couldn't imagine sitting through a long movie watching someone suffering and cutting his arm off. So, I said no anyway, even though he mentioned it four or five times. He was unhappy that I wouldn't go to this movie, but I just didn't want to sit through that kind of emotional drama.

With its portrayal of a less-than-ideal family, *Les Bougon* was a popular but controversial television show in Québec.

VISUAL SUMMARY 13.1   Selecting and Resisting Media

USES AND GRATIFICATIONS

Likes to watch Fox News	**Information**	Likes to watch MSNBC News
Likes to watch NFL games	**Personal Identity and Integration and Social Interaction**	Likes to watch reality shows
Likes comedies	**Entertainment**	Likes action/adventure films

RESISTING MEDIA

Avoids romance films Objects to violent images	**Taste Shaping Identities**	Avoids home decor shows Hates cooking shows

texts based on both their individual and social identities, and therefore, different social groups can consume the same text while being affected by it differently and interpreting it differently. However, all individual responses and choices occur in a larger social context. Thus, to provide a more complete picture, we now shift our attention to the role of media at the societal level.

TEST YOUR KNOWLEDGE

- What strategies do media consumers use to select and reject media texts?
- Why might audiences prefer to watch media texts that affirm the values and beliefs they already hold?

THE INDIVIDUAL, MASS MEDIA, AND SOCIETY

Why do media play such an important role in society? One reason is that they often serve as the voice of the community. In this way, media offer people a means of thinking about themselves, their places in the world, and the societal forces around them. As individuals, we can only choose from among the media choices available. Societal forces, including the government, economics, media organizations, and advertisers, largely determine which media options are available. In the following section we'll look at three important roles that media play in society: confirming social identities, helping people understand the world, and helping individuals understand important public events. And finally, because no discussion of media and society would be complete without a discussion of media violence and media economics, we will conclude with these topics.

content analysis
approach to understanding media that focuses on a specific aspect of the content of a text or group of texts

Confirming Social Identities

As we've noted, media representations influence our understanding of social identities, such as gender or age identity as well as the identities of others. This is one of the functions of media usage we examined as we discussed uses and gratifications. For example, images we see on television and in films, magazines, and newspapers shape our sense of what it is to be a man or woman. These views often create or enforce a hierarchy of identities, often portraying men as more powerful than women. Thus, media messages not only shape the way we understand social identities; they also show us which social identities are valued. For example, as Associated Press reviewer Christy Lemire (2005) noted in her review of the film *Deuce Bigalow: European Gigolo*, "Making fun of homosexuality seems to be the one area of humor that has yet to be ruled off-limits by political correctness; such jokes also appeared in the far superior *Wedding Crashers* earlier this summer." If Lemire's analysis is correct, this "permission" to joke about one particular social identity can reinforce a hierarchy in which heterosexuality is valued over homosexuality.

Content analysis can provide data on factors such as media representation of various groups, media violence, and the kinds of topics covered and the way in which they are covered in the media.

One approach to understanding how and what media communicate about various social identities is content analysis. **Content analysis** focuses on some specific aspect of a text's content. Bernard Berelson (1952/1971), a behavioral scientist, explains that content analysis took off during the late 1930s, with the work of Harold Laswell and his colleagues (see Chapter 2), who were concerned with "propaganda and public opinion and the emergence of radio as a great mass medium of communication."

How does content analysis work? To begin, a researcher might want to know how many non-White characters appear on the television show *Monk*, which is set in San Francisco, a very multiethnic and multicultural city, or on *NCIS: Los Angeles*, a show set in a city where Whites are a minority population. The researcher would thus watch a number of episodes, count the number of non-White characters, note the kinds of roles they play and which characters are central, and finally, draw conclusions based on these data. Recently, actress Geena Davis became quite concerned about the imbalance between males and females in media representations. In two large studies on television programs and films, males outnumbered females by 70 percent to 30 percent (Belkin, 2010). In order to try to understand these content differences and their impact on children, she founded the Geena Davis Institute on Gender and Media (http://www.thegeenadavisinstitute.org/). Further, researcher Caroline Aoyagi (2004) conducted a content analysis of TV shows set in the state of Hawaii and concluded the following:

No one can blame the big television networks for their love affair with the beautiful islands of Hawaii, but as several new shows are set to launch or are already on air, the lack of Asian Pacific Americans in the shows' casts have many wondering: what Hawaii is this?

In a state where Asian Pacific Islander Americans [APIA] make up more than 80 percent of the population and whites are considered the minority, a look at the new line-up of shows for FOX, the WB network, and NBC show no APIA lead actors and only one or two APIAs in supporting roles (p. 1).

Images of male beauty are socially constructed.

A content analysis of television shows, thus, can provide data on racial representation in media. Content analysis also can reveal the kinds of topics that arise most often, the way episodes and conflicts are resolved most frequently, the number and types of conflicts that occur, and many other issues. In their study of television news in Los Angeles and Orange County, California, Travis Dixon and Daniel Linz (2002) employed content analysis to determine whether correlations existed between pretrial publicity and race. Using the American Bar Association's definition of potentially prejudicial information, they found that "Blacks and Latinos are twice as likely as Whites to have prejudicial information aired about them, and Latinos are three times more likely than Whites to have prejudicial information aired when they victimize Whites" (p. 133). Through content analysis, then, these two scholars were able to show a strong correlation between the race of the accused and the reporting of prejudicial information in the news. Moreover, they found that reporting of prejudicial information dramatically increased when the crime victim was White. Here you can see how media confirm social identities.

Similarly, Cheryl Law and Magdala Peixoto Labre (2002) conducted a content analysis of images of male bodies in thirty years of popular magazines, specifically *GQ, Rolling Stone,* and *Sports Illustrated.* They found that "the images of men in popular magazines became more lean and muscular from 1967 to 1997, and that the V-shaped male figure also became more prevalent over time" (p. 705). As the researchers report, "this content analysis suggests that the new ideal seen in the mass media does not represent the body type most men have" (p. 706), and they speculate on the effect these images have on men's behavior, for example, their use of steroids, diets, and workouts. Because this was a content analysis and not a media-effects study, the researchers did not survey male readers of these magazines to find out whether they actually went on diets, used steroids, and so on. Instead, the point of the study is to highlight what media messages communicate to men (and women) about the ideal male image and male social identity.

Content analysis by itself does not reveal why viewers choose to watch particular television shows or consume other kinds of media messages. Collecting demographic information about an audience's racial, ethnic, or age composition may give some insight as to which groups are drawn to what kind of content, but, again, this is not the primary purpose of content analysis. For example, the study we mentioned earlier by Dixon and Linz did not try to explain whether or why southern Californians preferred pretrial television news coverage with prejudicial information about minorities, or why the television news industry produces this kind of news. What their data do confirm, however, is that Blacks and Latinos are represented more negatively in news programs.

Some studies use a more detailed analysis of media messages than content analysis does, and this approach can help us better understand which social identities are being confirmed and elevated. Such studies, which rely on textual analysis, typically focus on fewer media texts than content analyses do. Researchers who conduct textual analyses of media messages take an approach similar to literary critics when they explore meanings in a literary work. However, in textual analysis, any kind of media image can be considered a text. For example, in her study of the news coverage of Freaknik, a spring break event that used to draw African

American college students to Atlanta, Marian Meyers (2004) looked closely at the news reports of sexual violence against African American women perpetrated by African American men. "In essence," she wrote, "the news criminalized Black men primarily with respect to property damage while decriminalizing them concerning their abuse of women. The safety of Black women appears of less consequence than that of property" (p. 113). Thus, these news reports confirmed an identity of Black men as criminals while undermining the identity of Black women as crime victims.

In her study of masculinity, Helene Shugart (2008) focused on the media construction of the "metrosexual" in the context of commercialism. Metrosexuals are men who are meticulous about their appearance—not only their physiques, but also their clothing, hair styles, and so forth. In her textual analysis of the metrosexual, Shugart found that metrosexuality "bore all the hallmarks of a fad or a trend" (p. 295), but metrosexuality also "served a vital and strategic rhetoric function as part of a much larger and ongoing cultural discourse about masculinity(ies)" (p. 295). Because commercialism has threatened traditional masculinity by insisting on enhancing masculinity through the purchase of various products, metrosexuality helped to reconcile the contradiction between the commercial masculinity and a more traditional or normative masculinity.

Thus, what people see, hear, and read in the media can confirm identities, but so can their media choices. Although our social identities are not absolute predictors of media choices, trends do emerge if we look at the correlations between media consumption and various social identities. Nielsen Media Research has studied the most popular television shows among all U.S. Americans and among African Americans as a subgroup, revealing that their choices are similar in some respects and different in others, and thus, that racial identities do somewhat correlate with media consumption, as noted in *Did You Know? Nielsen Media Research*.

In addition, people often choose media images that not only confirm their identities but also help them deal with the various issues involved in any identity. For example, some women are drawn to the USA Network shows *Covert Affairs* and *In Plain Sight*, which feature strong women characters—one working as a CIA agent and the other as a U.S. marshal—who work in male-dominated environments. These characters help women envision how they can operate successfully in masculine environments and retain their gender identity.

How does media coverage favor some identities over others? The amount of coverage, as revealed by content analysis, is sometimes the controlling factor. For example, in their study of the Salt Lake City Olympics in 2002, Billings and Eastman (2003) found that NBC devoted more time to reporting on male athletes and White athletes than on other groups. The potential effect of this imbalance is that the identities of particular viewers are reinforced, while the identities of other viewers are undermined. Remember, however, that more extensive coverage can also have the opposite effect. For example, if an identity is portrayed with great frequency in a negative way, that identity can be undermined, as Dixon and Linz found in their analysis of pretrial coverage in southern California (2002).

As you learned in Chapter 3, social identities help shape individuals' outlook on the world; at the same time, individuals interpret media texts from their identity positions. Media critics have been instrumental in bringing to the public's attention these issues of identity confirmation and media bias in portraying identities. As a result, many with identities that media portray less positively have come to recognize their exclusion. The effect can be anger or disengagement when few, if any, images exist of one's own social group acting in positive ways.

Understanding the World

Media play a key role in helping people understand the world. Most people will never travel to the Ukraine, North Korea, Iraq, Palestine, Rwanda, Indonesia,

Did You Know?

Nielsen Media Research

What kinds of shows or movies do you like to watch, and which aspects of your social identities might guide these media choices? How might these choices sustain or challenge your social identities?

Nielsen ratings are widely used in the television industry to determine audience viewing, and they are used to set advertising rates. Note their findings on the top-rated television shows for African Americans and for the U.S. population at large, shown in the tables included here. How might social identities play a role in the popularity of some television shows?

The following were the highest-rated prime-time television programs in African American households for one week in June 2011:

Rank	Program	Network	Household Rating %
1	*The Voice*	NBC	6.2
2	*So You Think You Can Dance-Thu*	FOX	6.0
3	*America's Got Talent*	NBC	5.8
4	*Law and Order: L.A.*	NBC	5.7
5	*So You Think You Can Dance-Wed*	FOX	5.6
6	*America's Got Talent-Wed*	NBC	5.5
7	*America's Got Talent-Tue*	NBC	5.4
7	*NCIS: Los Angeles*	CBS	5.4
9	*The Voice: Results Show*	NBC	5.3
10	*Wipeout-Thurs*	ABC	4.8
10	*Criminal Minds*	CBS	4.8
10	*CSI: NY*	CBS	4.8

The following were the highest-rated prime-time television programs in all U.S. households (including African American homes) for one week in June 2011.

Rank	Program	Network	Household Rating %
1	*America's Got Talent-Wed*	NBC	7.5
2	*America's Got Talent-Tue*	NBC	7.1
3	*The Voice*	NBC	6.8
4	*NCIS*	CBS	6.2
5	*America's Got Talent (6/22)*	NBC	6.1
6	*The Voice: Results Show*	NBC	6.0
7	*NCIS: Los Angeles*	CBS	5.9
8	*The Mentalist*	CBS	5.2
9	*The Bachelorette*	ABC	5.1
9	*CSI*	CBS	5.1

SOURCE: Nielsen Media Research. (n.d.). Top primetime programs—African American homes. Retrieved July 12, 2011, from Nielsen Media Research. (n.d.). Television—Week of June 20, 2011. Retrieved July 12, 2011, from http://www.nielsen.com/us/en/insights/top10s/television.html

Somalia, or Brazil, but they can learn something about these places through media. They may see these distant regions on the Travel Channel or in *National Geographic* magazine, or they may see news about them on CNN, MSNBC, or other news channels.

However, the texts that media organizations produce can distort the images of faraway places as well as enhance them, especially if viewers have never been to the parts of the world represented. In her study of AP wire photographs of Afghan women—both during and after the Taliban regime—Shahira Fahmy (2004) found that "1 percent of [published] AP photographs portrayed women revealing their face and hair." Thus, even after the fall of the Taliban, Afghan women are depicted wearing their burqas—despite the fact that many photos exist that portray "images of Afghan women removing their burqas as a sign of liberation" (p. 110). In this study, Fahmy brings to light the discrepancy between the pool of available AP photographs and the ones selected for publication in the United States, noting that the ones that editors select shape and sometimes distort our impressions of the subject.

As another example of the media's power to shape knowledge and understanding, prior to the disappearance of Natalee Holloway in the spring of 2005, there had been little U.S. news coverage of the Caribbean island of Aruba. Many U.S. Americans did not know that Aruba was Dutch or that it operated under the Dutch legal system—much less what the technicalities of that system were. In contrast, media provide U.S. audiences with extensive detail on the British royal family. As another example, U.S. media coverage of weather typically stops at our northern and southern borders, as if weather didn't exist in Canada or Mexico. As you can see, by choosing what to cover and how extensively, media shape audience understanding of what is and isn't important in the world.

Agenda-Setting Capacity

This power of media coverage to influence individuals' view of the world is referred to as its **agenda-setting capacity.** Thus, in agenda-setting research, scholars focus on audience perceptions of reality and attempt to discover how or whether media coverage correlates with these audience perceptions. For example, Lowry, Nio, and Leitner (2003) studied correlations between crime rates, news coverage on crime, and public attitudes about crime from 1978 to 1998. Existing data indicated that in March 1992, only 5 percent of the public thought that crime was the most important problem. By August 1994, however, 52 percent felt that way. What accounted for this jump? By correlating the amount of television news coverage with the crime rates, the researchers found that the amount of news coverage was far more influential than actual crime rates in this change in public perception. By focusing so much attention on crime reporting, the theory goes, media set the public agenda for what was important. Agenda-setting studies often look at long time periods, as the crime-coverage study did, in order to correlate media coverage to changes in audience perceptions.

In another study using an agenda-setting perspective, Jochen Peter (2003) focused on the issue of fourteen European nations and their integration into the European Union (EU). Here, however, he did not find a simple correlation between more news coverage of EU integration and public attitudes about the importance of this issue. Instead he found that when political elites agreed about integration, public involvement or interest in the issue declined. Coverage of disagreement among political elites over EU integration did correlate, though, with public involvement in the issue. Thus, content and the degree of exposure play parts in setting the public's agenda.

agenda-setting capacity
the power of media coverage to influence individuals' view of the world

Cultivation Theory Media messages also play a critical role in acculturating individuals. **Cultivation theory** proposes that long-term immersion in a media environment leads to "cultivation," or enculturation, into shared beliefs about the world. Unlike other approaches that focus on specific media messages, television programs,

cultivation theory
idea that long-term immersion in a media environment leads to "cultivation," or enculturation, into shared beliefs about the world

Cultivation theory has been used to emphasize the role of news coverage of crime in the perceptions of crime rates.

movies, or other kinds of text, "Cultivation analysis is concerned with the more general and pervasive consequences of cumulative exposure to cultural media" (Morgan & Signorielli, 1990, p. 16). Initiated by George Gerbner (2002) and his colleagues, cultivation analysis seeks to uncover how television, in particular, influences those who are heavy viewers. Those who watch television news, the theory goes, will share certain beliefs or distortions about the world. Moreover, this theory argues that media coverage shapes attitudes about one's own society and the issues it faces. For example, although crime rates have gone down overall in recent years, many U.S. Americans feel more insecure than ever. In their study on fear of crime, Daniel Romer, Kathleen Hall Jamieson, and Sean Aday (2003) surveyed 2,300 Philadelphia residents. Within that population group, they found a relationship between the widespread belief that crime is a significant problem and the amount of local television news coverage of crimes. The point of the study is that Philadelphia media coverage cultivates attitudes and beliefs that shape everyday life in Philadelphia, with a key element of daily life being an exaggerated fear of crime.

In a recent cultivation study, Jeff Niederdeppe and his colleagues (2010) studied the ways that local television news covers cancer prevention because the "sheer volume of news coverage about cancer causes and prevention has led to broad speculation about its role in promoting fatalistic beliefs" (p. 231), Niederdeppe and colleagues developed three hypotheses comparing local television news coverage with local newspaper coverage of various cancer issues and their fourth hypothesis focused on the relationship between local TV news viewing and fatalistic beliefs about cancer prevention They found that there is "a tendency for local TV news to focus on aspects of cancer that are likely to cultivate the beliefs that everything causes cancer or that there are too many recommendations about cancer prevention" (p. 246). In both these studies, then, immersion in the television environment shaped, or cultivated, a particular view of the world.

Media Hegemony A different way of explaining how media influence how we understand the world is through **hegemony**. Hegemony refers to the process by which people consent to particular understandings as reflected in media representations. For instance, we come to understand what "mother" means through often idealized images of mothers on television programs, films, and other media. While there are no laws that regulate what a "mother" must do, we consent to these images of motherhood and we expect mothers to engage in certain behaviors, such as throwing birthday parties for their children. In contrast, our hegemonic understanding of "fathers" does not include that kind of activity. Fathers can, of course, throw birthday parties for their children, but it is not part of the hegemonic construction of fatherhood.

Masculinity, as represented in media content, has been a rich site for investigating how hegemony functions. For example, in his work on hegemony, communication scholar Nick Trujillo (1991) studied the media representations of Nolan Ryan, a baseball pitcher, to show how masculinity is constructed. He found five features of how Ryan was portrayed: (1) male athletic power, (2) ideal image of the capitalist worker, (3) family patriarch, (4) White rural cowboy, and (5) symbol of male (hetero)sexuality. Trujillo asks that we consider the negative consequences

hegemony
the process by which we consent to social constructions, rather than having them imposed on us

of this construction of masculinity. Additionally, in his study of the television show *thirtysomething*, Hanke (1990) analyzes the way that hegemonic masculinity shifts slightly to focus on men "who are more open to domestic concerns and interpersonal relationships" (p. 245). His analysis focuses on hegemony as a process in which masculinity shifts to respond to changing social needs. Hegemony is a process by which we all participate in the social construction of ourselves and others. If we violate these hegemonic notions, we risk alienation. This approach to the study of media content helps us better understand the contours and limits of how we might present ourselves and interpret others, as hegemony outlines what is acceptable, normal, or even ideal.

Interpreting Media Events

The term **media event** applies to those occasions or catastrophes that interrupt regular programming. Like rhetorical events, which we discussed in the previous chapter, media events create vast numbers of media messages. Examples include the funeral of John F. Kennedy, the Olympics, or the attacks of September 11, 2001. Media scholars are interested in the coverage of such events because such coverage can shape viewers' understanding of what has occurred and create powerful responses. For example, Daniel Dayan and Elihu Katz (1992) found that media events bring society closer together. As a new form of "high holidays of mass communication" (p. 1), these events both reinforce and celebrate national identity.

Some media events are staged by public relations officers to garner media attention on a particular issue. When the president of the United States calls a press conference, for example, he is creating a media event. Then, of course, the representatives of various news media are present to report what he says. In these cases, the president and his public relations staff carefully control many aspects of the conference—where it will be staged, what kinds of issues will be raised, who will be present, what video images will be shown, and so on. Other politicians, movie stars, and lawyers in high-profile cases also commonly create media events to bring attention to themselves and/or their causes.

Not everyone, however, can attract this kind of media attention. People seeking media attention who lack notoriety or celebrity must use other measures. For example, during the World Trade Organization meetings in Seattle in 1999, protestors used the Internet and alternative newspapers to plan a large march in downtown Seattle. The violence that erupted between police and some protesters drew considerable media attention and was broadcast widely (DeLuca & Peeples, 2002). More recently, when the Duke and Duchess of Cambridge visited Canada in June 2011, they aroused the anger of anti-monarchy activists; moreover, animal rights advocates were upset by their participation in a rodeo in Calgary. In various places during the tour, Canadian protestors created media events by staging large public protests.

Media events often focus on important rituals while promoting a variety of less obvious messages, or subtexts. Examples of rituals include royal marriages, state funerals, and presidential inaugurations. These events, media observers say, go well beyond the occasion to promote important cultural values through media coverage. For example, in their analysis of the British queen's Golden Jubilee, Claire Wardle and Emily West (2004) concluded that the British press framed the event not simply as an anniversary celebration for the queen, but as a sign of British national strength, thus converting it to a nationalistic celebration.

Media events are filled with messages that shape one's view of the world and invite one to view the world in a particular way. The funerals of Yasser Arafat and Ronald Reagan, the inaugurations of George W. Bush and Barack Obama, and many other media events are worthy of examination for the underlying assumptions and meanings they communicate beyond reporting the facts. For example, in addition to explaining what occurred, such events can stimulate nationalistic feelings,

media event
occasions or catastrophes that interrupt regular programming

celebrate a nation's history or values, or reinforce specific political beliefs and positions. Another example of a powerful media event was the 2010 earthquake in Haiti and the 2011 earthquake and tsunami in Japan. Media played a key role in bringing attention to these human tragedies, which in turn prompted huge numbers of people to make donations to relief organizations.

Monitoring Media Violence

Representations of violent acts in media are common and are an increasingly important area of research, as well as a concern among parents and other groups. As you might surmise, our society is ambivalent about **media violence,** as indicated by the range of responses to it. On the one hand, a large number of people must be entertained by it, or why would there be so many violent books, movies, and video games? On the other, media producers and editors make intentional decisions to keep certain violent images out of the public view (beheadings, coffins, bodies). In addition, we are inventing tools such as parental control devices for television to protect certain members of society from witnessing violence. These conflicting trends reveal tensions between the principles of censorship, freedom of the press, and protection of children.

While no clear-cut definition of violence exists, most people generally consider shootings, stabbings, and other kinds of killings and attempted killings to be violent. Slapping, hitting, and fighting of all types also constitute violence. Most of the concern about media violence focuses on its impact on children. The American Academy of Pediatrics, for example, is particularly concerned about the influence of media violence on children under 8 years of age. Based on current research (2002), they have concluded that media violence has the following effects on children:

- increased aggressiveness and antisocial behavior,
- increased fear of becoming victims,
- less sensitivity to violence and to victims of violence, and
- increased appetite for more violence in entertainment and in real life.

These concerns are not new. People, especially parents, began to worry about media violence in television almost as soon as broadcasting began in 1946. Also, as we noted earlier, numerous studies have shown that "media violence contributes to a more violent society" (Anderson & Bushman, 2002, p. 2377). Research has also demonstrated that although cartoons are far more violent than prime-time television, an intervention by parents and adults can influence how children respond to those violent images. For example, in her study of 5- to 7- and 10- to 12-year-old children, Amy Nathanson (2004) found that when parents and other adults simply discussed the production techniques of a program, this either had no effect on children or it increased the influence of the violent images. In contrast, when parents underscored the fictional nature of a program's characters, the children were better able to deal with the violence and were less afraid.

In response to concerns about children and television content, in 1998 the Federal Communications Commission (2003) mandated that half of all new televisions 13 inches or larger manufactured after July 1, 1999, and *all* sets 13 inches or larger manufactured after January 1, 2000 must have a **V-chip** installed. A V-chip identifies program ratings by content and can block programming that is designated by the owner, typically the parent(s). For example, a parent who does not want a child to watch programs with TV-14 ratings can block such programs from being shown. Similar systems have been developed to block access to certain kinds of Web sites on the Internet and other media.

Of course, not all violent images presented in media are fictional. Television news journalists must decide what is and is not too horrifying to broadcast. For

Parents play an important role in their children's media viewing, as well as the way in which their children interpret the programs they watch.

media violence
representations of violent acts in media

V-chip
device that identifies television program ratings by content and can block programming designated by the owner

example, recent Internet broadcasts of hostages in Iraq being beheaded have not been shown on U.S. network television. Images of people leaping to their deaths from the World Trade Center towers on September 11, 2001, also were considered too troubling to broadcast.

The Federal Communications Commission has oversight of the appropriateness of television programming, but it focuses more on the major network channels than on cable channels. Moreover, the commission can fine broadcasters for presenting inappropriate materials, but these fines are typically for indecency rather than violence. Sometimes broadcasters warn audiences that an upcoming image may not be suitable for all audiences—one approach to dealing with extremely violent images. For example, some television newscasters provided such warnings before showing the numerous bodies of victims of the 2004 Indian Ocean tsunami. Cable broadcasts, particularly pay-per-view, have more leeway in their programming, since the assumption is that viewers have actively sought out and paid for a particular type of programming.

Analyzing Media Economics

Mass communication today is dominated by the large corporations that produce and distribute media messages. Thus, the economics of media production shapes mass communication and gives it a unique and powerful role in our society. No individual can easily compete with a multinational corporation in producing and distributing media messages. Therefore, these huge media corporations determine which messages are available, and this ownership can have consequences for society in important ways. The Walt Disney Company, one of the world's largest media conglomerates, owns several television networks as well as TV and movie production and distribution companies; these, together with its publishing and merchandising divisions and Disney character licensing, give the company enormous influence on the messages that fill the media environment. An equally wide-reaching media conglomerate is News Corporation, headed by Australian-born entrepreneur Rupert Murdoch (see *Alternative View: Murdoch and the News Corporation Fallout*).

In the area of media studies concerned with economic issues, scholars focus on **political economy,** or the ways in which media institutions produce texts in a capitalist system and the legal and regulatory frameworks that shape their options for doing so. Political economists also examine how these media products are marketed in order to understand what they reveal about our society. This approach is an extension of the work of Karl Marx, the influential nineteenth-century socialist thinker, and it emphasizes the economics of media, rather than its messages or audiences, although all those components are interrelated. An example of this theory's application can be seen in one researcher's analysis of the recent decision by ABC to cease broadcasting the Miss America pageant. After all, the researcher noted, "a little more than a decade ago [this pageant] had copped about 27 million viewers; last month it drew a record-low 9.8 million" (de Moraes, 2004). With a small viewing audience, the demand for and price of advertising during the pageant also dropped. Thus, the theory goes, economic factors largely determine what media content people are exposed to.

Earlier in this chapter, we introduced the term *culture industries* to refer to organizations that produce, distribute, or show various media texts. In the United States, these culture industries most often are media corporations or media industries that operate for profit. In some other countries, however, culture industries are more like U.S. public television—meaning that they are nonprofit media organizations—and this economic structure affects content and programming. Consider for a moment how a nonprofit media organization might develop programming as compared with a for-profit organization. What factors might guide their decision making? PBS, for example, needs to please the public and the government, both of which fund it. In contrast, for-profit networks need to please shareholders and advertisers by drawing large audiences.

How well does the V-chip serve its intended purpose? What measures do you think society should take to limit children's exposure to inappropriate media content?

political economy
the ways in which media institutions produce texts in a capitalist system and the legal and regulatory frameworks that shape their options for doing so

Alternative **V I E W**
Murdoch and the News Corporation Fallout

How much attention should we pay to media owner-ship and the power of the media, especially in relation to politicians and other government officials? Can media organizations become too powerful?

News Corporation—popularly known as News Corp—originated from an Australian newspaper company that Rupert Murdoch inherited from his father in the 1950s; it grew to become "one of the world's largest media conglomerates. Created and still controlled by Rupert Murdoch, the company owns Fox News, The Wall Street Journal, The New York Post and 20th Century Fox film studio among other assets. The company also owns influential newspapers in Britain like The Times of London and The Sun" (News Corporation, 2011). In ad-dition, In the United States, its vast holdings include the Fox Network, *Dow Jones*, HarperCollins US, FX, and National Geographic Channel, among many others.

As News Corp. expanded into more and more coun-tries and media markets, concerns were raised about the consolidation of these media industries and the political power it could exert. Among these concerns were allega-tions that News Corp. reporters had obtained informa-tion for news stories through unethical and possibly illegal means. In particular, allegations and investigations into phone hacking had been aimed at News Corp.'s British tabloid newspaper, *News of the World*. By July 2011, a scandal broke out over the hacking into voice-mail messages left on phones of prominent public figures, victims of the 2005 London subway bombing, British soldiers killed in action, and—the example that truly outraged the public—a 13-year-old schoolgirl named Milly Dowler who had been kidnapped and later found dead. Evidence of bribing police for tips on stories also emerged. The anger over these breaches of journalistic

ethics led to the closure of *News of the World*, the withdrawal of News Corp.'s bid to buy British Sky Broadcasting, the arrests of a number of News Corp. em-ployees, the resignations of police officials, and further investigations into News Corp.'s activities.

The scandal had not yet faded from the headlines when British Prime Minister David Cameron fell un-der scrutiny for his own relationship with Murdoch. As *The Daily Beast* noted: "The tragedy of Cameron's position—that is the fatal decision from which all else flows—has its origins in the well-intentioned but disas-trous choice to hire former *News of the World* editor Andy Coulson to work as Cameron's communications director" (Massie, 2011). But the concerns were not lim-ited to the British prime minister. Questions were being asked about larger political influence, and not only in the United Kingdom.

Broader concerns, which should interest us as students of communication, focus on the organizational culture of News Corp. that may encourage unethical and illegal activities in pursuit of organizational goals: "Time and again in the United States and elsewhere, Mr. Murdoch's News Corporation has used blunt force spending to skate past judgment, agreeing to payments to settle legal cases and, undoubtedly more important, silence its crit-ics" (Carr, 2011). At issue here is the power of media conglomerates such as News Corp. and the influence they may have on society, politics, and everyday life. Some are now questioning whether transnational, capi-talist media organizations are in the best interests of any nation-state, or only in the best interests of the corpora-tion. Ultimately, "News Corporation's reputation may be under water, but the company itself is very liquid, with $11.8 billion in cash on hand and more than $2.5 billion of annual free cash flow" (Carr, 2011).

SOURCES: Carr, D. (2011, July 17). Troubles that money can't dispel. *New York Times*. Retrieved July 19, 2011, from http://www.nytimes.com/2011/07/18/business/media/for-news-corporation-troubles-that-money-cant-dispel.html?hp

Massie, A. (2011, July 18). Cameron on the ropes. *The Daily Beast*. Retrieved July 19, 2011, from http://www.thedailybeast.com/articles/2011/07/18/rupert-murdoch-scandal-threatens-prime-minister-cameron-s-government.html

News Corporation. (2011, September 20). *New York Times*. Retrieved October 5, 2011 from: http://topics.nytimes.com/top/news/business/companies/news_corporation/index.html

While television networks have historically been identified with specific nations—for example, CBC with Canada and BBC with Britain—globalization has recently sparked and sustained transnational television networks. Many media corpora-tions with significant financial backing are moving in this direction. Though initial attempts at transnational broadcasting in the early 1980s to mid-1990s faced many difficulties and most did not survive (Chalaby, 2003), today, transnational television networks are growing, and some of these include U.S.-based networks such as CNN International and MTV. Some are European-based, such as BBC World, Euronews, and Skynews. More studies need to be done to determine how this global flow of information and entertainment may be influencing societies.

In China, another kind of change has been occurring in the mass media system, related in part to globalization. As the Chinese economy has moved toward a capitalist or free-enterprise model, the state-owned mass media system has experienced changes, including the "rise of semi-independent newspapers and broadcasting stations, the proliferation of private Internet content providers and unlicensed cable networks, and increasing cross-investment by the media into other commercial enterprises, including joint ventures with international media giants" (Akhavan-Majid, 2004, p. 553). In her study of these new Chinese media, Akhavan-Majid argues that "non-state actors (e.g., citizens, journalists, entrepreneurs)" (2004, p. 554) have used loopholes in official Chinese policies to creatively open new media opportunities. As you can see, changes in political and economic structures can be intimately intertwined with changes in mass media.

Political economists also analyze the mergers and acquisitions that occur in the media industry as a way of understanding changes in programming. For example, when NBC acquired the Bravo channel (2001), it added performing arts and arts films to its roster as well as some riskier programs, including *Boy Meets Boy* (2003) and *Queer Eye for the Straight Guy* (2003–2007) (and *Girl* (2008)). In a news release related to this sale, Bob Wright, Vice Chairman of General Electric and Chairman and CEO of NBC, noted that "Bravo, with its desirable demographic, is a perfect strategic addition to our portfolio, providing a particularly good fit with NBC's network and cable viewers" (Cablevision, 2000). In analyzing these developments, a political economist might focus on the economic reasons behind this acquisition and the potential future revenues to be generated by appealing to this desirable demographic group. (*Desirable* typically refers to an audience with the size and demographic profile to bring in high advertising revenues.) As Bravo continues to search for desirable audiences, the network has moved to new television programming, including *Top Chef, Flipping Out, Million Dollar Decorators, Millionaire Matchmaker,* and *The Real Housewives of New Jersey.*

Of course, political economists cannot predict the kinds of media texts that will emerge from any specific merger. They know that television stations seek viewers who are more affluent so they can attract more advertisers, but political economists do not know (nor does anyone) what kinds of shows will attract affluent viewers. While television production companies try to create—and television networks try to buy—television programs that will draw large audiences, they do not always succeed. Political economists cannot and do not predict such successes, either. Instead, they focus on the ways that corporate media influence the information we get, the consequences of capitalist media corporations on society, and the demands that this political and economic structure places on journalists, broadcasters, and other media workers.

In the context of the 2003 Federation Communications Commission's decision to relax restrictions on ownership of media, understanding and unraveling the complex relationships among media economics, media ownership, and media content can be crucial. For example, because news is sold for profit, the profit motive shapes what readers consider "news." This commercial pressure influences the work of journalists as well as the way media organizations are run. One leading scholar in this area, Robert McChesney (1998), raised this alarm more than a decade ago:

The American media system is spinning out of control in a hyper-commercialized frenzy. Fewer than ten transnational media conglomerates dominate much of our media; fewer than two dozen account for the overwhelming majority of our newspapers, magazines, films, television, radio, and books. With every aspect of our media culture now fair game for commercial exploitation, we can look forward to the full-scale commercialization of sports, arts, and education, the disappearance of notions of public service from public discourse, and the degeneration of journalism, political coverage, and children's programming under commercial pressure. (p. 4)

By focusing on the political and economic structures in which media industries operate, political economists offer a unique perspective on the influence of media in our lives. Their analysis of areas that many people ignore reveals the potential consequences of the business of media on all of us.

Societal issues very much influence individuals' interactions with media. Moreover, both personal and social identities are key to one's interactions with media and how one interprets media violence. Given the profits to be made, media economics ensures that media violence will remain pervasive as long as people continue to purchase products with violent content.

TEST YOUR KNOWLEDGE

- How do media events reaffirm values and social identities?
- What role does the media play in how we understand the world?
- How do media events invite particular ways of viewing the world?
- What are common concerns about media violence, and how are these concerns being addressed?
- How are media influenced by the political and economic systems that they operate within?

ETHICS AND MASS MEDIA

Because media messages are so powerful, they can generate powerful responses. One potential response is **media activism,** or the practice of organizing to communicate displeasure with certain media images and messages, as well as to advocate for change in future media texts. The issues that media activists address are important because they highlight many significant ethical questions surrounding mediated communication. Media activism, of course, is not limited to the United States. Media activist groups have mobilized around the world to express ethical concerns about media coverage on a range of issues.

Voicing ethical concerns through media activism is not a recent phenomenon. People have been concerned about media content and images for centuries. The notions of freedom of speech and freedom of the press articulated in the U.S. Constitution reflect one response to media control. In the early twentieth century, as silent movies became popular entertainment, concerns about their racy content and the transition to talking movies led to calls for government regulation of media. In an attempt to avoid government regulation, Hollywood established the Hays Office to create its own system of regulation. The **Hays Code,** which was published in 1930, established strict rules for media content with the goal of wholesome entertainment (see *Did You Know? The Hays Code*). Some of the Hays regulations still apply today, such as the ban on exposing children's sex organs. Other regulations, however, have become outdated, such as the ban against portraying sexual relationships between interracial couples or using vulgar expressions or profanity, which the code specified as including the words "God, Lord, Jesus, Christ (unless used reverently); cripes; fairy (in a vulgar sense)."

The Hays code came about because of media activism in the 1920s, and it continued to set industry standards until the late 1960s, when the **MPAA** (Motion Picture Association of America) devised its rating codes. These codes have changed slightly since then, but most people are familiar with the G, PG, PG-13, R, and

media activism
the practice of organizing to communicate displeasure with certain media images and messages, as well as to force change in future media texts

Hays Code
self-imposed rules for Hollywood media content instituted in 1930 with the goal of creating "wholesome entertainment"

MPAA
Motion Picture Association of America

Did You Know?

The Hays Code

What kinds of restrictions do you believe are appropriate in mass media? Which of the Hays Code rules seem valid today? Should the media industry and/or government regulate the kinds of media messages that are available? Explain the reasons behind your answers.

All of the following regulations are taken from the Hays Code.

- Dances which emphasize indecent movements are to be regarded as obscene.
- Complete nudity is never permitted. This includes nudity in fact or in silhouette or licentious notice thereof by other characters in the picture.
- The use of the Flag shall be consistently respectful.
- No film or episode may throw ridicule on any religious faith.
- Adultery and Illicit Sex, sometimes necessary plot material, must not be explicitly treated, or justified, or presented attractively.
- Illegal drug traffic, and drug addiction, must never be presented.
- White slavery shall not be treated.

EXCERPTED FROM: Motion Picture Association of America, Inc. (1930–1955). *A Code to Govern the Making of Motion Pictures.*

NC-17 ratings. Today, media activism has concentrated largely on the ethics of four areas: children's programming, representations of cultural groups, news reporting, and alternative programming. Let's look at each of these in turn.

Complaints about content in television shows and its influence on children led to the creation of the **TV Parental Guidelines** (by the TV Parental Guidelines Monitoring Board), which are a self-regulating system of the television industry. These guidelines rate programs in terms of appropriateness for particular age groups. You have probably noticed the rating codes in the upper-left corner of the television screen. (An explanation of the ratings is available at www.tvguidelines. org/ratings.htm.) This kind of rating system is voluntary, so unless an adult activates the V-chip or an adult is present to change the channel or turn off the television, the rating system may not work as it was intended.

The second ethical focus of media activists has been distortions perpetrated or reinforced by media. The concern here is that such portrayals create stereotypes and misunderstandings. Minority groups, in particular, have had such concerns, as we can see in the number of media activist groups focused on media representations of racial and sexual minorities.

These activists argue that when people have limited contact with minority groups, they are likely to gain false impressions from media misrepresentations. In turn, these distorted images may lead to hate crimes or discriminatory government policies, such as racial profiling. Media activist groups that monitor media producers and challenge them to create responsible and accurate images include MANAA (Media Action Network for Asian Americans) and GLAAD (Gay and Lesbian Alliance Against Defamation) as well as organizations that have broader goals but that include a media activist focus, such as the National Organization for Women (NOW) and the League of United Latin American Citizens (LULAC).

TV Parental Guidelines
a self-regulating system of the television industry that rates programs in terms of appropriateness for particular age groups

The GLAAD Media Awards is an annual event that honors responsible and accurate media images of lesbians, gays, transgendered individuals, and bisexuals.

A third category of activist groups has focused on structural issues in media industries and the consequences for consumers. For example, organizations like FAIR (Fairness and Accuracy in Reporting, www.fair.org), the Annenberg Public Policy Center's factcheck.org, the Arthur W. Page Center for Integrity in Public Communication (thepagecenter.comm.psu.edu) and the National Public Radio program On the Media (www.onthemedia.org) are some of the organizations that focus on the news media and their accuracy and fairness in reporting various issues and the inclusion of diverse viewpoints.

The fourth ethical focus of media activists has been to find and provide media texts that offer alternatives to mainstream sources. For example, Clean Flicks was created by and for those who are concerned that movies have too much violence and sex. Clean Flicks offered alternatives that were free of profanity, graphic violence, nudity, and sexual content until they lost a court battle in 2006 and were prohibited from editing films. Many newspapers, radio programs, and Internet sites are available for those who want alternatives to mainstream news media coverage so that they can hear a diversity of voices and opinions. Earlier we discussed the alternative press, but there is also alternative radio programming, such as the Progressive Radio Network, and other alternative media outlets, such as Amy Goodman and Juan Gonzalez's daily television program *Democracy Now!* Other alternative views are expressed as humor in print, online in *The Onion*, and on television on *The Daily Show* and *The Colbert Report.*

Finally, some activists use media to communicate specific ethical concerns and messages to a wide audience. Thus, despite the fact that they lack the backing of huge media conglomerates, activists have used media to educate or influence audiences regarding cruelty to animals; the situations in Palestine, Guantánamo, and Afghanistan; violence against women; anti-Semitism; genocide; racism; and more. To get their messages out, these groups set up Web sites and Web casts, solicit funds to run advertisements on television or in mainstream newspapers or magazines, and sometimes organize demonstrations at strategic times and places.

As new media outlets develop (for example via the Internet, cable TV, and satellite radio) and the world continues to confront new challenges, new ethical issues and new ways of communicating will continue to emerge. We cannot forecast the future, but we do know that the ongoing process of change in the media environment shows no signs of abating. Media activists will continue to try to shape the media messages we receive, while at the same time, media producers will continue to try to sell what people are interested in purchasing. And so, bombarded as you are by media and the messages of a range of media activists, how can you become a responsible media consumer? Let's explore this topic next.

BECOMING A MORE EFFECTIVE MEDIA CONSUMER

As a potential consumer of practically nonstop messages coming from radio, television, newspapers, magazines, advertisements, movies, and so on, you need strategies for dealing with this complex media environment. The solution cannot be boiled down to a set of simple guidelines, of course, but here are some ideas to consider when interacting with media. To become more effective in your media consumption, be an active agent in your media choices, be mindful of the media choices you make, and speak out if you find media content offensive.

Be an Active Agent

How can you become an active consumer of media? First, don't just watch or read whatever is available. Make deliberate choices about media you expose yourself to so that you can better control the effect that media messages have on you. As you become more selective, you express a set of media-related values, which in turn indicates to media providers what type of media programming they should be providing.

As an active agent, then, seek out those media that meet your needs and avoid or resist others. In order to be a truly active agent, however, you have to think about the basis for your media choices. Are you avoiding some media messages simply because they challenge your beliefs? If so, this probably is not the best way to navigate through the media environment. Sometimes, you can benefit from being open-minded about the views and perspectives of others.

Broaden Your Media Horizons

People often live within the confines of a particular media environment and, like a fish in water, can't see the limits. With the vast possibilities now available via the Internet, in libraries, and through other media outlets, you have access to practically the whole world. Even if your only language is English, you have many media options available to you.

As an active media consumer, you can talk back to your television as well as discuss media messages with family and friends.

As you work to broaden your horizons, obtain a range of views on world events. Try to understand why other people view the world the way they do, no matter how different their views are from your own. Try to understand the rising anti-Americanism coming from around the world. You may disagree with what you hear, or even find it offensive, but by seeing the complexity of issues involved you can gain a better understanding of the world we live in.

Overall, being a responsible and effective consumer of media is not easy. It certainly extends far beyond lounging around watching whatever is on television. Becoming an active partner in this complex communication process is a challenge, one we hope you will take up.

How can media consumers find a range of media outlets from which to get news and information? How would you define an adequate and well-balanced "diet" of media consumption?

Talk Back

You can benefit from talking back or challenging the messages you receive via news commentators, politicians, reporters, or even characters in television programs. In other words, if you hear something you disagree with or that sounds wrong, point this out, even if only to yourself. For example, suppose you hear a reporter covering a natural disaster refer to "innocent victims." What, you might ask yourself, is a "guilty victim" in the context of an earthquake, or in any context for that matter? Questioning and noticing these kinds of empty phrases makes you a more active consumer of media. As you watch or listen, you might also consider why one news story is given more time than another one, or why a particular story is reported at all, and what that prioritizing and selection communicates about what is and isn't valued.

Talking back also includes being attentive to the ethical implications of media to which you are exposed, particularly if it promotes some social identities at the expense of others. More specifically, be aware of the ways that, for example, women and racial minorities, sexual minorities, and religious minorities are portrayed and what influences these images may have on the groups depicted. If you watch movies that mock particular cultural or religious groups, that denigrate women, or that misrepresent the experiences of certain individuals, consider the implications. You not only ratify this depiction by your attendance, but you also encourage the production of more of this type of media with your dollars.

Talking back, however, can involve much more than talking to the images that come to you in media or making choices about which images to support or resist. If you find something particularly objectionable, you can contact the television station, magazine, or newspaper that has offended you. For example, if you believe that specific programs manipulate or attempt to unfairly influence children, use the "contact us" information on the station's Web site to let the producers of those programs, and the companies that advertise in that medium, know exactly how you feel. Or you can complain to the Federal Communications Commission, the federal agency that regulates radio, television, wire, cable, and satellite. On the other hand, if you believe specific media have a positive influence and should be more widely produced or distributed, let advertisers and media companies know that as well. Certainly, praising a job well done is as important a form of talking back as raising objections.

In general, few consumers are sufficiently deliberate about the media messages they select. But because media messages have such a powerful impact on consumers, and because you can have some influence on the availability of specific types of media, you benefit society when you become an active and critical media consumer.

TEST YOUR KNOWLEDGE

- How do media activists respond to media messages they find objectionable?
- What are some concerns that contemporary media activists have raised?

SUMMARY

Media, in all their variety, play a powerful role in our lives. The entertainment and information they provide influence how we see ourselves and the world around us. We refer to the messages that come to us via media as *mediated communication* because they are mediated, or transmitted, through a channel, such as television, film, radio, or print. Mass media communication refers to communication that is directed at a mass audience. Individuals choose what types of media texts to watch, read, listen to, purchase, or avoid.

Media scholars are interested in how we make these decisions, and marketers and media producers also want to know how they might predict and characterize our choices: how we choose what to consume and how we resist the rest. Complicating our individual choices, however, are social forces that shape the media options that are available.

Media play a number of important roles in our lives as individuals as well as in our society: confirming our social identities, helping us understand the world, and helping us understand important public events. In addition, media shape the images of real and imagined violence and wield enormous economic influence.

Media activism—the practice of organizing to communicate displeasure with certain media images and messages—is one way that people express their ethical views and respond to objectionable media messages and powerful media corporations. Today, media activism has concentrated largely in four areas: children's programming, representations of cultural groups, news reporting, and alternative programming.

Finally, consumers of media can and should become more aware of their own media consumption habits. Guidelines for improving media consumption skills include being active in making media choices, broadening media horizons, and speaking out when media content is offensive.

HUMAN COMMUNICATION IN SOCIETY ONLINE

To review this chapter, use the MyCommunicationLab Web site to test your understanding of the following key terms, record your answers to the chapter review questions, and complete the suggested activities. Expand your learning and understanding of chapter concepts by completing additional activities and exercises online. Access code required. Go to www.mycommunicationlab.com for more information or to purchase standalone access.

KEY TERMS

media 351
mass media 351
culture industries 351
mass-market paperbacks 352
e-books 352
active agents 353
mass media effects 354
media text 355

selective exposure 355
uses and gratifications 357
content analysis 361
agenda-setting
    capacity 365
cultivation theory 365
hegemony 366
media event 367

media violence 368
V-chip 368
political economy 369
media activism 372
Hays Code 372
MPAA 372
TV Parental
    Guidelines 373

APPLY WHAT YOU KNOW

1. Research a popular media text—for example, a magazine, television show, or newspaper—that targets an identity group different from your own. What elements do you find in this text that differ from a text targeted at one of your identity groups?

2. Select and study a media event such as the Super Bowl, Miss America Pageant, or a famous murder trial, and identify the rituals that surround this event. How does the media event affirm U.S. cultural values?

3. Select a media activist group to study. Go to their Web page and identify their concerns about media. What strategies do they use to promote their messages? Who is their audience? How do they plan to change media in the ways that concern them?

4. Pick a major media event (whether a ritual event or a natural disaster) and compare how it was covered by several different media outlets. Look at news coverage overseas as well to help you compare the differences and similarities.

14
Communication and New Technologies

chapter outline

Since I got a smartphone, I've been discovering all the tons of cool things you can do with it, like the app for scanning barcodes to comparison shop and the Angry Birds game app, but I still mostly use it for text messaging and occasionally to check Facebook. Most of my friends and I use texting throughout the day to make plans or to talk about things like what happened at Jason's graduation party. I even get texts from my mom sometimes—she's just learning! Texting is more convenient than making phone calls because it doesn't stop you from doing other things. I can be at home, watching a movie with my friends, and respond to a text from someone without having to get up, pause the movie, and make everyone wait for my phone call to end. Texting just feels less invasive. I love it!

The way our student Claudia uses her mobile phone illustrates a number of issues we will address in this chapter. For example, how do people use technology to communicate in different contexts and with different people? How has the pervasiveness of technology impacted our identities and the way we communicate with others? And how does the potential constant "connectivity" to others affect our interpersonal relationships?

In the previous chapter we focused on mass media—one-way mediated communication produced by large industries intended for a large audience, like television, radio, and films. In this chapter we focus on **new media**, or mediated communication, which is more interactive and focused on interpersonal communication and which relies on more recent technologies like the Internet and mobile phones. First, we describe how new media play an increasingly important role in our lives and define what we mean by new media. Then we examine individuals' use of new media, including the identity issues and impacts on personal and work relationships. We then shift the focus to societal forces—examining how gender, race/ethnicity, and socioeconomic class impact new media use and who does (and does not) have access to new communication technologies. Finally, we discuss ethical issues related to new media use and conclude with suggestions for improving your own skills in using new communication technologies.

Once you have read this chapter, you will be able to:

- Identify and describe new media.
- Identify reasons for learning about new media.
- Explain differences between face-to-face and digitally mediated communication.

- Recognize issues that can arise in identity and relationship development when using new media.
- Understand the role of power and privilege in new media use.
- Describe the digital divide and other ethical challenges involving new media use.
- Discuss ways to improve your own mediated communication skills.

THE IMPORTANCE OF NEW MEDIA

New media are a constant reality in our lives and affect our daily activities in multiple ways. This pervasiveness provides the first and primary reason for learning more about this topic. A second reason is that understanding new media and having good media skills will help you be more successful personally and professionally.

First, we say that new media are pervasive because most of us now interact with these new communication technologies almost constantly. A recent study showed that children ages 8 to 18 spend almost 8 hours daily (every waking minute except for time in school) on some electronic communication device (smartphone, computer, television, and so on) (Rideout, Foehr, & Roberts, 2010). Similarly, another study showed that new media play a particularly important role in the lives of young people—especially college students. You are more likely to use the Internet and own more tech devices than any other population group (Smith, Rainie, & Zickuhr, 2011). In any one day, you probably use your computer or smartphone to communicate with friends and family via text messages, Twitter, and Facebook (as our student Claudia does). You may also communicate with a professor through email and post messages to other students in an online course discussion. And perhaps you also check up on breaking news on your favorite news Web site and perhaps play some computer games or download music.

Experts say that we now use new communication technologies for four specific purposes: 1) connecting with others, 2) searching for and exchanging information, 3) entertainment, and 4) financial transactions (Zickuhr, 2010). Let's look more closely at the many ways in which these technologies affect our daily activities.

The first and perhaps the most important impact of new media, particularly for young people, is the opportunities they provide for developing and maintaining relationships. A recent survey revealed that, indeed, the primary Internet activity (94 percent of Internet users) is sending and receiving messages (Zickuhr, 2010). Email is used much less by teens (ages 12 to 17) and young adults (ages 18 to 33) than other generations; like our student Claudia, they prefer to send text messages on their phone or keep in touch through social networking sites (SNSs) (Bennhold, 2011). Through SNSs, email, IM, and tweets we can stay in touch with old friends, maintain almost constant contact with current friends, and find new friends. By some accounts, people spend more time on SNSs than any other online activity (Hampton, Goulet, Rainie, & Purcell, 2011; Zickuhr, 2010). Throughout this chapter, we will examine how this pervasive connectivity affects our sense of identity as well as our romantic, work, and acquaintance relationships.

In terms of using new media for seeking information, the most frequently searched topics are health information, product information, and religious information (Zickuhr, 2010), Many people also follow news on commercial websites or **blogs** (short for weblogs). About 152 million blogs now exist worldwide ("Internet in numbers: 2010"). Blogging activity increased exponentially after 1999 partly because mainstream media increasingly recognized blog content as legitimate news sources and because blogging software, especially connected to Twitter, allows users the ability to update rapidly and easily—seen most dramatically in the coverage of the election protests in Iran (Sussman, 2009) and the 2011 uprisings in the

new media
a collection of mediated communication technologies that are digital and converging and tend to be interactive

blogs
short for weblogs; online diaries or news commentaries

Middle East during the "Arab Spring" (Griffin, 2011). In addition to major news blogs (e.g., *Huffington Post*), there are personal blogs in which people document their everyday activities and express their opinions, thoughts, feelings, and religious beliefs (Cheong, Halavais, & Kwon, 2008; Cheong & Poon, 2009). However, formal blogging seems to have peaked in 2010, probably because people are now doing blog-like things (posting jokes and links, reporting daily activities, expressing political opinions) in other new media spaces: social networking sites like Facebook and micro-blogging sites like Twitter (Zickuhr, 2010). Twitter is especially popular as it allows us to "follow" people we don't know and is being used by millions to disseminate marketing, political, news, and personal information as part of the larger web of social media. It has grown exponentially; five years since its invention, people are now sending 350 billion tweets a day! (Olivarez-Giles, 2011).

One of the most common information-gathering uses of new media for college students, however, is doing course research. Colleges and universities provide streaming audio or **podcasts** of various lecture series and important speakers on campus, and some textbooks come with audio summaries of chapters. In a 2010 study, 21 percent of all Internet users said they had downloaded a podcast to listen to or view at a later time (Zickuhr, 2010). Newspapers and magazines like *The Wall Street Journal* and *The Economist* and radio and TV networks like National Public Radio and Public Broadcasting Service offer daily podcasts of their publications and shows.

podcast
audio file stored digitally

New media forms are marrying the search function with connect opportunities. Through the Facebook service Connect, Facebook users have automatic access to information about their friends' activities. HuffPo Social News users can see what their friends have been reading and comment on it, Netflix users can see what films their friends have been watching, and Twitscoop allows people to see what topics their friends are talking about at the moment ("Global swap shops," 2010).

Some experts worry about our overreliance on the Internet for information; they say that we only "skim" on the Internet and don't make an effort to remember the information we find because it's always at our fingertips. As a result, they speculate, we are becoming less able to concentrate and recall information (Bennhold, 2011; Carr, 2008). The importance of Internet search activities in our lives may be seen in the fact that "Google" has become a verb. If we need a piece of information, we Google it.

The third most common new media activity is entertainment—for example, watching and downloading videos, playing video games, and downloading music. A recent and fast-growing form of entertainment available through new media is downloading and reading books and periodicals using e-readers like Kindle or tablet computers like iPads. As of 2011, the number of e-readers sold was doubling every six months (Purcell, 2011). The final common new media use is centered around financial transactions, including shopping, paying bills, and managing bank accounts and investment stock portfolios. These activities, once dominated by Generation X (ages 33 to 44), are now increasingly common across generations, although there are still significant differences between the youngest and oldest cohorts (Zickuhr, 2010).

Now that we've discussed the pervasiveness of new media in our lives, let's examine the second reason for studying about new media: the fact that an understanding of new media and good technological skills can help ensure personal and professional success. As we'll see later in the chapter, understanding the sometimes complex role that new media play in interpersonal relationships and employee–employer relationships is essential. Interpersonally, knowing about the specific characteristics of various new media and their effects on relationships is crucial. Understanding organizational rules and practices involving new media, including surveillance, privacy concerns, and "netiquette" (Wang & Kobsa, 2009), will serve you well. There are frequent news stories about employees who lost their jobs or were penalized due to not understanding the informal or formal rules about new media behavior in the workplace. It's easy to see that many everyday activities and transactions that used to be conducted face to face are now being carried out in cyberspace using new communication technologies. Before looking at how these media forms affect our everyday communication, our identity, and our relationships, let's discuss what we mean by the term "new media."

TEST YOUR KNOWLEDGE

* What are two major reasons for learning about new media?
* Why is it important to have communication technology skills in professional contexts?

WHAT ARE NEW MEDIA?

We define new media as a collection of mediated communication technologies that are digital and converging and tend to be interactive. Let's unpack this definition a little further and distinguish new media from mass media—the topic covered in Chapter 13. In contrast to face-to-face (FtF) communication, both mass media and new media are mediated forms of communication, meaning that the messages are carried through an *intervening* system of **digital** electronic storage before being transmitted between two or more people. Many of these messages are mediated through computers—termed **computer-mediated communication (CMC)**, sometimes used interchangeably with the term new media.

In contrast to mass media where messages are generally one-to-many, new media messages converge, meaning that they can be sent one-to-one, one-to-many, or many-to-many (think of email, Twitter, and Facebook) (Crosbie, 2002). Also in contrast to mass media, new media messages are generally interactive, meaning that communication goes both ways and permits individuals to connect and collaborate with others (e.g., in virtual teams) and even create new content (e.g., in wikis and cloud computing). However, it is easy to see how these distinctions between mass and new media are becoming increasingly blurred. For example, some mass media forms like television reality shows can be viewed on computers and allow for audience reaction and participation. And some new media, like podcasts, may not involve interaction. For the purposes of this chapter, we focus on the interactive elements of new media, where the "real give and take of social life" in **cyberspace** occurs (Walther & Parks, 2002, p. 3).

What are some specific examples of new media? Most new media are Internet- and Web-based. As you probably know, the **Internet** is a system of networks that connects millions of computers around the world, and the **World Wide Web (WWW)** is a system of interlinked hypertext documents contained on the Internet. Using a browser on your computer or smartphone, the WWW allows you view pages containing text, images, videos, and other multimedia and to navigate between them using hyperlinks. New media encompass a wide range of communication possibilities, from personal and commercial web pages to the more interactive email, text messages, tweets, **Social Networking Sites (SNSs)**, chats, and **MMOGs (Massively Multiplayer Online Games)**, all accessed on a variety of devices, from desktop and laptop computers, Personal Digital Assistants (PDAs), smartphones, and other mobile devices (see Table 14.1).

How does this mobility and constant connection with others through new media affect our communication choices? Before addressing this question, we need to understand how various communication technologies differ from face-to-face communication—the topic we turn to next.

TEST YOUR KNOWLEDGE

* What is the definition of new media?
* What is the difference between mass media and new media?

Text messages and instant messages are increasingly popular ways to communicate in the United States, particularly for adolescents and college students.

digital
information that is transmitted in a numerical format based on only two values (0 and 1)

computer-mediated communication (CMC)
the exchange of messages carried through an intervening system of digital electronic storage and transmitted between two or more people

cyberspace
the online world; often used synonymously with the Internet

Internet
a system of networks that connects millions of computers around the world

World Wide Web (WWW)
a system of interlinked hypertext documents contained on the Internet

Social Networking Sites (SNSs)
web-based service where people construct their profiles, identify others with whom they share a connection, and interact with others within the system

Massively Multiplayer Online Games (MMOGs)
text-based "virtual reality" games in which participants interact with enrichments, objects, and other participants

TABLE 14.1 New Communication Technologies

Email	Exchange of textual (word-based) messages between two or more parties.
Bulletin Board Systems	A form of email that communicates to a larger audience. Messages are sent to a single computer address where they are "posted" for others to read and respond to.
Chat	A real-time online discussion. Text-based messages sent to and simultaneously read by one or more people.
Social Networking Site (SNS)	An online community where users create personal profiles; organizations create pages. Allows users to maintain contact with friends, strengthen existing social networks, find new friends, and expand networks.
Applications (or "apps")	Software designed to help people perform a particular activity or set of activities. Some can be used for different platforms (Microsoft Office); others have narrower requirements (apps specifically for iPhones or for Facebook).
Wall or Comments	The space on an SNS page where a user's friends can post comments.
Mobile Phone	A hand-held communication device that uses wireless technology to send voice communication or data across distances to other devices. Web-enabled mobile devices allow access to the Internet.
Multimedia Services (MMS)	Audio, video, or picture images sent from one mobile phone to another.
Short Message Service (SMS)	Text message (less than 160 characters) sent from one mobile phone to another.
Real Simple Syndication (RSS)	A Web feed or reader that automatically notifies subscribers of new content available on Web sites or pages.
Twitter	A social networking service that allows people to share brief (140 characters or less) updates on their location, activities, thoughts, and so forth, with *followers*. Also referred to as microblogging.
Blog	A type of Web page where a person makes (or posts) regular entries (e.g., text, photos, videos) similar to an online journal. Readers can comment on posts.
Podcast	An audio or video file that is distributed over the Internet. The file can be accessed on a computer or an MP3 player.
Massively Multiplayer Online Game (MMOG)	Text-based virtual reality game. Real-time interaction. Participants interact with environment, objects, and other participants.

SOURCE: Thackaray, R., & Hunter, M. (2010). Empowering youth: Use of technology in advocacy to affect social change. *Journal of Computer-Mediated Communication, 15*, 577.

HOW DOES NEW MEDIA USE AFFECT OUR COMMUNICATION CHOICES?

Because new media are relatively recent and rapidly changing forms of communication, it is difficult to arrive at definitive conclusions about their exact role in everyday life. Researching these forms of communication can be like trying to hit a moving target. Still, with a basic understanding of what new media are, and some of the ways they can differ from face-to-face communication, we can get some sense of their increasingly important role.

To begin, consider this question: Have you ever tried to decide whether to communicate a message by a text message, by a phone call, or in person? Perhaps you had a difficult issue to discuss and were unsure what the most effective mode of communication would be. If so, you had good reason to feel unsure. Some forms of new media differ in important ways from face-to-face communication, and these differences can affect the outcome of your conversation.

When it comes to determining whether FtF communication is more useful than CMC (or vice versa), even scholars disagree. Early researchers proposed the

media deficit approach
a theoretical perspective that sees mediated communication as less useful than face-to-face communication

media augmentation approach
a theoretical perspective that sees views mediated communication as complementing or augmenting face-to-face communication

filtering
removing nonverbal cues

social presence
degree of psychological closeness or immediacy engendered by various media

social presence theory
suggests that face-to-face communication is generally high in this kind of social presence, and that media vary in the amount of social presence they convey

media richness theory
theory that describes the potential information-carrying capacity of a communication medium

media deficit approach, which suggests that mediated communication is often less useful than face to face communication. More recently, however, many communication scholars now emphasize the **media augmentation approach**, which suggests that mediated communication can play a complementing or augmenting role in our face-to-face communication. We'll consider each of these approaches.

Media Deficit Approach

The media deficit approach is based on two characteristics of early person-to-person mediated communication. First, some forms of new communication technologies are "filtered"—which means they lack the capability of carrying nonverbal cues. Second, some are also asynchronous in nature—which means a delay may occur between the time the message is sent and when it is responded to.

Filtered Communication   As we discussed in Chapter 6, nonverbal cues play an important role in understanding the totality of a person's message. When we speak face to face, we see the other person's gestures, facial expressions, and attire, we hear their sighs, accent, or dialect—these are just a few of the many cues we use to fully understand what a person means. Most new media, however—like text messages and tweets—are "cues-filtered-out" forms of communication. So when we communicate using these forms, because of **filtering** we are no longer able to consider all of those valuable cues that help us to determine what is being communicated.

Two "deficit" theories help us understand the impact of filtering on some forms of new media: social presence theory and media richness theory. **Social presence** refers to the feelings of psychological closeness or immediacy that people experience when they interact with each other (Short, Williams, & Christie, 1976). This closeness is communicated through nonverbal cues, like smiling, leaning forward, and relaxed body posture. **Social presence theory** suggests that face-to-face communication is generally high in this kind of social presence, and that media vary in the amount of social presence they convey. For example, talking on the telephone conveys less social presence than face-to-face interaction, but more than email communication—where all nonverbal cues are filtered out. The implication is that media low in social presence (like texting, emailing, and tweets) seem more impersonal, less sensitive, and less "relationship-focused."

Media richness theory describes the potential information-carrying capacity of a communication medium (Daft & Lengel, 1984, 1986). According to this theory, face-to-face communication is the richest medium for communicating—because you can see facial expressions and body gestures as well as hear the tone, speed, and quality of a person's voice. All these factors relay a tremendous amount of information and allow you to interpret and respond to messages more accurately. You not only hear the words, or the content of the message, but you also receive the relational messages that are being sent nonverbally and that reveal how that person feels about you. If the other person is smiling, leaning toward you, and maintaining eye contact, you probably infer that the person is happy or glad to talk with you. If the person is scowling and avoiding eye contact, you might infer that she or he is angry or unhappy with you.

According to media richness theory, some types of mediated communication do allow for a certain amount of richness. Consider video/audio communication, or Skype, an Internet-based video chat service. When you communicate using a webcam, you might miss some immediate context cues, such as body posture or gestures, but you have the benefit of seeing some of the nonverbal behaviors of the person you're communicating with. The telephone is a less rich medium. Conversation partners can process the audio information and discern some paralinguistic cues, but they don't see facial expression, eye gaze, or gestures.

Think of a recent conflict you had and describe how it might have been different if the communication media had been different. How might it have gone over the telephone? Face-to-face? Text messaging?

Media Richness Theory

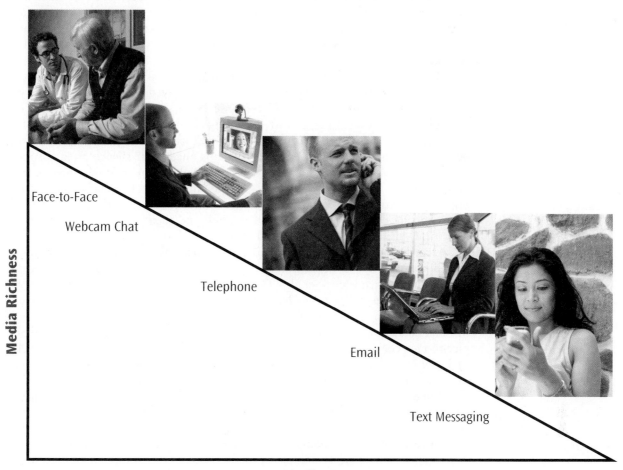

The least-rich media, according to media richness theory, are text-based messages—email, text messaging, and tweets (Timmerman & Madhavapeddi, 2008). But nonverbal cues aren't completely absent here, either. Some relational/nonverbal information *can* be communicated in these text-based media. For example, some people convey relational information by **emoticons**, or pictographs, such as the smiley face—: -)—or they use abbreviations like LOL (laughing out loud) or H&K (hugs and kisses). Messages can also be made "richer" in some technologies by altering the font color, using animation or icons (Sheer, 2011).

Of course, writing (including writing emails and text messages) is a form of communication that includes many techniques for expressing mood and feelings. For example, moods can be expressed by punctuation, by the length of sentences, and by numbers of adjectives or adverbs. Writers can also communicate intonation by emphasizing particular words in a sentence or by repetition.

emoticons
pictographs used to convey relational information in computer-mediated communication, such as the smiley face :-)

synchronous
communication in which messages are
sent and received at the same time

asynchronous
communication in which messages are
sent and received at different times

Asynchronous Interaction Another difference between face-to-face and some new media forms is the degree to which the exchange of messages is synchronous or asynchronous. Face-to-face communication and media like the telephone and online chats are **synchronous**; that is, messages are sent and received at the same time. However, email, online discussion messages, and video recordings are **asynchronous**; that is, messages may be received at a later time. Text messaging may be synchronous or not, depending on how quickly the other person acknowledges and/or responds to the message.

When you send a mediated message through an asynchronous medium, it is almost impossible to know if the other person has received your message—since you don't receive any "in the moment" response. Such silences or non-responses can be problematic. A challenge in text messaging is when to respond. In face-to-face interaction, silences can be meaningful and are usually interpreted by nonverbal cues to mean hesitation, reflection, or perhaps anger. But silence after posting a new Facebook status or sending a text message might mean anything, ranging from lack of interest to a technology glitch. Yet, the implications for relationships can be important (Pettigrew, 2010). One high school student describes the anxiety he feels when posting new music choices on Facebook and then anxiously waiting to see how (or if) his friends react (Bennhold, 2011).

According to media deficit theorists, asynchronicity may also create a lack of shared reality. That is, asynchronicity may impact personal relationships because the notion of friendship includes shared experiences, feelings, and activities. So, when you receive terrific news that you want to share with your best friend, telling him or her through an email message or delayed text message (if your friend does not immediately respond to your message) does not have the same impact that a face-to-face conversation would. See *Communication in Society: Love in the Age of Social Networking* to read how constant texting and lack of face-to-face contact may make relationships seem more distant and more complicated.

While there are few clear differences between FtF and CMC when it comes to social presence and media richness, deficit theorists emphasize the deficiencies of some communication technologies—that is, their lack of social presence and information-carrying richness compared with face-to-face communication. How do the characteristics of filtering and asynchronicity affect new media communication in everyday life? These are important questions and we'll explore them in the following sections, seeing that the answer depends on context and personal preferences and sometimes works well for some people and contexts and not for others.

Media Augmentation Approach

Most current new media experts emphasize the media augmentation approach, which suggests that mediated communication complements or augments face-to-face encounters. For example having prior information about a person can be helpful when you are interpreting their mediated relational messages. In this way, email and text messages are rendered less "lean." For example, suppose you and a classmate have been texting each other about a recent assignment:

Your Classmate: I bombed that last assignment. Most of the class did too. Maybe he'll grade on a curve. How'd u do?

You: Did okay. B+, i think.

Your Classmate: That's just great 4 u.

Interpreting the phrase "That's just great 4 u" is easier if you know something about the way your classmate usually communicates. Otherwise, her text response could mean anything from supportive of you ("That's just *great* for you!") to hostile that you succeeded when the rest of the class didn't—potentially ruining the

COMMUNICATION IN SOCIETY
Love in the Age of Social Networking

Have you ever gotten into an awkward situation with a romantic partner thanks to social networking? Do you think there are positive and negative ways to use social networking to build romantic relationships?

In a recent article, reporter Nicole Rosenleaf Ritter writes about the good and not-so-good sides of technology. According to Ritter, "When it comes to technology, young people and relationships, the interplay can perhaps best be summarized by a phrase familiar to Facebook users: 'It's complicated.'"

Ritter reports that most young people love the convenience of social networking sites like Facebook, MySpace, and Twitter and the ease of cell phone texting. They provide opportunities to make new friends, reconnect with old friends, and stay in constant contact with those we love.

However, according to the people Ritter interviewed, there are some downsides. Some young people say that all the technology use makes dating harder. That is, people are texting more than talking, and after all the texting, relationships seem more distant and less personal. Others mentioned "the speed of gossip" on social networking sites as a downside, explaining that there is no such thing as a private relationship or breakup on Facebook. When someone changes their "relationship status," it's there for everyone to see. According to one college counselor whom Ritter interviewed, while the constant contact gives young people an important sense of belonging, something might be lost in all the texting and new media use: human contact. "I think that some people are bypassing face-to-face bonding and missing the clues that they would get from sitting down with someone," he said. "There are no inflections and they are getting no feedback. That can cause misunderstandings."

All of this, Ritter concludes, points to just why teens and 20-somethings find technology and relationships "complicated." "While the technology is necessary and omnipresent, it can be difficult to navigate, especially when the rules still are being written."

SOURCE: Ritter, N. R. (2010, January 8). Love in the age of social networking too much text and not enough talk? *The Great Falls Tribune*. Retrieved July 25, 2011, from http://www.greatfallstribune.com/article/20090825/MT_HEALTH03/909090349/Love-age-social-networking

curve for everyone else ("That's just great for *you*.") —to sarcastic ("That's *just great* for *you*.") (Rooksby, 2002).

In addition, several media augmentation scholars point out that the asynchronicity of mediated messages can have also positive effects. For example, it can give people time to formulate a message, which can be very helpful for shy people and others as well (Baker & Oswald, 2010). In fact, in one study, young people explained that although there were often misunderstandings, they preferred mobile text messaging over other forms of communication partly because it gave them more time to ponder and think about what they were trying to express (Coyne, 2011). Asynchronicity, allowing the time to formulate thoughts into words, can also be very useful when communicating in a foreign language (Thompson & Ku, 2005).

Media scholars also point out that the reduced nonverbal cues can have a positive effect on communication, as these cues (e.g., appearance, accent) can sometimes trigger stereotypes. For example, viewing email or text messages, we may not be able to determine someone's race/gender/age/ability-disability and so are less likely to show prejudice or discrimination in online communication (Merryfield, 2003).

Further, according to media augmentation scholars, CMC and FtF communication are not necessarily two different realities. People simply use multiple media with varying degrees of social presence and media richness, in addition to face-to-face interaction, to fit their social needs and lifestyles (Boase, 2008; Sawhney, 2007). A recent study of Americans of all ages found that FtF contact "still trumps" all other means of communication—that is, people still spend more time in FtF communication than they do using cell phone, landline phone, text messaging, email and instant messaging, and visiting social networking sites (Hampton, Sessions, Her, & Rainie, 2009). Face-to-face conversations may be preferred in particular contexts. According to one study results, college students did not prefer email over FtF meetings with faculty members in advising sessions (Taylor, Jowi, Schreier & Bertelsen, 2011).

Media augmentation experts acknowledge that some skepticism about the impact of new communication technologies is understandable. Still, they caution, we should not assume that CMC is inferior to FtF communication.

Social Network Theory

Social network theory proposes that the patterns of connections among people affect their social behavior and communication. In short, the more that people are socially connected to each other, the more intensely they are likely to communicate using various media available to them. Indeed, one study found that people who had more frequent FtF social contacts also had more frequent online contacts—compared with those who had fewer FtF contacts (Bimie & Horvath, 2002). A more recent study found that the average user of a social networking site has more close friends and is half as likely to feel socially isolated as the average person; in addition, people who use mobile phones and instant messaging also have, on average, more friends (Hampton et al., 2011). At least one expert suggests that mobile phones can even restore the comfort and intimacy that was degraded by twentieth-century technologies, especially the television (Gergen, 2002).

These studies all come to similar conclusions—that is, new communication technologies do not weaken relationships, nor do they act as poor substitutes for FtF contact. Instead, individuals use various media to connect with different social networks (Boase, 2008). For example, people use mobile phones to stay in contact with people they already know well, and they use social media (Facebook, Twitter) to expand and maintain their social networks—getting to know people, reestablishing "dormant" relationships, and, more and more, using social networking sites to stay in touch with local friends (Hampton et al., 2011; Kim, Kim, Park, & Rice, 2007).

According to social network theory, the more that people are socially connected to each other, the more intensely they are likely to communicate using various media available to them.

Some media experts worry about the effects of all this constant connection, For example, one study found that many students, like Claudia in our opening vignette, preferred text messaging because it did not demand their total attention, thus allowing them to multitask (Coyne, 2011). Others are concerned not that people are too connected but that in the end, the problem is that we are "alone together" (see *Alternative View: Alone Together*).

While social presence and richness of various communication media (or lack thereof) are important, the differences between FtF and CMC are blurry, and the jury is still out on exactly how new media use affects our lives and relationships. What is clear is that they play an increasingly important role in our lives, and that people use multiple media in addition to face-to-face interactions to fit their social needs and lifestyles. Whether such communication undermines or enhances our connections and communications with others is yet to be seen. And this should not be a surprise, considering the pace of its development and how much we still have to learn about its capacities. With these thoughts in mind, let's look at a related topic—how personal identity is performed and managed in new media use.

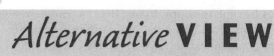

Alternative **V I E W**
Alone Together

Do you agree with Turkle's premise that pervasive connectivity actually makes us less connected to other people? Why or why not?

In a recent book, media expert Sherry Turkle challenges us to reexamine our assumptions about technology being the answer to intimacy and connections. She thinks that, although we are constantly in contact with each other, in fact *tethered* to our technology, we sometimes choose technologies that merely substitute for human intimacy. She offers as proof that adults would rather email, coworkers would rather leave voicemail messages, and teenagers would rather text. These technologies give us control over our relationships and actually distance us from others; as she puts it, "Technology makes it easy to communicate when we wish and to disengage at will" (p. 13). It's supposedly an efficient way to manage our time and relationships in our busy, hectic lives.

Turkle describes the story of Ellen, working in Paris, who used Skype to connect with her grandmother in Philadelphia. Twice a week they would talk for an hour.

But, unbeknownst to her grandmother, Ellen was multitasking during the conversation—typing away on her keyboard answering emails. So it wasn't a *real* connection because Ellen wasn't really present. And Ellen reportedly felt guilty about her actions.

Turkle gives other familiar examples: Attending a conference, she notes that people no longer talk with each other at breaks. Now they are all on smartphones, talking, answering email. Even during the presentation, they are on laptops and phones, only listening to the speaker from time to time. Of course there was some face-to-face networking, "but mostly what people wanted from the public space was to be alone with their personal networks" (p. 14). A 13-year-old tells her that she hates the phone and never listens to voicemail but finds texting just right.

Texting puts us in touch, but not too close. Maybe this is a response to being in constant connection. Answer one email, get ten back. Turkle concludes that we should continually examine the benefits and challenges of our "connectivity culture," always asking "how we got to this place and whether we are content to be here" (p. 2).

SOURCE: Turkle, S. (2011). *Alone together: Why we expect more from technology and less from each other.* New York: Basic Books.

TEST YOUR KNOWLEDGE
- What are two key differences between some new media and face-to-face communication?
- Describe the primary characteristics of social presence theory, media richness theory, and social network theory.

NEW MEDIA AND THE INDIVIDUAL

Clearly, the characteristics of new media can have a powerful impact on communication between individuals. The combined effects of filtering and asynchronicity have important implications for identity and, in turn, for personal relationships. Let's examine the way this works.

Managing Identity

The same characteristics that filter out nonverbal cues and make some new media a "leaner" form of communication add an interesting dimension to how communicators present themselves online. For example, when posting on an Internet forum, we can control the amount of information we disclose about ourselves, providing a fluidity to our identities that we don't have in face-to-face communication.

As we noted in Chapter 3, one's identity or self-concept is developed and expressed through communication with others. Early media researchers thought that online identities differed significantly from offline identities. However, as CMC has become the norm in our lives, researchers suggest that some mediated communication provides us the opportunity to express identities in ways not possible in FtF communication (Zywica & Danowski, 2008). Three of these identity issues are discussed below.

Anonymity and Psuedoanonymity

When you communicate via text messaging or in an online discussion forum, others may not know your age, gender, race, nationality, or many of the other cues that affect our perceptions of individuals. So new media technologies offers the possibility of withholding more aspects of your identity from public consideration than has ever before been possible.

This anonymity may be beneficial or detrimental, depending on how it is used. Communication researchers Andrew F. Wood and Matthew J. Smith (2005) identify three issues in the complex relationship between anonymity and identity in online communication. The first has to do with the informative aspect of the identity. On the one hand, knowing something about the person sending information gives a context for judging his or her messages. If you know, for example, that the person answering your medical question online is a doctor, that person seems more credible than a person who does not have a medical degree. On the other hand, because information on age, gender, and race can form the basis for stereotyping and prejudice, CMC can be remarkably free of prejudice.

A second issue regarding anonymity is its capacity to liberate speech. For example, without knowing who has issued a statement, the legal restrictions on speech are difficult to enforce. So if someone is **spoofing**, or misrepresenting oneself online, and makes racist or libelous statements, it is almost impossible to implement legal sanctions. On the other hand, anonymity can give people courage to express unpopular opinions or question conventional wisdom, which they might be afraid to do in FtF interaction. As an example, students often seem more willing to participate in discussions in online courses than in traditional classroom settings.

The third issue related to anonymity is that the combination has generated a new set of group norms. In some ways, the freedom that people feel as a result of their anonymity may lead them to be less responsible communicators. For example, professors have noted that, while online students are more participative, they can also be more rude and even aggressive than they would be in FtF classes (Smith, Ferguson, & Caris, 2001). Anonymity can also lead to bad behavior in virtual worlds. For example, two players were banned from Second Life for depicting sexual activity between an adult and a child ("Serious trouble," 2007). In addition, anonymity facilitates email rumors and hoaxes (e.g., warnings that canola oil can cause cancer or messages that companies like Microsoft will give away free money to people who forward the email message to five additional people). For information about evaluating these types of messages, check out Snopes.com.

Also annoying are the millions of **spam** messages (unwanted commercial messages and advertisements sent through email), which might be greatly reduced if addresses or spammers' identities were easier to trace. **Phishing**—the practice of trying fraudulently to get consumer banking and credit card information—is another problem for new media users. Increasing numbers of fake emails are showing up in email inboxes, "warning" users that their account information needs to be updated and then pointing to Web sites that ask the user to enter financial information. Although technology companies and banks aggressively pursue those who send spam and phishing messages, apprehending and prosecuting them is difficult (Lorentz, 2011).

Another form of bad behavior online is **cyberbullying**—"the deliberate and repeated misuse of communication technology by an individual or group to threaten or harm others" (Roberto & Eden, 2010, p. 198). Cyberbullying differs from traditional bullying partly because it is anonymous, it can occur anywhere (through voice, text, picture, or video messages on cell phones and through social

spoofing
misrepresenting oneself online

spam
unwanted commercial messages and advertisements sent through email

phishing
the practice of trying fraudulently to get consumer banking and credit card information

cyberbullying
the deliberate and repeated misuse of communication technology by an individual or group to threaten or harm others

networking sites, chat rooms, bulletin boards, and so on), and an infinite number of viewers can observe or participate. Research shows that cyberbullying can have many negative consequences for victims, ranging from psychological problems like depression, anxiety, and low self-esteem to disastrous consequences, as in the tragic case of Megan Meier, who committed suicide after being harassed on MySpace by a schoolmate's parent. Some experts report that 25 to 30 percent of minors are involved in cyberbullying, leading many schools to implement cyber-bullying prevention programs. Communities are also beginning to seriously enforce anti-cyberbullying laws (Waldman, 2011).

The final form of online bad behavior we'll discuss is deception. If you have represented yourself as something you are not on a discussion board or on your Facebook or MySpace profile, you are not alone. Forty-nine percent of young people say they put false information on their social networking site, and they give many reasons for doing so. Fabricating data on these sites may protect you from unwanted advances from strangers, or it can shield you from the watchful eye of your parents (boyd, 2007). Or you can find out what your "friends" think of you by starting an online conversation about yourself, using a false identity (Turkle, 2011). However, increasing numbers of children are lying about their age in order to create accounts on SNSs—most of which have an age limit of 13—leaving them open to fraud and predators (Richtel & Helft, 2011). We'll discuss online deception and new media further in the next section.

Beyond anonymity is a phenomenon made possible by new media—**pseudoanonymity,** or projecting a false identity. For example, people can invent identities through very acceptable means in MMOGs like "World of Warcraft," "EverQuest II," "Karaoke Revolution," and in virtual worlds like Second Life and Entropia Universe. The original multiplayer game was "Dungeons & Dragons," but hundreds of MMOGS now exist on the Internet—some for gaming and others, like Second Life, for socializing or pedagogical purposes or commercial ventures. In these virtual worlds, as many as 10,000 people—or their **avatars,** digital alter-egos/versions of themselves—can be present at the same time, engaged in activities from hanging out, to holding charity fundraisers, to operating sex clubs. Some universities have developed sites on Second Life where professors and students can interact, and a major American bank is using PIXELLearning's simulator for "diversity and inclusion training" ("Serious trouble," 2007).

Even though some of these communities are based on false identities, deception can still occur. For example, in one MMOG called Bluesky, a player and her boyfriend decided to take turns playing a character and see if other players would notice. When they decided to "confess" to the other players, some felt betrayed—even though identities in this game were understood to be assumed or false (Kendall, 2002). In this case, the outcome was relatively benign. In other cases, however, people have misrepresented themselves with far more significant results. In the case described in *It Happened to Me: Vivian*, both individuals used anonymity in deceptive ways, allowing the police officer to perform her job and resulting in an arrest for the teacher who had committed a crime.

pseudoanonymity
projecting a false identity

avatars
digital alter-egos or versions of oneself, used in MMOGs

Players of MMOGs invent new identities by creating avatars.

It Happened to Me: *Vivian*

At my high school, my math teacher was arrested and fired for communicating over the Internet with a 13-year-old girl. They formed a relationship, and when he went to meet her, he found a female police officer. So both participants were lying. The police officer told my teacher she was a young girl, and my math teacher told her he was a 16-year-old boy.

You may remember a few years ago that sites like MySpace were implicated in a series of sexual interactions between adults and minors, although some researchers now say that concerns about sexual predators on SNSs are greatly exaggerated (Pascoe, 2011).

Impression Management Online   With the rise of SNSs, the whole point is to be seen and known. But in using SNSs, you probably have made decisions about what kind of information to reveal about yourself. There seem to be three (overlapping) types of information that can be disclosed:

1. Standard information (e.g., name, gender, profile picture, email address);
2. Sensitive personal information—details that could be used to locate/identify and/or to threaten or harm (e.g., email address, birthday, birth year, employer, job position, profile picture, photo albums);
3. Potentially stigmatizing information—information that could result in stigmatization within society (e.g., religious views, political views, birth year, sexual orientation, photos).

How many personal details do you think people should disclose on their SNS pages? Is there any information that you think should be routinely disclosed? Never disclosed? How much do you disclose? Why?

How do you decide what type and how much information to reveal? Researchers have discovered that some decisions about what to reveal on SNSs are related to a person's age, their self-esteem, their relationship status, and their popularity. As it turns out, younger adolescents experiment more with online identities than young adults do and reveal more of all three types of information than do older people (Livingstone & Brake, 2010; Nosko, Wood, & Molema, 2010). Perhaps not surprisingly, people with low self-esteem tend to reveal more and present exaggerated information about themselves. For example, someone might say he plays in a band, when in reality his older brother plays in a band and he gets to play occasionally with them when they practice. In contrast, popular users tend to make strategic moves to enhance their popularity—for example, changing their profile picture in order to appear popular, changing their Facebook profiles to note new activities or interests, and adding friends (Zywica & Danowski, 2008). Additionally, single people tend to reveal more demographic and personal information, probably because they feel that information is needed to attract partners (Nosko et al., 2010).

Another aspect of self-presentation is listing friendship links, since "You are who you know." Unlike friends in the everyday sense, "friends" on SNSs can be used to provide context and to offer users a kind of imagined audience to interact with. But adding too many friends can have the opposite effect—raising doubts about one's popularity and desirability (Tong, Van Der Heide, Langwell, & Walther, 2008).

How much personal information to include in an SNS profile may also be determined by privacy and security concerns. Unfortunately, young people, especially teenagers, are not always aware of the public nature of the Internet, and they disclose too much information on SNSs—exposing themselves to possible identity theft or other criminal threats, such as cyberbullies or sexual predators (Turkle, 2011). In addition, many young people tend to accept at face value the online descriptions and profiles of others (Rybas, 2012). Experts say that two adolescent practices likely exacerbate online risk—the high disclosure of personal information and the experimental nature of peer communication. Which groups of young people are most at risk of online victimization? The answer is: those who communicate in multiple ways online, those who seek out opportunities to talk about sex with unknown people, and those who have unknown people in their buddy lists. Communicating in chatrooms and IMing tend to be more risky than SNSs (Livingstone & Brake, 2010). In addition, single people of any age are at risk, as they tend to disclose more information than those in committed relationships (Nosko et al., 2010).

There are other reasons to be careful about how much personal information to disclose; spammers have used freely accessible profile data from SNSs to craft phishing schemes that appear to originate from a friend on the network. Targets were much more likely to give away information to this "friend" than to a perceived "stranger" (boyd & Ellison, 2007). As we noted in Chapter 1, potential employers can also access profile information, and according to one study, 34 percent of employers surveyed admit to dismissing a candidate from consideration because of what they found on social networking sites (see *Did You Know? Employers Admit to Disqualifying Candidates Due to Facebook Content*).

To summarize, the anonymity of new communication technologies affords many possibilities for performing and managing identities, but these possibilities should be balanced with consideration of safety and ethical concerns. Let's now turn our attention to how relationships develop and are maintained through new media.

Did You Know?

Employers Admit to Disqualifying Candidates Due to Facebook Content

Does the information in this essay surprise you? How would you address the conflict between individuals' freedom of expression and employers' wish to find out about applicants before hiring them? If you were a legislator, are there employment laws regarding SNSs that you would advocate?

My conversations with dozens and perhaps even hundreds of employers who hire college students for internships and recent graduates for entry level jobs have led me to believe that about 75 percent are searching social networking sites such as Facebook and MySpace as part of their background checking process. But one question that was harder to answer was how many of those employers have declined to hire a candidate because of content on those sites.

Careerbuilder recently surveyed hiring managers and found that of those who admit to screening job candidates using Facebook, MySpace, and other social networking sites, 34 percent admit to dismissing a candidate from consideration because of what they found on the social networking sites. The top areas for concern among these hiring managers were:

- 41%—candidate posted information about them drinking or using drugs
- 40%—candidate posted provocative or inappropriate photographs or information
- 29%—candidate had poor communication skills
- 28%—candidate bad-mouthed their previous company or fellow employee
- 27%—candidate lied about qualifications
- 22%—candidate used discriminatory remarks related to race, gender, religion, etc.
- 22%—candidate's screen name was unprofessional
- 21%—candidate was linked to criminal behavior
- 19%—candidate shared confidential information from previous employers

I've said it before and I'll say it again: don't put anything on-line on any site unless you would feel comfortable sharing that information with your favorite grandmother. Posting information on-line is like getting a tattoo; there's nothing inherently wrong with it, but you have to understand that it is permanent and that people who you may not want to see it will at times see it.

SOURCE: CollegeRecruiter. Retrieved December 11, 2008, from http://www.collegerecruiter.com/weblog/2008/09/employers_admit.php

field of availables
potential partners and friends, typically much larger via CMC than via face-to-face relationships

Relationship Development

Today, most of us use new media to develop and maintain relationships. In fact, you probably have some relationships that exist only online, such as with acquaintances you met in an online course or on a bulletin board. Let's consider the impact of mediated communication on three types of relationships: friendships, romantic relationships, and relationships in the workplace.

Friendships While online and offline relationships have much in common, CMC affects our relational development in several ways: Online relationships offer a larger field of availables, and they overcome limits of time and space.

The phrase **field of availables** describes the fact that the universe of potential partners and friends accessible through new media is much larger than in traditional relationships. This is true for two reasons. First, you can come into contact with many more people online than you ever would in person. Moreover, when online, you have fewer reasons to dismiss someone as a potential friend/partner because initial physical cues are not present. The fact that you engage with someone in a chat room, over email, or on a discussion board means that you already have something in common, which is a powerful means of attraction.

Relationships that are initiated and/or maintained through new media also overcome limits of time and space. You do not have to (ever) be in close proximity to these people and you do not (ever) have to exchange messages at the same time. What are the implications of these characteristics for CMC relationships? It may be no surprise to you by now that the answer is—there are both positive and negative implications. On the positive side, these relationships may be more durable. For example, if you have a relationship that is strictly online and you relocate to a faraway place, the relationship may not be affected. As people are increasingly mobile, new communication technologies afford more continuity than was possible before.

On the other hand, online relationships can be somewhat more fragile, partly because they require some skepticism. As we discussed above, deception frequently occurs in initial stages of online relationships. There are also people who drop out because they find the pressures of SNS "performance" too stressful (agonizing over how to present themselves, which photos to post, whether their photos and music picks are "cool" enough, and so on). And some decide to stop participating in "the throwaway friendships of online life" (Turkle, 2011, p. 275).

How can you effectively navigate social networking sites, for example, where online relationships are developed? Since the information you post on SNSs is potentially accessed by hundreds of thousands of people, you should consider carefully how much and what type of information you post. For example, would you tell a complete stranger who you were with last night and what you did? Probably not, but if you post this info on a social networking site, you would be doing just that—unless you take some precautions. Therefore, when you go on Facebook or other SNSs, it's useful to ask yourself: Do you know who has access to the information? Do you know how it will be used? How much information do you want to share with others? For some guidelines, see *Communication in Society: Safe and Smart Use of SNSs.*

When you develop friendships online, more trust is required than in FtF relationships (Boyd, 2003; Rooksby, 2002). For this reason, many people who develop friendships on discussion boards or in chat rooms also exchange email addresses or phone numbers—or even meet in person—in order to establish more trust (Kendall, 2002).

A recent study showed that richer communication forms (webcam, MSN spaces) are helpful in creating first impressions, attracting acquaintances, and building new friendships—as the richness provides maximum information flow (audio and visual). This richness allows the quick superficial disclosure needed to build new relationships; however, texting or other in-depth communication is probably needed to develop close relationships (Sheer, 2011).

COMMUNICATION IN SOCIETY
Safe and Smart Use of SNSs

Do you believe SNSs pose more risks to personal safety and privacy than traditional FtF relationships? Why or why not? Do you disagree with any of the following suggestions? Explain your answer.

Here are several suggestions for being safe and smart on social networking sites:

1. Protect your identity. You probably know not to give out your Social Security number (not even the last four digits), home address, or PINs. However, you may not have realized that giving the state where you were born or posting your full résumé could enable others to obtain your Social Security number and other personal data. Google yourself from time to time to see how much of your personal information is available. Check a site's privacy policy to see what they do with your information. Facebook is free because the owners sell your information to advertisers.

2. Be careful what you say or show about yourself or anyone else. Don't post info or photos that show you or anyone else engaging in illegal, irresponsible, or indecent activities (including chugging pitchers of beer, even if you're over 21) because it may reflect poorly on you. Don't use profanity or say anything that you wouldn't want future in-laws, employers, clients, or customers to see. Don't write private messages on wall posts. It's embarrassing and rude and makes you look immature.

3. Know that "there are no erasers on the Internet." Once you post information on a site, it can be very difficult to remove it because of file sharing, archiving, and other considerations. Even if you unsubscribe to a site, the info may remain visible for a long time.

SOURCES: 50 social networking rules for college students. (2010, March 30). Retrieved July 29, 2011, from http://collegetimes.us/50-social-networking-rules-for-college-students/

Guidelines for using Social Networking Sites. (2006). Southampton Solent University. Retrieved January 26, 2010, from http://portal-live.solent.ac.uk/university/stay_safe/internet.aspx

---

In fact, communication researcher Joseph Walther (1996) suggests that online relationships can develop intimacy more quickly than those in FtF relationships. This may be because in mediated (lean, text-based) communication, participants place great importance on the cues that aren't filtered out. In fact, people receiving messages seem to "fill in the blanks" about the personality of the sender (Rosen, Cheever, Cummings & Felt, 2008). They can also take time to craft their own messages carefully. When replying to a newfound friend by texting or email, people tend to give the written words great meaning and to disclose more rapidly than they might in FtF interaction (McKenna, Green, & Gleason, 2002).

However, when moving an online relationship offline, the timing may be important; some experts suggest that it is better to move a relationship offline fairly soon after an initial meeting, before people develop an idealized notion of their online partner and have unrealistic expectations (Ramirez & Zhang, 2007).

Romantic Relationships Who becomes involved in online romantic relationships, and how does CMC-based romance differ from in-person romance? According to one survey, 50 percent of respondents said they knew someone who had met a romantic partner online (Friedman, 2011). Many online romance Web sites feature a scientific approach, which often includes compatibility and personality testing and seems to cover all ages and income levels. Some specialize in niche marketing focusing on religion (Jewish, Catholic, Christian), race/ethnicity (interracial, Black, Latino), or age.

Psychologists have identified three qualities of Internet communication that are particularly relevant to romantic relationships: the ease of finding similar others, of "getting past the gates," and of achieving intimate exchanges (McKenna et al., 2002).

"If you really want to know why I'm dumping you, you may want to check out my website where there's a long, detailed explanation posted."

To begin, it's easy to see how one can meet people with similar interests via online discussions boards or Web sites, where people gather precisely because they share an interest. In contrast, finding people with similar interests offline may be more difficult. And making that connection can be facilitated by new media, as it's easy to make that first connection. According to one student, "when you like a girl it's much easier to send a friend request than to ask for her phone number. Then you can check out her photos, her profile information and her posts....if you're still interested, chances are she's worth pursuing" (Bennhold, 2011).

Second, and perhaps even more important, when meeting online, it's easier to "get past the gates" that people sometimes close to each other because of features such as physical appearance, visible shyness, or lack of strong social skills. Getting past the gates can increase self-esteem and confidence, which, in turn, can lead to more ease in initiating relationships.

Third, online communication may give rise to easier, quicker self-disclosure and intimacy (as we have noted). For example, on Internet dating sites, profiles are set up to reveal extensive information about potential partners—describing their personality, interests (what they read, music they listen to, and so forth), ideal date, and political persuasion. It is easy to see how mediated communication in this context may lead to relationships in which people develop intimacy more quickly (Whitty, 2007).

However, developing online relationships poses dangers and can provide opportunities for deception and fraud (as described earlier in *It Happened to Me: Vivian*). In one study of online dating practices, researchers found that 50 percent of the participants admitted to lying about their looks, relationship status, age, weight, socioeconomic status, or interests (Whitty, 2007). Another found that older daters were more likely to misrepresent age, and men were more likely to misrepresent personal assets and interests, attributes, and relationship goals. Women were more likely to misrepresent weight (Hall, Park, Song, & Cody, 2010). However, online daters also report that they usually assume some deception and learn to "correct" for it: "One woman mentioned that if a profile said a man was 5'11" she would assume he was probably 5'9"; a man said that if a woman said she was "average" body type, he would assume she was slightly heavy" (Heino, Ellison, & Gibbs, 2010).

However, as noted earlier, more serious deception can occur—many people have been swindled out of money by criminals who pose as potential suitors and ask for money after gaining the trust and interest of dating partners (Mangla, 2008). It pays to be careful online; for suggestions on staying safe, see *Did You Know? Safety Tips for Dating Online*.

Despite the potential risks, people can and do form close, lasting relationships online. Many of the same things that make offline romantic relationships work are important in online relationships, like intimacy, trust, and communication satisfaction. But can these relationships survive face-to-face meetings? The answer depends on whether one has engaged in honest self-disclosure, communicated one's "true self," and established solid commonality (McKenna et al., 2002).

What role do new media play in maintaining romantic relationships? It appears that most people prefer to communicate with significant others by cell phone

Did You Know?
. . . .

Safety Tips for Online Dating

Do you think it is harder to build trust and loyalty with a partner one has met online than with partners met through traditional channels? Why or why not? Considering all the risks of online dating, what are some reasons why people continue to do it?

1. Before signing up with a dating site:
   - Evaluate potential dating sites very carefully. Some sites have questionable business practices or poor customer service.
   - Get references from others—preferably people you actually know. If you don't know anyone who has used the site, look for unbiased online customer reviews.
   - Read the terms and conditions carefully, and ask questions about anything you don't understand.
2. Whether you've met a potential partner through a dating site or a regular SNS, be aware of possible dishonesty. It is not unusual to encounter people who:
   - Have lied about their age, employment status, income level, marital status, or other characteristics.
   - Are using dating as a pretext for theft or other illegal activities.
   - Say they want a committed relationship but are really just looking for sex.
3. Before you agree to meet in person:
   - Verify the identity of the person. Find out as much as you can about them (for example, Google their user profile name).
   - Talk on the phone a few times. Listen to the noises in the background—do they match what you've been told (children, pets, roommates)? Don't use your own phone the first time you talk.
   - Ask for more than one photo. Some people use other people's photos.
4. If you decide to meet in person:
   - Meet in a public place and arrive (and leave) by your own transportation.
   - Tell a friend about your plans or bring a friend along the first time.
   - Don't leave your food or drink unattended.
   - When you leave, don't go directly home.
5. Above all, listen to your gut. If at any point something doesn't seem right, leave immediately.

(conversations) with text messaging a close second. Email, social networking sites, and instant messaging are all used, but not as frequently. One reason given is the easy access and the primary reason given for contacting was to express affection, so it would seem that new media provide a positive element to relationships. While not replacing face-to-face expressions of affection, a quick text message to say "I luv u :)" or a phone call while doing routine errands enables couples to continue expressing affection throughout the day. Interestingly, married couples used a larger variety of media (IM, social networking, blogs, and webcams) than dating couples (Coyne, 2011).

However, there are also downsides to the constant connectivity of new media in maintaining romantic relationships (Pettigrew, 2010). Experts have found that the use of Facebook is associated with increased jealousy in relationships (Muise, Christofides, & Desmarais, 2009). For example, one young man describes how he monitors his girlfriend's Facebook page to see what other guys write (Bennhold, 2011). Similarly, the connectedness of text messaging can be seen as stifling or even as harassing if one partner insists on constant communication (Duran, Kelly, & Rotaru, 2011; Pettigrew, 2010).

Work Relationships While most workers report that communication technologies have improved their ability to do their job, share ideas with coworkers, and work in a flexible way, there are some concerns. According to a recent study, many workers surveyed said that these technologies result in longer hours and increased stress levels, as many continue their work after they get home, and are expected to read email and be available for cell phone calls after work (Turkle, 2011). In any case, new media have had a huge impact on work relationships. The impact varies, however, depending on the type of relationship—whether it is a superior–subordinate relationship or a peer relationship.

Superior-Subordinate Communication The prevalence of new media in the workplace results in at least three areas of concern: status and boundary issues, surveillance issues, and confidentiality issues. A major impact of online communication in the workplace is its status-leveling effect. Before new media, gatekeepers like receptionists and secretaries controlled access to the boss. However, with email, anyone can have instant access to superiors. On the other hand, this status leveling can also raise boundary issues—how much online interaction is appropriate between boss and employees? Should you ask to friend your boss on Facebook? Should a supervisor request to friend a subordinate? (Wang & Kobsa, 2009).

New communication technologies also give superiors a way of checking up on subordinates. Messages sent through email may be stored forever on company servers, so management can monitor employees' correspondence. Many companies monitor employee email and Internet usage, and Web-based security cameras are increasingly common. Also, technologies such as GPS and employee badges with radio frequency identification (RFID) tags provide an even higher level of employee monitoring. These tracking systems can record, display, and archive the exact location of any employee, both inside and outside the office, at any time (James, 2003).

While most companies see the benefit of social networking sites as a way to advertise products and even bolster employee relationships (some large corporations have their own in-house versions of Facebook), they are skeptical of giving access to employees to social media during work hours ("A world of connections," 2010; Wang & Kobsa, 2009), partly due to fear of decreased productivity, also known as "social notworking." One study estimated that the personal use of SNSs was costing the British economy $2.3 billion annually, and another concluded that if companies banned employees from using Facebook, they could increase productivity by 1.5 percent ("Yammering away at the office," 2010).

Another new media concern for employers is losing control of their image, as in the case of a teacher who lost her job after posting negative comments on Facebook referring to her students and their parents (Heussner & Fahmy, 2010). Employers also worry about employees leaking confidential information through new media messages—loss of corporate, confidential, or customer information or making inappropriate public statements about the company (Ashley, 2008).

Another issue concerns decisions about what should be handled over CMC versus FtF. Communicating electronically gives workers the opportunity to think carefully about their communication before sending it, but it can result in misunderstandings. For an example of the type of workplace misunderstandings that can occur using email, read *It Happened to Me: Cruzita*.

It Happened to Me: *Cruzita*

I sent my manager an email requesting some time off, but she didn't receive it. When I found out that I did not get the weekend off, I was mad at her, but she had no idea I had sent her an email. If my manager and I had communicated face to face, we would not have had a mix up of this kind.

Peer Communication While the field of availables may increase through new media in work contexts, access to certain kinds of information often decreases when one relies on online communication. For example, in face-to-face work contexts, you can observe colleagues in the next office during meetings and talk with them in the halls or mailroom, but if you communicate online with a coworker at a different location, you have little information about them. This lack of information increases uncertainty as well as the potential for disagreements and misunderstanding, as one of our students describes in *It Happened to Me: Mei-Lin*. In order to minimize these misunderstandings and build trust among person-nel, some employers try to arrange periodic face-to-face meetings or even promote social networking commu-nication among coworkers (Wang & Kobsa, 2009).

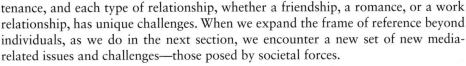

It Happened to Me: *Mei-Lin*

I sent an urgent email to a colleague requesting information for a report I was writ-ing. He didn't respond, and I became very irritated at his lack of response. A few days later, I found out that his child had been in a serious accident, and he missed work for several days. If we had been located in the same office, I would have known im-mediately what was wrong, would have responded more appropriately to his absence, and could have gotten the information I needed in some other way.

To summarize, new me-dia provides opportunities and challenges for relation-ship development and main-tenance, and each type of relationship, whether a friendship, a romance, or a work relationship, has unique challenges. When we expand the frame of reference beyond individuals, as we do in the next section, we encounter a new set of new media-related issues and challenges—those posed by societal forces.

TEST YOUR KNOWLEDGE

- Describe three identity concerns that result from anonymity afforded by some new media forms.
- What are some differences in how Internet relationships develop compared to in-person relationships?
- What are some guidelines for staying safe when using new media?

THE INDIVIDUAL, COMMUNICATION TECHNOLOGY, AND SOCIETY

All new media activities—whether for fun, socializing, or information-seeking—are enacted by humans within a social context and the larger society. These activities both reflect and influence larger societal norms. For example, some of the same social hierarchies that exist in the larger society also exist in the realm of new media. When we sort people out by various identities (e.g., gen-der, ethnicity, or race), we find differences not only in how many of them use communication technologies (see Tables 14.2 and 14.3) but also in how they are perceived to use new media. In this section, we'll first look at how various identities influence technology use and then examine the phenomenon known as the digital divide.

Gender, Age, Ethnicity, and Technology Use

Let's consider gender first. When college students were asked to identify various computer activities as either "masculine," "feminine," or "neutral," they identified arcade-style computer games as the most masculine activity, as well as high-tech peripherals (PDA, digital cameras), banking, and downloading music. In contrast, they identified emailing, Internet chat rooms, studying online, and shopping as feminine activities (Selwyn, 2007). These perceptions seem to represent traditional gender roles—men being more action oriented and females more interpersonally oriented. The authors conclude that "it is erroneous to presume that gender stereotyping of new technologies—and in particular the computer—has ceased to exist" (Selwyn, 2007, p. 534). How accurate are these stereotypes?

As it turns out, some of the perceptions are accurate. Males are more likely than females to play online games and to play a larger variety of games (Lenhart et al., 2008). Women tend to email more than men and to visit, post comments, and share photos on SNSs (except LinkedIn—visited by twice as many men as women) (Hampton et al., 2011), and they tend to communicate more in online discussions than men (Caspi, Chajut, & Saporta, 2008). Some evidence indicates that women are a bit more anxious about relatively advanced and complex computer technology and so are less likely to play complicated online games than men (Wang & Wang, 2008), although other evidence shows males and females having equal levels of computer skills (Cheong, 2008). Nevertheless, some of the stereotypes are unfounded. For example, males and females participate in online shopping equally (Horrigan, 2008). Taken together, then, this evidence suggests that communication technologies use only partially reinforces gender stereotypes.

How do other identities—such as age—interact with new media use? As one might expect, young people are much more comfortable with new technologies than older folks, and they tend to use communication technologies in different ways. As described at the beginning of the chapter, the younger you are, the more likely you are to IM, play online games, and download music. The same patterns extend to mobile phones and social networking sites; young people are more likely to text and tweet than are older people (Madden, 2010; Smith, 2011a). However, the stereotype of older people avoiding technology is inaccurate. In fact, the fastest-growing group of Internet users is older people (age 70+), and the number of older people (age 50+) who visit SNSs doubled in the years 2009–2010 (Madden, 2010). Moreover, a few online activities that were previously dominated by younger generations—searching for information and downloading videos—are now practiced more equally across all generations (Zickuhr, 2010).

Stereotypes of ethnic groups also persist online. Studies show that characters in video games are overwhelmingly White and male. Outside of sports video games, only a few Black characters exist; often they are portrayed as gangsters or street people. Latinos and Native Americans are extremely underrepresented as video game characters. While there are many White male game players, the population of gamers worldwide includes female gamers, people of different racial and cultural backgrounds, and gamers of varying ages. The typical gamer is not a White male adolescent, which seems to be the assumption of video game creators (Sinclair, 2009; Williams, Martins, Consalvo, & Ivory, 2009).

As you can see, not everyone is equally represented in the communication technology revolution, nor does everyone have access to digital life and cyberspace. The issue of access is perhaps the most important way that societal forces affect computer-mediated communication.

The fastest-growing group of Internet users is people age 70 and over.

digital divide
inequity of access between the technology "haves" and "have nots"

cultural capital
cultural knowledge and cultural competencies that people need to function effectively in society

Power, Access, and the Digital Divide

According to a recent Pew report on Internet and American Life, about 21 percent of Americans are not online (Zickuhr, 2010), and in many countries, only a tiny fraction of the population has access to computers and the Internet. This inequity of access between the technology "haves" and the "have nots" has been called the **digital divide**, and it exists within the United States and also on a global scale. While there is high Internet usage in Western Europe, North America, and east Asia, usage in developing countries—especially in Africa—is sparse. In Africa, Internet penetration is 11 percent, compared with 24 percent in Asia, 32 percent in the Middle East, 36 percent in Latin and South America, 58 percent in Europe, 60 percent in Oceania (Australia, New Zealand), and 78 percent in North America. Many developing countries lack landline services, but their mobile phone usage is growing exponentially and allowing people to connect in ways never possible before (Alzouma, 2012). As you can see in Table 14.2, there are pockets of low Internet use in many parts of the world.

Why do differences in access matter? In a global information society, information is an important commodity that everyone needs in order to function. In addition, to function effectively in society, people need **cultural capital** (Bourdieu, 1986), or certain bodies of cultural knowledge and cultural competencies. Those with the most power in a society decide what constitutes cultural capital, and it is passed down from parents to children, just as economic capital is.

In the United States and much of the world, cultural capital includes the ability to use new media in appropriate ways. This ability is especially important in an increasingly "networked" society. Without these skills and knowledge, one can feel disconnected from the center of society (van Dijk, 2004). For example, a researcher told of a man who had no experience with computers. When the man went for a haircut, he was told to check in at the computer terminal at the counter. He was too embarrassed to admit not knowing how to use the keyboard or cursor, so he left the shop without getting a haircut. Why is this man on the far side of the digital divide? What factors keep him, and so many others, from having access to the Internet?

Who Has Access to New Media? The digital divide does seem to be shrinking in some ways. For example, gender differences in online access—once a feature underlying the digital divide in the United States—have all but disappeared (Talukdar & Gauri, 2011). Racial and ethnic disparities are also shrinking for some media use, especially the more recent technologies. However, some experts say there is a widening digital divide based on income, education, and urban-rural groups as well as a new configuration of the digital divide (Brown, Campbell, & Ling, 2011). Let's look more closely at what they mean by this statement.

As shown in Table 14.3, African Americans and Latinos have much higher smartphone ownership rates than whites (44 percent vs. 30 percent). While all smartphone users can access the Internet by phone, Blacks and especially Latinos are more likely than whites to rely *only* on mobile phones because they are less likely to have access to a computer

TABLE 14.2 The Global Digital Divide

Percentage of Internet Users as of 2011*

Country	% of population
Iceland	97
Norway	94
S. Korea	81
Germany	80
Canada	79
Japan	78
U.S.A.	78
Spain	62
Chile	50
Morocco	41
China	35
Nigeria	28
Mexico	25
Egypt	24
Nicaragua	10
India	8
Cambodia	2
Somalia	.1

SOURCE: Internet World Stats. (2011, March 31). Retrieved September 13, 2011, from http://www.internetworldstats.com/stats.htm

Cultural capital includes the knowledge enabling people to make use of new media.

TABLE 14.3 The demographics of smartphone ownership (May 2011)

Percent of U.S. adults within each group who own a smartphone

All adults	35
Gender	
Men (n = 973)	39
Women (n = 1304)	31
Age	
18–29 (n = 337)	52
30–49 (n = 581)	45
50–64 (n = 659)	24
65 + (n = 637)	11
Race/Ethnicity	
White, non-Hispanic (n = 1637)	30
Black, non-Hispanic (n = 261)	44
Hispanic (n = 223)	44
Household Income	
Less than $30,000 (n = 671)	22
$30,000–$49,999 (n = 374)	40
$50,000–$74,999 (n = 276)	38
$75,000 + (n = 444)	59
Education Level	
No high school diploma (n = 229)	18
High school grad (n = 757)	27
Some college (n = 525)	38
College + (n = 746)	48
Geographic Location	
Urban (n = 618)	38
Suburban (n = 1113)	38
Rural (n = 465)	21

SOURCE: Smith, A. (2011b). 35% of American adults own a smartphone. *Pew Internet & American Life Project.* Retrieved July 21, 2011, from http://www.pewinternet.org/~/media//Files/Reports/2011/PIP_Smartphones.pdf

or broadband Internet at home (Livingston, 2011; Smith, 2011b). This difference remains even after controlling for income and education. What are the implications? It is difficult or impossible to accomplish some important activities with a smartphone, such as updating a résumé and conducting a job search online. Thus, these ethnic groups are at a disadvantage—a new configuration of the digital divide (Washington, 2011).

In addition, socioeconomic status and education level make a tremendous difference in Internet access, smartphone ownership, and Twitter use for all ethnic/racial groups (Talukdar & Gauri, 2011). People who make more than $75,000 a year are much more likely to be online, own a smartphone, and use Twitter than those making less than $30,000. Those with some college education are more than twice as likely to be online, own a smartphone, and use Twitter than those without a high school diploma (Smith, 2011a, 2011b; Livingston, 2011).

The rural/urban/suburban divide is also growing (Talukdar & Gauri, 2011). As you can see from Table 14.3, people in rural areas are about half as likely to own a smartphone as those in urban or suburban areas (21 percent vs. 38 percent). The same is true for Internet access and mobile phone ownership.

As we've mentioned, age is also a digital divide factor: 96 percent of young people ages 18 to 29 are online, compared with 77 percent of people ages 50 to 64 and only 46 percent of those 65 and older ("Demographics of Internet users," 2010). Older people are also less likely to be mobile phone and smartphone users. And disability is also associated with lower new media access and use—43 percent of those with a disability, compared with 81 percent of non-disabled, have Internet access. Even with analysis control for all demographic factors (age, income, education, and so on), people with disabilities are less likely to have Internet access and less likely than other Internet users to have high-speed access or wireless access (Fox, 2011).

Overall, then, in the United States, the people most likely to have access to and use new media:

■ Are young or middle-aged.

■ Have a college degree or are currently students.

■ Have a comfortable income.

■ Live in an urban or suburban area.

■ Are physically abled.

What Keeps People Offline? Twenty-one percent of Americans have never been online and are categorized as the "truly disconnected"; this number has remained constant for five years (Zickuhr, 2010). The primary reason given is that they have no desire to go online; the second most common reason is that it is too expensive. Other reasons are: It's too difficult, they have no computer, or they have no access (Zickuhr, 2010).

Some of these reasons may flow from the lack of a specific type of cultural capital—**technocapital**, or access to technological skills and resources. What hinders people from acquiring technocapital? One reason might be competing social and cultural influences.

According to one study, the factors that turned people away from computer use were family attitudes and resources, the educational system, peer pressure, and institutional factors (Jackson et al., 2004). This study investigated computer use in a low-income neighborhood in Austin, Texas—a technologically progressive city with a number of programs to ensure public access to new media and innovative training programs. Via interviews and surveys, researchers discovered that many of the poorest families in Austin—even though they had radios, cell phones, and televisions—did not own computers or have access to the Internet. Further, while some parents understood the importance of computer skills, they did not feel they had the time or energy to communicate this knowledge to their children. Although they owned other electronic devices, they did not feel they had the funds needed for computers. In addition, the neighborhood school, like most schools in poor neighborhoods, lacked adequate computer facilities and computer training (Jackson et al., 2004).

These inequities in educational resources, combined with parental attitudes, reinforce students' notion that computers and computer skills are "not for them," and so they acquire a negative attitude toward computer technology. A more recent study found similar results. This study tried to identify what determined people's "Internet connectedness" and found that, even more important than socioeconomic status, ethnicity or access to home computer were (1) the social environment—that is, whether people have family and friends who also use the Internet and who can help them resolve Internet-related problems and (2) whether they see the Internet as central to important activities (Jung, 2008). Just like the earlier study, this study showed that even though people may be avid video game players, they may still see computer skills as being for others and as irrelevant to their own lives (Bourdieu, 1986).

One theory that explains why some people accept new technologies and others don't is the **diffusion of innovations**, developed by Everett Rogers (2003). The theory suggests that in order for people to accept a new technology like the computer, they have to see it as useful and compatible with their vales and lifestyle. Moreover, if people important to the individual (e.g., an adolescent's peers) adopt the innovation first, then the individual is more likely to adopt it. So while giving people access to computers and the Internet is an important first step, it is not enough to close the digital divide.

Institutional structures also reinforce the social environment. Many of the very poor say that TV and billboard Internet ads are irrelevant to them. Indeed, most of these ads, often showing White, middle-class people (professionals or college students) touting the advantages of getting "connected," probably are not directed at them. They also don't use the free computers in public libraries because they regard libraries as unfriendly places (Rojas, Straubhaar, Rochowdhury, & Okur, 2004). Thus, the digital divide has deep societal and cultural roots—and arises from far more than a lack of access to computers.

Socioeconomic status and education are strong factors in the digital divide.

technocapital
access to technological skills and resources

diffusion of innovations
theory that suggests that in order for people to accept a new technology like the computer, they have to see it as useful and compatible with their vales and lifestyle

Globalization and the Digital Divide

Compared with those in the United States, even larger digital inequities exist on a global scale, as illustrated in Table 14.2. The issues of who does and does not have technocapital and whose culture dominates it are relevant in our current global economy. Why? Some activists and policymakers hope that facilitated by new communication technologies, economic globalization—meaning increased mobility of goods, services, labor, and capital—can lead to a more democratic and equitable world. And some evidence supports this hope. For example, outsourcing American jobs to overseas locations has provided income opportunities for many in English-speaking countries such as India. And, in spite of some governments' attempts to limit their citizens' access to new media, the Internet provides information, world news, and possibilities for interpersonal communication that were not available previously.

In addition, new media have been used successfully by advocates of social change. Social media like Facebook and Twitter enable organizers to reach many people quickly and can be used to recruit people, organize collective action, raise awareness and shape attitudes, raise money, and increase communication with decision makers. For example, on Facebook the application (Lil) Green Patch raises awareness about global warming and encourages people to take action to make a difference. Project 1200—organized by a group of Utah high school students and adults—was successfully used to fight legislation that would have cut $4 million from the Tobacco Prevention and Control Fund (Thackeray & Hunt, 2010).

However, other evidence suggests that new media technologies primarily benefit wealthy Western nations, promoting their cultural values and technology and enriching their countries. Evidence here includes the fact that Western countries control and profit from the majority of new media hardware and software. Furthermore, English has become the dominant language of the Internet, and most software is developed in English, even though only a small percentage of the world's population speaks English.

After examining Western domination of communication technology and media products (music, film, television), researcher Fernando Delgado (2002) makes the case that this domination enhances the digital divide and impacts interpersonal communication across cultures. Specifically, he argues that people in poorer countries are left behind by the new media revolution and resent the control wielded by Western technology.

Closing the Digital Divide

One recent theory—which is similar to the diffusions of innovations theory described above—is proposed by Dutch sociologist Jan van Dijk (2004) and addresses strategies for lessening the digital divide. Van Dijk emphasizes that access to computer hardware is only one part of exclusion from the digital world. To cross the digital divide, people must have access to four levels of technocapital: mental, material, skills, and usage. Furthermore, each level builds on the previous one.

Mental access—the first and perhaps most important level of technocapital—relates to motivation and acceptance of new media as meaningful. To cross the digital divide, people must be convinced that computer and Internet skills are important. As we noted earlier, however, older people and poor people often do not see the benefit for themselves. Thus, those concerned with minimizing the digital divide recommend that more attention and effort be directed to overcoming these mental-access barriers (Lenhart et al., 2003).

The second level of technocaptial—material access to computer hardware—is where most public policy currently focuses.

Providing access to computers is one way to overcome the digital divide in developing countries.

For example, one U.S. federal program uses telephone taxes to pay for Internet connections in elementary schools; state and local funds are used to pay for Internet connections at public libraries; and companies donating computer and technical training are given tax incentives (Lenhart et al., 2003; Marriot, 2006). On a more global scale, engineers at a British nonprofit agency have developed a small, sturdy $25 laptop with a powerful processor similar to those in high-end smartphones that can be connected to a TV screen. They hope to distribute them free of charge to British children and maybe then go global, like the One Laptop per Child project that has provided more than 2 million low-cost laptops in developing countries (Gaylord, 2011). Clearly, without access to hardware and Internet connections, acquiring technocapital can be impossible.

The third level of technocapital—skills access—is also critical. Many non-users view lack of training and lack of user-friendly technology as barriers, and frustration levels can be significant. In order to facilitate skills access, hardware and software developers must better understand the minds of users, taking into consideration their diverse cultural communication norms and practices. We need "technology that can think like the user" and that can think like users from many cultural backgrounds (Jackson et al., 2004, p. 180).

Finally, usage access means knowing how to use a variety of computer applications. For example, learning to use the Internet or build a Web site takes more know-how than using the computer to play games or send email. Even if people have computers, their lack of technological proficiency and social resources may frustrate them, leading to what some experts call a "secondary digital divide" (inequalities in Internet skills, problem-solving behaviors, and Internet usage patterns) in high-tech societies (Cheong, 2008).

People's computer usage knowledge is often related to their educational level. One study showed that even when people have the same access to computers, those with more education tend to have more usage knowledge and use the Internet for more varied applications. More important, they use the computer in ways that are professionally and personally enhancing; for example, they visit sites that provide useful information about national and international news, health and financial information, government services, and product information (Hargittai & Hinnant, 2008). Knowing how to use a broad range of applications would provide less educated and lower-income people with more technocapital and the social and economic opportunities that come with participation in the "connected" life (Jackson et al., 2004).

TEST YOUR KNOWLEDGE

- What is the digital divide? What are the most important factors that determine whether one has access to new media?
- What are some suggestions for closing the digital divide?

ETHICS AND NEW MEDIA

One message we hope you take from this chapter is that CMC, in itself, is neither better nor worse than FtF communication. It is simply different. However, these differences can allow for irresponsible, thoughtless, or even unethical communication. How can you become an ethical user of new media? There are at least three areas of ethical consideration: 1) presentation of identity online, 2) privacy issues, and 3) building online relationships.

Ethics and Online Identity

As we discussed earlier, the issue of identity and ethics online is complex, and one can take various positions on the issue. An extreme position would be that one should never misrepresent oneself. On the other hand, some new media (e.g.,

MMOGs) clearly offer legitimate opportunities to take on an entirely new identity. One general principle might be "Do no harm." In our earlier MMOG example, while some players felt betrayed, one could argue that the harm done to players was minimal. In the example of Vivian's teacher, who pretended to be a boy on the Internet, the behavior was clearly deceitful in addition to being criminal.

A final ethical issue is the incivility of messages on bulletin boards and blogs. When bloggers disclose their feelings and opinions, they become vulnerable to personal attacks via comments left by readers. Women seem to be frequent targets of vulgar or insulting comments—from death threats to manipulated photos (Stone, 2007). Some Web site and software developers have suggested that a set of guidelines for conduct be created and implemented to "bring civility to the Web" (Stone, 2007). They suggest that bloggers control if and when they will allow anonymous comments by strangers, and they also recommend that bloggers make it known on their page which behaviors they will tolerate.

Communication, of course, is interactive and reciprocal; it takes two people to engage in any interaction, and both have responsibility. Among the receiver's responsibilities is the duty to harbor a certain amount of skepticism for messages that may be questionable. In the case of new media, skepticism should focus on how people present their identity—particularly in certain contexts (for example, in SNSs, discussion forums, chat rooms, or other online venues).

Privacy Issues

A second ethical issue concerns online privacy, and the general guideline of doing no harm can also apply here. Specifically, ethical new media use includes respecting

Did You Know?

A Single Sign-on to Multiple Online Services

What do you think about the balance between privacy and Internet identity? What would be the advantages and disadvantages of a system like OpenID? Do you think current laws and policies about Internet identity are adequate? Why or why not?

To address identity problems related to anonymity on the Internet, some have proposed a mandatory Internet ID. One possibility is OpenID—a single sign-on to multiple online services and applications (Ashley, 2008). This fixed identity helps verify users identities and reduce impersonators and false identities.

Another solution would be a requirement that individuals use their real names for all online interaction. Several prominent Internet executives, including Facebook's marketing director and also a former Google CEO, have both called for an end to online anonymity, calling it "dangerous" and predicting that authorities will eventually demand it (Facebook's Randi Zuckerberg: Anonymity online has to go away, 2011). While the benefits of these solutions include decreasing some crime (particularly the exploitation of children) and some unethical behavior and may promote more civil online dialogue (IntenseDebate uses OpenID), it raises the issue of basic privacy rights. Moreover, for some people, as noted earlier, anonymity is part of the "fun" of online communication. It would also be challenging to find a way to implement an effective ID that would protect everyone and *not* be susceptible to fraud or identity theft.

One possible solution would be to tailor the ID requirements to the context. For example, some sites could require ID while others would not, and the users at those sites would follow a "buyer beware" guideline. Internet users could then choose their sites based on their own comfort levels.

others' privacy and not snooping around emails and text messages that are not intended for you. There is increasing opportunity for privacy violation as we own more new media devices (desktop, laptop, tablet, phones, and so on).

In addition, if you accidentally access private information, you should consider carefully the consequences of sharing this information with others—would the owner of the information want this information to be shared? Will others be harmed by sharing the information? Of course, the harm could be mild (sharing news about a friend that she or he would not want shared) to much more drastic consequences (sharing personal identity information that could result in cyberbullying or identity theft).

Building Ethical Mediated Relationships

The first step in building ethical relationships is to remember how some new media forms differ from face-to-face communication. First, when nonverbal cues are filtered, you need to provide as much information as you can to help the receiver know who you are. You need to present yourself as honestly and truthfully as you can and behave as you would in real life. How you act online may be the most direct way that people—including potential employers as well as love interests—will perceive you. You also need to give recipients of your message enough information to discern the "tone" of your message For example, you may have to explain in words (or emoticons) the humorous tone that in person you would communicate with facial expressions or gestures.

A second step is to consider which form of communication is appropriate for your message. Here, relevant factors are your relationship with the receiver and the purpose of the message. For example, in a work context, a lean email message can convey essential information. However, personal messages may be better delivered in person, especially if miscommunication is likely and you need immediate feedback to make sure you are understood.

TEST YOUR KNOWLEDGE

- What are ethical guidelines in presenting one's identity online?
- What are suggestions for ethical communication in mediated relationships?

IMPROVING YOUR MEDIATED COMMUNICATION SKILLS

What should you take from this chapter that can help you be a better communicator? First, you can strive to communicate more politely, following guidelines for new media "netiquette." Second, you can use social media effectively in job hunting.

New Media Etiquette

Just as we have norms of courtesy for traditional, face-to-face communication, we also have etiquette for computer-mediated communication. Let's look at several new media forms and the challenges they pose for communicating politely.

Email Because email is prevalent in work, at school (e.g., contacting professors), and in some social contexts, it is worth considering how to increase its effectiveness. The most important guideline is to think before writing a message and hitting the send button. Remember that what you put in writing can never be unwritten and that others besides the intended recipient may see it. Here are a few specific suggestions:

- Send email only to those who will want or need to use it. Don't forward the latest joke or YouTube video to everyone you know. Those who don't share your sense of humor—or are too busy to laugh—might lose respect for you.

- Give your email a context. Don't just write "FYI" or "Hi" in the subject field; let the recipient know specifically what you're writing about. This is especially important in work contexts. Because of the status-leveling effects of email, people get many more messages now than they ever did by telephone, so they want to know the subject of those messages.

- Address the recipient appropriately. If the recipient is your professor, address him or her by title unless you are securely on a first-name basis. It's always better to err on the formal side rather than the informal. Abruptly starting with "Hey!" "Hi there," or "I need to talk with you about my grade" is not very respectful.

- Check your spelling carefully. Sending emails full of typos and grammar mistakes communicates a lack of respect for yourself and the recipient.

Mobile Phones As a society, we are still figuring out how to use mobile phones in ways that promote smooth and effective relational communication. A recent survey found that nearly all U.S. adults (91 percent) say that they've seen people misuse mobile technology, and 75 percent think that mobile manners are becoming worse. The most common forms of misbehavior are: using mobile devices while driving (which, it's important to note, is illegal in many states) and talking on a device loudly in public places ("New Intel survey," 2011). (For a description of laws regarding cell phone use, visit www.statehighwaysafety.org/html/stateinfo/laws/cellphone_laws.html). Here are some general guidelines:

- Be respectful of others' schedules. Don't assume that because you are awake, working, or not busy, that the person you're calling or texting is, too.

- Ask permission to use the phone when appropriate. For example, if you are expecting a call or text message during a meeting, inform others at the beginning of the meeting that you are expecting an important message and get their permission to take the call or respond to the text message.

- In public places, avoid talking where you may be distracting to others—for example, in places of business (waiting rooms, banks) or in restaurants.

- When talking on the phone, using a lower-than-normal voice will allow you to be heard by the caller and not by others in the room.

- When you're with friends, keep the voice conversations short and limit your use of your PDA or smartphone. Contrary to popular belief, composing a text message or surfing the Internet while in a face-to-face conversation with someone is as rude as taking a voice call.

Text Messaging Here are some additional guidelines that apply specifically to text messaging:

- Remember that text messages are informal. They shouldn't be used for formal invitations or to dump your girlfriend or boyfriend—the casualness reduces the impact and meaning of the message.

- Don't get upset if you don't get a reply. Before you text someone and get frustrated at the lack of a response, consider reasons for their not responding: maybe they don't have text capability, they may be out of range, their phone may not be working, they may be busy and not able to text, and so on.

- Be aware of your tone. Just as with email, what seems to you to be a completely inoffensive message may be grossly misinterpreted by the recipient, causing possible discomfort and even irreparable harm to your relationship. For example, using capital letters counts as shouting and some people avoid this to keep from offending others.

Surveys report that loud cell phone conversations in public places are one of the top complaints about bad manners with regard to CMC.

- Consider whether to use slang. Don't expect your stodgy superiors at work to know text messaging lingo. And don't expect to win points with your kids by trying to be cool, either.

ADAPTED FROM: Cell phone etiquette, mobile phone manners, mobile phone etiquette. (2000). *Indianchild.com*. Retrieved July 25, 2011, from http://www.indianchild.com/cell_phone_etiquette.htm and Top 10 list of SMS etiquette. (n.d.). *The Wireless Developer Network*. Retrieved July 25, 2011, from http://www.wirelessdevnet.com/newswire-less/thefeature04.html

Microblogging As microblogging services such as Twitter have grown in popularity, they pose etiquette challenges of their own. Here are some suggestions:

- Use your real name. Staying connected on social media is about being honest. A pseudonym can also turn off your professional contacts.
- Don't use automation tools. Social media is about staying actively engaged. Sending an automatic message every time someone follows you just makes you look lazy and unengaged.
- Keep tabs on your ratio. Since people use ratio to make decisions about following you, keep it balanced to avoid looking desperate or snobbish.
- Keep private what's private. Use the private messages function for private conversations.
- Be savvy. Be skeptical and careful not to get taken in by scams or deceptive information. Don't pass information on unless you have checked its accuracy.
- Share other people's work. Be generous. Don't just tweet your own stuff; tweet other people's work as well.
- Don't ask to be retweeted. If something you tweet is worth passing on, it will be.

SOURCE: 50 social networking rules for college students. (2010, March 30). *College Times*. Retrieved July 29, 2011, from http://collegetimes.us/50-social-networking-rules-for-college-students/

As you can see, the overarching principle in CMC etiquette is to be considerate of others' time and convenience. Put yourself in the place of the person receiving your message and ask yourself, "Would I appreciate the way this message has been worded and transmitted?" If the answer is yes, you are probably doing all right.

Using Social Media in Job Hunting

New media are playing an increasingly important role in job searches for both employers and job applicants. How can you use mediated messages effectively in searching for employment?

First of all, network. Get the word out that you're looking (but, of course, be very discreet if you don't want your current employer to know). Use as many media forms as possible—Facebook, Twitter, LinkedIn. LinkedIn allows you to search by people, jobs, and companies; you can also join groups related to your industry and participate in job-related discussions. Twitter provides Twello, which allows you to search people's bios and URLs. Google Plus allows you to categorize your relationships into "circles," controlling who gets to see what content you post. In general, the more visible you are, the more likely you are to make the contacts that will lead to a job while meeting a lot of professionals who share your same career aspirations. And you never know where *the* contact might happen.

Post your résumé—making sure that it is up to date, professional looking, and relevant to your career goal. Useful résumé-building Web sites include Emurse, VisualCV, Carbonmade, and Gigtide. Consider posting a short video résumé on YouTube in which you briefly explain your skills and the story of your background. If you're using LinkedIn, be sure that your profile is accurate and reflects your current job status. Consider starting a blog if you don't already have one—it can give potential employers a better sense of who you are and, depending on your field, may show that you have relevant skills. Most job applications ask for a Web site address or blog site.

Learn about potential employers. Read about trends in your chosen industry, search for news items that mention companies and their executives, explore company Web sites. When you meet someone online who works (or has worked) for a potential employer, ask them to tell you about the company.

Follow up: Be thoughtful and considerate in contacting and following up with potential employers. After a meeting or interview, it's good to follow up with a short thank-you email. Similarly, be sure to thank anyone who helps you by giving you leads or recommendations. However, don't continue to try to get in touch after that. If you push too hard, you'll look like a stalker rather than an eager applicant.

Help others: A final suggestion is to remember to help others. In your job search, you may come across information or contacts that may not be relevant to your search but might be helpful to a friend, colleague, or online acquaintance. What goes around comes around—the person you help today may be in a position to do you a favor next week or next year.

As we move forward, new media will inevitably be a part of our lives. It is deeply imbedded in the way we do business and research and in the ways we socialize and connect with others. Clearly, we have much to think about as we use these tools in every context to communicate responsibly, ethically, equitably, and with social awareness.

TEST YOUR KNOWLEDGE

- What are some guidelines for improving your CMC etiquette?
- How might you use social media in a job search?

SUMMARY

New media are now a constant reality in our lives and impact our daily activities in multiple ways. This pervasiveness provides the first and primary reason for learning more about this topic. A second reason is that understanding new media and having good media skills will help you be more successful personally and professionally.

New media are defined as a collection of mediated communication technologies that are digital and converging and tend to be interactive. In contrast to mass media where messages are generally one-to-many, new media messages converge, meaning they can be sent one-to-one, one-to-many, or many-to-many.

Communication scholars offer two views of the relationship between new media and face-to-face communication: the media deficit approach and the media augmentation approach. Specifically, some new media filter out most nonverbal cues used in face-to-face communication and can be conducted asynchronously—leading early experts to propose a media deficit approach. However, now the lines between face-to-face and mediated communication are rather blurred, leading scholars to emphasize the media augmentation approach. Compared with face-to-face communication, some new media afford more control over how people present themselves. Specifically, online one can perform multiple identities, be rather anonymous, or even assume a false identity (pseudoanonymity). In addition, mediated relationships differ from in-person relationships in that new media afford access to many more potential relationships, and these relationships are not bound by time or space.

These characteristics make mediated relationships somewhat more durable but also somewhat more fragile.

New media uses are also affected by societal forces and, especially by who has access to them. The digital divide—the differential access to new media by various income, educational, and national groups—separates those who have access from those who do not. Power also comes into play in the digital divide, as it does in other parts of society, as the most powerful are the ones who develop and define computer literacy and expertise—sometimes excluding those from less powerful groups.

Communicating ethically using new media is especially important in presentation of identity online, in respecting others' privacy, and in building online relationships. Suggestions for communicating effectively using new media include following email, mobile phone, and micro-blogging etiquette and using social media effectively when job hunting.

KEY TERMS

new media 379
blogs 380
podcast 381
digital 382
computer-mediated communication (CMC) 382
cyberspace 382
Internet 382
World Wide Web (WWW) 382
Social Networking Sites (SNSs) 382
Massively Multiplayer Online Games (MMOGs) 382

media deficit approach 384
media augmentation approach 384
filtering 384
social presence 384
social presence theory 384
media richness theory 384
emoticons 385
synchronous 386
asynchronous 386
social network theory 388

spoofing 390
spam 390
phishing 390
cyberbullying 390
pseudoanonymity 391
avatars 391
field of availables 394
digital divide 401
cultural capital 401
technocapital 403
diffusion of innovations 403

APPLY WHAT YOU KNOW

1. Don't use any new media for 24 hours and then answer the following questions. To what extent did you miss these forms of communication? What did you miss most/least? What might you conclude about the role new media play in *your* everyday life and relationships? How do you view those who have limited access to new communication technologies?

2. Select any personal Web page from the Internet and describe the identity you think the person is trying to project. Describe the elements that contribute to this identity. What kind of information is presented? What information is missing?

3. Visit an MMOG (go to www.mudconnector.com for a list and access to many MMOGs). Log in and participate for a while. Then answer the following questions: Did you enjoy the experience? Why or why not? Did you try to project a different identity than you usually do? Describe your interaction with other players. How did your communication with them differ from other contexts—for example, online discussions and text messaging. Why?

Glossary

absolute pertaining to the belief that there is a single correct moral standard that holds for everyone, everywhere, every time

action-oriented listening style that reflects a preference for error-free and well-organized speaking

active agents seekers of various media messages and resisters of others

adaptors gestures used to manage emotions

age identity a combination of self-perception of age along with what others understand that age to mean

agenda-setting capacity the power of media coverage to influence individuals' view of the world

analysis paralysis potential pitfall in small group interaction; occurs when excessive analysis prevents a group from moving toward a solution

artifacts clothing and other accessories

artistic proofs artistic skills of a rhetor that influence effectiveness

assertiveness expressing one's opinions forcefully without offending others

assimilation the communicative, behavioral, and cognitive processes that influence individuals to join, identify with, become integrated into, and (occasionally) exit an organization

asynchronous communication in which messages are sent and received at different times

attachment an emotional tie, such as the closeness young children develop with their caregivers

attraction theory a theory that explains the primary forces that draw people together

attractiveness the appeal one person has for another, based on physical appearance, personalities, and/or behavior

attribution theory explanation of the processes we use to judge our own and others' behavior

attributional bias the tendency to attribute one's own negative behavior to external causes and one's positive actions to internal states

audience analysis the process of determining what an audience already knows or wants to know about a topic, who they are, what they know or need to know about the speaker, and what their expectations might be for the presentation

authoritarian leader leader who takes charge, makes all the decisions, and dictates strategies and work tasks

avatars digital alter-egos or versions of oneself, used in MMOGs

avoiding stage of romantic relational dissolution in which couples try not to interact with each other

behaviorism the focus on the study of behavior as a science

blogs short for weblogs; online diaries or news commentaries

bonding stage of romantic relational development characterized by public commitment

border dwellers people who live between cultures and often experience contradictory cultural patterns

brainstorm to generate as many ideas as possible without critiquing them

bullying repeated hostile behaviors that are or are percieved to be intended to harm parties who are unable to defend themselves

burnout a chronic condition that results from the accumulation of daily stress, which manifests itself in a very specific set of characteristics, including exhaustion, cynicism, and ineffectiveness

categorization a cognitive process used to organize information by placing it into larger groupings of information

cause–effect pattern one used to create understanding and agreement, and sometimes to argue for a specific action

channel the means through which a message is transmitted

charismatic leadership a leadership style in which extremely self-confident leaders inspire unusual dedication to themselves by relying upon their strong personalities and charm

chronemics the study of the way people use time as a message

chronological pattern one that follows a timeline

circumscribing stage of romantic relational dissolution in which couples discuss safe topics

cocultural group a significant minority group within a dominant majority that does not share dominant group values or communication patterns

cocultural theory explores the role of power in daily interactions

cognitive complexity the degree to which a person's constructs are detailed, involved, or numerous

cognitive representation the ability to form mental models of the world

cohort effect the influence of shared characteristics of a group that was born and reared in the same general period

cohort effect the process by which historical events influence the perceptions of people who grew up in a given generation and time period

collectivistic orientation a value orientation that stresses the needs of the group

communicating information using nonverbal behaviors to help clarify verbal messages and reveal attitudes and moods

communication ethics the standards of right and wrong that one applies to messages that are sent and received

computer-mediated communication (CMC) the exchange of messages carried through an intervening system of digital electronic storage and transmitted between two or more people

conclusion closing material of a speech where the speaker reviews the main points, may challenge the audience to act, and leaves the audience with a positive view of speaker and topic

confirming communication comments that validate positive self-images of others

congruent verbal and nonverbal messages that express the same meaning

connotative meaning the affective or interpretive meanings attached to a word

constructive marginal people people who thrive in a border-dweller life, while recognizing its tremendous challenges

constructs categories people develop to help them organize information

content analysis approach to understanding communication that focuses on specific aspects of the content of a text or group of texts

content analysis approach to understanding media that focuses on a specific aspect of the content of a text or group of texts

content meaning the concrete meaning of the message, and the meanings suggested by or associated with the message and the emotions triggered by it

content-oriented a listening style that reflects an interest in detailed and complex information, simply for the content itself

contingent employees individuals who work in temporary positions, part-time or as subcontractors

contradicting verbal and nonverbal messages that send conflicting messages

critical approach an approach used not only to understand human behavior but ultimately to change society

critical listening listening skills that are useful in a wide variety of situations—particularly those involving persuasive speaking

cultivation theory idea that long-term immersion in a media environment leads to "cultivation," or enculturation, into shared beliefs about the world

cultural capital cultural knowledge and cultural competencies that people need to function effectively in society

cultural values beliefs that are so central to a cultural group that they are never questioned

culture learned patterns of perceptions, values, and behaviors shared by a group of people

culture learned patterns of perceptions, values, and behaviors shared by a group of people

culture industries large organizations in the business of mass communication that produce, distribute, or show various media texts (cultural products) as an industry

culture shock a feeling of disorientation and discomfort due to the lack of familiar environmental cues

cyberbullying the deliberate and repeated misuse of communication technology by an individual or group to threaten or harm others

cyberspace the online world; often used synonymously with the Internet

deception concealment, distortion, or lying in communication

decoding receiving a message and interpreting its meaning

deliberative rhetoric the type of rhetoric used to argue what a society should do in the future

delivery the presentation of a speech before an audience

demand touching a type of touch used to establish dominance and power

demand-withdrawal an interaction pattern in which one partner criticizes or tries to change the other partner, who responds by becoming defensive and then disengaging—either psychologically or physically

democratic leader leader whose style is characterized by considerable input from group members

demographic analysis the portion of an audience analysis that considers the ages, races, sexes, sexual orientations, religions, and social class of the audience

denotative meaning the dictionary, or literal, meaning of a word

dialect a variation of a language distinguished by its vocabulary, grammar, and pronunciation

dialectic approach recognizes that things need not be perceived as "either/or," but may be seen as "both/and"

diaspora group of immigrants, sojourners, slaves, or strangers living in new lands while retaining strong attachments to their homelands

dichotomous thinking thinking in which things are perceived as "either/or"—for example, "good or bad," "big or small," "right or wrong"

differentiating stage of romantic relational dissolution in which couples increase their interpersonal distance

diffusion of innovations theory that suggests that in order for people to accept a new technology like the computer, they have to see it as useful and compatible with their vales and lifestyle

digital information that is transmitted in a numerical format based on only two values (0 and 1)

digital divide inequity of access between the technology "haves" and "have nots"

disability identity identification with physical or mental impairment that substantially impact everyday life

disconfirming communication comments that reject or invalidate a positive or negative self-image of our conversational partners

downward communication in a traditional conduit model of communication, communication with subordinates

e-books electronic books read on a computer screen instead of a printed page

Ebonics a version of English that has its roots in West African, Caribbean, and U.S. slave languages

ego-defensive function the role prejudice plays in protecting individuals' sense of self-worth

elocutionists scholars in the 19th century who promoted the study of the mechanics of public speaking, including proper pronunciation, grammar, and gestures

emblems gestures that stand for a specific verbal meaning

emergence phase the third phase of the decision-making process; occurs when group members express a cooperative attitude

emoticons pictographs used to convey relational information in computer-mediated communication, such as the smiley face :-)

empowerment employees' feelings of self-efficacy

enacting identities performing scripts deemed proper for particular identities

encapsulated marginal people people who feel disintegrated by having to shift cultures

encoding taking ideas and converting them into messages

establishing social control using nonverbal behavior to exercise influence over other people

ethics standards of what is right and wrong, good and bad, moral and immoral

ethnic identity identification with a particular group with which one shares some or all of these characteristics: national or tribal affiliation, religious beliefs, language, and/or cultural and traditional origins and background

ethnocentrism the tendency to view one's own group as the standard against which all other groups are judged

ethnographic relating to studies in which researchers actively engage with participants

ethos the rhetorical construction of character

evaluating assessing your reaction to a message

experimenting stage of romantic relational development in which both people seek to learn about each other

expressing and managing intimacy using nonverbal behaviors to help convey attraction and closeness

eye contact looking directly into the eyes of another

feedback the response to a message

field of availables potential partners and friends, typically much larger via CMC than via face-to-face relationships

field of experience the education, life events, and cultural background that a communicator possesses

filtering removing nonverbal cues

forensic rhetoric rhetoric that addresses events that happened in the past with the goal of setting things right after an injustice has occurred

formal structure officially designated channels of communication, reflecting explicit or desired patterns of interaction

frame a structure that shapes how people interpret their perceptions

friendship touch touch that is more intimate than social touch and usually conveys warmth, closeness, and caring

function the goals and effects of communication

functional (situational) theory a theory that assumes leadership behaviors can be learned

functional touch the least intimate type of touch; used by certain workers such as dentists, hairstylists, and hospice workers, as part of their livelihood; also known as *professional touch*

fundamental attribution error the tendency to attribute others' negative behavior to internal causes and their positive behaviors to external causes

gender identity how and to what extent one identifies with the social construction of masculinity and femininity

general purpose whichever of three goals—to inform, persuade, or entertain—dominates a speech

general systems theory theory that organizations are a system composed of many subsystems and embedded in larger systems, and that organizations should develop communication strategies that serve both

generalized other the collection of roles, rules, norms, beliefs, and attitudes endorsed by the community in which a person lives

gestures nonverbal communication made with part of the body, including actions such as pointing, waving, or holding up a hand to direct people's attention

globalization the increasing connectedness of the world in economic, political, and cultural realms

grammar the structural rules that govern the generation of meaning in a language

group processes the methods, including communication, by which a group accomplishes a task

group roles the shared expectations group members have regarding each individual's communication behavior in the group

grouphate the distaste and aversion that people feel toward working in groups

groupthink a negative, and potentially disastrous, group process characterized by "excessive concurrence thinking"

haptics the study of the communicative function of touch

hate speech use of verbal communication to attack others based upon some social category

Hays Code self-imposed rules for Hollywood media content instituted in 1930 with the goal of creating "wholesome entertainment"

hegemony the process by which we consent to social constructions, rather than having them imposed on us

heterogeneous diverse

heuristic use of language to acquire knowledge and understanding

hierarchy a power structure in which some members exercise authority over others

homogeneity a high degree of similarity

horizontal communication in a traditional conduit model of communication, communication with peers

hostile work environment an intimidating, hostile, or offensive workplace atmosphere created by unwelcome and inappropriate sexually based behavior; one of two types of sexual harassment recognized by federal law

human communication a process in which people generate meaning through the exchange of verbal and nonverbal messages in specific contexts, influenced by individual and social forces, and embedded in culture

human relations approach to management that holds that the job of management is actually to educate, interact, and integrate

human–nature value orientation the perceived relationship between humans and nature

humanism a system of thought that celebrates human nature and its potential

hurtful messages messages that criticize, tease, reject, or otherwise cause an emotional injury to another

identity who a person is; composed of individual and social categories a person identifies with, as well as the categories that others identify with that person

illustrators signals that accompany speech to clarify or emphasize the verbal messages

imaginative use of language to express oneself artistically or creatively

immediacy how close or involved people appear to be with each other

individual roles roles that focus more on individuals' own interests and needs than on those of the group

individualist orientation a value orientation that respects the autonomy and independence of individuals

informal structure unspoken but understood channels of communication, reflecting patterns that develop spontaneously

informational listening listening skills that are useful in situations requiring attention to content

informative use of language to communicate information or report facts

ingratiation behavior and communication designed to increase liking

initiating stage of romantic relational development in which both people behave so as to appear pleasant and likeable

innovation a function of organizational communication by means of which systems are changed

instrumental use of language to obtain what you need or desire

integrating stage of romantic relational development in which both people portray themselves as a couple

intensifying stage of romantic relational development in which both people seek to increase intimacy and connectedness

interactional use of language to establish and define social relationships

intercultural communication communication that occurs in interactions between people who are culturally different

Internet a system of networks that connects millions of computers around the world

interpersonal violence physical violence against a partner or child

interpretation the act of assigning meaning to sensory information

interpretive approach contemporary term for humanistic (rhetorical) study

intimate distance (0 to 18 inches) the space used when interacting with those with whom one is very close

introduction opening material of a speech from which the audience members gain a first impression of the speech's content and of the speaker

involuntary long-term travelers people who are border dwellers permanently but not by choice, such as those who relocate to escape war

involuntary short-term travelers people who are border dwellers not by choice and only for a limited time, such as refugees forced to move

jargon the specialized terms that develop in many professions

jealousy a complex and often painful emotion that occurs when a person perceives a threat to an existing relationship

kinesics nonverbal communication sent by the body, including gestures, posture, movement, facial expressions, and eye behavior

Knapp's stage model model of relationship development that views relationships as occurring in "stages" and that focuses on how people communicate as relationships develop and decline

label a name assigned to a category based on one's perception of the category

laissez-faire a leadership style characterized by complete freedom for the group in making decisions

lexical choice vocabulary

listening the process of receiving, constructing meaning from, and responding to spoken and/or nonverbal messages

listening style a set of attitudes, beliefs, and predispositions about the how, where, when, who, and what of the information receiving and encoding process

logos rational appeals; the use of rhetoric to help the audience see the rationale for a particular conclusion

long-term orientation a value orientation in which people stress the importance of virtue

long-term versus short-term orientation the dimension of a society's value orientation that reflects its attitude toward virtue or truth

looking-glass self the idea that self-image results from the images others reflect back to an individual

love-intimate touch the touch most often used with one's romantic partners and family

Machiavellian tactics having a third party convey one's unhappiness about a relationship

maintenance a function of organizational communication in which the stability of existing systems is preserved

mass media mediated communication intended for large audiences

mass media effects the influence that media have on people's everyday lives

mass-market paperbacks popular books addressed to a large audience and widely distributed

Massively Multiplayer Online Games (MMOGs) text-based "virtual reality" games in which participants interact with enrichments, objects, and other participants

matching hypothesis the tendency to develop relationships with people who are approximately as attractive as we are

media the plural form of *medium*, a channel of communication

media activism the practice of organizing to communicate displeasure with certain media images and messages, as well as to force change in future media texts

media augmentation approach a theoretical perspective that sees views mediated communication as complementing or augmenting face-to-face communication

media deficit approach a theoretical perspective that sees mediated communication as less useful than face-to-face communication

media event occasions or catastrophes that interrupt regular programming

media richness theory theory that describes the potential information-carrying capacity of a communication medium

media text a television show, advertisement, movie, or other media event

media violence representations of violent acts in media

mediation peaceful third-party intervention

messages the building blocks of communication events

methods the specific ways that scholars collect and analyze data which they then use to prove or disprove their theories

monochronically engaging in one task or behavior at a time

monotheistic belief in one god

motivation feeling personally invested in accomplishing a specific activity or goal

MPAA Motion Picture Association of America

multiracial identity one who self-identifies as having more than one racial identity

mutable subject to change

national identity a person's citizenship

naturalistic relating to everyday, real-life situations, such as a classroom, café, or shopping mall

new media a collection of mediated communication technologies that are digital and converging and tend to be interactive

new social contract assumes that loyalty is not expected by workers or organizations and that job security is unlikely

noise any stimulus that can interfere with, or degrade, the quality of a message

nominalists those who argue that any idea can be expressed in any language and that the structure and vocabulary of the language do not influence the speaker's perception of the world

nonverbal behavior all the nonverbal actions people perform

nonverbal codes distinct, organized means of expression that consists of symbols and rules for their use

nonverbal communication nonverbal behavior that has symbolic meaning

openness a state in which communicators are willing to share their ideas as well as listen to others in a way that avoids conveying negative or disconfirming feedback

orator a public speaker

organization the process by which one recognizes what sensory input represents

organizational culture a pattern of shared beliefs, values, and behaviors

organizational identification the stage of assimilation that occurs when an employee's values overlap with the organization's values

organizations the set of interactions that members of purposeful groups use to accomplish their individual and common goals

paradigm belief system that represents a particular worldview

paralinguistics all aspects of spoken language except the words themselves; includes rate, volume, pitch, stress

participants the people interacting during communication

particular others the important people in an individual's life whose opinions and behavior influence the various aspects of identity

passing away the process by which relationships decline over time

pathos the rhetorical use of emotions to affect audience decision making

people-oriented a listening style that is associated with friendly, open communication and an interest in establishing ties with others

performance of identity the process or means by which we show the world who we think we are

persona the identity one creates through one's public communication efforts

personal distance (18 inches to 4 feet) the space used when interacting with friends and acquaintances

personal language use of language to express individuality and personality

phishing the practice of trying fraudulently to get consumer banking and credit card information

phonology the study of the sounds that compose individual languages and how those sounds communicate meaning

podcast audio file stored digitally

political economy the ways in which media institutions produce texts in a capitalist system and the legal and regulatory frameworks that shape their options for doing so

polychronically engaging in multiple activities simultaneously

polytheistic belief in more than one god

power distance a value orientation that refers to the extent to which less powerful members of institutions and organizations within a culture expect and accept an unequal distribution of power

pragmatics field of study that emphasizes how language is used in specific situations to accomplish goals

predicted outcome theory a theory that attempts to explain how reducing uncertainty can lead to attraction or repulsion

preferred personality a value orientation that expresses whether it is more important for a person to "do" or to "be"

prejudice experiencing aversive or negative feelings toward a group as a whole or toward an individual because she or he belongs to a group

primary groups groups that provide members with a sense of belonging and affection

primary tension the uncertainty commonly felt in the beginning phase of decision making

problem–solution pattern one in which the speaker describes various aspects of a problem and then proposes solutions

production a function of organizational communication in which activity is coordinated toward accomplishing tasks

professional touch type of touch used by certain workers, such as dentists, hairstylists, and hospice workers, as part of their livelihood; also known as *functional touch*

prototype an idealized schema

proxemics the study of how people use spatial cues, including interpersonal distance, territoriality, and other space relationships, to communicate

proximity how physically close one is to others

pseudoanonymity projecting a false identity

public distance (12 to 25 feet) the distance used for public ceremonies such as lectures and performances

public sphere the arena in which deliberative decision making occurs through the exchange of ideas and arguments

qualitative methods methods in which researchers study naturally occurring communication rather than assembling data and converting it to numbers

quantitative methods methods that convert data to numerical indicators, and then analyze these numbers using statistics to establish relationships among the concepts

quid pro quo requests for sexual favors as a condition of getting or keeping a job or benefit; one of two types of sexual harassment recognized by federal law

racial identity identification with a particular racial group

rationality the ability to communicate through reasoning, bargaining, coalition building, and assertiveness

reflected appraisals the idea that people's self-images arise primarily from the ways that others view them and from the many messages they have received from others about who they are

regulating interaction using nonverbal behaviors to help manage conversational interaction

regulators gestures used to control conversation

regulatory use of language to control or regulate the behaviors of others

reinforcement phase the final phase of the decision-making process when group members reach consensus, and members feel a sense of accomplishment

relational maintenance behaviors that couples perform that help maintain their relationships

relational roles roles that help establish a group's social atmosphere

relational trajectory models relationship development models that view relationship development as more variable than stage models

relationship meaning what a message conveys about the relationship between the parties

relative pertaining to the belief that moral behavior varies among individuals, groups, and cultures and across situations

relativists those who argue that language serves not only as a way for us to voice our ideas but "is itself the shaper of ideas, the guide for the individual's mental activity"

relaxation the degree of tension displayed by one's body

religious identity aspect of identity defined by one's spiritual beliefs

responding showing others how you regard their message

reverse culture shock/reentry shock culture shock experienced by travelers upon returning to their home country

rhetor a person or institution that addresses a large audience; the originator of a communication message but not necessarily the one delivering it

rhetoric communication that is used to influence the attitudes or behaviors of others; the art of persuasion

rhetoric communication that is used to influence the attitudes or behaviors of others; the art of persuasion

rhetorical analysis used by researchers to examine texts or public speeches as they occur in society with the aim of interpreting textual meaning

rhetorical audience those people who can take the appropriate action in response to a message

rhetorical critic an informed consumer of rhetorical discourse who is prepared to analyze rhetorical texts

rhetorical event any event that generates a significant amount of public discourse

rhetoricians scholars who study the art of public speaking and the art of persuasion

role expectations the expectation that one will perform in a particular way because of the social role occupied

Sapir-Whorf hypothesis idea that the language people speak determines the way they see the world (a relativist perspective)

schemas cognitive structures that represent an individual's understanding of a concept or person

script a relatively fixed sequence of events that functions as a guide or template for communication or behavior

secondary (recurring) tension conflict or tension found in the second or conflict phase of the decision-making process

secondary groups groups that meet principally to solve problems

selection the process of choosing which sensory information to focus on

selective attention consciously or unconsciously attending to just a narrow range of the full array of sensory information available

selective exposure the idea that people seek media messages and/or interpret media texts in ways that confirm their beliefs and, conversely, resist or avoid messages that challenge their beliefs

self-concept the understanding of one's unique characteristics as well as the similarities to, and differences from, others

self-esteem part of one's self-concept; arises out of how one perceives and interprets reflected appraisals and social comparisons

self-fulfilling prophecy when an individual expects something to occur, the expectation increases the likelihood that it will

self-respect treating others, and expecting to be treated, with respect and dignity

self-serving bias the tendency to give one's self more credit than is due when good things happen and to accept too little responsibility for those things that go wrong

semantic-information distance describes the gap in information and understanding between supervisors and subordinates on specific issues

semantics the study of meaning

sensing the stage of listening most people refer to as "hearing"; when listeners pick up the sound waves directed toward them

servant leadership a leadership style that seeks to ensure that other people's highest priority needs are being served in order to increase teamwork and personal involvement

service-task functions using nonverbal behavior to signal close involvement between people in impersonal relationships and contexts

setting the physical surroundings of a communication event

sexual coercion physically nonviolent pressure to engage in unwanted sex

sexual identity which of the various categories of sexuality one identifies with

shared (collaborative or distributed) leadership a type of leadership style where functional leadership is extended to an organizational level; all members are equal partners and share responsibility for the work of the group

short-term orientation a value orientation that stresses the importance of possessing one fundamental truth

signposts transitions in a speech that help an audience understand the speaker's organization, making it easier for them to follow

similarity degree to which people share the same values, interests, and background

small group communication communication among a small number of people who share a common purpose or goal, who feel connected to each other, and who coordinate their behavior

social class identity an informal ranking of people in a culture based on their income, occupation, education, dwelling, child-rearing habits, and other factors

social distance (4 to 12 feet) the distance most U.S. Americans use when they interact with unfamiliar others

social facilitation the tendency for people to work harder and do better when others are around

social movement a large, organized body of people who are attempting to create social change

social network theory theory that proposes that the patterns of connections among people affect their social behavior and communication

Social Networking Sites (SNSs) web-based service where people construct their profiles, identify others with whom they share a connection, and interact with others within the system

social penetration theory a theory that proposes relationships develop through increases in self-disclosure

social position place in the social hierarchy, which comes from the way society is structured

social presence degree of psychological closeness or immediacy engendered by various media

social presence theory suggests that face-to-face communication is generally high in this kind of social presence, and that media vary in the amount of social presence they convey

social role the specific position or positions one holds in a society

social science approach contemporary term for the behaviorist approach

social-polite touch touch that is part of daily interaction in the United States; it is more intimate than professional touch but is still impersonal

sophists the first group to teach persuasive speaking skills in the Greek city-states

soundscape the everyday sounds in our environments

spam unwanted commercial messages and advertisements sent through email

spatial pattern one that arranges points by location and can be used to describe something small

special-occasion speeches evocative speeches intended to entertain, inspire, celebrate, commemorate, or build community

specific purpose what a speaker wants to inform or persuade an audience about, or the type of feelings the speaker wants to evoke

speech act theory branch of pragmatics that suggests that when people communicate, they do not just say things, they also *do* things with their words

spoofing misrepresenting oneself online

stagnating stage of romantic relational dissolution in which couples try to prevent change

stereotype threat process in which reminding individuals of stereotypical expectations regarding important identities can impact their performance

stereotyping creating schemas that overgeneralize attributes of a specific group

strategic communication communication on that is purpose directed

strategy control assessing the available information and options in order to increases one's understanding of the conflict and the other party before engaging in conflict communication

structure recurring patterns of interaction among organizational members

style theory theory that asserts that a leader's manner or style determines his or her success

sudden death the process by which relationships end without prior warning for at least one participant

supporting materials information that supports the speaker's ideas

supportive listening listening skills focused not only on understanding information but also "listening" to others' feelings

supportiveness refers to supervisors who provide their subordinates with access to information and resources

symbol something that represents something else and conveys meaning

synchronous communication in which messages are sent and received at the same time

Synergetic Model of Communication a transactional model based on the roles individual and societal forces, contexts, and culture play in the communication process

syntax the rules that govern word order

task roles roles that are directly related to the accomplishment of group goals

technocapital access to technological skills and resources

terminating stage of romantic relational dissolution in which couples end the relationship

textual analysis similar to rhetorical analysis; used to analyze cultural "products," such as media and public speeches

theory a set of statements that explains a particular phenomenon

thesis statement a statement of the topic of a speech and the speaker's position on it

time-oriented a listening style that prefers brief, concise speech

topical pattern one that has no innate organization except that imposed by the speaker

trait theory leadership theory that suggests that leaders are born

transformational leadership a leadership style that empowers group members to work independently from the leader by encouraging group cohesion

truth bias the tendency to not suspect one's intimates of deception

turning point model a model of relationship development in which couples move both toward and away from commitment over the course of their relationship

TV Parental Guidelines a self-regulating system of the television industry that rates programs in terms of appropriateness for particular age groups

uncertainty reduction theory a theory that argues relationship development is facilitated or derailed by participants' efforts to reduce their uncertainty about each other

understanding interpreting the messages associated with sounds or what the sounds mean

upward communication in a traditional conduit model of communication, communication with superiors

upward distortion occurs when subordinates are hesitant to communicate negative news and present information to superiors in a more positive light than is warranted

urgent organizations companies that try to shorten the time it takes to develop new products and respond to customer demands

uses and gratifications the idea that people use media messages and find various types of gratifications in some media texts rather than in others

V-chip device that identifies television program ratings by content and can block programming designated by the owner

value-expressive function the role played by prejudice in allowing people to view their own values, norms, and cultural practices as appropriate and correct

view of human nature a value orientation that expresses whether humans are fundamentally good, evil, or a mixture

visual aids audiovisual materials that help a speaker reach intended speech goals

vocalizations uttered sounds that do not have the structure of language

voice qualities qualities such as speed, pitch, rhythm, vocal range, and articulation that make up the "music" of the human voice

voluntary long-term travelers people who are border dwellers by choice and for an extended time, such as immigrants

voluntary short-term travelers people who are border dwellers by choice and for a limited time, such as study-abroad students or corporate personnel

withdrawal/avoidance a friendship termination strategy in which friends spend less time together, don't return phone calls, and avoid places where they are likely to see each other

World Wide Web (WWW) a system of interlinked hypertext documents contained on the Internet

References

Chapter 1

Alberts, J. K., Yoshimura, C. G., Rabby, M. K., & Loschiavo, R. (2005). Mapping the topography of couples' daily interaction. *Journal of Social and Personal Relationships, 22,* 299–323.

Andersen, P. A., Lustig, M. W., & Andersen, J. F. (1990). Changes in latitude, changes in attitude: The relationship between climate and interpersonal communication predispositions. *Communication Quarterly, 38,* 291–311.

Barnlund, D. C. (1962). Consistency of emergent leadership in groups with changing tasks and members. *Speech Monographs, 29,* 45–52.

Buller, D. B., & Burgoon, J. K. (1996). Interpersonal deception theory. *Communication Theory, 6,* 203–242.

Buck, R., & VanLear, C. A. (2002). Verbal and nonverbal communication: Distinguishing symbolic, spontaneous and pseudo-spontaneous nonverbal behavior. *Journal of Communication, 52,* 522–541.

Christians, C., & Traber, M. (Eds.). (1997). *Communication ethics and universal values.* Thousand Oaks, CA: Sage.

Dickens, T. E. (2003). General symbol machines: The first stage in the evolution of symbolic communication. *Evolutionary Psychology, 1,* 192–209.

Diener, M. (2002, January). Fair enough: To be a better negotiator, learn to tell the difference between a lie and a *lie. Entrepreneur Magazine.* Retrieved March 16, 2006, from http://www. Entrepreneurmagazine.com

Dixon, M., & Duck, S. W. (1993). Understanding relationship processes: Uncovering the human search for meaning. In S. W. Duck (Ed.), *Understanding relationship processes, Vol. 1: Individuals in relationships* (pp. 175–206). Newbury Park, CA: Sage.

Duck, S. (1994). *Meaningful relationships: Talking, sense and relating.* Newbury Park, CA: Sage.

Eisenberg, E. M., Goodall, H. L., Jr., & Trethewey, A. (2010). *Organizational communication: Balancing creativity and constraints.* New York: St. Martin's.

Emanuel, R. (2007). Humanities: Communication's core discipline. *American Communication Journal, 9*(2). Retrieved March 11, 2009, from http://www.acjournal.org/holdings/vol9/summer/articles/discipline.html

FoxNews.com (2010, November 24). Tom DeLay convicted of money laundering. Retrieved February 17, 2011, from http://www.foxnews.com/politics/2010/ 11/24/jury-convicts-delay-money-laundering-trial/

Gergen, K. J. (1982). *Toward transformation in social knowledge.* New York: Springer.

Johannesen, R. (1990). *Ethics in human communication.* Prospect Heights, IL: Waveland.

Jones, A., & Koppel, N. (2010, August 7). Ethical lapses felled long list of company executives. WallStreetJournal.com. Retrieved February 17, 2011, from http://online.wsj.com/article/SB1 0001424052748703309704575413842089375632.html

Kant, I. (1949). *Fundamental principles of the metaphysic of morals* (tr. by T. K. Abbott, Trans.). Indianapolis: Bobbs-Merrill. (Original work published 1785)

Laswell, H. D. (1948). The structure and function of communication in society. In L. Bryson Ed.), *The Communication of Ideas.* New York: Harper.

Leventhal, R. (2011, February 16). Victims respond after Madoff points fingers at banks in first interview from prison. FoxNews.com. Retrieved February 17, 2011, from http://www.foxnews.com/us/2011/02/16/victims-respond-madoff-points-fingers-banks-interview/

Martin, J. N., & Nakayama, T. K. (2005). *Experiencing intercultural communication* (2nd ed.). Boston: McGraw-Hill.

McCabe, D. L., & Trevino, L. K. (1996). What we know about cheating in college: Longitudinal trends and recent developments. *Change, 28,* 28–33.

McCord, L. B., Greenhalgh, K., & Magasin, M. (2004). Businesspersons beware: Lying is a crime. *Graziadio Business Report, 7*(23). Pepperdine University. Retrieved December 30, 2009, from http://gbr.pepperdine.edu/043/lying.html

McCornack, S. A., & Parks, M. R. (1986). Deception detection and relationship development: The other side of trust. In M. L. McLaughlin (Ed.), *Communication Yearbook 9* (pp. 377–389). Newbury Park, CA: Sage. Retrieved March 16, 2006, from http://www.natcom.org/policies/External/EthicalComm

Mead, G. H. (1934). *Mind, self, and society.* Chicago: University of Chicago Press.

National Communication Association (2003). What is communication? *Pathways.* Retrieved October 24, 2008, from http://www.natcom.org/nca/Template2.asp?bid=339

Passer, M. W., & Smith, R. E. (2004). *Psychology: The science of mind and behavior* (2nd ed.). New York: McGraw-Hill.

Paul, R., & Elder, L. (2008). *The miniature guide to critical thinking concepts and tools.* Dillon Beach, CA: Foundation for Critical Thinking Press.

Robinson-Smith, G. (2004). Verbal indicators of depression in conversations with stroke survivors. *Perspectives in Psychiatric Care, 40,* 61–69.

Rogers, E. M., & Chafee, S. H. (1983). Communication as an academic discipline: A dialogue. *Journal of Communication, 3,* 18–30.

Sartre, J. P. (1973). *Existentialism and humanism* (P. Mairet, Trans.) London: Methuen Ltd. (Original work published 1946)

Schirato, T., & Yell, S. (1996). *Communication & cultural literacy: An introduction.* St. Leonards, Australia: Allen & Unwin.

Shannon, C. E., & Weaver, W. (1949). *A mathematical model of communication.* Urbana, IL: University of Illinois Press.

Tolhuizen, J. H. (1990, November). *Deception in developing dating relationships.* Paper presented at the Speech Communication Association Convention, Chicago, IL.

Warren, S. F. & Yoder, P. J. (1998). Facilitating the transition to intentional communication. In A. Wetherby, S. Warren, & J. Reichle (Eds.). *Transitions in Prelinguistic Communication* (pp. 39–58). Baltimore: Brookes Publishing

Watzlawick, P., Beavin, J., & Jackson, D. D. (1967). *Pragmatics of human communication.* New York: W. W. Norton.

Wokutch, R. E., & Carson, T. L. (1981). The ethics and profitability of bluffing in business. In Lewickis, Saunders, & Minton (Eds.), *Negotiation: Readings, exercises, and cases* (pp. 341–353). Boston: Irwin/McGraw-Hill.

Chapter 2

Alberts, J. K. (1988). An analysis of couples' conversational complaint interactions. *Communication Monographs, 5*, 184–197.

Alcoff, L. (Winter 1991–1992). The problem of speaking for others. *Cultural Critique, 20*, 5–32.

Bartholomew, K. (1990). Avoidance of intimacy: An attachment perspective. *Journal of Social and Personal Relationships, 7*, 147–178.

Becker, J. A. H., Ellevold, B., & Stamp, G. H. (2008). The creation of defensiveness in social interaction II: A model of defensive communication among romantic couples. *Communication Monographs, 75*(1), 86–110.

Bowlby, J. (1982). Attachment and loss: Vol I: Attachment (2nd ed.). New York: Basic Books.

Borda, J. L. (2002). The woman suffrage parades of 1910–1913: Possibilities and limitations of an early feminist rhetorical strategy. *Western Journal of Communication, 66*, 25–52.

Bormann, E. G. (1980). *Communication theory*. New York: Holt, Rinehart and Winston.

Burrell, G., & Morgan, G. (1988). *Sociological paradigms and organizational analysis*. Portsmouth, NH: Heinemann.

Calafell, B. M., & Delgado, F. P. (2004). Reading Latina/o images: Interrogating Americanos. *Critical Studies in Media Communication, 21*, 1–21.

Campbell, K. K. (1994). *Women public speakers in the United States, 1925–1993: A bio-critical sourcebook*. Westport, CT: Greenwood

Carbaugh, D. (1990). Communication rules in Donahue discourse. In D. Carbaugh (Ed.), Cultural communication and intercultural contact (pp. 119–149). Hillsdale, NJ: Lawrence Erlbaum.

Carbaugh, D. (1999). "Just listen": "Listening" and landscape among the Blackfeet. *Western Journal of Communication, 63*, 250–270.

Carbaugh, D., & Berry, M. (2001). Communicating history, Finnish and American discourses: An ethnographic contribution to intercultural communication inquiry. *Communication Theory, 11*, 352–366.

Caughlin, J. P., & Vangelisti, A. L. (1999). Desire for change in one's partner as a predictor of the demand/withdraw pattern of marital communication. *Communication Monographs, 66*(1), 66–89.

Christensen, A. (1987). Detection of conflict patterns in couples. In K. Hahlweg & M. J. Goldstein (Eds.), *Understanding major mental disorder: The contribution of family interaction research* (pp. 250–265). New York: Family Process Press.

Christensen, A. (1988). Dysfunctional interaction patterns in couples. In P. Noller & M. A. Fitzpatrick (Eds.), *Perspectives in marital interaction* (pp. 31–52). Philadelphia: Multilingual Matters Ltg.

Christensen, A., & Heavey, C. L. (1990). Gender and social structure in the demand/withdraw pattern of marital conflict. *Journal of Personality and Social Psychology, 59*, 73–81.

Cloud, D. L. (2010). The irony bribe and reality television: Investment and detachment in *The Bachelor. Critical Studies in Media Communication, 27*(5), 413–437.

Cohen, H. (1994). *The history of speech communication: The emergence of a discipline, 1914–1945*. Annandale, VA: Speech Communication Association.

Craig, R. T. (1999). Communication theory as a field. *Communication Theory, 9*, 119–161.

Denzin, N. K. & Lincoln, Y. S. (Eds.). (2005), *Handbook of qualitative research* (3rd ed). Thousand Oaks, CA: Sage.

Dues, M., & Brown, M. (2004). *Boxing Plato's shadow: An introduction to the study of human communication*. Boston: McGraw-Hill.

Eldridge, K. A., Sevier, M., Jones, J., Atkins, D. C., & Christensen, A. (2007). Demand-withdraw communication in severely distressed, moderately distressed, and nondistressed couples: Rigidity and polarity during relationship and personal problem discussions. *Journal of Family Psychology, 21*, 218–226.

Eldridge, K. A., & Christensen, A. (2002). Demand-withdraw communication during couple conflict: A review and analysis. In P. Noller & J. A. Feeney (Eds.), *Understanding marriage: Developments in the study of couple interaction* (pp. 289–322). Cambridge: Cambridge University Press.

Ellis, C. (2007). Telling secrets, revealing lives: Relational ethics in research with intimate others, *Qualitative Inquiry, 13*(1), 3–29.

Engels, J. (2009). Uncivil speech: Invective and the rhetorics of democracy in the early republic. *Quarterly Journal of Speech, 95*(3), 311–334.

Fowler, C., & Dillow, M. R. (2011). Attachment dimensions and the Four Horsemen of the Apocalypse. *Communication Research Reports, 28*(1), 16–26.

Glaser, B. G., & Strauss, A. (1967). *Discovery of grounded theory: Strategies for qualitative research*. Chicago: Aldine de Gruyter.

González, M. C. (2000). The four seasons of ethnography: A creation centered ontology for ethnography. *International Journal of Intercultural Relations, 24*, 525–539.

Guerrero, L. K., Farinelli, L., & McEwan, B. (2009) Attachment and relational satisfaction: The mediating effect of emotional communication. *Communication Monographs, 76*(4), 487–514.

Hill, L. (2010). Gender and genre: Situating *Desperate Housewives. Journal of Popular Film and Television, 38*(4), 162–169.

Jacobson, N. S. (1989). The politics of intimacy. *Behavior Therapist, 12*, 29–32.

Jacobson, N. S. (1990). Commentary: Contribution from psychology to an understanding of marriage. In F. D. Fincham & T. N. Bradbury (Eds.), *The psychology of marriage*. New York: Guilford Press.

Kraybill, D. B. (2001). *The riddle of Amish culture (revised ed.)* Baltimore: Johns Hopkins University Press.

Kraybill, D. B., Nolt, S. M., & Weaver-Zercher, D. L. (2010). *Amish grace: How forgiveness transcended tragedy*. San Francisco, Ca: John Wiley.

Lazard, L. (2009). V. 'You'll Like This—It's Feminist!' Representations of strong women in horror fiction. *Feminism in Psychology, 19*(11), 132–136.

Lindlof, T. R., & Taylor, B. C. (2002). *Qualitative communication research methods* (2nd ed.). Thousand Oaks: Sage.

Lindsley, S. L. (1999). A layered model of problematic intercultural communication in U.S.-owned *maquiladoras* in Mexico. *Communication Monographs, 66*(2), 145–168.

Litwin, A. H., & Hallstein, L. O. (2007). Shadows and silences: How women's positioning and unspoken friendship rules in organizational settings cultivate difficulties among some women at work. *Women's Studies in Communication, 30*(1), 111–142.

Martin, J. N., & Butler, R. L. W. (2001). Towards an ethic of intercultural communication research. In V. H. Milhouse, M. K. Asante, & P. O. Nwosu (Eds.), *Transcultural realities: Interdisciplinary perspectives on cross-cultural relations* (pp. 283–298). Thousand Oaks, CA: Sage.

Milburn, T. (2010). The relevance of cultural communication: For whom and in what respect? *Communication Monographs, 77*(4), 439–441.

Miller, W. L., & Crabtree, B. F. (2005). Clinical Research. In N. K. Denzin & Y. S. Lincoln (Eds.), *Handbook of qualitative research* (3rd ed., pp. 605–640). Thousand Oaks, CA: Sage.

Mumby, D. (1997). Modernism, postmodernism, and communication studies: A rereading of ongoing debates. *Communication Theory, 7*, 1–28.

Mumby, D. (2005). Theorizing resistance in organization studies: A dialectical approach. *Management Communication Quarterly, 19*(1), 19–44.

Noller, P. (1993). Gender and emotional communication in marriage: Different cultures or differential social power? *Journal of Language and Social Psychology, 12*, 132–152.

Papp, L. M., Kouros, C. D., & Cummings, M. (2009). Demand-withdraw patterns in marital conflict in the home. *Personal Relationships, 16*, 285–300.

Piliavin, I. M., Rodin, J., and Piliavin, J. A. (1969). Good samaritanism: An underground phenomenon? *Journal of Personality and Social Psychology, 13*, 289–299.

Rholes, W. S., Simpson, J. A., Tran, S., Martin III, A. M., & Friedman, M. (2007). Attachment and information seeking in romantic relationships. *Personality and Social Psychology Bulletin, 33*, 422–438.

Shugart, H. (2008). Managing masculinities: The metrosexual moment. *Communication and Critical/Cultural Studies, 5*(3), 280–300.

Sommerson, W. (2004). White men on the edge: Rewriting the borderlands in *Lone Star. Men and Masculinities, 6*(3), 215–239.

Strauss, A., & Corbin, J. (1998). *Basics of qualitative research: Techniques and procedures for developing grounded theory* (2nd ed.). Newbury Park, CA: Sage.

Suter, E. A. (2004). Tradition never goes out of style: The role of tradition in women's naming practices. *Communication Review, 7*, 57–87.

Tanno, D. (1997). *Communication and identity across cultures.* Thousand Oaks, CA: Sage.

Trethewey, A. (1997). Resistance, identity, and empowerment: A postmodern feminist analysis of clients in a human service organization. *Communication Monographs, 64*, 281–301.

Zaeske, S. (2002). Signature of citizenship: The rhetoric of women's antislavery petitions. *Quarterly Journal of Speech, 88*, 147–168.

Chapter 3

Abrams, J., O'Connor, J., & Giles, H. (2002). Identity and intergroup communication. In W. B. Gudykunst & B. Mody (Eds.), *Handbook of international and intercultural communication* (2nd ed., pp. 225–240). Thousand Oaks, CA: Sage.

Allen, B. (2004). *Difference matters: Communicating social identity.* Long Grove, IL: Waveland.

Americans with Disabilities Act of 1990, as amended with Amendments of 2008. Retrieved May 13, 2011, from: http://www.ada.gov/pubs/adastatute08.htm

Arana, M. (2008, November 30). He's not black. *Washington Post*, p. B1. Retrieved December 31, 2008, from www.washingtonpost.com/wp-dyn/content/article/2008/11/28/AR2008112802219.html

Azuri, L. (2006, November 17). Public debate in Saudi Arabia on employment opportunities for women. *Inquiry and Analysis 300*. Retrieved March 16, 2009, from www.memri.org/bin/articles.cgi?Area=ia&ID=IA30006&Page=archives

Baker, C. (2003, November 30). What is middle class? *The Washington Times*. Retrieved January 16, 2005, from www.washtimes.com/specialreport/200311291058557412r.htm

Bennett-Haigney, B. (1995, August). Faulkner makes history at the Citadel. *NOW Newsletter*. Retrieved March 1, 2006, from www.now.org/nnt/08-95/citadel.html

Blumer, H. (1969). *Symbolic interactionism: Perspective and method.* Englewood Cliffs, NJ: Prentice Hall.

Bock, G. (1989), Women's history and gender history: Aspects of an international debate. *Gender & History, 1*: 7–30.

Bourdieu, P. (1984). *Distinction: A social critique of the judgment of taste.* (R. Nice, Trans.). London: Routledge & Kegan Paul.

Butler, J. (1990). *Gender trouble: Feminism and the subversion of identity.* New York: Routledge.

Butler, J. (1993). *Bodies that matter: On the discursive limits of "sex."* New York: Routledge.

Candiotti, S., Koppel, A., Zarrella, J., & Bash, D. (2006, October 3). Attorney: Clergyman molested Foley as teen. *CNN*. Retrieved December 31, 2008, from www.cnn.com/2006/POLITICS/10/03/foley.scandal/index.htm

Carbaugh, D. (2007). Cultural discourse analysis: Communication practices and intercultural encounters. *Journal of Intercultural Communication Research, 36*, 167–182.

Cardillo, L. W. (2010). Empowering narratives: Making sense of the experience of growing up with chronic illness or disability. *Western Journal of Communication, 74*(5), 525–546.

Cauchon, D. (2010, September 14). Gender pay gap is smallest on record. *USA Today*. Retrieved on March 22, 2011, from: http://www.usatoday.com/money/workplace/2010-09-13-wage-gaps_N.htm

Cohen, A. (2010, September 22). Justice Scalia Mouths Off on Sex Discrimination. *Time*. Retrieved May 12, 2011, from: http://www.time.com/time/nation/article/0,8599,2020667,00.html

Cooley, C. H. (1902). *Human nature and the social order.* New York: Scribner's.

Corey, F. C. (2004). A letter to Paul. *Text and Performance Quarterly, 24*, 185–190.

Corey, F. C., & Nakayama, T. K. (2004). Introduction. Special issue "Religion and Performance." *Text and Performance Quarterly, 24*, 209–211.

Cornell University. (2004). Fear factor: 44 percent of Americans queried in Cornell national poll favor curtailing some liberties for Muslim Americans. *Cornell News*. Retrieved December 6, 2006, from www.news.cornell.edu/releases/Dec04/Muslim.Poll.bpf.html

Croizet, J., & Claire, T. (1998). Extending the concept of stereotype threat to social class: The intellectual underperformance of students from low socioeconomic backgrounds. *Personality and Social Psychology, 24*(5), 588–594.

Daigle, K. (2011, February 12). India's census counts 'third gender.' Edge Boston. Retrieved March 22, 2011, from: http://www.edgeboston.com/?116206

Davies, R., & Ikeno, O. (Eds.). (2002). *The Japanese mind: Understanding contemporary culture.* Boston: Tuttleman.

Drum Major Institute for Public Policy. (2005). Middle class 2004: How Congress voted. Retrieved June 12, 2006, from www.drummajorinstitute.org/library/report.php?ID=4

Edwards, R. (1990). Sensitivity to feedback and the development of the self. *Communication Quarterly, 38*, 101–111.

El Nasser, H. (2010, March 15). Multiracial no longer boxed in by the Census, *USA Today*. Retrieved May 12, 2011, from: http://www.usatoday.com/news/nation/census/2010-03-02-census-multi-race_N.htm

Erickson, A. L. (1993). *Women and property in early modern England.* London: Routlege.

Fassett, D. L., & Morella, D. L. (2008). Remaking (the) discipline: Marking the performative accomplishment of (dis)ability. *Text and Performance Quarterly, 28*(1–2), 139–156.

Foucault, M. (1988). *History of sexuality* (R. Hurley, Trans.). New York: Vintage Books.

Fussell, P. (1992). *Class: A guide through the American status system.* New York: Touchstone.

Guzman, I. M., & Valdivia, A. N. (2004). Brain, brow, and booty: Latina iconicity in U.S. popular culture. *Communication Review, 7,* 205–221.

Hacker, A. (2003). *Two nations: Black and White, separate, hostile, unequal.* New York: Scribner.

Harwood, J. (2006). Communication as social identity. In G. J. Shepherd, J. St. John, & T. Striphas (Eds.), *Communication as...: Perspectives on theory* (pp. 84–90). Thousand Oaks, CA: Sage.

Hecht, M. L. (1993). 2002—A research odyssey. *Communication Monographs, 60,* 76–82.

Hecht, M. L., Jackson R. L., III, & Ribeau, S. A. (2003). *African American communication: Exploring identity and culture.* (2nd ed). Mahwah, NJ: Lawrence Erlbaum Associates.

Henderson, B., & Ostrander, R. N. (2008). Introduction to special issue on disability studies/performance studies. *Text and Performance Quarterly, 28*(1–2), 1–5.

Hirschman, C. (2003, May). The rise and fall of the concept of race. Paper presented at the Annual Meeting of the Population Association of America, Minneapolis, MN.

Hutcheson, J., Domke, D., Billeaudeaux, A., & Garland, P. (2004). U.S. national identity, political elites, and a patriotic press following September 11. *Political Communication, 21,* 27–50.

Johnson, A. G. (2001). *Privilege, power and difference.* Boston: McGraw-Hill.

Jones, N. A., & Smith, A. S. (2001). The two or more races population. *Census 2000 Brief (U.S. Census Bureau Publication No. C2KBR/01-6).* Washington, DC: U.S. Government Printing Office.

Kimmel, M. S. (2005). *The history of men: Essays in the history of American and British masculinities.* Albany: State University of New York Press.

Koshy, S. (2004). *Sexual naturalization: Asian Americans and miscegenation.* Stanford, CA: Stanford University Press.

Kraybill, D. B. (1989). *The riddle of Amish culture.* Baltimore: Johns Hopkins University Press.

Lagarde, D. (2005, September 22–28). Afghanistan: La loi des tribus. *L'Express International,* 30–37.

Lengel, L., & Warren, J. T. (2005). Introduction: Casting gender. In L. Lengel & J. T. Warren (Eds.), *Casting gender: Women and performance in intercultural contexts* (pp. 1–18). New York: Peter Lang.

Lindemann, K. (2008). "I can't be standing up out there": Communicative performances of (dis)ability in wheelchair rugby. *Text and Performance Quarterly, 28*(1–2), 98–115.

Lerner, M. (2008, November 18). Minnesota disciplines four doctors, two for inappropriate contact. *Star-Tribune.* Retrieved May 3, 2011, from: http://www.startribune.com/lifestyle/34691559.html?page=all&prepage=1&c=y#continue

Loden, M., & Rosener, J. B. (1991). *Workforce America: Managing workforce diversity as a vital resource.* Homewood, IL: Business One Irwin.

Lucas, K. (2011). Socializing messages in blue-collar families: Communication pathways to social mobility and reproduction. *Western Journal of Communication, 75*(1), 95–121.

Manczak, D. W. (1999, July 1). Raising your child's self-esteem. *Clinical Reference Systems,* 1242.

Marshall, G. A. (1993). Racial classification: Popular and Scientific. In S. G. Harding (Ed.), *The "racial" economy of science: Toward a democratic future* (pp. 116–127). Bloomington: Indiana University Press.

Martin, J. N., & Harrell, T. (1996). Reentry training for intercultural sojourners. In D. Landis & R. S. Bhagat (Eds.), *Handbook of intercultural training* (2nd ed., pp. 307–326). Thousand Oaks, CA: Sage.

McGlone, M. S., & Aronson, J. (2006). Stereotype threat, identity salience, and spatial reasoning. *Journal of Applied Development Psychology, 27*(5), 486–493.

Mead, G. H. (1934). *Mind, self, and society.* Chicago: University of Chicago Press.

Mikkelsen, E. G., & Einarsen, S. (2001). Bullying in Danish worklife: Prevalence and health correlates. *European Journal of Work and Organizational Psychology, 10,* 393–413.

Milbank, D. (2007, August 29). A senator's wide stance. "I am not gay." *Washington Post,* p. A2. Retrieved December 31, 2008, from www.washingtonpost.com/wp-dyn/content/article/2007/08/28/AR2007082801664.html

Noy, C. (2004). Performing identity: Touristic performances of self-change. *Text and Performance Quarterly, 24*(2), 115–138.

Office for National Statistics. Retrieved July 8, 2009, from www.ons.gov.uk/about-statistics/classifications/archived/ethnic-interim/presenting-data/index.html

Online Glossary. (2005, January). Prentice Hall. Retrieved January 16, 2005, from www.prenhall.com/rm_student/html/glossary/a_gloss.html

Palladino, G. (1996). *Teenagers: An American history.* New York: Basic Books.

Papalia, D. E., Olds, S. W., & Feldman, R. D. (2002). *A child's world: Infancy through adolescence.* New York: McGraw-Hill.

Pew Forum on Religion and Public Life. (2008, November 20). *How the News Media Covered Religion in the General Election.* Retrieved December 31, 2008, from http://pewforum.org/docs/?DocID=372

Phelps, J. L., Belsky, J., & Crnic, K. (1998). Earned security, daily stress, and parenting: A comparison of five alternative models. *Development and Psychology, 10,* 21–38.

Philipsen, G. (1992). *Speaking culturally: Explorations in social communication.* Albany, NY: SUNY Press.

Rawls, J. (1995). Self-respect, excellence, and shame. In R. S. Dillon (Ed.), *Dignity, character, and self-respect* (pp. 125–131). New York: Routledge.

Roland, C. E., & Foxx, R. M. (2003). Self-respect: A neglected concept. *Philosophical Psychology. 16*(2) 247–288.

Rosenblith, J. F. (1992). *In the beginning: Development from conception to age two.* Newbury Park, CA: Sage.

Sanders, W. B. (1994). *Gangbangs and drive-bys: Grounded culture and juvenile gang violence.* New York: Aldine de Gruyter.

Sen. Craig restroom tanking as tourist destination. (2008, December 28). *Washington Post.* Retrieved December 31, 2008, from www.cbsnews.com/stories/2008/12/28/ap/strange/main4688671.shtml

Sheridan, V. (2004, November). *From Vietnamese refugee to Irish citizen: Politics, language, culture and identity.* Paper presented at the International Association of Languages and Intercultural Communication, Dublin City University, Dublin, Ireland.

Shih, M., Pittinsky, T. L., & Ambady, N. (1999). Stereotype susceptibility: Identity salience and shifts in quantitative performance. *Psychological Science. 10*(1), 80–83.

Sloop, J. M. (2004). *Disciplining gender: Rhetoric of sex identity in contemporary U.S. culture.* Amherst: University of Massachusetts Press.

Smith, J. L., & White, P. H. (2002). An examination of implicitly activated, explicitly activated, and nullified stereotypes on mathematical performance: It's not just a women's issue. *Sex Roles, 47*(3–4), 179–191.

Steele, C. M., & Aronson, J. (1995). Stereotype threat and intellectual test performance of African Americans. *Journal of Personality and Social Psychology, 69*(5), 797–811.

Sullivan, H. S. (1953). *The interpersonal theory of psychology.* New York: Norton.

Sullivan, T. A., Warren, E., & Westbrook, J. (2001). *The fragile middle class: Americans in debt.* New Haven: Yale University Press.

Taylor, J. (2005, June 6). *Between two worlds.* How many Americans really attend church each week? Retrieved January 30, 2006, from http://theologica.blogspot.com/2005/06/how-many-americans-really-attend.html

Ting-Toomey, S. (1999). *Communicating across cultures.* New York: Guilford.

Trethewey, A. (2001). Reproducing and resisting the master narrative of decline: Midlife professional women's experiences of aging. *Management Communication Quarterly, 15,* 183–226.

Venkat, V. (2008, Feb. 16–29). Gender issues: From the shadows. *Frontline, India's National Magazine, 25*(4). Retrieved March 3, 2011, from http://www.frontlineonnet.com/Fl2504/Stories/20080229607610000.htm

Vevea, N., "Body Art: Performing Identity Through Tattoos and Piercing," *Paper presented at the annual meeting of the NCA 94th Annual Convention, TBA, San Diego, CA Online.* Retrieved March 11, 2011, from http://www.allacademic.com/meta/p258244_index.html

Waters, M. C. (1990). *Ethnic options: Choosing identities in America.* Berkeley: University of California Press.

Wax, E. (2005, September 26–October 2). Beyond the pull of the tribe: In Kenya, some teens find unity in contemporary culture. *Washington Post,* National Weekly Edition, 22(49), 8.

Zinzer, L. (2010, July 7). South African cleared to compete as a woman. *New York Times.* Retrieved May 13, 2011, from: http://query.nytimes.com/gst/fullpage.html?res=9803E2DE1430F934A35754C0A9669D8B63&ref=castersemenya

Chapter 4

Applegate, J. (1982). The impact of construct system development on communication and impression formation in persuasive contexts. *Communication Monographs, 49,* 277–289.

Bradbury, T. N., & Fincham, F. D. (1988). Individual difference variables in close relationships: A contextual model of marriage as an integrative framework. *Journal of Personality and Social Psychology, 54,* 713–721.

Braithwaite, C. (1990). Communicative silence: A cross-cultural study of Basso's hypothesis. In D. Carbaugh (Ed.), *Cultural communication and intercultural contact* (pp. 321–327). Hillsdale NJ: Lawrence Erlbaum Associates.

Brislin, R. (2000). *Understanding culture's influence on behavior* (2nd ed.). Belmont, CA: Wadsworth.

Bruner, J. (1991). *Acts of meaning,* Cambridge: Harvard University Press.

Bruner, J. S. (1958). Neural mechanisms in perception. Research Publication of the Association for Research in Nervous and Mental Disease, 36, 118–143.

Burgoon, J. K., Berger, C. R., & Waldron, V. R. (2000). Mindfulness and interpersonal communication. *Journal of Social Issues, 56,* 105–127.

Burleson, B. R., & Caplan, S. E. (1998). Cognitive complexity. In J. C. McCroskey, J. Daly, & M. M. Martin (Eds.), *Communication and personality: Trait perspectives.* Cresskill, NJ: Hampton.

Chaiken, S. (1986). Physical appearance and social influence. In C. P. Herman, M. P. Zanna, & E. T. Higgins (Eds.), *Physical appearance, stigma, and social behavior: The Ontario Symposium* (Vol. 3, pp. 143–144). Hillsdale, NJ: Erlbaum.

Chapin, J. (2001). It won't happen to me: The role of optimistic bias in African American teens' risky sexual practices. *Howard Journal of Communications, 12,* 49–59.

Classen, C. (1990). Sweet colors, fragrant songs: Sensory models of the Andes and the Amazon. *American Ethnologist, 14,* 722–735.

Deutsch, F. M., Sullivan, L., Sage, C., & Basile, N. (1991). The relations among talking, liking, and similarity between friends. *Personality and Social Psychology Bulletin, 17,* 406–411.

Dijk, T. A., van (1977). *Text and context: Explorations in the semantics and pragmatics of discourse.* London: Longman.

Dillard, J. P., Solomon, D. H., & Samp, J. A. (1996). Framing social reality: The relevance of relational judgments. *Communication Research, 23,* 703–723.

Douglas, W. (1990). Uncertainty, information-seeking, and liking during initial interaction. *Western Journal of Speech Communication, 54,* 66–81.

Douthat, R. (2005, November). Does meritocracy work? *Atlantic,* 120–126.

Ehrenreich, B. (2001). *Nickel and dimed: On (not) getting by in America.* New York: Metropolitan Books.

Estroff, H. (2004, September/October). Cupid's comeuppance. *Psychology Today.* Retrieved March 15, 2006, from www.psychologytoday.com/articles/pto-20040921-000001.html

Fisher, K. (1997). Locating frames in the discursive universe. *Sociological Research Online, 2*(3). Retrieved October 25, 2008, from www.socresonline.org.uk/2/3/4.html

Fiske, S. T., & Taylor, S. E. (1991). *Social cognition* (2nd ed.). New York: McGraw-Hill.

Greenough, W. T., Black, J. E., & Wallace, C. S. (1987). Experience and brain development. *Child Development, 58,* 539–559.

Griffin, E. (1994). *A first look at communication theory.* New York: McGraw-Hill.

Gueguen, N., & De Gail, M. (2003). The effect of smiling on helping behavior: Smiling and good Samaritan behavior. *Communication Reports, 16*(2), 133–140.

Hacker, A. (2003). *Two nations: Black and White, separate, hostile, unequal.* New York: Scribner.

Heider, F. (1958). *The psychology of interpersonal relations,* New York: Wiley.

Heine, S. J., & Lehman, D. R. (2004). Move the body, change the self: Acculturative effects on self-concept. In A. Schaller & C. Crandall (Eds.), *The psychological foundations of culture* (pp. 305–31). Hillsdale, NJ: Erlbaum.

Herz, R. S., & Inzlicht, M. (2002). Sex differences in response to physical and social factors involved in human mate selection: The importance of smell for women. *Evolution and Human Behavior, 23,* 359–364.

Hurley R. W., & Adams, M. C. B. (2008). Sex, gender and pain: An overview of a complex field. *Anesthesia and Analgesia. 107,* 309–17

Jong, P. F. de, Koomen, W., & Mellenbergh, G. J. (1988). Structure of causes for success and failure: A multidimensional scaling analysis of preference judgments. *Journal of Personality and Social Psychology, 55,* 718–725.

Kanizsa, G. (1979). *Organization in vision*. New York: Praeger.

Kellerman, K. (2004). A goal-direct approach to compliance-gaining: Relating differences among goals to differences in behavior. *Communication Research, 31*, 345–347.

Kelley, H. H. (1973). The processes of causal attribution. *American Psychologist, 28*, 107–128.

Kim, M. S. (2002). *Non-Western perspectives on human communication*. Thousand Oaks, CA: Sage.

Kirouac, G., & Hess, U. (1999). Group membership and the decoding of nonverbal behavior. In R. S. Feldman & P. Philippot (Eds.), *The social context of nonverbal behavior* (pp.182–210). New York: Cambridge University Press.

Krivonos, P. D., & Knapp, M. L. (1975). Initiating communication: What do you say when you say hello? *Central States Speech Journal, 26*, 115–125.

Lakoff, G. (1987). *Women, fire, and dangerous things: What categories reveal about the mind*. Chicago: University of Chicago Press.

Langer, E. J. (1978). Rethinking the role of thought in social interaction. In J. H. Harvey, W. Ickes, & R. F. Kidd (Eds.), *New directions in attribution research* (Vol. 2, pp. 3–58). New York: Wiley.

Levinthal, D., & Gavetti, G. (2000, March). Looking forward and looking backward: Cognition and experiential search. *Administrative Science Quarterly*, 1–9.

Link, B. G., & Phelan, J. C. (August, 2001). Conceptualizing stigma. *Annual Review of Sociology, 27*, 363–385.

Lupfer, M. B., Weeks, M., & Dupuis, S. (2000). How pervasive is the negativity bias in judgments based on character appraisal? *Personality and Social Psychology Bulletin, 26*, 1353–1366.

Manusov, V., & Spitzberg, B. (2008). Attributes of attribution theory: Finding good cause in the search for a theory. In D. O. Braithwaite & L. A. Baxter (Eds.), *Engaging theories in interpersonal* (pp. 37–49). Thousand Oaks, CA: Sage.

Markus, H. R., Mullally, P. R., & Kitayama, S. (1997). Selfways: Diversity in modes of cultural participation. In U. Neisser & D. A. Jopling (Eds.), *The conceptual self in context* (pp. 13–59). Cambridge, UK: Cambridge University Press.

McCoy, N. L., & Pitino, L. (2002). Pheromonal influences on sociosexual behavior in young women. *Physiology and Behavior, 75*, 367–375.

"Middle of the Class" (2005, July 14). Survey: America. *Economist*. Retrieved March 10, 2006, from www.economist.com/displayStory.cfm?Story_id=4148885

Morgan, M. J. (1977). *Molyneux's question : Vision, touch and the philosophy of perception*. Cambridge, NY: Cambridge University Press.

Neale, M. A., & Bazerman, M. H. (1991). *Cognition and rationality in negotiation*. New York: Free Press.

Pearce, W. B. (1994). *Interpersonal communication: Making social worlds*. New York: HarperCollins.

Pew Research Center for People and the Press. (2005, September 8). Huge racial divide over Katrina and its consequences. Retrieved June 1, 2006, from http://people-press.org/reports/pdf/255.pdf

Planalp, S. (1993). Communication, cognition, and emotion. *Communication Monographs, 60*, 3–9.

Putnam, L. L., & Holmer, M. (1992). Framing, reframing and issue development. In L. L. Putnam & M. E. Roloff (Eds.), *Communication and negotiation* (pp. 128–155). Newbury Park, CA: Sage.

Ross, L. (1977). The intuitive psychologist and his shortcomings: Distortions in the attribution process. In L. Berkowitz (Ed.), *Advances in experimental social psychology* (Vol. 10, pp. 173–220). New York: Academic Press.

Rothenberg, P. S. (1992). *Race, class, and gender in the United States*. New York: St. Martin's Press.

Samter, W., & Burleson, B. R. (1984). Cognitive and motivational influences on spontaneous comforting behavior. *Human Communication Research, 11*, 231–260.

Scollon, R., & Wong-Scollon, S. (1990). Athabaskan-English interethnic communication. In D. Carbaugh (Ed.), *Cultural communication and intercultural contact* (pp. 259–287). Hillsdale, NJ: Erlbaum.

Seligman, M. (1998). *Learned optimism*. New York: Simon & Schuster.

Shore, B. (1996). *Culture in mind: Cognition, culture and the problem of meaning*. New York: Oxford University Press.

Sillars, A. L, Roberts, L. J., Leonard, K. E., & Dun, T. (2000). Cognition during marital conflict: The relationship of thought and talk. *Journal of Social and Personal Relationships, 17*, 479–502.

Sillars, A. L, Roberts, L. J., Leonard, K. E., & Dun, T. (2002). Cognition and communication during marital conflicts: How alcohol affects subjective coding of interaction in aggressive and nonaggressive couples. In P. Noller & J. A. Feeney (Eds.), *Understanding marriage: Developments in the study of couples' interaction* (p. 85–112). Cambridge, U.K.: Cambridge University Press.

Singh, D., & Bronstad, P. M. (2001). Female body odour is a potential cue to ovulation. *Proceedings of the Royal Society: Biological Science, 268*, 797–801.

Siu, W. L. W., & Finnegan, J. R. (2004, May). An exploratory study of the interaction of affect and cognition in message evaluation. Paper presented at the International Communication Association Convention, San Francisco, CA.

Smith, S. W., Kopfman, J. E., Lindsey, L., Massi, Y. J., & Morrison, K. (2004). Encouraging family discussion on the decision to donate organs: The role of the willingness to communicate scale. *Health Communication. 16*, 333–346.

Snyder, M. (1998). Self-fulfilling stereotypes. In P. S. Rothenberg (Ed.), *Race, class and gender in the U.S.: An integrated study* (pp. 452–457). New York: St. Martin's Press.

Stephan, C., & Stephan, W. (1992). Reducing intercultural anxiety through intercultural contact. *International Journal of Intercultural Relations, 16*, 89–106.

Ting-Toomey, S. (1999). *Communicating across cultures*. New York: Guilford.

U.S. National Research Council. (1989). *Improving risk communication*. Committee on risk perception and communication. Washington, DC: National Academy Press.

Weick, K. (1995). *Sensemaking in organizations*. Thousand Oaks, CA: Sage.

Wilson, G., & Nias, D. (1999). Beauty can't be beat. In J. A. DeVito & L. Guerrero, (Eds.), *The nonverbal communication reader: Classic and contemporary readings* (2nd ed., pp. 92–132). Prospect Heights, IL: Waveland Press.

Chapter 5

American Civil Liberties Union (1994). Free speech: Hate speech on campus. Retrieved May 31, 2011, from http://www.aclu.org/free-speech/hate-speech-campus

American Heritage Dictionary of the English Language. 4th ed, (2000). Boston: Houghton-Mifflin. Retrieved June 12, 2006, from http://www.bartleby.com/cgibin/texis/webinator/ahdsearch?search_type=enty&query=wise&db=ahd&submit=Search

Aries, E. (1996). *Men and women in interaction: Reconsidering the differences*. New York: Oxford University Press.

Austin, J. L. (1975). *How to do things with words* (2nd ed.). Cambridge, MA: Harvard University Press.

Aylor, B., & Dainton, M. (2004). Biological sex and psychological gender as predictors of routine and strategic relational maintenance. *Sex Roles: A Journal of Research, 50,* 689–697.

Baker, M. (1991). Gender and verbal communication in professional settings: A review of research. *Management Communication Quarterly, 5,* 36–63.

Bippus, A. M., & Young, S. L. (2005). Owning your emotions: Reactions to expressions of self versus other-attributed positive and negative emotions. *Journal of Applied Communication Research, 33,* 26–45.

Bowen, S. P. (2003). Jewish and/or woman: Identity and communicative styles. In A. González, M. Houston, & V. Chen (Eds.), *Our voices: Essays in culture, ethnicity, and communication* (4th ed.). Los Angeles: Roxbury.

Boxer, D. (2002). Nagging: The familial conflict arena. *Journal of Pragmatics, 34,* 49–61.

Burrell, N. A., Donohue, W. A., & Allen, M. (1988). Gender-based perceptual biases in mediation. *Communication Research, 15,* 447–469.

Canary, D. J., & Emmers-Sommer, T. M. (1997). *Sex and gender differences in personal relationships.* New York: Guilford.

Canary, D. J., & Hause, K. S. (1993). Is there any reason to research sex difference in communication? *Communication Quarterly, 41,* 129–144.

Caughlin, J. P. (2002). The demand/withdraw pattern of communication as a predictor of marital satisfaction over time: Unresolved issues and future directions. *Human Communication Research, 28,* 49–85.

Chomsky, N. (1957). *Syntactic Structures,* The Hague/Paris: Mouton.

Coltri, L. S. (2004). *Conflict diagnosis and alternative dispute resolution.* Upper Saddle River, NJ: Prentice Hall.

Crystal, D. (2003). *The Cambridge encyclopedia of the English language.* New York: Cambridge University Press.

Dance, F. E. X., & Larson, C. E. (1976). *The functions of human communication.* New York: Holt, Rinehart, & Winston.

Duke, M.P., Fivush, R., Lazarus, A., & Bohanek, J. (2003). Of ketchup and kin: Dinnertime conversations as a major source of family knowledge, family adjustment, and family resilience (Working Paper #26). Retrieved September 6, 2011 from http://www.marial.emory.edu/research/

Edwards, J. V. (2004). Foundations of bilingualism. In T. K. Bhatia & W. C. Ritchie (Eds.), *The handbook of bilingualism* (pp. 7–31). Malden, MA: Blackwell.

Ellis, A., & Beattie, G. (1986). The language channel. *The psychology of language.* New York: Guilford.

Fromkin, V., & Rodman, R. (1983). *An introduction to language.* New York: Holt, Rinehart, and Winston.

Gong, G. (2004). When Mississippi Chinese talk. In A. González, M. Houston, & V. Chen (Eds.), *Our voices: Essays in culture, ethnicity, and communication* (4th ed.). Los Angeles: Roxbury.

Gray, J. (1992). *Men are from Mars, women are from Venus.* New York: HarperCollins.

Hannah, A. & Murachver, T. (2007). Gender preferential responses to speech. *Journal of Language and Social Psychology, 26*(3), 274–290.

Hecht, M. L., Jackson, R. L. II, & Ribeau, S. A. (2003). *African American communication.* Mahwah, NJ: Lawrence Erlbaum Associates.

Hegarty, P., & Buechel, C. (2006). Androcentric reporting of gender differences in APA journals: 1965–2004. *Review of General Psychology, 10*(4), 377–389.

Heilman, M. E. (2001). Description and prescription: How gender stereotypes prevent women's ascent up the organizational ladder. In "Gender, hierarchy and leadership," Ed. L. Carli & A. Eagly. *Journal of Social Issues, 57*(4), 657–674.

Heilman, M. E., Caleo, S., & Halim, M. L. (2010), Just the thought of it! Effects of anticipating computer-mediated communication on gender stereotyping. *Journal of Experimental Social Psychology, 46*(4), 672–675.

Hoijer, H. (1994). The Sapir-Whorf hypothesis. In L. Samovar & R. E. Porter (Eds.), *Intercultural communication: A reader* (pp. 194–200). Belmont, CA: Wadsworth.

Hudson, R. A. (1983). *Sociolinguistics.* London: Cambridge University Press.

Hyde, J. S. (2006). Gender similarities still rule. *American Psychologist, 61*(6), 641–642.

Jacobson, C. (2008). Some notes on gender-neutral language. Retrieved May 23, 2008, from http://www.english.upenn.edu/~cjacobso/gender.html

Kenneally, C. (2008, April 22). When language can hold the answer. *New York Times,* p. F1.

Kikoski, J. F., & Kikoski, C. K. (1999). *Reflexive communication in the culturally diverse workplace.* Westport, CT: Praeger.

Kim, M. S. (2002). *Non-Western perspectives on human communication.* Thousand Oaks, CA: Sage.

Knott, K., & Natalle, E. (1997). Sex differences, organizational level, and superiors evaluations of managerial leadership. *Management Communication Quarterly, 10*(4), 523–540.

Koerner, F. F. K. (2000). Towards a "full pedigree" of the "Sapir-Whorf hypothesis." In M. Putz & M. H. Verspoor (Eds.), *Explorations in linguistic relativity* (pp. 1–23). Amsterdam: John Benjamins.

Kohonen, S. (2004). Turn-taking in conversation: Overlaps and interruptions in intercultural talk. *Cahiers, 10.1,* 15–32.

Krieger, L. (2004, February 26). Like, what dew you mean, tha-yt I hav-yvee an accent? *Detroit Free Press,* p. 16A.

Kubany, E. S., Bauer, G. B., Muraoka, M., Richard, D. C., & Read, P. (1995). Impact of labeled anger and blame in intimate relationships. *Journal of Social and Clinical Psychology, 14,* 53–60.

Labov, W. (1980). The social origins of sound change. In W. Labov (Ed.), *Locating language in time and space* (pp. 251–265). New York: Academic Press.

Labov, W. (Ed.). (2005). *Atlas of North American English.* New York: Walter De Gruyter.

Leaper, C., & Ayres, M. M. (2007). A meta-analytic review of gender variation in adults' language use: Talkativeness, affiliative speech, and assertive speech. *Personality and Social Psychology Review, 11*(4), 328–363.

Li, P., & Gleitman, L. (2002). Turning the tables: Language and spatial reasoning. *Cognition, 83,* 265–294.

Liptak, A. (2008). Hate speech or free speech? What much of West bans is protected in U.S. *New York Times.* Retrieved May 31, 2011, from http://www.nytimes.com/2008/06/11/world/americas/11iht-hate.4.13645369.html

Martin, J. N., Krizek, R. L., Nakayama, T. K., & Bradford, L. (1999). What do White people want to be called? A study of self-labels for White Americans. In T. K. Nakayama & J. N. Martin (Eds.), *Whiteness: The communication of social identity* (pp. 27–50). Thousand Oaks, CA: Sage.

Media Awareness Network (n.d.). Criminal code of Canada: Hate provisions—summary. Retrieved May 30, 2011, from http://www.media-awareness.ca/english/resources/legislation/canadian_law/federal/criminal_code/criminal_code_hate.cfm

Mehl, M. R., & Pennebaker, J. W. (2003). The sounds of social life: A psychometric analysis of students' daily social environments and natural conversations. *Journal of Personality and Social Psychology, 84*, 857–70.

Mey, J. L. (2001). *Pragmatics: An introduction* (2nd ed.). Oxford, UK: Blackwell Publishing.

Mulac, A., Bradac. J. J., & Gibbons, P. (2001). Empirical support for the gender-as-culture hypothesis: An intercultural analysis of male/female language differences. *Human Communication Research, 27*, 121–152.

Nofsinger, R. (1999). *Everyday conversation.* Prospect Heights, IL: Waveland.

Orbe, M. P. (1998). *Constructing co-cultural theory: An explication of culture, power, and communication.* Thousand Oaks, CA: Sage.

Paramasivam, S. (2007). Managing disagreement while managing not to disagree: Polite disagreement in negotiation discourse. *Journal of Intercultural Communication Research, 36*(2), 91–116.

Pennebaker, J. W., & Stone, L. D. (2003). Words of wisdom: Language use across the life span. *Journal of Personality and Social Psychology, 82*, 291–301.

Philips, S. U. (1990). Some sources of cultural variability in the regulation of talk. In D. Carbaugh (Ed.), *Cultural communication and intercultural contact* (pp. 329–344). Hillsdale, NJ: Erlbaum.

Piaget, J. (1952). *The origins of intelligence in children.* New York: International Universities Press.

Pinker, S. (2007). *The stuff of thought: Language as a window into human nature.* New York: Viking.

Pinto, D., & Raschio, R. (2007) A comparative study of requests in heritage speaker Spanish, L1 Spanish, and L1 English. *International Journal of Bilingualism, 11*(2), 135–155.

Preston, D. R. (2003). Where are the dialects of American English at anyhow? *American Speech, 78*, 235–254.

"Prison ferme pour deux négationnistes." (2008, June 20). *Le soir.* Retrieved May 16, 2011, from http://archives.lesoir.be/?action=nav&gps=608066

Ramírez-Esparza, N., Gosling, S. D., Benet-Martínez, V., Potter, J. D., & Pennebaker, J. W. (2006). Do bilinguals have two personalities? A special case of cultural frame switching. *Journal of Research in Personality, 40*, 99–120.

Reid, S. A., Keerie, N., & Palomares, N. A. (2003). Language, gender salience, and social influence. *Journal of Language and Social Psychology, 22*, 210–233.

Rose, C. (1995). Bargaining and gender. *Harvard Journal of Law and Public Policy, 18*, 547–65.

Ruben, D. L. (2003). Help! My professor (or doctor or boss) doesn't talk English! In J. N. Martin, T. K. Nakayama, & L. A. Flores (Eds.). *Readings in intercultural communication* (2nd ed., pp. 127–138). Boston: McGraw-Hill.

Sacks, H., Schegloff, E., & Jefferson, G. (1978). A simplest systematics for the organization of turn-taking for conversation. In J. Schenkein (Ed.), *Studies in the organization of conversational interaction* (pp. 7–55). New York: Academic Press.

Sagrestano, L. M., Heavey, C. L., & Christensen, A. (1998). Theoretical approaches to understanding sex differences and similarities in conflict behavior. In D. J. Canary & K. Dindia (Eds.), *Sex differences and similarities in communication: Critical essays and empirical investigations on sex and gender in interaction* (pp. 287–302). Mahwah, NJ: Erlbaum.

Sbisa, M. (2002). Speech act in context, *Language & Communication, 22*, 421–436.

Schegloff, E. A. (2000) Overlapping talk and the organization of turn-taking for conversation, *Language in Society, 29*, 1–63.

Scheibel, D. (1995). Making waves with Burke: Surf Nazi culture and the rhetoric of localism. *Western Journal of Communication, 59*(4), 253–269.

Sellers, J. G., Woolsey, M. D., & Swann, J. B. (2007). Is silence more golden for women than men? Observers derogate effusive women and their quiet partners. *Sex Roles, 57*(7–8), 477–482.

Shutiva, C. (2004). Native American culture and communication through humor. In A. González, M. Houston, & V. Chen (Eds.), *Our voices: Essays in culture, ethnicity, and communication* (4th ed.). Los Angeles: Roxbury.

Weger, H., Jr. (2005). Disconfiming communication and self-verification in marriage: Associations among the demand/withdraw interaction pattern, feeling understood, and marital satisfaction. *Journal of Social and Personal Relationships, 22*, 19–31.

Wiest, L. R., Abernathy, T. V., Obenchain, K. M., & Major, E. M. (2006). Researcher study thyself: AERA participants' speaking times and turns by gender. *Equity & Excellence in Education, 39*(4), 313–323.

Wolfram, W., Adger, C. T., & Christian, D. (1999). *Dialects in schools and communities.* Mahwah, NJ: Erlbaum.

Wood, J. T. (2002). *Gendered lives: Communication, gender and cultures.* Belmont, CA: Wadsworth.

Wood, J. T., & Dindia, K. (1998). What's the differences? A dialogue about differences and similarities between men and women. In D. J. Canary & K. Dindia (Eds.), *Sex differences and similarities in communication: Critical essays and empirical investigations on sex and gender in interaction* (pp. 19–39). Mahwah, NJ: Erlbaum.

Chapter 6

Abu-Ghazzeh, T. M. (2000). Environmental messages in multiple family housing: Territory and personalization. *Landscape Research, 25*, 97–114.

Als, H. (1977). The newborn communicates. *Journal of Communication, 2*, 66–73.

Axtell, R. (1993). *Do's and taboos around the world.* New York: Wiley.

Becker, F. D. (1973). Study of special markers. *Journal of Personality and Social Psychology, 26*, 429–445.

Birdwhistell, R. L. (1985). Kinesics and context: Essays in body motion communication. Philadelphia: University of Philadelphia Press.

Boone, R. T., & Cunningham, J. G. (1998). Children's decoding of emotion in expressive body movement: The development of cue attunement. *Developmental Psychology, 34*, 1007–1016.

Briton, N. J., & Hall, J. A. (1995). Beliefs about female and male nonverbal communication. *Sex Roles, 32*, 79–90.

Burgoon, J. K., Buller, D. B., & Woodall, W. G. (1996). *Nonverbal communication: The unspo-ken dialogue.* New York: Harper & Row.

Burgoon, J. K., & Guerrero, L. K. (1994). Nonverbal communication. In M. Burgoon, F. G. Hunsaker, & E. J. Dawson (Eds.), *Human communication* (pp. 122–171). Thousand Oaks, CA: Sage.

Capella, J. (1985). The management of conversations. In M. L. Knapp & G. R. Miller (Eds.), *Handbook of interpersonal communication* (pp. 393–435). Beverly Hills, CA: Sage.

Carvajal, D. (2006, February 7). Primping for the cameras in the name of research. *New York Times*. Retrieved February 23, 2006, from http://www.nytimes.com/2006/02/07/business/07hair.html?ex=1139979600&en=f5f94cb9d81a9fa8&ei=5070&emc=eta1

Chartrand T. L., & Bargh J. A. (1999). The chameleon effect: The perception-behavior link and social interaction. *Journal of Personality and Social Psychology, 76*, 893–910.

Chiang, L. H. (1993, October). Beyond the language: Native Americans' nonverbal communication. Paper presented at the Annual Meeting of the Midwest Association of Teachers of Educational Psychology, Anderson, IN: October 1–2.

Cicca, A. H., Step, M., & Turkstra, L. (2003, December 16). Show me what you mean: Nonverbal communication theory and application. *ASHA Leader, 34*, 4–5.

Dié, L. (2008, November, 9). Obama: Speech patterns analyzed. *News Flavor: U. S. Politics*. Retrieved May 31, 2011, from http://newsflavor.com/category/politics/us-politics/

Dijksterhuis, A., & Smith, P. K. (2005). What do we do unconsciously? And how? *Journal of Consumer Psychology 15*(3), 225–229.

Duke, L. (2002). Get real! Cultural relevance and resistance to the mediated feminine ideal. *Psychology and Marketing, 19*, 211–234.

Eibl-Eibesfeld, I. (1972). Similarities and differences between cultures in expressive movement. In R. A. Hinde (Ed.), *Nonverbal communication* (pp. 297–314). Cambridge: Cambridge University Press.

Ekman, P. (2003). *Emotions revealed: Recognizing faces and feelings to improve communication and emotional life*. New York: Times Books.

Ekman, P., & Friesen, W. V. (1969). The repertoire of nonverbal behavior: Categories, origins, usage and coding. *Semiotica, 1*, 49–98.

Ekman, P., & Friesen, W. V. (1986). A new pan-cultural expression of emotion. *Motivation and Emotion, 10*(2), 159–168.

Elfenbein, H. A. (2006). Learning in emotion judgments: Teaching and the cross-cultural understanding of facial expressions. *Journal of Nonverbal Communication, 30*, 21–36.

Elfenbein, H. A., Maw, D. F., White, J., Tan, H. H., & Aik, V. C. (2007). Reading your counter-part: The benefit of emotion recognition accuracy for effectiveness in negotiation. *Journal of Nonverbal Behavior, 31*, 205–223.

Eskritt, M., & Lee, K. (2003) Do actions speak louder than words? Preschool children's use of the verbal-nonverbal consistency principle during inconsistent communication. *Journal of Nonverbal Behavior, 27*, 25–41.

Field, T. (2002). Infants' need for touch. *Human Development, 45*, 100–104.

Fussell, P. (1992). *Class: A guide through the American status system*. New York: Touchstone Books.

Givens, D. B. (2005). *The nonverbal dictionary of gestures, signs, and body language cues*. Spokane, WA: Center for Nonverbal Studies Press.

Grammer, K., Fink, B., Joller, A., & Thornhill, R. (2003). Darwinian aesthetics: Sexual selection and the biology of beauty. *Biological Reviews, 78*, 385–408.

Guerrero, L. K., & Andersen, P. A. (1991). The waxing and waning of relational intimacy: Touch as a function of relational stage, gender, and touch avoidance. *Journal of Social and Personal Relationships, 8*, 147–165.

Guerrero, L. K., & Andersen, P. A. (1994). Patterns of matching and initiation: Touch behavior and touch avoidance across romantic relationship stages. *Journal of Nonverbal Behavior, 18*, 137–153.

Guerrero, L. K., & Ebesu, A. S. (1993, May). While at play: An observational analysis of children's touch during interpersonal interaction. Paper presented at the annual conference of the International Communication Association, Washington, D.C.

Gundersen, D. F. (1990). Uniforms: Conspicuous invisibility. In J. A. Devito & M. L. Hecht (Eds.), *The nonverbal communication reader* (pp. 172–178). Prospect Heights, IL: Waveland.

Hall, E. T. (1966). *The hidden dimension*. New York: Doubleday.

Hall, E. T. (1983). *The dance of life*. Garden City, NY: Doubleday.

Hall, E. T., & Hall, M. R. (1987). *Hidden differences: Doing business with the Japanese*. Garden City, NY: Anchor.

Hall, E. T., & Hall, M. R. (1990). *Understanding cultural differences: Germans, French and Americans*. Yarmouth, ME: Intercultural Press.

Hanzal, A., Segrin, C., & Dorros, S. M. (2008). The role of marital status and age on men's and women's reactions to touch from a relational partner. *Journal of Nonverbal Behavior, 32*, 21–35.

Isaacson, L. A. (1998). Student dress codes. *ERIC Digest, 117*. Retrieved June 15, 2006, from http://eric.uoregon.edu/publications/digests/digest117.html

Johnson, A. G. (2001). *Privilege, power, and difference*. Boston: McGraw-Hill.

Jones, S. E., & LeBaron, C. D. (2002). Research on the relationship between verbal and nonver-bal communication: Emerging integration. *Journal of Communication, 52*, 499–521.

Kemmer, S. (1992). Are we losing our touch? *Total Health, 14*, 46–49.

Knapp, M. L., & Hall, J. A. (1992). *Nonverbal communication in human interaction* (3rd ed.). New York: Holt, Rinehart and Winston.

Knapp, M. L., & Hall, J. A. (2001). *Nonverbal communication in human interaction*. Belmont, CA: Wadsworth.

Kraus, M., & Keltner, D. (2009). Signs of socio-economic status: A thin-slicing approach. *Psychological Science, 20*, 99–106.

Manusov, V. (1995). Reacting to changes in nonverbal behaviors: Relational satisfaction and adaptation patterns in romantic dyads. *Human Communication Research, 21*, 456–477.

Manusov, V., & Patterson, M. (2006). *Handbook of nonverbal communication*. Thousand Oaks, CA: Sage

Mast, M. S., & Hall, J. A., (2004). Who is the boss and who is not? Accuracy of judging status. *Journal of Nonverbal Behavior, 28*, 145–165.

Matsumoto, D. (2006). Culture and nonverbal behavior. In *Handbook of nonverbal communication*, V. Manusov & M. Patters (eds.). Thousand Oaks, CA: Sage.

Mehrabian, A. (2007). *Nonverbal communication*. Chicago, IL: Aldine de Gruyter.

Mehrabian, A., & Weiner, M. (1967). Decoding of inconsistent communication. *Journal of Personality and Social Psychology, 6*, 109–-104.

Mehrabian, A., & Ferris, S. R. (1967). Influence of attitudes from nonverbal communication in two channels. *Journal of Consulting Psychology, 31*, 248–252.

Mehrabian, A. (1971). *Nonverbal communication*. Chicago: Aldine-Atherton.

Meltzoff, A. N., & Prinz, W. (2002). *The imitative mind: Development, evolution, and brain bases*. Cambridge, England: Cambridge University Press.

Montepare, J. M., Goldstein, S. B., & Clausen, A. (1987). The identification of emotions from gait information. *Ethology and Sociobiology, 6*, 237–247.

Newport, F. (1999). Americans agree that being attractive is a plus in American society. Gallup Poll Monthly, 408, 45–49.

Parasuram, T. V. (2003, October 23). Sikh shot and injured in Arizona hate crime. *Sikh Times*. Retrieved February 24, 2006, from http://www.sikhtimes.com/news_052103a.html

Patterson, M. L. (1982). A sequential functional model of nonverbal exchange. *Psychological Bulletin, 89*, 231–249.

Patterson, M. L. (1983). *Nonverbal behavior.* New York: Springer.

Patterson, M. L. (2003). Commentary. Evolution and nonverbal behavior: Functions and mediating processes. *Journal of Nonverbal Behavior, 27*, 201–207.

Richards, V., Rollerson, B., & Phillips, J. (1991). Perceptions of submissiveness: Implications for victimization. *Journal of Psychology, 125*(4), 407–411.

Richeson, J. A., & Shelton, J. N. (2005). Brief report: Thin slices of racial bias. *Journal of Non-verbal Behavior, 29*, 75–86.

Samovar, L. & Porter, R. (2004). *Communication between cultures.* Thomson, Wadsworth.

Schwartz, L. M., Foa, U. G., & Foa, E. B. (1983) Multichannel nonverbal communication: Evidence for combinatory rules. *Journal of Personality and Social Psychology, 45*, 274–281.

Segerstrale, U., & Molnár, P. (1997) (Eds.), *Nonverbal communication: Where nature meets culture* (pp. 27–46). Mahwah, NJ: Erlbaum.

Shelp, S. (2002). Gaydar: Visual detection of sexual orientation among gay and straight men. *Journal of Homosexuality, 44*, 1–14.

Tiedens, L., & Fragale, A. (2003). "Power moves: Complementarity in dominant and submissive nonverbal behavior." *Journal of Personality and Social Psychology, 84*, 558–568.

Watson, O. & Graves, T. (1966). Quantitative research in proxemic behavior. *American Anthropologist, 68*, 971–985.

Wise, T. (2005, October 23). Opinions on NBA dress code are far from uniform. *Washington Post,* p. A01. Retrieved February 24, 2006, from http://www.washingtonpost.com/wp-dyn/content/article/2005/10/22/AR2005102201386.html

Wolburg, J. M. (2001). Preserving the moment, commodifying time, and improving upon the past: Insights into the depiction of time in American advertising. *Journal of Communication, 51*, 696–720.

Young, R. L. (1999). *Understanding misunderstandings.* Austin, TX: University of Texas Press.

Zezima, K. (2005, December 3). Military, police now more strict on tattoos. *The San Diego Un-ion-Tribune.* Retrieved February 22, 2006, from http://www.signonsandiego.com/uniontrib/20051203/news_1n3tattoo.html

Chapter 7

Aurand, T., Ridnour, R., Timm, S. & Kaminski, P. (2000). The listening process: measuring listening competence. In S. Hall & D. Martin (Eds), *Proceedings of the American Society of Business and Behavioral Sciences Conference, 7*(4), 391–399.

Barker, L., & Watson, K. (2000). *Listen up: How to improve relationships, reduce stress, and be more productive by using the power of listening.* New York: St. Martin's Press.

Battell, C. (2006). *Effective listening.* ASTD Press

Beall, M. L., Gill-Rosier, J., Tate, J., & Matten, A. (2008). State of the context: Listening in education. *The International Journal of Listening, 22*, 123–132.

Beard, D. (2009). A broader understanding of the ethics of listening: Philosophy, Cultural Studies, Media Studies and the ethical listening subject. *The International Journal of Listening, 23*(1), 7–20.

Bodie, G. D. (2010). Treating listening ethically. *International Journal of Listening, 24*(3), 185–188.

Bodie, G. D., & Worthington, D. L. (2010). Revisiting the Listening Styles Profile (LSP-16): A confirmatory factor analytic approach to scale validation and reliability estimation. *International Journal of Listening, 24*(2), 69–88.

Bommelje, R., Houston, J. M., & Smither, R. (2003). Personality characteristics of effective listeners: A five factor perspective. *International Journal of Listening, 17*, 32–46.

Brownell, J. (1990). Perceptions of Effective Listeners: A management study. *Journal of Business Communication, 27*, 401–415.

Brownell, J. (1994). Managerial listening and career development in the hospitality industry. *The International Journal of Listening, 8*, 31–49.

Brownell, J. (2002). *Listening: Attitudes, principles and skills.* Boston: Allyn-Bacon.

Clark. A. (2005). Listening to and involving young children: A review of research and practice. *Early Child Development and Care. 175*(6), 489–505.

Cooper, L. O., & Buchanan, T. (2010). Listening competency on campus: A psychometric analysis of student listening. *International Journal of Listening, 24*(3), 141–163.

Davis, J., Foley, A., Crigger, N., & Brannigan, M. C. (2008). Healthcare and listening: A relationship for caring. *The International Journal of Listening, 22*, 168–175.

Diamond, L. E. (2007). *Rule #1: Stop talking!: A guide to listening.* Cupertino, CA: Listeners Press.

Dillon, R. K., & McKenzie, N. J. (1998). The influence of ethnicity on listening, communication competence, approach, and avoidance. *The International Journal of Listening, 12*, 106–121.

Emanuel, R., Adams, J., Baker, K., Daufin, E. K., Ellington, C., Fitts, E., Himsel, J., Holladay, L., & Okeowo, D. (2008). How college students spend their time communicating. *The International Journal of Listening, 22*(1), 13–28.

Floyd, J. (2010). Provocation: Dialogic listening as reachable goal. *International Journal of Listening, 24*(3), 170–173.

Flynn, J., Valikoski, T. R., & Grau, J. (2008). Listening in the business context: Reviewing the state of research. *The International Journal of Listening, 22*, 141–151.

Fowler, K. (2005). Mind tools on active listening. Retrieved December 7, 2009, from http://www.mindtools.com/CommSkll/Mind%20Tools%20Listening.pdf

Fujii, Y. (2008). You must have a wealth of stories': Cross-linguistic differences between addressee support behaviour in Australian and Japanese. *Multilingua, 27*(4) 325–370.

Holmes, F. (2007). If you listen, the patient will tell you the diagnosis. *The International Journal of Listening, 21*(2), 156–161.

Imhof, M. (2001). How to listen more efficiently: Self-monitoring strategies in listening. *The International Journal of Listening, 5*, 2–19.

Imhof, M. (2004). Who are we as we listen?: Individual listening profiles in varying contexts. *The International Journal of Listening, 18*, 39–44.

Imhof, M. (2010). Listening to voices and judging people. *International Journal of Listening, 24*(1), 19–33.

International Listening Association (1995, April). An ILA Definition of Listening. *ILA Listening Post, 53*, 1–4.

Jalongo, M. (2010). Listening in early childhood: An interdisciplinary review of the literature. *International Journal of Listening, 24*(1), 1–18.

Janusik, L. A., & Wolvin, A. D. (2009). 24 hours in a day: A listening update to the time studies. *International Journal of Listening, 23*(2), 104–120.

Johnston, M. K., Weaver, J. B., Watson, K.W., & Barker, L. L. (2000). Listening styles: Biological or psychological differences? *International Journal of Listening, 14,* 32–46.

Kiewitz, C., Weaver, J. B., Brosius, H. B., & Weimann, G. (1997), Cultural differences in listening style preferences: A comparison of young adults in Germany, Israel, and the United States. *International Journal of Public Opinion, 9,* 233–248.

Kotter, J. P. (1982). What do effective managers really do? *Harvard Business Review, 60*(6), 156–167.

Lynch, J. J. (1985). *Language of the heart: The body's response to human dialogue.* New York: Basic Books.

McCormick, J., & Matusitz, J. (2010). The impact on U.S. society of noise-induced and music-induced hearing loss caused by personal media players. *International Journal of Listening, 24*(2), 125–140.

Mooney, D. (1996) Improving your listening skills. Retrieved December 7, 2009. from http://suicideand mentalhealthassociationinternational.org/improvlisten.html

Nichols, M. P. (2009). *The lost art of listening.* New York: The Guilford Press.

Pearce, C. G., Johnson, I. W., & Barker, R. T. (2003). Assessment of the Listening Styles Inventory: Progress in establishing reliability and validity. *Journal of Business and Technical Communication, 17*(1), 84–113.

Robertson K. (2005). Active listening: More than just paying attention. *Australian Family Physician, 34* (12): 1053–1055

Rosenfeld, L. B., & Berko, R. (1990). *Communicating with competency.* Glenview, IL: Scott, Foresman/Little.

Salem, R. (2003). Empathic listening. In G. Burgess and H. Burgess (Eds.), *Beyond Intractability.* Conflict Research Consortium, University of Colorado, Boulder. Retrieved December 14, 2009, from http://www.beyondintractability.org/essay/empathic_listening/

Shafir, R. Z. (2000). *The Zen of listening.* Wheaton, IL: Quest Books.

Shotter, J. (2009). Listening in a way that recognizes/realizes the world of "the other." T*he International Journal of Listening, 23*(1), 21–43.

Silverman, J. (1970). Attentional styles and the study of sex differences. In D. I. Mostofsky (Ed.). *Attention: Contemporary theory and analysis* (pp. 61–79). New York: Appleton-Century-Crofts.

Stoltz, M. (2010). Response: Choice and ethics in listening situations. *International Journal of Listening, 24*(3), 177–178.

Sypher, B. D. (1984). The importance of social cognition abilities in organizations. In R. Bostrom (Ed.), *Competence in communication* (pp. 103–128). Beverly Hills, CA: Sage.

Thomlison, T. D. (1996). Intercultural listening. In D. Borisoff & M. Purdy (Eds.), *Listening in everyday life: A personal and professional approach* (2nd ed., pp. 79–120). New York: University Press of America.

Villaume, W. A., & Bodie, G. D. (2007). Discovering the listener within us: The impact of trait-like personality variables and communicator styles on preferences for listening style. *International Journal of Listening, 21*(2), 102–123.

Watson, K. W., Barker, L. L., & Weaver, J. B. (1995). The Listening Styles Profile (LSP-16): Development and validation of an instrument to assess four listening styles. *Journal of the International Listening Association, 9,* 1–13.

Chapter 8

Adler, P. (1975). The transitional experience: An alternative view of culture shock. *Journal of Humanistic Psychology, 15,* 13–23.

Alexie, S. (2003). *Ten little Indians.* New York: Grove Press.

Allen, B. (2003). *Difference matters: Communicating social identity.* Waveland Press.

Anderson, E. (2010, August 26). One town's post-Katrina diaspora. *msnbc.msn.com.* Retrieved September 7, 2011 from http://www.msnbc.msn.com/id/38851079/ns/us_news-katrina_five_years_later/t/one-towns-post katrina-diaspora/

Anzaldúa, G. (1999). *Borderlands/La frontera: The new mestiza.* San Francisco: Aunt Lute Books.

Bahk, M., & Jandt, F. E. (2004). Being white in America: Development of a scale. *Howard Journal of Communications, 15,* 57–68.

Bellah, R. N., Madsen, R., Sullivan, W. M., Swidler, A., & Tipton, S. M. (1996). *Habits of the heart: Individualism and commitment in American life.* Los Angeles: University of California Press.

Bennett, J. M. (1998). Transition shock: Putting culture shock in perspective. In M. J. Bennett (Ed.), *Basic concepts in intercultural communication: Selected readings* (pp. 215–224). Yarmouth, ME: Intercultural Press. First published in 1977, in N. C. Jain (Ed.), *International and Intercultural Communication Annual, 4,* 45–52.

Bercovitch, J., & Derouen, K. (2004). Mediation in internationalized ethnic conflicts, *Armed Forces & Society, 30,* 147–170.

Bernal, V. (2005). Eritrea on-line: Diaspora, cyberspace, and the public sphere. *American Ethnologist, 32,* 660–675.

Berry, J. W. (2005) Acculturation: Living successfully in two cultures. *International Journal of Intercultural Relations, 29,* 697–712.

Bertrand, O. (2011). What goes around, comes around: Effects of offshore outsourcing on the export performance of firms. *International Business Studies, 42*(2), 334–344.

Bhatia, S. (2008). 9/11 and the Indian diaspora: Narratives of race, place and immigrant identity. *Journal of Intercultural Studies, 29*(1), 21–39.

Blair, C., Brown, J. R., & Baxter, L. A. (1994). Disciplining the feminine. *Quarterly Journal of Speech, 80,* 383–409.

Bond, M. (1991). *Beyond the Chinese face.* Hong Kong: Oxford University Press.

Bond, M. (Ed.) (1996). *The handbook of Chinese psychology.* Hong Kong: Oxford University Press.

Broome, B. J. (2004). Building a shared future across the divide: Identity and conflict in Cyprus. In M. Fong and R. Chuang (Eds.), *Communicating ethnic and cultural identity* (pp. 275–294). Lanham, MD: Rowman and Littlefield, Publishers.

Budelman, R. (n.d.). *Indian Cultural Tips.* Retrieved June 13, 2006, from http://www.stylusinc.com/business/india/americans_independant.htm

Chinese Culture Connection (1987). Chinese values and the search for culture-free dimensions of culture. *Journal of Cross-Cultural Psychology, 18,* 143–164.

Chisholm, G. C. (2008). Relations between African-Americans and Whites in the United States. *Human Development, 29*(3), 15–18.

Clark-Ibanez, M. K., & Felmlee, D. (2004). Interethnic relationships: The role of social network diversity. *Journal of Marriage and Family, 66,* 229–245.

Cowan, G. (2005). Interracial interactions of racially diverse university campuses. *Journal of Social Psychology, 14,* 49–63.

Deggans, E. (2004, October 24). TV reality not often apoken of: Race. *St. Petersburg Times.*

Dunbar, R. A. (1997). Bloody footprints: Reflections on growing up poor white. In M. Wray & A. Newitz (Eds.), *White trash: Race and class in America* (pp. 73–86). New York: Routledge.

Dyson, M. E. (2009). An American man, an American moment. *Ebony, 64*(3), 90–94.

Ewing, K. P. (2004). Migration, identity negotiation, and self-experience. In J. Friedman & S. Randeria, (Eds.), *Worlds on the move: Globalization, migration, and cultural security* (pp. 117–140). London: I. B. Tauris.

Fiebert, M. S., Nugent, D., Hershberger, S. L., & Kasdan, M. (2004). Dating and commitment choices as a function of ethnicity among American college students in California. *Psychological Reports, 94*, 1293–1300.

Finn, H. K. (2003). The case for cultural diplomacy. *Foreign Affairs, 82*, 15.

Flores, L. A. (1996). Creating discursive space through a rhetoric of difference: Chicana feminists craft a homeland. *Quarterly Journal of Speech, 82*, 142–156.

Gudykunst, W. B., & Lee, C. M. (2002). Cross-cultural communication theories. In W. B. Gudykunst & B. Mody (Eds.), *Handbook of international and intercultural communication* (2nd ed., pp. 25–50). Thousand Oaks, CA: Sage.

Hall, B. J. (1997). Culture, ethics and communication. In F. L. Casmir (Ed.), *Ethics in intercultural and international communication* (pp. 11–41). Mahwah, NJ: Erlbaum.

Hall, E. T., & Hall, M. (1990). *Understanding cultural differences: Germans, French and Americans.* Yarmouth, ME: Intercultural Press.

Halualani, R. T. (2008). How do multicultural university students define and make sense of intercultural contact? A qualitative study. *International Journal of Intercultural Relations, 32*, 1–16.

Hecht, M., Sedano, M., & Ribeau, S. (1993). Understanding culture, communication, and research: Application to Chicanos and Mexican Americans. *International Journal of Intercultural Relations, 17*, 157–165.

Hecht, M. L., Jackson R. L., II, & Ribeau, S. (2002). *African American Communication: Exploring identity and culture* (2nd ed.). Hillsdale, NJ: Erlbaum.

Hegde, R. S. (1998). Swinging the trapeze: The negotiation of identity among Asian Indian immigrant women in the United States. In D. V. Tanno & A. González (Eds.), *Communication of identity across cultures* (pp. 34–55). Thousand Oaks, CA: Sage.

Hegde, R. S. (2000). Hybrid revivals: Defining Asian Indian ethnicity through celebration. In A. González, M. Houston, V. Chen (Eds.), *Our voices: Essays in culture, ethnicity and communication* (pp. 133–138). Los Angeles: Roxbury.

Hemmingsen, J. (2002) Klamath talks begin. *Indian Country Today, 21*, A1.

Herbert, B. (2005, June 6). The mobility myth. *New York Times.* Retrieved October 7, 2005, from http://www.commondreams.org/views05/0606-27.htm

Ho, M. K. (1987). *Family therapy with ethnic minorities.* Newbury Park, CA: Sage.

Hofstede, G. (1997). *Cultures and organizations: Software of the mind* (Rev. ed.). New York: McGraw-Hill.

Hofstede, G. (1998). *Masculinity and femininity.* Thousand Oaks, CA: Sage.

Hofstede, G. (2001). *Culture's consequences* (2nd ed.). Thousand Oaks, CA: Sage.

Hulse, E. (1996). Example of the English Puritans. *Reformation Today, 153.* Retrieved June 13, 2006, from http://www.puritansermons.com/banner/hulse1.htm

Institute of International Education (2010a). *Open Doors 2010: International students in the U.S.* Retrieved February 7, 2011, from http://www.iie.org/en/Research-and-Publications/Open-Doors

Institute of International Education (2010b). *Open Doors 2010: American students studying abroad.* Retrieved February, 7, 2011, from http://www.iie.org/en/Research-and-Publications/Open-Doors

Johnson, A. G. (2006). *Privilege, power and difference.* Thousand Oaks, CA: Sage.

Johnson, B. R., & Jacobson, C. K. (2005). Context in contact: An examination of social settings on Whites' attitudes toward interracial marriage. *Journal of Social Psychology, 68*, 387–399.

Jung, E., Hecht, M. L., & Wadsworth, B. C. (2007). The role of identity in international students' psychological well-being in the United States: A model of depression level, identity gaps, discrimination, and acculturation. *International Journal of Intercultural Relations, 31*, 605–624.

Kashima, E. S., & Loh, E. (2006) International students' acculturation: Effects of international, conational, and local ties and need for closure. *International Journal of Intercultural Relations, 30*, 471–486.

Kreager, D. A. (2008). Guarded borders: Adolescent interracial romance and peer trouble at school. *Social Forces, 87*(2), 887–910.

Kikoski, J. F., & Kikoski, C. K. (1999). *Reflexive communication in the culturally diverse workplace.* Westport, CT: Praeger.

Kim, Y. Y. (2005). Adapting to a new culture: An integrative communication theory. In W. B. Gudykunst (Ed.), *Theorizing about intercultural communication* (pp. 375–400). Thousand Oaks, CA: Sage.

Koinova, M. (2010). Diasporas and secessionist conflicts: The mobilization of the Armenian, Albanian, and Chechen diasporas. *Ethnic and Racial Studies, 34*, 333–356.

Kluckhohn, F., & Strodtbeck, F. (1961). *Variations in value orientations.* Chicago: Row, Peterson & Co.

Kohls, R. L. (2001). *Survival kit for overseas living* (4th ed.). Yarmouth, ME: Nicholas Brealey/Intercultural Press.

Levin, S., Taylor, P. L., & Caudle, E. (2007). Interethnic and interracial dating in college: A longitudinal study. *Journal of Social and Personal Relationships, 24*(3), 323–341.

Lee, J. J., & Rice, C. (2007). Welcome to America? International student perceptions of discrimination, *Higher Education, 53*, 381–409.

Lin, C. (2006). Culture shock and social support: An investigation of a Chinese student organization on a U.S. campus. *Journal of Intercultural Communication Research, 35*(2), 117–137.

Loewen, J. W. (1995). *Lies my teacher told me.* New York: Simon & Schuster.

Martin, J. N., & Nakayama, T. K. (2008). *Experiencing intercultural communication: An introduction* (3rd ed.). Boston: McGraw-Hill.

Martin, J. N., Trego, A., & Nakayama, T. K., (2010). The relationship between college students' racial attitudes and friendship diversity. *Howard Journal of Communications, 21*(2), 97–118.

Matsumoto, D. (2002). *The new Japan: Debunking seven cultural stereotypes.* Yarmouth, ME: Intercultural Press.

McGoldrick, M., Giordano, J., & Pearce, J. K. (Eds.). (1996). *Ethnicity and family therapy* (2nd ed.). New York: Guilford Press.

McKinnon, S. (2004, September 1). Spotted owl habitat plan ruffles feathers. *Arizona Republic*, B1.

Melmer, D. (2004). Buffalo and Lakota are kin. *Indian Country Today, 23*, B1.

Numbers. (2008, February 4). *Time*, 18.

Orbe, M. P. (1998). *Constructing co-cultural theory: An explication of culture, power, and communication*. Thousand Oaks, CA: Sage.

Passel, J. S., & Cohn, D. V. (2008, February 11). U.S. populations projections: 2005–2050. Retrieved March 20, 2009, from http://pewhispanic.org/files/reports/85.pdf

Pendery, D. (2008). Identity development and cultural production in the Chinese diaspora to the United States, 1850–2004: new perspectives, *Asian Ethnicity, 9*(3), 201–218

Porter, T. (2002). The words that come before all else. *Native Americas, 19*, 7–10.

Rabbi: My radio show pulled because of racism (2005, September 27). *The Associated Press*. Retrieved October 10, 2005, from http://www.newsmax.com/archives/ic/2005/9/22/173035.shtml

Reiter, M. J., & Gee, C. B. (2009). Open communication and partner support in intercultural and interfaith romantic relationship: A relational maintenance approach. *Journal of Social and Personal Relationships. 25*(4), 539–599.

Root, M. P. P. (2001). *Love's revolution: Interracial marriage.* Philadelphia, PA: Temple University Press.

Rosenstone, R. A. (2005). My wife, the Muslim. *Antioch Review, 63*, 234–246.

Schneider, S. C., & Barsoux, J. L. (2003). *Managing across cultures.* New York: Prentice Hall.

Shelden, R. G. (2004). The imprisonment crisis in America: An introduction. *Review of Policy Research, 21*, 5–13.

Shim, Y-J., Kim, M-S., & Martin, J. N. (2008) *Changing Korea: Understanding culture and communication.* New York: Peter Lang.

Simpson, J. L. (2008). The color-blind double bind. Communication Theory, 18(1), 880,139–159.

Snyder, M. (2001). Self-fulfilling stereotypes. In P. S. Rothenberg (Ed.), *Race, class & gender in the U.S.* (5th ed., pp. 511–517). New York: Worth.

Stewart, E. C., & Bennett, M. J. (1991). *American cultural patterns: A cross-cultural perspective.* Yarmouth, ME: Intercultural Press.

Tai, S. H. C., & Lau, L. B. Y. (2009). Export of American fantasy world to the Chinese. *International Journal of Case Studies in Management (Online), 7*(2), 1. Retrieved July 28, 2011 from http://login.ezproxy1.lib.asu.edu/login?url=http://search.proquest.com/docview/197457950?accountid=4485

Taylor, P., Funk, C., & Craighill, P. (2006). *Guess who's coming to dinner.* Pew Research Center Social Trends Report. Washington, DC: Pew Research Center.

Ting-Toomey, S. (1999). *Communicating across cultures.* New York: Guilford.

Tourism Highlights (2010). Retrieved February 7, 2011, from http://www.unwto.org/facts/eng/pdf/highlights/UNWTO_Highlights10_en_HR.pdf

Triandis, H. (1995). *Individualism and collectivism.* Boulder, CO: Westview Press.

Trompenaars, F., & Hampden-Turner, C. (1997). *Riding the waves of culture: Understanding diversity in global business.* Boston: McGraw-Hill.

United Nations High Commissioner for Refugees (2009). *UNHCR Statistical Yearbook 2009.* Retrieved February 7, 2011, from http://www.unhcr.org/4ce530889.html

Ward, C. (2008). Thinking outside the Berry boxes: New perspectives on identity, acculturation and intercultural relations. *International Journal of Intercultural Relations, 32*, 105–114.

Waterston, A. (2005). Bringing the past into the present: Family narratives of Holocaust, exile, and diaspora: The story of my story: An anthropology of violence, dispossession, and diaspora. *Anthropological Quarterly, 78*, 43–61.

Wells, S. (2002). *The journey of man: A genetic odyssey.* Princeton, NJ: Princeton University Press.

Yamato, G. (2001). Something about the subject makes it hard to name. In M. L. Andersen & P. H. Collins (Eds.), *Race, class, and gender: An anthology* (4th ed., pp. 90–94). Belmont, CA: Wadsworth.

Yen, H. (2011, February 3). Census estimates show big gains for US minorities. Yahoo News. Retrieved February 6, 2011, from http://news.yahoo.com/s/ap/20110203/ap_on_re_us/us_census2010_population

Zuni eagle aviary is a beautiful sign (2002, July 31). [Editorial.] Retrieved March 20, 2009, from http://www.highbeam.com/doc/1P179291291.html

Chapter 9

Abbey, A. (1982). Sex differences in attributions for friendly behavior: Do males misperceive female's friendliness? *Journal of Personality and Social Psychology, 42*, 830–838.

Abbey, A. (1991). Misperceptions as an antecedent of Acquaintance Rape: A Consequence of Ambiguity in communication between men and women. In *Acquaintance rape: The hidden crime*, ed. A. Parrot and L. Bechhofer. New York: Wiley.

Aboud, F. E., & Mendelson, M. J. (1996). Determinants of friendship selection and quality: Developmental perspectives. In W. M. Bukowski, A. F. Newcomb, & W. W. Hartup (Eds.), *The company they keep: Friendship in childhood and adolescence* (pp. 87–112). New York: Cambridge University Press.

Alberts, J., Yoshimura, C., Rabby, M., & Loschiavo, R. (2005). Mapping the topography of couples' everyday interaction. *Journal of Social and Personal Relationships, 22*, 299–322.

Allan, G. (1977). Class variation in friendship patterns. *British Journal of Sociology, 28*, 389–393.

Altman, I., & Taylor, D. A. (1973). *Social penetration: The development of interpersonal relationships.* New York: Holt, Rinehart & Winston.

Altman, I., & Taylor, D. (1987). Communication in interpersonal relationships: Social penetration theory. In M. E. Roloff and G. R. Miller (Eds.), *Interpersonal processes: New directions in communication research* (pp. 257–277). Newbury Park, CA: Sage.

Altman, I., Vinsel, A., & Brown, B. B. (1981). Dialectic conceptions in social psychology: An application to social penetration and privacy regulation. In L. Berkowitz (Ed.), *Advances in experimental social psychology* (Vol. 14, pp. 107–160). New York: Academic Press.

American Psychological Association. (1996). *Violence and the family: Report of the American Psychological Association presidential task force on violence and the family.* Retrieved June 15, 2006, from http://www.apa.org/pi/viol&fam.html

Andersen, P., Eloy, S. V., Guerrero, L. K., & Spitzberg, B. H. (1995). Romantic jealousy and relational satisfaction: A look at the impact of jealousy experience and expression. *Communication Reports, 8*, 77–85.

Anglin, K., & Holtzworth-Munroe, A. (1997). Comparing the responses of maritally violent and nonviolent spouses to problematic marital and nonmarital situations: Are the skills deficits of physically aggressive husbands and wives global? *Journal of Family Psychology, 11*, 301–313.

Argyle, M., & Henderson, M. (1984). The rules of friendship. *Journal of Social and Personal Relationships, 1,* 211–237.

Atkinson, M. P., & Glass, B. L. (1985). Marital age, heterogamy and homogamy, 1900 to 1980. *Journal of Marriage and the Family, 47*(3), 685–700.

Aune, K. S., & Comstock, J. (1991) Experience and expression of jealousy: Comparison between friends and romantics. *Psychological Reports, 69,* 315–319.

Baxter, L. A. (1982). Strategies for ending relationships: Two studies. *Western Journal of Speech Communication, 46,* 233–242.

Baxter, L. A. (1988). A dialectical perspective on communication strategies in relationship development. In S. W. Duck, D. F. Hay, S. E. Hobfoll, W. Ickes, & B. Montgomery (Eds.), *Handbook of personal relationships* (pp. 257–273). London: Wiley.

Baxter, L. A. (1991). Gender differences in the heterosexual relationship rules embedded in break-up accounts. *Journal of Social and Personal Relationships, 3,* 289–306.

Baxter, L. A., & Bullis, C. (1986). Turning points in developing romantic relationships. *Human Communication Research, 12,* 469–493.

Becker, J. A. H., Johnson, A. J., Craig, E. A., Gilchrist, E., Haigh, M. M., & Lane, L. L. (2009). Friendships are flexible not fragile: Turning points in geographically-close and long-distance friendships. *Journal of Social and Personal Relationships, 26*(4), 347–369.

Berg, J. H., & Piner, K. E. (1990). Social relationships and the lack of social relationships. In S. Duck & R. C. Silver (Eds.), *Personal relationships and social support* (pp. 140–158). London: Sage Publications.

Berger, C. R., & Calabrese, R. J. (1975). Some explorations in initial interaction and beyond: Toward a developmental theory of interpersonal communication. *Human Communication Theory, 1,* 99–112.

Berger, C. R. & Kellerman, N. (1994). Acquiring social information. In J. Daly & J. Wiemann (Eds.), *Strategic interpersonal communication* (pp. 1–31). Hillsdale, NJ: Lawrence Erlbaum.

Berscheid, E., & Reis, H. T. (1998). Attraction and close relationships. In D. Gilbert, S. Fiske, & G. Lindzey (Eds.), *Handbook of social psychology* (Vol. 2., 4th ed., pp. 193–281). New York: McGraw-Hill.

Blieszner, R., & Adams, R. G. (1992). *Adult friendship.* Newbury Park, CA: Sage.

Bok, S. (1978). *Lying: Moral choice in public and private life.* New York: Random House.

Bowker, A. (2004). Predicting friendship stability during early adolescence. *Journal of Early Adolescence, 24,* 85–112.

Bradshaw, C., Kahn, A. S., Saville, B. K. (2010). To hook up or date: Which gender benefits? *Sex Roles, 9–10,* 661–669.

Bramlett, M. D., & Mosher, W. D. (2002). Cohabitation, marriage, divorce, and remarriage in the United States. *National Center for Health Statistics.* Vital Health Stat, 23(22).

Buller, D. B., & Burgoon, J. K. (1996). Interpersonal deception theory. *Communication Theory, 6,* 203–242.

Bureau of Justice Statistics. (1995, August). *Special Report: Violence against women: Estimates from the Redesigned Survey* (NCJ-154348), 3.

Burgoon, J. K., & Bacue, A. E. (2003). Nonverbal communication skills. In J.O. Greene & B. R. Burleson (Eds.) *Handbook of communication and social interaction skills.* Mawah, NJ: Lawrence Erlbaum.

Burgoon, J. K., Buller, D. B., Ebesu, A., & Rockwell, P. (1994). Interpersonal deception: 5. Accuracy in deception detection. *Communication Monographs, 61,* 303–325.

Burleson, B. R., & Samter, W. (1996). Similarity in the communication skills of young adults: Foundations of attraction, friendship, and relationship satisfaction. *Communication Reports, 9,* 127–137.

Burleson, B. R., & Samter, W. (1996). (2006). Cognitive and motivational influences on spontaneous comforting behavior. *Human Communication Research, 11* (2), 231–260. Retrieved May 16, 2011 from http://onlinelibrary.wiley.com/doi/10.1111/j.1468-2958.1984.tb00047.x/abstract.

Buss, D. M. (1985). Human mate selection. *American Scientist, 73,* 47–51.

Buss, D. M. (1988). From vigilance to violence: Tactics of mate retention in American undergraduates. *Ethology and Sociobiology, 9,* 291–317.

Buss, D.M. (2003). *The evolution of desire: Strategies of human mating.* New York: Basic Books.

Buss, D. M., Shackelford, T. K., Kirkpatrick, L. A., & Larsen, R. J. (2001). A half century of mate preferences: The cultural evolution of values. *Journal of Marriage and the Family, 63,* 491–503.

Byrne, D. (1997). An overview (and underview) of research and theory within the attraction paradigm. *Journal of Social and Personal Relationships, 14,* 417–431.

Canary, D. J., & Spitzberg, B. H. (1985). Loneliness and relationally competent communication. *Journal of Social and Personal Relationships, 2,* 387–402.

Canary, D. J., & Stafford, L. (1994). Maintaining relationships through strategic and routine interaction. In D. J. Canary & L. Stafford (Eds.), *Communication and relational maintenance* (pp. 3–22). San Diego: Academic Press.

Canary, D. J., Stafford, L., Hause, K. S., & Wallace, L. A. (1993). An inductive analysis of relational maintenance strategies: Comparisons among lovers, relatives, friends, and others. *Communication Research Reports, 10,* 5–14.

Cano, A., & O'Leary, K. D. (1997). Romantic jealousy and affairs: Research and implications for couples' therapy. *Journal of Sex and Marital Therapy, 23,* 249–275.

Cash, T. F., & Derlega, V. J. (1978). The matching hypothesis: Physical attractiveness among same-sex friends. *Personality and Social Psychology Bulletin, 4,* 240–243.

Cauffman, E., Feldman, S., Jensen, L., & Arnett, J. (2000). The (Un)acceptability of violence against peers and dates. *Journal of Adolescent Research, 15,* 652–673.

Centers for Disease Control and Prevention. (2002). Youth risk behavior surveillance—United States, 2001. In CDC Surveillance Summaries, June 28, 2002. MMWR, 51(SS-4), 5–6.

Chambers, V. J., Christiansen, J. R., & Kunz, P. R. (1983). Physiognomic homogamy: A test of physical similarity as a factor in mate selection process. *Social Biology, 30,* 151–157.

Cody, M. J. (1982). A typology of disengagement strategies and an examination of the role intimacy, reactions to inequity and relational problems play in strategy selection. *Communication Monographs, 49,* 148–170.

Cordova, J. V., Jacobsen, N. S., Gottman, J. M., Rushe, R., & Cox, G. (1993). Negative reciprocity and communication in couples with a violent husband. *Journal of Abnormal Psychology, 102,* 559–564.

Dainton, M. A., Zelley, E., & Langan, E. (2003). Maintaining friendships throughout the lifespan. In D. J. Canary & M.

Dainton (Eds.), *Maintaining relationships through communication* (pp. 79–102). Mahwah, NJ: Erlbaum.

Donaghue, N., & Fallon, B. J. (2003) Gender-role self-stereotyping and the relationship between equity and satisfaction in close relationships. *Sex Roles, 48,* 217–230.

Duck, S. (1991). *Understanding relationships.* New York: Guilford Press.

Duck, S. W. (1982). Social and cognitive features of the dissolution of commitment to relationships. In S. W. Duck (Ed.), *Personal relationships 4: Dissolving personal relationships,* (pp. 51–73). London: Academic Press.

Duck, S. W. (1988). *Relating to others.* Chicago: Dorsey Press.

Dunleavy, K. N., Goodboy, A. K., Booth-Butterfield, M., & Sidelinger, S. B. (2007). Repairing hurtful messages in marital relationships. *Communication Quarterly, 57*(1), 67–84.

Edgell, P. (2003). In rhetoric and practice: Defining the "good family" in local congregations. In M. Dillon (Ed.), *Handbook of the sociology of religion.* New York: Cambridge University Press.

Emmers-Sommers, T. M. (2004). The effect of communication quality and quantity indicators on intimacy and relational satisfaction. *Journal of Social and Personal Relationships, 21*(4), 399–411.

Essau, C. A., Conradt, J., & Petermann, F. (1999). Frequency and comorbidity of social phobia and fears in adolescents. *Behavior Research and Therapy, 37,* 831–843.

Fehr, B. (2000). The life cycle of friendship. In C. Hendrick & S. S. Hendrick (Eds.), *Close relationships: A source book* (pp. 71–82). Thousand Oaks: CA: Sage.

Felmlee, D. H. (1995). Fatal attractions: Affections and disaffections in intimate relationships. *Journal of Social and Personal Relationships, 12,* 295–311.

Ferraro, K. (1996). *The dance of dependency: A genealogy of domestic violence discourse.* Hypattia, 11, 72–91.

Folkes, V. S. (1982). Communicating the causes of social rejection. *Journal of Experimental Social Psychology, 18,* 235–252.

Galassi, J. P., & Galassi, M. D. (1979). Modifications of heterosexual skills deficits. In A. S. Bellack & M. Hersen (Eds.), *Research and practice in social skills training* (pp. 131–188). New York: Plenum.

Gierveld, J., & Tilburg, T. (1995). Social relationships, integration and loneliness. In C. P. M. Knipscheer, J. Gierveld, T. Tilburg, & P. A. Dykstra (Eds.), *Living arrangements and social networks among older adults.* Amsterdam: VU University Press.

Glen, N., & Marquardt, E. (2001). "Hooking up," hanging out and hoping for Mr. Right. A report conducted by the Institute for American Values for the Independent Women's Forum. Retrieved May 22, 2011 from http://www.americanvalues.org/Hooking_Up.pdf.

Goodwin, R., & Tang, D. (1991). Preferences for friends and close relationships partners: A cross-cultural comparison. *Journal of Social Psychology, 131,* 579–581.

Grotpeter, J. K., & Crick, N. R. (1996). Relational aggression, overt aggression, and friendship. *Child Development, 67,* 2328–2338.

Guerrero, L. K., & Afifi, W. A. (1999). Toward a goal-centered approach for understanding strategic communicative responses to jealousy. *Western Journal of Communication, 63,* 216–248.

Guerrero, L. K., & Andersen, P. A. (1998). Jealousy experience and expression in romantic relationships. In L. K. Guerrero & P. A. Andersen (Eds.), *Communication and emotion: Theory, research and application* (pp. 155–188). San Diego, CA: Academic Press.

Guerrero, L. K., Eloy, S. V., & Wabnik, A. I. (1993). Linking maintenance strategies to relationship development and disengagement: A reconceptualization. *Journal of Social and Personal Relationships, 10,* 273–283.

Haas, S. M., & Stafford, L. (1998). An initial examination of relationship maintenance behaviors in gay and lesbian relationships. *Journal of Social and Personal Relationships, 15,* 846–855.

Hays, R. B. (1988). Friendship. In S. W. Duck (Eds.), *Handbook of personal relationships* (pp. 391–408). New York: Wiley.

Hinsz, V. B. (1989). Facial resemblance in engaged and married couples. *Journal of Social and Personal Relationships, 6,* 223–229.

Holt-Lunstad, J., Birmingham, W., & Jones, B. Q. (2008) Is there something unique about marriage? The relative impact of marital status, relationship quality, and network support on ambulatory blood pressure and mental health. *Annals of Behavioral Medicine, 35,* 239–244.

Holt-Lunstad J., Smith, T.B., & Layton, J. B. (2010). Social relationships and mortality risk: A meta-analytic review. *PLoS Medicine, 7*(7). Retrieved May 25, 2011, from http://www.plosmedicine.org/article/info%3Adoi%2F10.1371%2Fjournal.pmed.1000316

Infante, D. A., Chandler, T.A., & Rudd, J. E. (1989). A test of an argumentative skill deficiency model of interspousal violence. *Communication Monographs, 56,* 163–177.

Janz, T. A. (2000). The evolution and diversity of relationships in Canadian families. *Canadian Journal of Higher Education.* Retrieved June 15, 2006, from http://www.lcc.gc.ca/research_project/00_diversity_1-en.asp

Johnson, A. J. (2000, July). *A role theory approach to examining the maintenance of geographically close and long-distance friendships.* Paper presented at the International Network on Personal Relationships Conference, Prescott, AZ.

Johnson, A. J., Wittenberg, E., Haigh, M., & Wigley, S. (2004). The process of relationship development and deterioration: Turning points in friendships that have terminated. *Communication Quarterly, 52,* 54–68.

Kalmijin, M. (1994). Assortative mating by cultural and economic occupational status. *American Journal of Sociology, 100,* 422–452.

Kelley, H. H., Berscheid, E., Christensen, A., Harvey, J., Huston, T., Levinger, G., McClintock, E., Peplau, L. A., & Peterson, D. (1983). *Close relationships.* San Francisco: Freeman.

Kenrick, D., & Trost, M. R. (1996). Evolutionary approaches to relationships. In S. Duck (Ed.), *Handbook of personal relationships* (2nd ed.). London: Wiley.

Kimmel, M. S. (2002). Male victims of domestic violence: A substantive and methodological research review. *Violence Against Women, 8*(11), 1332–1363.

Knapp, M. L. (1978). *Social intercourse: From greeting to goodbye.* Boston: Allyn & Bacon.

Knapp, M. L., & Vangelisti, A. (1997). *Interpersonal communication and relationships* (2nd ed.). Boston: Allyn & Bacon.

Knox, D., Schacht, C., Holt, J., & Turner, J. (1993). Sexual lies among university students. *College Student Journal, 27*(2), 269–272.

Kowalski, R., Valentine, S., Wilkinson, R., Queen, A., & Sharpe, B. (2003). Lying, cheating, complaining, and other aversive interpersonal behaviors: A narrative examination of the dark side of relationships. *Journal of Social and Personal Relationships, 20,* 471–490.

Kramer, D., & Moore, M. (2001). Gender roles, romantic fiction and family therapy. *Family Therapy, 12*(24), 1–8.

Kurdek, L.A. (1991). The dissolution of gay and lesbian couples. *Journal of Social and Personal Relationships, 8,* 265–78.

Kurt, J. E., & Sherker, J. L. (2003). Relationship quality, trait similarity, and self-other agreement on personality ratings in college roommates. *Journal of Personality, 71,* 21–40.

LaFollette, H. (1996). *Personal relationships: Love, identity, and morality.* Cambridge, MA: Blackwell Publishers.

Lim, G. Y., & Roloff, M. (1999). Attributing sexual consent. *Journal of Applied Communication Research, 27,* 1–23.

Lloyd, S. A. (1990). Conflict types and strategies in violent marriages. *Journal of Family Violence, 5,* 269–284.

Lloyd, S. A. (1999). The interpersonal and communication dynamics of wife battering. In X. Arriaga & S. Oskamp (Eds.), *Violence in intimate relationships* (pp. 91–111). Thousand Oaks, CA: Sage.

Lloyd, S. A., & Emery, B. C. (2000). The context and dynamics of intimate aggression against women. *Journal of Social and Personal Relationships, 17*(4–5), 503–521.

Mare, R. D. (1991). Five decades of educational assortative mating. *American Sociological Review, 56,* 15–32.

Becker, J. A. H., Johnson, McCormick, N. B., & Jones, J. J. (1989). Gender differences in nonverbal flirtation. *Journal of Sex Education and Therapy, 15,* 271–282.

McCornack, S. A., & Parks, M. R. (1986). Deception detection and relationship development: The other side of trust. In M. L. McLaughlin (Ed.), *Communication Yearbook, 9,* 377–389. Newbury Park, CA: Sage.

McCoy, K., & Oelschlager, J. (n.d.) Sexual coercion awareness and prevention. *Florida Institute of Technology.* Retrieved May 17, 2011 from http://www.fit.edu/caps/documents/SexualCoercion_000.pdf

McEwen, W. J., & Greenberg, B. S. (1970). The effects of message intensity on receiver revaluations of source, message, and topic. *Journal of Communication, 20,* 340–350.

McCroskey, L. L., McCroskey, J. C., & Richmond, V. P. (2006.) Analysis and improvement of the measurement of interpersonal attraction and homophily. *Communication Quarterly, 54*(1), 1–31.

Messman, S. J., Canary, D. J., & Hause, K. S. (2000). Motives to remain platonic, equity, and the use of maintenance strategies in opposite-sex friendships. *Journal of Social and Personal Relationships, 17,* 67–94.

Miller, C. W., & Roloff, M. (2005). Gender and willingness to confront hurtful messages from romantic partners. *Communication Quarterly, 53*(3), 323–337.

Miller, R. S. (1997). We always hurt the ones we love: Aversive interactions in close relationships. In R. M. Kowalski (Ed.), *Aversive interpersonal behaviors* (pp. 12–29). New York: Plenum.

Miller, R. S. (2002). Suicidal and death ideation in older primary care patients with depression, anxiety, and at-risk. *American Journal of Geriatric Psychiatry, 10,* 417–427.

Mills, R. S. L., Nazar, J., & Farrell, H. M. (2002). Child and parent perceptions of hurtful messages. *Journal of Social and Personal Relationships, 19,* 731–754.

Mongeau, P. A., Ramirez, R., & Vorell, M. (2003). *Friends with benefits: An initial exploration of a sexual but not romantic relationship.* Paper presented at the Western States Communication Association. Salt Lake, UT.

MSNBC News. (2004, March 8). *Lip-lock could mean lockup in Indonesia.* Retrieved March 8, 2006, from http://www.msnbc.msn.com/id/4478875/

Muehlenhard, C. L. (1989). Misinterpreted dating behaviors and the risk of date rape. In M. A. Pirog-Good & J. E. Stets (Eds.), *Violence in dating relationships: Emerging social issues* (pp. 241–256). New York: Praeger.

Muehlenhard, C. L., & Hollabough, L. C. (1988). Do women sometimes say no when they mean yes?: The prevalence and correlates of women's token resistance to sex. *Journal of Personality and Social Psychology, 54,* 872–879.

Muehlenhard, C. L., & Linton, M. A. (1987). Date rape and sexual aggression in dating: Incidence and risk factors. *Journal of Personality and Social Psychology, 34,* 186–196.

Muehlenhard, C. L., & McFalls, M. C. (1981). Dating initiation from a woman's perspective. *Behavior Therapy, 14,* 626–636.

Muehlenhard, C. L., & Miller, E. N. (1988). Traditional and non-traditional men's responses to women's dating initiation. *Behavior Modification, 12*(3), 385–403.

Mullen, P. E., & Maack, L. H. (1985). Jealousy, pathological jealousy, and aggression. In D. P. Farrington & J. Gunn (Eds.), *Aggression and dangerousness* (pp. 103–126). New York: Wiley.

Myers, S. A., & Schrodt, P. & Rittenour, C. E. (2006). The impact of parents' use of hurtful messages on adult children's self-esteem and educational motivation. In L. H. Turner & R. West (Eds), *The family communication sourcebook* (pp. 425–446). Thousand Oaks, CA: Sage Publications.

Nardi, P. M. (1992). That's what friends are for: Friends as family in the gay and lesbian community. In K. Plummer (Ed.), *Modern homosexualities: Fragments of lesbian and gay experience* (pp. 108–120). New York: Routledge.

Nardi, P. M. (2007). Friendship, sex, and masculinity. In M. Kimmel (ed.), *The sexual self* (pp. 49–60). Nashville, TN: Vanderbilt University Press.

Noller, P., & Fitzpatrick, M. A. (1990). Marital communication in the eighties. *Journal of Marriage and the Family, 52,* 832–843.

O'Brien, E., & Foley, L. (1999). The dating game: An exercise illustrating the concepts of homogamy, heterogamy, hyperogamy, and hypogamy. *Teaching Sociology, 27*(2), 145–149.

Owen, W. F. (1987). The verbal expression of love by women and men as a critical communication event in personal relationships. *Women's Studies in Communication, 10,* 15–24.

Pogrebin, L. C. (1992). The same and different: Crossing boundaries of color, culture, sexual preference, disability, and age. In W. B. Gudykunst, & Y. Y. Kim (Eds.), *Readings on communicating with strangers* (pp. 318–336). New York: McGraw-Hill.

Psarska, A. D. (1970). Jealousy factor in homicide in forensic material. *Polish Medical Journal, 9,* 1504–1510.

Rawlins, W. K. (1992). *Friendship matters.* New York: Aline de Guyter.

Reeder, H. (1996). *What Harry and Sally didn't tell you.* Unpublished doctoral dissertation, Arizona State University, Tempe.

Rennison, C. M., & Welchans, S. (2000). *Intimate Partner Violence Special Report,* NCJ 178247. Washington, DC: U.S. Department of Justice.

Rindfuss, R. R., & Stephen, E. H. (1990). Marital noncohabitation: Separation does not make the heart grow fonder. *Journal of Marriage and the Family, 52,* 259–270.

Root, M. P. (2001). *Love's revolution: Interracial marriage.* Philadelphia, PA: Temple University Press.

Rose, S. M. (1984). How friendships end: Patterns among young adults. *Journal of Social and Personal Relationships, 1,* 267–277.

Roth, M., & Parker, J. (2001). Affective and behavioral responses to friends who neglect their friends for dating partners: Influences of gender, jealousy and perspective. *Journal of Adolescence, 24,* 281–296.

Sabourin, T. C. (1996). The role of communication in verbal abuse between spouses. In D. D. Cahn & S. A. Lloyd (Eds.), *Family violence from a communication perspective* (pp. 199–217). Thousand Oaks, CA: Sage.

Sagarin, B. J., Rhoads, K. L., & Cialdini, R. B. (1998). Deceiver's distrust: Denigration as a consequence of undiscovered deception. *Personality and Social Psychology Bulletin. 24,* 1167–1176.

Sailer, S. (2003, March 14). *Interracial marriage gender gap grows.* United Press International (UPI). Retrieved June 28, 2004, from http://www.modelminority.com/article338.html

Schafer, R. B., & Keith, P. M. (1990). Matching by weight in married couples: A life cycle perspective. *Journal of Social Psychology, 130*(5), 657–664.

Segrin, C., & Givertz, M. (2003). Methods of social skills training and development. In J. O. Green & B. R. Burleson (Eds.), *Handbook of communication and social interaction skills* (pp. 135–176). Mahwah, NJ: Erlbaum.

Shehan, C. L., Bock, E. W., & Lee, G. R., (1990). Religious heterogamy, religiosity, and marital happiness: The case of Catholics. *Journal of Marriage and the Family, 52,* 73–79.

Sias, P. M., & Cahill, D. J. (1998). From coworkers to friends: The development of peer friendships in the workplace. *Western Journal of Communication, 62,* 273–299.

Sollors, W. (Ed.). (2000). *Interracialism: Black and white intermarriage in American history, literature and law.* New York: Oxford University Press.

Spitzberg, B. (1998). Sexual coercion in courtship relationships. In B. Spitzberg & W. Cupach (Eds.), *The dark side of close relationships.* Hillsdale, NJ: Erlbaum.

Sprecher, S. (1998). Insiders' perspectives on reasons for attraction to a close other. *Social Psychology Quarterly, 61,* 287–300.

Sprecher, S., & Regan, P. (2002). Liking some things (in some people) more than others: Partner preferences in romantic relationships and friendships. *Journal of Social and Personal Relationships, 19,* 463–481.

Stiff, J. B., Kim, H. J., & Ramesh, C. N. (1989). *Truth biases and aroused suspicion in relational deception.* Paper presented at the annual meeting of the Interpersonal Communication Association (May), San Francisco, CA.

Struckman-Johnson, C. J., Struckman-Johnson, B. L., & Anderson, B. (2003). Tactics of sexual coercion: When men and women won't take no for an answer. *Journal of Sex Research, 40*(1), 76–86.

Sunnafrank, M. (1986). Predicted outcome value in initial conversations. *Communication Research Reports, 5*(2), 169–172.

Surra, C. (1987). Reasons for changes in commitment: Variations by courtship type. *Journal of Social and Personal Relationships, 4,* 17–33.

Times Square Travels. (2004). *Travel in Japan.* Retrieved June 15, 2006, from http://www.taveltst.ca/index.php?tpl=vacation-guides_japan-guide_introduction

Tolhuizen, J. H. (1990). *Deception in developing dating relationships.* Paper presented at the Speech Communication Association Convention, Chicago, IL.

Tracy, K., Van Dusen, D., & Robinson, S. (1987). "Good" and "bad" criticism: A descriptive analysis. *Journal of Communication, 37*(2), 46–59.

Trost, M. R., & Kenrick, D. T. (1993). An evolutionary perspective on interpersonal communication. In S. Petronio, J. K. Alberts, M. Hecht, & J. Buley (Eds.), *Contemporary perspectives on interpersonal communication* (pp. 120–124). Madison, WI: Brown & Benchmark.

Turner, R. E., Edgley, C., & Olmstead, G. (1975). Information control in conversations: Honesty is not always the best policy. *Kansas Journal of Sociology, 11,* 69–89.

U.S. Bureau of the Census. (1998, October 10). *Race of wife by race of husband, 1960, 1970, 1980, 1990, 1992.* Retrieved June 28, 2004, from http://www.census.gov/population/socdemo/race/interractab1.txt

Vangelisti, A. L. (1994). Messages that hurt. In W. R. Cupach, & B. H. Spitzberg (Eds.), *The dark side of interpersonal communication* (pp. 53–82). Hillsdale, NJ: Erlbaum.

Vangelisti, A. L. (2007). Communicating hurt. In B. Spitzberg & W. Cupach (Eds.), *The dark side of close relationships* (pp. 121–142). Mahwah, NJ: Erlbaum.

Vorauer, J., & Ratner, R. (1996). Who's going to make the first move? *Journal of Social and Personal Relationships, 13,* 483–506.

Weber, A. L. (1998). Losing, leaving and letting go: Coping with nonmarital breakups. In B. H. Spitzberg & W. R. Cupach (Eds.), *The dark side of close relationships* (pp. 267–306). Mawah, NJ: Erlbaum.

White, G. L. (1980) Physical attractiveness and courtship progress. *Personality and Social Psychology, 39,* 660–668.

White, G. L., & Mullen, P. E. (1989). *Jealousy.* New York: Guilford Press.

Willan, V. J., & Pollard, P. (2003). Likelihood of acquaintance rape as a function of males' sexual expectations, disappointment, and adherence to rape-conducive attitudes. *Journal of Social and Personal Relationships, 20,* 637–661.

Wolcott, J. (2004). Is dating dead on college campuses? *Christian Science Monitor.* Retrieved May 25, 2011, from http://www.csmonitor.com/2004/0302/p11s01-legn.html

World Travels. (2004). Kuwait travel guide. Retrieved March 16, 2006, from http://www.worldtravelguide.net/country/141/country_guide/Middle-East/Kuwait.html

Wright, D. E. (1999). *Personal relationships: An interdisciplinary approach.* Mountain View, CA: Mayfield Publishing.

Young, J. E. (1981). Cognitive therapy and loneliness. In G. Emery, S. D. Hollon, & R. C. Bed-rosian (Eds.), *New directions in cognitive therapy: A casebook* (pp. 139–159). New York: Guilford Press.

Young, S. L., & Bippus, A. M. (2001). Does it make a difference if they hurt you in a funny way?: Humorously and non-humorously phrased hurtful messages in personal relationships. *Communication Quarterly, 49,* 35–52.

Chapter 10

Adams, K., & Galanes, G. J. (2003). *Communicating in groups: Applications and skills.* Boston: McGraw-Hill.

Allen, T. H., & Plax, T. G. (2002). Exploring consequences of group communication in the classroom. In L. R. Frey (Ed.), *New directions in group communication* (pp. 219–234). Thousand Oaks, CA: Sage.

Alsop, R. (2003, September 9). Playing well with others. *Wall Street Journal* (Eastern Edition), p. R11.

Arrow, H., McGrath, J. E., & Berdahl, J. L. (2000). *Small groups as complex systems.* Thousand Oaks, CA: Sage.

Baldoni, J. (2004). Powerful leadership communication. *Leader to Leader, 32,* 20–21.

Bantz, C. R. (1993). Cultural diversity and group cross-cultural team research. *Journal of Applied Communication Research, 21,* 1–20.

Barge, J. K. (1989). Leadership as medium: A leaderless group discussion model. *Communication Quarterly, 37,* 237–247.

Barnard, C. (1938). *The functions of an executive.* Cambridge, MA: Harvard University Press.

Barnlund, D. C., & Haiman, S. (1960). *The dynamics of discussion.* Boston: Houghton-Mifflin.

Benne, K. D., & Sheats, P. (1948). Functional roles of group members. *Journal of Social Issues, 4,* 41–49.

Bensimon, E. M. & Neumann, A. (1994). *Redesigning collegiate leadership: Teams and teamwork in higher education.* Baltimore, MD: Johns Hopkins University Press.

Bock, W. (2006). Three star leadership. Retrieved March 30, 2011, from http://www.threestarleadership.com/articles/4mistakes.htm

Bonito, J. A., DeCamp, M. H. & Ruppel, E. K. (2008). The process of information sharing in small groups: Application of a local model. *Communication Monographs, 75,* 171–192.

Bono, J. E., & Judge, T. A. (2004). Personality and transformational and transactional leadership: A meta-analysis. *Journal of Applied Psychology, 89*(5), 901–910.

Bormann, E. G. (1975). *Discussion and group methods* (2nd ed.). New York: Harper & Row.

Bowers, C. A., Pharmer, J. A., & Salas, E. (2000). When member homogeneity is needed in work teams: A meta-analysis. *Small Group Research, 31,* 305–327.

Broome, B. J., & Chen, M. (1992). Guidelines for computer-assisted problem solving: Meeting the challenges of complex issues, *Small Group Research, 23,* 216–236.

Broome, B. J., & Fulbright, L. (1995). A multistage influence model of barriers to group problem solving: A participant-generated agenda for small group research, *Small Group Research, 26,* 24–55.

Brown, S. (2007, April 12). It's teamwork, not solos, that make for discoveries, research finds. *The Chronicle of Higher Education.* Retrieved April 17, 2011, from http://chronicle.com/article/Its-Teamwork-Not-Solos-That/38549/

Cady, S. H., & Valentine, J. (1999). Team innovation and perceptions of consideration: What difference does diversity make? *Small Group Research, 30,* 730–750.

Connaughton, S. L., & Shuffler, M. (2007). Multinational and multicultural distributed teams: A review and future agenda. *Small Group Research, 38*(1), 387–412.

Covey, S. R. (1989). *The seven habits of highly effective people: Restoring the character ethic.* New York: Simon and Schuster.

Cox, T. (1994). *Cultural diversity in organizations: Theory, research and practice.* San Francisco: Berrett-Kochler.

Cragan, J. F., & Wright, D. W. (1999). *Communication in small groups: Theory, process, skills* (5th ed.). Belmont, CA: Wadsworth.

Crown, D. F. (2007). The use of group and groupcentric individual goals for culturally heterogeneous and homogeneous task groups: An assessment of European work teams. *Small Group Research, 38*(4), 489–508.

Daft, R. L. (2010). *The leadership experience* (5th ed.). Mason, OH: Thomson Higher Education.

Denhardt, R. B. & Denhardt, J. V. (2004). *The dance of leadership.* Armonk, NJ: M. E. Sharpe.

Engleberg, I. N., & Wynn, D. R. (2010). *Working in groups: Communication principles and strategies* (5th ed.). Boston: Allyn-Bacon.

Eysenbach, G., Powell, J., Englesakis, M., Rizo, C., & Stern, A. (2004). Health related virtual communities and electronic support groups: Systematic review of the effects of online peer to peer interactions. *BMJ Journal.* Retrieved April 2, 2011, from http://www.bmj.com/content/328/7449/1166.short

Fisher, B. A. (1970). *Decision emergence: Phases in group decision-making. Speech Monographs, 37,* 53–66.

Fisher, B. A. (1980). *Small group decision making: Communication and the group process* (2nd ed.). New York: McGraw-Hill.

Fisher, B. A. & Ellis, D. G. (1993). *Small group decision making: Communication and the group process.* Boston: McGraw Hill

Foels, R., Driskell, J. E., Mullen, B., & Salas, E. (2000). The effects of democratic leadership on group member satisfaction: An integration. *Small Group Research, 31,* 676–701.

French, J. R., Jr., & Raven, B. H. (1959). The bases of social power. In D. Cartwright (Ed.), *Studies in social power* (pp. 150–167). Ann Arbor, MI: Institute for Social Research.

Frey, L. R. (1994). The call of the field: Studying communication in natural groups. In L. R. Frey (Ed.), *Group communication in context: Studies of natural groups* (pp. ix–xiv). Hillsdale, NJ: Erlbaum.

Gagné, M., & Zuckerman, M. (1999). Performance and learning goal orientations as moderators of social loafing and social facilitation. *Small Group Research, 30,* 524–541.

Gastil, J. (1994). A meta-analytic review of the productivity and satisfaction of democratic and autocratic leadership. *Small Group Research, 25,* 384–399.

Gladwell, M. (2008). *Outliers.* NY: Little, Brown and Company.

Gokhale, A. (1995). Collaborative learning enhances critical thinking. *Journal of Technology Education, 7,* 22–30.

Gollent, M. (2007, June 6). Why are leadership skills important—for everyone? Retrieved March 30, 2011, from http://ezinearticles.com/?why-are-leadership-skills-important—for-everyone?&id=591333

Gouran, D. S., Hirokawa, R., & Martz, A. (1986). A critical analysis of factors related to the decisional processes involved in the *Challenger* disaster. *Central States Speech Journal,* 119–135.

Greenleaf, R. (1970/1991). *The servant as leader.* Indianapolis: The Robert K. Greenleaf Center, 1–37.

Greenleaf, R. K. (2002). *Servant leadership: A journey into the nature of legitimate power and greatness.* 25th anniversary edition. New York: Paulist Press.

Groutage, H. (1999, October 10). Mother of slain student calls for tolerance. *Salt Lake Tribune,* p. A4.

Hansen, R. S. & Hansen, K. (2003, November 17). What do employers *really* want? *QuintZine, 4*(23). Retrieved March 25, 2011, from http://www.quintcareers.com/job_skills_values.html

Hargrove, R. (1998). *Mastering the art of creative collaboration.* New York: BusinessWeek Books.

Haslett, B. B., & Ruebush, J. (1999). What differences do individual differences in groups make? The effects of individuals, culture, and group composition. In L. R. Frey, D. S. Gouran, & M. S. Poole (Eds.), *The handbook of group communication theory and research* (pp. 115–138). Thousand Oaks, CA: Sage.

Henningsen, D. D., & Henningsen, M. L. M. (2006). Examining the symptoms of groupthink and retrospective sensemaking. *Small Group Research, 37*(1), 36–64.

Hirokawa, R. Y., & Salazar, A. J. (1999). Task-group communication and decision-making performance. In L. R. Frey, D. S. Gouran, & M. S. Poole (Eds.), The *handbook of group communication theory and research* (pp. 167–191). Thousand Oaks, CA: Sage.

Hughes, L. (2003). How to be an effective team player. *Women in Business, 55,* 22.

Ilgen, D. R., Hollenbeck, J. R., Johnson, M., & Jundt, D. (2005). Teams in organizations: From input-process-output models to IMOI models. *Annual Review of Psychology, 56,* 517–543.

Judge, T. A., Bono, J. E., Ilies, R., & Gerhardt, M. W. (2002). Personality and leadership: A qualitative and quantitative review. *Journal of Applied Psychology, 87,* 765–780.

Judge, T. A., & Cable, D. M. (2004). The effect of physical height on workplace success and income: Preliminary test of a theoretical model. *Journal of Applied Psychology, 89,* 428–441.

Judge, T. A., Colbert, A. E., & Ilies, R. (2004). Intelligence and leadership: A quantitative review and test of theoretical propositions. *Journal of Applied Psychology, 89,* 542–552.

Jung, D. I., & Sosik, J. J. (2002). Transformational leadership in work groups: The role of empowerment, cohesiveness, and collective-efficacy on perceived group performance. *Small Group Research, 33,* 313–336.

Kent, M. V. (1994). The presence of others. In A. P. Hare, H. H. Blumberg, M. F. Davies, & M. V. Kent. *Small group research: A handbook* (pp. 81–106). Norwood, NJ: Ablex.

Keyton, J., Harmon, N., & Frey, L. R. (1996, November). Grouphate: Implications for teaching group communication. Paper presented at the annual meeting of the National Communication Association, San Diego, CA.

Keyton, J. (1999). Relational communication in groups. In L. R. Frey, D. S. Gouran, & M. S. Poole (Eds.), *Handbook of group communication theory and research* (pp. 199–222). Thousand Oaks, CA: Sage.

Keyton, J. (2000). Introduction: The relational side of groups. *Small Group Research, 34,* 387–396.

King, N., & Anderson, N. (1990). Innovation in working groups. In M. A. West & J. F. Farr (Eds.), *Innovation and creativity at work: Psychological and organizational strategies* (pp. 110–135). Chichester, UK: Wiley.

Klocke, U. (2007). How to improve decision making in small groups: Effects of dissent and training interventions. *Small Group Research, 38(3),* 437–468.

Komives, S. R., Lucas, N. & McMahon, T. (1998). Exploring leadership for college students who want to make a difference. San Francisco: Jossey-Bass Publishers.

Landy, F. J., & Conte, J. M. (2010). *Work in the 21st Century: An Introduction to Industrial & Organizational Psychology* (3rd ed.). Hoboken: John Wiley & Sons.

Larson, J. R. (2007). Deep diversity and strong synergy: Modeling the impact of variability in members' problem solving strategies on group problem-solving performance, *Small Group Research, 38(3),* 413–436.

Levine, K. J. , Muenchen, R. A. & Brooks, A. M. (2010). Measuring transformational and charismatic leadership: Why isn't charisma measured? *Communication Monographs, 77(4),* 576–591.

Lewin, K., Lippit, R., & White, R. K. (1939). Patterns of aggressive behavior in experimentally created "social climates." *Journal of Social Psychology, 10,* 271–279.

Lewis, L. K., Isbell, M. G., & Koschmann, M. A. (2010). Collaborative tensions: Practitioners' experiences of interorganizational relationships. *Communication Monographs, 77(4),* 462-481.

Li, D. C. S. (2007). Computer-mediated communication and group decision making: A functional perspective. *Small Group Research 38(5),* 593–614.

Littlejohn, S. W. (2002). *Theories of human communication* (7th ed.). Belmont, CA: Wadsworth.

Lowry, P. B., Roberts, T. L., Romano, N. C., Cheney, P. D., & Hightower R. T. (2006). The impact of group size and social presence on small-group communication: Does computer-mediated communication make a difference? *Small Group Research, 37(6),* 631–661.

MacNeil, A., & McClanahan, A. (2005). Shared leadership, The Connexions Project. Retrieved May 21, 2008, from http://cnx.org/content/m12923/latest/

Matha, B. & Boehm, M. (2008). Beyond the Babble: Leadership communication that drives results. San Francisco, CA: Jossey-Bass.

Maznevski, M., & Chudoba, C. (2000). Bridging space over time: Global virtual team dynamics and effectiveness. *Organization Science, 11(5),* 473–492.

McLeod, P. L., Lobel, S. A., & Cox, T. H. (1996). Ethnic diversity and creativity in small groups. *Small Group Research, 27,* 248–264.

Meade, R. (1985). Experimental studies of authoritarian and democratic leadership in four cultures: American, Indian, Chinese and Chinese-American. *High School Journal, 68,* 293–295.

Moore, R. M., III. (2000). Creativity of small groups and of persons working alone. *Journal of Social Psychology, 140,* 143–144.

Myers, S. A., & Goodboy, A. K. (2005). A study of grouphate in a course on small group communication. *Psychological Reports, 97(2),* 381–386.

Northouse, P. G. (2010). *Leadership: Theory and practice.* Thousand Oaks, CA: Sage.

Oetzel, J. G. (1998). Explaining individual communication processes in homogeneous and heterogeneous group through individual-collectivism and self-construal, *Human Communication Research, 25,* 202–224.

Oetzel, J. G. (2001). Self-construals, communication processes, and group outcomes in homogeneous and heterogeneous groups, *Small Group Research, 32,* 19–54.

Oetzel, J. G. (2005). Effective intercultural workgroup communication theory. In W. B. Gudykunst (Ed.), *Theorizing about intercultural communication* (pp. 351–371). Thousand Oaks, CA: Sage.

Paletz, S. B. F., Peng, K., Erez, M., & Maslach, C. (2004). Ethnic composition and its differential impact on group processes in diverse teams. *Small Group Research, 35,* 128–158.

Pavitt, C. (1999). Theorizing about the group communication-leadership relationship. In L. R. Frey, D. S. Gouran, & M. S. Poole (Eds.), *Handbook of group communication theory and research* (pp. 313–334). Thousand Oaks, CA: Sage.

Peterson, R. S., & Behfar, K. J. (2003). The dynamic relationship between performance feedback, trust, and conflict in groups: A longitudinal study. *Organizational Behavior and Human Decision Processes, 92,* 102–112.

Polzer, J. T., Milton, L. P., & Swann, W. B., Jr. (2002). Capitalizing on diversity: Interpersonal congruence in small work groups. *Administrative Science Quarterly, 47,* 296–324.

Poole, M. S. (1983). Decision development in small groups: A study of multiple sequences in decision-making. *Communication Monographs, 50,* 206–232.

Poole, M. S. (1999). Group communication theory. In L. R. Frey, D. S. Gouran, & M. S. Poole (Eds.), *Handbook of group communication theory and research* (pp. 37–70). Thousand Oaks, CA: Sage.

Poole, M. S. & Garner, J. T. (2006). Workgroup conflict and communication. In J. G. Oetzel & S. Ting-Toomey (Eds.), *The Sage handbook of conflict communication* (pp. 267–292). Thousand Oaks, CA: Sage.

Propp, K. M. (1999). Collective information processing in groups. In L. R. Frey, D. S. Gouran, & M. S. Poole (Eds.), *Handbook of group communication theory and research* (pp. 225–250). Thousand Oaks, CA: Sage.

Putnam, L. L., & Stohl, C. (1996). Bona fide groups: An alternative perspective for communication and small group decision-making. In R. Y. Hirokawa & M. S. Poole (Eds.), *Communication and group decision-making* (2nd ed., pp. 147–178). Thousand Oaks, CA: Sage.

Rauch, C. F., Jr., & Behling, O. (1984). Functionalism: Basis for alternative approach to the study of leadership. In J. G. Hunt, D.-M. H. Hosking, C. A. Schriesheim, & R. Stewart (Eds.), *Leaders and managers: International perspectives on managerial behavior and leadership* (pp. 45–62). New York: Pergamon.

Reeves, R., (2004, March). Enough of the 't'-word. *Management Today*, 29.

Riddle, B. L., Anderson, C. M., & Martin, M. M. (2000). Small group socialization scale: Development and validity. *Small Group Research, 31*, 554–572.

Rost, J. C. (2008). Leadership definition. In a. Marturano & J. Gosling (Eds.), *Leadership: The key concepts* (pp. 96–99). New York: Routledge.

Rothwell, J. D. (1995). *In mixed company: Small group communication* (2nd ed.). Fort Worth, TX: Harcourt Brace.

Rowold, J. & Heinitz, K. (2007). Transformational and charismatic leadership: Assessing the convergent, divergent and criterion validity of the MLQ and the CKS. *The Leadership Quarterly, 18*, 121–133.

Salazar, A. J. (1997). Communication effects in small group decision-making: Homogeneity and task as moderators of the communication performance relationship. *Western Journal of Communication, 61*, 35–65.

Sargent, L. D., & Sue-Chan, C. (2001). Does diversity affect group efficacy? *Small Group Research, 32*, 426–450.

Savič, B. S., & Pagon, M. (2008). Individual involvement in health care organizations: Differences between professional groups, leaders and employees. *Stress and Health, 24*, 71–84.

Schiller, S. Z., & Mandviwalla, M. (2007). Virtual team research: An analysis of theory use and a framework for theory appropriation. *Small Group Research, 38*(1), 12–59.

Schultz, B. G. (1999). Improving group communication performance. In L. R. Frey, D. S. Gouran, & M. S. Poole (Eds.), *Handbook of group communication theory and research* (pp. 371–394). Thousand Oaks, CA: Sage.

Scott, C. R. (1999). Communication technology and group communication. In L. R. Frey, D. S. Gouran, & M. S. Poole (Eds.), *The handbook of group communication theory research* (pp. 432–472). Thousand Oaks, CA: Sage.

Sell, J., Lovaglia, M. J., Mannix, E. A., Samuelson, C. D., & Wilson, R. K. (2004). Investigating conflict, power, and status within and among groups. *Small Group Research, 35*, 44–72.

Smith, P. G. (2001). Communication holds global teams together. *Machine Design, 73*, 70–73.

Stogdill, R. M. (1974). *Handbook of leadership: A survey of theory and research*. New York: Free Press.

Support Groups: Do I Really Need One? (n.d.) Adoption.com. Retrieved April 2, 2011 from http://library.adoption.com/articles/support-groups-.html

Uhl-Bien, M. (2006). Relational leadership theory: Exploring the social processes of leadership and organizing. *The Leadership Quarterly, 17*, 654–676.

Valenti, M. A., & Rockett, R. (2008). The effects of demographic differences on forming intragroup relationships. *Small Group Research, 39*(2), 179–202.

van Knippenberg, D., De Dreu, C. K. W., & Homan, A. C. (2004). Work group diversity and group performance: An integrative model and research agenda. *Journal of Applied Psychology, 89*(6), 1008–1022.

van Swol, L. M. (2009). Discussion and perception of information in groups and judge-advisor systems. *Communication Monographs, 76*(1), 99-120.

Wellen, J. M., & Neale, M. (2006). Deviance, self-typicality and group cohesion: The corrosive effects of the bad apples on the barrel. *Small Group Research, 37*(2), 165–186.

Wheelan, S. A., Davidson, B., & Tilin, F. (2003). Group development across time: Reality or illusion? *Small Group Research, 34*, 223–245.

Chapter 11

Aeberhard-Hodges, J. (1996). Sexual harassment in employment: Recent judicial and arbitral trends. *International Labor Review, 135*(5), 499–533.

Alberts, J. K., Lutgen-Sandvik, P., & Tracy, S. J. (2005, May). Bullying in the workplace: A case of escalated incivility. *Organizational Communication Division*. The International Communication Association Convention, New York, NY.

Alberts, J. K., Tracy, S., & Trethewey, A. (2011). An integrative theory of the division of domestic labor: Threshold level, social organizing, and sensemaking. *Journal of Family Communication, 11*, 271–238.

American Management Association. (2005, May 18). *2005 electronic monitoring & surveillance survey: Many companies monitoring, recording, videotaping, and firing employees*. Retrieved June 16, 2006, from http://www.amanet.org/press/amanews/ems05.htm

Barley, S. R., & Kunda, G. (1992). Design and devotion: Surges of rational and normative ideologies of control in managerial discourse. *Administrative Science Quarterly, 37*, 363–399.

Berger, C. (1979). Beyond initial interaction. In H. Giles & R. St. Clair (Eds.), *Language and psychology* (pp. 122–144). Oxford, UK: Basil Blackwell.

Bertalanffy, L. von. (1968). *General systems theory*. New York: Braziller.

Belous, R. (1989). *The contingent economy: The growth of the temporary, part-time and subcontracted workforce*. Washington, DC: The National Planning Association.

Blau, P. M., & Meyer, M. W. (1987). *Bureaucracy in modern society* (3rd ed). New York: Random House.

Brown, M. (1989, Winter). Ethics in organizations. *Issues in Ethics, 2*(1). Santa Clara University: Markkula Center for Applied Ethics. Retrieved March 15, 2006, from http://www.scu.edu/ethics/publications/iie/v2n1/homepage.html

Bullis, C., & Tompkins, P. K. (1989). The forest ranger revisited: A study of control practices and identification. *Communication Monographs, 56*, 287–306.

Canary, D., & Lakey, S. L. (2012). *Strategic conflict. New York:*, Routledge.

Casey, M. K. (1998). *Communication, stress and burnout: Use of resource replacement strategies in response to conditional demands in community-based organizations*. Unpublished doctoral dissertation, Michigan State University, East Lansing, MI.

Chambers, B., Moore, A. B., & Bachtel, D. (1998). *Role conflict, role ambiguity and job satisfaction of county extension agents in the Georgia Cooperative Extension Service.* AERC Proceedings. Retrieved September 15, 2006, from http://www.edst.educ.ubc .ca/aercd1998/98chambers.htm

Cheney, G. (1995). Democracy in the workplace: Theory and practice from the perspective of communication. *Journal of Applied Communication Research, 23,* 167–200.

Cheney, G., Christensen, L. T., Zorn, T. E., Jr., & Ganesh, S. (2004). *Organizational communication in an age of globalizations: Issues, reflections, practices.* Prospect Heights, IL: Waveland.

Chiles, A., & Zorn, T. (1995). Empowerment in organizations: Employees' perceptions of the influences on empowerment. *Journal of Applied Communication Research, 23,* 1–25.

Chilton, K., & Weidenbaum, M. (1994, November). *A new social contract for the American workplace: From paternalism to partnering.* St. Louis, MO: Center for the Study of American Business.

Clair, R. (1996). The political nature of a colloquialism, "A real job": Implications for organizational assimilation. *Communication Monographs, 63,* 249–267.

Conrad, C., & Poole, M. S. (2005). *Strategic organizational communication* (6th ed.). Belmont, CA: Wadsworth.

Conrad, C., & Witte, K. (1994). Is emotional expression repression oppression? *Communication Yearbook, 17,* 417–428. Thousand Oaks: Sage.

Coy, P., Conlin, M., & Herbst, M. (2010, Jan. 7). The disposable worker. *Bloomberg Business Week.* Retrieved September 17, 2011 from http://www.businessweek.com/magazine/content/10_03/b4163032935448.htm.

Daniels, T. D., Spiker, B. K., & Papa, M. J. (1996). *Perspectives on organizational communication* (4th ed.). Madison, WI: Brown & Benchmark.

Dansereau, F. D., & Markham, S. E. (1987). Superior–subordinate communication: Multiple levels of analysis. In F. Jablin, L. Putnam, K. Roberts, & L. Porter (Eds.), *Handbook of organizational communication* (pp. 343–386). Newbury Park, CA: Sage.

Deetz, S. (1992). *Democracy in an age of corporate colonization: Developments in communication and the politics of everyday life.* Albany, NY: SUNY Press.

DiTecco, D., Cwitco, G., Arsenault, A., & Andre, M. (1992). Operator stress and monitoring practices. *Applied Ergonomics, 23(1),* 29–34.

Dockery, T. M., & Steiner, D. D. (1990). The role of the initial interaction in leader-member exchange. *Group and Organization Studies, 15,* 395–413.

Eisenberg, E., Goodall, H. L., & Trethewey, A. (2010). *Organizational communication: Balance, creativity and constraint.* Boston, MA: Bedford/St. Martin's.

Eisenberg, E. M., Monge, P. R., & Farace, R. V. (1984). Coorientation on communication rules in managerial dyads. *Human Communication Research, 11,* 261–271.

Equal Employment Opportunity Commission. (1980). Guidelines on discrimination because of sex (Sect. 1604.11). *Federal Register, 45,* 74676–74677.

Everbach, T. (2007). The culture of a women-led newspaper: An ethnographic study of the Sarasota Herald-Tribune. *Journalism and Mass Communication Quarterly, 83,* 477–493.

Fishman, C. (2006). *The Wal-Mart effect.* NY: Penguin Press.

Follett, M. P. (1942). *Dynamic administration.* New York: Harper & Row.

Ganesh, S., Zoller, H. & Cheney, G. (2005). Transforming resistance, broadening our boundaries: Critical organization meets globalization from below. *Communication Monographs, 72(2),* 169–191.

Glisson, C., & Durick, M. (1988). Predictors of job satisfaction and organizational commitment in human service organizations. *Administrative Quarterly, 33,* 61–81.

Golembiewski, R. T., Boudreau, R. A., Sun, B. C., & Luo, H. (1998). Estimates of burnout in public agencies: Worldwide how many employees have which degrees of burnout, and with what consequences? *Public Administration Review, 58,* 59–65.

Gossett, L. (2001). The long-term impact of short-term workers. *Management Communication Quarterly, 15(1),* 115–120.

Graen, G., & Graen, J. (2006). *Sharing network leadership.* Greenwich, CT: Information Age Publishing.

Gruber, J. E., & Smith, M. D. (1995). Women's responses to sexual harassment: A multivariate analysis. *Basic and Applied Social Psychology, 17,* 543–562.

Hewlitt, S. (2007). *Off-ramps and on-ramps: Keeping talented women on the road to success.* Harvard, MA: Harvard Business School Publishing.

Highgate, P., & Upton, J. (2005). War, militarism, and masculinities. In M.S. Kimmel, J. Hearn, & R. W. Connell (Eds.), *Handbook of studies on men and masculinities* (pp. 432–447). Thousand Oaks, CA: Sage.

Hochschild, A. (1983). *The managerial heart.* Berkeley: University of California Press.

Howard-Grenville, J. A. (2006). Inside the "black box": How organizational culture and subcultures inform interpretations and actions on environmental issues. *Organization & Environment, 19(1),* 46–73.

Igbaria, M., & Guimaraes, T. (1993). Antecedents and consequences of job satisfaction among information center employees. *Journal of Management Information Systems, 9(4),* 145–155.

Jablin, F. M. (1979). Superior-subordinate communication: The state of the art. *Psychological Bulletin, 86,* 1201–1222.

Jablin, F. M., & Krone, K. J. (1987). Organizational assimilation. In C. R. Berger & S. H. Chafee (Eds.), *Handbook of communication science* (pp. 711–746). Newbury Park, CA: Sage.

Jablin, F. M., & Sias, P. M. (2001). Communication competence. In F. M. Jablin & L. Putnam (Eds.), *The new handbook of organizational communication* (pp. 819–864). Thousand Oaks, CA: Sage.

Jenner, L. (1994). *Work-family programs: Looking beyond written programs.* HR Focus, 71, 19–20.

Kirby, E. L., & Krone, K. J. (2002). "The policy exists but you can't really use it": Communication and the structuration of work-family polices. *Journal of Applied Communication Research, 30,* 50–77.

Koniarek, J., & Dudek, B. (1996). Social support as a barrier in the stress–burnout relationship. *International Journal of Stress Management, 3,* 99–106.

Kram, K. E., & Isabella, L. A. (1985). Mentoring alternatives: The role of peer relationships in career development. *Academy of Management Journal, 28,* 110–132.

Kreps, G. (1991). *Organizational communication: Theory and practice* (2nd ed.). New York: Longman.

Krugman, P. (2002). *The great unraveling: Losing our way in the new century.* New York: W. W. Norton.

Larson, J., Jr. (1989). The dynamic interplay between employees: Feedback-seeking strategies and supervisors' delivery of performance feedback. *Academy of Management Review, 14,* 408–422.

Lipson, S. (2011, January 2). Perma-lancing. *The Fiscal Times.* Retrieved July 13, 2011, from http://www .thefiscaltimes.com/Articles/2011/01/02/Permalancing-The-New-Disposable-Workforce.aspx

Lutgen-Sandvik, P., Tracy, S., & Alberts, J. (2005, February*). Burned by bullying in the American workplaces: A first time study of U.S. prevalence and delineation of bullying "degree."* Presented at the Western States Communication Convention, San Francisco, CA.

Martin, J. (2002). *Organizational culture: Mapping the terrain.* Thousand Oaks, CA: Sage.

Maslach, C. (2003). Job burnout: New directions in research and intervention. *Current Directions in Psychological Science, 12*(5), 189–192.

Maslach, C., & Leiter, M. (1997). *The truth about burnout: How organizations cause personal stress and what to do about it.* San Francisco: Josey-Bass.

McGrath J. E. (1976). Stress and behavior in organizations. In M. D. Dunnette (Ed.), *Handbook of industrial and organizational psychology.* Palo Alto, CA: Consulting Psychologists Press.

McNamara, C. (2008). *Field guide to leadership and supervision.* Minneapolis, MN: Authenticity Publishing.

Miller, K. (2009). *Organizational communication: Approaches and processes* (5th ed.). Belmont, CA: Wadsworth.

Miller, V. D., & Jablin, F. (1991). Information seeking during organizational entry: Influence, tactics and a model of the process. *Academy of Management Review, 16,* 522–541.

Morgan, H., & Milliken, F. J. (1992). Keys to action: Understanding differences in organizations' responsiveness to work-and-family issues. *Human Resource Management, 31,* 227–248.

MSNBC.com News Service. (2011, July 14). FBI probes Murdoch empire over 9/11 hacking claims. Retrieved August 9, 2011, from http://www.msnbc.msn.com/id/43750733/ns/world_news-europe/t/fbi-probes-murdoch-empire-over-hacking-claims/

Prokokos, A., & Padavik, I. (2002). "There ought to be a law against bitches": Masculinity lessons in police academy training. *Gender, Work and Organization, 9*(4), 439–459.

Putnam, L. L., Phillips, N., & Chapman, P. (1996). Metaphors of communication and organization. In S. R. Clegg, C. Hardy, & W. R. Nord (Eds.), *Handbook of organization studies* (pp. 375–408). London: Sage.

Rapoport, R., & Bailyn, L. (1996). *Relinking life and work.* New York: Ford Foundation.

Rawlins, W. K. (1994). Being there and growing apart: Sustaining friendships during adulthood. In D. Canary & L. Stafford, *Communication and relational maintenance* (pp. 275–294). San Diego, CA: Academic.

Richardsen, A. M., & Martinussen, M. (2004). The Maslach burnout inventory: Factorial validity and consistency across occupational groups in Norway. *Journal of Occupational and Organizational Psychology, 77,* 1–20.

Richmond, V. P., McCroskey, J. C., & Davis, L. M. (1986). The relationship of supervisor use of power and affinity-seeking strategies with subordinate satisfaction. *Communication Quarterly, 34,* 178–193.

Rizzo, J. R., House, R. J., & Lirtzman, S. L. (1970). Role conflict and ambiguity in complex organizations. *Administrative Science Quarterly, 15,* 150–163.

Roberts, B. S., & Mann, R. A. (2000, December 5). *Sexual harassment in the workplace: A primer.* Retrieved September 12, 2006, from http://www3.uakron.edu/lawrev/robert1.html

Roy, D. F. (1995). Banana time: Job satisfaction and informal interaction. In S. R. Corman, S. P. Banks, C. R. Bantz, & M. E. Mayer (Eds.), *Foundations of Organizational Communication: A Reader* (pp. 111–120). White Plains, NY: Longman.

Rudman, L.A., Borgida, E., & Robertson, B. A. (1995). Suffering in silence: Procedural justice versus gender socialization issues in university sexual harassment grievance procedures. *Basic and Applied Social Psychology, 17,* 519–541.

Schein, E. H. (2002). *Organizational culture and leadership.* San Francisco, CA: Josey-Bass.

Schor, J. B. (1992). *The overworked American: The unexpected decline of leisure.* New York: BasicBooks.

Scott, C., & Myers, K. (2005). The emotion of socialization and assimilation: Learning emotion management at the firehouse. *Journal of Applied Communication Research, 33*(1), 67–92.

Shuler, S., & Sypher, B. D. (2000). Seeking emotion labor: When managing the heart enhances the work experience. *Management Communication Quarterly, 14,* 50–89.

Sias, P. M. (2005). Workplace relationship quality and employee information experiences. *Communication Studies, 56*(4), 375–395.

Sias, P. M., & Cahill, D. J. (1998). From coworkers to friends: The development of peer friendships in the workplace. *Western Journal of Communication, 62,* 273–279.

Sias, P. M., & Jablin, F. M. (1995). Differential superior-subordinate relations: Perceptions of fairness, and coworker communication. *Human Communication Research, 22,* 5–38.

Sias, P. M., Smith, G., & Avdeyeva, T. (2003). Sex and sex-composition differences and similarities in peer workplace friendship development. *Communication Studies, 54,* 322–340.

Sigal, J., Braden-Maguire, J., Patt, I., Goodrich, C., & Perrino, C. S. (2003). Effect of coping response, setting, and social context on reactions to sexual harassment. *Sex Roles, 48*(3–4), 157–166.

Solomon, C. (1994). Work/family's failing grade: Why today's initiatives aren't enough. *Personnel Journal, 73*(5), 72–87.

Stanton, J. M., & Julian, A. L. (2002). The impact of electronic monitoring on quality and quantity of performance. *Computers in Human Behavior, 18*(1), 85–113.

Taylor, J. R., & Van Every, J. F. (1993). *The vulnerable fortress: Bureaucratic organizations and management in the information age.* Toronto, Canada: University of Toronto Press.

Thurnell, R., & Parker, A. (2008). Men, masculinities and firefighting: Occupational identity, shop-floor culture and organisational change. *Emotion, Space and Society, 1*(2), 127–134.

Tracy, S. J. (2000). Becoming a character for commerce: Emotion labor, self-subordination and discursive construction of identity in a total institution. *Management Communication Quarterly, 14,* 90–128.

Tracy, S. J. (2005). Locking up emotion: Moving beyond dissonance for understanding emotion labor discomfort. *Communication Monographs, 72,* 261–238.

Trethewey, A., & Corman, S. (2001). Anticipating k-commerce: E-Commerce, knowledge management, and organizational communication. *Management Communication Quarterly, 14,* 619–628.

U.S. Department of Labor. (2008, October). Fact finding. *Report from the commission on the future of worker-management relations.* Retrieved November 12, 2008, from http://www .dol.gov/_sec/media/reports/dunlop/summary/htm

U.S. General Accounting Office. (2000, June). *Contingent Workers: Income and benefits lag behind those of rest of workforce.* Retrieved November 12, 2008, from http://www. gao.gov/cgi-bin/getrpt?GAO/HEHS-00-76

Vault. (2003). *Vault office romance survey.* Retrieved March 10, 2006, from http://www.vault.com/nr/newsmain.jsp>nr_page=3dch_id=420d.article_id=16513021

Waldron, V. R. (1994). Once more, with feeling: Reconsidering the role of emotion in work. In S. Deetz (Ed.), *Communication Yearbook, 17,* 388–416). Thousand Oaks, CA: Sage.

Wayne, S. G., & Ferris, G. R. (1990). Influence tactics, affect and exchange quality in supervisor-subordinate interactions: A laboratory experiment and field study. *Journal of Applied Psychology, 75,* 487–499.

Westman, M., & Etzion, D. (2005). The crossover of work- family conflict from one spouse to the other. *Journal of Applied Social Psychology, 35*(9), 1936–1957.

Whetton, D. A., & Cameron, K. S. (2002). *Developing managerial skills* (6th ed.). Upper Saddle River, NJ: Prentice Hall.

Zuckerman, M. B. (2011, June 20). Why the job situation is worse than it looks. *U.S. News and World Report.* Retrieved September, 17, 2011 from http://www.usnews.com/opinion/mzuckerman/articles/2011/06/20/why-the-jobs-situation-is-worse-than-it-looks

Chapter 12

Aristotle. (1991). *On rhetoric: A theory of civic discourse* (G. A. Kennedy, Trans.). New York: Oxford University Press. (Original work written about 350 B.C.E.)

Behnke, R., & Sawyer, C. (1999). Milestones of anticipatory public speaking anxiety. *Communication Education, 48,* 165–173.

Behnke, R., & Sawyer, C. (2004). Public speaking anxiety as a function of sensitization and habituation processes. *Communication Education, 53,* 164–173.

Bitzer, L. (1968). The rhetorical situation. *Philosophy and Rhetoric, 1,* 1–14.

Bush, G. W. (2001, September 12). "Today … our very freedom came under attack." Boston Globe. Retrieved September 14, 2011 from: http://www.boston.com/news/packages/underattack/globe_stories/0912/_Today_our_very_freedom_came_under_attack_+.shtml

Conley, T. (1994). *Rhetoric in the European tradition.* Chicago: University of Chicago Press.

Darsey, J. (1991). From "gay is good" to the scourge of AIDS: The evolution of gay liberation rhetoric, 1977–1990. *Communication Studies, 42,* 43–66.

Darsey, J. (1994). Must we all be rhetorical theorists?: An anti-democratic inquiry. *Western Journal of Communication, 58,* 164–181.

Dehghan, S. K. (2011, July 31). Iranian woman blinded by acid attack pardons assailant as he faces same fate. *Guardian.* Retrieved July 31, 2011, from http://www.guardian.co.uk/world/2011/jul/31/iran-acid-woman-pardons-attacker

Delgado, F. (1995). Chicano movement rhetoric: An ideographic interpretation. *Communication Quarterly, 43,* 446–455.

DeLuca, K. M. (1999). *Image politics: The new rhetoric of environmental activism.* New York: Guilford.

Ehninger, D. (1967) On rhetoric and rhetorics. *Western Speech, 31,* 242–249.

Erdbrink. T. (2008, December 14). Woman blinded by spurned man invokes Islamic retribution. *Washington Post,* p. A1.

Gayle, B. M. (2004). Transformations in a civil discourse public speaking class: Speakers' and listeners' attitude change. *Communication Education, 53,* 174–185.

Infante, D. A., Rancer, A. S., & Womack, D. F. (1990). *Building communication theory.* Prospect Heights, IL: Waveland.

Johannesen, R. L. (1997). Diversity, freedom, and responsibility in tension. In J. M. Makau & R. C. Arnett (Eds.),

Communication ethics in an age of diversity (pp. 157–186). Urbana: University of Illinois Press.

Kennedy, G. A. (1998). *Comparative rhetoric: An historical and cross-cultural introduction.* New York: Oxford University Press.

King, J. L. (2002). Cultural differences in the perceptions of sports mascots: A rhetorical study of Tim Giago's newspaper columns. In J. N. Martin, T. K. Nakayama, & L. A. Flores (Eds.), *Readings in intercultural communication: Experiences and contexts* (pp. 205–212). New York: McGraw-Hill.

Levasseur, D. G., Dean, K. W., & Pfaff, J. (2004). Speech pedagogy beyond the basics: A study of instructional methods in the advanced public speaking course. *Communication Education. 53,* 234–252.

Lucaites, J. L., Condit, C. M., & Caudill, S. (1999). *Contemporary rhetorical theory: A reader.* New York. Guilford.

Maffesoli, M. (1996). *The time of the tribes: The decline of individualism in mass society.* Thousand Oaks, CA: Sage.

Makau, J. M. (1997). Embracing diversity in the classroom. In J. M. Makau & R. C. Arnett (Eds.), *Communication ethics in an age of diversity* (pp. 48–67). Urbana: University of Illinois Press.

McKerrow, R. E., Gronbeck, B. E., Ehninger, D., & Monroe, A. H. (2003). *Principles of public speaking* (15th ed.). Boston: Allyn & Bacon.

O'Hair, D., Stewart, R., & Rubenstein, H. (2004). *A speaker's guidebook* (2nd ed.). Boston: Bedford/St. Martin's.

Osterman, R. (2005, May 23). "Soft skills" top list of what area employers desire. *Sacramento Bee,* D1.

Pew Forum on Religion and Public Life. (2008, December 18). Many Americans say other faiths can lead to eternal life. Retrieved January 7, 2009, from http://pewresearch.org/pubs/1062/many-americans-say-other-faiths-can-lead-to-eternal-life

Pew Research Center for People and the Press. (2005, September 8). Huge racial divide over Katrina and its consequences: Two-in-three critical of Bush's relief efforts. Retrieved June 26, 2006, from http://people-press.org/reports/pdf/255.pdf

Sanow, A. (2005, March 3). How I overcame the fear of public speaking. Retrieved June 26, 2006, from http://www.expertclick.com/NewsReleaseWire/default.cfm?Action=ReleaseDetail&ID=8372&NRWid=1698

Sprague, J. & Stuart, D. (2005). *The speaker's handbook.* Belmont, CA: Wadsworth/Thomson.

U.S. Census Bureau. (2003, February 25). Census 2000. Table 5: Detailed list of languages spoken at home for the population 5 years and over by state. Retrieved March 27, 2009, from http://www.census.gov/population/www.cen2000/briefs/phc-t20/tab05.pdf

Witt, R. (2011, March 15). Rush Limbaugh suggests tsunami hit Japan because they make electric cars. *Examiner.com.* Retrieved July 30, 2011, from http://www.examiner.com/political-buzz-in-national/rush-limbaugh-suggests-tsunami-hit-japan-because-they-make-electric-cars-audio

Chapter 13

Akhavan-Majid, R. (2004). Mass media reform in China: Toward a new analytical perspective. *Gazette: The International Journal for Communication Studies, 66,* 553–565.

American Academy of Pediatrics. (2002). Some things you should know about media violence and media literacy. Retrieved June 1, 2006, from http://www.aap.org/advocacy/childhealthmonth/media.htm

Anderson, C. A., & Bushman, B. J. (2002, March 29). The effects of media violence on society. *Science, 295*, 2377–2378. Retrieved May 1, 2006, from http://www.psychology.iastate.edu/faculty/caa/abstracts/2000-2004/02AB2.pdf

Aoyagi, C. (2004, July 2–15). TV networks' current fascination with Hawaii often doesn't translate into more roles for APAs. *Pacific Citizen, 139*, 1.

Aubin, B. (2004, March 1). Why Quebecers feel especially betrayed. *Macleans*. Retrieved May 10, 2006, from http://www.macleans.ca/topstories/politics/article.jsp?content=20040301_76248_76248

Belkin, L. (2010, December 14). Wanted: More girls on screen. *New York Times*. Retrieved July 19, 2011, from http://parenting.blogs.nytimes.com/2010/12/14/wanted-more-girls-on-screen/

Berelson, B. (1971). *Content analysis in communication research.* New York: Hafner Publishing Co. (Originally published in 1952.)

Billings, A. C., & Eastman, S. T. (2003). Framing identities: Gender, ethnic, and national parity in network announcing of the 2002 Olympics. *Journal of Communication, 53*, 569–586.

Bissell, K. L., & Zhou, P. (2004). Must-see TV or ESPN: Entertainment and sports media exposure and body-image distortion in college women. *Journal of Communication, 54*, 5–21.

Boorstin, D. J. (1965). *The Americans: The national experience.* New York: Random House.

Bryant, J., & Miron, D. (2004). Theory and research in mass communication. *Journal of Communication, 54*, 662–704.

Bushman, B. J., & Gibson, B. (2011). Violent video games cause an increase in aggression long after the game has been turned off. *Social Psychological and Personality Science, 2*, 29–32.

Cablevision. (2000, November 4). NBC to acquire Bravo from Cablevision Systems Corporation. Retrieved June 24, 2006, from http://www.cablevision.com/index.jhtml?id=2002_11_04

Cernetig, M. (2004, January 13). Radio-Canada satire strikes nerve. *Toronto Star*. Retrieved June 24, 2006, from http://www.ondespubliques.ca/index_f.php?page=96342876

Chalaby, J. K. (2003). Television for a new global order: Transnational television networks and the formation of global systems. *Gazette: The International Journal for Communication Studies, 65*, 457–472.

Chapman, J. (2005). *Comparative media history.* Malden, MA: Polity Press.

Cho, H., & Boster, F. J. (2008). Effect of gain versus loss frame antidrug ads on adolescents. *Journal of Communication, 58*, 428–446.

Cohen, J. (2002). Television viewing preferences: Programs, schedules, and the structure of viewing choices made by Israeli adults. *Journal of Broadcasting & Electronic Media, 46*, 204–221.

comScore. (2011, June 8). Television and fixed Internet found to be most important information sources in Japan following earthquake and tsunami. Press release. Retrieved July 14, 2011, from http://www.comscore.com/Press_Events/Press_Releases/2011/6/Television_and_Fixed_Internet_Found_to_be_Most_Important_Information_Sources_in_Japan_Following_Earthquake_and_Tsunami

Dayan, D., & Katz, E. (1992). *Media events: The live broadcasting of history.* Cambridge, MA: Harvard University Press.

DeLuca, K. M., & Peeples, J. (2002). From public sphere to public screen: Democracy, activism, and the "violence" of Seattle. *Critical Studies in Media Communication, 19*, 125–151.

de Moraes, L. (2004, October 21). No more Miss America pageantry for ABC. *Washington Post*, p. C7. Retrieved June 24, 2006, from http://www.washingtonpost.com/wp-dyn/articles/A50114-2004Oct20.html

Dixon, T. L., & Linz, D. (2002). Television news, prejudicial pretrial publicity, and the depiction of race. *Journal of Broadcasting & Electronic Media, 46*, 112–136.

Durham, M. G. (2004). Constructing the "new ethnicities": Media, sexuality, and diaspora identity in the lives of South Asian immigrant girls. *Critical Studies in Media Communication, 21*, 140–161.

Dwyer, D., & Jones, L. (2010, May 20). Rape kit testing backlog thwarts justice for victims. *ABC News*. Retrieved July 14, 2011, from http://abcnews.go.com/Politics/sexual-assault-victims-congress-solve-rape-kit-backlog/story?id=10701295

Fahmy, S. (2004). Picturing Afghan women: A content analysis of AP wire photographs during the Taliban regime and after the fall of the Taliban regime. *Gazette: The International Journal for Communication Studies, 66*, 91–112.

Federal Communications Commission. (2003, July 8). V-chip: Viewing television responsibly. Retrieved June 24, 2006, from http://www.fcc.gov/vchip/

Gerbner, G. (2002). *Against the mainstream: The selected works of George Gerbner.* M. Morgan (ed.). New York: Peter Lang.

Glaister, D. (2005, January 15). Wives or sluts? US viewers in love-hate match with TV hit. *Guardian*. Retrieved June 24, 2006, from http://www.guardian.co.uk/usa/story/0,12271,1391061,00.html

Hanke, R. (1990). Hegemonic masculinity in *thirtysomething. Critical Studies in Mass Communication, 7*, 231–248.

Hightower, K. & Sedensky, M. (2011, July 10). Anger over Casey Anthony verdict pours out online. *USA Today*. Retrieved August 1, 2011, from http://www.usatoday.com/news/topstories/2011-07-09-2575323558_x.htm

Jhally, S., & Lewis, J. (1992). *Enlightened racism: The Cosby show, audiences, and the myth of the American dream.* Boulder, CO: Westview Press.

Kennedy, M. G., O'Leary, A., Beck, V., Pollard, K., & Simpson, P. (2004). Increases in calls to the CDC National STD and AIDS Hotline following AIDS-related episodes in a soap opera. *Journal of Communication, 54*, 287–301.

Krauss, C. (2004, December 27). A twisted sitcom makes the Simpsons look like saints. *New York Times*, A4.

Law, C., & Labre, M. P. (2002). Cultural standards of attractiveness: A thirty-year look at changes in male images in magazines. *Journalism and Mass Communication Quarterly, 79*, 697–711.

Lazarsfeld, P. F., Berelson, B., & Gaudet, H. (1948). *The people's choice: How the voter makes up his mind in a presidential campaign.* New York: Columbia University Press.

Lemire, C. (2005, August 10). Even trashing "Deuce Bigalow" a tired cliché. MSNBC. Retrieved June 24, 2006, from http://msnbc.msn.com/id/8887672

Lowry, D. T., Nio, T. C. J., & Leitner, D. W. (2003). Setting the public fear agenda: A longitudinal analysis of network TV crime reporting, public perceptions of crime and FBI crime statistics. *Journal of Communication, 53*, 61–73.

McChesney, R. (1998). Making media democratic. *Boston Review, 23*, 4–10, 20. Retrieved June 24, 2006, from http://www.bostonreview.net/BR23.3/mcchesney.html

McQuail, D. et al. (1972). The television audience: a revised perspective. In McQuail, D. (ed.)., *Sociology of Mass Communication* (pp. 135–165). New York: Penguin.

McQuail, D. (1987). *Mass communication theory: An introduction* (2nd ed.). Newbury Park, CA: Sage Publications.

Meyers, M. (2004). African American women and violence: Gender, race, and class in the news. *Critical Studies in Media Communication, 21*, 95–118.

Morgan, M., & Signorielli, N. (1990). Cultivation analysis: Conceptualization and methodology. In N. Signorielli & M. Morgan (Eds.), *Cultivation analysis: New directions in media effects research* (pp. 13–34). Newbury Park, CA: Sage Publications.

Nathanson, A. (2004). Factual and evaluative approaches to modifying children's responses to violent television. *Journal of Communication, 54*, 321–336.

Niederdeppe, J., Fowler, E. F., Goldstein, K. & Pribble, J. (2010). Does local television news coverage cultivate fatalistic beliefs about cancer prevention? *Journal of Communication, 60*: 230-253.

Nielsen Media Research. (2005, September 29) Nielsen reports Americans watch TV at record levels. Retrieved June 26, 2006, from http://www.nielsenmedia.com/newsreleases/2005/AvgHoursMinutes92905.pdf

Peter, J. (2003). Country characteristics as contingent conditions of agenda setting: The moderating influence of polarized elite opinion. *Communication Research, 30*, 683–712.

Romer, D., Jamieson, K. H., & Aday, S. (2003). Television news and the cultivation of fear of crime. *Journal of Communication, 53*, 88–104.

Rubin, S. (2010, October 6). Rape kit backlog hits primetime on "SVU." *Ms. Magazine.* Retrieved July 14, 2011, from http://msmagazine.com/blog/blog/2010/10/06/rape-kit-backlog-hits-primetime-on-svu/

Shugart, H. (2008). Managing masculinities: The metrosexual moment. *Communication and Critical/Cultural Studies, 5*, 280–300.

Slater, M. D., Henry, K. L., Swaim, R. C., & Anderson, L. L. (2003). Violent media content and aggressiveness in adolescents: A downward spiral model. *Communication Research, 30*, 713–736.

Sproule, J. M. (1989). Progressive propaganda critics and the magic bullet myth. *Critical Studies in Mass Communication, 6*, 225–246.

Trujillo, N. (1991). Hegemonic masculinity on the mound: Media representations of Nolan Ryan and American sports culture. *Critical Studies in Mass Communication, 8*, 290–308.

TV Parental Guidelines Monitoring Board. (n.d.) Understanding the TV ratings. Retrieved June 24, 2006, from http://www.tvguidelines.org/ratings.htm

Wardle, C., & West, E. (2004). The press as agents of nationalism in the Queen's Golden Jubilee: How British newspapers celebrated a media event. *European Journal of Communication, 19*, 195–219.

Washington State Department of Health. (n.d.) *Media literacy: fast facts.* Retrieved June 24, 2006, from http://depts.washington.edu/thmedia/view.cgi?section=medialiteracy&page=fastfacts

Wolf, N. (2002). *The beauty myth: How images of beauty are used against women.* New York: HarperCollins. Originally published 1991.

Chapter 14

Alzouma, G. (2012). Far away from home…with a mobile phone! Reconnecting and regenerating the extended family in Africa. In P. H. Cheong, J. N. Martin, & L. P. Macfadyen (Eds.), *New media and intercultural communication: Identity, communication and politics* (pp. 193–208). New York: Peter Lang.

Ashley, M. (2008, Oct 11). Converging on Microsoft: 12 tips for safe social networking [Web log post]. *Network World.* Retrieved July 21, 2011, from http://www.networkworld.com/community/tips-for-safe-social-networking?page=0%2C0

Baker, L. R., & Oswald, D. L. (2010). Shyness and online social networking services. *Journal of Social and Personal Relationships, 27*, 873–889.

Bennhold, K. (2011, June 23). Generation FB. *The New York Times.* Retrieved July 21, 2011, from http://www.nytimes.com/2011/06/24/opinion/global/24iht-June24-ihtmag-bennhold-22.html?_r=1&scp=11&sq=youth%20social%20media&st=cse

Bimie, S. A., & Horvath, P. (2002). Psychological predictors of Internet social communication. *Journal of Computer-Mediated Communication, 7*, 1–25.

Boase, J. (2008). Personal networks and the personal communication system. *Information, Communication & Society, 11*(4), 490–508.

Bourdieu, P. (1986). The forms of capital. In J. G. Richardson (Eds.), *Handbook of theory and research for the sociology of education* (pp. 241–258). Westport, CT: Greenwood.

boyd, d. m. (2007). Why youth (heart) social network sites: The role of networked publics in teenage social life. In D. Buckingham (Ed). *Youth, identity, and digital media* (MacArthur Foundation Series on Digital Learning). Cambridge, MA: MIT Press.

boyd, d. m., & Ellison, N.B. (2007). Social network sites: Definition, history, and scholarship. *Journal of Computer-Mediated Communication, 13*(1), 210–230.

Boyd, J. (2003). The rhetorical construction of trust online. *Communication Theory, 13*, 392–410.

Brown, K., Campbell, S. W., & Ling, R. (2011). Mobile phones bridging the digital divide for teens in the US? *Future Internet, 3*, 144–158.

Carr, N. (2008, July/August). Is Google making us stupid?: What the Internet is doing to our brains. *The Atlantic, 302*(1), 56–63.

Caspi, A., Chajut, E., & Saporta, K. (2008). Participation in class and in online discussions: Gender differences. *Computers & Education, 50*, 718–724.

Cheong, P. H. (2008). The young and techless? Investigating internet use and problem-solving behaviors of young adults in Singapore. *New Media & Society, 10*(5), 771–791.

Cheong, P. H., Halavais, A., & Kwon, K. (2008). The chronicles of me: Understanding blogging as a religious practice. *Journal of Media and Religion, 7*, 107–131.

Cheong, P., & Poon, J. (2009). Weaving webs of faith: Examining Internet use and religious communication among Chinese Protestant transmigrants. *Journal of International and Intercultural Communication, 2*(3), 189–207.

Coyne, S. M., Stockdale, L., Busby, D., Iverson, B., & Grant, D.M. (2011). "I luv u :)!": A descriptive study of the media use of individuals in romantic relationships, *Family Relations, 60*, 150 – 162.

Crosbie, V. (2002). What is "new media." Retrieved July 25, 2011, from http://www.sociology.org.uk/as4mm3a.pdf

Daft, R. L., & Lengel, R. H. (1984). Information richness: A new approach to managerial behavior and organization design. *Research in Organizational Behavior, 6*, 191–233.

Daft, R. L., & Lengel, R. H. (1986). A proposed integration among organizational information requirements, media richness, and structural design. *Management Science, 32*(5), 544–571.

Delgado, F. (2002). Mass-Mediated Communication. In J. N. Martin, T. K. Nakayama, & L. A. Flores (Eds.). *Readings in intercultural communication* (2nd ed., pp. 351–360). Boston: McGraw-Hill.

Demographics of Internet users (2010, December). *Pew Internet & American Life Project*. Retrieved July 26, 2011, from http://pewinternet.org/Static-Pages/Trend-Data/Whos-Online.aspx

Duran, R. L. , Kelly, L.& Rotaru, T. (2011). Mobile phones in romantic relationships and the dialectic of autonomy versus connection, *Communication Quarterly, 59*(1), 19-36.

Facebook's Randi Zuckerberg: Anonymity online has to go away. (2011, July 27). *Huffingtonpost.com*. Retrieved July 29, 2011, from http://www.huffingtonpost.com/2011/07/27/randi-zuckerberg-anonymity-online_n_910892.html

Fox, S. (2011, January 21). Americans with disabilities and their technology use. *Pew Internet & American Life Project*. Retrieved July 26, 2011, from http://pewinternet.org/Reports/2011/Disability.aspx

Friedman, M. (2011, March 28). How do I love thee? Let me tweet the ways. *Time, 177*(12), 62–65.

Gaylord, C. (2011, July 12). Raspberry Pi: Rise of the $25 computer. *Christian Science Monitor. Retrieved September 7, 2011 from* http://www.csmonitor.com/Innovation/Responsible-Tech/2011/0712/Raspberry-Pi-Rise-of-the-25-computer

Gergen, K. J. (2002). The challenge of absent-presence. In J. Katz & M. Aakhus (Eds.), *Perpetual contact: Mobile communication, private talk, public performance* (pp. 223–227). Cambridge, UK: Cambridge University Press.

Global swap shops: Special report: Social networking. (2010, January 30). *The Economist, 394*(8667), 6–8.

Griffin, G. (2011, April 20). Egypt's uprising: Tracking the social media factor. *PBS NewsHour.com*. Retrieved May 6, 2011, from http://www.pbs.org/newshour/updates/middle_east/jan-june11/revsocial_04-19.html

Hall, J. A., Park, N., Song, H., & Cody, M. J. (2010). Strategic misrepresentation in online dating: The effects of gender, self-monitoring, and personality traits. *Journal of Social and Personal Relationships, 27*, 117–135.

Hampton, K. N., Goulet, L. S., Rainie, L. & Purcell, K. (2011). Social networking sites and our lives. *Pew Internet & American Life Project*. Retrieved July 22, 2011, from http://www.pewinternet.org/Reports/2011/Technology-and-social-networks.aspx

Hampton, K. N., Sessions, L. F., Her, E. J., & Rainie, L. (2009). Social isolation and new technology. *Pew Internet & American Life Project*. Retrieved December 13, 2009, from http://www.pewinternet.org/~/media//Files/Reports/2009/PIP_Tech_and_Social_Isolation.pdf

Hargittai, W., & Hinnant, A. (2008). Digital inequality: Differences in young adults' use of the Internet. *Communication Research, 35*(5), 602–621.

Heino, R. D., Ellison, N. B., & Gibbs, J. L. (2010). Relationshopping: Investigating the market metaphor in online dating. *Journal of Social and Personal Relationships, 27*, 427–447.

Heussner, K. M., & Fahmy, D. (2010, August 19). Teacher loses job after commenting about students, parents on Facebook. *ABCNews Online/Technology*. Retrieved July 21, 2011, from http://abcnews.go.com/Technology/facebook-firing-teacher-loses-job-commenting-students-parents/story?id=11437248

Horrigan, J. (2008). The Internet and consumer choice. *Pew Internet & American Life Project*. Retrieved December 15, 2008, from http://www.pewinternet.org/pdfs/PIP_Online%20Shopping.pdf

Internet in numbers: 2010. Stephanslighthouse.com. Retrieve May 13, 2011, from http://stephenslighthouse.com/2011/01/15/the-internet-in-numbers-2010/

Jackson, L. A., Barbatsis, G., Biocca, F. A., von Eye, A., Zhao, Y., & Fitzgerald, H. E. (2004). Home Internet use in low-income families: Is access enough to eliminate the digital divide? In E. P. Bucy & J. E. Newhagen (Eds.), *Media access: Social and psychological dimensions of new technology use* (pp. 155–186). Mahwah, NJ: Erlbaum.

James, G. (2003, March 1). Can't hide your prying eyes. *Computerworld, 38*, 35–37.

Jung, J-Y. (2008). Internet connectedness and its social origins: An ecological approach to postaccess digital divides. *Communication Studies, 59*(4), 322–339.

Kendall, L. (2002). *Hanging out in the virtual pub: Masculinities and relationships online*. Berkeley: University of California Press.

Kim, H., Kim, G. J., Park, H. W., & Rice, R. E. (2007). Configurations of relationships in different media: FtF, email, instant messenger, mobile phone, and SMS. *Journal of Computer-Mediated Communication, 12*, 1183–1207.

Lenhart, A., Horrigan, J., Rainie, L., Allen, K., Boyce, A., Madden, M., & O'Grady, E. (2003, April 16). *The ever-shifting Internet population: A new look at Internet access and the digital divide*. Retrieved March 30, 2009, from http://www.pewinternet.org/Reports/2003/The-EverShifting-Internet-Population-A-new-look-at-Internet-access-and-the-digital-divide.aspx

Livingston, G. (2011, February 9). Latinos and digital technology, 2010. *Pew Hispanic Center*. Retrieved July 25, 2011, from http://pewhispanic.org/files/reports/134.pdf

Livingstone, S., & Brake, D. R. (2010). On the rapid rise of social networking sites: New findings and policy implications. *Children and Society, 24*, 75–83.

Lorentz, D. (2011). Review of litigation under the CAN-Spam Act. *Review of Litigation, 30*(3), 559–605.

Madden, M. (2010, August 27). Older adults and social media. *Pew Internet & American Life Project*. Retrieved July 22, 2011, from http://www.pewinternet.org/Reports/2010/Older-Adults-and-Social-Media.aspx

Mangla, I. S. (2008). Bye-bye love, bye-bye bank account. *Money, 37*(10), 18.

Marriot, M. (2006, March 31). Blacks turn to Internet highway, and digital divide starts to close. *The New York Times*,A1.

McKenna, K. Y. A., Green, A. S., & Gleason, M. E. J. (2002). Relationship formation on the Internet: What's the big attraction? *Journal of Social Issues, 58*, 9–31.

Merryfield, M. (2003). Like a veil: Cross-cultural experiential learning online. *Contemporary Issues in Technology and Teacher Education, 3*(2), 146–171.

Muise, A., Christofides, E. & Desmarais, S. (2009). More information than you ever wanted: Does Facebook bring out the green-eyed monster of jealousy? *CyberPsychology & Behavior, 12*(4), 441-444.

New Intel survey finds "mobile etiquette" mishaps are running rampant (2011, February 25). *Businesswire.com*. Retrieved July 25, 2011, from http://www.businesswire.com/news/home/20110225005074/en/Intel-Survey-Finds-'Mobile-Etiquette'-Mishaps-Running

Nosko, A., Wood, E., Molema, S. (2010). All about me: Disclosure in online social networking profiles: The case of Facebook. *Computers in Human Behavior, 26*, 406–418.

Olivarez-Giles, N. (2011, July 15). Twitter, launched five years ago, delivers 350 billion tweets a day. *Los Angeles Times/Business*. Retrieved July 23, 2011, from http://latimesblogs.latimes.com/technology/2011/07/twitter-delivers-350-billion-tweets-a-day.html

Pascoe, C. J. (2011). Resource and risk: Youth sexuality and new media use. *Sexuality Research and Social Policy, 8*, 5–17.

Pettigrew, J. (200). Text messaging and connectedness within close interpersonal relationships. *Marriage & Family Review, 45*, 697–716,

Purcell, K. (2011, June 27). E-reader ownership doubles in 6 months. *Pew Internet & American Life Project.* Retrieved July 22, 2011, from http://www.pewinternet.org/Reports/2011/E-readers-and-tablets.aspx

Rainie, L., Fox, S., Horrigan, J., Fallows, D., Lenhart, A., Madden, M., Cornfield, M., Carter-Sykes, C. (2005). Internet: the mainstreaming of online life. Retrieved September 13, 2011 from http://www.pewinternet.org/~/media/Files/Reports/2005/Internet_Status_2005.pdf.pdf

Ramirez, A., & Zhang, S. (2007). When online meets offline: The effect of modality switching on relational communication. *Communication Monographs, 74*(3), 287–310.

Richtel, M., & Helft, M. (2011, March 11). Facebook users who are underage raise concerns. The New York Times. Retrieved July 21, 2011, from http://www.nytimes.com/2011/03/12/technology/internet/12underage.html

Rideout, V. J., Foehr, U. G., & Roberts, D. F. (2010). *Generation M2: Media in the lives of 8- to 18-year-olds* (A Kaiser Family Foundation Study). Menlo Park, CA: Henry J. Kaiser Family Foundation.

Roberto, A. J., & Eden, J. (2010). Cyberbullying: Aggressive communication in the digital age. In T.A. Avtgis & A. S. Rancer (Eds.), *Arguments, aggression, and conflict: New directions in theory and research* (pp. 198–216). New York: Routledge.

Rogers, E. M. (2003). *Diffusion of innovations* (5th ed.). New York: The Free Press.

Rojas, V., Straubhaar,J., Roychowdhury, D., & Okur, O. (2004). Communities, cultural capital, and the digital divide. In E. P. Bucy & J. E. Newhagen (Eds.), *Media access: Social and Psychological dimensions of new technology use* (pp. 107–130). Mahwah, NJ: Erlbaum.

Rybas, N. (2012). Producing the self at the digital interface. In P. H. Cheong, J. N. Martin, & L P. Macfadyen (Eds.), *New media and intercultural communication: Identity, communication and politics* (pp. 99–107). New York: Peter Lang.

Rooksby, E. (2002). *Email and ethics: Style and ethical relations in computer-mediated communication.* New York: Routledge.

Rosen, L. D., Cheever, N. A., Cummings, C., & Felt, J. (2008). The impact of emotionality and self-disclosure on online dating versus traditional dating. *Computers in Human Behavior, 24,* 2124–2157.

Sawhney, H. (2007). Strategies for increasing the conceptual yield of new technologies research. *Communication Monographs, 74*(3), 395–401.

Selwyn, N. (2007). Guy-tech?: an exploration of undergraduate students' gendered perceptions of information and communication technologies, *Sex Roles, 56,* 525–536.

Serious trouble. (2007, December 8). *The Economist* (Technology Quarterly), 3–4.

Sheer, V. (2011). Teenagers' use of MSN features, discussion topic and online friendship development: The impact of media richness and communication control. *Communication Quarterly, 59*(1), 82–103.

Sinclair, B. (2009, September 23). Study: Minorities underrepresented in games. *Gamespot.* Retrieved July 25, 2010, from http://www.gamespot.com/news/6229016.html

Smith, A. (2010a, July 7). Mobile access 2010. *Pew Internet & American Life Project.* Retrieved July 23, 2011, from http://www.pewinternet.org/~/media/Files/Reports/2010/PIP_Mobile_Access_2010.pdf.

Smith, A. (2011a, June 1). Twitter update 2011. *Pew Internet & American Life Project.* Retrieved July 21, 2011, from http://www.pewinternet.org/~/media/Files/Reports/2011/Twitter%20Update%202011.pdf

Smith, A. (2011b). 35% of American adults own a smartphone. *Pew Internet & American Life Project.* Retrieved July 21, 2011, from http://www.pewinternet.org/~/media/Files/Reports/2011/PIP_Smartphones.pdf

Smith, A., Rainie, L., & Zickuhr, K. (2011, July 19). College students and technology. *Pew Internet & American Life Project.* Retrieved July 21, 2011, from http://www.pewinternet.org/Reports/2011/College-students-and-technology.aspx

Smith, G. G., Ferguson, D., & Caris, M. (2001). Teaching college courses online vs face-to-face. *The Journal, 28,* 18–26.

Sussman, M. (2009). Day 5: Twitter, global Impact and the future of blogging—SOTB 2009. *Technocrati.com.* Retrieved December 13, 2009, from http://technorati.com/blogging/article/day-5-twitter-global-impact-and/

Stone, B. (2007, April 9). A call for manners in the world of nasty blogs. *The New York Times.* Retrieved March 30, 2009, from http://www.nytimes.com/2007/04/09/technology/09blog.html

Talukdar, D., & Gauri, D. K. (2011). Home Internet access and usage in the USA: Trends in the socio-economic digital divide. *Communications of the Association for Information Systems, 28,* article 7.

Taylor, M., Jowi, D., Schreier, H., & Bertelsen, D. (2011). Students' perception of e-mail interaction during student-professor advising sessions: The pursuit of interpersonal goals. *Journal of Computer-Mediated Communication, 16,* 307–330.

Thackaray, R. & Hunter, M. (2010). Empowering youth: Use of technology in advocacy to affect social change. *Journal of Computer-Mediated Communication, 15,* 575–591.

Thompson, L., & Ku, H-Y. (2005). Chinese graduate students' experiences and attitudes toward online learning. *Educational Media International, 42*(1), 33–47.

Timmerman, C. E., & Madhavapeddi, S. N. (2008). Perceptions of organizational media richness: Channel expansion effects for electronic and traditional media across richness dimensions, *IEEE Transactions on Professional Communication, 5*(1), 18–32.

Tong, S. T., Van Der Heide, B., Langwell, L., & Walther, J. B. (2008). Too much of a good thing? The relationship between number of friends and interpersonal impressions on Facebook. *Journal of Computer-Mediated Communication, 13,* 531–549.

Turkle, S. (2011). *Alone together: Why we expect more from technology and less from each other.* New York: Basic Books.

van Dijk, J. (2004). Divides in succession: Possession, skills, and use of new media for societal participation. In E. P. Bucy & J. E. Newhagen (Eds.), *Media access: Social and psychological dimensions of new technology use* (pp. 233–254). Mahwah, NJ: Erlbaum.

Waldman, S. (2011, June 16). Teen charged under cyberbullying law. *TimesUnion.com.* Retrieved July 18, 2011, from http://www.timesunion.com/local/article/Teen-charged-under-cyberbullying-law-1427634.php

Walther, J. B. (1996). Computer-mediated communication: Impersonal, interpersonal, and hyper-personal interaction. *Communication Research, 23,* 3–43.

Walther, J. B., & Parks, M. R. (2002). Cues filtered out, cues filtered in: Computer-mediated communication and relationships. In M. L. Knapp & J. A. Daly (Eds.), *Handbook of interpersonal communication* (pp. 529–563). Thousand Oaks, CA: Sage.

Wang, Y., & Kobsa, A. (2009). Privacy in online social networking at workplace. *Computational Science and Engineering, 4,* 975–978.

Wang, H-Y., & Wang, Y-S. (2008). Gender differences in the perception and acceptance of online games. *British Journal of Educational Technology, 39*(5) 787–806.

Washington, J. (2011, January 10). For minorities, new digital divide seen. *USAToday.com.* Retrieved July 26, 2011, from http://www.usatoday.com/tech/news/2011-01-10-minorities-online_N.htm

Whitty, M. T. (2007). Revealing the "real" me, searching for the "actual" you: Presentations of self on an Internet dating site. *Computers in Human Behavior, 24,* 1707–1723.

Williams, D., Martins, N., Consalvo, M., & Ivory, J. (2009). The virtual census: representations of gender, race, and age in video games. *New Media & Society, 11*(5), 815–834.

Wood, A. F., & Smith, M. J. (2005). *Online communication: Linking technology, identity and culture* (2nd ed.). Mahwah, NJ: Erlbaum.

A world of connections: Special report: Social networking. (2010, January 30). *The Economist, 394*(8667), 3–4.

Yammering away at the office: Special report: Social networking. (2010, January 30). *The Economist, 394*(8667), 14.

Zywica, J., & Danowski, J. (2008). The faces of Facebookers: Investigating social enhancement and social compensation hypotheses: Predicting Facebook and offline popularity from sociability and self-esteem, and mapping the meaning of popularity with semantic networks. *Journal of Computer-Mediated Communication, 14,* 1–34.

Zickuhr, K. (2010, December 16). Generations 2010. *Pew Internet & American Life Project.* Retrieved July 23, 2011, from http://www.pewinternet.org/Reports/2010/Generations-2010.aspx

Photo Credits

Index

I-4INDEX